ORACLE®

Oracle Press™

S0-AEQ-417

OCP Java™ SE 8 Programmer II Exam Guide

(Exam 1Z0-809)

Oracle Press™

OCP Java™ SE 8 Programmer II Exam Guide

(Exam 1Z0-809)

Kathy Sierra
Bert Bates
Elisabeth Robson

New York Chicago San Francisco
Athens London Madrid
Mexico City Milan New Delhi
Singapore Sydney Toronto

Cataloging-in-Publication Data is on file with the Library of Congress

McGraw-Hill Education books are available at special quantity discounts to use as premiums and sales promotions, or for use in corporate training programs. To contact a representative, please visit the Contact Us pages at www.mhprofessional.com.

OCP Java™ SE 8 Programmer II Exam Guide (Exam 1Z0-809)

1 2 3 4 5 6 7 8 9   LCR   21 20 19 18

ISBN: Book p/n 978-1-260-11735-6 and CD p/n 978-1-260-11736-3
of set 978-1-260-11738-7

MHID: Book p/n 1-260-11735-9 and CD p/n 1-260-11736-7
of set 1-260-11738-3

Sponsoring Editor Lisa McClain	**Copy Editor** LeeAnn Pickrell	**Composition** Cenveo® Publisher Services
Editorial Supervisors Jody McKenzie and Janet Walden	**Proofreader** Lisa McCoy	**Illustration** Cenveo Publisher Services
Project Editor LeeAnn Pickrell	**Indexer** Ted Laux	**Art Director, Cover** Jeff Weeks
Acquisitions Coordinator Claire Yee	**Production Supervisor** James Kussow	

About the Authors

Kathy Sierra was a lead developer for the SCJP exam for Java 5 and Java 6. Kathy worked as a Sun "master trainer," and in 1997, founded JavaRanch.com, the world's largest Java community website. Her bestselling Java books have won multiple *Software Development Magazine* awards, and she is a founding member of Oracle's Java Champions program.

These days, Kathy is developing advanced training programs in a variety of domains (from horsemanship to computer programming), but the thread that ties all of her projects together is helping learners reduce cognitive load.

Bert Bates was a lead developer for many of Sun's Java certification exams, including the SCJP for Java 5 and Java 6. Bert was also one of the lead developers for Oracle's OCA 7 and OCP 7 exams and a contributor to the OCP 8 exam. He is a forum moderator on JavaRanch.com and has been developing software for more than 30 years (argh!). Bert is the co-author of several best-selling Java books, and he's a founding member of Oracle's Java Champions program. Now that the book is done, Bert plans to go whack a few tennis balls around and once again start riding his beautiful Icelandic horse, Eyrraros fra Gufudal-Fremri.

Elisabeth Robson has an MSc in Computer Science and was a software programmer and engineering manager at The Walt Disney Company for many years. Since 2012 she has been a freelance writer and instructor. She produces online training and has written four best-selling books, including *Head First Design Patterns* (O'Reilly).

About the Technical Review Team

This is the fifth edition of the book that we've cooked up. The first version we worked on was for Java 2. Then we updated the book for the SCJP 5, again for the SCJP 6, then for the OCA 7 and OCP 7 exams, and now for the OCA 8 and OCP 8 exams. Every step of the way, we were unbelievably fortunate to have fantastic JavaRanch.com-centric technical review teams at our sides. Over the course of the last 15 years, we've been "evolving" the book more than rewriting it. Many sections from our original work on the Java 2 book are still intact. On the following pages, we'd like to acknowledge the members of the various technical review teams who have saved our bacon over the years.

About the Java 2 Technical Review Team

Johannes de Jong has been the leader of our technical review teams forever and ever. (He has more patience than any three people we know.) For the Java 2 book, he led our biggest team ever. Our sincere thanks go out to the following volunteers who were knowledgeable, diligent, patient, and picky, picky, picky!

Rob Ross, Nicholas Cheung, Jane Griscti, Ilja Preuss, Vincent Brabant, Kudret Serin, Bill Seipel, Jing Yi, Ginu Jacob George, Radiya, LuAnn Mazza, Anshu Mishra, Anandhi Navaneethakrishnan, Didier Varon, Mary McCartney, Harsha Pherwani, Abhishek Misra, and Suman Das.

About the SCJP 5 Technical Review Team

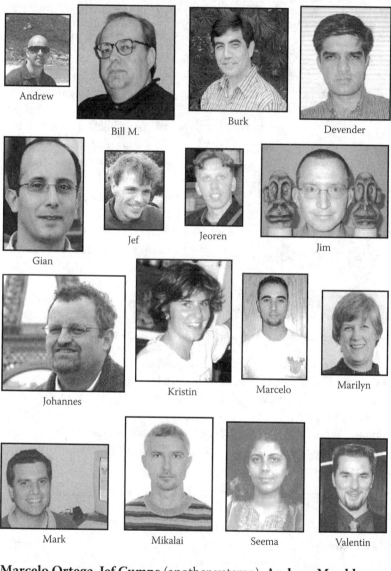

Andrew

Bill M.

Burk

Devender

Gian

Jef

Jeoren

Jim

Johannes

Kristin

Marcelo

Marilyn

Mark

Mikalai

Seema

Valentin

We don't know who burned the most midnight oil, but we can (and did) count everybody's edits—so in order of most edits made, we proudly present our Superstars.

Our top honors go to **Kristin Stromberg**—every time you see a semicolon used correctly, tip your hat to Kristin. Next up is **Burk Hufnagel** who fixed more code than we care to admit. **Bill Mietelski** and **Gian Franco Casula** caught every kind of error we threw at them— awesome job, guys! **Devender Thareja** made sure we didn't use too much slang, and **Mark Spritzler** kept the humor coming. **Mikalai Zaikin** and **Seema Manivannan** made great catches every step of the way, and **Marilyn de Queiroz** and **Valentin Crettaz** both put in another stellar performance (saving our butts yet again).

Marcelo Ortega, **Jef Cumps** (another veteran), **Andrew Monkhouse**, and **Jeroen Sterken** rounded out our crew of Superstars—thanks to you all. **Jim Yingst** was a member of the Sun exam creation team, and he helped us write and review some of the twistier questions in the book (bwa-ha-ha-ha).

As always, every time you read a clean page, thank our reviewers, and if you do catch an error, it's most certainly because your authors messed up. And oh, one last thanks to **Johannes**. You rule, dude!

About the SCJP 6 Technical Review Team

Fred

Marc P.

Marc W.

Mikalai

Christophe

Since the upgrade to the Java 6 exam was like a small surgical strike we decided that the technical review team for this update to the book needed to be similarly fashioned. To that end, we hand-picked an elite crew of JavaRanch's top gurus to perform the review for the Java 6 exam.

Our endless gratitude goes to **Mikalai Zaikin**. Mikalai played a huge role in the Java 5 book, and he returned to help us out again for this Java 6 edition. We need to thank Volha, Anastasia, and Daria for letting us borrow Mikalai. His comments and edits helped us make huge improvements to the book. Thanks, Mikalai!

Marc Peabody gets special kudos for helping us out on a double header! In addition to helping us with Sun's new SCWCD exam, Marc pitched in with a great set of edits for this book—you saved our bacon this winter, Marc! (BTW, we didn't learn until late in the game that Marc, Bryan Basham, and Bert all share a passion for ultimate Frisbee!)

Like several of our reviewers, not only does **Fred Rosenberger** volunteer copious amounts of his time moderating at JavaRanch, he also found time to help us out with this book. Stacey and Olivia, you have our thanks for loaning us Fred for a while.

Marc Weber moderates at some of JavaRanch's busiest forums. Marc knows his stuff and uncovered some really sneaky problems that were buried in the book. While we really appreciate Marc's help, we need to warn you all to watch out—he's got a Phaser!

Finally, we send our thanks to **Christophe Verre**—if we can find him. It appears that Christophe performs his JavaRanch moderation duties from various locations around the globe, including France, Wales, and most recently Tokyo. On more than one occasion Christophe protected us from our own lack of organization. Thanks for your patience, Christophe! It's important to know that these guys all donated their reviewer honorariums to JavaRanch! The JavaRanch community is in your debt.

The OCA 7 and OCP 7 Team

Contributing Authors

Tom   Jeanne

The OCA 7 exam is primarily a useful repackaging of some of the objectives from the SCJP 6 exam. On the other hand, the OCP 7 exam introduced a vast array of brand-new topics. We enlisted several talented Java gurus to help us cover some of the new topics on the OCP 7 exam. Thanks and kudos to **Tom McGinn** for his fantastic work in creating the massive JDBC chapter. Several reviewers told us that Tom did an amazing job channeling the informal tone we use throughout the book. Next, thanks to **Jeanne Boyarsky**. Jeanne was truly a renaissance woman on this project. She contributed to several OCP chapters; she wrote some questions for the master exams; she performed some project management activities; and as if that wasn't enough, she was one of our most energetic technical reviewers. Jeanne, we can't thank you enough. Our thanks go to **Matt Heimer** for his excellent work on the concurrency chapter. A really tough topic, nicely handled! Finally, **Roel De Nijs** and **Roberto Perillo** made some nice contributions to the book *and* helped out on the technical review team—thanks, guys!

Technical Review Team

Roel   Mikalai

Vijitha   Roberto

Roel, what can we say? Your work as a technical reviewer is unparalleled. Roel caught so many technical errors, it made our heads spin. Between the printed book and all the material on the CD, we estimate that there are over 1,500 pages of "stuff" here. It's huge! Roel grinded through page after page, never lost his focus, and made this book better in countless ways. Thank you, Roel!

In addition to her other contributions, **Jeanne** provided one of the most thorough technical reviews we received. (We think she enlisted her team of killer robots to help her!)

It seems like no K&B book would be complete without help from our old friend **Mikalai Zaikin**. Somehow, between earning 812 different Java certifications, being a husband and father (thanks to **Volha**, **Anastasia**, **Daria**, and **Ivan**), and being a "theoretical fisherman" [sic], Mikalai made substantial contributions to the quality of the book; we're honored that you helped us again, Mikalai.

Next up, we'd like to thank **Vijitha Kumara**, JavaRanch moderator and tech reviewer extraordinaire. We had many reviewers help out during the long course of writing this book, but Vijitha was one of the few who stuck with us from Chapter 1 all the way through the master exams and on to Chapter 15. Vijitha, thank you for your help and persistence!

Finally, thanks to the rest of our review team: **Roberto Perillo** (who also wrote some killer exam questions), **Jim Yingst** (was this your fourth time?), other repeat offenders: **Fred Rosenberger**, **Christophe Verre**, **Devaka Cooray**, **Marc Peabody**, and newcomer **Amit Ghorpade**—thanks, guys!

The OCP 8 Team

Approximately two-thirds of the OCP 8 exam's objectives are the same as the OCP 7 exam, and about one-third are new topics focused on all of the amazing new features introduced in Java 8. This time around, our entire review team was composed of veterans. In addition, it's about time that we give thanks to all of the folks on JavaRanch who took time to share errata with us. Because of our amazing review team and the generosity of JavaRanchers (we know "CodeRanch"), this book was improved immensely.

Between the printed book and the two final mock exams, this book has well over 900 pages of material. One way of looking at this book is that every page is a series of factual claims. It's hard to estimate, but perhaps there are 20 such claims on every page. That means we're making about 18,000 factual claims in this book! This makes us authors feel better about saying that our various reviewers found hundreds of errors or areas in which our explanations could have been better. Hundreds out of 18,000 isn't too bad is it?

When we're in the mode of incorporating our reviewers' feedback, we often have to make tough choices. We know that our job isn't to restate the Java Language Spec. We have to make many decisions about how deeply to go into the topics on the exam. You should know that our reviewers constantly challenge us to go deeper. That's a good thing. If you feel as though we haven't covered a topic as deeply as you'd like or that we've oversimplified an explanation, the fault almost certainly lies with us authors, not with the reviewers!

With all of that said, it's time to thank the members of our amazing review team individually.

Technical Review Team

Mikalai

Campbell

Paweł

Frits

Roberto

Vijitha

Tim

Mikalai, wow, wow, wow! This is the fourth time (at least?) that Mikalai Zaikin has been one of our reviewers. Mikalai is a real expert, and he pushes us and makes us think. Mikalai is first and foremost a family man (hooray!), but he's also a geek, and—not satisfied with being only a Java expert—he also pursues other programming approaches as well. It wouldn't surprise us at all if he was into functional programming and other such wackiness. You all have a huge debt to pay to **Campbell**. Campbell Ritchie is a JavaRanch moderator and another true expert. Campbell is passionate about Java, and his edits really taught us a thing or two. Thanks for all your time Campbell! **Paweł Baczyński**, gave us a TON of good feedback. Paweł, send our thanks to your wife and kids; we appreciate their patience! Our next thanks go to veteran reviewer and JavaRanch moderator **Frits Walraven**. Frits is a published mock-exam-question creator (awesome), husband, father, and serial Java certificate holder. Get some sleep, Frits! Once again, we were honored to have **Roberto Perillo** on our review team. This is at least the third time Roberto has helped out. Given what a thankless job this is, Roberto, we can't thank you enough. Roberto is a dad, hooray, and from what we hear he plays a mean guitar. With over 4000 JavaRanch posts to his credit, moderator **Vijitha Kumara** proved once again to be "in it for the long haul!" In addition to traveling and community service, Vijitha was with us right to the final mock exam. Vijitha, thanks for all your help! Last but not least, our thanks go to yet another JavaRanch moderator **Tim Cooke**. Rumor has it that Tim's cat Polly (an Erlang aficionado!?), was at Tim's side throughout the editing process. This might explain some of the attitude that came through in Tim's edits. Tim focused his energies on editing the new FP-ish additions to the exam. Tim, thanks so much for all of your help!

For Jim, Joe, and Solveig

CONTENTS AT A GLANCE

CONTENTS

ACKNOWLEDGMENTS

Kathy and Bert (and in the cases of McGraw-Hill Education and JavaRanch, Elisabeth) would like to thank the following people:

- All the incredibly hard-working folks at McGraw-Hill Education: Tim Green (who's been putting up with us for 15 years now), LeeAnn Pickrell (and team), Lisa McClain, Jody McKenzie, and Jim Kussow. Thanks for all your help, and for being so responsive, patient, flexible, and professional, and the nicest group of people we could hope to work with.

- All of our friends at Kraftur (and our other horse-related friends) and most especially to Sherry; Steinar; Stina and the girls, Jec, Lucy, Cait, and Jennifer; Leslie and David; Annette and Bruce; Kacie; DJ; Gabrielle; and Mary. Thanks to Pedro and Ely, who can't believe it can take so long to finish a book.

- Some of the software professionals and friends who helped us in the early days: Tom Bender, Peter Loerincs, Craig Matthews, Leonard Coyne, Morgan Porter, and Mike Kavenaugh.

- Dave Gustafson and Marc Hedlund for their continued support, insights, and coaching.

- Our good friend at Oracle, Yvonne Prefontiane.

- The crew at Oracle who worked hard to build these exams: Tom McGinn, Matt Heimer, Mike Williams, Stuart Marks, and Mikalai Zaikin.

- Our old wonderful and talented certification team at Sun Educational Services, primarily the most persistent get-it-done person we know, Evelyn Cartagena.

- Our great friends and gurus, Simon Roberts, Bryan Basham, and Kathy Collina.

- Stu, Steve, Burt, and Eric for injecting some fun into the process.

- To Eden and Skyler, for being horrified that adults—out of school—would study this hard for an exam.

- To the JavaRanch Trail Boss Paul Wheaton, for running the best Java community site on the Web, and to all the generous and patient JavaRanch moderators.

■ To all the past and present Sun Ed Java instructors for helping to make learning Java a fun experience, including (to name only a few) Alan Petersen, Jean Tordella, Georgianna Meagher, Anthony Orapallo, Jacqueline Jones, James Cubeta, Teri Cubeta, Rob Weingruber, John Nyquist, Asok Perumainar, Steve Stelting, Kimberly Bobrow, Keith Ratliff, and the most caring and inspiring Java guy on the planet, Jari Paukku.

■ Our furry and feathered friends Eyra, Kara, Draumur, Vafi, Boi, Niki, and Bokeh.

■ Finally, to Elisabeth Robson (our amazing new co-author) and Eric Freeman, for your continued inspiration.

Though this book's primary objective is to help you prepare for and pass Oracle's OCP Java SE 8 Programmer II certification exam.

If you already have an SCJP 6 or OCP 7 certification and want to take an upgrade exam, all of the topics covered in the OCP 7 and SCJP 6 Upgrade exams are covered here as well.

This book follows closely both the breadth and the depth of the real exams. For instance, after reading this book, you probably won't emerge as an NIO.2 guru, but if you study the material and do well on the Self Tests, you'll have a basic understanding of NIO.2, and you'll do well on the exam. After completing this book, you should feel confident that you have thoroughly reviewed all of the objectives that Oracle has established for these exams.

In This Book

This book is organized to optimize your learning of the topics covered by the OCP 8 exam. Whenever possible, we've organized the chapters to parallel the Oracle objectives, but sometimes we'll mix up objectives or partially repeat them in order to present topics in an order better suited to learning the material.

In the Chapters

We've created a set of chapter components that call your attention to important items, reinforce important points, and provide helpful exam-taking hints. Take a look at what you'll find in the chapters:

- Every chapter begins with the **Certification Objectives**—what you need to know in order to pass the section on the exam dealing with the chapter topic. The Certification Objective headings identify the objectives within the chapter, so you'll always know an objective when you see it!

- **On the Job** callouts discuss practical aspects of certification topics that might not occur on the exam, but that will be useful in the real world.

e x a m

watch   Exam Watch *notes call attention to information about, and potential pitfalls in, the exam. Since we were on the team that created these exams, we know what you're about to go through!*

- ■ **Exercises** help you master skills that are likely to be an area of focus on the exam. Don't just read through the exercises; they are hands-on practice that you should be comfortable completing. Learning by doing is an effective way to increase your competency with a product.

- ■ The **Certification Summary** is a succinct review of the chapter and a restatement of salient points regarding the exam.

✓ ■ The **Two-Minute Drill** at the end of every chapter is a checklist of the main points of the chapter. It can be used for last-minute review.

Q&A ■ The **Self Test** offers questions similar to those found on the certification exam, including multiple-choice and pseudo drag-and-drop questions. The answers to these questions, as well as explanations of the answers, can be found at the end of every chapter. By taking the Self Test after completing each chapter, you'll reinforce what you've learned from that chapter, while becoming familiar with the structure of the exam questions.

Organization

This book is organized in such a way as to serve as an in-depth review for the OCP Java SE 8 Programmer II exam for both experienced Java professionals and those in the early stages of experience with Java technologies. Each chapter covers at least one major aspect of the exam, with an emphasis on the "why" as well as the "how to" of programming in the Java language.

Throughout this book and supplemental digital material, you'll find support for three exams:

- OCP Java SE 8 Programmer II
- Upgrade to Java SE 8 Programmer from Java SE 7
- Upgrade to Java SE 8 Programmer from Java SE 6

What This Book Is Not

You will not find a beginner's guide to learning Java in this book. All 900+ pages of this book are dedicated solely to helping you pass the exams. Since you cannot take this exam without another Java certification under your belt, in this book, we assume you have a working knowledge of everything covered in the OCA 8 exam. We do not, however, assume any level of prior knowledge of the individual topics covered. In other words, for any given topic (driven exclusively by the actual exam objectives), we start with the assumption that you are new to that topic. So we assume you're new to the individual topics, but we assume that you are not new to Java.

We also do not pretend to be both preparing you for the exam and simultaneously making you a complete Java being. This is a certification exam study guide, and it's very clear about its mission. That's not to say that preparing for the exam won't help you become a better Java programmer! On the contrary, even the most experienced Java developers often claim that having to prepare for the certification exam made them far more knowledgeable and well-rounded programmers than they would have been without the exam-driven studying.

About the Digital Content

You'll receive access to online practice exam software with the equivalent of two 85-question exams for OCP Java SE 8 candidates. The digital content included with the book includes three chapters that complete the coverage necessary for the OCP 7 and SCJP 6 upgrade certifications. We've also included an Online Appendix, "Creating Streams from Files Methods," describing additional methods for processing files and directories.

Please see the Appendix for details on accessing the digital content and online practice exams.

Some Pointers

Once you've finished reading this book, set aside some time to do a thorough review. You might want to return to the book several times and make use of all the methods it offers for reviewing the material:

1. *Re-read all the Two-Minute Drills, or have someone quiz you.* You also can use the drills as a way to do a quick cram before the exam. You might want to make some flash cards out of 3×5 index cards that have the Two-Minute Drill material on them.

2. *Re-read all the Exam Watch notes.* Remember that these notes are written by authors who helped create the exam. They know what you should expect— and what you should be on the lookout for.

3. *Re-take the Self Tests.* Taking the tests right after you've read the chapter is a good idea because the questions help reinforce what you've just learned. However, it's an even better idea to go back later and do all the questions in the book in one sitting. Pretend that you're taking the live exam. (Whenever you take the Self Tests, mark your answers on a separate piece of paper. That way, you can run through the questions as many times as you need to until you feel comfortable with the material.)

4. *Complete the exercises.* The exercises are designed to cover exam topics, and there's no better way to get to know this material than by practicing. Be sure you understand why you are performing each step in each exercise. If there is something you are not clear on, re-read that section in the chapter.

5. *Write lots of Java code.* We'll repeat this advice several times. When we wrote this book, we wrote hundreds of small Java programs to help us do our research. We have heard from hundreds of candidates who have passed the exam, and in almost every case, the candidates who scored extremely well on the exam wrote lots of code during their studies. Experiment with the code samples in the book, create horrendous lists of compiler errors—put away your IDE, crank up the command line, and write code!

A Note About the Certification Objectives

Some of the OCP 8 Certification Objectives are not exactly the most clearly written objectives. You may, as we sometimes did, find yourself squinting a little sideways at an objective when attempting to parse what exactly the objective is about and what the objective might be leaving unsaid. We've done our best to cover all the topics we *think* the objective writers meant to include. And, as a reminder, we do try to teach about 115 percent of what we think you'll need to know for the exam, just to cover all our (and your) bases. That said, there are some gray areas here and there. So look carefully at each objective, and if you think there's something we missed, go study that on your own (and do let us know!).

Introduction to the Material in the Book

The OCP 8 exam is considered one of the hardest in the IT industry, and we can tell you from experience that a large chunk of exam candidates goes in to the test unprepared. As programmers, we tend to learn only what we need to complete our current project, given the insane deadlines we're usually under.

But this exam attempts to prove your complete understanding of the Java language, not just the parts of it you've become familiar with in your work.

Experience alone will rarely get you through this exam with a passing mark, because even the things you think you know might work just a little differently than you imagined. It isn't enough to be able to get your code to work correctly; you must understand the core fundamentals in a deep way and with enough breadth to cover virtually anything that could crop up in the course of using the language.

Who Cares About Certification?

Employers do. Headhunters do. Programmers do. Passing this exam proves three important things to a current or prospective employer: you're smart; you know how to study and prepare for a challenging test; and, most of all, you know the Java language. If an employer has a choice between a candidate who has passed the exam and one who hasn't, the employer knows that the certified programmer does not have to take time to learn the Java language.

But does it mean that you can actually develop software in Java? Not necessarily, but it's a good head start.

Taking the Programmer's Exam

In a perfect world, you would be assessed for your true knowledge of a subject, not simply how you respond to a series of test questions. But life isn't perfect, and it just isn't practical to evaluate everyone's knowledge on a one-to-one basis.

For the majority of its certifications, Oracle evaluates candidates using a computer-based testing service operated by Pearson VUE. To discourage simple memorization, Oracle exams present a potentially different set of questions to different candidates. In the development of the exam, hundreds of questions are compiled and refined using beta testers. From this large collection, questions are pulled together from each objective and assembled into many different versions of the exam.

Each Oracle exam has a specific number of questions, and the test's duration is designed to be generous. The time remaining is always displayed in the corner of the testing screen. If time expires during an exam, the test terminates, and incomplete answers are counted as incorrect.

exam

ⓦatch *Many experienced test-takers do not go back and change answers unless they have a good reason to do so. Only change an answer when you feel you may have misread or misinterpreted the question the first time. Nervousness may make you second-guess every answer and talk yourself out of a correct one.*

Question Format

Oracle's Java exams pose questions in multiple-choice format.

Multiple-Choice Questions

In earlier versions of the exam, when you encountered a multiple-choice question, you were not told how many answers were correct, but with each version of the exam, the questions have become more difficult, so today, each multiple-choice question tells you how many answers to choose. The Self Test questions at the end of each chapter closely match the format, wording, and difficulty of the real exam questions, with two exceptions:

■ Whenever we can, our questions will *not* tell you how many correct answers exist (we will say "Choose all that apply"). We do this to help you master the material. Some savvy test-takers can eliminate wrong answers when the number of correct answers is known. It's also possible, if you know how many answers are correct, to choose the most plausible answers. Our job is to toughen you up for the real exam!

■ The real exam typically numbers lines of code in a question. Sometimes we do not number lines of code—mostly so that we have the space to add comments at key places. On the real exam, when a code listing starts with line 1, it means that you're looking at an entire source file. If a code listing starts at a line number greater than 1, that means you're looking at a partial source file. When looking at a partial source file, assume that the code you can't see is correct. (For instance, unless explicitly stated, you can assume that a partial source file will have the correct import and package statements.)

exam

ⓦatch   *When you find yourself stumped answering multiple-choice questions, use your scratch paper (or whiteboard) to write down the two or three answers you consider the strongest, then underline the answer you feel is most likely correct. Here is an example of what your scratch paper might look like when you've gone through the test once:*

■ *21. B or C*

■ *33. A or C*

This is extremely helpful when you mark the question and continue on. You can then return to the question and immediately pick up your thought process where you left off. Use this technique to avoid having to re-read and rethink questions. You will also need to use your scratch paper during complex, text-based scenario questions to create visual images to better understand the question. This technique is especially helpful if you are a visual learner.

Tips on Taking the Exam

The number of questions and passing percentages for every exam are subject to change. Always check with Oracle before taking the exam, at www.Oracle.com.

You are allowed to answer questions in any order, and you can go back and check your answers after you've gone through the test. There are no penalties for wrong answers, so it's better to at least attempt an answer than to not give one at all.

A good strategy for taking the exam is to go through once and answer all the questions that come to you quickly. You can then go back and do the others. Answering one question might jog your memory for how to answer a previous one.

Be very careful on the code examples. Check for syntax errors first: count curly braces, semicolons, and parentheses and then make sure there are as many left ones as right ones. Look for capitalization errors and other such syntax problems before trying to figure out what the code does.

Many of the questions on the exam will hinge on subtleties of syntax. You will need to have a thorough knowledge of the Java language in order to succeed.

This brings us to another issue that some candidates have reported. The testing center is supposed to provide you with sufficient writing implements so you can work problems out "on paper." In some cases, the centers have provided inadequate markers and dry-erase boards that are too small and cumbersome to use effectively. We recommend that you call ahead and verify that you will be supplied with a sufficiently large whiteboard, sufficiently fine-tipped markers, and a good eraser. What we'd really like to encourage is for everyone to complain to Oracle and Pearson VUE and have them provide actual pencils and at least several sheets of blank paper.

Tips on Studying for the Exam

First and foremost, give yourself plenty of time to study. Java is a complex programming language, and you can't expect to cram what you need to know into a single study session. It is a field best learned over time, by studying a subject and then applying your knowledge. Build yourself a study schedule and stick to it, but be reasonable about the pressure you put on yourself, especially if you're studying in addition to your regular duties at work.

One easy technique to use in studying for certification exams is the 15-minutes-per-day effort. Simply study for a minimum of 15 minutes every day. It is a small but significant commitment. If you have a day where you just can't focus, then give up at 15 minutes. If you have a day where it flows completely for you, study longer. As long as you have more of the "flow days," your chances of succeeding are excellent.

We strongly recommend you use flash cards when preparing for the programmer's exams. A flash card is simply a 3×5 or 4×6 index card with a question on the front and the answer on the back. You construct these cards yourself as you go through a chapter, capturing any topic you think might need more memorization or practice time. You can drill yourself with them by reading the question, thinking through the answer, and then turning the card over to see if you're correct. Or you can get another person to help you by holding up the card with the question facing you and then verifying your answer. Most of our students have found these to be tremendously helpful, especially because they're so portable that while you're in study mode, you can take them everywhere. Best not to use them while driving, though, except at red lights. We've taken ours everywhere—the doctor's office, restaurants, theaters, you name it.

Certification study groups are another excellent resource, and you won't find a larger or more willing community than on the JavaRanch.com Big Moose Saloon certification forums. If you have a question from this book, or any other mock exam question you may have stumbled upon, posting a question in a certification forum will get you an answer in nearly all cases within a day—usually, within a few hours. You'll find us (the authors) there several times a week, helping those just starting out on their exam preparation journey. (You won't actually think of it as anything as pleasant sounding as a "journey" by the time you're ready to take the exam.)

Finally, we recommend that you write a lot of little Java programs! During the course of writing this book, we wrote hundreds of small programs, and if you listen to what the most successful candidates say (you know, those guys who got 98 percent), they almost always report that they wrote a lot of code.

Scheduling Your Exam

You can purchase your exam voucher from Oracle or Pearson VUE. Visit Oracle.com (follow the training/certification links) or visit PearsonVue.com for exam scheduling details and locations of test centers.

Arriving at the Exam

As with any test, you'll be tempted to cram the night before. Resist that temptation. You should know the material by this point, and if you're groggy in the morning, you won't remember what you studied anyway. Get a good night's sleep.

Arrive early for your exam; it gives you time to relax and review key facts. Take the opportunity to review your notes. If you get burned out on studying, you can usually start your exam a few minutes early. We don't recommend arriving late. Your test could be cancelled, or you might not have enough time to complete the exam.

When you arrive at the testing center, you'll need to provide current, valid photo identification. Visit PearsonVue.com for details on the ID requirements. They just want to be sure that you don't send your brilliant Java guru next-door neighbor who you've paid to take the exam for you.

Aside from a brain full of facts, you don't need to bring anything else to the exam room. In fact, your brain is about all you're allowed to take into the exam!

All the tests are closed book, meaning you don't get to bring any reference materials with you. You're also not allowed to take any notes out of the exam room. The test administrator will provide you with a small marker board. If you're allowed to, we do recommend that you bring a water bottle or a juice bottle (call ahead for details of what's allowed). These exams are long and hard, and your brain functions much better when it's well hydrated. In terms of hydration, the ideal approach is to take frequent, small sips. You should also verify how many "bio-breaks" you'll be allowed to take during the exam!

Leave your pager and telephone in the car or turn them off. They only add stress to the situation, since they are not allowed in the exam room, and can sometimes still be heard if they ring outside of the room. Purses, books, and other materials must be left with the administrator before entering the exam.

Once in the testing room, you'll be briefed on the exam software. You might be asked to complete a survey. The time you spend on the survey is *not* deducted from your actual test time—nor do you get more time if you fill out the survey quickly. Also, remember that the questions you get on the exam will *not* change depending on how you answer the survey questions. Once you're done with the survey, the real clock starts ticking and the fun begins.

The testing software allows you to move forward and backward between questions. Most important, there is a Mark check box on the screen—this will prove to be a critical tool, as explained in the next section.

Test-Taking Techniques

Without a plan of attack, candidates can become overwhelmed by the exam or become sidetracked and run out of time. For the most part, if you are comfortable with the material, the allotted time is more than enough to complete the exam. The trick is to keep the time from slipping away during any one particular problem.

Your obvious goal is to answer the questions correctly and quickly, but other factors can distract you. Here are some tips for taking the exam more efficiently.

Size Up the Challenge

First, take a quick pass through all the questions in the exam. "Cherry-pick" the easy questions, answering them on the spot. Briefly read each question, noticing the type of question and the subject. As a guideline, try to spend less than 25 percent of your testing time in this pass.

This step lets you assess the scope and complexity of the exam, and it helps you determine how to pace your time. It also gives you an idea of where to find potential answers to some of the questions. Sometimes the wording of one question might lend clues or jog your thoughts for another question.

If you're not entirely confident in your answer to a question, answer it anyway, but check the Mark box to flag it for later review. In the event that you run out of time, at least you've provided a "first guess" answer, rather than leaving it blank.

Second, go back through the entire test, using the insight you gained from the first go-through. For example, if the entire test looks difficult, you'll know better than to spend more than a minute or two on each question. Create a pacing with small milestones—for example, "I need to answer 10 questions every 15 minutes."

At this stage, it's probably a good idea to skip past the time-consuming questions, marking them for the next pass. Try to finish this phase before you're 50 to 60 percent through the testing time.

Third, go back through all the questions you marked for review, using the Review Marked button in the question review screen. This step includes taking a second look at all the questions you were unsure of in previous passes, as well as tackling the time-consuming ones you deferred until now. Chisel away at this group of questions until you've answered them all.

If you're more comfortable with a previously marked question, unmark the Review Marked button now. Otherwise, leave it marked. Work your way through the time-consuming questions now, especially those requiring manual calculations. Unmark them when you're satisfied with the answer.

By the end of this step, you've answered every question in the test, despite having reservations about some of your answers. If you run out of time in the next step, at least you won't lose points for lack of an answer. You're in great shape if you still have 10 to 20 percent of your time remaining.

Review Your Answers

Now you're cruising! You've answered all the questions, and you're ready to do a quality check. Take yet another pass (yes, one more) through the entire test, briefly re-reading each question and your answer.

Carefully look over the questions again to check for "trick" questions. Be particularly wary of those that include a choice of "Does not compile." Be alert for last-minute clues. You're pretty familiar with nearly every question at this point, and you may find a few clues that you missed before.

The Grand Finale

When you're confident with all your answers, finish the exam by submitting it for grading. After you finish your exam, you'll receive an e-mail from Oracle giving you a link to a page where your exam results will be available. As of this writing, you must ask for a hard copy certificate specifically or one will not be sent to you.

Retesting

If you don't pass the exam, don't be discouraged. Try to have a good attitude about the experience, and get ready to try again. Consider yourself a little more educated. You'll know the format of the test a little better, and you'll have a good idea of the difficulty level of the questions you'll get next time around.

If you bounce back quickly, you'll probably remember several of the questions you might have missed. This will help you focus your study efforts in the right area.

Ultimately, remember that Oracle certifications are valuable because they're hard to get. After all, if anyone could get one, what value would it have? In the end, it takes a good attitude and a lot of studying, but you can do it!

OCP 8 Objectives Map

The following table for the OCP Java SE 8 Programmer II Exam describes the objectives and where you will find them in the book.

Oracle Certified Professional Java SE 8 Programmer II (Exam IZ0-804)

(Note: Some of the OCP objectives detailed here are similar to or duplicates of OCA 8 objectives. If you've read our *OCA 8 Java SE 8 Programmer I Exam Guide*, you will recognize some of the material covering those objectives, particularly material in Chapters 1 and 2.)

Official Objective	Exam Guide Coverage
Java Class Design	
Implement encapsulation (1.1)	Chapter 1
Implement inheritance including visibility modifiers and composition (1.2)	Chapter 1
Implement polymorphism (1.3)	Chapter 1
Override the hashcode, equals, and toString methods from Object class (1.4)	Chapter 1
Create and use singleton classes and immutable classes (1.5)	Chapter 1
Develop code that uses the static keyword on initialize blocks, variables, methods, and classes (1.6)	Chapter 1
Advanced Java Class Design	
Develop code that uses abstract classes and methods (2.1)	Chapter 2
Develop code that uses the final keyword (2.2)	Chapter 2
Create inner classes including static inner class, local class, nested class, and anonymous inner class (2.3)	Chapter 2
Use enumerated types including methods, and constructors in an enum type (2.4)	Chapter 2
Develop code that declares, implements and/or extends interfaces and use the @Override annotation (2.5)	Chapter 2
Create and use Lambda expressions (2.6)	Chapters 6, 7, and 8
Generics and Collections	
Create and use a generic class (3.1)	Chapter 6
Create and use ArrayList, TreeSet, TreeMap, and ArrayDeque objects (3.2)	Chapter 6
Use java.util.Comparator and java.lang.Comparable interfaces (3.3)	Chapter 6
Collections Streams and Filters (3.4)	Chapter 6
Iterate using forEach methods of Streams and List (3.5)	Chapters 8 and 9
Describe Stream interface and Stream pipeline (3.6)	Chapter 9
Filter a collection by using lambda expressions (3.7)	Chapter 9
Use method references with Streams (3.8)	Chapter 9

Official Objective	Exam Guide Coverage
Lambda Built-in Functional Interfaces	
Use the built-in interfaces included in the java.util.function package such as Predicate, Consumer, Function, and Supplier (4.1)	Chapter 8
Develop code that uses primitive versions of functional interfaces (4.2)	Chapter 8
Develop code that uses binary versions of functional interfaces (4.3)	Chapter 8
Develop code that uses the UnaryOperator interface (4.4)	Chapter 8
Java Stream API	
Develop code to extract data from an object using peek() and map() methods including primitive versions of the map() method (5.1)	Chapter 9
Search for data by using search methods of the Stream classes including findFirst, findAny, anyMatch, allMatch, noneMatch (5.2)	Chapter 9
Develop code that uses the Optional class (5.3)	Chapter 9
Develop code that uses Stream data methods and calculation methods (5.4)	Chapter 9
Sort a collection using Stream API (5.5)	Chapter 9
Save results to a collection using the collect method and group/partition data using the Collectors class (5.6)	Chapter 9
Use flatMap() methods in the Stream API (5.7)	Chapter 9
Exceptions and Assertions	
Use try-catch and throw statements (6.1)	Chapter 3
Use catch, multi-catch, and finally clauses (6.2)	Chapter 3
Use Autoclose resources with a try-with-resources statement (6.3)	Chapter 3
Create custom exceptions and Autocloseable resources (6.4)	Chapter 3
Test invariants by using assertions (6.5)	Chapter 3
Use Java SE 8 Date/Time API	
Create and manage date-based and time-based events including a combination of date and time into a single object using LocalDate, LocalTime, LocalDateTIme, Instant, Period, and Duration (7.1)	Chapter 4
Work with dates and times across timezones and manage changes resulting from daylight savings including Format date and times values (7.2)	Chapter 4
Define and create and manage date-based and time-based events using Instant, Period, Duration, and TemporalUnit (7.3)	Chapter 4
Java I/O Fundamentals	
Read and write data from the console (8.1)	Chapter 5
Use BufferedReader, BufferedWriter, File, FileReader, FileWriter, FileInputStream, FileOutputStream, ObjectOutputStream, ObjectInputStream, and PrintWriter in the java.io package (8.2)	Chapter 5

The document identifies this as page 43, Introduction xliii.

Official Objective	Exam Guide Coverage
Java File I/O (NIO.2)	
Use Path interface to operate on file and directory paths (9.1)	Chapter 5
Use Files class to check, read, delete, copy, move, manage metadata of a file or directory (9.2)	Chapter 5
Use Stream API with NIO.2 (9.3)	Chapters 5, 9, and Online Appendix
Java Concurrency	
Create worker threads using Runnable, Callable and use an ExecutorService to concurrently execute tasks (10.1)	Chapters 10, 11
Identify potential threading problems among deadlock, starvation, livelock, and race conditions (10.2)	Chapter 10
Use synchronized keyword and java.util.concurrent.atomic package to control the order of thread execution (10.3)	Chapters 10, 11
Use java.util.concurrent collections and classes including CyclicBarrier and CopyOnWriteArrayList (10.4)	Chapter 11
Use parallel Fork/Join Framework (10.5)	Chapter 11
Use parallel Streams including reduction, decomposition, merging processes, pipelines and performance (10.6)	Chapter 11
Building Database Applications with JDBC	
Describe the interfaces that make up the core of the JDBC API including the Driver, Connection, Statement, and ResultSet interfaces and their relationships to provider implementations (11.1)	Chapter 12
Identify the components required to connect to a database using the DriverManager class including the JDBC URL (11.2)	Chapter 12
Submit queries and read results from the database including creating statements, returning result sets, iterating through the results, and properly closing result sets, statements, and connections (11.3)	Chapter 12
Localization	
Read and set the locale using the Locale object (12.1)	Chapter 4
Create and read a Properties file (12.2)	Chapter 4
Build a resource bundle for each locale and load a resource bundle in an application (12.3)	Chapter 4

Taking the Java SE 7 or Java 6 Upgrade Exam

For those of you who have your OCP 7 or SCJP 6 certification and want to take the upgrade exam to get your OCP 8 certification, this book contains everything you'll need to study. To be fair, there is a lot in this book that you won't need to study, but by comparing the upgrade objectives to the Table of Contents, you should be able to determine which chapters apply to you. There are a handful of objectives that do NOT overlap with the OCP 8 exam, and you can find coverage for those objectives in the included digital content. The digital content contains chapters that include coverage for

- Java 6, Objective 1.1, Develop code that uses String objects in the switch statement, binary literals, and numeric literals, including underscores in literals
- Java 7, Objective 6.2, Develop code that uses Java SE 8 I/O improvements, including Files.find(), Files.walk(), and lines() methods

Please refer to the Appendix for details on accessing the additional digital content.

1
Declarations, Access Control, and Enums

- Declare Classes and Interfaces
- Declare Class Members
- Declare Constructors and Arrays
- Create static Class Members

- Use enums
- ✓ Two-Minute Drill
- Q&A Self Test

W e assume that most of our readers have earned their OCA 8 Java certification and are reading this book in pursuit of the OCP 8 Java certification. If that's you, congratulations on earning your OCA 8! If you're NOT pursuing an Oracle Java certification, we'd like to think you might still find this book helpful. Oracle's certification exams are well regarded in the industry, and understanding the concepts in this book will make you a better Java programmer. But make no mistake, this book is REALLY focused on helping you pass the OCP 8.

Java Class Design and Object Orientation: A Refresher

If you compare the exam objectives of the OCA 8 exam and the OCP 8 exam, you'll notice some overlapping concepts. Specifically, many of the objectives in OCA 8 section 6 (Working with Methods and Encapsulation) and OCA 8 section 7 (Working with Inheritance) overlap heavily with the objectives in OCP 8 section 1 (Java Class Design) and OCP 8 section 2 (Advanced Java Class Design). This chapter is focused on most of those areas of conceptual overlap:

- ■ 1.2 Inheritance, visibility, and composition (HAS-A)
- ■ 1.6 The static keyword and init blocks
- ■ 2.1 Abstract classes
- ■ 2.2 The final keyword
- ■ 2.4 Enums
- ■ 2.5 Interfaces

You could consider this chapter a bit of a refresher from the OCA 8 exam, and if you feel really solid on the objectives listed above, you could consider skipping this chapter.

CERTIFICATION OBJECTIVE

Define Classes and Interfaces
(OCP Objectives 1.2, 2.1, and 2.2)

1.2   Implement inheritance including visibility modifiers and composition.
2.1   Develop code that uses abstract classes and methods.
2.2   Develop code that uses the final keyword.

Class Declarations and Modifiers

The class declarations we'll discuss in this section are limited to top-level classes. In addition to top-level classes, Java provides for another category of class known as *nested classes* or *inner classes*. Inner classes will be covered in Chapter 7. You're going to love learning about inner classes. No, really. Seriously.

The following code is a bare-bones class declaration:

```
class MyClass { }
```

This code compiles just fine, but you can also add modifiers before the class declaration. In general, modifiers fall into two categories:

- Access modifiers (`public`, `protected`, `private`)
- Nonaccess modifiers (including `strictfp`, `final`, and `abstract`)

We'll look at access modifiers first, so you'll learn how to restrict or allow access to a class you create. Access control in Java is a little tricky because there are four access *controls* (levels of access) but only three access *modifiers*. The fourth access control level (called *default* or *package* access) is what you get when you don't use any of the three access modifiers. In other words, *every* class, method, constructor, and instance variable you declare has an access *control,* whether you explicitly type one or not. Although all four access *controls* (which means all three *modifiers*) work for most method and variable declarations, a class can be declared with only `public` or *default* access; the other two access control levels don't make sense for a class, as you'll see.

Java is a package-centric language; the developers assumed that for good organization and name scoping, you would put all your classes into packages. They were right, and you should. Imagine this nightmare: Three different programmers, in the same company but working on different parts of a project, write a class named `Utilities`*. If those three* `Utilities` *classes have not been declared in any explicit package and are in the classpath, you won't have any way to tell the compiler or JVM which of the three you're trying to reference. Oracle recommends that developers use reverse domain names, appended with division and/or project names. For example, if your domain name is* `geeksanonymous.com` *and you're working on the client code for the TwelvePointOSteps program, you would name your package something like* `com.geeksanonymous.steps.client`*. That would essentially change the name of your class to* `com.geeksanonymous.steps.client.Utilities`*. You might still have name collisions within your company if you don't come up with your own naming schemes, but you're guaranteed not to collide with classes developed outside your company (assuming they follow Oracle's naming convention, and if they don't, well, Really Bad Things could happen).*

Class Access

What does it mean to access a class? When we say code from one class (class A) has access to another class (class B), it means class A can do one of three things:

■ Create an *instance* of class B.

■ *Extend* class B (in other words, become a subclass of class B).

■ *Access* certain methods and variables within class B, depending on the access control of those methods and variables.

In effect, access means *visibility*. If class A can't *see* class B, the access level of the methods and variables within class B won't matter; class A won't have any way to access those methods and variables.

Default Access   A class with default access has *no* modifier preceding it in the declaration! It's the access control you get when you don't type a modifier in the class declaration. Think of *default* access as *package*-level access, because a class with default access can be seen only by classes within the same package. For example, if class A and class B are in different packages, and class A has default access, class B won't be able to create an instance of class A or even declare a variable or return type of class A. In fact, class B has to pretend that class A doesn't even exist, or the compiler will complain. Look at the following source file:

```
package cert;
class Beverage { }
```

Now look at the second source file:

```
package exam.stuff;
import cert.Beverage;
class Tea extends Beverage { }
```

As you can see, the superclass (`Beverage`) is in a different package from the subclass (`Tea`). The `import` statement at the top of the `Tea` file is trying (fingers crossed) to import the `Beverage` class. The `Beverage` file compiles fine, but when we try to compile the `Tea` file, we get *something like* this:

```
Can't access class cert.Beverage. Class or interface must be public, in same
package, or an accessible member class.
import cert.Beverage;
```

Note: For various reasons, the error messages we show throughout this book might not match the error messages you get. Don't worry, the real point is to understand when you're apt to get an error of some sort.

`Tea` won't compile because its superclass, `Beverage`, has default access and is in a different package. You can do one of two things to make this work. You could put both classes in the same package, or you could declare `Beverage` as `public`, as the next section describes.

When you see a question with complex logic, be sure to look at the access modifiers first. That way, if you spot an access violation (for example, a class in package A trying to access a default class in package B), you'll know the code won't compile so you don't have to bother working through the logic. It's not as if you don't have anything better to do with your time while taking the exam. Just choose the "Compilation fails" answer and zoom on to the next question.

Public Access

A class declaration with the `public` keyword gives all classes from all packages access to the `public` class. In other words, *all* classes in the Java Universe (JU) have access to a `public` class. Don't forget, though, that if a `public` class you're trying to use is in a different package from the class you're writing, you'll still need to import the `public` class or use the fully qualified name.

In the example from the preceding section, we may not want to place the subclass in the same package as the superclass. To make the code work, we need to add the keyword `public` in front of the superclass (`Beverage`) declaration, as follows:

```
package cert;
public class Beverage { }
```

This changes the `Beverage` class so it will be visible to all classes in all packages. The class can now be instantiated from all other classes, and any class is now free to subclass (extend from) it—unless, that is, the class is also marked with the nonaccess modifier `final`. Read on.

Other (Nonaccess) Class Modifiers

You can modify a class declaration using the keyword `final`, `abstract`, or `strictfp`. These modifiers are in addition to whatever access control is on the class, so you could, for example, declare a class as both `public` and `final`. But you can't always mix nonaccess modifiers. You're free to use `strictfp` in combination with `final`, for example, but you must never, ever, ever mark a class as both `final` *and* `abstract`. You'll see why in the next two sections.

You won't need to know how `strictfp` works, so we're focusing only on modifying a class as `final` or `abstract`. For the exam, you need to know only that `strictfp` is a keyword and can be used to modify a class or a method, but never a variable. Marking a class as `strictfp` means that any method code in the class will conform strictly to the IEEE 754 standard rules for floating points.

Without that modifier, floating points used in the methods might behave in a platform-dependent way. If you don't declare a class as `strictfp`, you can still get `strictfp` behavior on a method-by-method basis by declaring a method as `strictfp`. If you don't know the IEEE 754 standard, now's not the time to learn it. You have, as they say, bigger fish to fry.

Final Classes

When used in a class declaration, the `final` keyword means the class can't be subclassed. In other words, no other class can ever extend (inherit from) a `final` class, and any attempts to do so will result in a compiler error.

So why would you ever mark a class `final`? After all, doesn't that violate the whole OO notion of inheritance? You should make a `final` class only if you need an absolute guarantee that none of the methods in that class will ever be overridden. If you're deeply dependent on the implementations of certain methods, then using `final` gives you the security that nobody can change the implementation out from under you.

You'll notice many classes in the Java core libraries are `final`. For example, the `String` class cannot be subclassed. Imagine the havoc if you couldn't guarantee how a `String` object would work on any given system your application is running on! If programmers were free to extend the `String` class (and thus substitute their new `String` subclass instances where `java.lang.String` instances are expected), civilization—as we know it—could collapse. So use `final` for safety, but only when you're certain that your `final` class has, indeed, said all that ever needs to be said in its methods. Marking a class `final` means, in essence, your class can't ever be improved upon, or even specialized, by another programmer.

There's a benefit to having nonfinal classes in this scenario: Imagine that you find a problem with a method in a class you're using, but you don't have the source code. So you can't modify the source to improve the method, but you can extend the class and override the method in your new subclass and substitute the subclass everywhere the original superclass is expected. If the class is `final`, though, you're stuck.

Let's modify our `Beverage` example by placing the keyword `final` in the declaration:

```
package cert;
public final class Beverage {
    public void importantMethod() { }
}
```

Now let's try to compile the `Tea` subclass:

```
package exam.stuff;
import cert.Beverage;
class Tea extends Beverage { }
```

We get an error—something like this:

```
Can't subclass final classes: class
cert.Beverage class Tea extends Beverage{
1 error
```

In practice, you'll almost never make a final class. A final class obliterates a key benefit of OO—extensibility. Unless you have a serious safety or security issue, assume that someday another programmer will need to extend your class. If you don't, the next programmer forced to maintain your code will hunt you down and <insert really scary thing>.

Abstract Classes   An abstract class can never be instantiated. Its sole purpose, mission in life, *raison d'être,* is to be extended (subclassed). (Note, however, that you can compile and execute an abstract class, as long as you don't try to make an instance of it.) Why make a class if you can't make objects out of it? Because the class might be just too, well, *abstract.* For example, imagine you have a class Car that has generic methods common to all vehicles. But you don't want anyone actually creating a generic abstract Car object. How would they initialize its state? What color would it be? How many seats? Horsepower? All-wheel drive? Or more importantly, how would it behave? In other words, how would the methods be implemented?

No, you need programmers to instantiate actual car types such as BMWBoxster and SubaruOutback. We'll bet the Boxster owner will tell you his car does things the Subaru can do "only in its dreams." Take a look at the following abstract class:

```
abstract class Car {
   private double price;
   private String model;
   private String year;
   public abstract void goFast();
   public abstract void goUpHill();
   public abstract void impressNeighbors();
   // Additional, important, and serious code goes here
}
```

The preceding code will compile fine. However, if you try to instantiate a Car in another body of code, you'll get a compiler error, something like this:

```
AnotherClass.java:7: class Car is an abstract
class. It can't be instantiated.
     Car x = new Car();
1 error
```

Notice that the methods marked abstract end in a semicolon rather than curly braces.

Look for questions with a method declaration that ends with a semicolon, rather than curly braces. If the method is in a class—as opposed to an interface—then both the method and the class must be marked abstract. You might get a question that asks how you could fix a code sample that includes a method ending in a semicolon, but without an abstract modifier on the class or method. In that case, you could either mark the method and class abstract or change the semicolon to code (like a curly brace pair). Remember if you change a method from abstract to nonabstract, don't forget to change the semicolon at the end of the method declaration into a curly brace pair!

We'll look at abstract methods in more detail later in this objective, but always remember that if even a single method is abstract, the whole class must be declared abstract. One abstract method spoils the whole bunch. You can, however, put nonabstract methods in an abstract class. For example, you might have methods with implementations that shouldn't change from Car type to Car type, such as getColor() or setPrice(). By putting nonabstract methods in an abstract class, you give all concrete subclasses (*concrete* just means *not abstract*) inherited method implementations. The good news there is that concrete subclasses get to inherit functionality and need to implement only the methods that define subclass-specific behavior.

(By the way, if you think we misused *raison d'être* earlier, don't send an e-mail. We'd like to see *you* work it into a programmer certification book.)

Coding with abstract class types (including interfaces, discussed later in this chapter) lets you take advantage of *polymorphism* and gives you the greatest degree of flexibility and extensibility. You'll learn more about polymorphism in Chapter 2.

You can't mark a class as both abstract and final. They have nearly opposite meanings. An abstract class must be subclassed, whereas a final class must not be subclassed. If you see this combination of abstract and final modifiers used for a class or method declaration, the code will not compile.

EXERCISE 1-1

Creating an Abstract Superclass and Concrete Subclass

The following exercise will test your knowledge of public, default, final, and abstract classes. Create an abstract superclass named Fruit and a concrete subclass named Apple. The superclass should belong to a package called food, and the subclass can belong to the default package (meaning it isn't put into a package explicitly). Make the superclass `public` and give the subclass default access.

1. Create the superclass as follows:

   ```
   package food;
   public abstract class Fruit{ /* any code you want */}
   ```

2. Create the subclass in a separate file as follows:

   ```
   import food.Fruit;
   class Apple extends Fruit{ /* any code you want */}
   ```

3. Create a directory called `food` off the directory in your classpath setting.

4. Attempt to compile the two files. If you want to use the `Apple` class, make sure you place the `Fruit.class` file in the `food` subdirectory.

CERTIFICATION OBJECTIVE

Use Interfaces (OCP Objective 2.5)

2.5   Develop code that declares, implements, and/or extends interfaces and use the @Override annotation.

Declaring an Interface

In general, when you create an interface, you're defining a contract for *what* a class can do, without saying anything about *how* the class will do it.

Note: As of Java 8, you can now also describe the *how*, but you usually won't. Until we get to Java 8's new interface-related features—`default` and `static` methods—we will discuss interfaces from a traditional perspective, which is, again, defining a contract for *what* a class can do.

An interface is a contract. You could write an interface `Bounceable`, for example, that says in effect, "This is the `Bounceable` interface. Any concrete class type that implements this interface must agree to write the code for the `bounce()` and `setBounceFactor()` methods."

By defining an interface for `Bounceable`, any class that wants to be treated as a `Bounceable` thing can simply implement the `Bounceable` interface and provide code for the interface's two methods.

Interfaces can be implemented by any class and from any inheritance tree. This lets you take radically different classes and give them a common characteristic. For example, you might want both a `Ball` and a `Tire` to have bounce behavior, but `Ball` and `Tire` don't share any inheritance relationship; `Ball` extends `Toy` whereas `Tire` extends only `java.lang.Object`. But by making both `Ball` and `Tire` implement `Bounceable`, you're saying that `Ball` and `Tire` can be treated as "Things that can bounce," which in Java translates to "Things on which you can invoke the `bounce()` and `setBounceFactor()` methods." Figure 1-1 illustrates the relationship between interfaces and classes.

FIGURE 1-1

The relationship between interfaces and classes

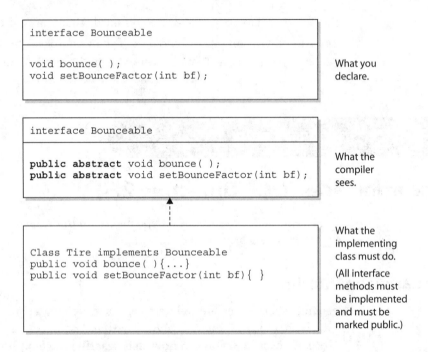

```
interface Bounceable

void bounce( );
void setBounceFactor(int bf);
```
What you declare.

```
interface Bounceable

public abstract void bounce( );
public abstract void setBounceFactor(int bf);
```
What the compiler sees.

```
Class Tire implements Bounceable
public void bounce( ){...}
public void setBounceFactor(int bf){ }
```
What the implementing class must do.

(All interface methods must be implemented and must be marked public.)

Think of an interface as a 100-percent `abstract` class. Like an `abstract` class, an interface defines abstract methods that take the following form:

```
abstract void bounce();   // Ends with a semicolon rather than
                          // curly braces
```

But although an `abstract` class can define both `abstract` and nonabstract methods, an interface *generally* has only `abstract` methods. Another way interfaces differ from `abstract` classes is that interfaces have very little flexibility in how the methods and variables defined in the interface are declared. These rules are strict:

- All interface methods are implicitly `public`. Unless declared as `default` or `static`, they are also implicitly `abstract`. In other words, you do not need to actually type the `public` or `abstract` modifiers in the method declaration, but the method is still always `public` and `abstract`.
- All variables defined in an interface must be `public`, `static`, and `final`—in other words, interfaces can declare only constants, not instance variables.
- Interface methods cannot be marked `final`, `strictfp`, or `native`. (More on these modifiers later in the chapter.)
- An interface can *extend* one or more other interfaces.
- An interface cannot extend anything but another interface.
- An interface cannot implement another interface or class.
- An interface must be declared with the keyword `interface`.
- Interface types can be used polymorphically (see Chapter 2 for more details).

The following is a legal interface declaration:

```
public abstract interface Rollable { }
```

Typing in the `abstract` modifier is considered redundant; interfaces are implicitly abstract whether you type `abstract` or not. You just need to know that both of these declarations are legal and functionally identical:

```
public abstract interface Rollable { }
public interface Rollable { }
```

The `public` modifier is required if you want the interface to have `public` rather than default access.

We've looked at the interface declaration, but now we'll look closely at the methods within an interface:

```
public interface Bounceable {
    public abstract void bounce();
    public abstract void setBounceFactor(int bf);
}
```

Typing in the `public` and `abstract` modifiers on the methods is redundant, though, because all interface methods are implicitly `public` and `abstract`.

Given that rule, you can see the following code is exactly equivalent to the preceding interface:

```
public interface Bounceable {
      void bounce();                      // No modifiers
      void setBounceFactor(int bf);  // No modifiers
}
```

You must remember that all interface methods not declared `default` or `static` are `public` and `abstract` regardless of what you see in the interface definition.

Look for interface methods declared with any combination of `public`, `abstract`, or no modifiers. For example, the following five method declarations, if declared within their own interfaces, are legal and identical!

```
void bounce();
public void bounce();
abstract void bounce();
public abstract void bounce();
abstract public void bounce();
```

The following interface method declarations won't compile:

```
final void bounce();          // final and abstract can never be used
                              // together, and abstract is implied
private void bounce();        // interface methods are always public
protected void bounce();      // (same as above)
```

Declaring Interface Constants

You're allowed to put constants in an interface. By doing so, you guarantee that any class implementing the interface will have access to the same constant. By placing the constants right in the interface, any class that implements the interface has direct access to the constants, just as if the class had inherited them.

You need to remember one key rule for interface constants. They must always be

```
public static final
```

So that sounds simple, right? After all, interface constants are no different from any other publicly accessible constants, so they obviously must be declared `public`, `static`, and `final`. But before you breeze past the rest of this discussion, think about the implications: **Because interface constants are defined in an interface, they don't have to be *declared* as `public`, `static`, or `final`. They must be `public`, `static`, and `final`, but you don't actually**

have to declare them that way. Just as interface methods are always `public` and `abstract` whether you say so in the code or not, any variable defined in an interface must be—and implicitly is—a `public` constant. See if you can spot the problem with the following code (assume two separate files):

```
interface Foo {
   int BAR = 42;
   void go();
}

class Zap implements Foo {
   public void go() {
      BAR = 27;
   }
}
```

You can't change the value of a constant! Once the value has been assigned, the value can never be modified. The assignment happens in the interface itself (where the constant is declared), so the implementing class can access it and use it, but as a read-only value. So the `BAR = 27` assignment will not compile.

e x a m
ⓦ a t c h
Look for interface definitions that define constants, but without explicitly using the required modifiers. For example, the following are all identical:

```
public int x = 1;            // Looks non-static and non-final,
                             // but isn't!
int x = 1;                   // Looks default, non-final,
                             // non-static, but isn't!
static int x = 1;            // Doesn't show final or public
final int x = 1;             // Doesn't show static or public
public static int x = 1;     // Doesn't show final
public final int x = 1;      // Doesn't show static
static final int x = 1;      // Doesn't show public
public static final int x = 1; // what you get implicitly
```

Any combination of the required (but implicit) modifiers is legal, as is using no modifiers at all! On the exam, you can expect to see questions you won't be able to answer correctly unless you know, for example, that an interface variable is `final` *and can never be given a value by the implementing (or any other) class.*

Declaring `default` Interface Methods

As of Java 8, interfaces can include inheritable* methods with concrete implementations. (*The strict definition of "inheritance" has gotten a little fuzzy with Java 8; we'll talk more about inheritance in the next chapter.) These concrete methods are called `default` methods. Later in the book (mostly in Chapter 2), we'll talk a lot about the various OO-related rules that are impacted because of `default` methods. For now, we'll just cover the simple declaration rules:

- `default` methods are declared by using the `default` keyword. The `default` keyword can be used only with interface method signatures, not class method signatures.
- `default` methods are `public` by definition, and the `public` modifier is optional.
- `default` methods **cannot** be marked as `private`, `protected`, `static`, `final`, or `abstract`.
- `default` methods must have a concrete method body.

Here are some examples of legal and illegal `default` methods:

```
interface TestDefault {
  default int m1(){ return 1; }          // legal
  public default void m2(){ ; }          // legal
  // static default void m3(){ ; }       // illegal: default cannot be marked static
  // default void m4();                  // illegal: default must have a method body
}
```

Declaring `static` Interface Methods

As of Java 8, interfaces can include `static` methods with concrete implementations. As with interface `default` methods, there are OO implications that we'll discuss later in the chapter.

For now, we'll focus on the basics of declaring and using `static` interface methods:

- `static` interface methods are declared by using the `static` keyword.
- `static` interface methods are public, by default, and the `public` modifier is optional.
- `static` interface methods cannot be marked as `private`, `protected`, `final`, or `abstract`.
- `static` interface methods must have a concrete method body.
- When invoking a `static` interface method, the method's type (interface name) MUST be included in the invocation.

Here are some examples of legal and illegal static interface methods and their use:

```
interface StaticIface {
  static int m1(){ return 42; }      // legal
  public static void m2(){ ; }       // legal
  // final static void m3(){ ; }     // illegal: final not allowed
  // abstract static void m4(){ ; }  // illegal: abstract not allowed
  // static void m5();               // illegal: needs a method body
}

public class TestSIF implements StaticIface {
  public static void main(String[] args) {
    System.out.println(StaticIface.m1());   // legal: m1()'s type
                                            // must be included
    new TestSIF().go();
    // System.out.println(m1());            // illegal: reference to interface
                                            // is required
  }
  void go() {
    System.out.println(StaticIface.m1());   // also legal from an instance
  }
}
```

which produces this output:

```
42
42
```

Later, we'll return to our discussion of default methods and static methods for interfaces.

Declare Class Members (OCP Objectives 1.2, 1.6, 2.1, and 2.2)

1.2 Implement inheritance including visibility modifiers and composition.
1.6 Develop code that uses static keyword on initialize blocks, variables, methods, and classes.
2.1 Develop code that uses abstract classes and methods.
2.2 Develop code that uses the final keyword.

We've looked at what it means to use a modifier in a class declaration, and now we'll look at what it means to modify a method or variable declaration.

Methods and instance (nonlocal) variables are collectively known as *members*. You can modify a member with both access and nonaccess modifiers, and you have more modifiers to choose from (and combine) than when you're declaring a class.

Access Modifiers

Because method and variable members are usually given access control in exactly the same way, we'll cover both in this section.

Whereas a *class* can use just two of the four access control levels (default or `public`), members can use all four:

- `public`
- `protected`
- default
- `private`

Default protection is what you get when you don't type an access modifier in the member declaration. The default and `protected` access control types have almost identical behavior, except for one difference that we will mention later.

Note: As of Java 8, the word `default` can ALSO be used to declare certain methods in interfaces. When used in an interface's method declaration, `default` has a different meaning than what we are describing in this section of this chapter.

It's crucial that you know access control inside and outside for the exam. There will be quite a few questions in which access control plays a role. Some questions test several concepts of access control at the same time, so not knowing one small part of access control could mean you blow an entire question.

What does it mean for code in one class to have access to a member of another class? For now, ignore any differences between methods and variables. If class A has access to a member of class B, it means that class B's member is visible to class A. When a class does not have access to another member, the compiler will slap you for trying to access something that you're not even supposed to know exists!

You need to understand two different access issues:

- Whether method code in one class can *access* a member of another class
- Whether a subclass can *inherit* a member of its superclass

The first type of access occurs when a method in one class tries to access a method or a variable of another class, using the dot operator (.) to invoke a method or retrieve a variable. For example:

```
class Zoo {
  public String coolMethod() {
    return "Wow  baby";
  }
}
class Moo {
  public void useAZoo() {
    Zoo z = new Zoo();
    // If the preceding line compiles Moo has access
    // to the Zoo class
    // But... does it have access to the coolMethod()?
    System.out.println("A Zoo says, " + z.coolMethod());
    // The preceding line works because Moo can access the
    // public method
  }
}
```

The second type of access revolves around which, if any, members of a superclass a subclass can access through inheritance. We're not looking at whether the subclass can, say, invoke a method on an instance of the superclass (which would just be an example of the first type of access). Instead, we're looking at whether the subclass *inherits* a member of its superclass. Remember, if a subclass *inherits* a member, it's exactly as if the subclass actually declared the member itself. In other words, if a subclass *inherits* a member, the subclass *has* the member. Here's an example:

```
class Zoo {
  public String coolMethod() {
    return "Wow  baby";
  }
}
```

```
  }
class Moo extends Zoo {
  public void useMyCoolMethod() {
    // Does an instance of Moo inherit the coolMethod()?
    System.out.println("Moo says, " + this.coolMethod());
    // The preceding line works because Moo can inherit the
    // public method
    // Can an instance of Moo invoke coolMethod() on an
    // instance of Zoo?
    Zoo z = new Zoo();
    System.out.println("Zoo says, " + z.coolMethod());
    // coolMethod() is public, so Moo can invoke it on a Zoo
    // reference
  }
}
```

Figure 1-2 compares a class inheriting a member of another class and accessing a member of another class using a reference of an instance of that class.

Much of access control (both types) centers on whether the two classes involved are in the same or different packages. Don't forget, though, that if class A *itself* can't be accessed by class B, then no members within class A can be accessed by class B.

You need to know the effect of different combinations of class and member access (such as a default class with a `public` variable). To figure this out, first look at the access level of the class. If the class itself will not be visible to another class, then none of the members will be visible either, even if the member is declared `public`. Once you've confirmed that the class is visible, then it makes sense to look at access levels on individual members.

Public Members

When a method or variable member is declared `public`, it means all other classes, regardless of the package they belong to, can access the member (assuming the class itself is visible).

Look at the following source file:

```
package book;
import cert.*;   // Import all classes in the cert package
class Goo {
  public static void main(String[] args) {
    Sludge o = new Sludge();
    o.testIt();
  }
}
```

FIGURE 1-2

Comparison of
inheritance vs.
dot operator for
member access

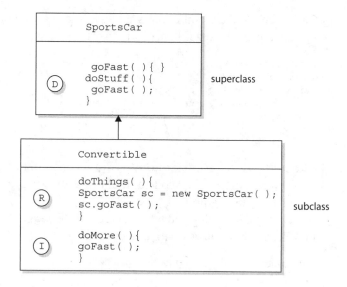

Three ways to access a method:

(D) Invoking a method declared in the same class

(R) Invoking a method using a reference of the class

(I) Invoking an inherited method

Now look at the second file:

```
package cert;
public class Sludge {
  public void testIt() { System.out.println("sludge"); }
}
```

As you can see, Goo and Sludge are in different packages. However, Goo can
invoke the method in Sludge without problems because both the Sludge class
and its testIt() method are marked public.

For a subclass, if a member of its superclass is declared `public`, the subclass inherits that member regardless of whether both classes are in the same package:

```
package cert;
public class Roo {
  public String doRooThings() {
    // imagine the fun code that goes here
    return "fun";
  }
}
```

The Roo class declares the `doRooThings()` member as `public`. So if we make a subclass of Roo, any code in that Roo subclass can call its own inherited `doRooThings()` method.

Notice in the following code that the `doRooThings()` method is invoked without having to preface it with a reference:

```
package notcert;    // Not the package Roo is in
import cert.Roo;
class Cloo extends Roo {
  public void testCloo() {
    System.out.println(doRooThings());
  }
}
```

Remember, if you see a method invoked (or a variable accessed) without the dot operator (`.`), it means the method or variable belongs to the class where you see that code. It also means that the method or variable is implicitly being accessed using the `this` reference. So in the preceding code, the call to `doRooThings()` in the Cloo class could also have been written as `this.doRooThings()`. The reference `this` always refers to the currently executing object—in other words, the object running the code where you see the `this` reference. Because the `this` reference is implicit, you don't need to preface your member access code with it, but it won't hurt. Some programmers include it to make the code easier to read for new (or non) Java programmers.

Besides being able to invoke the `doRooThings()` method on itself, code from some other class can call `doRooThings()` on a Cloo instance, as in the following:

```
package notcert;
class Toon {
  public static void main(String[] args) {
    Cloo c = new Cloo();
    System.out.println(c.doRooThings()); // No problem; method
                                         // is public

  }
}
```

Private Members

Members marked `private` can't be accessed by code in any class other than the class in which the `private` member was declared. Let's make a small change to the `Roo` class from an earlier example:

```
package cert;
public class Roo {
  private String doRooThings() {
    // imagine the fun code that goes here, but only the Roo
    // class knows
    return "fun";
  }
}
```

The `doRooThings()` method is now `private`, so no other class can use it. If we try to invoke the method from any other class, we'll run into trouble:

```
package notcert;
import cert.Roo;
class  UseARoo {
  public void testIt() {
    Roo r = new Roo(); //So far so good; class Roo is public
    System.out.println(r.doRooThings()); // Compiler error!
  }
}
```

If we try to compile `UseARoo`, we get a compiler error, something like this:

```
cannot find symbol
symbol  : method doRooThings()
```

It's as if the method `doRooThings()` doesn't exist, and as far as any code outside of the `Roo` class is concerned, this is true. A `private` member is invisible to any code outside the member's own class.

What about a subclass that tries to inherit a `private` member of its superclass? When a member is declared `private`, a subclass can't inherit it. For the exam, you need to recognize that a subclass can't see, use, or even think about the `private` members of its superclass. You can, however, declare a matching method in the subclass. But regardless of how it looks, *it is not an overriding method!* It is simply a method that happens to have the same name as a `private` method (which you're not supposed to know about) in the superclass. The rules of overriding do not apply, so you can make this newly declared-but-just-happens-to-match method declare new exceptions, or change the return type, or do anything else you want it to do.

```
package cert;
public class Roo {
   private String doRooThings() { // do fun, secret stuff
      return "fun";
} }
```

The doRooThings() method is now off limits to all subclasses, even those in the same package as the superclass:

```
package cert;                        // Cloo and Roo are in the same package
class Cloo extends Roo {             // Still OK, superclass Roo is public
  public void testCloo() {
    System.out.println(doRooThings()); // Compiler error!
  }
}
```

If we try to compile the subclass Cloo, the compiler is delighted to spit out an error, something like this:

```
%javac Cloo.java
Cloo.java:4: Undefined method: doRooThings()
      System.out.println(doRooThings());
1 error
```

Can a private method be overridden by a subclass? That's an interesting question, but the answer is no. Because the subclass, as we've seen, cannot inherit a private method, it, therefore, cannot override the method—overriding depends on inheritance. We'll cover the implications of this in more detail a little later in this chapter, but for now, just remember that a method marked private cannot be overridden. Figure 1-3 illustrates the effects of the public and private modifiers on classes from the same or different packages.

Protected and Default Members

Note: Just a reminder, in the next several sections, when we use the word "default," we're talking about access control. We're NOT talking about the new kind of Java 8 interface method that can be declared default.

The protected and default access control levels are almost identical, but with one critical difference: a *default* member may be accessed only if the class accessing the member belongs to the same package, whereas a protected member can be accessed (through inheritance) by a subclass *even if the subclass is in a different package*. Take a look at the following two classes:

```
package certification;
public class OtherClass {
  void testIt() {    // No modifier means method has default
                     // access
    System.out.println("OtherClass");
  }
}
```

FIGURE 1-3

Effects of
`public` and
`private` access

The effect of private access control

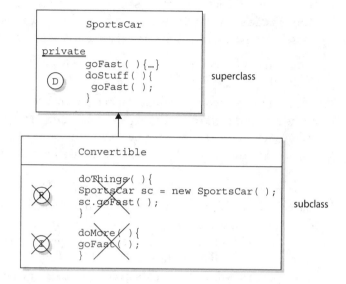

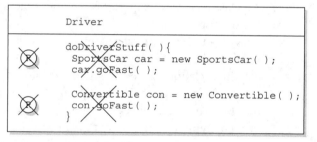

Three ways to access a method:

(D) Invoking a method declared in the same class

(R) Invoking a method using a reference of the class

(I) Invoking an inherited method

In another source code file, you have the following:

```
package somethingElse;
import certification.OtherClass;
class AccessClass {
static public void main(String[] args) {
OtherClass o = new OtherClass();
o.testIt();
}
}
```

As you can see, the `testIt()` method in the first file has *default* (think *package-level*) access. Notice also that class `OtherClass` is in a different package from the `AccessClass`. Will `AccessClass` be able to use the method `testIt()`? Will it cause a compiler error? Will Daniel ever marry Francesca? Stay tuned.

```
No method matching testIt() found in class
certification.OtherClass.    o.testIt();
```

From the preceding results, you can see that `AccessClass` can't use the `OtherClass` method `testIt()` because `testIt()` has default access and `AccessClass` is not in the same package as `OtherClass`. So `AccessClass` can't see it, the compiler complains, and we have no idea who Daniel and Francesca are.

Default and protected behavior differ only when we talk about subclasses. If the `protected` keyword is used to define a member, any subclass of the class declaring the member can access it *through inheritance*. It doesn't matter if the superclass and subclass are in different packages; the `protected` superclass member is still visible to the subclass (although visible only in a very specific way, as you'll see a little later). This is in contrast to the default behavior, which doesn't allow a subclass to access a superclass member unless the subclass is in the same package as the superclass.

Whereas default access doesn't extend any special consideration to subclasses (you're either in the package or you're not), the `protected` modifier respects the parent-child relationship, even when the child class moves away (and joins a new package). So when you think of *default* access, think *package* restriction. No exceptions. But when you think `protected`, think *package + kids*. A class with a `protected` member is marking that member as having package-level access for all classes, but with a special exception for subclasses outside the package.

But what does it mean for a subclass-outside-the-package to have access to a superclass (parent) member? It means the subclass inherits the member. It does not, however, mean the subclass-outside-the-package can access the member using a reference to an instance of the superclass. In other words, `protected` = inheritance. `Protected` does not mean the subclass can treat the `protected` superclass member as though it were public. So if the subclass-outside-the-package gets a reference to the superclass (by, for example, creating an instance of the superclass somewhere in the subclass's code), the subclass cannot use the dot operator on the superclass reference to access the `protected` member. To a subclass-outside-the-package, a `protected` member might as well be default (or even `private`), when the subclass is using a reference to the superclass. **The subclass can see the `protected` member only through inheritance.**

Are you confused? Hang in there and it will all become clearer with the next batch of code examples.

Protected Details

Let's take a look at a `protected` instance variable (remember, an instance variable is a member) of a superclass.

```
package certification;
public class Parent {
    protected int x = 9; // protected access
}
```

The preceding code declares the variable x as `protected`. This makes the variable *accessible* to all other classes *inside* the certification package, as well as *inheritable* by any subclasses *outside* the package.

Now let's create a subclass in a different package and attempt to use the variable x (that the subclass inherits):

```
package other;                          // Different package
import certification.Parent;
class Child extends Parent {
    public void testIt() {
        System.out.println("x is " + x); // No problem; Child
                                         // inherits x
    }
}
```

The preceding code compiles fine. Notice, though, that the `Child` class is accessing the `protected` variable through inheritance. Remember, any time we talk about a subclass having access to a superclass member, we could be talking about the subclass inheriting the member, not simply accessing the member through a reference to an instance of the superclass (the way any other nonsubclass would access it). Watch what happens if the subclass `Child` (outside the superclass's package) tries to access a `protected` variable using a `Parent` class reference:

```
package other;
import certification.Parent;
class Child extends Parent {
   public void testIt() {
      System.out.println("x is " + x);        // No problem; Child
                                               // inherits x

      Parent p = new Parent();                 // Can we access x using
                                               // the p reference?
      System.out.println("x in parent is " + p.x); // Compiler error!

   }
}
```

The compiler is more than happy to show us the problem:

```
%javac -d . other/Child.java
other/Child.java:9: x has protected access in certification.Parent
System.out.println("x in parent is " + p.x);
                                          ^
```

```
1 error
```

So far, we've established that a `protected` member has essentially package-level or default access to all classes except for subclasses. We've seen that subclasses outside the package can inherit a `protected` member. Finally, we've seen that subclasses outside the package can't use a superclass reference to access a protected member. ***For a subclass outside the package, the protected member can be accessed only through inheritance.***

But there's still one more issue we haven't looked at: What does a `protected` member look like to other classes trying to use the subclass-outside-the-package to get to the subclass's inherited `protected` superclass member? For example, using our previous `Parent`/`Child` classes, what happens if some other class—`Neighbor`, say—in the same package as the `Child` (subclass) has a reference to a `Child` instance and wants to access the member variable x? In other words, how does that `protected` member behave once the subclass has inherited it? Does it maintain its `protected` status, such that classes in the `Child`'s package can see it?

No! Once the subclass-outside-the-package inherits the `protected` member, that member (as inherited by the subclass) becomes private to any code outside the subclass, with the exception of subclasses of the subclass. So if class `Neighbor` instantiates a `Child` object, then even if class `Neighbor` is in the same package as class `Child`, class `Neighbor` won't have access to the `Child`'s inherited (but `protected`) variable x. Figure 1-4 illustrates the effect of `protected` access on classes and subclasses in the same or different packages.

FIGURE 1-4   Effects of `protected` access

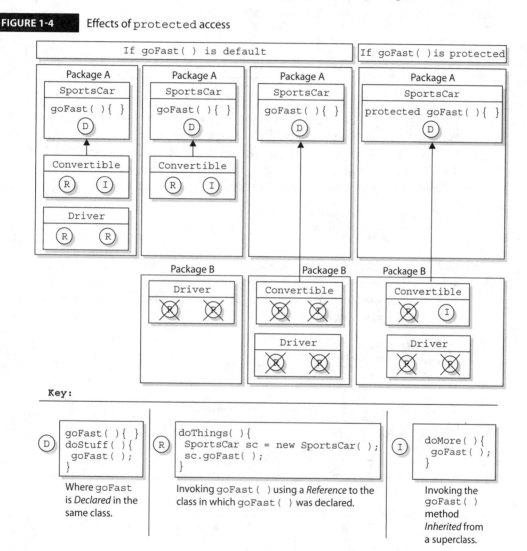

Whew! That wraps up `protected`, the most misunderstood modifier in Java. Again, it's used only in very special cases, but you can count on it showing up on the exam. Now that we've covered the `protected` modifier, we'll switch to default member access, a piece of cake compared to `protected`.

Default Details

Let's start with the default behavior of a member in a superclass. We'll modify the Parent's member x to make it default:

```
package certification;
public class Parent {
   int x = 9; // No access modifier, means default
              // (package) access
}
```

Notice we didn't place an access modifier in front of the variable x. Remember, if you don't type an access modifier before a class or member declaration, the access control is default, which means package level. We'll now attempt to access the default member from the Child class that we saw earlier.

When we try to compile the Child.java file, we get an error something like this:

```
Child.java:4: Undefined variable: x
      System.out.println("x is " + x);
1 error
```

The compiler gives an error as when a member is declared as private. The subclass Child (in a different package from the superclass Parent) can't see or use the default superclass member x! Now, what about default access for two classes in the same package?

```
package certification;
public class Parent{
   int x = 9; // default access
}
```

And in the second class you have the following:

```
package certification;
class Child extends Parent{
   static public void main(String[] args) {
     Child sc = new Child();
     sc.testIt();
   }
   public void testIt() {
     System.out.println("Variable x is " + x); // No problem;
   }
}
```

The preceding source file compiles fine, and the class Child runs and displays the value of x. Just remember that default members are visible to subclasses only if those subclasses are in the same package as the superclass.

Local Variables and Access Modifiers

Can access modifiers be applied to local variables? NO!

There is never a case where an access modifier can be applied to a local variable, so watch out for code like the following:

```
class Foo {
  void doStuff() {
    private int x = 7;
    this.doMore(x);
  }
}
```

You can be certain that any local variable declared with an access modifier will not compile. In fact, there is only one modifier that can ever be applied to local variables—final.

That about does it for our discussion on member access modifiers. Table 1-1 shows all the combinations of access and visibility; you really should spend some time with it. Next, we're going to dig into the other (nonaccess) modifiers that you can apply to member declarations.

TABLE 1-1   Determining Access to Class Members

Visibility	Public	Protected	*Default*	Private
From the same class	Yes	Yes	Yes	Yes
From any class in the same package	Yes	Yes	Yes	No
From a subclass in the same package	Yes	Yes	Yes	No
From a subclass outside the same package	Yes	Yes, *through inheritance*	No	No
From any nonsubclass class outside the package	Yes	No	No	No

Nonaccess Member Modifiers

We've discussed member access, which refers to whether code from one class can invoke a method (or access an instance variable) from another class. That still leaves a boatload of other modifiers you can use on member declarations. Two you're already familiar with—final and abstract—because we applied them to class declarations earlier in this chapter. But we still have to take a quick look at transient and synchronized, and then a long look at the Big One, static, much later in the chapter.

We'll look first at modifiers applied to methods, followed by a look at modifiers applied to instance variables. We'll wrap up this section with a look at how `static` works when applied to variables and methods.

Final Methods

The `final` keyword prevents a method from being overridden in a subclass and is often used to enforce the API functionality of a method. For example, the `Thread` class has a method called `isAlive()` that checks whether a thread is still active. If you extend the `Thread` class, though, there is really no way that you can correctly implement this method yourself (it uses native code, for one thing), so the designers have made it `final`. Just as you can't subclass the `String` class (because we need to be able to trust in the behavior of a String object), you can't override many of the methods in the core class libraries. This can't-be-overridden restriction provides for safety and security, but you should use it with great caution. Preventing a subclass from overriding a method stifles many of the benefits of OO, including extensibility through polymorphism. A typical `final` method declaration looks like this:

```
class SuperClass{
  public final void showSample() {
    System.out.println("One thing.");
  }
}
```

It's legal to extend `SuperClass`, since the *class* isn't marked `final`, but we can't override the `final` *method* `showSample()`, as the following code attempts to do:

```
class SubClass extends SuperClass {
  public void showSample() { // Try to override the final
                             // superclass method
    System.out.println("Another thing.");
  }
}
```

Attempting to compile the preceding code gives us something like this:

```
%javac FinalTest.java
FinalTest.java:5: The method void showSample() declared in class
SubClass cannot override the final method of the same signature
declared in class SuperClass.
Final methods cannot be overridden.
    public void showSample() { }
1 error
```

Final Arguments

Method arguments are the variable declarations that appear in between the parentheses in a method declaration. A typical method declaration with multiple arguments looks like this:

```
public Record getRecord(int fileNumber, int recNumber) {}
```

Method arguments are essentially the same as local variables. In the preceding example, the variables `fileNumber` and `recNumber` will both follow all the rules applied to local variables. This means they can also have the modifier `final`:

```
public Record getRecord(int fileNumber, final int recNumber) {}
```

In this example, the variable `recNumber` is declared as `final`, which, of course, means it can't be modified within the method. In this case, "modified" means reassigning a new value to the variable. In other words, a `final` parameter must keep the same value as the argument had when it was passed into the method. In the case of reference variables, what this means is that you might be able to change the values in the object the `final` reference variable refers to, but you CANNOT force the `final` reference variable to refer to a different object.

Abstract Methods

An `abstract` method is a method that's been *declared* (as `abstract`) but not *implemented*. In other words, the method contains no functional code. And if you recall from the earlier section "Abstract Classes," an `abstract` method declaration doesn't even have curly braces, but instead closes with a semicolon. In other words, *it has no method body.* You mark a method `abstract` when you want to force subclasses to provide the implementation. For example, if you write an `abstract` class `Car` with a method `goUpHill()`, you might want to force each subtype of `Car` to define its own `goUpHill()` behavior, specific to that particular type of car.

```
public abstract void showSample();
```

Notice that the `abstract` method ends with a semicolon instead of curly braces. **It is illegal to have even a single `abstract` method in a class that is not explicitly declared `abstract`!** Look at the following illegal class:

```
public class IllegalClass {
  public abstract void doIt();
}
```

The preceding class will produce the following error if you try to compile it:

```
IllegalClass.java:1: class IllegalClass must be declared
abstract.
It does not define void doIt() from class IllegalClass.
public class IllegalClass{
1 error
```

You can, however, have an `abstract` class with no `abstract` methods. The following example will compile fine:

```
public abstract class LegalClass {
   void goodMethod() {
      // lots of real implementation code here
   }
}
```

In the preceding example, `goodMethod()` is not `abstract`. Three different clues tell you it's not an `abstract` method:

- The method is not marked `abstract`.
- The method declaration includes curly braces, as opposed to ending in a semicolon. In other words, the method has a method body.
- The method **might** provide actual implementation code inside the curly braces.

Any class that extends an `abstract` class must implement all `abstract` methods of the superclass, unless the subclass is *also* `abstract`. The rule is this: **The first concrete subclass of an `abstract` class must implement *all* `abstract` methods of the superclass.**

Concrete just means nonabstract, so if you have an `abstract` class extending another `abstract` class, the `abstract` subclass doesn't need to provide implementations for the inherited `abstract` methods. Sooner or later, though, somebody's going to make a nonabstract subclass (in other words, a class that can be instantiated), and that subclass will have to implement all the `abstract` methods from up the inheritance tree. The following example demonstrates an inheritance tree with two `abstract` classes and one concrete class:

```
public abstract class Vehicle {
  private String type;
  public abstract void goUpHill();   // Abstract method
  public String getType() {          // Non-abstract method
    return type;
  }
}
```

```
public abstract class Car extends Vehicle {
  public abstract void goUpHill();   // Still abstract
  public void doCarThings() {
    // special car code goes here
  }
}

public class Mini extends Car {
  public void goUpHill() {
    // Mini-specific going uphill code
  }
}
```

So how many methods does class Mini have? Three. It inherits both the getType() and doCarThings() methods because they're public and concrete (nonabstract). But because goUpHill() is abstract in the superclass Vehicle and is never implemented in the Car class (so it remains abstract), it means class Mini—as the first concrete class below Vehicle—must implement the goUpHill() method. In other words, class Mini can't pass the buck (of abstract method implementation) to the next class down the inheritance tree, but class Car can, because Car, like Vehicle, is abstract. Figure 1-5 illustrates the effects of the abstract modifier on concrete and abstract subclasses.

Look for concrete classes that don't provide method implementations for abstract methods of the superclass. The following code won't compile:

```
public abstract class A {
  abstract void foo();
}
class B extends A {
  void foo(int i) { }
}
```

Class B won't compile because it doesn't implement the inherited abstract method foo(). Although the foo(int i) method in class B might appear to be an implementation of the superclass's abstract method, it is simply an overloaded method (a method using the same identifier, but different arguments), so it doesn't fulfill the requirements for implementing the superclass's abstract method. We'll look at the differences between overloading and overriding in detail in Chapter 2.

A method can never, ever, ever be marked as both abstract and final, or both abstract and private. Think about it—abstract methods must be implemented (which essentially means overridden by a subclass), whereas final and private methods cannot ever be overridden by a subclass. Or to phrase

FIGURE 1-5

The effects of
the `abstract`
modifier on
concrete and
abstract
subclasses

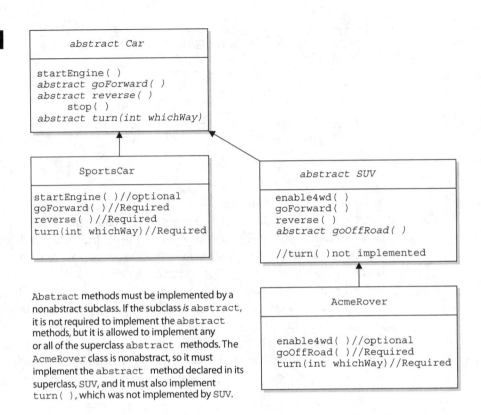

```
                  abstract Car

        startEngine( )
        abstract goForward( )
        abstract reverse( )
              stop( )
        abstract turn(int whichWay)
```

```
             SportsCar

   startEngine( )//optional
   goForward( )//Required
   reverse( )//Required
   turn(int whichWay)//Required
```

```
              abstract SUV

      enable4wd( )
      goForward( )
      reverse( )
      abstract goOffRoad( )

      //turn( )not implemented
```

```
              AcmeRover

   enable4wd( )//optional
   goOffRoad( )//Required
   turn(int whichWay)//Required
```

Abstract methods must be implemented by a
nonabstract subclass. If the subclass *is* `abstract`,
it is not required to implement the `abstract`
methods, but it is allowed to implement any
or all of the superclass `abstract` methods. The
AcmeRover class is nonabstract, so it must
implement the `abstract` method declared in its
superclass, SUV, and it must also implement
`turn( )`, which was not implemented by SUV.

it another way, an `abstract` designation means the superclass doesn't know
anything about how the subclasses should behave in that method, whereas a `final`
designation means the superclass knows everything about how all subclasses
(however far down the inheritance tree they may be) should behave in that method.
The `abstract` and `final` modifiers are virtually opposites. Because `private`
methods cannot even be seen by a subclass (let alone inherited), they, too, cannot
be overridden, so they, too, cannot be marked `abstract`.

Finally, you need to know that—for top-level classes—the `abstract` modifier
can never be combined with the `static` modifier. We'll cover `static` methods
later in this objective, but for now just remember that the following would be illegal:

```
abstract static void doStuff();
```

And it would give you an error that should be familiar by now:

```
MyClass.java:2: illegal combination of modifiers: abstract and static
    abstract static void doStuff();
```

Synchronized Methods

The synchronized keyword indicates that a method can be accessed by only one thread at a time. In Chapter 10, we'll study the synchronized keyword extensively, but for now...all we're concerned with is knowing that the synchronized modifier can be applied only to methods—not variables, not classes, just methods. A typical synchronized declaration looks like this:

```
public synchronized Record retrieveUserInfo(int id) { }
```

You should also know that the synchronized modifier can be matched with any of the four access control levels (which means it can be paired with any of the three access modifier keywords).

Methods with Variable Argument Lists (var-args)

Java allows you to create methods that can take a variable number of arguments. Depending on where you look, you might hear this capability referred to as "variable-length argument lists," "variable arguments," "var-args," "varargs," or our personal favorite (from the department of obfuscation), "variable arity parameters." They're all the same thing, and we'll use the term "var-args" from here on out.

As a bit of background, we'd like to clarify how we're going to use the terms "argument" and "parameter" throughout this book.

■ **arguments**   The things you specify between the parentheses when you're *invoking* a method:

```
doStuff("a", 2);  // invoking doStuff, so "a" & 2 are
                  // arguments
```

■ **parameters**   The things in the *method's signature* that indicate what the method must receive when it's invoked:

```
void doStuff(String s, int a) { }   // we're expecting two
                                    // parameters:
                                    // String and int
```

Let's review the declaration rules for var-args:

■ **Var-arg type**   When you declare a var-arg parameter, you must specify the type of the argument(s) this parameter of your method can receive. (This can be a primitive type or an object type.)

■ **Basic syntax**   To declare a method using a var-arg parameter, you follow the type with an ellipsis (. . .), a space (preferred but optional), and then the name of the array that will hold the parameters received.

■ **Other parameters**   It's legal to have other parameters in a method that uses a var-arg.

■ **Var-arg limits   The var-arg must be the last parameter in the method's signature, and you can have only one var-arg in a method.**

Let's look at some legal and illegal var-arg declarations:

Legal:

```
void doStuff(int... x) { }              // expects from 0 to many ints
                                        // as parameters
void doStuff2(char c, int... x)  { }    // expects first a char,
                                        // then 0 to many ints
void doStuff3(Animal...animal) { }      // 0 to many Animal objects
                                        // (no space before the argument is legal)
```

Illegal:

```
void doStuff4(int x...) { }                  // bad syntax
void doStuff5(int... x, char... y) { }   // too many var-args
void doStuff6(String... s, byte b) { }   // var-arg must be last
```

Constructor Declarations

In Java, objects are constructed. Every time you make a new object, at least one constructor is invoked. Every class has a constructor, although if you don't create one explicitly, the compiler will build one for you. There are tons of rules concerning constructors, and we're saving our detailed discussion for Chapter 2. For now, let's focus on the basic declaration rules. Here's a simple example:

```
class Foo {
  protected Foo() { }        // this is Foo's constructor
  protected void Foo() { }   // this is a badly named, but legal, method
}
```

The first thing to notice is that constructors look an awful lot like methods. A key difference is that a constructor can't ever, ever, ever, have a return type...ever! Constructor declarations can, however, have all of the normal access modifiers, and they can take arguments (including var-args), just like methods. The other BIG RULE to understand about constructors is that they must have the same name as the class in which they are declared. Constructors can't be marked `static` (they are, after all, associated with object instantiation), and they can't be marked `final` or `abstract` (because they can't be overridden). Here are some legal and illegal constructor declarations:

```
class Foo2 {
  // legal constructors
  Foo2() { }
  private Foo2(byte b) { }
  Foo2(int x) { }
  Foo2(int x, int... y) { }
  // illegal constructors
  void Foo2() { }             // it's a method, not a constructor
  Foo() { }                   // not a method or a constructor
  Foo2(short s);              // looks like an abstract method
  static Foo2(float f) { }    // can't be static
  final Foo2(long x) { }      // can't be final
  abstract Foo2(char c) { }   // can't be abstract
  Foo2(int... x, int t) { }   // bad var-arg syntax
}
```

Variable Declarations

There are two types of variables in Java:

■ **Primitives**   A primitive can be one of eight types: `char`, `boolean`, `byte`, `short`, `int`, `long`, `double`, or `float`. Once a primitive has been declared, its primitive type can never change, although in most cases its value can change.

■ **Reference variables**   A reference variable is used to refer to (or access) an object. A reference variable is declared to be of a specific type, and that type can never be changed. A reference variable can be used to refer to any object of the declared type or of a *subtype* of the declared type (a compatible type). We'll talk a lot more about using a reference variable to refer to a subtype in Chapter 2, when we discuss polymorphism.

Declaring Primitives and Primitive Ranges

Primitive variables can be declared as class variables (statics), instance variables, method parameters, or local variables. You can declare one or more primitives, of the same primitive type, in a single line. Here are a few examples of primitive variable declarations:

```
byte b;
boolean myBooleanPrimitive;
int x, y, z;                              // declare three int primitives
```

First, let's review the concepts.

All six number types in Java are made up of a certain number of 8-bit bytes and are *signed*, meaning they can be negative or positive. The leftmost bit (the most significant digit) is used to represent the sign, where a 1 means negative and 0 means positive, as shown in Figure 1-6. The rest of the bits represent the value, using two's complement notation.

FIGURE 1-6

The sign bit for a byte

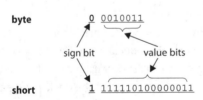

sign bit: 0 = positive
 1 = negative

value bits:

byte: 7 bits can represent 2^7 or 128 different values:
0 thru 127 -or- –128 thru –1

short: 15 bits can represent 2^{15} or 32768 values:
0 thru 32767 -or- –32768 thru –1

Table 1-2 shows the primitive types with their sizes and ranges. Figure 1-6 shows that with a byte, for example, there are 256 possible numbers (or 2^8). Half of these are negative, and half − 1 are positive. The positive range is one less than the negative range because the number 0 is stored as a positive binary number. We use the formula $-2^{(bits-1)}$ to calculate the negative range, and we use $2^{(bits-1)} - 1$ for the positive range. Again, if you know the first two columns of this table, you'll be in good shape for the exam.

TABLE 1-2		Ranges of Numeric Primitives		
Type	**Bits**	**Bytes**	**Minimum Range**	**Maximum Range**
byte	8	1	-2^7	$2^7 - 1$
short	16	2	-2^{15}	$2^{15} - 1$
int	32	4	-2^{31}	$2^{31} - 1$
long	64	8	-2^{63}	$2^{63} - 1$
float	32	4	n/a	n/a
double	64	8	n/a	n/a

Determining the range for floating-point numbers is complicated, but luckily you don't need to know these for the exam (although you are expected to know that a double holds 64 bits and a float 32).

There is not a range of boolean values; a boolean can be only true or false. If someone asks you for the bit depth of a boolean, look them straight in the eye and say, "That's virtual-machine dependent." They'll be impressed.

The char type (a character) contains a single, 16-bit Unicode character. Although the extended ASCII set known as ISO Latin-1 needs only 8 bits (256 different characters), a larger range is needed to represent characters found in languages other than English. Unicode characters are actually represented by unsigned 16-bit integers, which means 2^{16} possible values, ranging from 0 to 65535 ($2^{16} - 1$). Remember from the OCA 8 exam that because a char is really an integer type, it can be assigned to any number type large enough to hold 65535 (which means anything larger than a short; although both chars and shorts are 16-bit types, remember that a short uses 1 bit to represent the sign, so fewer positive numbers are acceptable in a short).

Declaring Reference Variables

Reference variables can be declared as static variables, instance variables, method parameters, or local variables. You can declare one or more reference variables, of the same type, in a single line:

```
Object o;
Dog myNewDogReferenceVariable;
String s1, s2, s3;                      // declare three String vars.
```

Instance Variables

Instance variables are defined inside the class, but outside of any method, and are initialized only when the class is instantiated. Instance variables are the fields that belong to each unique object. For example, the following code defines fields (instance variables) for the name, title, and manager for employee objects:

```
class Employee {
    //  define fields (instance variables) for employee instances
    private String name;
    private String title;
    private String manager;
    // other code goes here including access methods for private
    // fields
}
```

The preceding `Employee` class says that each employee instance will know its own name, title, and manager. In other words, each instance can have its own unique values for those three fields. For the exam, you need to know that instance variables

- Can use any of the four access *levels* (which means they can be marked with any of the three access *modifiers*)
- Can be marked `final`
- Can be marked `transient`
- Cannot be marked `abstract`
- Cannot be marked `synchronized`
- Cannot be marked `strictfp`
- Cannot be marked `native`
- Cannot be marked `static` because then they'd become class variables

Figure 1-7 compares the way in which modifiers can be applied to methods versus variables.

FIGURE 1-7

Comparison of modifiers on variables vs. methods

Local Variables	Variables (nonlocal)	Methods
final	final	final
	public	public
	protected	protected
	private	private
	static	static
	transient	
	volatile	abstract
		synchronized
		strictfp
		native

Local (Automatic/Stack/Method) Variables

A local variable is a variable declared within a method. That means the variable is not just initialized within the method, but also declared within the method. Just as the local variable starts its life inside the method, it's also destroyed when the method has completed. Local variables are always on the stack, not the heap. Although the value of the variable might be passed into, say, another method that then stores the value in an instance variable, the variable itself lives only within the scope of the method.

Just don't forget that while the local variable is on the stack, if the variable is an object reference, the object itself will still be created on the heap. There is no such thing as a stack object, only a stack variable. You'll often hear programmers use the phrase "local object," but what they really mean is "locally declared reference variable." So if you hear programmers use that expression, you'll know that they're just too lazy to phrase it in a technically precise way. You can tell them we said that—unless they know where we live.

Local variable declarations can't use most of the modifiers that can be applied to instance variables, such as `public` (or the other access modifiers), `transient`, `volatile`, `abstract`, or `static`, but as you saw earlier, local variables can be marked `final`. Remember, before a local variable can be *used*, it must be *initialized* with a value. For instance:

```
class TestServer {
  public void logIn() {
    int count = 10;
  }
}
```

Typically, you'll initialize a local variable in the same line in which you declare it, although you might still need to reassign it later in the method. The key is to remember that a local variable must be initialized before you try to use it. The compiler will reject any code that tries to use a local variable that hasn't been assigned a value because—unlike instance variables—local variables don't get default values.

A local variable can't be referenced in any code outside the method in which it's declared. In the preceding code example, it would be impossible to refer to the variable count anywhere else in the class except within the scope of the method logIn(). Again, that's not to say that the value of count can't be passed out of the method to take on a new life. But the variable holding that value, count, can't be accessed once the method is complete, as the following illegal code demonstrates:

```
class TestServer {
  public void logIn() {
    int count = 10;
  }
  public void doSomething(int i) {
    count = i;   // Won't compile! Can't access count outside
                 // method logIn()
  }
}
```

It is possible to declare a local variable with the same name as an instance variable. It's known as *shadowing*, as the following code demonstrates:

```
class TestServer {
    int count = 9;          // Declare an instance variable named count
    public void logIn() {
        int count = 10;     // Declare a local variable named count
        System.out.println("local variable count is " + count);
    }
    public void count() {
        System.out.println("instance variable count is " + count);
    }
    public static void main(String[] args) {
        new TestServer().logIn();
        new TestServer().count();
    }
}
```

The preceding code produces the following output:

```
local variable count is 10
instance variable count is 9
```

Why on Earth (or the planet of your choice) would you want to do that? Normally, you won't. But one of the more common reasons is to name a parameter with the same name as the instance variable to which the parameter will be assigned.

The following (wrong) code is trying to set an instance variable's value using a parameter:

```
class Foo {
   int size = 27;
   public void setSize(int size) {
      size = size;  // ??? which size equals which size???
   }
}
```

So you've decided that—for overall readability—you want to give the parameter the same name as the instance variable its value is destined for, but how do you resolve the naming collision? Use the keyword this. The keyword this always, always, always refers to the object currently running. The following code shows this in action:

```
class Foo {
   int size = 27;
   public void setSize(int size) {
      this.size = size;   // this.size means the current object's
                          // instance variable, size. The size
                          // on the right is the parameter
   }
}
```

Array Declarations

In Java, arrays are objects that store multiple variables of the same type or variables that are all subclasses of the same type. Arrays can hold either primitives or object references, but an array itself will always be an object on the heap, even if the array is declared to hold primitive elements. In other words, there is no such thing as a primitive array, but you can make an array of primitives.

Arrays are efficient, but many times you'll want to use one of the Collection types from java.util (including `HashMap`, `ArrayList`, and `TreeSet`). Collection classes offer more flexible ways to access an object (for insertion, deletion, reading, and so on) and, unlike arrays, can expand or contract dynamically as you add or remove elements. There are Collection types for a wide range of needs. Do you need a fast sort? A group of objects with no duplicates? A way to access a name-value pair? Java provides a wide variety of Collection types to address these situations, and Chapter 6 discusses Collections in more detail.

Arrays are declared by stating the type of elements the array will hold (an object or a primitive), followed by square brackets to either side of the identifier.

Declaring an Array of Primitives:

```
int[] key;        // Square brackets before name (recommended)
int key [];       // Square brackets after name (legal but less
                  // readable)
```

Declaring an Array of Object References:

```
Thread[] threads;   // Recommended
Thread threads [];  // Legal but less readable
```

When declaring an array reference, you should always put the array brackets immediately after the declared type, rather than after the identifier (variable name). That way, anyone reading the code can easily tell that, for example, `key` is a reference to an `int` array object, not an `int` primitive.

We can also declare multidimensional arrays, which are, in fact, arrays of arrays. This can be done in the following manner:

```
String[][][] occupantName;
String[] managerName [];
```

The first example is a three-dimensional array (an array of arrays of arrays), and the second is a two-dimensional array. Notice in the second example, we have one square bracket before the variable name and one after. This is perfectly legal to the compiler, proving once again that just because it's legal doesn't mean it's right.

It is never legal to include the size of the array in your declaration. Yes, we know you can do that in some other languages, which is why you might see a question or two that include code similar to the following:

```
int[5] scores;
```

The preceding code won't compile. Remember, the JVM doesn't allocate space until you actually instantiate the array object. That's when size matters.

Final Variables

Declaring a variable with the `final` keyword makes it impossible to reassign that variable once it has been initialized with an explicit value (notice we said "explicit" rather than "default"). For primitives, this means that once the variable is assigned a value, the value can't be altered. For example, if you assign 10 to the `int` variable x, then x is going to stay 10, forever. So that's straightforward for primitives, but what does it mean to have a `final` object reference variable? A reference variable marked `final` can never be reassigned to refer to a different object. The data within the object can be modified, but the reference variable cannot be changed. In other words, a `final` reference still allows you to modify the state of the object it refers to, but you can't modify the reference variable to make it refer to a different object. Burn this in: there are no `final` objects, only `final` references.

We've now covered how the `final` modifier can be applied to classes, methods, and variables. Figure 1-8 highlights the key points and differences of the various applications of `final`.

Effect of `final` on variables, methods, and classes

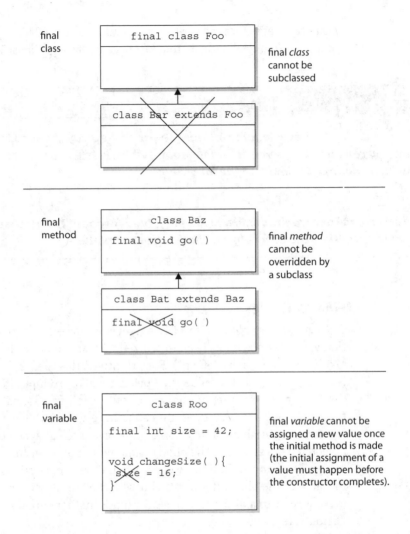

final class

final *class* cannot be subclassed

final method

final *method* cannot be overridden by a subclass

final variable

final *variable* cannot be assigned a new value once the initial method is made (the initial assignment of a value must happen before the constructor completes).

Transient Variables

If you mark an instance variable as `transient`, you're telling the JVM to skip (ignore) this variable when you attempt to serialize the object containing it. Serialization is one of Java's coolest features; it lets you save (sometimes called "flatten") an object by writing its state (in other words, the value of its instance variables) to a special type of I/O stream. With serialization, you can save an object to a file or even ship it over a wire for reinflating (deserializing) at the other end in another JVM. In Chapter 5, we'll do a deep dive into serialization.

Static Variables and Methods

Note: The discussion of static in this section DOES NOT include the new `static` interface method discussed earlier in this chapter. Don't you just love how the Java 8 folks reused important Java terms?

The `static` modifier is used to create variables and methods that will exist independently of any instances created for the class. All `static` members exist before you ever make a new instance of a class, and there will be only one copy of a `static` member regardless of the number of instances of that class. In other words, all instances of a given class share the same value for any given `static` variable. We'll cover `static` members in great detail in the next chapter.

Things you can mark as `static`:

- Methods
- Variables
- A class nested within another class, but not within a method
- Initialization blocks

Things you can't mark as `static`:

- Constructors (makes no sense; a constructor is used only to create instances)
- Classes (unless they are nested)
- Interfaces (unless they are nested)
- Method local inner classes (not on the OCA 8 exam)
- Inner class methods and instance variables (not on the OCA 8 exam)
- Local variables

CERTIFICATION OBJECTIVE

Declare and Use enums (OCP Objective 2.4)

2.4   Use enumerated types including methods, and constructors in an enum type.

Declaring enums

Java lets you restrict a variable to having one of only a few predefined values—in other words, one value from an enumerated list. (The items in the enumerated list are called, surprisingly, enums.)

Using enums can help reduce the bugs in your code. For instance, imagine you're creating a commercial-coffee-establishment application, and in your coffee shop application, you might want to restrict your CoffeeSize selections to BIG, HUGE, and OVERWHELMING. If you let an order for a LARGE or a GRANDE slip in, it might cause an error. enums to the rescue. With the following simple declaration, you can guarantee that the compiler will stop you from assigning anything to a CoffeeSize except BIG, HUGE, or OVERWHELMING:

```
enum CoffeeSize { BIG, HUGE, OVERWHELMING };
```

From then on, the only way to get a CoffeeSize will be with a statement something like this:

```
CoffeeSize cs = CoffeeSize.BIG;
```

It's not required that enum constants be in all caps, but, borrowing from the Oracle code convention that constants are named in caps, it's a good idea.

The basic components of an enum are its constants (that is, BIG, HUGE, and OVERWHELMING), although in a minute you'll see that there can be a lot more to an enum. enums can be declared as their own separate class or as a class member; however, they must not be declared within a method!

Here's an example declaring an enum *outside* a class:

```
enum CoffeeSize { BIG, HUGE, OVERWHELMING }  // this cannot be
                                             // private or protected
class Coffee {
   CoffeeSize size;
}
public class CoffeeTest1 {
   public static void main(String[] args) {
```

```
        Coffee drink = new Coffee();
        drink.size = CoffeeSize.BIG;            // enum outside class
    }
}
```

The preceding code can be part of a single file (or, in general, enum classes can exist in their own file like `CoffeeSize.java`). But remember, in this case the file must be named `CoffeeTest1.java` because that's the name of the `public` class in the file. The key point to remember is that an enum that isn't enclosed in a class can be declared with only the `public` or default modifier, just like a non-inner class. Here's an example of declaring an enum *inside* a class:

```
class Coffee2 {
    enum CoffeeSize {BIG, HUGE, OVERWHELMING }
    CoffeeSize size;
}
public class CoffeeTest2 {
    public static void main(String[] args) {
        Coffee2 drink = new Coffee2();
        drink.size = Coffee2.CoffeeSize.BIG;    // enclosing class
                                                // name required
    }
}
```

The key points to take away from these examples are that enums can be declared as their own class or enclosed in another class, and that the syntax for accessing an enum's members depends on where the enum was declared.

The following is NOT legal:

```
public class CoffeeTest1 {
    public static void main(String[] args) {
        enum CoffeeSize { BIG, HUGE, OVERWHELMING } // WRONG! Cannot
                                                    // declare enums
                                                    // in methods

        Coffee drink = new Coffee();
        drink.size = CoffeeSize.BIG;
    }
}
```

To make it more confusing for you, the Java language designers made it optional to put a semicolon at the end of the enum declaration (when no other declarations for this enum follow):

```
public class CoffeeTest1 {
    enum CoffeeSize { BIG, HUGE, OVERWHELMING }; // <--semicolon
                                                 // is optional here
    public static void main(String[] args) {
        Coffee drink = new Coffee();
        drink.size = CoffeeSize.BIG;
    }
}
```

So what gets created when you make an enum? The most important thing to remember is that enums are not `String`s or `int`s! Each of the enumerated `CoffeeSize` values is actually an instance of `CoffeeSize`. In other words, `BIG` is of type `CoffeeSize`. Think of an enum as a kind of class that looks something (but not exactly) like this:

```
// conceptual example of how you can think
// about enums
class CoffeeSize {
   public static final CoffeeSize BIG =
                              new CoffeeSize("BIG", 0);
   public static final CoffeeSize HUGE =
                              new CoffeeSize("HUGE", 1);
   public static final CoffeeSize OVERWHELMING =
                              new CoffeeSize("OVERWHELMING", 2);

   CoffeeSize(String enumName, int index) {
      // stuff here
   }
   public static void main(String[] args) {
     System.out.println(CoffeeSize.BIG);
   }
}
```

Notice how each of the enumerated values, `BIG`, `HUGE`, and `OVERWHELMING`, is an instance of type `CoffeeSize`. They're represented as `static` and `final`, which, in the Java world, is thought of as a constant. Also notice that each enum value knows its index or position—in other words, the order in which enum values are declared matters. You can think of the `CoffeeSize` enums as existing in an array of type `CoffeeSize`, and as you'll see in a later chapter, you can iterate through the values of an enum by invoking the `values()` method on any enum type.

Declaring Constructors, Methods, and Variables in an enum

Because an enum really is a special kind of class, you can do more than just list the enumerated constant values. You can add constructors, instance variables, methods, and something really strange known as a *constant specific class body*. To understand why you might need more in your enum, think about this scenario: Imagine you want to know the actual size, in ounces, that map to each of the three `CoffeeSize` constants. For example, you want to know that `BIG` is 8 ounces, `HUGE` is 10 ounces, and `OVERWHELMING` is a whopping 16 ounces.

You could make a lookup table using some other data structure, but that would be a poor design and hard to maintain. The simplest way is to treat your enum values (BIG, HUGE, and OVERWHELMING) as objects, each of which can have its own instance variables. Then you can assign those values at the time the enums are initialized by passing a value to the enum constructor. This takes a little explaining, but first look at the following code:

```
enum CoffeeSize {
    // 8, 10 & 16 are passed to the constructor
    BIG(8), HUGE(10), OVERWHELMING(16);
    CoffeeSize(int ounces) {    // constructor
        this.ounces = ounces;
    }

    private int ounces;          // an instance variable
    public int getOunces() {
        return ounces;
    }
}

class Coffee {
    CoffeeSize size;             // each instance of Coffee has an enum

    public static void main(String[] args) {
        Coffee drink1 = new Coffee();
        drink1.size = CoffeeSize.BIG;

        Coffee drink2 = new Coffee();
        drink2.size = CoffeeSize.OVERWHELMING;

        System.out.println(drink1.size.getOunces());  // prints 8
        for(CoffeeSize cs: CoffeeSize.values())
            System.out.println(cs + " " + cs.getOunces());
    }
}
```

which produces:

```
8
BIG 8
HUGE 10
OVERWHELMING 16
```

Note: Every enum has a static method, values(), that returns an array of the enum's values in the order they're declared.

The key points to remember about enum constructors are

- You can NEVER invoke an enum constructor directly. The enum constructor is invoked automatically with the arguments you define after the constant value. For example, BIG(8) invokes the CoffeeSize constructor that takes an int, passing the int literal 8 to the constructor. (Behind the scenes, of course, you can imagine that BIG is also passed to the constructor, but we don't have to know—or care—about the details.)

- You can define more than one argument to the constructor, and you can overload the enum constructors, just as you can overload a normal class constructor. We discuss constructors in much more detail in Chapter 2. To initialize a CoffeeSize with both the number of ounces and, say, a lid type, you'd pass two arguments to the constructor as BIG(8, "A"), which means you have a constructor in CoffeeSize that takes both an int and a String.

And, finally, you can define something really strange in an enum that looks like an anonymous inner class. It's known as a *constant specific class body,* and you use it when you need a particular constant to override a method defined in the enum.

Imagine this scenario: you want enums to have two methods—one for ounces and one for lid code (a String). Now imagine that most coffee sizes use the same lid code, "B", but the OVERWHELMING size uses type "A". You can define a getLidCode() method in the CoffeeSize enum that returns "B", but then you need a way to override it for OVERWHELMING. You don't want to do some hard-to-maintain if/then code in the getLidCode() method, so the best approach might be to somehow have the OVERWHELMING constant override the getLidCode() method.

This looks strange, but you need to understand the basic declaration rules:

```
enum CoffeeSize {
    BIG(8),
    HUGE(10),
    OVERWHELMING(16) {          // start a code block that defines
                                // the "body" for this constant

        public String getLidCode() {   // override the method
                                       // defined in CoffeeSize

        return "A";
      }
    };    // the semicolon is REQUIRED when more code follows
```

```
CoffeeSize(int ounces) {
  this.ounces = ounces;
}

private int ounces;

public int getOunces() {
  return ounces;
}
public String getLidCode() {       // this method is overridden
                                   // by the OVERWHELMING constant

  return "B";                      // the default value we want to
                                   // return for CoffeeSize constants

}
}
```

CERTIFICATION SUMMARY

After absorbing the material in this chapter, you should be familiar with some of the nuances of the Java language. You may also be experiencing confusion around why you ever wanted to take this exam in the first place. That's normal at this point. If you hear yourself asking, "What was I thinking?" just lie down until it passes. We would like to tell you that it gets easier...that this was the toughest chapter and it's all downhill from here.

Let's briefly review what you'll need to know for the exam:

You now have a good understanding of access control as it relates to classes, methods, and variables. You've looked at how access modifiers (public, protected, and private) define the access control of a class or member.

You learned that abstract classes can contain both abstract and nonabstract methods, but that if even a single method is marked abstract, the class must be marked abstract. Don't forget that a concrete (nonabstract) subclass of an abstract class must provide implementations for all the abstract methods of the superclass, but that an abstract class does not have to implement the abstract methods from its superclass. An abstract subclass can "pass the buck" to the first concrete subclass.

We covered interface implementation. Remember that interfaces can extend another interface (even multiple interfaces) and that any class that implements an interface must implement all methods from all the interfaces in the inheritance tree of the interface the class is implementing.

You've also looked at the other modifiers, including `static`, `final`, `abstract`, `synchronized`, and so on. You've learned how some modifiers can never be combined in a declaration, such as mixing `abstract` with either `final` or `private`.

Keep in mind that there are no `final` objects in Java, unless you go out of your way to develop your class to create "immutable objects," which is a design approach we'll discuss in Chapter 2. A reference variable marked `final` can never be changed, but the object it refers to can be modified. You've seen that `final` applied to methods means a subclass can't override them, and when applied to a class, the `final` class can't be subclassed.

Methods can be declared with a var-arg parameter (which can take from zero to many arguments of the declared type), but that you can have only one var-arg per method, and it must be the method's last parameter.

Remember that although the values of nonfinal variables can change, a reference variable's type can never change.

You also learned that arrays are objects that contain many variables of the same type. Arrays can also contain other arrays.

Remember what you've learned about `static` variables and methods, especially that `static` members are per-class as opposed to per-instance. Don't forget that a `static` method can't directly access an instance variable from the class it's in because it doesn't have an explicit reference to any particular instance of the class.

Finally, we covered `enums`. An `enum` is a safe and flexible way to implement constants. Because they are a special kind of class, `enums` can be declared very simply, or they can be quite complex—including such attributes as methods, variables, constructors, and a special type of inner class called a constant specific class body.

Before you hurl yourself at the practice test, spend some time with the following optimistically named "Two-Minute Drill." Come back to this particular drill often, as you work through this book and especially when you're doing that last-minute cramming. Because—and here's the advice you wished your mother had given you before you left for college—it's not what you know, it's when you know it.

For the exam, knowing what you can't do with the Java language is just as important as knowing what you can do. Give the sample questions a try! They're very similar to the difficulty and structure of the real exam questions and should be an eye opener for how difficult the exam can be. Don't worry if you get a lot of them wrong. If you find a topic that you are weak in, spend more time reviewing and studying. Many programmers need two or three serious passes through a chapter (or an individual objective) before they can answer the questions confidently.

TWO-MINUTE DRILL

Remember that in this chapter, when we talk about classes, we're referring to non-inner classes, in other words, *top-level* classes.

Class Access Modifiers (OCP Objective 1.2)

- ☐ There are three access modifiers: `public`, `protected`, and `private`.
- ☐ There are four access levels: `public`, `protected`, default, and `private`.
- ☐ Classes can have only `public` or default access.
- ☐ A class with default access can be seen only by classes within the same package.
- ☐ A class with `public` access can be seen by all classes from all packages.
- ☐ Class visibility revolves around whether code in one class can
  - ☐ Create an instance of another class
  - ☐ Extend (or subclass) another class
  - ☐ Access methods and variables of another class

Class Modifiers (Nonaccess) (OCP Objectives 1.2, 2.1, and 2.2)

- ☐ Classes can also be modified with `final`, `abstract`, or `strictfp`.
- ☐ A class cannot be both `final` and `abstract`.
- ☐ A `final` class cannot be subclassed.
- ☐ An `abstract` class cannot be instantiated.
- ☐ A single `abstract` method in a class means the whole class must be `abstract`.
- ☐ An `abstract` class can have both `abstract` and nonabstract methods.
- ☐ The first concrete class to extend an `abstract` class must implement all of its `abstract` methods.

Interface Implementation (OCP Objectives 1.2, 2.1, 2.2, and 2.5)

- ☐ Usually, interfaces are contracts for what a class can do, but they say nothing about the way in which the class must do it.
- ☐ Interfaces can be implemented by any class from any inheritance tree.
- ☐ Usually, an interface is like a 100-percent `abstract` class and is implicitly abstract whether or not you type the `abstract` modifier in the declaration.
- ☐ Usually interfaces have only `abstract` methods.
- ☐ Interface methods are, by default, `public` and usually `abstract`—explicit declaration of these modifiers is optional.
- ☐ Interfaces can have constants, which are always implicitly `public`, `static`, and `final`.
- ☐ Interface constant declarations of `public`, `static`, and `final` are optional in any combination.
- ☐ As of Java 8, interfaces can have concrete methods declared as either `default` or `static`.

Note: This section uses some concepts that we HAVE NOT yet covered. Don't panic: once you've read through the entire book, this section will make sense as a reference.

- ☐ A legal nonabstract implementing class has the following properties:
  - ☐ It provides concrete implementations for the interface's methods.
  - ☐ It must follow all legal override rules for the methods it implements.
  - ☐ It must not declare any new checked exceptions for an implementation method.
  - ☐ It must not declare any checked exceptions that are broader than the exceptions declared in the interface method.
  - ☐ It may declare runtime exceptions on any interface method implementation regardless of the interface declaration.
  - ☐ It must maintain the exact signature (allowing for covariant returns) and return type of the methods it implements (but does not have to declare the exceptions of the interface).
- ☐ A class implementing an interface can itself be `abstract`.

- ☐ An `abstract`-implementing class does not have to implement the interface methods (but the first concrete subclass must).
- ☐ A class can extend only one class (no multiple inheritance), but it can implement many interfaces.
- ☐ Interfaces can extend one or more other interfaces.
- ☐ Interfaces cannot extend a class or implement a class or interface.
- ☐ When taking the exam, verify that interface and class declarations are legal before verifying other code logic.

Member Access Modifiers (OCP Objective 1.2)

- ☐ Methods and instance (nonlocal) variables are known as "members."
- ☐ Members can use all four access levels: `public`, `protected`, default, and `private`.
- ☐ Member access comes in two forms:
  - ☐ Code in one class can access a member of another class.
  - ☐ A subclass can inherit a member of its superclass.
- ☐ If a class cannot be accessed, its members cannot be accessed.
- ☐ Determine class visibility before determining member visibility.
- ☐ `public` members can be accessed by all other classes, even in other packages.
- ☐ If a superclass member is `public`, the subclass inherits it—regardless of package.
- ☐ Members accessed without the dot operator (`.`) must belong to the same class.
- ☐ `this.` always refers to the currently executing object.
- ☐ `this.aMethod()` is the same as just invoking `aMethod()`.
- ☐ `private` members can be accessed only by code in the same class.
- ☐ `private` members are not visible to subclasses, so `private` members cannot be inherited.

- ☐ Default and `protected` members differ only when subclasses are involved:
  - ☐ Default members can be accessed only by classes in the same package.
  - ☐ `protected` members can be accessed by other classes in the same package, plus subclasses regardless of package.
  - ☐ `protected` = package + kids (kids meaning subclasses).
  - ☐ For subclasses outside the package, the `protected` member can be accessed only through inheritance; a subclass outside the package cannot access a `protected` member by using a reference to a superclass instance. (In other words, inheritance is the only mechanism for a subclass outside the package to access a `protected` member of its superclass.)
  - ☐ A `protected` member inherited by a subclass from another package is not accessible to any other class in the subclass package, except for the subclass's own subclasses.

Local Variables (OCP Objective 2.2)

- ☐ Local (method, automatic, or stack) variable declarations cannot have access modifiers.
- ☐ `final` is the only modifier available to local variables.
- ☐ Local variables don't get default values, so they must be initialized before use.

Other Modifiers—Members (OCP Objectives 2.1 and 2.2)

- ☐ `final` methods cannot be overridden in a subclass.
- ☐ `abstract` methods are declared with a signature, a return type, and an optional `throws` clause, but they are not implemented.
- ☐ `abstract` methods end in a semicolon—no curly braces.
- ☐ Three ways to spot a nonabstract method:
  - ☐ The method is not marked `abstract`.
  - ☐ The method has curly braces.
  - ☐ The method **MIGHT** have code between the curly braces.
- ☐ The first nonabstract (concrete) class to extend an `abstract` class must implement all of the `abstract` class's `abstract` methods.

- ☐ The `synchronized` modifier applies only to methods and code blocks.
- ☐ `synchronized` methods can have any access control and can also be marked `final`.
- ☐ `abstract` methods must be implemented by a subclass, so they must be inheritable. For that reason
    - ☐ `abstract` methods cannot be `private`.
    - ☐ `abstract` methods cannot be `final`.

Methods with var-args (OCP Objective 1.2)

- ☐ Methods can declare a parameter that accepts from zero to many arguments, a so-called var-arg method.
- ☐ A var-arg parameter is declared with the syntax `type... name`, for instance: `doStuff(int... x) { }`.
- ☐ A var-arg method can have only one var-arg parameter.
- ☐ In methods with normal parameters and a var-arg, the var-arg must come last.

Constructors (OCP Objectives 1.2 and 2.4)

- ☐ Constructors must have the same name as the class
- ☐ Constructors can have arguments, but they cannot have a return type.
- ☐ Constructors can use any access modifier (even `private`!).

Variable Declarations (OCP Objectives 2.1 and 2.2)

- ☐ Instance variables can
    - ☐ Have any access control
    - ☐ Be marked `final` or `transient`
- ☐ Instance variables can't be `abstract` or `synchronized`.
- ☐ It is legal to declare a local variable with the same name as an instance variable; this is called "shadowing."

☐ `final` variables have the following properties:

   ☐ `final` variables cannot be reassigned once assigned a value.

   ☐ `final` reference variables cannot refer to a different object once the object has been assigned to the `final` variable.

   ☐ `final` variables must be initialized before the constructor completes.

☐ There is no such thing as a `final` object. An object reference marked `final` does NOT mean the object itself can't change.

☐ The `transient` modifier applies only to instance variables.

☐ The `volatile` modifier applies only to instance variables.

Array Declarations (OCP Objective 1.2)

☐ Arrays can hold primitives or objects, but the array itself is always an object.

☐ When you declare an array, the brackets can be to the left or to the right of the variable name.

☐ It is never legal to include the size of an array in the declaration.

☐ An array of objects can hold any object that passes the IS-A (or `instanceof`) test for the declared type of the array. For example, if `Horse` extends `Animal`, then a `Horse` object can go into an `Animal` array.

Static Variables and Methods (OCP Objective 1.6)

☐ They are not tied to any particular instance of a class.

☐ No class instances are needed in order to use `static` members of the class or interface.

☐ There is only one copy of a `static` variable/class and all instances share it.

☐ `static` methods do not have direct access to nonstatic members.

enums (OCP Objective 2.4)

☐ An enum specifies a list of constant values assigned to a type.

☐ An enum is NOT a `String` or an `int`; an enum constant's type is the enum type. For example, `SUMMER` and `FALL` are of the enum type `Season`.

☐ An enum can be declared outside or inside a class, but NOT in a method.

☐ An enum declared outside a class must NOT be marked `static`, `final`, `abstract`, `protected`, or `private`.

☐ enums can contain constructors, methods, variables, and constant specific class bodies.

☐ enum constants can send arguments to the enum constructor, using the syntax `BIG(8)`, where the `int` literal 8 is passed to the enum constructor.

☐ enum constructors can have arguments and can be overloaded.

☐ enum constructors can NEVER be invoked directly in code. They are always called automatically when an enum is initialized.

☐ The semicolon at the end of an enum declaration is optional. These are legal:

```
enum Foo { ONE, TWO, THREE}
enum Foo { ONE, TWO, THREE};
```

☐ `MyEnum.values()` returns an array of `MyEnum`'s values.

SELF TEST

The following questions will help measure your understanding of the material presented in this chapter. Read all the choices carefully, as there may be more than one correct answer. Choose all correct answers for each question. Stay focused.

If you have a rough time with these at first, don't beat yourself up. Be positive. Repeat nice affirmations to yourself: "I am smart enough to understand enums," and "OK, so that other guy knows enums better than I do, but I bet he can't <insert something you *are* good at> like me."

1. Which are true? (Choose all that apply.)
   A. "X extends Y" is correct if and only if X is a class and Y is an interface
   B. "X extends Y" is correct if and only if X is an interface and Y is a class
   C. "X extends Y" is correct if X and Y are either both classes or both interfaces
   D. "X extends Y" is correct for all combinations of X and Y being classes and/or interfaces

2. Given:

```
class Rocket {
  private void blastOff() { System.out.print("bang "); }
}
public class Shuttle extends Rocket {
  public static void main(String[] args) {
    new Shuttle().go();
  }
  void go() {
    blastOff();
    // Rocket.blastOff();  // line A
  }
  private void blastOff() { System.out.print("sh-bang "); }
}
```

Which are true? (Choose all that apply.)
A. As the code stands, the output is bang
B. As the code stands, the output is sh-bang
C. As the code stands, compilation fails
D. If line A is uncommented, the output is bang bang
E. If line A is uncommented, the output is sh-bang bang
F. If line A is uncommented, compilation fails

3. Given:

```
1. enum Animals {
2.    DOG("woof"), CAT("meow"), FISH("burble");
3.    String sound;
4.    Animals(String s) { sound = s; }
5. }
6. class TestEnum {
7.    static Animals a;
8.    public static void main(String[] args) {
9.      System.out.println(a.DOG.sound + " " + a.FISH.sound);
10.   }
11. }
```

What is the result?

A. `woof burble`

B. Multiple compilation errors

C. Compilation fails due to an error on line 2

D. Compilation fails due to an error on line 3

E. Compilation fails due to an error on line 4

F. Compilation fails due to an error on line 9

4. Given two files:

```
1. package pkgA;
2. public class Foo {
3. int a = 5;
4. protected int b = 6;
5. public int c = 7;
6. }
```

```
3. package pkgB;
4. import pkgA.*;
5. public class Baz {
6.    public static void main(String[] args) {
7.      Foo f = new Foo();
8.      System.out.print(" " + f.a);
9.      System.out.print(" " + f.b);
10.     System.out.println(" " + f.c);
11.   }
12. }
```

What is the result? (Choose all that apply.)

A. `5 6 7`

B. 5 followed by an exception

C. Compilation fails with an error on line 7

D. Compilation fails with an error on line 8

E. Compilation fails with an error on line 9

F. Compilation fails with an error on line 10

5. Given:

```
1. public class Electronic implements Device
     { public void doIt() { } }
2.
3. abstract class Phone1 extends Electronic { }
4.
5. abstract class Phone2 extends Electronic
     { public void doIt(int x) { } }
6.
7. class Phone3 extends Electronic implements Device
     { public void doStuff() { } }
8.
9. interface Device { public void doIt(); }
```

What is the result? (Choose all that apply.)

A. Compilation succeeds

B. Compilation fails with an error on line 1

C. Compilation fails with an error on line 3

D. Compilation fails with an error on line 5

E. Compilation fails with an error on line 7

F. Compilation fails with an error on line 9

6. Given:

```
3. public class TestDays {
4.    public enum Days { MON, TUE, WED };
5.    public static void main(String[] args) {
6.       for(Days d : Days.values() )
7.          ;
8.       Days [] d2 = Days.values();
9.       System.out.println(d2[2]);
10.   }
11. }
```

What is the result? (Choose all that apply.)

A. TUE

B. WED

C. The output is unpredictable

D. Compilation fails due to an error on line 4

E. Compilation fails due to an error on line 6

F. Compilation fails due to an error on line 8

G. Compilation fails due to an error on line 9

7. Given:

```
 4. public class Frodo extends Hobbit {
 5.    public static void main(String[] args) {
 6.       int myGold = 7;
 7.       System.out.println(countGold(myGold, 6));
 8.    }
 9. }
10. class Hobbit {
11.    int countGold(int x, int y) { return x + y; }
12. }
```

What is the result?

A. 13

B. Compilation fails due to multiple errors

C. Compilation fails due to an error on line 6

D. Compilation fails due to an error on line 7

E. Compilation fails due to an error on line 11

8. Given:

```
interface Gadget {
  void doStuff();
}
abstract class Electronic {
  void getPower() { System.out.print("plug in "); }
}
public class Tablet extends Electronic implements Gadget {
  void doStuff() { System.out.print("show book "); }
  public static void main(String[] args) {
    new Tablet().getPower();
    new Tablet().doStuff();
  }
}
```

Which are true? (Choose all that apply.)

A. The class Tablet will NOT compile

B. The interface Gadget will NOT compile

C. The output will be plug in show book

D. The abstract class Electronic will NOT compile

E. The class Tablet CANNOT both extend and implement

9. Given:

```
interface MyInterface {
   // insert code here
   }
```

Which lines of code—inserted independently at `insert code here`—will compile? (Choose all that apply.)

A. `public static m1() {;}`

B. `default void m2() {;}`

C. `abstract int m3();`

D. `final short m4() {return 5;}`

E. `default long m5();`

F. `static void m6() {;}`

SELF TEST ANSWERS

1. ☑ **C** is correct.
   ☒ **A** is incorrect because classes implement interfaces, they don't extend them. **B** is incorrect because interfaces only "inherit from" other interfaces. **D** is incorrect based on the preceding rules. (OCP Objectives 1.2 and 2.5)

2. ☑ **B** and **F** are correct. Since `Rocket.blastOff()` is `private`, it can't be overridden, and it is invisible to class `Shuttle`.
   ☒ **A, C, D,** and **E** are incorrect based on the above. (OCP Objective 1.2 and 1.3)

3. ☑ **A** is correct; enums can have constructors and variables.
   ☒ **B, C, D, E,** and **F** are incorrect; these lines all use correct syntax. (OCP Objective 2.4)

4. ☑ **D** and **E** are correct. Variable a has default access, so it cannot be accessed from outside the package. Variable b has protected access in `pkgA`.
   ☒ **A, B, C,** and **F** are incorrect based on the above information. (OCP Objective 1.2)

5. ☑ **A** is correct; all of these are legal declarations.
   ☒ **B, C, D, E,** and **F** are incorrect based on the above information. (OCP Objectives 1.2, 2.1, and 2.5)

6. ☑ **B** is correct. Every enum comes with a `static values()` method that returns an array of the enum's values in the order in which they are declared in the enum.
   ☒ **A, C, D, E, F,** and **G** are incorrect based on the above information. (OCP Objectives 1.6 and 2.4)

7. ☑ **D** is correct. The `countGold()` method cannot be invoked from a static context.
   ☒ **A, B, C,** and **E** are incorrect based on the above information. (OCP Objective 1.6)

8. ☑ **A** is correct. By default, an interface's methods are `public` so the `Tablet.doStuff` method must be public, too. The rest of the code is valid.
   ☒ **B, C, D,** and **E** are incorrect based on the above. (OCP Objectives 1.2 and 2.5)

9. ☑ **B, C,** and **F** are correct. As of Java 8, interfaces can have `default` and `static` methods.
   ☒ **A, D,** and **E** are incorrect. **A** has no return type; **D** cannot have a method body; and **E** needs a method body. (OCP Objective 2.5)

2
Object Orientation

This chapter will prepare you for many of the object-oriented objectives and questions you'll encounter on the exam. As with Chapter 1, most of this chapter is a refresher of some of the topics you learned while studying for the OCA 8 exam. Apart from the discussions of the @Override annotation, the singleton pattern, and immutable classes, if you feel you mastered the OCA 8 section 6 objectives (Working with Methods and Encapsulation) and the section 7 objectives (Working with Inheritance) while studying for the OCA 8, you might be able to skip this chapter. If you're not sure, try your hand at the Self Test at the end of the chapter.

CERTIFICATION OBJECTIVE

Encapsulation (OCP Objective 1.1)

1.1   Implement encapsulation.

Imagine you wrote the code for a class and another dozen programmers from your company all wrote programs that used your class. Now imagine that later on, you didn't like the way the class behaved, because some of its instance variables were being set (by the other programmers from within their code) to values you hadn't anticipated. *Their* code brought out errors in *your* code. (Relax, this is just hypothetical.) Well, it is a Java program, so you should be able to ship out a newer version of the class, which they could replace in their programs without changing any of their own code.

This scenario highlights two of the promises/benefits of an object-oriented (OO) language: flexibility and maintainability. But those benefits don't come automatically. You have to do something. You have to write your classes and code in a way that supports flexibility and maintainability. So what if Java supports OO? It can't design your code for you. For example, imagine you made your class with `public` instance variables, and those other programmers were setting the instance variables directly, as the following code demonstrates:

```
public class BadOO {
   public int size;
   public int weight;
   ...
```

```
  }
public class ExploitBadOO {
  public static void main (String [] args) {
    BadOO b = new BadOO();
    b.size = -5; // Legal but bad!!
  }
}
```

And now you're in trouble. How are you going to change the class in a way that lets you handle the issues that come up when somebody changes the `size` variable to a value that causes problems? Your only choice is to go back in and write method code for adjusting `size` (a `setSize(int a)` method, for example) and then insulate the `size` variable with, say, a private access modifier. But as soon as you make that change to your code, you break everyone else's!

The ability to make changes in your implementation code without breaking the code of others who use your code is a key benefit of encapsulation. You want to hide implementation details behind a public programming interface. By *interface,* we mean the set of accessible methods your code makes available for other code to call—in other words, your code's API. By hiding implementation details, you can rework your method code (perhaps also altering the way variables are used by your class) without forcing a change in the code that calls your changed method.

If you want maintainability, flexibility, and extensibility (and, of course, you do), your design must include encapsulation. How do you do that?

- Keep instance variables hidden (with an access modifier, often `private`).

- Make `public` accessor methods, and force calling code to use those methods rather than directly accessing the instance variable. These so-called accessor methods allow users of your class to **set** a variable's value or **get** a variable's value.

- For these accessor methods, use the most common naming convention of `set<SomeProperty>` and `get<SomeProperty>`.

Figure 2-1 illustrates the idea that encapsulation forces callers of our code to go through methods rather than accessing variables directly.

We call the access methods *getters* and *setters,* although some prefer the fancier terms *accessors* and *mutators.* (Personally, we don't like the word "mutate.") Regardless of what you call them, they're methods that other programmers must

FIGURE 2-1 The nature of encapsulation

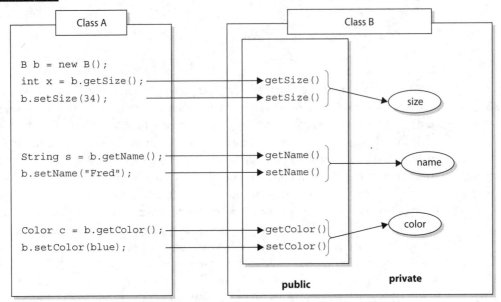

Class A cannot access Class B instance variable data without going through getter and setter methods. Data is marked private; only the accessor methods are public.

go through in order to access your instance variables. They look simple, and you've probably been using them forever:

```
public class Box {
    // hide the instance variable; only an instance
    // of Box can access it
    private int size;
    // Provide public getters and setters
    public int getSize() {
        return size;
    }
}
```

```
public void setSize(int newSize) {
  size = newSize;
}
}
```

Wait a minute. How useful is the previous code? It doesn't even do any validation or processing. What benefit can there be from having getters and setters that add no functionality? The point is, you can change your mind later and add more code to your methods without breaking your API. Even if today you don't think you really need validation or processing of the data, good OO design dictates that you plan for the future. To be safe, force calling code to go through your methods rather than going directly to instance variables. *Always*. Then you're free to rework your method implementations later, without risking the wrath of those dozen programmers who know where you live.

exam
ⓦatch
Look out for code that appears to be asking about the behavior of a method, when the problem is actually a lack of encapsulation. Look at the following example, and see if you can figure out what's going on:

```
class Foo {
  public int left = 9;
  public int right = 3;
  public void setLeft(int leftNum) {
    left = leftNum;
    right = leftNum/3;
  }
  // lots of complex test code here
}
```

Now consider this question: Is the value of right always going to be one-third the value of left? It looks like it will, until you realize that users of the Foo *class don't need to use the* setLeft() *method! They can simply go straight to the instance variables and change them to any arbitrary* int *value.*

CERTIFICATION OBJECTIVE

Inheritance and Polymorphism (OCP Objectives 1.2 and 1.3)

1.2   Implement inheritance including visibility modifiers and composition.
1.3   Implement polymorphism.

Inheritance is everywhere in Java. It's safe to say that it's almost (almost?) impossible to write even the tiniest Java program without using inheritance. To explore this topic, we're going to use the `instanceof` operator. This code:

```
class Test {
  public static void main(String [] args) {
    Test t1 = new Test();
    Test t2 = new Test();
    if (!t1.equals(t2))
      System.out.println("they're not equal");
    if (t1 instanceof Object)
      System.out.println("t1's an Object");
  }
}
```

produces this output:

```
they're not equal
t1's an Object
```

Where did that `equals` method come from? The reference variable `t1` is of type `Test`, and there's no `equals` method in the `Test` class. Or is there? The second `if` test asks whether `t1` is an instance of class `Object`, and because it *is* (more on that soon), the `if` test succeeds.

Hold on...how can `t1` be an instance of type `Object`, when we just said it was of type `Test`? I'm sure you're way ahead of us here, but it turns out that every class in Java is a subclass of class `Object` (except, of course, class `Object` itself). In other words, every class you'll ever use or ever write will inherit from class `Object`. You'll always have an `equals` method, `notify` and `wait` methods, and others available to use. Whenever you create a class, you automatically inherit all of class `Object`'s methods.

Why? Let's look at that `equals` method, for instance. Java's creators correctly assumed that it would be common for Java programmers to want to compare instances of their classes to check for equality. If class `Object` didn't have an `equals` method, you'd have to write one yourself—you and every other Java programmer. That one `equals` method has been inherited billions of times. (To be fair, `equals` has also been *overridden* billions of times, but we're getting ahead of ourselves.)

The Evolution of Inheritance

Until Java 8, when the topic of inheritance was discussed, it usually revolved around subclasses inheriting methods from their superclasses. While this simplification was never perfectly correct, it became less correct with the new features available in Java 8. As Table 2-1 shows, it's now possible to inherit concrete methods from interfaces. This is a big change. For the rest of the chapter, when we talk about inheritance generally, we will tend to use the terms "subtypes" and "supertypes" to acknowledge that both classes and interfaces need to be accounted for. We will tend to use the terms "subclass" and "superclass" when we're discussing a specific example that's under discussion. Inheritance is a key aspect of most of the topics we'll be discussing in this chapter, so be prepared for LOTS of discussion about the interactions between supertypes and subtypes!

As you study Table 2-1, you'll notice that, as of Java 8, interfaces can contain two types of concrete methods: `static` and `default`. We'll discuss these important additions later in this chapter.

Table 2-1 summarizes the elements of classes and interfaces relative to inheritance.

TABLE 2-1   Inheritable Elements of Classes and Interfaces

Elements of Types	Classes	Interfaces
Instance variables	Yes	Not applicable
Static variables	Yes	Only constants
Abstract methods	Yes	Yes
Instance methods	Yes	Java 8, default methods
Static methods	Yes	Java 8, inherited no, accessible yes
Constructors	No	Not applicable
Initialization blocks	No	Not applicable

For the exam, you'll need to know that you can create inheritance relationships in Java by *extending* a class or by implementing an interface. It's also important to understand that the two most common reasons to use inheritance are

■ To promote code reuse

■ To use polymorphism

Let's start with reuse. A common design approach is to create a fairly generic version of a class with the intention of creating more specialized subclasses that inherit from it. For example:

```
class GameShape {
  public void displayShape() {
    System.out.println("displaying shape");
  }
  // more code
}

class PlayerPiece extends GameShape {
  public void movePiece() {
    System.out.println("moving game piece");
  }
  // more code
}


public class TestShapes {
  public static void main (String[] args) {
    PlayerPiece shape = new PlayerPiece();
    shape.displayShape();
    shape.movePiece();
  }
}
```

outputs:

```
displaying shape
moving game piece
```

Notice that the `PlayerPiece` class inherits the generic `displayShape()` method from the less-specialized class `GameShape` and also adds its own method, `movePiece()`. Code reuse through inheritance means that methods with generic functionality—such as `displayShape()`, which could apply to a wide range of different kinds of shapes in a game—don't have to be reimplemented. That means all specialized subclasses of `GameShape` are guaranteed to have the capabilities of the more general superclass. You don't want to have to rewrite the `displayShape()` code in each of your specialized components of an online game.

But you knew that. You've experienced the pain of duplicate code when you make a change in one place and have to track down all the other places where that same (or very similar) code exists.

The second (and related) use of inheritance is to allow your classes to be accessed polymorphically—a capability provided by interfaces as well, but we'll get to that in a minute. Let's say that you have a `GameLauncher` class that wants to loop through a list of different kinds of `GameShape` objects and invoke `displayShape()` on each of them. At the time you write this class, you don't know every possible kind of `GameShape` subclass that anyone else will ever write. And you sure don't want to have to redo *your* code just because somebody decided to build a dice shape six months later.

The beautiful thing about polymorphism ("many forms") is that you can treat any *subclass* of `GameShape` as a `GameShape`. In other words, you can write code in your `GameLauncher` class that says, "I don't care what kind of object you are as long as you inherit from (extend) `GameShape`. And as far as I'm concerned, if you extend `GameShape`, then you've definitely got a `displayShape()` method, so I know I can call it."

Imagine we now have two specialized subclasses that extend the more generic GameShape class, `PlayerPiece` and `TilePiece`:

```
class GameShape {
  public void displayShape() {
    System.out.println("displaying shape");
  }
  // more code
}

class PlayerPiece extends GameShape {
  public void movePiece() {
    System.out.println("moving game piece");
  }
  // more code
}

class TilePiece extends GameShape {
  public void getAdjacent() {
    System.out.println("getting adjacent tiles");
  }
  // more code
}
```

Now imagine a test class has a method with a declared argument type of
GameShape, which means it can take any kind of GameShape. In other words,
any subclass of GameShape can be passed to a method with an argument of type
GameShape. This code:

```
public class TestShapes {
  public static void main (String[] args) {
    PlayerPiece player = new PlayerPiece();
    TilePiece tile = new TilePiece();
    doShapes(player);
    doShapes(tile);
  }

  public static void doShapes(GameShape shape) {
    shape.displayShape();
  }
}
```

outputs:

```
displaying shape
displaying shape
```

The key point is that the doShapes() method is declared with a GameShape
argument but can be passed any subtype (in this example, a subclass) of
GameShape. The method can then invoke any method of GameShape, without
any concern for the actual runtime class type of the object passed to the method.
There are implications, though. The doShapes() method knows only that the
objects are a type of GameShape since that's how the parameter is declared. And
using a reference variable declared as type GameShape—regardless of whether the
variable is a method parameter, local variable, or instance variable—means that
only the methods of GameShape can be invoked on it. The methods you can call
on a reference are totally dependent on the *declared* type of the variable, no matter
what the actual object is, that the reference is referring to. That means you can't use
a GameShape variable to call, say, the getAdjacent() method even if the object
passed in *is* of type TilePiece. (We'll see this again when we look at interfaces.)

IS-A and HAS-A Relationships

Note: As of early 2018, the OCP 8 exam doesn't mention IS-A and HAS-A
relationships explicitly, but inheritance and polymorphism are all about IS-A
relationships, and composition is another way of saying "HAS-A."

IS-A

In OO, the concept of IS-A is based on inheritance (or interface implementation). IS-A is a way of saying, "This thing is a type of that thing." For example, a Mustang is a type of Horse, so in OO terms we can say, "Mustang IS-A Horse." Subaru IS-A Car. Broccoli IS-A Vegetable (not a very fun one, but it still counts). You express the IS-A relationship in Java through the keywords extends (for *class* inheritance) and implements (for *interface* implementation).

```
public class Car {
  // Cool Car code goes here
}

public class Subaru extends Car {
  // Important Subaru-specific stuff goes here
  // Don't forget Subaru inherits accessible Car members which
  // can include both methods and variables.
}
```

A Car is a type of Vehicle, so the inheritance tree might start from the Vehicle class as follows:

```
public class Vehicle { ... }
public class Car extends Vehicle { ... }
public class Subaru extends Car { ... }
```

In OO terms, you can say the following:

Vehicle is a superclass of Car.
Car is a subclass of Vehicle.
Car is a superclass of Subaru.
Subaru is a subclass of Vehicle.
Car inherits from Vehicle.
Subaru inherits from both Vehicle and Car.
Subaru is derived from Car.
Car is derived from Vehicle.
Subaru is derived from Vehicle.
Subaru is a subtype of both Vehicle and Car.

Returning to our IS-A relationship, the following statements are true:

"Car extends Vehicle" means "Car IS-A Vehicle."
"Subaru extends Car" means "Subaru IS-A Car."

And we can also say:

"Subaru IS-A Vehicle"

because a class is said to be "a type of" anything further up in its inheritance tree. If the expression (`Foo instanceof Bar`) is `true`, then class `Foo` IS-A `Bar`, even if `Foo` doesn't directly extend `Bar`, but instead extends some other class that is a subclass of `Bar`. Figure 2-2 illustrates the inheritance tree for `Vehicle`, `Car`, and `Subaru`. The arrows move from the subclass to the superclass. In other words, a class's arrow points toward the class from which it extends.

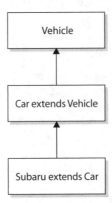

HAS-A

HAS-A relationships are based on use, rather than inheritance. In other words, class A HAS-A B if code in class A has a reference to an instance of class B. For example, you can say the following:

A `Horse` IS-A `Animal`. A `Horse` HAS-A `Halter`.

The code might look like this:

```
public class Animal { }
public class Horse extends Animal {
   private Halter myHalter;
}
```

In this code, the `Horse` class has an instance variable of type `Halter` (a halter is a piece of gear you might have if you have a horse), so you can say that a "`Horse` HAS-A `Halter`." In other words, `Horse` has a reference to a `Halter`. `Horse` code can use that `Halter` reference to invoke methods on the `Halter` and get `Halter` behavior without having `Halter`-related code (methods) in the `Horse` class itself. Figure 2-3 illustrates the HAS-A relationship between `Horse` and `Halter`.

FIGURE 2-3

HAS-A
relationship
between Horse
and Halter

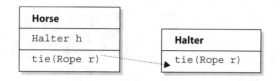

Horse class has a Halter, because Horse
declares an instance variable of type Halter.
When code invokes tie() on a Horse instance,
the Horse invokes tie() on the Horse
object's Halter instance variable.

HAS-A relationships allow you to design classes that follow good OO practices
by not having monolithic classes that do a gazillion different things. Classes
(and their resulting objects) should be specialists. As our friend Andrew says,
"Specialized classes can actually help reduce bugs." The more specialized the class,
the more likely it is that you can reuse the class in other applications. If you put all
the Halter-related code directly into the Horse class, you'll end up duplicating
code in the Cow class, UnpaidIntern class, and any other class that might need
Halter behavior. By keeping the Halter code in a separate specialized Halter
class, you have the chance to reuse the Halter class in multiple applications.

Users of the Horse class (that is, code that calls methods on a Horse instance)
think that the Horse class has Halter behavior. The Horse class might have a
tie(LeadRope rope) method, for example. Users of the Horse class should
never have to know that when they invoke the tie() method, the Horse object
turns around and delegates the call to its Halter class by invoking myHalter
.tie(rope). The scenario just described might look like this:

```
public class Horse extends Animal {
  private Halter myHalter = new Halter();
  public void tie(LeadRope rope) {
    myHalter.tie(rope);   // Delegate tie behavior to the
                          // Halter object
  }
}
public class Halter {
  public void tie(LeadRope aRope) {
    // Do the actual tie work here
  }
}
```

FROM THE CLASSROOM

Object-Oriented Design

IS-A and HAS-A relationships and encapsulation are just the tip of the iceberg when it comes to OO design. Many books and graduate theses have been dedicated to this topic. The reason for the emphasis on proper design is simple: money. The cost to deliver a software application has been estimated to be as much as ten times more expensive for poorly designed programs.

Even the best OO designers (often called "architects") make mistakes. It is difficult to visualize the relationships between hundreds, or even thousands, of classes. When mistakes are discovered during the implementation (code writing) phase of a project, the amount of code that must be rewritten can sometimes mean programming teams have to start over from scratch.

The software industry has evolved to aid the designer. Visual object modeling languages, such as the Unified Modeling Language (UML), allow designers to design and easily modify classes without having to write code

first because OO components are represented graphically. This allows designers to create a map of the class relationships and helps them recognize errors before coding begins. Another innovation in OO design is design patterns. Designers noticed that many OO designs were applied consistently from project to project and that it was useful to apply the same designs because it reduced the potential to introduce new design errors. OO designers then started to share these designs with each other. Now there are many catalogs of these design patterns both on the Internet and in book form.

Although passing the Java certification exam does not require you to understand OO design this thoroughly, hopefully this background information will help you better appreciate why the test writers chose to (tacitly) include encapsulation and IS-A and HAS-A relationships on the exam.

—Jonathan Meeks,
Sun Certified Java Programmer

In OO, we don't want callers to worry about which class or object is actually doing the real work. To make that happen, the `Horse` class hides implementation details from `Horse` users. `Horse` users ask the `Horse` object to do things (in this case, tie itself up), and the `Horse` will either do it or, as in this example, ask something else (like perhaps an inherited `Animal` class method) to do it. To the caller, though, it always appears that the `Horse` object takes care of itself. Users of a `Horse` should not even need to know that there is such a thing as a `Halter` class.

Polymorphism (OCP Objective 1.3)

1.3   Implement polymorphism.

Remember, any Java object that can pass more than one IS-A test can be considered polymorphic. Other than objects of type `Object`, *all* Java objects are polymorphic in that they pass the IS-A test for their own type and for class `Object`.

Remember, too, that the only way to access an object is through a reference variable. There are a few key things you should know about references:

- A reference variable can be of only one type, and once declared, that type can never be changed (although the object it references can change).
- A reference is a variable, so it can be reassigned to other objects (unless the reference is declared `final`).
- A reference variable's type determines the methods that can be invoked on the object the variable is referencing.
- A reference variable can refer to any object of the same type as the declared reference, or—this is the big one—**it can refer to any** *subtype* **of the declared type!**
- A reference variable can be declared as a class type or an interface type. If the variable is declared as an interface type, it can reference any object of any class that *implements* the interface.

Earlier we created a `GameShape` class that was extended by two other classes, `PlayerPiece` and `TilePiece`. Now imagine you want to animate some of the shapes on the gameboard. But not *all* shapes are able to be animated, so what do you do with class inheritance?

Could we create a class with an `animate()` method and have only *some* of the `GameShape` subclasses inherit from that class? If we can, then we could have `PlayerPiece`, for example, extend *both* the `GameShape` class and `Animatable` class, whereas the `TilePiece` would extend only `GameShape`. But no, this won't work! Java supports only single class inheritance! That means a class can have only one immediate superclass. In other words, if `PlayerPiece` is a class, there is no way to say something like this:

```
class PlayerPiece extends GameShape, Animatable { // NO!
  // more code
}
```

A *class* cannot *extend* more than one class: that means one parent per class. A class *can* have multiple ancestors, however, because class B could extend class A, and class C could extend class B, and so on. So any given class might have multiple classes up its inheritance tree, but that's not the same as saying a class directly extends two classes.

on the **job**

Some languages (such as C++) allow a class to extend more than one other class. This capability is known as "multiple inheritance." The reason that Java's creators chose not to allow multiple class inheritance is that it can become quite messy. In a nutshell, the problem is that if a class extended two other classes, and both superclasses had, say, a doStuff() method, which version of doStuff() would the subclass inherit? This issue can lead to a scenario sometimes called the "Deadly Diamond of Death," because of the shape of the class diagram that can be created in a multiple inheritance design. The diamond is formed when classes B and C both extend A and both B and C inherit a method from A. If class D extends both B and C, and both B and C have overridden the method in A, class D has, in theory, inherited two different implementations of the same method. Drawn as a class diagram, the shape of the four classes looks like a diamond.

e x a m

ⓦa t c h *To reiterate, as of Java 8, interfaces can have concrete methods (marked `default` or `static` methods). This allows for a form of multiple inheritance, which we'll discuss later in the chapter.*

So if that doesn't work, what else could you do? You could simply put the `animate()` code in `GameShape`, and then disable the method in classes that can't be animated. But that's a bad design choice for many reasons—it's more error-prone; it makes the `GameShape` class less cohesive; and it means the `GameShape` API "advertises" that all shapes can be animated when, in fact, that's not true since only some of the `GameShape` subclasses will be able to run the `animate()` method successfully.

So what *else* could you do? You already know the answer—create an
`Animatable` *interface* and have only the `GameShape` subclasses that can be
animated implement that interface. Here's the interface:

```
public interface Animatable {
  public void animate();
}
```

And here's the modified `PlayerPiece` class that implements the interface:

```
class PlayerPiece extends GameShape implements Animatable {
  public void movePiece() {
    System.out.println("moving game piece");
  }
  public void animate() {
    System.out.println("animating...");
  }
  // more code
}
```

So now we have a `PlayerPiece` that passes the IS-A test for both the
GameShape class and the `Animatable` interface. That means a `PlayerPiece`
can be treated polymorphically as one of four things at any given time, depending
on the declared type of the reference variable:

- An `Object` (since any object inherits from `Object`)
- A `GameShape` (since `PlayerPiece` extends `GameShape`)
- A `PlayerPiece` (since that's what it really is)
- An `Animatable` (since `PlayerPiece` implements `Animatable`)

The following are all legal declarations. Look closely:

```
PlayerPiece player = new PlayerPiece();
Object o = player;
GameShape shape = player;
Animatable mover = player;
```

There's only one object here—an instance of type `PlayerPiece`—but there
are four different types of reference variables, all referring to that one object on
the heap. Pop quiz: Which of the preceding reference variables can invoke the
`displayShape()` method? Hint: Only two of the four declarations can be used to
invoke the `displayShape()` method.

Remember that method invocations allowed by the compiler are based solely
on the declared type of the reference, regardless of the object type. So looking

at the four reference types again—Object, GameShape, PlayerPiece, and
Animatable—which of these four types know about the displayShape()
method?

You guessed it—both the GameShape class and the PlayerPiece class are
known (by the compiler) to have a displayShape() method, so either of those
reference types can be used to invoke displayShape(). Remember that to the
compiler, a PlayerPiece IS-A GameShape, so the compiler says, "I see that the
declared type is PlayerPiece, and since PlayerPiece extends GameShape,
that means PlayerPiece inherited the displayShape() method. Therefore,
PlayerPiece can be used to invoke the displayShape() method."

Which methods can be invoked when the PlayerPiece object is being
referred to using a reference declared as type Animatable? Only the animate()
method. Of course, the cool thing here is that any class from any inheritance tree
can also implement Animatable, so that means if you have a method with an
argument declared as type Animatable, you can pass in PlayerPiece objects,
SpinningLogo objects, and anything else that's an instance of a class that
implements Animatable. And you can use that parameter (of type Animatable)
to invoke the animate() method but not the displayShape() method (which
it might not even have), or anything other than what is known to the compiler
based on the reference type. The compiler always knows, though, that you can
invoke the methods of class Object on any object, so those are safe to call
regardless of the reference—class or interface—used to refer to the object.

We've left out one big part of all this, which is that even though the compiler only
knows about the declared reference type, the Java Virtual Machine (JVM) at runtime
knows what the object really is. And that means even if the PlayerPiece object's
displayShape() method is called using a GameShape reference variable, if the
PlayerPiece overrides the displayShape() method, the JVM will invoke
the PlayerPiece version! The JVM looks at the real object at the other end of
the reference, "sees" that it has overridden the method of the declared reference
variable type, and invokes the method of the object's actual class. But there is one
other thing to keep in mind:

> **Polymorphic method invocations apply only to *instance methods*. You can
> always refer to an object with a more general reference variable type (a
> superclass or interface), but at runtime, the ONLY things that are dynami-
> cally selected based on the actual *object* (rather than the *reference* type)
> are instance methods. Not *static* methods. Not *variables*. Only overridden
> instance methods are dynamically invoked based on the real object's type.**

Because this definition depends on a clear understanding of overriding and the distinction between static methods and instance methods, we'll cover those later in the chapter.

Overriding/Overloading (OCP Objectives 1.2, 1.3, and 2.5)

1.2   Implement inheritance including visibility modifiers and composition.
1.3   Implement polymorphism.
2.5   Develop code that declares, implements and/or extends interfaces and use the @Override annotation.

The exam will use overridden and overloaded methods on many, many questions. These two concepts are often confused (perhaps because they have similar names?), but each has its own unique and complex set of rules. It's important to get really clear about which "over" uses which rules!

Overridden Methods

Any time a type inherits a method from a supertype, you have the opportunity to override the method (unless, as you learned earlier, the method is marked `final`). The key benefit of overriding is the ability to define behavior that's specific to a particular subtype. The following example demonstrates a `Horse` subclass of `Animal` overriding the `Animal` version of the `eat()` method:

```
public class Animal {
  public void eat() {
    System.out.println("Generic Animal Eating Generically");
  }
}
class Horse extends Animal {
  public void eat() {
    System.out.println("Horse eating hay, oats, "
                       + "and horse treats");
  }
}
```

For abstract methods, you inherit from a supertype; you have no choice: You *must* implement the method in the subtype ***unless the subtype is also abstract.*** Abstract methods must be *implemented* by the first concrete subclass, but this is a lot like saying the concrete subclass *overrides* the abstract methods of the supertype(s). So you could think of abstract methods as methods you're forced to override—eventually.

The `Animal` class creator might have decided that for the purposes of polymorphism, all `Animal` subtypes should have an `eat()` method defined in a unique way. Polymorphically, when an `Animal` reference refers not to an `Animal` instance but to an `Animal` subclass instance, the caller should be able to invoke `eat()` on the `Animal` reference; however, the actual runtime object (say, a `Horse` instance) will run its own specific `eat()` method. Marking the `eat()` method abstract is the `Animal` programmer's way of saying to all subclass developers, "It doesn't make any sense for your new subtype to use a generic `eat()` method, so you have to come up with your *own* `eat()` method implementation!" A (nonabstract) example of using polymorphism looks like this:

```
public class TestAnimals {
  public static void main (String [] args) {
    Animal a = new Animal();
    Animal b = new Horse();  // Animal ref, but a Horse object
    a.eat(); // Runs the Animal version of eat()
    b.eat(); // Runs the Horse version of eat()
  }
}
class Animal {
  public void eat() {
    System.out.println("Generic Animal Eating Generically");
  }
}
class Horse extends Animal {
  public void eat() {
    System.out.println("Horse eating hay, oats, "
                     + "and horse treats");
  }
  public void buck() { }
}
```

In the preceding code, the test class uses an `Animal` reference to invoke a method on a `Horse` object. Remember, the compiler will allow only methods in class `Animal` to be invoked when using a reference to an `Animal`. The following would not be legal given the preceding code:

```
Animal c = new Horse();
c.buck();  // Can't invoke buck();
           // Animal class doesn't have that method
```

To reiterate, the compiler looks only at the reference type, not the instance type. Polymorphism lets you use a more abstract supertype (including an interface) reference to one of its subtypes (including interface implementers).

The overriding method cannot have a more restrictive access modifier than the method being overridden (for example, you can't override a method marked public and make it protected). Think about it: If the Animal class advertises a public eat() method and someone has an Animal reference (in other words, a reference declared as type Animal), that someone will assume it's safe to call eat() on the Animal reference regardless of the actual instance that the Animal reference is referring to. If a subtype were allowed to sneak in and change the access modifier on the overriding method, then suddenly at runtime—when the JVM invokes the true object's (Horse) version of the method rather than the reference type's (Animal) version—the program would die a horrible death. (Not to mention the emotional distress for the one who was betrayed by the rogue subtype.)

Let's modify the polymorphic example you saw earlier in this section:

```
public class TestAnimals {
  public static void main (String [] args) {
    Animal a = new Animal();
    Animal b = new Horse();    // Animal ref, but a Horse object
    a.eat();                   // Runs the Animal version of eat()
    b.eat();                   // Runs the Horse version of eat()
  }
}
class Animal {
  public void eat() {
    System.out.println("Generic Animal Eating Generically");
  }
}
class Horse extends Animal {
  private void eat() {         // whoa! - it's private!
    System.out.println("Horse eating hay, oats, "
                     + "and horse treats");
  }
}
```

If this code compiled (which it doesn't), the following would fail at runtime:

```
Animal b = new Horse();  // Animal ref, but a Horse
                         // object, so far so good
b.eat();                 // Meltdown at runtime!
```

The variable b is of type Animal, which has a public eat() method. But remember that at runtime, Java uses virtual method invocation to dynamically select the actual version of the method that will run, based on the actual instance. An Animal reference can always refer to a Horse instance because Horse

IS-A(n) `Animal`. What makes that supertype reference to a subtype instance possible is that the subtype is guaranteed to be able to do everything the supertype can do. Whether the `Horse` instance overrides the inherited methods of `Animal` or simply inherits them, anyone with an `Animal` reference to a `Horse` instance is free to call all accessible `Animal` methods. For that reason, an overriding method must fulfill the contract of the superclass.

Note: In Chapter 3 we will explore exception handling in detail. Once you've studied Chapter 3, you'll appreciate this single handy list of overriding rules. The rules for overriding a method are as follows:

- The argument list must exactly match that of the overridden method. If they don't match, you can end up with an overloaded method you didn't intend.

- The return type must be the same as, or a subtype of, the return type declared in the original overridden method in the superclass. (More on this in a few pages when we discuss covariant returns.)

- The access level can't be more restrictive than that of the overridden method.

- The access level CAN be less restrictive than that of the overridden method.

- Instance methods can be overridden only if they are inherited by the subtype. A subtype within the same package as the instance's supertype can override any supertype method that is not marked `private` or `final`. A subtype in a different package can override only those nonfinal methods marked `public` or `protected` (since `protected` methods are inherited by the subtype).

- The overriding method CAN throw any unchecked (runtime) exception, regardless of whether the overridden method declares the exception.

- The overriding method must NOT throw checked exceptions that are new or broader than those declared by the overridden method. For example, a method that declares a `FileNotFoundException` cannot be overridden by a method that declares a `SQLException`, `Exception`, or any other non-runtime exception unless it's a subclass of `FileNotFoundException`.

- The overriding method can throw narrower or fewer exceptions. Just because an overridden method "takes risks" doesn't mean that the overriding subtype's exception takes the same risks. Bottom line: an overriding method doesn't have to declare any exceptions that it will never throw, regardless of what the overridden method declares.

- You cannot override a method marked `final`.

- You cannot override a method marked `static`. We'll look at an example in a few pages when we discuss `static` methods in more detail.
- If a method can't be inherited, you cannot override it. Remember that overriding implies that you're reimplementing a method you inherited! For example, the following code is not legal, and even if you added an `eat()` method to `Horse`, it wouldn't be an override of `Animal`'s `eat()` method.

```
public class TestAnimals {
  public static void main (String [] args) {
    Horse h =  new Horse();
    h.eat(); // Not legal because Horse didn't inherit eat()
  }
}
class Animal {
  private void eat() {
    System.out.println("Generic Animal Eating Generically");
  }
}
class Horse extends Animal { }
```

Invoking a Supertype Version of an Overridden Method

Often, you'll want to take advantage of some of the code in the supertype version of a method, yet still override it to provide some additional specific behavior. It's like saying, "Run the supertype version of the method, and then come back down here and finish with my subtype additional method code." (Note that there's no requirement that the supertype version run before the subtype code.) It's easy to do in code using the keyword `super` as follows:

```
public class Animal {
  public void eat() { }
  public void printYourself() {
    // Useful printing code goes here
  }
}
class Horse extends Animal {
  public void printYourself() {
    // Take advantage of Animal code, then add some more
    super.printYourself();  // Invoke the superclass
                            // (Animal) code
                            // Then do Horse-specific
                            // print work here
  }
}
```

In a similar way, you can access an interface's overridden method with the syntax:

```
InterfaceX.super.doStuff();
```

Note: Using super to invoke an overridden method applies only to instance methods. (Remember that static methods can't be overridden.) And you can use super only to access a method in a type's supertype, not the supertype of the supertype—that is, you **cannot** say super.super.doStuff() and you **cannot** say InterfaceX.super.super.doStuff().

exam
watch

If a method is overridden but you use a polymorphic (supertype) reference to refer to the subtype object with the overriding method, the compiler assumes you're calling the supertype version of the method. If the supertype version declares a checked exception, but the overriding subtype method does not, the compiler still thinks you are calling a method that declares an exception. Let's look at an example:

```
class Animal {
  public void eat() throws Exception {
                     // throws an Exception
  }
}
class Dog2 extends Animal {
  public void eat() { /* no Exceptions */}
  public static void main(String [] args) {
    Animal a = new Dog2();
    Dog2 d = new Dog2();
    d.eat();          // ok
    a.eat();          // compiler error -
                      // unreported exception
  }
}
```

This code will not compile because of the exception declared on the Animal eat() method. This happens even though, at runtime, the eat() method used would be the Dog version, which does not declare the exception.

Examples of Illegal Method Overrides

Let's take a look at overriding the eat() method of Animal:

```
public class Animal {
  public void eat() { }
}
```

Table 2-2 lists examples of illegal overrides of the Animal eat() method, given the preceding version of the Animal class.

TABLE 2-2   Examples of Illegal Overrides

Illegal Override Code	Problem with the Code
`private void eat() { }`	Access modifier more restrictive
`public void eat() throws IOException { }`	Declares a checked exception not defined by superclass version
`public void eat(String food) { }`	A legal overload, not an override, because the argument list changed
`public String eat() { }`	Not an override because of the return type, and not an overload either because there's no change in the argument list

Using @Override

Java 5 introduced the @Override annotation, which you can use to help catch errors with overriding or implementing at compile time. If you intend to override a method in a superclass or implement a method in an interface, you can annotate that method with @Override, like this:

```
public class Animal {
    public void eat() {
        System.out.println("Generic Animal Eating Generically");
    }
}

class Horse extends Animal {
    @Override                              // ask the compiler for verification
    public void eat() {
        System.out.println("Horse eating hay, oats, "
                + "and horse treats");
    }
}
```

Now, if you make a mistake in how you override the eat() method, the compiler will warn you. For instance, let's say you accidentally add a parameter to the eat() method:

```
public void eat(int j) {
    System.out.println("Horse eating hay, oats, "
            + "and horse treats");
}
```

Without the @Override, the Java compiler is fine with this code, but what you've done is *overload* the eat() method, not *override* it. If you then call the eat()

method on a Horse, without passing in an int, you'll get the Animal's eat() method, not the Horse's eat() method, as you intended.

Add the @Override, however, and, you'll see a compiler error something like:

```
Animal.java:7: error: method does not override or implement a method from a supertype
@Override
^
```

This also works if you, let's say, misspell the name of the method you want to override:

```
public class Animal {
    public void eat() {
        System.out.println("Generic Animal Eating Generically");
    }
    public void walk() { }              // method you intend to override
}
class Horse extends Animal {
    @Override
    public void eat() {
        System.out.println("Horse eating hay, oats, "
                + "and horse treats");
    }
    @Override
    public void walkie() { } // you meant to override, but spelled it wrong
}
```

Again, you'll see a compiler error indicating that something is wrong.

@Override is not required when overriding or implementing, but it can help prevent mistakes, and it also makes it easier for other programmers reading your code to know what you intended.

Overloaded Methods

Over*loaded* methods let you reuse the same method name in a class, but with different arguments (and, optionally, a different return type). Overloading a method often means you're being a little nicer to those who call your methods because your code takes on the burden of coping with different argument types rather than forcing the caller to do conversions prior to invoking your method. The rules aren't too complex:

- Overloaded methods MUST change the argument list.
- Overloaded methods CAN change the return type.
- Overloaded methods CAN change the access modifier.
- Overloaded methods CAN declare new or broader checked exceptions.

■   A method can be overloaded in the *same* type or in a *subtype*. In other words, if class A defines a doStuff(int i) method, then subclass B could define a doStuff(String s) method without overriding the superclass version that takes an int. So two methods with the same name but in different types can still be considered overloaded if the subtype inherits one version of the method and then declares another overloaded version in its type definition.

e x a m

ⓦ a t c h   *Less experienced Java developers are often confused about the subtle differences between overloaded and overridden methods. Be careful to recognize when a method is overloaded rather than overridden. You might see a method that appears to be violating a rule for overriding, but that is actually a legal overload, as follows:*

```
public class Foo {
  public void doStuff(int y, String s) { }
  public void moreThings(int x) { }
}
class Bar extends Foo {
  public void doStuff(int y, long s) throws IOException { }
}
```

It's tempting to see the IOException as the problem because the overridden doStuff() method doesn't declare an exception and IOException is checked by the compiler. But the doStuff() method is not overridden! Subclass Bar overloads the doStuff() method by varying the argument list, so all the code, including the IOException, is fine.

Legal Overloads

Let's look at a method we want to overload:

```
public void changeSize(int size, String name, float pattern) { }
```

The following methods are legal overloads of the changeSize() method:

```
public void changeSize(int size, String name) { }
private int changeSize(int size, float pattern) { }
public void changeSize(float pattern, String name)
                       throws IOException { }
```

Invoking Overloaded Methods

When a method is invoked, more than one method of the same name might exist for the object type you're invoking a method on. For example, the Horse class might have three methods with the same name but with different argument lists, which means the method is overloaded.

Decide which of the matching methods to invoke based on the arguments. If you invoke the method with a String argument, the overloaded version that takes a String is called. If you invoke a method of the same name but pass it a float, the overloaded version that takes a float will run. If you invoke the method of the same name but pass it a Foo object and there isn't an overloaded version that takes a Foo, then the compiler will complain that it can't find a match. The following are examples of invoking overloaded methods:

```
class Adder {
  public int addThem(int x, int y) {
    return x + y;
  }

  // Overload the addThem method to add doubles instead of ints
  public double addThem(double x, double y) {
    return x + y;
  }
}
  // From another class, invoke the addThem() method
public class TestAdder {
  public static void main (String [] args) {
    Adder a = new Adder();
    int b = 27;
    int c = 3;
    int result = a.addThem(b,c);            // Which addThem is invoked?
    double doubleResult = a.addThem(22.5,9.3); // Which addThem?
  }
}
```

In this TestAdder code, the first call to a.addThem(b,c) passes two ints to the method, so the first version of addThem()—the overloaded version that takes two int arguments—is called. The second call to a.addThem(22.5, 9.3) passes two doubles to the method, so the second version of addThem()—the overloaded version that takes two double arguments—is called.

Invoking overloaded methods that take object references rather than primitives is a little more interesting. Say you have an overloaded method such that one version takes an Animal and one takes a Horse (subclass of Animal). If you pass a Horse object in the method invocation, you'll invoke the overloaded version that takes a Horse. Or so it looks at first glance:

```
class Animal { }
class Horse extends Animal { }
class UseAnimals {
  public void doStuff(Animal a) {
    System.out.println("In the Animal version");
  }
  public void doStuff(Horse h) {
    System.out.println("In the Horse version");
  }
  public static void main (String [] args) {
    UseAnimals ua = new UseAnimals();
    Animal animalObj = new Animal();
    Horse horseObj = new Horse();
    ua.doStuff(animalObj);
    ua.doStuff(horseObj);
}}
```

The output is what you expect:

```
In the Animal version
In the Horse version
```

But what if you use an `Animal` reference to a `Horse` object?

```
Animal animalRefToHorse = new Horse();
  ua.doStuff(animalRefToHorse);
```

Which of the overloaded versions is invoked? You might want to answer, "The one that takes a `Horse` since it's a `Horse` object at runtime that's being passed to the method." But that's not how it works. The preceding code would actually print this:

```
in the Animal version
```

Even though the actual object at runtime is a `Horse` and not an `Animal`, the choice of which overloaded method to call (in other words, the signature of the method) is NOT dynamically decided at runtime.

Just remember—the *reference* type (not the object type) determines which overloaded method is invoked!

To summarize, which over*ridden* version of the method to call (in other words, from which class in the inheritance tree) is decided at *runtime* based on *object* type, but which over*loaded* version of the method to call is based on the *reference* type of the argument passed at *compile* time.

If you invoke a method passing it an `Animal` reference to a `Horse` object, the compiler knows only about the `Animal`, so it chooses the overloaded version of the method that takes an `Animal`. It does not matter that, at runtime, a `Horse` is actually being passed.

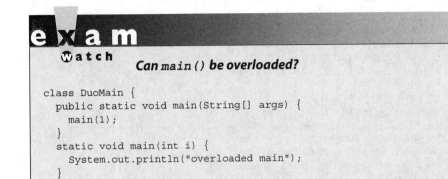

Can `main()` *be overloaded?*

```
class DuoMain {
  public static void main(String[] args) {
    main(1);
  }
  static void main(int i) {
    System.out.println("overloaded main");
  }
}
```

Absolutely! But the only `main()` **with JVM superpowers is the one with the signature you've seen about 100 times already in this book.**

Polymorphism in Overloaded and Overridden Methods   How does polymorphism work with overloaded methods? From what we just looked at, it doesn't appear that polymorphism matters when a method is overloaded. If you pass an `Animal` reference, the overloaded method that takes an `Animal` will be invoked, even if the actual object passed is a `Horse`. Once the `Horse` masquerading as `Animal` gets in to the method, however, the `Horse` object is still a `Horse` despite being passed into a method expecting an `Animal`. So it's true that polymorphism doesn't determine which overloaded version is called; polymorphism does come into play when the decision is about which overridden version of a method is called. But sometimes a method is both overloaded and overridden. Imagine that the `Animal` and `Horse` classes look like this:

```
public class Animal {
  public void eat() {
    System.out.println("Generic Animal Eating Generically");
  }
}
public class Horse extends Animal {
  public void eat() {
    System.out.println("Horse eating hay ");
  }
  public void eat(String s) {
    System.out.println("Horse eating " + s);
  }
}
```

Notice that the `Horse` class has both overloaded and overridden the `eat()` method. Table 2-3 shows which version of the three `eat()` methods will run depending on how they are invoked.

TABLE 2-3   Examples of Legal and Illegal Overrides

Method Invocation Code	Result
`Animal a = new Animal();` `a.eat();`	`Generic Animal Eating Generically`
`Horse h = new Horse();` `h.eat();`	`Horse eating hay`
`Animal ah = new `**`Horse();`** `ah.eat();`	`Horse eating hay` Polymorphism works—the actual object type (`Horse`), not the reference type (`Animal`), is used to determine which `eat()` is called.
`Horse he = new Horse();` `he.eat("Apples");`	`Horse eating Apples` The overloaded `eat(String s)` method is invoked.
`Animal a2 = new Animal();` `a2.eat("treats");`	Compiler error! Compiler sees that the `Animal` class doesn't have an `eat()` method that takes a `String`.
`Animal ah2 = new `**`Horse();`** `ah2.eat("Carrots");`	Compiler error! Compiler still looks only at the reference and sees that `Animal` doesn't have an `eat()` method that takes a `String`. Compiler doesn't care that the actual object might be a `Horse` at runtime.

e x a m

w a t c h   *Don't be fooled by a method that's overloaded but not overridden by a subclass. It's perfectly legal to do the following:*

```
public class Foo {
  void doStuff() { }
}
class Bar extends Foo {
  void doStuff(String s) { }
}
```

The `Bar` class has two `doStuff()` methods: the no-arg version it inherits from `Foo` (and does not override) and the overloaded `doStuff(String s)` defined in the `Bar` class. Code with a reference to a `Foo` can invoke only the no-arg version, but code with a reference to a `Bar` can invoke either of the overloaded versions.

Table 2-4 summarizes the difference between overloaded and overridden methods.

TABLE 2-4   Differences Between Overloaded and Overridden Methods

	Overloaded Method	**Overridden Method**
Argument(s)	Must change.	Must not change.
Return type	Can change.	Can't change except for covariant returns. (Covered later this chapter.)
Exceptions	Can change.	Can reduce or eliminate. Must not throw new or broader checked exceptions.
Access	Can change.	Must not make more restrictive (can be less restrictive).
Invocation	*Reference* type determines which overloaded version (based on declared argument types) is selected. Happens at *compile* time. The actual *method* that's invoked is still a virtual method invocation that happens at runtime, but the compiler will already know the *signature* of the method to be invoked. So at runtime, the argument match will already have been nailed down, just not the *class* in which the method lives.	*Object* type (in other words, *the type of the actual instance on the heap*) determines which method is selected. Happens at *runtime*.

We'll cover constructor overloading later in the chapter, where we'll also cover the other constructor-related topics that are on the exam. Figure 2-4 illustrates the way overloaded and overridden methods appear in class relationships.

FIGURE 2-4

Overloaded
and overridden
methods in class
relationships

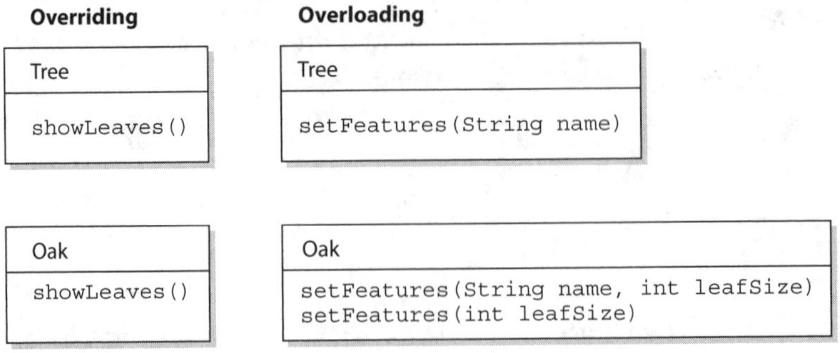

Casting (OCP Objectives 1.2 and 1.3)

1.2   Implement inheritance including visibility modifiers and composition.
1.3   Implement polymorphism.

You've seen how it's both possible and common to use general reference variable types to refer to more specific object types. It's at the heart of polymorphism. For example, this line of code should be second nature by now:

```
Animal animal = new Dog();
```

But what happens when you want to use that `animal` reference variable to invoke a method that only class `Dog` has? You know it's referring to a `Dog`, and you want to do a `Dog`-specific thing? In the following code, we've got an array of `Animals`, and whenever we find a `Dog` in the array, we want to do a special `Dog` thing. Let's agree for now that all this code is okay, except we're not sure about the line of code that invokes the `playDead` method:

```
class Animal {
  void makeNoise() {System.out.println("generic noise"); }
}
class Dog extends Animal {
  void makeNoise() {System.out.println("bark"); }
  void playDead() { System.out.println("roll over"); }
}

class CastTest2 {
  public static void main(String [] args) {
    Animal [] a = {new Animal(), new Dog(), new Animal() };
    for(Animal animal : a) {
      animal.makeNoise();
      if(animal instanceof Dog) {
        animal.playDead();        // try to do a Dog behavior?
      }
    }
  }
}
```

When we try to compile this code, the compiler says something like this:

```
cannot find symbol
```

The compiler is saying, "Hey, class `Animal` doesn't have a `playDead()` method." Let's modify the `if` code block:

```
if(animal instanceof Dog) {
  Dog d = (Dog) animal;        // casting the ref. var.
  d.playDead();
}
```

The new and improved code block contains a cast, which in this case is sometimes called a *downcast*, because we're casting down the inheritance tree to a more specific class. Now the compiler is happy. Before we try to invoke `playDead`, we cast the `animal` variable to type `Dog`. What we're saying to the compiler is, "We know it's really referring to a `Dog` object, so it's okay to make a new `Dog` reference variable to refer to that object." In this case we're safe, because before we ever try the cast, we do an `instanceof` test to make sure.

It's important to know that the compiler is forced to trust us when we do a downcast, even when we screw up:

```
class Animal { }
class Dog extends Animal { }
class DogTest {
  public static void main(String [] args) {
    Animal animal = new Animal();
    Dog d = (Dog) animal;              // compiles but fails later
  }
}
```

It can be maddening! This code compiles! But when we try to run it, we'll get an exception, something like this:

```
java.lang.ClassCastException
```

Why can't we trust the compiler to help us out here? Can't it see that `animal` is of type `Animal`? All the compiler can do is verify that the two types are in the same inheritance tree, so depending on whatever code might have come before the downcast, it's possible that `animal` is of type `Dog`. The compiler must allow things that might possibly work at runtime. However, if the compiler knows with certainty that the cast could not possibly work, compilation will fail. The following replacement code block will NOT compile:

```
Animal animal = new Animal();
Dog d = (Dog) animal;
String s = (String) animal;    // animal can't EVER be a String
```

In this case, you'll get an error something like this:

```
inconvertible types:Animal cannot be converted to a String
```

Unlike downcasting, *upcasting* (casting *up* the inheritance tree to a more general type) works implicitly (that is, you don't have to type in the cast) because when you upcast you're implicitly restricting the number of methods you can invoke, as opposed to *down*casting, which implies that later on you might want to invoke a more *specific* method. Here's an example:

```
class Animal { }
class Dog extends Animal { }

class DogTest {
  public static void main(String [] args) {
    Dog d = new Dog();
    Animal a1 = d;              // upcast ok with no explicit cast
    Animal a2 = (Animal) d;   // upcast ok with an explicit cast
  }
}
```

Both of the previous upcasts will compile and run without exception because a Dog IS-A(n) Animal, which means that anything an Animal can do, a Dog can do. A Dog can do more, of course, but the point is that anyone with an Animal reference can safely call Animal methods on a Dog instance. The Animal methods may have been overridden in the Dog class, but all we care about now is that a Dog can always do at least everything an Animal can do. The compiler and JVM know it, too, so the implicit upcast is always legal for assigning an object of a subtype to a reference of one of its supertype classes (or interfaces). If Dog implements Pet and Pet defines beFriendly(), then a Dog can be implicitly cast to a Pet, but the only Dog method you can invoke then is beFriendly(), which Dog was forced to implement because Dog implements the Pet interface.

One more thing...if Dog implements Pet, then, if Beagle extends Dog but Beagle does not *declare* that it implements Pet, Beagle is still a Pet! Beagle is a Pet simply because it extends Dog, and Dog's already taken care of the Pet parts for itself and for all its children. The Beagle class can always override any method it inherits from Dog, including methods that Dog implemented to fulfill its interface contract.

And just one more thing...if Beagle does declare that it implements Pet, just so that others looking at the Beagle class API can easily see that Beagle IS-A

Pet without having to look at Beagle's superclasses, Beagle still doesn't need to implement the beFriendly() method if the Dog class (Beagle's superclass) has already taken care of that. In other words, if Beagle IS-A Dog and Dog IS-A Pet, then Beagle IS-A Pet and has already met its Pet obligations for implementing the beFriendly() method since it inherits the beFriendly() method. The compiler is smart enough to say, "I know Beagle already IS a Dog, but it's okay to make it more obvious by adding a cast."

So don't be fooled by code that shows a concrete class that declares it implements an interface but doesn't implement the *methods* of the interface. Before you can tell whether the code is legal, you must know what the supertypes of this implementing class have declared. If any supertype in its inheritance tree has already provided concrete (that is, nonabstract) method implementations, then regardless of whether the supertype declares that it implements the interface, the subclass is under no obligation to reimplement (override) those methods.

exam

watch *The exam creators will tell you that they're forced to jam tons of code into little spaces "because of the exam engine." Although that's partially true, they also like to obfuscate. The following code*

```
Animal a = new Dog();
Dog d = (Dog) a;
d.doDogStuff();
```

can be replaced with this easy-to-read bit of fun:

```
Animal a = new Dog();
((Dog)a).doDogStuff();
```

In this case the compiler needs all those parentheses; otherwise, it thinks it's been handed an incomplete statement.

Implementing an Interface (OCP Objective 2.5)

2.5   Develop code that declares, implements and/or extends interfaces and use the @Override annotation (sic*).

* This objective tests for two different concepts: the use of interfaces in general and the use of the @Override annotation. As we mentioned in the introduction, some of the official objectives aren't very well worded. When in doubt about how broadly the exam covers a topic, we suggest that you assume a broader scope, rather than a narrower scope.

When you implement an interface, you're agreeing to adhere to the contract defined in the interface. That means you're agreeing to provide legal implementations for every abstract method defined in the interface, and that anyone who knows what the interface methods look like (not how they're implemented, but how they can be called and what they return) can rest assured that they can invoke those methods on an instance of your implementing class.

For example, if you create a class that implements the Runnable interface (so your code can be executed by a specific thread), you must provide the public void run() method. Otherwise, the poor thread could be told to go execute your Runnable object's code and—surprise, surprise—the thread then discovers the object has no run() method! (At which point, the thread would blow up and the JVM would crash in a spectacular yet horrible explosion.) Thankfully, Java prevents this meltdown from occurring by running a compiler check on any class that claims to implement an interface. If the class says it's implementing an interface, it darn well better have an implementation for each abstract method in the interface (with a few exceptions that we'll look at in a moment).

Assuming an interface Bounceable, with two methods, bounce() and setBounceFactor(), the following class will compile:

```
public class Ball implements Bounceable {  // Keyword
                                           // 'implements'
  public void bounce() { }
  public void setBounceFactor(int bf) { }
}
```

Okay, we know what you're thinking: "This has got to be the worst implementation class in the history of implementation classes." It compiles, though. And it runs.

The interface contract guarantees that a class will have the method (in other words, others can call the method subject to access control), but it never guaranteed a good implementation—or even any actual implementation code in the body of the method. (Keep in mind, though, that if the interface declares that a method is NOT void, your class's implementation code has to include a return statement.) The compiler will never say, "Um, excuse me, but did you really mean to put nothing between those curly braces? HELLO. This is a method after all, so shouldn't it do something?"

Implementation classes must adhere to the same rules for method implementation as a class extending an `abstract` class. To be a legal implementation class, a nonabstract implementation class must do the following:

- Provide concrete (nonabstract) implementations for all abstract methods from the declared interface.
- Follow all the rules for legal overrides, such as the following:
  - Declare no checked exceptions on implementation methods other than those declared by the interface method, or subclasses of those declared by the interface method.
  - Maintain the signature of the interface method, and maintain the same return type (or a subtype). (But it does not have to declare the exceptions declared in the interface method declaration.)

watch *Implementation classes are NOT required to implement an interface's static or default methods. We'll discuss this in more depth later in the chapter.*

But wait, there's more! An implementation class can itself be `abstract`! For example, the following is legal for a class `Ball` implementing `Bounceable`:

```
abstract class Ball implements Bounceable { }
```

Notice anything missing? We never provided the implementation methods. And that's okay. If the implementation class is `abstract`, it can simply pass the buck to its first concrete subclass. For example, if class `BeachBall` extends `Ball` and `BeachBall` is not `abstract`, then `BeachBall` has to provide an implementation for all the abstract methods from `Bounceable`:

```
class BeachBall extends Ball {
    // Even though we don't say it in the class declaration above,
    // BeachBall implements Bounceable, since BeachBall's abstract
    // superclass (Ball) implements Bounceable
```

```
    public void bounce() {
    // interesting BeachBall-specific bounce code

    }
    public void setBounceFactor(int bf) {
    // clever BeachBall-specific code for setting
    // a bounce factor

    }
    // if class Ball defined any abstract methods,
    // they'll have to be
    // implemented here as well.
}
```

Look for classes that claim to implement an interface but don't provide the correct method implementations. Unless the implementing class is abstract, the implementing class must provide implementations for all abstract methods defined in the interface.

You need to know two more rules, and then we can put this topic to sleep (or put you to sleep; we always get those two confused):

1. A class can implement more than one interface. It's perfectly legal to say, for example, the following:

   ```
   public class Ball implements Bounceable, Serializable, Runnable { ... }
   ```

   You can extend only one class, but you can implement many interfaces (which, as of Java 8, means a form of multiple inheritance, which we'll discuss shortly). In other words, subclassing defines who and what you are, whereas implementing defines a role you can play or a hat you can wear, despite how different you might be from some other class implementing the same interface (but from a different inheritance tree). For example, a Person extends HumanBeing (although for some, that's debatable). But a Person may also implement Programmer, Snowboarder, Employee, Parent, or PersonCrazyEnoughToTakeThisExam.

2. An interface can itself extend another interface. The following code is perfectly legal:

   ```
   public interface Bounceable extends Moveable { }    // ok!
   ```

What does that mean? The first concrete (nonabstract) implementation class of Bounceable must implement all the abstract methods of Bounceable, plus all the abstract methods of Moveable! The subinterface, as we call it, simply adds more requirements to the contract of the superinterface. You'll see this concept applied in many areas of Java, especially Java EE, where you'll often have to build your own interface that extends one of the Java EE interfaces.

Hold on, though, because here's where it gets strange. An interface can extend more than one interface! Think about that for a moment. You know that when we're talking about classes, the following is illegal:

```
public class Programmer extends Employee, Geek { } // Illegal!
```

As we mentioned earlier, a class is not allowed to extend multiple classes in Java. An interface, however, is free to extend multiple interfaces:

```
interface Bounceable extends Moveable, Spherical {    // ok!
  void bounce();
  void setBounceFactor(int bf);
}
interface Moveable {
  void moveIt();
}
interface Spherical {
  void doSphericalThing();
}
```

In the next example, `Ball` is required to implement `Bounceable`, plus all abstract methods from the interfaces that `Bounceable` extends (including any interfaces those interfaces extend, and so on, until you reach the top of the stack— or is it the bottom of the stack?). So `Ball` would need to look like the following:

```
class Ball implements Bounceable {

  public void bounce() { }              // Implement Bounceable's methods
  public void setBounceFactor(int bf) { }

  public void moveIt() { }              // Implement Moveable's method

  public void doSphericalThing() { }    // Implement Spherical
}
```

If class `Ball` fails to implement any of the abstract methods from `Bounceable`, `Moveable`, or `Spherical`, the compiler will jump up and down wildly, red in the face, until it does. Unless, that is, class `Ball` is marked `abstract`. In that case, `Ball` could choose to implement some, all, or none of the abstract methods from any of the interfaces, thus leaving the rest of the implementations to a concrete subclass of `Ball`, as follows:

```
abstract class Ball implements Bounceable {
  public void bounce() { ... }    // Define bounce behavior
  public void setBounceFactor(int bf) { ... }
  // Don't implement the rest; leave it for a subclass
}
```

```
class SoccerBall extends Ball {   // class SoccerBall must
                                  // implement the interface
                                  // methods that Ball didn't
    public void moveIt() { ... }
    public void doSphericalThing() { ... }
    // SoccerBall can choose to override the Bounceable methods
    // implemented by Ball
    public void bounce() { ... }
}
```

Figure 2-5 compares concrete and `abstract` examples of extends and implements, for both classes and interfaces.

FIGURE 2-5   Comparing concrete and *abstract* examples of extends and implements

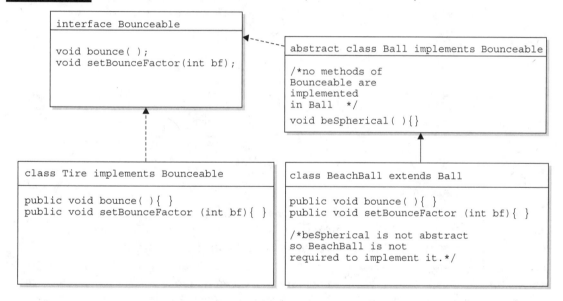

Because `BeachBall` is the first concrete class to implement `Bounceable`, it must provide implementations for all methods of `Bounceable`, except those defined in the abstract class `Ball`. Because `Ball` did not provide implementations of `Bounceable` methods, `BeachBall` was required to implement all of them.

Look for illegal uses of `extends` and `implements`. The following shows examples of legal and illegal class and interface declarations:

```
class Foo { }                            // OK
class Bar implements Foo  { }            // No! Can't implement a class
interface Baz { }                        // OK
interface Fi { }                         // OK
interface Fee implements Baz { }         // No! an interface can't
                                         // implement an interface
interface Zee implements Foo { }         // No! an interface can't
                                         // implement a class
interface Zoo extends Foo { }            // No! an interface can't
                                         // extend a class
interface Boo extends Fi { }             // OK. An interface can extend
                                         // an interface
class Toon extends Foo, Button { }       // No! a class can't extend
                                         // multiple classes
class Zoom implements Fi, Baz { }        // OK. A class can implement
                                         // multiple interfaces
interface Vroom extends Fi, Baz { }      // OK. An interface can extend
                                         // multiple interfaces
class Yow extends Foo implements Fi { }  // OK. A class can do both
                                         // (extends must be 1st)
class Yow extends Foo implements Fi, Baz { } // OK. A class can do all three
                                         // (extends must be 1st)
```

Burn these into your memory, and watch for abuses in the questions you get on the exam. Regardless of what the question appears to be testing, the real problem might be the class or interface declaration. Before you get caught up in, say, tracing a complex threading flow, check to see if the code will even compile. (Just that tip alone may be worth your putting us in your will!) (You'll be impressed by the effort the exam developers put into distracting you from the real problem.) (How did people manage to write anything before parentheses were invented?)

Java 8—Now with Multiple Inheritance!

It might have already occurred to you that since interfaces can now have concrete methods and classes can implement multiple interfaces, the specter of multiple inheritance and the Deadly Diamond of Death can rear its ugly head! Well, you're partly correct. A class CAN implement interfaces with duplicate, concrete method signatures! But the good news is that the compiler's got your back, and if you DO want to implement both interfaces, you'll have to provide an overriding method in your class. Let's look at the following code:

```
interface I1 {
  default int doStuff() { return 1; }
}
interface I2 {
  default int doStuff() { return 2; }
}
public class MultiInt implements I1, I2 {  // needs to override doSruff
  public static void main(String[] args) {
    new MultiInt().go();
  }
  void go() {
    System.out.println(doStuff());
  }
// public int doStuff() {
//    return 3;
// }
}
```

As the code stands, it WILL NOT COMPILE because it's not clear which version of doStuff() should be used. In order to make the code compile, you need to override doStuff() in the class. Uncommenting the class's doStuff() method would allow the code to compile and, when run, produce the output:

3

CERTIFICATION OBJECTIVE

Legal Return Types (OCP Objectives 1.2 and 1.3)

1.2   Implement inheritance including visibility modifiers and composition.
1.3   Implement polymorphism.

This section covers two aspects of return types: what you can declare as a return type and what you can actually return as a value. What you can and cannot declare is pretty straightforward, but it all depends on whether you're overriding an inherited method or simply declaring a new method (which includes overloaded methods). We'll take just a quick look at the difference between return type rules for overloaded and overriding methods, because we've already covered that in this chapter. We'll cover a small bit of new ground, though, when we look at polymorphic return types and the rules for what is and is not legal to actually return.

Return Type Declarations

This section looks at what you're allowed to declare as a return type, which depends primarily on whether you are overriding, overloading, or declaring a new method.

Return Types on Overloaded Methods

Remember that method overloading is not much more than name reuse. The overloaded method is a completely different method from any other method of the same name. So if you inherit a method but overload it in a subtype, you're not subject to the restrictions of overriding, which means you can declare any return type you like. What you can't do is change *only* the return type. To overload a method, remember, you must change the argument list. The following code shows an overloaded method:

```
public class Foo{
  void go() { }
}
public class Bar extends Foo {
  String go(int x) {
    return null;
  }
}
```

Notice that the Bar version of the method uses a different return type. That's perfectly fine. As long as you've changed the argument list, you're overloading the method, so the return type doesn't have to match that of the supertype version. What you're NOT allowed to do is this:

```
public class Foo{
  void go() { }
}
public class Bar extends Foo {
  String go() { // Not legal! Can't change only the return type
    return null;
  }
}
```

Overriding and Return Types and Covariant Returns

When a subtype wants to change the method implementation of an inherited method (an override), the subtype must define a method that matches the inherited version exactly. Or, since Java 5, you're allowed to change the return type in the overriding method as long as the new return type is a *subtype* of the declared return type of the overridden (superclass) method.

Let's look at a covariant return in action:

```
class Alpha {
  Alpha doStuff(char c) {
    return new Alpha();
  }
}
class Beta extends Alpha {
  Beta doStuff(char c) {     // legal override since Java 1.5
    return new Beta();
  }
}
```

Since Java 5, this code compiles. If you were to attempt to compile this code with a 1.4 compiler or with the source flag as follows,

```
javac -source 1.4 Beta.java
```

you would get a compiler error like this:

```
attempting to use incompatible return type
```

Other rules apply to overriding, including those for access modifiers and declared exceptions, but those rules aren't relevant to the return type discussion.

watch *For the exam, be sure you know that overloaded methods can change the return type, but overriding methods can do so only within the bounds of covariant returns. Just that knowledge alone will help you through a wide range of exam questions.*

Returning a Value

You have to remember only six rules for returning a value:

1. You can return `null` in a method with an object reference return type.

```
public Button doStuff() {
  return null;
}
```

2. An array is a perfectly legal return type.

```
public String[] go() {
  return new String[] {"Fred", "Barney", "Wilma"};
}
```

3. In a method with a primitive return type, you can return any value or variable that can be implicitly converted to the declared return type.

```
public int foo() {
  char c = 'c';
  return c;  // char is compatible with int
}
```

4. In a method with a primitive return type, you can return any value or variable that can be explicitly cast to the declared return type.

```
public int foo() {
  float f = 32.5f;
  return (int) f;
}
```

5. You must *not* return anything from a method with a void return type.

```
public void bar() {
  return "this is it";  // Not legal!!
}
```

(Although you can say `return;`)

6. In a method with an object reference return type, you can return any object type that can be implicitly cast to the declared return type.

```
public Animal getAnimal() {
  return new Horse();  // Assume Horse extends Animal
}

public Object getObject() {
  int[] nums = {1,2,3};
  return nums;          // Return an int array, which is still an object
}

public interface Chewable { }
public class Gum implements Chewable { }

public class TestChewable {
  // Method with an interface return type
  public Chewable getChewable() {
    return new Gum();  // Return interface implementer
  }
}
```

e**x**a**m**

ⓦatch

Watch for methods that declare an abstract class or interface return type, and know that any object that passes the IS-A test (in other words, would test true using the `instanceof` operator) can be returned from that method. For example:

```
public abstract class Animal { }
public class Bear extends Animal { }
public class Test {
  public Animal go() {
    return new Bear();  // OK, Bear "is-a" Animal
  }
}
```

This code will compile, and the return value is a subtype.

CERTIFICATION OBJECTIVE

Constructors and Instantiation (OCP Objectives 1.2 and 1.3)

1.2   Implement inheritance including visibility modifiers and composition.

1.3   Implement polymorphism.

Objects are constructed. You CANNOT make a new object without invoking a constructor. In fact, you can't make a new object without invoking not just the constructor of the object's actual class type, but also the constructor of each of its superclasses! Constructors are the code that runs whenever you use the keyword new. (Okay, to be a bit more accurate, there can also be initialization blocks that run when you say new, and we're going to cover initialization blocks and their static initialization counterparts after we discuss constructors.) We've got plenty to talk about here—we'll look at how constructors are coded, who codes them, and how they work at runtime. So grab your hardhat and a hammer, and let's do some object building.

Constructor Basics

Every class, *including abstract classes,* MUST have a constructor. Burn that into your brain. But just because a class must have a constructor doesn't mean the programmer has to type it. A constructor looks like this:

```
class Foo {
  Foo() { } // The constructor for the Foo class
}
```

Notice what's missing? There's no return type! Two key points to remember about constructors are that they have no return type and their names must exactly match the class name. Typically, constructors are used to initialize the instance variable state, as follows:

```
class Foo {
  int size;
  String name;
  Foo(String name, int size) {
    this.name = name;
    this.size = size;
  }
}
```

In the preceding code example, the Foo class does not have a no-arg constructor. That means the following will fail to compile,

```
Foo f = new Foo();          // Won't compile, no matching constructor
```

but the following will compile:

```
Foo f = new Foo("Fred", 43);  // No problem. Arguments match
                              // the Foo constructor.
```

So it's very common (and desirable) for a class to have a no-arg constructor, regardless of how many other overloaded constructors are in the class (yes, constructors can be overloaded). You can't always make that work for your classes; occasionally you have a class where it makes no sense to create an instance without supplying information to the constructor. A java.awt.Color object, for example, can't be created by calling a no-arg constructor. That would be like saying to the JVM, "Make me a new Color object, and I really don't care what color it is... you pick." Do you seriously want the JVM making your style decisions?

Constructor Chaining

We know that constructors are invoked at runtime when you say new on some class type as follows:

```
Horse h = new Horse();
```

But what *really* happens when you say new Horse()? (Assume Horse extends Animal and Animal extends Object.)

1. The Horse constructor is invoked. Every constructor invokes the constructor of its superclass with an (implicit) call to super(), unless the constructor invokes an overloaded constructor of the same class (more on that in a minute).

2. The Animal constructor is invoked (Animal is the superclass of Horse).

3. The Object constructor is invoked (Object is the ultimate superclass of all classes, so class Animal extends Object even though you don't actually type "extends Object" into the Animal class declaration; it's implicit.) At this point we're on the top of the stack.

4. If class Object had any instance variables, then they would be given their explicit values. By *explicit* values, we mean values that are assigned at the time the variables are declared, such as int x = 27, where 27 is the explicit value (as opposed to the default value) of the instance variable.

5. The Object constructor completes.

6. The Animal instance variables are given their explicit values (if any).

7. The Animal constructor completes.

8. The Horse instance variables are given their explicit values (if any).

9. The Horse constructor completes.

Figure 2-6 shows how constructors work on the call stack.

FIGURE 2-6

Constructors on the call stack

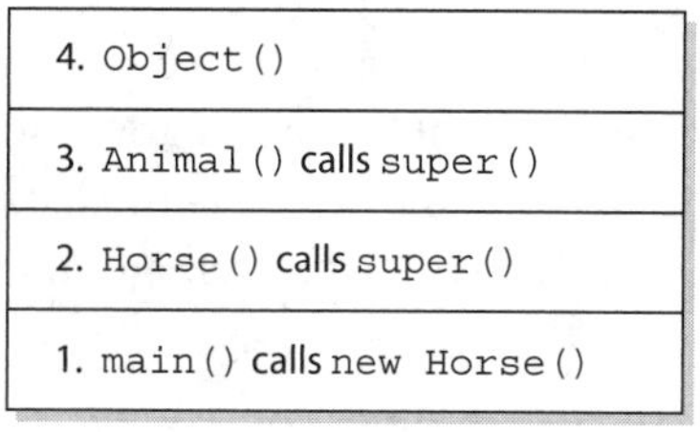

4. Object()
3. Animal() calls super()
2. Horse() calls super()
1. main() calls new Horse()

Rules for Constructors

The following list summarizes the rules you'll need to know for the exam (and to understand the rest of this section). You MUST remember these, so be sure to study them more than once.

- Constructors can use any access modifier, including `private`. (A `private` constructor means only code within the class itself can instantiate an object of that type, so if the `private` constructor class wants to allow an instance of the class to be used, the class must provide a static method or variable that allows access to an instance created from within the class.)
- The constructor name must match the name of the class.
- Constructors must not have a return type.
- It's legal (but stupid) to have a method with the same name as the class, but that doesn't make it a constructor. If you see a return type, it's a method rather than a constructor. In fact, you could have both a method and a constructor with the same name—the name of the class—in the same class, and that's not a problem for Java. Be careful not to mistake a method for a constructor—be sure to look for a return type.
- If you don't type a constructor into your class code, a default constructor will be automatically generated by the compiler.
- The default constructor is ALWAYS a no-arg constructor.
- If you want a no-arg constructor and you've typed any other constructor(s) into your class code, the compiler won't provide the no-arg constructor (or any other constructor) for you. In other words, if you've typed in a constructor with arguments, you won't have a no-arg constructor unless you typed it in yourself!
- Every constructor has, as its first statement, either a call to an overloaded constructor (`this()`) or a call to the superclass constructor (`super()`), although remember this call can be inserted by the compiler.
- If you do type in a constructor (as opposed to relying on the compiler-generated default constructor) and you do not type in the call to `super()` or a call to `this()`, the compiler will insert a no-arg call to `super()` for you as the very first statement in the constructor.
- A call to `super()` can either be a no-arg call or can include arguments passed to the super constructor.

- A no-arg constructor is not necessarily the default (that is, compiler-supplied) constructor, although the default constructor is always a no-arg constructor. The default constructor is the one the compiler provides! Although the default constructor is always a no-arg constructor, you're free to put in your own no-arg constructor.

- You cannot make a call to an instance method or access an instance variable until after the super constructor runs.

- Only static variables and methods can be accessed as part of the call to `super()` or `this()`. (Example: `super(Animal.NAME)` is OK, because `NAME` is declared as a static variable.)

- Abstract classes have constructors, and those constructors are always called when a concrete subclass is instantiated.

- Interfaces do not have constructors. Interfaces are not part of an object's inheritance tree.

- The only way a constructor can be invoked is from within another constructor. In other words, you can't write code that actually calls a constructor as follows:

```
class Horse {
  Horse() { } // constructor
  void doStuff() {
    Horse();  // calling the constructor - illegal!
  }
}
```

Determine Whether a Default Constructor Will Be Created

The following example shows a `Horse` class with two constructors:

```
class Horse {
  Horse() { }
  Horse(String name) { }
}
```

Will the compiler put in a default constructor for this class? No!
How about for the following variation of the class?

```
class Horse {
  Horse(String name) { }
}
```

Now will the compiler insert a default constructor? No!

What about this class?

```
class Horse { }
```

Now we're talking. The compiler will generate a default constructor for this class because the class doesn't have any constructors defined.

Okay, what about this class?

```
class Horse {
  void Horse() { }
}
```

It might look like the compiler won't create a constructor, since one is already in the Horse class. Or is it? Take another look at the preceding Horse class.

What's wrong with the Horse() constructor? It isn't a constructor at all! It's simply a method that happens to have the same name as the class. Remember, the return type is a dead giveaway that we're looking at a method, not a constructor.

How do you know for sure whether a default constructor will be created?   Because you didn't write any constructors in your class.

How do you know what the default constructor will look like?   Because...

- ■ The default constructor has the same access modifier as the class.
- ■ The default constructor has no arguments.
- ■ The default constructor includes a no-arg call to the super constructor (super()).

Table 2-5 shows what the compiler will (or won't) generate for your class.

What happens if the super constructor has arguments?   Constructors can have arguments just as methods can, and if you try to invoke a method that takes, say, an int, but you don't pass anything to the method, the compiler will complain as follows:

```
class Bar {
  void takeInt(int x) { }
}

class UseBar {
  public static void main (String [] args) {
    Bar b = new Bar();
    b.takeInt();  // Try to invoke a no-arg takeInt() method
  }
}
```

TABLE 2-5   Compiler-Generated Constructor Code

Class Code (What You Type)	Compiler-Generated Constructor Code (in Bold)

`class Foo { }`	`class Foo {`
	  `Foo() {`
	    `super();`
	  `}`
	`}`

`class Foo {`
 `Foo() { }`
`}`
	`class Foo {`
	 `Foo() {`
	    `super();`
	  `}`
	`}`

`public class Foo { }`	`public class Foo {`
	  `public Foo() {`
	    `super();`
	  `}`
	`}`

`class Foo {`
 `Foo(String s) { }`
`}`
	`class Foo {`
	 `Foo(String s) {`
	    `super();`
	  `}`
	`}`

`class Foo {`
 `Foo(String s) {`
  `super();`
 `}`
`}`
	Nothing; compiler doesn't need to insert anything.

`class Foo {`
 `void Foo() { }`
`}`
	`class Foo {`
	 `void Foo() { }`
	  `Foo() {`
	    `super();`
	  `}`
	`}`
	(`void Foo()` is a method, not a constructor.)

The compiler will complain that you can't invoke `takeInt()` without passing an `int`. Of course, the compiler enjoys the occasional riddle, so the message it spits out on some versions of the JVM (your mileage may vary) is less than obvious:

```
UseBar.java:7: takeInt(int) in Bar cannot be applied to ()
   b.takeInt();
    ^
```

But you get the idea. The bottom line is that there must be a match for the method. And by match, we mean the argument types must be able to accept the values or variables you're passing and in the order you're passing them. Which brings us back to constructors (and here you were thinking we'd never get there), which work exactly the same way.

So if your super constructor (that is, the constructor of your immediate superclass/parent) has arguments, you must type in the call to super(), supplying the appropriate arguments. Crucial point: if your superclass does not have a no-arg constructor, you must type a constructor in your class (the subclass) because you need a place to put in the call to super() with the appropriate arguments.

The following is an example of the problem:

```
class Animal {
  Animal(String name) { }
}

class Horse extends Animal {
  Horse() {
    super();  // Problem!
  }
}
```

And once again the compiler treats us with something like the stunning lucidity below:

```
Horse.java:7: cannot resolve symbol
symbol  : constructor Animal  ()
location: class Animal
  super();  // Problem!
      ^
```

If you're lucky (and it's a full moon), *your* compiler might be a little more explicit. But again, the problem is that there just isn't a match for what we're trying to invoke with super()—an Animal constructor with no arguments.

Another way to put this is that if your superclass does *not* have a no-arg constructor, then in your subclass you will not be able to use the default constructor supplied by the compiler. It's that simple. Because the compiler can *only* put in a call to a no-arg super(), you won't even be able to compile something like this:

```
class Clothing {
  Clothing(String s) { }
}
class TShirt extends Clothing { }
```

Trying to compile this code gives us exactly the same error we got when we put a constructor in the subclass with a call to the no-arg version of super():

```
Clothing.java:4: cannot resolve symbol
symbol  : constructor Clothing  ()
location: class Clothing
class TShirt extends Clothing { }
  ^
```

In fact, the preceding Clothing and TShirt code is implicitly the same as the following code, where we've supplied a constructor for TShirt that's identical to the default constructor supplied by the compiler:

```
class Clothing {
  Clothing(String s) { }
}
class TShirt extends Clothing {
              // Constructor identical to compiler-supplied
              // default constructor
  TShirt() {
    super();   // Won't work!
  }            // tries to invoke a no-arg Clothing constructor
              // but there isn't one

}
```

One last point on the whole default constructor thing (and it's probably very obvious, but we have to say it or we'll feel guilty for years), ***constructors are never inherited.*** They aren't methods. They can't be overridden (because they aren't methods, and only instance methods can be overridden). So the type of constructor(s) your superclass has in no way determines the type of default constructor you'll get. Some folks mistakenly believe that the default constructor somehow matches the super constructor, either by the arguments the default constructor will have (remember, the default constructor is always a no-arg) or by the arguments used in the compiler-supplied call to super().

So although constructors can't be overridden, they can—and often are—overloaded (which you've already seen).

Overloaded Constructors

Overloading a constructor means typing in multiple versions of the constructor, each having a different argument list, like the following examples:

```
class Foo {
  Foo() { }
  Foo(String s) { }
}
```

The preceding `Foo` class has two overloaded constructors: one that takes a string and one with no arguments. Because there's no code in the no-arg version, it's actually identical to the default constructor the compiler supplies—but remember, since there's already a constructor in this class (the one that takes a string), the compiler won't supply a default constructor. If you want a no-arg constructor to overload the with-args version you already have, you're going to have to type it yourself, just as in the `Foo` example.

Overloading a constructor is typically used to provide alternative ways for clients to instantiate objects of your class. For example, if a client knows the animal name, they can pass that to an `Animal` constructor that takes a string. But if they don't know the name, the client can call the no-arg constructor and that constructor can supply a default name. Here's what it looks like:

```
1.  public class Animal {
2.     String name;
3.     Animal(String name) {
4.        this.name = name;
5.     }
6.
7.     Animal() {
8.        this(makeRandomName());
9.     }
10.
11.    static String makeRandomName() {
12.       int x = (int) (Math.random() * 5);
13.       String name = new String[] {"Fluffy", "Fido",
                                      "Rover", "Spike",
                                      "Gigi"} [x];
14.       return name;
15.    }
16.
17.    public static void main (String [] args) {
18.       Animal a = new Animal();
19.       System.out.println(a.name);
20.       Animal b = new Animal("Zeus");
21.       System.out.println(b.name);
22.    }
23. }
```

Running the code four times produces output something like this:

```
% java Animal
Gigi
Zeus
```

```
% java Animal
Fluffy
Zeus

% java Animal
Rover
Zeus

% java Animal
Fluffy
Zeus
```

There's a lot going on in the preceding code. Figure 2-7 shows the call stack for constructor invocations when a constructor is overloaded. Take a look at the call stack, and then let's walk through the code straight from the top.

FIGURE 2-7

Overloaded
constructors on
the call stack

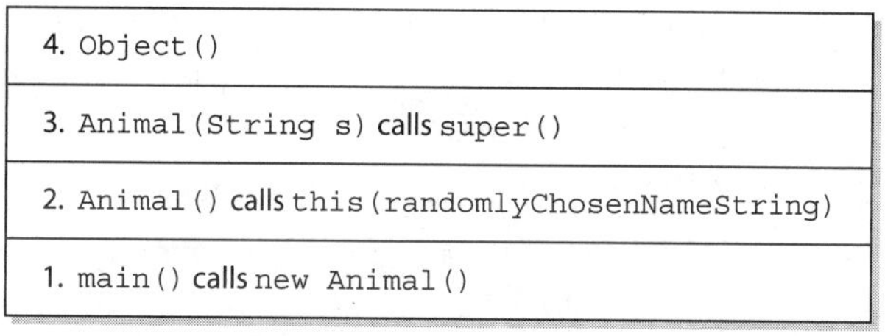

4. `Object()`
3. `Animal(String s)` calls `super()`
2. `Animal()` calls `this(randomlyChosenNameString)`
1. `main()` calls `new Animal()`

- **Line 2**   Declare a `String` instance variable name.
- **Lines 3–5**   Constructor that takes a `String` and assigns it to an instance variable name.
- **Line 7**   Here's where it gets fun. Assume every animal needs a name, but the client (calling code) might not always know what the name should be, so the `Animal` class will assign a random name. The no-arg constructor generates a name by invoking the `makeRandomName()` method.
- **Line 8**   The no-arg constructor invokes its own overloaded constructor that takes a `String`, in effect calling it the same way it would be called if client code were doing a `new` to instantiate an object, passing it a `String` for the name. The overloaded invocation uses the keyword `this`, but uses it as though it were a method named `this()`. So line 8 is simply calling the constructor on line 3, passing it a randomly selected `String` rather than a client-code chosen name.

■ **Line 11** Notice that the makeRandomName() method is marked static! That's because you cannot invoke an instance (in other words, nonstatic) method (or access an instance variable) until after the super constructor has run. And because the super constructor will be invoked from the constructor on line 3, rather than from the one on line 7, line 8 can use only a static method to generate the name. If we wanted all animals not specifically named by the caller to have the same default name, say, "Fred," then line 8 could have read this("Fred"); rather than calling a method that returns a string with the randomly chosen name.

■ **Line 12** This doesn't have anything to do with constructors, but since we're all here to learn, it generates a random integer between 0 and 4.

■ **Line 13** Weird syntax, we know. We're creating a new String object (just a single String instance), but we want the string to be selected randomly from a list. Except we don't have the list, so we need to make it. So in that one line of code we

1. Declare a String variable name.
2. Create a String array (anonymously—we don't assign the array itself to a variable).
3. Retrieve the string at index [x] (x being the random number generated on line 12) of the newly created String array.
4. Assign the string retrieved from the array to the declared instance variable name. (Throwing in unusual syntax, especially for code wholly unrelated to the real question, is in the spirit of the exam. Don't be startled! Okay, be startled, but then just say to yourself, "Whoa!" and get on with it.)

■ **Line 18** We're invoking the no-arg version of the constructor (causing a random name from the list to be passed to the other constructor).

■ **Line 20** We're invoking the overloaded constructor that takes a string representing the name.

The key point to get from this code example is in line 8. Rather than calling super(), we're calling this(), and this() always means a call to another constructor in the same class. Okay, fine, but what happens after the call to this()? Sooner or later the super() constructor gets called, right? Yes, indeed. A call to this() just means you're delaying the inevitable. Some constructor, somewhere, must make the call to super().

Key Rule: The first line in a constructor must be a call to super() or a call to this().

No exceptions. If you have neither of those calls in your constructor, the compiler will insert the no-arg call to super(). In other words, if constructor A() has a call to this(), the compiler knows that constructor A() will not be the one to invoke super().

The preceding rule means a constructor can never have both a call to super() and a call to this(). Because each of those calls must be the first statement in a constructor, you can't legally use both in the same constructor. That also means the compiler will not put a call to super() in any constructor that has a call to this().

Thought question: What do you think will happen if you try to compile the following code?

```
class A {
  A() {
    this("foo");
  }
  A(String s) {
    this();
  }
}
```

Java 8 compilers should catch the problem in this code and report an error, something like:

```
Error:
recursive constructor invocation
```

Older compilers may not actually catch the problem. They might assume you know what you're doing. Can you spot the flaw? Given that a super constructor must always be called, where would the call to super() go? Remember, the compiler won't put in a default constructor if you've already got one or more constructors in your class. And when the compiler doesn't put in a default constructor, it still inserts a call to super() in any constructor that doesn't explicitly have a call to the super constructor—unless, that is, the constructor already has a call to this(). So in the preceding code, where can super() go? The only two constructors in the class both have calls to this(), and, in fact, you'll get exactly what you'd get if you typed the following method code:

```
public void go() {
  doStuff();
}

public void doStuff() {
  go();
}
```

Now can you see the problem? Of course you can. The stack explodes! It gets higher and higher and higher until it just bursts open and method code goes spilling out, oozing from the JVM right onto the floor. Two overloaded constructors both calling `this()` are two constructors calling each other—over and over and over, resulting in this:

```
% java A
Exception in thread "main" java.lang.StackOverflowError
```

The benefit of having overloaded constructors is that you offer flexible ways to instantiate objects from your class. The benefit of having one constructor invoke another overloaded constructor is to avoid code duplication. In the `Animal` example, there wasn't any code other than setting the name, but imagine if after line 4 there was still more work to be done in the constructor. By putting all the other constructor work in just one constructor, and then having the other constructors invoke it, you don't have to write and maintain multiple versions of that other important constructor code. Basically, each of the other not-the-real-one overloaded constructors will call another overloaded constructor, passing it whatever data it needs (data the client code didn't supply).

Constructors and instantiation become even more exciting (just when you thought it was safe) when you get to inner classes, but we know you can stand to have only so much fun in one chapter, and besides, you don't have to deal with inner classes until Chapter 7.

CERTIFICATION OBJECTIVE

Singleton Design Pattern (OCP Objective 1.5)

1.5 Create and use singleton classes and immutable classes.

We just finished discussing how constructors play a role whenever new objects are created. In this section, we'll discuss the singleton design pattern that allows us to ensure we only have one instance of a class within an application. (Note: These days not everyone is a fan of the singleton pattern, but that's a discussion for another time.) *Singleton* is called a creational design pattern because it deals with creating objects. But wait, what's this "design pattern"?

What Is a Design Pattern?

Wikipedia currently defines a design pattern as "a general reusable solution to a commonly occurring problem within a given context." What does that mean? Programmers often encounter the same problem repeatedly. Rather than have everyone come up with their own solution to common programming issues, we use a "best practice"–type solution that has been documented and proven to work. The word "general" is important. We can't just copy and paste a design pattern into our code. It's just an idea. We should write an implementation for it and put that in our code.

Using a design pattern has a few advantages. We get to use a solution that is known to work. The tradeoffs, if any, are well documented, so we don't stumble over problems that have already been solved. Design patterns also serve as communication aids. Your boss can say, "We will use a singleton," and that one word is enough to tell you what is expected.

When books or web pages document patterns, they do so using a consistent format. We pay homage to this universal format by including sections for the "Problem," "Solution," and "Benefits" of the singleton pattern. The "Problem" section explains why we need the pattern—what problem we are trying to solve. The "Solution" section explains how to implement the pattern. The "Benefits" section reviews why we need the pattern and how it has helped us solve the problem. Some of the benefits are hinted at in the "Problem" section. Others are additional benefits that come from the pattern.

on the job

The OCP 8 exam covers only one pattern; this is just to get your feet wet. Whole books have been written on the topic of design patterns. Head First Design Patterns *(O'Reilly Media, 2004) covers more patterns. And the most famous book on patterns—*Design Patterns: Elements of Reusable Object-Oriented Software *(Addison-Wesley Professional, 1994), also known as "Gang of Four"— covers 23 design patterns. You may notice that these books are more than 10 years old. That's because the classic patterns haven't changed.*

Problem

Let's suppose we're putting on a show. We're going to perform the show once, and we only have a few seats in the theater.

```
import java.util.*;

public class Show {
  private Set<String> availableSeats;
```

```
public Show() {
  availableSeats = new HashSet<String>();
  availableSeats.add("1A");
  availableSeats.add("1B");
}
public boolean bookSeat(String seat) {
  return availableSeats.remove(seat);
}
public static void main(String[] args) {
  ticketAgentBooks("1A");
  ticketAgentBooks("1A");
}
private static void ticketAgentBooks(String seat) {
  Show show = new Show();              // a new Show gets created
                                       // each time we call the method
  System.out.println(show.bookSeat(seat));
}
}
```

This code prints out true twice. That's a problem. We just put two people in the
same seat. Why? We created a new Show object every time we needed it. Even
though we want to use the same theater and seats, Show deals with a new set of
seats each time, which means we've double-booked seats.

Solution

There are a few ways to implement the singleton pattern. Here's the simplest:

```
import java.util.*;

public class Show {
  private static final Show INSTANCE    // store one instance
          = new Show();                 // (this is the singleton)
  private Set<String> availableSeats;

  public static Show getInstance() { // callers can get to
    return INSTANCE;                  // the instance
  }
  private Show() {                          // callers can't create
                                           // directly anymore.
                                           // Must use getInstance()

    availableSeats = new HashSet<String>();
    availableSeats.add("1A");
    availableSeats.add("1B");
  }
  public boolean bookSeat(String seat) {
    return availableSeats.remove(seat);
  }
```

```
public static void main(String[] args) {
  ticketAgentBooks("1A");
  ticketAgentBooks("1A");
}
private static void ticketAgentBooks(String seat) {
  Show show = Show.getInstance();
  System.out.println(show.bookSeat(seat));
}
}
```

Now the code prints `true` and `false`. Much better! We are no longer going to have two people sitting in the same seat. The bolded bits in the code call attention to the implementation of the singleton pattern.

The key parts of the singleton pattern are

- A private static variable to store the single instance called the singleton. This variable is usually final to keep developers from accidentally changing it.
- A public static method for callers to get a reference to the instance.
- A private constructor so no callers can instantiate the object directly.

Remember, the code doesn't create a new `Show` each time, but merely returns the singleton instance of `Show` each time `getInstance()` is called.

To understand this a little better, let's consider what happens if we change parts of the code.

If the constructor weren't private, we wouldn't have a singleton. Callers would be free to ignore `getInstance()` and instantiate their own instances, which would leave us with multiple instances in the program and defeat the purpose entirely.

If `getInstance()` weren't public, we would still have a singleton. However, it wouldn't be as useful because only methods in the same package would be able to use the singleton.

If `getInstance()` weren't static, we'd have a bigger problem. Callers couldn't instantiate the class directly, which means they wouldn't be able to call `getInstance()` at all.

If `INSTANCE` weren't static and final, we could have multiple instances at different points in time. These keywords signal that we assign the field once and it stays that way for the life of the program.

When talking about design patterns, it is also common to communicate the pattern in diagram form. The singleton pattern diagram looks like this:

Show
private static Show INSTANCE
private Show() public static Show getInstance()

The diagrams use a format called Unified Modeling Language (UML). The diagrams in this book use some aspects of UML, such as a box with three sections representing each class. Actual UML uses more notation, such as showing public versus private visibility. You can think of this as faux-UML.

As long as the method in the diagram keeps the same signature, we can change our logic to other implementations of the singleton pattern. One "feature" of the above implementation is that it creates the Show object before we need it. This is called *eager initialization,* which is good if the object isn't expensive to create or we know it will be needed every time the program runs. Sometimes, however, we want to create the object only on the first use. This is called *lazy* initialization.

```
private static Show INSTANCE;
private Set<String> availableSeats;
public static Show getInstance() {
  if (INSTANCE == null) {
    INSTANCE = new Show();
  }
  return INSTANCE;
}
```

In this case, INSTANCE isn't set to be a Show until the first time getInstance() is called. Walking through what happens, the first time getInstance() is called, Java sees INSTANCE is still null and creates the singleton. The second time getInstance() is called, Java sees INSTANCE has already been set and simply returns it. In this example, INSTANCE isn't final because that would prevent the code from compiling.

The singleton code here assumes you are only running one thread at a time. It is NOT thread-safe. What if this were a web site and two users managed to be booking a seat at the exact same time? If getInstance() were running at the exact same time, both of them could see that INSTANCE was null and create a new Show at the same time. There are a few ways to solve this. One is to add synchronized *to the* getInstance() *method. This works, but comes with a small performance hit. We're getting way beyond the scope of the exam, but you can Google "double checked locked pattern" for more information.*

You might have noticed that the code for `getInstance()` can get a bit complicated. Java 5 gave us a much shorter way of creating a singleton:

```java
public enum ShowEnum {                    // this is an enum
  INSTANCE;                               // instead of a class

  private Set<String> availableSeats;
  private ShowEnum() {
    availableSeats = new HashSet<String>();
    availableSeats.add("1A");
    availableSeats.add("1B");
  }
  public boolean bookSeat(String seat) {
    return availableSeats.remove(seat);
  }
  public static void main(String[] args) {
    ticketAgentBooks("1A");
    ticketAgentBooks("1A");
  }

  private static void ticketAgentBooks(String seat) {
    ShowEnum show = ShowEnum.INSTANCE;   // we don't even
                                         // need a method to
                                         // get the instance
    System.out.println(show.bookSeat(seat));
  }
}
```

Short and sweet. By definition, there is only one instance of an enum constant. You are probably wondering why we've had this whole discussion of the singleton pattern when you can write it so easily. The main reason is that enums were introduced with Java 5, and there is a ton of older code out there that you need to be able to understand. Another reason is that sometimes you still need the older versions of the pattern.

Benefits

Benefits of the singleton pattern include the following:

- The primary benefit is that there is only one instance of the object in the program. When an object's instance variables are keeping track of information that is used across the program, it's useful. For example, consider a web site visitor counter. You only want one count that is shared.
- Another benefit is performance. Some objects are expensive to create; for example, maybe we need to make a database call to look up the state for the object.

CERTIFICATION OBJECTIVE

Immutable Classes (OCP Objective 1.5)

1.5   Create and use singleton classes and immutable classes.

Immutable classes aren't a new idea, but they're new to the OCP exam. Because they are inherently thread-safe, immutable classes are particularly useful in applications that include concurrency and/or parallelism. In this world of big data and fast data, the need for concurrency and parallelism is on the rise, so adding immutable classes to the exam is a timely choice.

You're already familiar with so-called "immutable classes" because String is a great example of one! One way of looking at the String class is that you might want to create an object that has a string value AND you want to allow others to have access to your string's value, but you don't want to let anyone (including you) change the object's value. That's exactly what a String object allows.

You can create your own "immutable classes" whenever you have a design goal similar to the one described above—in other words, whenever you want to create a class whose objects' values are immutable. In addition, usually when you want a type that creates only immutable objects, you won't want people to be able to extend your class and undo your immutability goal, so immutable classes should be marked `final`. Again, this is just like the String class (which is also a `final` class).

Other than the immutability of values and their "final-ness," there is nothing unique about these classes. You can design them to be instantiated via constructors or by using a factory method. They can have behavior like the String class has. The only difference is that—by definition—the class's object's variables can't be changed. Let's look at what steps are necessary to develop an immutable class.

Imagine your team is developing an audio synthesizer app for Android. An important part of the synth software is the ADSR envelope. (ADSR stands for attack, decay, sustain, and release.) A given ADSR envelope describes a unique sound. You want your users to be able to create, save, and share the custom ADSR envelope objects they've created, but your users don't want anyone to be able to alter their unique sonic creations. Below is the code for our ADSR immutable class. (Note: For the sake of brevity, we omitted the code for the sustain and release values, but it will be the same as the code we show for attack and decay.)

```
final class ADSR {                         // final class, can't be
extended
  private final StringBuilder name;
  private final int attack;
```

```
    private final int decay;
    // sustain and release code omitted (for brevity)

    public ADSR(StringBuilder n,              // public constructor
                int a, int d) {
      this.name = n;
      this.attack = a;
      this.decay = d;
    }

    // Notice there are NO SETTERS !

    public StringBuilder getName() {          // return a new object
                                              // not the original
      StringBuilder nameCopy = new StringBuilder(name);
      return nameCopy;
    }
    public ADSR getADSR() { return this; }  // return an immutable object
}
```

The code above allows the following:

- You can build your own immutable ADSR objects with secret values.
- You can share your ADSR objects.
- Your users can read the name field of your objects, but they can't mutate your objects.

Does this all make sense? Does the code look bulletproof? There is a problem with the way we implemented the ADSR class! Let's look at a test class:

```
public class TestADSR {
  public static void main(String[] args) {
    StringBuilder sb = new StringBuilder("a1 ");
    ADSR a1 = new ADSR(sb, 5, 7);
    ADSR a2 = a1.getADSR();
    System.out.println(a1.getName());
    sb.append("alter the name ");
    System.out.println(a1.getName());
  }
}
```

which produces the output:

```
a1
a1 alter the name
```

Oops! Our constructor is using the same `StringBuilder` object as the one used by the method that invoked the constructor. (Note: If you're thinking "Don't use a `StringBuilder`, use a `String`" to give yourself extra points. We used a

`StringBuilder` to demonstrate how to deal with instance variables that are of a mutable, nonprimitive type.) So we gotta fix that! Here's the fixed version of the ADSR class:

```
// immutable class - version 2
final class ADSR {                          // final class, can't be extended
  private final StringBuilder name;
  private final int attack;
  private final int decay;
  // sustain and release code omitted (for brevity)

  public ADSR(StringBuilder n,              // public constructor
              int a, int d) {
    name = new StringBuilder(n);            // make a new object for the name
!
    this.attack = a;
    this.decay = d;
  }
  public StringBuilder getName() {          // return a new object
                                            // not the original
    StringBuilder nameCopy = new StringBuilder(name);
    if(nameCopy != name)
      System.out.println("different objects");
    return nameCopy;
  }
  public ADSR getADSR() { return this; }
}
public class TestADSR {
  public static void main(String[] args) {
    StringBuilder sb = new StringBuilder("a1 ");
    ADSR a1 = new ADSR(sb, 5, 7);
    ADSR a2 = a1.getADSR();
    System.out.println(a1.getName());
    sb.append("alter the name ");
    System.out.println(a1.getName());
  }
}
```

which produces:

```
a1
a1
```

Much better! Here's a list of things to do to create an immutable class:

1. Mark the class final so that it cannot be extended.

2. Mark its variables private and final.

3. If the constructor takes any mutable objects as arguments, make new copies of those objects in the constructor.

4. Do NOT provide any setter methods!

5. If any of the getter methods return a mutable object reference, make a copy of the actual object, and return a reference to the copy.

Notice that points 3 and 5 both discuss making copies of objects. This idea is an aspect of what is sometimes referred to as "defensive copying." If some of this section reminds you of ideas in the "Encapsulation" section earlier in this chapter, congratulations! An immutable class is—by definition—extremely well encapsulated.

In the real world there are some more advanced ideas associated with immutable classes, but if you understand this section, you'll be fine for the exam.

on the Job

In this section we've often put quotes around the phrase "immutable class" because it's a bit of a misnomer. More accurately, what we're talking about here are classes whose objects are immutable.

CERTIFICATION OBJECTIVE

Initialization Blocks (OCP Objective 1.6)

1.6   Develop code that uses static keyword (sic) on initialize blocks, variables, methods, and classes.

We've talked about two places in a class where you can put code that performs operations: methods and constructors. There is also a third place in a Java program where operations can be performed: initialization blocks. Static initialization blocks run when the class is first loaded, and instance initialization blocks run whenever an instance is created (a bit similar to a constructor). Let's look at an example:

```
class SmallInit {
static int x;
int y;

static { x = 7 ; }       // static init block
{ y = 8; }               // instance init block
}
```

As you can see, the syntax for initialization blocks is pretty terse. They don't have names, they can't take arguments, and they don't return anything. A *static* initialization block runs *once* when the class is first loaded. An *instance* initialization block runs once *every time a new instance is created*. Remember when we talked about the order in which constructor code executed? Instance `init` block code runs right after the call to `super()` in a constructor and before any of the other code in the constructor—in other words, after all `super` constructors have run.

You can have many initialization blocks in a class. It is important to note that unlike methods or constructors, *the order in which initialization blocks appear in a class matters*. When it's time for initialization blocks to run, if a class has more than one, they will run in the order in which they appear in the class file—in other words, from the top down. Based on the rules we just discussed, can you determine the output of the following program?

```
class Init {
  Init(int x) { System.out.println("1-arg const"); }
  Init() { System.out.println("no-arg const"); }
  static { System.out.println("1st static init"); }
  { System.out.println("1st instance init"); }
  { System.out.println("2nd instance init"); }
  static { System.out.println("2nd static init"); }

  public static void main(String [] args) {
    new Init();
    new Init(7);
  }
}
```

To figure this out, remember these rules:

- `init` blocks execute in the order in which they appear.
- Static `init` blocks run once, when the class is first loaded.
- Instance `init` blocks run every time a class instance is created.
- Instance `init` blocks run after the constructor's call to `super()`.

With those rules in mind, the following output should make sense:

```
1st static init
2nd static init
1st instance init
2nd instance init
no-arg const
1st instance init
2nd instance init
1-arg const
```

As you can see, the instance `init` blocks each ran twice. Instance `init` blocks are often used as a place to put code that all the constructors in a class should share. That way, the code doesn't have to be duplicated across constructors.

Finally, if you make a mistake in your static `init` block, the JVM can throw an `ExceptionInInitializerError`. Let's look at an example:

```
class InitError {
  static int [] x = new int[4];
  static { x[4] = 5; }              // bad array index!
  public static void main(String [] args) { }
}
```

It produces something like this:

```
Exception in thread "main" java.lang.ExceptionInInitializerError
Caused by: java.lang.ArrayIndexOutOfBoundsException: 4
        at InitError.<clinit>(InitError.java:3)
```

By convention, `init` blocks usually appear near the top of the class file, somewhere around the constructors. However, this is the OCP exam we're talking about. Don't be surprised if you find an `init` block tucked in between a couple of methods, looking for all the world like a compiler error waiting to happen!

CERTIFICATION OBJECTIVE

Statics (OCP Objective 1.6)

1.6 Develop code that uses static keyword (sic) on initialize blocks, variables, methods, and classes.

Static Variables and Methods

The `static` modifier has such a profound impact on the behavior of a method or variable that we're treating it as a concept entirely separate from the other modifiers. To understand the way a `static` member works, we'll look first at a reason for using one. Imagine you've got a utility class or interface with a method that always runs the same way; its sole function is to return, say, a random number. It wouldn't matter which instance of the class performed the method—it would always behave exactly the same way. In other words, the method's behavior has no dependency on the state (instance variable values) of an object. So why, then, do you need an object when the method will never be instance-specific? Why not just ask the type itself to run the method?

Let's imagine another scenario: Suppose you want to keep a running count of all instances instantiated from a particular class. Where do you actually keep that variable? It won't work to keep it as an instance variable within the class whose instances you're tracking, because the count will just be initialized back to a default value with each new instance. The answer to both the utility-method-always-runs-the-same scenario and the keep-a-running-total-of-instances scenario is to use the static modifier. Variables and methods marked static belong to the type, rather than to any particular instance. In fact, for classes, you can use a static method or variable without having any instances of that class at all. You need only have the type available to be able to invoke a static method or access a static variable. static variables, too, can be accessed without having an instance of a class. But if there are instances, a static variable of a class will be shared by all instances of that class; there is only one copy.

The following code declares and uses a static counter variable:

```
class Frog {
  static int frogCount = 0;   // Declare and initialize
                              // static variable
  public Frog() {
    frogCount += 1;           // Modify the value in the constructor
  }
  public static void main (String [] args) {
    new Frog();
    new Frog();
    new Frog();
    System.out.println("Frog count is now " + frogCount);
  }
}
```

In the preceding code, the static frogCount variable is set to zero when the Frog class is first loaded by the JVM, before any Frog instances are created! (By the way, you don't actually need to initialize a static variable to zero; static variables get the same default values instance variables get, but it's good practice to initialize them anyway.) Whenever a `Frog` instance is created, the `Frog` constructor runs and increments the `static frogCount` variable. When this code executes, three `Frog` instances are created in `main()`, and the result is

```
Frog count is now 3
```

Now imagine what would happen if `frogCount` were an instance variable (in other words, nonstatic):

```
class Frog {
  int frogCount = 0;   // Declare and initialize
                       // instance variable
  public Frog() {
    frogCount += 1;    // Modify the value in the constructor
  }
  public static void main (String [] args) {
    new Frog();
    new Frog();
    new Frog();
    System.out.println("Frog count is now " + frogCount);
  }
}
```

When this code executes, it should still create three `Frog` instances in `main()`, but the result is...a compiler error! We can't get this code to compile, let alone run.

```
Frog.java:11: nonstatic variable frogCount cannot be referenced
from a static context
   System.out.println("Frog count is " + frogCount);
                                         ^
   1 error
```

The JVM doesn't know which Frog object's `frogCount` you're trying to access. The problem is that `main()` is itself a `static` method and thus isn't running against any particular instance of the class; instead it's running on the class itself. A `static` method can't access a nonstatic (instance) variable because there is no instance! That's not to say there aren't instances of the class alive on the heap, but rather that even if there are, the `static` method doesn't know anything about them. The same applies to instance methods; a `static` method can't directly invoke a nonstatic method. Think static = class, nonstatic = instance. Making the method called by the JVM (`main()`) a `static` method means the JVM doesn't have to create an instance of your class just to start running code.

e x a m

w a t c h   *One of the mistakes most often made by new Java programmers is attempting to access an instance variable (which means nonstatic variable) from the static* `main()` *method (which doesn't know anything about any instances, so it can't access the variable). The following code is an example of illegal access of a nonstatic variable from a* `static` *method:*

```
class Foo {
  int x = 3;
    public static void main (String [] args) {
      System.out.println("x is " + x);
  }
}
```

Understand that this code will never compile, because you can't access a nonstatic (instance) variable from a `static` *method. Just think of the compiler saying, "Hey, I have no idea which* `Foo` *object's x variable you're trying to print!" Remember, it's the class running the* `main()` *method, not an instance of the class.*

   Of course, the tricky part for the exam is that the question won't look as obvious as the preceding code. The problem you're being tested for—accessing a nonstatic variable from a `static` *method—will be buried in code that might appear to be testing something else. For example, the preceding code would be more likely to appear as*

```
class Foo {
  int x = 3;
  float y = 4.3f;
  public static void main (String [] args) {
    for (int z = x; z < ++x; z--, y = y + z)
    // complicated looping and branching code
  }
}
```

   So while you're trying to follow the logic, the real issue is that x and y can't be used within `main()` *because x and y are instance, not* `static`, *variables! The same applies for accessing nonstatic methods from a* `static` *method. The rule is that a* `static` *method of a class can't access a nonstatic (instance) method or variable of its own class.*

Accessing Static Methods and Variables

Since you don't need to have an instance in order to invoke a static method or access a static variable, how do you invoke or use a `static` member? What's the syntax? We know that with a regular old instance method, you use the dot operator on a reference to an instance:

```
class Frog {
  int frogSize = 0;
  public int getFrogSize() {
    return frogSize;
  }
  public Frog(int s) {
    frogSize = s;
  }
  public static void main (String [] args) {
    Frog f = new Frog(25);
    System.out.println(f.getFrogSize()); // Access instance
                                         // method using f
  }
}
```

In the preceding code, we instantiate a `Frog`, assign it to the reference variable `f`, and then use that `f` reference to invoke a method on the `Frog` instance we just created. In other words, the `getFrogSize()` method is being invoked on a specific `Frog` object on the heap.

But this approach (using a reference to an object) isn't appropriate for accessing a `static` method because there might not be any instances of the class at all! So the way we access a `static` method (or `static` variable) is to use the dot operator on the type name, as opposed to using it on a reference to an instance, as follows:

```
class Frog {
  private static int frogCount = 0;  // static variable
  static int getCount() {            // static getter method
    return frogCount;
  }
  public Frog() {
    frogCount += 1;         // Modify the value in the constructor
  }
}
class TestFrog {
  public static void main (String [] args) {
    new Frog();
    new Frog();
    new Frog();
    System.out.println("from static " + Frog.getCount());   // static context
    new Frog();
```

```
    new TestFrog().go();
    Frog f = new Frog();
    System.out.println("use ref var " + f.getCount());       // use reference var
  }
  void go() {
    System.out.println("from instance " + Frog.getCount());  // instance context
  }
}
```

which produces the output:

```
from static 3
from instance 4
use ref var 5
```

But just to make it really confusing, the Java language also allows you to use an object reference variable to access a static member. Did you catch the last line of main()? It included this invocation:

f.getCount(); // Access a static using an instance variable

In the preceding code, we instantiate a Frog, assign the new Frog object to the reference variable f, and then use the f reference to invoke a static method! But even though we are using a specific Frog instance to access the static method, the rules haven't changed. This is merely a syntax trick to let you use an object reference variable (but not the object it refers to) to get to a static method or variable, but the static member is still unaware of the particular instance used to invoke the static member. In the Frog example, the compiler knows that the reference variable f is of type Frog, and so the Frog class static method is run with no awareness or concern for the Frog instance at the other end of the f reference. In other words, the compiler cares only that reference variable f is declared as type Frog.

Invoking static methods from interfaces is almost the same as invoking static methods from classes, except the "instance variable syntax trick" just discussed works only for static methods in classes. The following code demonstrates how interface static methods can and cannot be invoked:

```
interface FrogBoilable {
  static int getCtoF(int cTemp) {                  // interface static method
    return (cTemp * 9 / 5) + 32;
  }
  default String hop() { return "hopping"; }       // interface default method
}

public class DontBoilFrogs implements FrogBoilable {
  public static void main(String[] args) {
    new DontBoilFrogs().go();
  }
```

```
void go() {
  System.out.println(hop());               // 1 - ok for default method
  // System.out.println(getCtoF(100));      // 2 - cannot find symbol

  System.out.println(
      FrogBoilable.getCtoF(100));           // 3 - ok for static method
  DontBoilFrogs dbf = new DontBoilFrogs();
  // System.out.println(dbf.getCtoF(100));  // 4 - cannot find symbol
  }
}
```

Let's review the code:

- **Line 1** is a legal invocation of an interface's `default` method.
- **Line 2** is an **illegal** attempt to invoke an interface's `static` method.
- **Line 3** is THE legal way to invoke an interface's `static` method.
- **Line 4** is another **illegal** attempt to invoke an interface's `static` method.

Figure 2-8 illustrates the effects of the `static` modifier on methods and variables.

FIGURE 2-8

The effects of `static` on methods and variables

```
class Foo

int size = 42;
static void doMore( ){
  int x = size;
}
```
static method cannot access an instance (nonstatic) variable

```
class Bar

void go(){}
static void doMore( ){
  go( );
}
```
static method cannot access a nonstatic method

```
class Baz

static int count;
static void woo( ){ }
static void doMore( ){
  woo( );
  int x = count;
}
```
static method *can* access a static method or variable

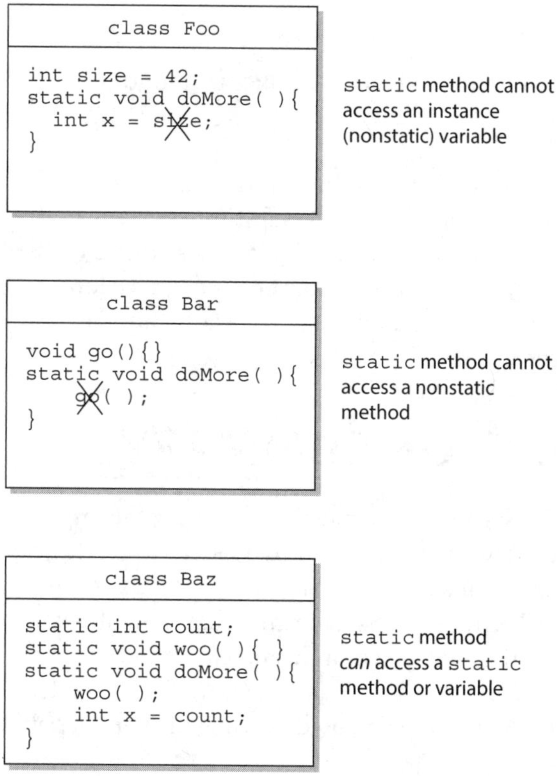

Finally, remember that *static methods can't be overridden*! This doesn't mean they can't be redefined in a subclass, but redefining and overriding aren't the same thing. Let's look at an example of a redefined (remember, not overridden) static method:

```
class Animal {
  static void doStuff() {
    System.out.print("a ");
  }
}
class Dog extends Animal {
  static void doStuff() {               // it's a redefinition,
                                        // not an override
    System.out.print("d ");
  }
  public static void main(String [] args) {
    Animal [] a = {new Animal(), new Dog(), new Animal()};
    for(int x = 0; x < a.length; x++) {
      a[x].doStuff();                   // invoke the static method
    }
    Dog.doStuff();                      // invoke using the class name
  }
}
```

Running this code produces this output:

```
a a a d
```

Remember, the syntax a [x].doStuff() is just a shortcut (the syntax trick)—the compiler is going to substitute something like Animal.doStuff() instead. Notice also that you can invoke a static method by using the class name.

We also didn't use the enhanced for loop here, even though we could have. Expect to see a mix of both Java 1.4 and Java 5–8 coding styles and practices on the exam.

CERTIFICATION SUMMARY

We started the chapter by discussing the importance of encapsulation in good OO design, and then we talked about how good encapsulation is implemented: with private instance variables and public getters and setters.

Next, we covered the importance of inheritance, so that you can grasp overriding, overloading, polymorphism, reference casting, return types, and constructors.

We covered IS-A and HAS-A. IS-A is implemented using inheritance, and HAS-A is implemented by using instance variables that refer to other objects.

Polymorphism was next. Although a reference variable's type can't be changed, it can be used to refer to an object whose type is a subtype of its own. We learned how to determine what methods are invocable for a given reference variable.

We looked at the difference between overridden and overloaded methods, learning that an overridden method occurs when a subtype inherits a method from a supertype and then reimplements the method to add more specialized behavior. We learned that, at runtime, the JVM will invoke the subtype version on an instance of a subtype and the supertype version on an instance of the supertype. `Abstract` methods must be "overridden" (technically, `abstract` methods must be implemented, as opposed to overridden, since there really isn't anything to override).

We saw that overriding methods must declare the same argument list and return type or they can return a subtype of the declared return type of the supertype's overridden method), and that the access modifier can't be more restrictive. The overriding method also can't throw any new or broader checked exceptions that weren't declared in the overridden method. You also learned that the overridden method can be invoked using the syntax `super.doSomething();`.

Overloaded methods let you reuse the same method name in a class, but with different arguments (and, optionally, a different return type). Whereas overriding methods must not change the argument list, overloaded methods must. But unlike overriding methods, overloaded methods are free to vary the return type, access modifier, and declared exceptions any way they like.

We ended our discussions of overriding by looking at the `@Override` annotation. You can use this annotation to tell the compiler that you intend for the method that follows the annotation to either be an override of a superclass method or an implementation of an interface method. The compiler will tell you if you're doing it wrong.

We learned the mechanics of casting (mostly downcasting) reference variables and when it's necessary to do so.

Implementing interfaces came next. An interface describes a *contract* that the implementing class must follow. The rules for implementing an interface are similar to those for extending an `abstract` class. As of Java 8, interfaces can have concrete methods, which are labeled `default` or `static`. Also, remember that a class can implement more than one interface and that interfaces can extend another interface.

We also looked at method return types and saw that you can declare any return type you like (assuming you have access to a class for an object reference return type), unless you're overriding a method. Barring a covariant return, an overriding method must have the same return type as the overridden method of the superclass. We saw that, although overriding methods must not change the return type, overloaded methods can (as long as they also change the argument list).

Finally, you learned that it is legal to return any value or variable that can be implicitly converted to the declared return type. So, for example, a `short` can be returned when the return type is declared as an `int`. And (assuming `Horse` extends `Animal`), a `Horse` reference can be returned when the return type is declared an `Animal`.

We covered constructors in detail, learning that if you don't provide a constructor for your class, the compiler will insert one. The compiler-generated constructor is called the default constructor, and it is always a no-arg constructor with a no-arg call to `super()`. The default constructor will never be generated if even a single constructor exists in your class (regardless of the arguments of that constructor); so if you need more than one constructor in your class and you want a no-arg constructor, you'll have to write it yourself. We also saw that constructors are not inherited and that you can be confused by a method that has the same name as the class (which is legal). The return type is the giveaway that a method is not a constructor because constructors do not have return types.

We saw how all the constructors in an object's inheritance tree will always be invoked when the object is instantiated using `new`. We also saw that constructors can be overloaded, which means defining constructors with different argument lists. A constructor can invoke another constructor of the same class using the keyword `this()`, as though the constructor were a method named `this()`. We saw that every constructor must have either `this()` or `super()` as the first statement (although the compiler can insert it for you).

After constructors, we did a quick introduction to design patterns, focusing on a common pattern, the singleton. You use the singleton pattern whenever you want to make sure that only one instance of a class can ever be created.

After singleton, we introduced immutable classes. The phrase "immutable class" is a bit misleading; you should think of these as thread-safe classes whose objects are made immutable through the generous use of the `private` and `final` keywords and by not providing any setter methods.

Next, we discussed the two kinds of initialization blocks and how and when their code runs.

We looked at `static` methods and variables. `static` members are tied to the class or interface, not an instance, so there is only one copy of any `static` member. A common mistake is to attempt to reference an instance variable from a `static` method. Use the respective class or interface name with the dot operator to access `static` members.

And, once again, you learned that the exam includes tricky questions designed largely to test your ability to recognize just how tricky the questions can be.

TWO-MINUTE DRILL

Here are some of the key points from each certification objective in this chapter.

Encapsulation, IS-A, HAS-A* (OCP Objectives 1.1 and 1.2)

- ☐ Encapsulation helps hide implementation behind an interface (or API).
- ☐ Encapsulated code has two features:
    - ☐ Instance variables are kept protected (usually with the `private` modifier).
    - ☐ Getter and setter methods provide access to instance variables.
- ☐ IS-A refers to inheritance or implementation.
- ☐ IS-A is expressed with the keyword `extends` or `implements`.
- ☐ IS-A, "inherits from," and "is a subtype of" are all equivalent expressions.
- ☐ HAS-A means an instance of one class "has a" reference to an instance of another class or another instance of the same class. *HAS-A is NOT on the exam, but it's good to know.

Inheritance (OCP Objective 1.2)

- ☐ Inheritance allows a type to be a subtype of a supertype and thereby inherit `public` and `protected` variables and methods of the supertype.
- ☐ Inheritance is a key concept that underlies IS-A, polymorphism, overriding, overloading, and casting.
- ☐ All classes (except class `Object`) are subclasses of type `Object`, and therefore they inherit `Object`'s methods.

Polymorphism (OCP Objective 1.3)

- ☐ Polymorphism means "many forms."
- ☐ A reference variable is always of a single, unchangeable type, but it can refer to a subtype object.
- ☐ A single object can be referred to by reference variables of many different types—as long as they are the same type or a supertype of the object.

☐ The reference variable's type (not the object's type) determines which methods can be called!

☐ Polymorphic method invocations apply only to overridden *instance* methods.

Overriding and Overloading (OCP Objectives 1.2 and 1.3)

☐ Methods can be overridden or overloaded; constructors can be overloaded but not overridden.

☐ With respect to the method it overrides, the overriding method

   ☐ Must have the same argument list

   ☐ Must have the same return type or a subclass (known as a covariant return)

   ☐ Must not have a more restrictive access modifier

   ☐ May have a less restrictive access modifier

   ☐ Must not throw new or broader checked exceptions

   ☐ May throw fewer or narrower checked exceptions, or any unchecked exception

☐ `final` methods cannot be overridden.

☐ Only inherited methods may be overridden, and remember that private methods are not inherited.

☐ A subclass uses `super.overriddenMethodName()` to call the superclass version of an overridden method.

☐ A subclass uses `MyInterface.super.overriddenMethodName()` to call the super interface version on an overridden method.

☐ Overloading means reusing a method name but with different arguments.

☐ Overloaded methods

   ☐ Must have different argument lists

   ☐ May have different return types, if argument lists are also different

   ☐ May have different access modifiers

   ☐ May throw different exceptions

☐ Methods from a supertype can be overloaded in a subtype.

☐ Polymorphism applies to overriding, not to overloading.

☐ Object type (not the reference variable's type) determines which overridden method is used at runtime.

☐ Reference type determines which overloaded method will be used at compile time.

@Override Annotation (OCP Objective 2.5)

- ☐ The @Override annotation can be used to ask the compiler to verify that you've properly overridden a method.
- ☐ The @Override annotation can be used to ask the compiler to verify that you've properly implemented an interface method.

Reference Variable Casting (OCP Objectives 1.2 and 1.3)

- ☐ There are two types of reference variable casting: downcasting and upcasting.
  - ☐ **Downcasting** If you have a reference variable that refers to a subtype object, you can assign it to a reference variable of the subtype. You must make an explicit cast to do this, and the result is that you can access the subtype's members with this new reference variable.
  - ☐ **Upcasting** You can assign a reference variable to a supertype reference variable explicitly or implicitly. This is an inherently safe operation because the assignment restricts the access capabilities of the new variable.

Implementing an Interface (OCP Objective 2.5)

- ☐ When you implement an interface, you are fulfilling its contract.
- ☐ You implement an interface by properly and concretely implementing all the abstract methods defined by the interface.
- ☐ A single class can implement many interfaces.

Return Types (OCP Objectives 1.2 and 1.3)

- ☐ Overloaded methods can change return types; overridden methods cannot, except in the case of covariant returns.
- ☐ Object reference return types can accept `null` as a return value.
- ☐ An array is a legal return type, both to declare and return as a value.
- ☐ For methods with primitive return types, any value that can be implicitly converted to the return type can be returned.
- ☐ Nothing can be returned from a `void`, but you can return nothing. You're allowed to simply say `return` in any method with a `void` return type to bust out of a method early. But you can't return nothing from a method with a non-`void` return type.

☐ Methods with an object reference return type can return a subtype.

☐ Methods with an interface return type can return any implementer.

Constructors and Instantiation (OCP Objectives 1.2 and 1.3)

☐ A constructor is always invoked when a new object is created.

☐ When a new object is created, a constructor for each superclass in the object's inheritance tree will be invoked.

☐ Every class, even an abstract class, has at least one constructor.

☐ Constructors must have the same name as the class.

☐ Constructors don't have a return type. If you see code with a return type, it's a method with the same name as the class; it's not a constructor.

☐ Typical constructor execution occurs as follows:

   ☐ The constructor calls its superclass constructor, which calls its superclass constructor, and so on, all the way up to the `Object` constructor.

   ☐ The `Object` constructor executes and then returns to the calling constructor, which runs to completion and then returns to its calling constructor, and so on, back down to the completion of the constructor of the actual instance being created.

☐ Constructors can use any access modifier (even `private`!).

☐ The compiler will create a default constructor if you don't create any constructors in your class.

☐ The default constructor is a no-arg constructor with a no-arg call to `super()`.

☐ The first statement of every constructor must be a call either to `this()` (an overloaded constructor) or to `super()`.

☐ The compiler will add a call to `super()` unless you have already put in a call to `this()` or `super()`.

☐ Instance members are accessible only after the `super` constructor runs.

☐ `Abstract` classes have constructors that are called when a concrete subclass is instantiated.

☐ Interfaces do not have constructors.

- ☐ If your superclass does not have a no-arg constructor, you must create a constructor and insert a call to `super()` with arguments matching those of the superclass constructor.
- ☐ Constructors are never inherited; thus, they cannot be overridden.
- ☐ A constructor can be directly invoked only by another constructor (using a call to `super()` or `this()`).
- ☐ Regarding issues with calls to `this()`:
  - ☐ They may appear only as the first statement in a constructor.
  - ☐ The argument list determines which overloaded constructor is called.
  - ☐ Constructors can call constructors, and so on, but sooner or later one of them better call `super()` or the stack will explode.
  - ☐ Calls to `this()` and `super()` cannot be in the same constructor. You can have one or the other, but never both.

Singleton Design Pattern (OCP Objective 1.5)

- ☐ A design pattern is "a general reusable solution to a commonly occurring problem within a given context."
- ☐ Having only one instance of the object allows a program to share its state.
- ☐ This pattern might improve performance by not repeating the same work.
- ☐ This pattern often stores a single instance as a static variable.
- ☐ We can instantiate right away (eager) or when needed (lazy).

Immutable Classes (OCP Objective 1.5)

- ☐ Since they are thread-safe, they are great for concurrent and/or parallel applications.
- ☐ They should be built using the following guidelines:
  - ☐ Mark the class final
  - ☐ Mark the variables private and final
  - ☐ Do NOT provide setter methods
  - ☐ Whenever references to mutable types are sent or received, a defensive copy should be used.
- ☐ Unlike singletons, many instances of an immutable class can be made.

Initialization Blocks (OCP Objective 1.6)

☐ Use `static init` blocks—`static { /* code here */ }`—for code you want to have run once, when the class is first loaded. Multiple blocks run from the top down.

☐ Use normal `init` blocks—`{ /* code here }`—for code you want to have run for every new instance, right after all the super constructors have run. Again, multiple blocks run from the top of the class down.

Statics (OCP Objective 1.6)

☐ Use `static` methods to implement behaviors that are not affected by the state of any instances.

☐ Use `static` variables to hold data that is class specific as opposed to instance specific—there will be only one copy of a `static` variable.

☐ All `static` members belong to the class, not to any instance.

☐ A `static` method can't access an instance variable directly.

☐ Use the dot operator to access `static` members, but remember that using a reference variable with the dot operator is really a syntax trick, and the compiler will substitute the class name for the reference variable; for instance:

```
d.doStuff();
```

becomes

```
Dog.doStuff();
```

☐ To invoke an interface's static method, use `MyInterface.doStuff()` syntax.

☐ `static` methods can't be overridden, but they can be redefined.

SELF TEST

1. Given:

```
public abstract interface Frobnicate { public void twiddle(String s); }
```

Which is a correct class? (Choose all that apply.)

A. `public abstract class Frob implements Frobnicate {`
   `    public abstract void twiddle(String s) { }`
   `}`

B. `public abstract class Frob implements Frobnicate { }`

C. `public class Frob extends Frobnicate {`
   `    public void twiddle(Integer i) { }`
   `}`

D. `public class Frob implements Frobnicate {`
   `    public void twiddle(Integer i) { }`
   `}`

E. `public class Frob implements Frobnicate {`
   `    public void twiddle(String i) { }`
   `    public void twiddle(Integer s) { }`
   `}`

2. Given:

```
class Top {
  public Top(String s) { System.out.print("B"); }
}
public class Bottom2 extends Top {
  public Bottom2(String s) { System.out.print("D"); }
  public static void main(String [] args) {
    new Bottom2("C");
    System.out.println(" ");
  }
}
```

What is the result?

A. BD

B. DB

C. BDC

D. DBC

E. Compilation fails

3. Given:

```
class Clidder {
  private final void flipper() { System.out.println("Clidder"); }
}
public class Clidlet extends Clidder {
  public final void flipper() { System.out.println("Clidlet"); }
  public static void main(String [] args) {
    new Clidlet().flipper();
  }
}
```

What is the result?

A. `Clidlet`

B. `Clidder`

C. `Clidder`
   `Clidlet`

D. `Clidlet`
   `Clidder`

E. Compilation fails

Special Note: The next question crudely simulates a "drag-and-drop" style of question that you probably will NOT encounter on the exam, but just in case, we've left a few drag-and-drop questions in the book.

4. Using the **fragments** below, complete the following **code** so it compiles. Note that you may not have to fill in all of the slots.

Code:

```
class AgedP {
  _____  _____   _____   _____

  public AgedP(int x) {
    _____  _____   _____   _____

  }}
public class Kinder extends AgedP {
  _____   _____   _____   _____

  public Kinder(int x) {
    _____   _____   _____   _____   _____ ();
  }}
```

Fragments: Use the following fragments zero or more times:

AgedP	super	this	
(	)	{	}
;			

5. Given:

```
class Bird {
   { System.out.print("b1 "); }
   public Bird() { System.out.print("b2 "); }
}
class Raptor extends Bird {
   static { System.out.print("r1 "); }
   public Raptor() { System.out.print("r2 "); }
   { System.out.print("r3 "); }
   static { System.out.print("r4 "); }
}
class Hawk extends Raptor {
   public static void main(String[] args) {
      System.out.print("pre ");
      new Hawk();
      System.out.println("hawk ");
   }
}
```

What is the result?

A. pre b1 b2 r3 r2 hawk

B. pre b2 b1 r2 r3 hawk

C. pre b2 b1 r2 r3 hawk r1 r4

D. r1 r4 pre b1 b2 r3 r2 hawk

E. r1 r4 pre b2 b1 r2 r3 hawk

F. pre r1 r4 b1 b2 r3 r2 hawk

G. pre r1 r4 b2 b1 r2 r3 hawk

H. The order of output cannot be predicted

I. Compilation fails

Note: You'll probably never see this many choices on the real exam!

6. Given the following:

```
1. class X { void do1() { } }
2. class Y extends X { void do2() { } }
3.
4. class Chrome {
5.    public static void main(String [] args) {
```

```
 6.      X x1 = new X();
 7.      X x2 = new Y();
 8.      Y y1 = new Y();
 9.      // insert code here
10. } }
```

Which of the following, inserted at line 9, will compile? (Choose all that apply.)

A.   x2.do2();

B.   (Y)x2.do2();

C.   ((Y)x2).do2();

D.   None of the above statements will compile

7.   Given:

```
public class Locomotive {
   Locomotive() { main("hi"); }

   public static void main(String[] args) {
     System.out.print("2 ");
   }
   public static void main(String args) {
     System.out.print("3 " + args);
   }
}
```

What is the result? (Choose all that apply.)

A.   2 will be included in the output

B.   3 will be included in the output

C.   hi will be included in the output

D.   Compilation fails

E.   An exception is thrown at runtime

8.   Given:

```
 3. class Dog {
 4.    public void bark() { System.out.print("woof "); }
 5. }
 6. class Hound extends Dog {
 7.    public void sniff() { System.out.print("sniff "); }
 8.    public void bark() { System.out.print("howl "); }
 9. }
10. public class DogShow {
11.    public static void main(String[] args) { new DogShow().go(); }
12.    void go() {
13.      new Hound().bark();
14.      ((Dog) new Hound()).bark();
```

```
15.     ((Dog) new Hound()).sniff();
16.   }
17. }
```

What is the result? (Choose all that apply.)

A. `howl howl sniff`

B. `howl woof sniff`

C. `howl howl` followed by an exception

D. `howl woof` followed by an exception

E. Compilation fails with an error at line 14

F. Compilation fails with an error at line 15

9. Given:

```
3. public class Redwood extends Tree {
4.    public static void main(String[] args) {
5.      new Redwood().go();
6.    }
7.    void go() {
8.      go2(new Tree(), new Redwood());
9.      go2((Redwood) new Tree(), new Redwood());
10.   }
11.   void go2(Tree t1, Redwood r1) {
12.      Redwood r2 = (Redwood)t1;
13.      Tree t2 = (Tree)r1;
14.   }
15. }
16. class Tree { }
```

What is the result? (Choose all that apply.)

A. An exception is thrown at runtime

B. The code compiles and runs with no output

C. Compilation fails with an error at line 8

D. Compilation fails with an error at line 9

E. Compilation fails with an error at line 12

F. Compilation fails with an error at line 13

10. Given:

```
3. public class Tenor extends Singer {
4.    public static String sing() { return "fa"; }
5.    public static void main(String[] args) {
6.      Tenor t = new Tenor();
7.      Singer s = new Tenor();
8.      System.out.println(t.sing() + " " + s.sing());
```

```
 9.    }
10.  }
11.  class Singer { public static String sing() { return "la"; } }
```

What is the result?

A. fa fa

B. fa la

C. la la

D. Compilation fails

E. An exception is thrown at runtime

11. Given:

```
 3. class Alpha {
 4.    static String s = " ";
 5.    protected Alpha() { s += "alpha "; }
 6. }
 7. class SubAlpha extends Alpha {
 8.    private SubAlpha() { s += "sub "; }
 9. }
10. public class SubSubAlpha extends Alpha {
11.    private SubSubAlpha() { s += "subsub "; }
12.    public static void main(String[] args) {
13.       new SubSubAlpha();
14.       System.out.println(s);
15.    }
16. }
```

What is the result?

A. subsub

B. sub subsub

C. alpha subsub

D. alpha sub subsub

E. Compilation fails

F. An exception is thrown at runtime

12. Given:

```
 3. class Building {
 4.    Building() {  System.out.print("b ");  }
 5.    Building(String name) {
 6.       this();   System.out.print("bn " + name);
 7.    }
 8. }
 9. public class House extends Building {
10.    House() {  System.out.print("h ");   }
11.    House(String name) {
12.       this();   System.out.print("hn " + name);
13.    }
```

```
14.    public static void main(String[] args) { new House("x "); }
15. }
```

What is the result?

A. h hn x

B. hn x h

C. b h hn x

D. b hn x h

E. bn x h hn x

F. b bn x h hn x

G. bn x b h hn x

H. Compilation fails

13. Given:

```
3. class Mammal {
4.    String name = "furry ";
5.    String makeNoise() { return "generic noise"; }
6. }
7. class Zebra extends Mammal {
8.    String name = "stripes ";
9.    String makeNoise() { return "bray"; }
10. }
11. public class ZooKeeper {
12.    public static void main(String[] args) { new ZooKeeper().go(); }
13.    void go() {
14.       Mammal m = new Zebra();
15.       System.out.println(m.name + m.makeNoise());
16.    }
17. }
```

What is the result?

A. furry bray

B. stripes bray

C. furry generic noise

D. stripes generic noise

E. Compilation fails

F. An exception is thrown at runtime

14. Given:

```
1. interface FrogBoilable {
2.    static int getCtoF(int cTemp) {
3.       return (cTemp * 9 / 5) + 32;
4.    }
5.    default String hop() { return "hopping "; }
6. }
```

```
 7. public class DontBoilFrogs implements FrogBoilable {
 8.    public static void main(String[] args) {
 9.       new DontBoilFrogs().go();
10.    }
11.    void go() {
12.       System.out.print(hop());
13.       System.out.println(getCtoF(100));
14.       System.out.println(FrogBoilable.getCtoF(100));
15.       DontBoilFrogs dbf = new DontBoilFrogs();
16.       System.out.println(dbf.getCtoF(100));
17.    }
18. }
```

What is the result? (Choose all that apply.)

A. hopping 212

B. Compilation fails due to an error on line 2

C. Compilation fails due to an error on line 5

D. Compilation fails due to an error on line 12

E. Compilation fails due to an error on line 13

F. Compilation fails due to an error on line 14

G. Compilation fails due to an error on line 16

15. Given:

```
interface I1 {
   default int doStuff() { return 1; }
}
interface I2 {
   default int doStuff() { return 2; }
}
public class MultiInt implements I1, I2 {
   public static void main(String[] args) {
      new MultiInt().go();
   }
   void go() {
      System.out.println(doStuff());
   }
   int doStuff() {
      return 3;
   }
}
```

What is the result?

A. 1

B. 2

C. 3

D. The output is unpredictable

E. Compilation fails

F. An exception is thrown at runtime

16. Given:

```
interface MyInterface {
  default int doStuff() {
    return 42;
  }
}
public class IfaceTest implements MyInterface {
  public static void main(String[] args) {
    new IfaceTest().go();
  }
  void go() {
    // INSERT CODE HERE
  }
  public int doStuff() {
    return 43;
  }
}
```

Which line(s) of code, inserted independently at // INSERT CODE HERE, will allow the code to compile? (Choose all that apply.)

A. `System.out.println("class: " + doStuff());`

B. `System.out.println("iface: " + super.doStuff());`

C. `System.out.println("iface: " + MyInterface.super.doStuff());`

D. `System.out.println("iface: " + MyInterface.doStuff());`

E. `System.out.println("iface: " + super.MyInterface.doStuff());`

F. None of the lines, A–E, will allow the code to compile

17. Given:

```
interface i1 {
  void doStuff(int x);
}
class Patton {
  void stuff(String s) {
    System.out.println("stuff ");
  }
}
public class override extends Patton implements i1 {
  public static void main(String[] args) {
    new override().doStuff(1);
    new override().stuff("x");
  }
  @Override
  void doStuff(int x) {
```

```
      System.out.print("doStuff ");
    }
    @Override
    void stuff(String s) {
      System.out.println("my stuff ");
    }
  }
```

What is the result? (Choose all that apply.)

A. `Stuff stuff`

B. `doStuff stuff`

C. `doStuff my stuff`

D. An exception is thrown at runtime

E. Compilation fails due to an `@Override`-related error

F. Compilation fails due to an error other than an `@Override`-related error

18. Which statements about singletons are true? (Choose all that apply.)

A. The singleton pattern ensures that no two objects of the same class will have duplicate state.

B. A class that properly implements a singleton must have a constructor marked either private or protected.

C. Typically, a singleton's public-facing API has only one method.

D. The singleton pattern is considered a creational design pattern.

E. A properly designed singleton must declare at least one enum.

19. Which statements about immutable classes are true? (Choose all that apply.)

A. They should be marked `final` so that they cannot be subclassed.

B. Their fields should allow updates only via setter methods.

C. Their objects must be instantiated via factory methods.

D. None of their fields can be of mutable types.

E. Reference variables sent in as instantiation arguments must be dealt with defensively.

F. Reference variables returned in getters must be dealt with defensively.

G. Properly designed immutable classes are well encapsulated.

SELF TEST ANSWERS

1. ☑ **B** and **E** are correct. **B** is correct because an `abstract` class need not implement any or all of an interface's methods. **E** is correct because the class implements the interface method and additionally overloads the `twiddle()` method.

   ☒ **A, C,** and **D** are incorrect. **A** is incorrect because `abstract` methods have no body. **C** is incorrect because classes implement interfaces; they don't extend them. **D** is incorrect because overloading a method is not implementing it. (OCP Objectives 1.2, 1.3, and 2.5)

2. ☑ **E** is correct. The implied `super()` call in `Bottom2`'s constructor cannot be satisfied because there is no no-arg constructor in `Top`. A default no-arg constructor is generated by the compiler only if the class has no constructor defined explicitly.

   ☒ **A, B, C,** and **D** are incorrect based on the above. (OCP Objectives 1.2 and 1.3)

3. ☑ **A** is correct. Although a `final` method cannot be overridden, in this case, the method is private and, therefore, hidden. The effect is that a new, accessible method flipper is created. Therefore, no polymorphism occurs in this example; the method invoked is simply that of the child class; and no error occurs.

   ☒ **B, C, D,** and **E** are incorrect based on the preceding. (OCP Objectives 1.3 and 2.2)

   Special Note: This next question crudely simulates a style of question known as "drag-and-drop." Up through the SCJP 6 exam, drag-and-drop questions were included. As of early 2018, Oracle DOES NOT include any drag-and-drop questions on its Java exams, but just in case Oracle's policy changes, we left a few in the book.

4. Here is the answer:

   ```
   class AgedP {
     AgedP() {}
     public AgedP(int x) {
     }
   }
   public class Kinder extends AgedP {
     public Kinder(int x) {
       super();
     }
   }
   ```

   As there is no droppable tile for the variable x and the parentheses (in the `Kinder` constructor) are already in place and empty, there is no way to construct a call to the superclass constructor that takes an argument. Therefore, the only remaining possibility is to create a call to the no-arg superclass constructor. This is done as `super();`. The line cannot be left blank, as the parentheses are already in place. Further, since the superclass constructor called is the no-arg version, this constructor must be created. It will not be created by the compiler because another constructor is already present. (OCP Objectives 1.2 and 1.3)

5. ☑ **D** is correct. Static `init` blocks are executed at class loading time; instance `init` blocks run right after the call to `super()` in a constructor. When multiple `init` blocks of a single type occur in a class, they run in order, from the top down.
☒ **A, B, C, E, F, G, H,** and **I** are incorrect based on the above. Note: You'll probably never see this many choices on the real exam! (OCP Objective 2.6)

6. ☑ **C** is correct. Before you can invoke `Y`'s `do2` method, you have to cast `x2` to be of type `Y`.
☒ **A, B,** and **D** are incorrect based on the preceding. **B** looks like a proper cast, but without the second set of parentheses, the compiler thinks it's an incomplete statement. (OCP Objectives 1.2 and 1.3)

7. ☑ **A** is correct. It's legal to overload `main()`. Because no instances of `Locomotive` are created, the constructor does not run and the overloaded version of `main()` does not run.
☒ **B, C, D,** and **E** are incorrect based on the preceding. (OCP Objectives 1.2 and 1.3)

8. ☑ **F** is correct. Class `Dog` doesn't have a `sniff` method.
☒ **A, B, C, D,** and **E** are incorrect based on the above information. (OCP Objectives 1.2 and 1.3)

9. ☑ **A** is correct. A `ClassCastException` will be thrown when the code attempts to downcast a `Tree` to a `Redwood`.
☒ **B, C, D, E,** and **F** are incorrect based on the above information. (OCP Objectives 1.2 and 1.3)

10. ☑ **B** is correct. The code is correct, but polymorphism doesn't apply to `static` methods.
☒ **A, C, D,** and **E** are incorrect based on the above information. (OCP Objectives 1.3 and 1.6)

11. ☑ **C** is correct. Watch out, because `SubSubAlpha` extends `Alpha`! Because the code doesn't attempt to make a `SubAlpha`, the private constructor in `SubAlpha` is okay.
☒ **A, B, D, E,** and **F** are incorrect based on the above information. (OCP Objectives 1.2 and 1.3)

12. ☑ **C** is correct. Remember that constructors call their superclass constructors, which execute first, and that constructors can be overloaded.
☒ **A, B, D, E, F, G,** and **H** are incorrect based on the above information. (OCP Objectives 1.2 and 1.3)

13. ☑ **A** is correct. Polymorphism is only for instance methods, not instance variables.
☒ **B, C, D, E,** and **F** are incorrect based on the above information. (OCP Objective 1.3)

14. ☑ **E** and **G** are correct. Neither of these lines of code uses the correct syntax to invoke an interface's static method.
☒ **A, B, C, D,** and **F** are incorrect based on the above information. (OCP Objective 2.5)

15. ☑ **E** is correct. This is kind of a trick question; the implementing method must be marked `public`. If it was, all the other code is legal, and the output would be 3. If you understood all the multiple inheritance rules and just missed the access modifier, give yourself half credit.

☒ **A, B, C, D,** and **F** are incorrect based on the above information. (OCP Objective 2.5)

16. ☑ **A** and **C** are correct. **A** uses correct syntax to invoke the class's method, and **C** uses the correct syntax to invoke the interface's overloaded `default` method.

☒ **B, D, E,** and **F** are incorrect based on the above information. (OCP Objective 2.5)

17. ☑ **F** is correct. The `@Override` methods are properly overridden, but interface methods are public, so the compiler will complain about weaker access privileges. This question could be called a "misdirection" question. On the surface, it appears to be about `@Override`, but you might get bitten by another problem. We agree that these are tricky, but you will encounter this sort of tricky question on the real exam.

☒ **A, B, C, D,** and **E** are incorrect based on the above information. (OCP Objective 2.5)

18. ☑ **D** is a correct statement about singletons.

☒ **A, B, C,** and **E** are incorrect. **A** is simply incorrect. **B** is almost right; a singleton's constructor can only be marked private. **C** is simply incorrect; a singleton usually has many methods. **E** is incorrect because, although you can implement a singleton using an enum, using an enum is not required. (OCP Objective 1.5)

19. ☑ **A, E, F,** and **G** are correct statements about immutable classes.

☒ **B** is incorrect because immutable classes cannot have any setter methods. **C** is incorrect because immutable classes can also use constructors. **D** is incorrect because fields can be of mutable types, but they must be dealt with defensively. (OCP Objective 1.5)

3

Assertions and Java Exceptions

T he assertion mechanism gives you a way to do testing and debugging checks on conditions you expect to smoke out while developing, when you don't want the runtime overhead associated with exception handling.

When you do need to use exception handling, you can take advantage of two features added to exception handling in Java 7. First, multi-catch gives you a way of dealing with two or more exception types at once, and second, try-with-resources lets you close your resources very easily.

CERTIFICATION OBJECTIVE

Working with the Assertion Mechanism (OCP Objective 6.5)

6.5   *Test invariants by using assertions.*

You know you're not supposed to make assumptions, but you can't help it when you're writing code. You put them in comments:

```
if (x > 2) {
  // do something
} else if (x < 2) {
  // do something
} else {
  // x must be 2
  // do something else
}
```

You write print statements with them:

```
while (true) {
  if (x > 2) {
    break;
  }
  System.out.print("If we got here " +
                   "something went horribly wrong");
}
```

Assertions let you test your assumptions during development, without the expense (in both your time and program overhead) of writing exception handlers, for exceptions that you assume will never happen once the program is out of development and fully deployed.

For the OCP 8 exam, you're expected to know the basics of how assertions work, including how to enable them, how to use them, and how *not* to use them.

Assertions Overview

Suppose you assume that a number passed into a method (say, methodA()) will never be negative. While testing and debugging, you want to validate your assumption, but you don't want to have to strip out print statements, runtime exception handlers, or if/else tests when you're done with development. But leaving any of those in is, at the least, a performance hit. Assertions to the rescue! Check out the following code:

```
private void methodA(int num) {
  if (num >= 0) {
    useNum(num + x);
  } else {  // num < 0 (this should never happen!)
    System.out.println("Yikes! num is a negative number! " + num);
  }
}
```

Because you're so certain of your assumption, you don't want to take the time (or program performance hit) to write exception-handling code. And at runtime, you don't want the if/else either because if you do reach the else condition, it means your earlier logic (whatever was running prior to this method being called) is flawed.

Assertions let you test your assumptions during development, but the assertion code basically evaporates when the program is deployed, leaving behind no overhead or debugging code to track down and remove. Let's rewrite methodA() to validate that the argument was not negative:

```
private void methodA(int num) {
  assert (num>=0);   // throws an AssertionError
                     // if this test isn't true
  useNum(num + x);
}
```

Not only do assertions make code stay cleaner and tighter, but also, because assertions are inactive unless specifically "turned on" (enabled), the code will run as though it were written like this:

```
private void methodA(int num) {
  useNum(num + x);  // we've tested this;
                    // we now know we're good here
}
```

Assertions work quite simply. You always assert that something is `true`. If it is, no problem. Code keeps running. But if your assertion turns out to be wrong (`false`), then a stop-the-world `AssertionError` is thrown (which you should never, ever handle!) right then and there, so you can fix whatever logic flaw led to the problem.

Assertions come in two flavors: *really simple* and *simple,* as follows:

Really simple:

```
private void doStuff() {
  assert (y > x);
  // more code assuming y is greater than x
}
```

Simple:

```
private void doStuff() {
  assert (y > x): "y is " + y + " x is " + x;
  // more code assuming y is greater than x
}
```

The difference between the two is that the simple version adds a second expression separated from the first (boolean expression) by a colon—this expression's string value is added to the stack trace. Both versions throw an immediate `AssertionError`, but the simple version gives you a little more debugging help, whereas the really simple version tells you only that your assumption was false.

on the
job

Assertions are typically enabled when an application is being tested and debugged, but disabled when the application is deployed. The assertions are still in the code, although ignored by the JVM, so if you do have a deployed application that starts misbehaving, you can always choose to enable assertions in the field for additional testing.

Assertion Expression Rules

Assertions can have either one or two expressions, depending on whether you're using the "simple" or the "really simple." The first expression (we'll call it expression1) must always result in a `boolean` value! Follow the same rules you use for `if` and `while` tests. The whole point is to assert aTest, which means you're asserting that aTest is `true`. If it is `true`, no problem. If it's not `true`, however, then your assumption was wrong and you get an `AssertionError`.

The second expression (expression2), used only with the simple version of an `assert` statement, can be anything that results in a value. Remember, the second expression is used to generate a `String` message that displays in the stack trace to give you a little more debugging information. It works much like `System.out .println()` in that you can pass it a primitive or an object and it will convert it into a `String` representation. It must resolve to a value!

The following code lists legal and illegal expressions for both parts of an `assert` statement. Remember, expression2 (the value to print in the stack trace) is used only with the simple `assert` statement; the second expression exists solely to give you a little more debugging detail:

```
void noReturn() { }
int aReturn() { return 1; }
void go() {
  int x = 1;
  boolean b = true;

  // the following six are legal assert statements
  assert(x == 1);
  assert(b);
  assert true;
  assert(x == 1) : x;
  assert(x == 1) : aReturn();
  assert(x == 1) : new ValidAssert();

  // the following six are ILLEGAL assert statements
  assert(x = 1);                   // none of these are booleans
  assert(x);
  assert 0;
  assert(x == 1) : ;               // none of these return a value
  assert(x == 1) : noReturn();
  assert(x == 1) : ValidAssert va;
}
```

e x a m

ⓦ a t c h

If you see the word "expression" in a question about assertions and the question doesn't specify whether it means expression1 (the boolean test) or expression2 (the value to print in the stack trace), always assume the word "expression" refers to expression1, the boolean test. For example, consider the following question:

Exam Question: An `assert` expression must result in a `boolean` value, true or false?

Assume that the word "expression" refers to expression1 of an `assert`, so the question statement is correct. If the statement were referring to expression2, however, the statement would be incorrect because expression2 can be anything that results in a value, not just a `boolean`.

Using Assertions

If you want to use assertions, the first step is to put them in your code. Next, every time you run your code, you can choose whether to enable the assertions or not.

Running with Assertions

Here's where it gets cool. Once you've written your assertion-aware code, you can choose to enable or disable your assertions at runtime! The first thing to remember is that at runtime assertions are **disabled by default**.

Enabling Assertions at Runtime

You enable assertions at runtime with a command like this:

```
java -ea com.geeksanonymous.TestClass
```

or

```
java -enableassertions com.geeksanonymous.TestClass
```

The preceding command-line switches tell the JVM to run with assertions enabled.

Disabling Assertions at Runtime

You must also know the command-line switches for disabling assertions:

```
java -da com.geeksanonymous.TestClass
```

or

```
java -disableassertions com.geeksanonymous.TestClass
```

Because assertions are disabled by default, using the disable switches might seem unnecessary. Indeed, using the switches the way we do in the preceding example just gives you the default behavior (in other words, you get the same result, regardless of whether you use the disabling switches). But...you can also selectively enable and disable assertions in such a way that they're enabled for some classes and/or packages and disabled for others while a particular program is running.

Selective Enabling and Disabling

The command-line switches for assertions can be used in various ways:

- **With no arguments (as in the preceding examples)** Enables or disables assertions in all classes, except for the system classes.

- **With a package name**   Enables or disables assertions in the package specified and in any packages below this package in the same directory hierarchy (more on that in a moment).
- **With a class name**   Enables or disables assertions in the class specified.

You can combine switches to, say, disable assertions in a single class but keep them enabled for all others as follows:

```
java -ea  -da:com.geeksanonymous.Foo
```

The preceding command line tells the JVM to enable assertions in general, but disable them in the class com.geeksanonymous.Foo. You can do the same selectivity for a package as follows:

```
java -ea -da:com.geeksanonymous...
```

The preceding command line tells the JVM to enable assertions in general, but disable them in the package com.geeksanonymous and all of its subpackages! You may not be familiar with the term "subpackages," since that term wasn't used much prior to assertions. A subpackage is any package in a subdirectory of the named package. For example, look at the following directory tree:

```
com
   |_geeksanonymous
                  |_Foo.class
                  |_twelvesteps
                              |_StepOne.class
                              |_StepTwo.class
```

This tree lists three directories:

```
com
geeksanonymous
twelvesteps
and three classes:
com.geeksanonymous.Foo
com.geeksanonymous.twelvesteps.StepOne
com.geeksanonymous.twelvesteps.StepTwo
```

The subpackage of com.geeksanonymous is the twelvesteps package. Remember that in Java, the com.geeksanonymous.twelvesteps package is treated as a completely distinct package that has no relationship with the packages above it (in this example, the com.geeksanonymous package), except they just happen to share a couple of directories. Table 3-1 lists examples of command-line switches for enabling and disabling assertions.

Command-Line Example	What It Means
`java -ea` `java -enableassertions`	Enable assertions.
`java -da` `java -disableassertions`	Disable assertions (the default behavior).
`java -ea:com.foo.Bar`	Enable assertions in class `com.foo.Bar`.
`java -ea:com.foo...`	Enable assertions in package `com.foo` and any of its subpackages.
`java -ea -dsa`	Enable assertions in general, but disable assertions in system classes.
`java -ea -da:com.foo...`	Enable assertions in general, but disable assertions in package `com.foo` and any of its subpackages.

Using Assertions Appropriately

Not all legal uses of assertions are considered appropriate. As with so much of Java, you can abuse the intended use of assertions, despite the best efforts of Oracle's Java engineers to discourage you from doing so. For example, you're never supposed to handle an assertion failure. That means you shouldn't catch it with a `catch` clause and attempt to recover. Legally, however, `AssertionError` is a subclass of `Throwable`, so it can be caught. But just don't do it! If you're going to try to recover from something, it should be an exception. To discourage you from trying to substitute an assertion for an exception, the `AssertionError` doesn't provide access to the object that generated it. All you get is the `String` message.

So who gets to decide what's appropriate? Oracle. The exam uses Oracle's "official" assertion documentation to define appropriate and inappropriate uses.

Don't Use Assertions to Validate Arguments to a public Method

The following is an inappropriate use of assertions:

```
public void doStuff(int x) {
  assert (x > 0);               // inappropriate !
  // do things with x
}
```

If you see the word "appropriate" on the exam, do not mistake that for "legal." "Appropriate" always refers to the way in which something is supposed to be used, according to either the developers of the mechanism or best practices officially embraced by Oracle. If you see the word "correct" in the context of assertions, as in "Line 3 is a correct use of assertions," you should also assume that correct is referring to how assertions SHOULD be used rather than how they legally COULD be used.

A `public` method might be called from code that you don't control (or from code you have never seen). Because `public` methods are part of your interface to the outside world, you're supposed to guarantee that any constraints on the arguments will be enforced by the method itself. But since assertions aren't guaranteed to actually run (they're typically disabled in a deployed application), the enforcement won't happen if assertions aren't enabled. You don't want publicly accessible code that works only conditionally, depending on whether assertions are enabled.

If you need to validate `public` method arguments, you'll probably use exceptions to throw, say, an `IllegalArgumentException` if the values passed to the `public` method are invalid.

Do Use Assertions to Validate Arguments to a private Method

If you write a `private` method, you almost certainly wrote (or control) any code that calls it. When you assume that the logic in code calling your `private` method is correct, you can test that assumption with an assertion as follows:

```
private void doMore(int x) {
  assert (x > 0);
  // do things with x
}
```

The only difference that matters between the preceding example and the one before it is the access modifier. So, do enforce constraints on `private` methods' arguments, but do not enforce constraints on `public` methods. You're certainly free to compile assertion code with an inappropriate validation of `public` arguments, but for the exam (and real life), you need to know that you shouldn't do it.

Don't Use Assertions to Validate Command-Line Arguments

This is really just a special case of the "Do not use assertions to validate arguments to a `public` method" rule. If your program requires command-line arguments, you'll probably use the exception mechanism to enforce them.

Do Use Assertions, Even in public Methods, to Check for Cases That You Know Are Never, Ever Supposed to Happen

This can include code blocks that should never be reached, including the default of a `switch` statement as follows:

```
switch(x) {
  case 1: y = 3; break;
  case 2: y = 9; break;
  case 3: y = 27; break;
  default: assert false; // we're never supposed to get here!
}
```

If you assume that a particular code block won't be reached, as in the preceding example where you assert that x must be 1, 2, or 3, then you can use `assert false` to cause an `AssertionError` to be thrown immediately if you ever do reach that code. So in the `switch` example, we're not performing a boolean test—we've already asserted that we should never be there, so just getting to that point is an automatic failure of our assertion/assumption.

Don't Use assert Expressions That Can Cause Side Effects!

The following would be a very bad idea:

```
public void doStuff() {
  assert (modifyThings());
  // continues on
}
public boolean modifyThings() {
  y = x++;
  return true;
}
```

The rule is that an `assert` expression should leave the program in the same state it was in before the expression! Think about it. `assert` expressions aren't guaranteed to always run, so you don't want your code to behave differently depending on whether assertions are enabled. Assertions must not cause any side effects. If assertions are enabled, the only change to the way your program runs is that an `AssertionError` can be thrown if one of your assertions (think *assumptions*) turns out to be false.

Using assertions that cause side effects can cause some of the most maddening and hard-to-find bugs known to man or woman! When a hot-tempered QA analyst is screaming at you that your code doesn't work, trotting out the old "well, it works on MY machine" excuse won't get you very far.

CERTIFICATION OBJECTIVE

Working with Exception Handling (OCP Objectives 6.1, 6.2, 6.3, and 6.4)

6.1   Use try-catch, and throw statements.
6.2   Use catch, multi-catch, and finally clauses.
6.3   Use Autoclose resources with a try-with-resources statement.
6.4   Create custom exceptions and Auto-closeable resources.

You should already know the basics of try, catch, and throw, but if you need a refresher, head back to Chapter 5 of the *OCA Java SE 8 Programmer I Exam Guide*. For this section, we're assuming you know that material, so we're going to dive right into Java's more advanced exception-handling features.

Use the try Statement with multi-catch and finally Clauses

Sometimes we want to handle different types of exceptions the same way. Especially when all we can do is log the exception and declare defeat. But we don't want to repeat code. So what to do? When you were studying for the OCA 8 exam, you already saw that having a single catch-all exception handler is a bad idea. Prior to Java 7, the best we could do was

```
try {
  // access the database and write to a file
} catch (SQLException e) {
  handleErrorCase(e);
} catch (IOException e) {
  handleErrorCase(e);
}
```

You may be thinking that it is only one line of duplicate code. But what happens when you are catching six different exception types? That's a lot of duplication.

Luckily, Java 7 made handling this sort of situation nice and easy with a feature called multi-`catch`:

```
try {
  // access the database and write to a file
} catch (SQLException | IOException e) {
  handleErrorCase(e);
}
```

No more duplication. This is great. As you might imagine, multi-`catch` is short for "multiple `catch`." You just list out the types you want the multi-`catch` to handle separated by pipe (|) characters. This is easy to remember because | is the "or" operator in Java, which means the `catch` can be read as "SQLException or IOException e."

e x a m

ⓦ a t c h   *You can't use the variable name multiple times in a* `multi`-*catch. The following won't compile:*

```
catch(Exception1 e1 | Exception2 e2)
```

It makes sense that this example doesn't compile. After all, the code in the exception handler needs to know which variable name to refer to.

```
catch(Exception1 e | Exception2 e)
```

This one is tempting. When we declare variables, we normally put the variable name right after the type. Try to think of it as a list of types. We are declaring variable e *to be caught and it must be one of* Exception1 *or* Exception2 *types.*

With multi-`catch`, order doesn't matter. The following two snippets are equivalent to each other:

```
catch(SQLException | IOException e)    // these two statements are
                                       // equivalent
catch(IOException | SQLException e)
```

Just like with exception matching in a regular `catch` block, you can't just throw any two exceptions together. With multi-`catch`, you have to make sure a given exception can only match one type. The following will not compile:

```
catch(FileNotFoundException | IOException e)
catch(IOException | FileNotFoundException e)
```

You'll get a compiler error that looks something like:

```
The exception FileNotFoundException is already caught by the
alternative IOException
```

Since `FileNotFoundException` is a subclass of `IOException`, we could have just written that in the first place! There was no need to use multi-`catch`. The simplified and working version simply says:

```
catch(IOException e)
```

Remember, multi-`catch` is only for exceptions in different inheritance hierarchies. To make sure this is clear, what do you think happens with the following code?

```
catch(IOException | Exception e)
```

That's right. It won't compile because `IOException` is a subclass of `Exception`. Which means it is redundant and the compiler won't accept it.

To summarize, we use multi-`catch` when we want to reuse an exception handler. We can list as many types as we want so long as none of them have a superclass/subclass relationship with each other.

Multi-catch and catch Parameter Assignment

There is one tricky thing with multi-`catch`. And we know the exam creators like tricky things!

The following LEGAL code demonstrates assigning a new value to the single catch parameter:

```
try {
  // access the database and write to a file
} catch (IOException e) {
  e = new IOException();
}
```

*Don't assign a new value to the `catch` parameter. It is **not** good practice and creates confusing, hard-to-maintain code. But it is legal Java code to assign a new value to the `catch` block's parameter when there is only one type listed, and it will compile.*

The following ILLEGAL code demonstrates trying to assign a value to the final multi-`catch` parameter:

```
try {
  // access the database and write to a file
} catch (SQLException | IOException e) {
  e = new IOException();
}
```

At least you get a clear compiler error if you try to do this. The compiler tells you:

```
The parameter e of a multi-catch block cannot be assigned
```

Since multi-catch uses multiple types, there isn't a clearly defined type for the variable that you can set. Java solves this by making the catch parameter final when that happens. And then the code doesn't compile because you can't assign a new value to a final variable.

Rethrowing Exceptions

Sometimes we want to do something with the thrown exceptions before we rethrow them:

```
public void couldThrowAnException() throws IOException, SQLException {}

public void rethrow() throws SQLException, IOException {
  try {
    couldThrowAnException();
  } catch (SQLException | IOException e) {
    log(e);
    throw e;
  }
}
```

This is a common pattern called "handle and declare." We want to do something with the exception—log it. We also want to acknowledge we couldn't completely handle it, so we declare it and let the caller deal with it. (As an aside, many programmers believe that logging an exception and rethrowing it is a bad practice, but you never know—you might see this kind of code on the exam.)

You may have noticed that couldThrowAnException() doesn't actually throw an exception. The compiler doesn't know this. The method signature is key to the compiler. It can't assume that no exception gets thrown, as a subclass could override the method and throw an exception.

There is a bit of duplicate code here. We have the list of exception types thrown by the methods we call typed twice. Multi-catch was introduced to avoid having duplicate code, yet here we are with duplicate code.

Lucky for us, Java helps us out here as well with a feature added in Java 7. This example is a nicer way of writing the previous code:

```
1. public void rethrow() throws SQLException, IOException {
2.   try {
3.     couldThrowAnException();
4.   } catch (Exception e) {    // watch out: this isn't really
```

```
5.                                    // catching all exception subclasses
6.      log(e);
7.      throw e;                      // note: won't compile in Java 6
8.    }
9.  }
```

Notice the multi-`catch` is gone and replaced with `catch(Exception e)`. It's not bad practice here, though, because we aren't really catching all exceptions. The compiler is treating `Exception` as "any exceptions that the called methods happen to throw." (You'll see this idea of code shorthand again with the diamond operator when you get to generics.)

This is very different from Java 6 code that catches `Exception`. In Java 6, we'd need the `rethrow()` method signature to be `throws Exception` in order to make this code compile.

In Java 7 and later, `} catch (Exception e) {` doesn't really catch ANY `Exception` subclass. The code may say that, but the compiler is translating for you. The compiler says, "Well, I know it can't be just any exception because the throws clause won't let me. I'll pretend the developer meant to only catch `SQLException` and `IOException`. After all, if any others show up, I'll just fail compilation on `throw e;`—just like I used to in Java 6." Tricky, isn't it?

At the risk of being too repetitive, remember that `catch (Exception e)` doesn't necessarily catch all `Exception` subclasses. In Java 7 and later, it means catch all `Exception` subclasses that would allow the method to compile.

Got that? Now why on earth would Oracle do this to us? It sounds more complicated than it used to be! Turns out they were trying to solve another problem at the same time they were changing this stuff. Suppose the API developer of `couldThrowAnException()` decided the method will never throw a `SQLException` and removes `SQLException` from the signature to reflect that.

Imagine we were using the Java 6 style of having one `catch` block per exception or even the multi-`catch` style of

```
} catch (SQLException | IOException e) {
```

Our code would stop compiling with an error like:

```
Unreachable catch block for SQLException
```

It is reasonable for code to stop compiling if we add exceptions to a method. But we don't want our code to break if a method's implementation gets LESS brittle. And that's the advantage of using

```
} catch (Exception e) {
```

Java infers what we mean here and doesn't say a peep when the API we are calling removes an exception.

on the job

Don't go changing your API signatures on a whim. Most code was written before Java 7 and will break if you change signatures. Your callers won't thank you when their code suddenly fails compilation because they tried to use your new, shiny, "cleaner" API.

You've probably noticed by now that Oracle values backward compatibility and doesn't change the behavior or "compiler worthiness" of code from older versions of Java. That still stands. In Java 6, we can't write `catch (Exception e)` and merely throw specific exceptions. If we tried, the compiler would still complain:

```
Unhandled exception type Exception.
```

Backward compatibility only needs to work for code that compiles! It's OK for the compiler to get less strict over time.

To make sure you understand what is going on here, think about what happens in this example:

```
public class A extends Exception{}
public class B extends Exception{}
public void rain() throws A, B {}
```

Table 3-2 summarizes handling changes to the exception-related parts of method signatures in Java 6, Java 7, and Java 8.

There is one more trick. If you assign a value to the `catch` parameter, the code no longer compiles:

```
public void rethrow() throws SQLException, IOException {
  try {
     couldThrowAnException();
  } catch (Exception e) {
    e = new IOException();
    throw e;
  }
}
```

As with multi-`catch`, you shouldn't be assigning a new value to the `catch` parameter in real life anyway. The difference between this and multi-`catch` is where the compiler error occurs. For multi-`catch`, the compiler error occurs on the line where we attempt to assign a new value to the parameter, whereas here, the compiler error occurs on the line where we `throw e`. It is different because code written prior to Java 7 still needs to compile. Because the multi-`catch` syntax is still relatively new, there is no legacy code to worry about.

TABLE 3-2   Exceptions and Signatures

	What happens if rain() adds a new checked exception?	What happens if rain() removes a checked exception from the signature?
| Java 6 style:<br><br>```java
public void ahh() throws A, B {
  try {
    rain();
  } catch (A e) {
    throw e;
  } catch (B e) {
    throw e;
  }
}
``` | Add another `catch` block to handle the new exception. | Remove a `catch` block to avoid compiler error about unreachable code. |
| Java 7 and 8, with duplication:<br><br>```java
public void ahh() throws A, B {
  try {
    rain();
  } catch (A | B e) {
    throw e;
  }
}
``` | Add another exception to the multi-`catch` block to handle the new exception. | Remove an expression from the multi-`catch` block to avoid compiler error about unreachable code. |
| Java 7 and 8, without duplication:<br><br>```java
public void ahh() throws A, B {
  try {
    rain();
  } catch (Exception e) {
    throw e;
  }
}
``` | Add another exception to the method signature to handle the new exception that can be thrown. | No code changes needed. |

AutoCloseable Resources with a try-with-resources Statement

The `finally` block is a good place for closing files and assorted other resources, but real-world clean-up code is easy to get wrong. And when correct, it is verbose. Let's look at the code to close our one resource when closing a file:

```java
1: Reader reader = null;
2: try {
3:   // read from file
```
```

```
 4: } catch(IOException e) {
 5:    log(); throw e;
 6: } finally {
 7:    if (reader != null) {
 8:      try {
 9:        reader.close();
10:      } catch (IOException e) {
11:      // ignore exceptions on closing file
12:      }
13:    }
14: }
```

That's a lot of code just to close a single file! But it's all necessary. First, we need to check if the reader is null on line 7. It is possible the `try` block threw an exception before creating the reader, or while trying to create the reader if the file we are trying to read doesn't exist. It isn't until line 9 that we get to the one line in the whole `finally` block that does what we care about—closing the file. Lines 8 and 10 show a bit more housekeeping. We can get an `IOException` on attempting to close the file. While we could try to handle that exception, there isn't much we can do, thus making it common to just ignore the exception. This gives us nine lines of code (lines 6–14) just to close a file.

Developers typically write a helper class to close resources, or they use the open-source Apache Commons helper to get this mess down to three lines:

```
 6: } finally {
 7:    HelperClass.close(reader);
 8: }
```

Which is still three lines too many.

Lucky for us, we have *Automatic Resource Management* using "try-with-resources" to get rid of even these three lines. The following code is equivalent to the previous example:

```
1:  try (Reader reader =
2:    new BufferedReader(new FileReader(file))) {   // note the new syntax
3:    // read from file
4:  } catch (IOException e) { log(); throw e;}
```

No `finally` left at all! We don't even mention closing the reader. Automatic Resource Management takes care of it for us. Let's take a look at what happens here. **We start out by declaring the reader inside the `try` declaration. Think of the parentheses as a `for` loop in which we declare a loop index variable that is scoped to just the loop. Here, the reader is scoped to just the `try` block. Not the `catch` block, just the `try` block.**

The actual `try` block does the same thing as before. It reads from the file. Or, at least, it comments that it would read from the file. The `catch` block also does the same thing as before. And just like in our traditional `try` statement, `catch` is optional.

Remember that a `try` must have `catch` or `finally`. Time to learn something new about that rule.

This is ILLEGAL code because it demonstrates a `try` without a `catch` or `finally`:

```
1: try {
2:   // do stuff
3: } // need a catch or finally here
```

The following LEGAL code demonstrates a `try`-with-resources with no `catch` or `finally`:

```
1:   try (Reader reader =
2:      new BufferedReader(new FileReader(file))) {
3:      // do stuff
4:   }
```

What's the difference? The legal example does have a `finally` block; you just don't see it. **The `try`-with-resources statement is logically calling a `finally` block to close the reader.** And just to make this even trickier, you can add your own `finally` block to `try`-with-resources as well. Both will get called. We'll take a look at how this works shortly.

Since the syntax is inspired from the `for` loop, we get to use a semicolon when declaring multiple resources in the `try`. For example:

```
try (MyResource mr = MyResource.createResource();   // first resource
    MyThingy mt = mr.createThingy()) {              // second resource
  // do stuff
}
```

There is something new here. Our declaration calls methods. Remember that the `try`-with-resources is just Java code. It is restricted to only declarations. This means if you want to do anything more than one statement long, you'll need to put it into a method.

To review, Table 3-3 lists the big differences that are new for `try`-with-resources.

AutoCloseable and Closeable

Because Java is a statically typed language, it doesn't let you declare just any type in a `try`-with-resources statement. The following code will not compile:

```
try (String s = "hi") {}
```

TABLE 3-3	Comparing Traditional `try` Statement to `try-with-resources`

	try-catch-finally	**try-with-resources**
Resource declared	Before `try` keyword	In parentheses within `try` declaration
Resource initialized	In `try` block	In parentheses within `try` declaration
Resource closed	In `finally` block	Nowhere—happens automatically
Required keywords	`try` One of `catch` or `finally`	`try`

You'll get a compiler error that looks something like:

```
The resource type String does not implement java.lang.AutoCloseable
```

`AutoCloseable` only has one method to implement. Let's take a look at the simplest code we can write using this interface:

```
public class MyResource implements AutoCloseable {
  public void close() {
    // take care of closing the resource
  }
}
```

There's also an interface called `java.io.Closeable`, which is similar to `AutoCloseable` but with some key differences. Why are there two similar interfaces, you may wonder? The `Closeable` interface was introduced in Java 5. When `try-with-resources` was invented in Java 7, the language designers wanted to change some things but needed backward compatibility with all existing code. So they created a superinterface with the rules they wanted.

One thing the language designers wanted to do was make the signature more generic. `Closeable` allows implementors to throw only an `IOException` or a `RuntimeException`. `AutoCloseable` allows any `Exception` at all to be thrown. Look at some examples:

```
// ok because AutoCloseable allows throwing any Exception
class A implements AutoCloseable { public void close() throws Exception{}}

// ok because subclasses or implementing methods can throw
// a subclass of Exception or none at all
class B implements AutoCloseable { public void close() {}}
class C implements AutoCloseable { public void close() throws IOException {}}
```

```
// ILLEGAL - Closeable only allows IOExceptions or subclasses
class D implements Closeable { public void close() throws Exception{}}

// ok because Closeable allows throwing IOException
class E implements Closeable { public void close() throws IOException{}}
```

In your code, Oracle recommends throwing the narrowest `Exception` subclass that will compile. However, they do limit `Closeable` to `IOException`, and you must use `AutoCloseable` for anything more.

The next difference is even trickier. What happens if we call the `close()` multiple times? It depends. For classes that implement `Closeable`, the implementation is required to be *idempotent*—which means you can call `close()` over and over again and nothing will happen the second time and beyond. It will not attempt to close the resource again and it will not blow up. For classes that implement `AutoCloseable`, there is no such guarantee.

If you look at the JavaDoc, you'll notice many classes implement both `AutoCloseable` and `Closeable`. These classes use the stricter signature rules and are idempotent. They still need to implement `Closeable` for backward compatibility, but added `AutoCloseable` for the new contract.

To review, Table 3-4 shows the differences between `AutoCloseable` and `Closeable`. Remember the exam creators like to ask about "similar but not quite the same" things!

TABLE 3-4   Comparing `AutoCloseable` and `Closeable`

	AutoCloseable	Closeable
Extends	None	`AutoCloseable`
`close` method throws	`Exception`	`IOException`
Must be idempotent (can call more than once without side effects)	No, but encouraged	Yes

A Complex try-with-resources Example   The following example is as complicated as `try`-with-resources gets:

```
1: class One implements AutoCloseable {
2:    public void close() {
3:       System.out.println("Close - One");
4: } }
5: class Two implements AutoCloseable {
6:    public void close() {
7:       System.out.println("Close - Two");
8: } }
```

```
 9: class TryWithResources {
10:   public static void main(String[] args) {
11:     try (One one = new One(); Two two = new Two()) {
12:       System.out.println("Try");
13:       throw new RuntimeException();
14:     } catch (Exception e) {
15:       System.out.println("Catch");
16:     } finally {
17:       System.out.println("Finally");
18: } } }
```

Running the preceding code will print:

```
Try
Close - Two
Close - One
Catch
Finally
```

It's actually more logical than it looks at first glance. We first enter the `try` block on line 11, and Java creates our two resources. Line 12 prints `Try`. When we throw an exception on line 13, the first interesting thing happens. The `try` block "ends," and Automatic Resource Management automatically cleans up the resources before moving on to the `catch` or `finally`. The resources get cleaned up, "backward" printing `Close - Two` and then `Close - One`. The `close()` method gets called in the reverse order in which resources are declared to allow for the fact that resources might depend on each other. Then we are back to the regular `try` block order, printing `Catch` and `Finally` on lines 15 and 17.

If you only remember two things from this example, remember that try-with-resources is part of the `try` block, and resources are cleaned up in the reverse order in which they were created.

Suppressed Exceptions

We're almost done with exceptions. There's only one more wrinkle to cover in exception handling. Now that we have an extra step of closing resources in the `try`, it is possible for multiple exceptions to get thrown. Each `close()` method can throw an exception in addition to the `try` block itself.

```
1: public class Suppressed {
2:   public static void main(String[] args) {
3:     try (One one = new One()) {
4:       throw new Exception("Try");
5:     } catch (Exception e) {
```

```
6:         System.err.println(e.getMessage());
7:         for (Throwable t : e.getSuppressed()) {
8.          System.err.println("suppressed:" + t);
9. } } } }

class One implements AutoCloseable {
  public void close() throws IOException {
    throw new IOException("Closing");
} }
```

We know that after the exception in the `try` block gets thrown on line 4, the `try`-with-resources still calls `close()` on line 3 and the `catch` block on line 5 catches one of the exceptions. Running the code prints:

```
Try
suppressed:java.io.IOException: Closing
```

This tells us the exception we thought we were throwing still gets treated as most important. Java also adds any exceptions thrown by the `close()` methods to a suppressed array in that main exception. The `catch` block or caller can deal with any or all of these. If we remove line 4, the code just prints `Closing`.

In other words, the exception thrown in `close()` doesn't always get suppressed. It becomes the main exception if there isn't already one existing. As one more example, think about what the following prints:

```
class Bad implements AutoCloseable {
  String name;
  Bad(String n) { name = n; }
  public void close() throws IOException {
    throw new IOException("Closing - "  + name);
} }

public class Suppressed {
  public static void main(String[] args) {
    try (Bad b1 = new Bad("1"); Bad b2 = new Bad("2")) {
      // do stuff
    } catch (Exception e) {
      System.err.println(e.getMessage());
      for (Throwable t : e.getSuppressed()) {
        System.err.println("suppressed:" + t);
} } } }
```

The answer is:

```
Closing - 2
suppressed:java.io.IOException: Closing - 1
```

Until `try-with-resources` calls `close()`, everything is going just dandy. When Automatic Resource Management calls `b2.close()`, we get our first exception. This becomes the main exception. Then, Automatic Resource Management calls `b1.close()` and throws another exception. Since there was already an exception thrown, this second exception gets added as a second exception.

If the `catch` or `finally` block throws an exception, no suppressions happen. The last exception thrown gets sent to the caller rather than the one from the `try`—just like before `try-with-resources` was created.

CERTIFICATION SUMMARY

Assertions are a useful debugging tool. You learned how you can use them for testing by enabling them but keep them disabled when the application is deployed.

You learned how `assert` statements always include a boolean expression, and if the expression is `true`, the code continues on, but if the expression is false, an `AssertionError` is thrown. If you use the two-expression `assert` statement, then the second expression is evaluated, converted to a `String` representation, and inserted into the stack trace to give you a little more debugging info. Finally, you saw why assertions should not be used to enforce arguments to public methods and why `assert` expressions must not contain side effects!

Exception handling was enhanced in Java version 7, making exceptions easier to use. First you learned that you can specify multiple exception types to share a `catch` block using the new multi-`catch` syntax. The major benefit is in reducing code duplication by having multiple exception types share the same exception handler. The variable name is listed only once, even though multiple types are listed. You can't assign a new exception to that variable in the `catch` block. Then you saw the "handle and declare" pattern where the exception types in the multi-`catch` are listed in the method signature and Java translates "`catch Exception e`" into that exception type list.

Next, you learned about the `try-with-resources` syntax where Java will take care of calling `close()` for you. The objects are scoped to the `try` block. Java treats them as a `finally` block and closes these resources for you in the opposite order to which they were opened. If you have your own `finally` block, it is executed after `try-with-resources` closes the objects. You also learned the difference between `AutoCloseable` and `Closeable`. `Closeable` was introduced in Java 5, allowing only `IOException` (and `RuntimeException`) to be thrown. `AutoCloseable` was added in Java 7, allowing any type of `Exception`.

TWO-MINUTE DRILL

Here are some of the key points from the certification objectives in this chapter.

Test Invariants Using Assertions (OCP Objective 6.5)

- ☐ Assertions give you a way to test your assumptions during development and debugging.
- ☐ Assertions are typically enabled during testing but disabled during deployment.
- ☐ Assertions are disabled at runtime by default. To enable them, use a command-line flag: `-ea` or `-enableassertions`.
- ☐ Selectively disable assertions by using the `-da` or `-disableassertions` flag.
- ☐ If you enable or disable assertions using the flag without any arguments, you're enabling or disabling assertions in general. You can combine enabling and disabling switches to have assertions enabled for some classes and/or packages, but not others.
- ☐ You can enable and disable assertions on a class-by-class basis, using the following syntax:
  ```
  java -ea -da:MyClass TestClass
  ```
- ☐ You can enable and disable assertions on a package-by-package basis, and any package you specify also includes any subpackages (packages further down the directory hierarchy).
- ☐ Do not use assertions to validate arguments to `public` methods.
- ☐ Do not use `assert` expressions that cause side effects. Assertions aren't guaranteed to always run, and you don't want behavior that changes depending on whether assertions are enabled.
- ☐ Do use assertions—even in `public` methods—to validate that a particular code block will never be reached. You can use `assert false;` for code that should never be reached so that an assertion error is thrown immediately if the `assert` statement is executed.

Use the try Statement with Multi-catch and finally Clauses (OCP Objective 6.2)

- ☐ If two `catch` blocks have the same exception handler code, you can merge them with multi-`catch` using `catch (Exception1 | Exception2 e)`.
- ☐ The types in a multi-`catch` list must not extend one another.
- ☐ When using multi-`catch`, the `catch` block parameter is final and cannot have a new value assigned in the `catch` block.
- ☐ If you catch a general exception as shorthand for specific subclass exceptions and rethrow the caught exception, you can still list the specific subclasses in the method signature. The compiler will treat it as if you had listed them out in the catch.

AutoCloseable Resources with a try-with-resources Statement (OCP Objectives 6.3 and 6.4)

- ☐ `try-with-resources` automatically calls `close()` on any resources declared in the `try` as `try(Resource r = new Foo())`.
- ☐ A `try` must have at least a `catch` or `finally` unless it is a `try-with-resources`. For `try-with-resources`, it can have neither, one, or both of the keywords.
- ☐ `AutoCloseable`'s `close()` method throws `Exception` and may be but is not required to be idempotent. `Closeable`'s `close()` throws `IOException` and must be idempotent.
- ☐ `try-with-resources` are closed in reverse order of creation and before going on to `catch` or `finally`.
- ☐ If more than one exception is thrown in a `try-with-resources` block, it gets added as a suppressed exception.
- ☐ The type used in a `try-with-resources` statement must implement `AutoCloseable`.

SELF TEST

The following questions will help you measure your understanding of the material presented in this chapter. Read all of the choices carefully, as there may be more than one correct answer. Choose all correct answers for each question. Stay focused.

1. Which are true? (Choose all that apply.)
   A. It is appropriate to use assertions to validate arguments to methods marked `public`
   B. It is appropriate to catch and handle assertion errors
   C. It is NOT appropriate to use assertions to validate command-line arguments
   D. It is appropriate to use assertions to generate alerts when you reach code that should not be reachable
   E. It is NOT appropriate for assertions to change a program's state

2. Given:

```
3. public class Clumsy {
4.    public static void main(String[] args) {
5.       int j = 7;
6.       assert(++j > 7);
7.       assert(++j > 8): "hi";
8.       assert(j > 10): j=12;
9.       assert(j==12): doStuff();
10.      assert(j==12): new Clumsy();
11.   }
12.   static void doStuff() { }
13. }
```

Which are true? (Choose all that apply.)
   A. Compilation succeeds
   B. Compilation fails due to an error on line 6
   C. Compilation fails due to an error on line 7
   D. Compilation fails due to an error on line 8
   E. Compilation fails due to an error on line 9
   F. Compilation fails due to an error on line 10

3. Given:

```
class AllGoesWrong {
  public static void main(String[] args) {
    AllGoesWrong a = new AllGoesWrong();
    try {
      a.blowUp();
      System.out.print("a");
```

```
      } catch (IOException e | SQLException e) {
        System.out.print("c");
      } finally {
        System.out.print("d");
      }
    }
  void blowUp() throws IOException, SQLException {
    throw new SQLException();
  }
}
```

What is the result?

A. ad

B. acd

C. cd

D. d

E. Compilation fails

F. An exception is thrown at runtime

4. Given:

```
class BadIO {
  public static void main(String[] args) {
    BadIO a = new BadIO();
    try {
      a.fileBlowUp();
      a.databaseBlowUp();
      System.out.println("a");
    } // insert code here
      System.out.println("b");
    } catch (Exception e) {
      System.out.println("c");
  } }
  void databaseBlowUp() throws SQLException {
    throw new SQLException();
  }
  void fileBlowUp() throws IOException {
    throw new IOException();
  }
} }
```

Which, inserted independently at `// insert code here`, will compile and produce the output b? (Choose all that apply.)

A. `catch(Exception e) {`

B. `catch(FileNotFoundException e) {`

C. `catch(IOException e) {`

D. `catch(IOException | SQLException e) {`

E. `catch(IOException e | SQLException e) {`

F. `catch(SQLException e) {`

G. `catch(SQLException | IOException e) {`

H. `catch(SQLException e | IOException e) {`

5. Given:

```
class Train {
  class RanOutOfTrack extends Exception { }
  class AnotherTrainComing extends Exception { }

  public static void main(String[] args) throws RanOutOfTrack,
      AnotherTrainComing {
    Train a = new Train();
    try {
      a.drive();
      System.out.println("toot! toot!");
    } // insert code here
      System.out.println("error locomoting");
      throw e;
    }
  }
  void drive() throws RanOutOfTrack, AnotherTrainComing {
    throw new RanOutOfTrack();
} }
```

Which, inserted independently at `// insert code here`, will compile and produce the output `error driving` before throwing an exception? (Choose all that apply.)

A. `catch(AnotherTrainComing e) {`

B. `catch(AnotherTrainComing | RanOutOfTrack e) {`

C. `catch(AnotherTrainComing e | RanOutOfTrack e) {`

D. `catch(Exception e) {`

E. `catch(IllegalArgumentException e) {`

F. `catch(RanOutOfTrack e) {`

G. None of the above—code fails to compile for another reason

6. Given:

```
class Conductor {
  static String s = "-";
  class Whistle implements AutoCloseable {
    public void toot() {     s += "t";   }
    public void close() {     s += "c";   }
  }
  public static void main(String[] args) {
    new Conductor().run();
    System.out.println(s);
```

```
    }
    public void run() {
        try (Whistle w = new Whistle()) {
            w.toot();
            s += "1";
            throw new Exception();
        } catch (Exception e) { s += "2";
        } finally { s += "3"; }
    } }
```

What is the result?

A. `-t123t`

B. `-t12c3`

C. `-t123`

D. `-t1c3`

E. `-t1c23`

F. None of the above; `main()` throws an exception

G. Compilation fails

7. Given:

```
public class MultipleResources {
    class Lamb implements AutoCloseable {
        public void close() throws Exception {
            System.out.print("l");
    } }
    class Goat implements AutoCloseable {
        public void close() throws Exception {
            System.out.print("g");
    } }
    public static void main(String[] args) throws Exception {
        new MultipleResources().run();
    }
    public void run() throws Exception {
        try (Lamb l = new Lamb();
            System.out.print("t");
            Goat g = new Goat();) {
            System.out.print("2");
        } finally {
            System.out.print("f");
    } } }
```

What is the result?

A. `2glf`

B. `2lgf`

C. `tglf`

D. `t2lgf`

E. `t2lgf`

F.   None of the above; `main()` throws an exception

G.   Compilation fails

8.   Given:

```
1: public class Animals {
2:    class Lamb {
3:      public void close() throws Exception { }
4:    }
5:    public static void main(String[] args) throws Exception {
6:      new Animals().run();
7:    }
8:
9:    public void run() throws Exception {
10:     try (Lamb l = new Lamb();) {
11:     }
12:   }
13: }
```

And the following possible changes:

C1. Replace line 2 with class `Lamb` implements `AutoCloseable` {

C2. Replace line 2 with class `Lamb` implements `Closeable` {

C3. Replace line 11 with } `finally {}`

What change(s) allow the code to compile? (Choose all that apply.)

A.   Just C1 is sufficient

B.   Just C2 is sufficient

C.   Just C3 is sufficient

D.   Both C1 and C3 are required

E.   Both C2 and C3 are required

F.   The code compiles without any changes

9.   Given:

```
public class Animals {
  class Lamb implements Closeable {
    public void close() {
      throw new RuntimeException("a");
    } }
  public static void main(String[] args)  {
    new Animals().run();
  }
  public void run()  {
    try (Lamb l = new Lamb();) {
      throw new IOException();
    } catch(Exception e) {
      throw new RuntimeException("c");
} } }
```

Which exceptions will the code throw?

A. `IOException` with suppressed `RuntimeException` a

B. `IOException` with suppressed `RuntimeException` c

C. `RuntimeException` a with no suppressed exception

D. `RuntimeException` c with no suppressed exception

E. `RuntimeException` a with suppressed `RuntimeException` c

F. `RuntimeException` c with suppressed `RuntimeException` a

G. Compilation fails

10. Given:

```
public class Animals {
  class Lamb implements AutoCloseable {
    public void close() {
      throw new RuntimeException("a");
  } }
  public static void main(String[] args) throws IOException {
    new Animals().run();
  }
  public void run() throws IOException {
    try (Lamb l = new Lamb();) {
      throw new IOException();
    } catch(Exception e) {
      throw e;
} } }
```

Which exceptions will the code throw?

A. `IOException` with suppressed `RuntimeException` a

B. `IOException` with suppressed `Exception` e

C. `RuntimeException` a with no suppressed exception

D. `Exception` e with no suppressed exception

E. `RuntimeException` a with suppressed `Exception` e

F. `RuntimeException` c with suppressed `RuntimeException` a

G. Compilation fails

11. Given:

```
public class Concert {
  static class PowerOutage extends Exception {}
  static class Thunderstorm extends Exception {}
  public static void main(String[] args) {
    try {
    new Concert().listen();
    System.out.print("a");
```

```
      } catch(PowerOutage | Thunderstorm e) {
        e = new PowerOutage();
        System.out.print("b");
      } finally { System.out.print("c"); }
    }
    public void listen() throws PowerOutage, Thunderstorm{ }
  }
```

What will this code print?

A. a

B. ab

C. ac

D. abc

E. bc

F. Compilation fails

SELF TEST ANSWERS

1. ☑ **C, D,** and **E** are correct statements.
   ☒ **A** is incorrect. It is acceptable to use assertions to test the arguments of `private` methods. **B** is incorrect. While assertion errors can be caught, Oracle discourages you from doing so. (OCP Objective 6.5)

2. ☑ **E** is correct. When an `assert` statement has two expressions, the second expression must return a value. The only two-expression `assert` statement that doesn't return a value is on line 9.
   ☒ **A, B, C, D,** and **F** are incorrect based on the above. (OCP Objective 6.5)

3. ☑ **E** is correct. `catch (IOException e | SQLException e)` doesn't compile. While multiple exception types can be specified in the multi-`catch`, only one variable name is allowed. The correct syntax is `catch (IOException | SQLException e)`. Other than this, the code is valid. Note that it is legal for `blowUp()` to have `IOException` in its signature even though that `Exception` can't be thrown.
   ☒ **A, B, C, D,** and **F** are incorrect based on the above. If the `catch` block's syntax error were corrected, the code would output `cd`. The multi-`catch` would catch the `SQLException` from `blowUp()` since it is one of the exception types listed. And, of course, the `finally` block runs at the end of the `try/catch`. (OCP Objective 6.2)

4. ☑ **C, D,** and **G** are correct. Since order doesn't matter, both **D** and **G** show correct use of the multi-`catch` block. And **C** catches the `IOException` from `fileBlowUp()` directly. Note that `databaseBlowUp()` is never called at runtime. However, if you remove the call, the compiler won't let you catch the `SQLException` since it would be impossible to be thrown.
   ☒ **A, B, E, H,** and **F** are incorrect. **A** is incorrect because it will not compile. Since there is already a `catch` block for `Exception`, adding another will make the compiler think there is unreachable code. **B** is incorrect because it will print `c` rather than `b`. Since `FileNotFoundException` is a subclass of `IOException`, the thrown `IOException` will not match the `catch` block for `FileNotFoundException`. **E** and **H** are incorrect because they are invalid syntax for multi-`catch`. The catch parameter `e` can only appear once. **F** is incorrect because it will print `c` rather than `b`. Since the `IOException` thrown by `fileBlowUp()` is never caught, the thrown exception will match the `catch` block for `Exception`. (OCP Objective 6.2)

5. ☑ **B, D,** and **F** are correct. **B** uses multi-`catch` to identify both exceptions `drive()` may throw. **D** still compiles since it uses the new enhanced exception typing to recognize that `Exception` may only refer to `AnotherTrainComing` and `RanOutOfTrack`. **F** is the simple case that catches a single exception. Since `main` declares that it can throw `AnotherTrainComing`, the `catch` block doesn't need to handle it.

☒   **A, C, E,** and **G** are incorrect. **A** and **E** are incorrect because the `catch` block will not handle `RanOutOfTrack` when `drive()` throws it. The `main` method will still throw the exception, but the `println()` will not run. **C** is incorrect because it is invalid syntax for multi-`catch`. The `catch` parameter `e` can only appear once. **G** is incorrect because of the above. (OCP Objective 6.2)

6.   ☑   **E** is correct. After the exception is thrown, Automatic Resource Management calls `close()` before completing the `try` block. From that point, `catch` and `finally` execute in the normal order.
☒   **F** is incorrect because the `catch` block catches the exception and does not rethrow it. **A, B, C, D,** and **G** are incorrect because of the above. (OCP Objective 6.3)

7.   ☑   **G** is correct. `System.out.println` cannot be in the declaration clause of a `try`-with-resources block because it does not declare a variable. If the `println` was removed, the answer would be **A** because resources are closed in the opposite order in which they are created.
☒   **A, B, C, D, E,** and **F** are incorrect because of the above. (OCP Objective 6.3)

8.   ☑   **A** is correct. If the code is left with no changes, it will not compile because `try`-with-resources requires `Lamb` to implement `AutoCloseable` or a subinterface. If C2 is implemented, the code will not compile because `close()` throws `Exception` instead of `IOException`. Unlike the traditional `try`, `try`-with-resources does not require `catch` or `finally` to be present.
☒   **B, C, D, E,** and **F** are incorrect because of the above. (OCP Objective 6.3)

9.   ☑   **D** is correct. While the exception caught by the `catch` block matches choice **A,** it is ignored by the `catch` block. The `catch` block just throws `RuntimeException c` without any suppressed exceptions.
☒   **A, B, C, E, F,** and **G** are incorrect because of the above. (OCP Objective 6.3)

10.   ☑   **A** is correct. After the `try` block throws an `IOException`, Automatic Resource Management calls `close()` to clean up the resources. Since an exception was already thrown in the `try` block, `RuntimeException a` gets added to it as a suppressed exception. The `catch` block merely rethrows the caught exception. The code does compile, even though the `catch` block catches an `Exception` and the method merely throws an `IOException`. In Java 7, the compiler is able to pick up on this.
☒   **B, C, D, E, F,** and **G** are incorrect because of the above. (OCP Objective 6.3)

11.   ☑   **F** is correct. The exception variable in a `catch` block may not be reassigned when using multi-`catch`. It CAN be reassigned if we are only catching one exception.
☒   **C** would have been correct if `e = new PowerOutage();` were removed. **A, B, D,** and **E** are incorrect because of the above. (OCP Objectives 6.2 and 6.4)

4

Dates, Times, Locales, and Resource Bundles

T his chapter focuses on the exam objectives related to working with date- and time-related events, formatting dates and times, and using resource bundles for localization and internationalization tasks. Many of these topics could fill an entire book. Fortunately, you won't have to become a guru to do well on the exam. The intention of the exam team was to include just the basic aspects of these technologies, and in this chapter, we cover *more* than you'll need to get through the related objectives on the exam.

CERTIFICATION OBJECTIVE

Dates, Times, and Locales (OCP Objectives 7.1, 7.2, 7.3, and 12.1)

7.1   Create and manage date-based and time-based events including a combination of date and time into a single object using LocalDate, LocalTime, LocalDateTime, Instant, Period, and Duration.

7.2   Work with dates and times across timezones and manage changes resulting from daylight savings including Format date and times values.

7.3   Define, create and manage date-based and time-based events using Instant, Period, Duration, and TemporalUnit.

12. 1   Read and set the locale by using the Locale object.

The Java API provides an extensive (perhaps a little *too* extensive) set of classes to help you work with dates and times. The exam will test your knowledge of the basic classes and methods you'll use to work with dates and such. When you've finished this section, you should have a solid foundation in tasks such as creating date and time objects, and creating, manipulating, and formatting dates and times, and doing all of this for locations around the globe. In fact, a large part of why this section was added to the exam was to test whether you can do some basic internationalization (often shortened to "i18n").

Note: In this section, we'll introduce the `Locale` class. Later in the chapter, we'll be discussing resource bundles, and you'll learn more about `Locale` then.

Working with Dates and Times

If you want to work with dates and times from around the world (and who doesn't?), you'll need to be familiar with several classes from the `java.time` package. `java.time` is new in Java 8, so if you're looking for the old familiar `java.util.Date` and `java.util.Calendar`, you won't find them on the exam, although we'll briefly mention them here for comparison purposes.

Here's an overview of how the classes in `java.time` are organized:

- **Local dates and times**   These dates and times are local to your time zone and so don't have time-zone information associated with them. These are represented by classes `java.time.LocalDate`, `java.time.LocalTime`, and `java.time.LocalDateTime`.

- **Zoned dates and times**   These dates and times include time-zone information. They are represented by classes `java.time.ZonedDateTime` and `java.time.OffsetDateTime`.

- **Formatters for dates and times**   With `java.time.format.DateTimeFormatter`, you can parse and print dates and times with patterns and in a variety of styles.

- **Adjustments to dates and times**   With `java.time.temporal.TemporalAdjusters` and `java.time.temporal.ChronoUnit`, you can adjust and manipulate dates and times by handy increments.

- **Periods, Durations, and Instants**   `java.time.Periods` and `java.time.Durations` represent an amount of time, periods for days or longer and durations for shorter periods like minutes or seconds. `java.time.Instants` represent a specific instant in time, so you can, say, compute the number of minutes between two instants.

If you're used to working with `java.util.Date`, `java.util.Calendar`, and `java.text.DateFormat`, you're going to have to forget most of what you've learned and start over (although the concepts are similar, so you have a bit of a head start). All those classes are still around (although some methods are marked as deprecated), but they are considered "old," and the classes in `java.time` are designed to replace them completely. Hopefully this design will stick!

The `Date` Class

The API design of the `java.util.Date` class didn't do a good job of handling internationalization and localization situations, so it's been largely replaced by the classes in `java.time`, like `java.time.localDateTime` and `java.time`

.ZonedDateTime. You might find Date used in legacy code, but, for the most part, it's time to leave it behind.

The Calendar Class

Likewise, the java.util.Calendar class has largely been replaced with the classes in java.time. You'll still find plenty of legacy Calendar code around, but if you've worked with Calendar before, you'll likely find the java.time classes easier and less convoluted to work with.

With that, we'll dive right into the java.time classes.

The java.time.* Classes for Dates and Times

To make learning about dates and times more fun, let's imagine you are a solar eclipse hunter. You love chasing solar eclipses around the country and around the world. This example will be U.S.-centric, but you can easily apply all these ideas to dates and times in other countries too (and doing so is great practice for the exam).

Let's begin by figuring out the current date and time where you are, right now:

```
import java.time.*;
public class Eclipse {
  public static void main(String[] args) {
    LocalDate nowDate = LocalDate.now();
    LocalTime nowTime = LocalTime.now();
    LocalDateTime nowDateTime = LocalDateTime.of(nowDate, nowTime);
    System.out.println("It's currently " + nowDateTime + " where I am");
  }
}
```

Here we're using the static method LocalDate.now() to get the current date. It has no time zone, so think of it as a description of "the date," whatever that date is for you today, wherever you are, as you try this code. Similarly, we're using the static method LocalTime.now() to get the current time, so that will be whatever the time is for you right now, wherever you are, as you try this code. We then use the date and time of "now" to create a LocalDateTime object using the of() static method and then display it.

When we run this code we see

```
It's currently 2017-10-11T14:51:19.982 where I am
```

The string 2017-10-11T14:51:19.982 represents the date, October 11, 2017, and time, 14:51:19.982, which is 2:51 PM and 19 seconds and 982 milliseconds.

Notice that Java displays a "T" between the date and the time when converting the LocalDateTime to a string.

Of course, you'll see a completely different date and time because you're running this code in your own date and time, wherever and whenever that is.

We could also write:

```
LocalDateTime nowDateTime = LocalDateTime.now();
```

to get the current date and time of now as a LocalDateTime.

What if you want to set a specific date and time rather than "now"?

Let's say you went to Madras, Oregon, in the United States to see the solar eclipse on August 21, 2017. Here are a couple of ways you can set that specific date:

```
// The day of the eclipse in Madras, OR
LocalDate eclipseDate1 = LocalDate.of(2017, 8, 21);
LocalDate eclipseDate2 = LocalDate.parse("2017-08-21");
System.out.println("Eclipse date: " + eclipseDate1 + ", " +
eclipseDate2);
```

We're creating the same date in two slightly different ways: first, by specifying a year, month, and day as arguments to the LocalDate.of() static method; and second, by using the LocalDate.parse() method to parse a string that matches the date. LocalDate represents a date in the ISO-8601 calendar system (which specifies a format of YYYY-MM-DD). You don't need to know that, except to know the kinds of strings that the parse() method can parse correctly. (For a full list of the formats of the dates and times that can be parsed and represented, check out the documentation for java.time.format.DateTimeFormatter, which we'll talk more about in a little bit. See https://docs.oracle.com/javase/8/docs/api/java/time/format/DateTimeFormatter.html.)

When we run this code, we see the default display (using that ISO format) for both dates:

```
Eclipse date: 2017-08-21, 2017-08-21
```

An eclipse happens at a specific time of day. The eclipse begins awhile before *totality* (when the moon almost completely obscures the sun), so let's create LocalTime objects to represent the time the eclipse begins and the time of totality:

```
// Eclipse begins in Madras, OR
LocalTime begins = LocalTime.of(9, 6, 43);          // 9:06:43
// Totality starts in Madras, OR
LocalTime totality = LocalTime.parse("10:19:36");   // 10:19:36
System.out.println("Eclipse begins at " + begins +
   " and totality is at " + totality);
```

As with `LocalDate`, a `LocalTime` has no time zone associated with it, so in this case, we need to know that we're creating times that are valid in Madras, OR (on U.S. Pacific time). For these times, we again use the static `of()` and `parse()` methods to demonstrate two different ways to create `LocalTime` objects.

When we print the times, we see:

```
Eclipse begins at 09:06:43 and totality is at 10:19:36
```

If you want to be precise about the format of the date and time you're parsing into a `LocalDate` or `LocalTime` or `LocalDateTime`, you can use `DateTimeFormatter`. You can either use one of several predefined formats or create your own format for parsing using a sequence of letters and symbols. In the following example, we create a date and time in a string and then tell the `LocalDateTime` how to parse that using a `DateTimeFormatter`:

```
String eclipseDateTime = "2017-08-21 10:19";
DateTimeFormatter formatter =
   DateTimeFormatter.ofPattern("yyyy-MM-dd HH:mm");
LocalDateTime eclipseDay =
   LocalDateTime.parse(eclipseDateTime, formatter); // use formatter
System.out.println("Eclipse day: " + eclipseDay);
```

This creates a `LocalDateTime` object from the string, formatted using the pattern we specified, and when we print out the `LocalDateTime`, we see the correct date and time, printed in the standard ISO format we saw before:

```
Eclipse day: 2017-08-21T10:19
```

Of course, you can also use `DateTimeFormatter` to change the format of the output (again using letters and symbols):

```
System.out.println("Eclipse day, formatted: " +
   eclipseDay.format(DateTimeFormatter.ofPattern("dd, mm, yy hh, mm")));
```

This code results in the output:

```
Eclipse day, formatted: 21, 19, 17 10, 19
```

We'll come back to `DateTimeFormatter` in a bit.

`LocalDateTime` has several methods that make it easy to add to and subtract from dates and times. For instance, let's say your Mom calls from Nashville, TN (on U.S. Central time) and asks, "What time will it be here when you're seeing the eclipse there?" You know that Central time is two hours ahead of Pacific time, so to answer that question you can write:

```
System.out.println("Mom time: " + eclipseDay.plusHours(2));
```

which reveals that it will be 12:19 PM where she is in Tennessee when you're watching the eclipse at 10:19 AM in Oregon:

```
Mom time: 2017-08-21T12:19:36
```

Then she asks, "When are you coming home?" You can tell her, "In three days" by writing the following code:

```
System.out.println("Going home: " + eclipseDay.plusDays(3));
```

which means you'll be going home on August 24:

```
Going home: 2017-08-24T10:19:36
```

Of course, there are loads of other handy methods too, like getDayOfWeek() to find out what day of the week the eclipse occurs:

```
System.out.println("What day of the week is eclipse? " +
    eclipseDay.getDayOfWeek());
```

which lets you know the eclipse was on a Monday:

```
What day of the week is eclipse? MONDAY
```

Zoned Dates and Times

Local dates and times are great when you don't need to worry about the time zone, but sometimes we need to share dates and times with people in other time zones, so knowing which time zone you're in or they're in becomes important.

exam

ⓦatch *You don't need to know too much about time zones for the exam, except, of course, to understand what a time zone is and that different places in different parts of the world are on different time zones. For instance, in Madras, Oregon, you are in the U.S. Pacific time zone, whereas your Mom in Tennessee is in the U.S. Central time zone.*

All time zones are based on *Greenwich Mean Time (GMT)*, the time in Greenwich, England. GMT is a time zone. The name of the time standard that uses GMT as the basis for all other time zones is *Coordinated Universal Time (UTC)*.

Your time zone will either be ahead of or behind GMT. For instance, in Madras, OR, for the eclipse, you are GMT-7, meaning you are seven hours behind GMT.

That's for summer; in winter, you'll be GMT-8, or eight hours behind GMT because the United States has daylight savings time in summer and standard time in winter. Yes, zoned dates and times can get complicated fast, but rest assured, the exam is not about your depth of understanding of time zones. As long as you know the basics and you can create and use zoned dates and times, you'll be fine.

Let's create a zoned date and time for the date and time of the eclipse:

```
ZonedDateTime zTotalityDateTime =
    ZonedDateTime.of(eclipseDay, ZoneId.of("US/Pacific"));
System.out.println("Date and time totality begins with time zone: "
    + zTotalityDateTime);
```

Looking at the output, we see:

```
Date and time totality begins with time zone:
2017-08-21T10:19:36-07:00[US/Pacific]
```

A `ZonedDateTime` is a `LocalDateTime` plus a time zone, which is represented as a `ZoneId`. In this example, the `ZoneId` is "US/Pacific," which happens to be GMT-7 (which you may also see written as UTC-7). You can use either "US/Pacific" or "GMT-7" as the `ZoneId`.

You might be asking: How did you know the name of the `ZoneId`? Good question. The names of the zones are not listed in the documentation page for `ZoneId`, so one good way to find them is to write some code to display them:

```
Set<String> zoneIds = ZoneId.getAvailableZoneIds();
List<String> zoneList = new ArrayList<String>(zoneIds);
Collections.sort(zoneList);
for (String zoneId : zoneList) {
    if (zoneId.contains("US")) {
        System.out.println(zoneId);
    }
}
```

With this code, we're displaying only the U.S. `zoneIds`. If you, say, want to display the `zoneIds` for Great Britain, then use `"GB"` in place of `"US"`. The list includes some `zoneIds` by country, some by city, and some by other names.

Let's get back to daylight savings time. Recall that the U.S. Pacific time zone is either GMT-7 (in winter, standard time) or GMT-8 (in summer, daylight savings time). That means when you're creating a `ZonedDateTime` for Madras, Oregon (or any other place that uses daylight savings), you're going to need to know if you're currently in daylight savings time.

You can find out if you're in daylight savings time by using `ZoneRules`. All you need to know about `ZoneRules` is that the class captures the current rules about daylight savings in various parts of the world. Unfortunately, this tends to change (as politicians tend to change their minds—what a shocker!) so the rules are, as the documentation states, only as accurate as the information provided. Let's assume the rules are up to date (as you should for the exam) and write some code to find out if the `"US/Pacific"` time zone is currently in daylight savings time:

```
ZoneId pacific = ZoneId.of("US/Pacific");
// pacific.getRules() returns a ZoneRules object that has all the rules
// about time zones, including daylight savings and standard time.
System.out.println("Is Daylight Savings in effect at time of totality: " +
    pacific.getRules().isDaylightSavings(zTotalityDateTime.toInstant()));
```

In this code, we first get the `ZoneId` for the `"US/Pacific"` time zone. We can then use that `ZoneId` to get the `ZoneRules` with the `getRules()` method. A `ZoneRules` object has a method `isDaylightSavings()`, which takes an `Instant` and determines whether that `Instant` is currently in daylight savings. We'll discuss `Instant`s in more detail shortly; for now, just know that we can convert the `ZonedDateTime` representing the date and time of the eclipse into an `Instant` with the `toInstant()` method. The result is

```
Is Daylight Savings in effect at time of totality: true
```

The result is `true` because the date of the eclipse, `zTotalityDateTime` (that is, August 21, 2017, in the U.S. Pacific zone), was in daylight savings time (summer time).

Date and Time Adjustments

Once you've created a `LocalDateTime` or `ZonedDateTime`, you can't modify it. The documentation describes datetime objects as "immutable." However, you can create a new datetime object from an existing datetime object, and `java.time.*` provides plenty of adjusters that make it easy to do so. In other words, rather than modifying an existing datetime, you just make a new datetime from the existing one.

Let's say you want to find the date of the Thursday following the eclipse. We can take the `ZonedDateTime` for the eclipse we made above, `zTotalityDateTime`, and create a new `ZonedDateTime` from it to represent "the following Thursday" like this:

```
ZonedDateTime followingThursdayDateTime =
    zTotalityDateTime.with(TemporalAdjusters.next(   // adjust date time
        DayOfWeek.THURSDAY));                        // to next Thursday
System.out.println("Thursday following the totality: " +
    followingThursdayDateTime);
```

The output is:

```
Thursday following the totality: 2017-08-24T10:19:36-07:00[US/Pacific]
```

We can see that the Thursday following the eclipse (which, remember, was on Monday, August 21, 2017) is August 24.

The class `TemporalAdjusters` has a whole slew of handy methods to make a `TemporalAdjuster` for a variety of scenarios, such as `firstDayOfNextYear()`, `lastDayOfMonth()`, and more.

You've already seen how you can add days and hours from a datetime; many other adjustments, including `plusMinutes()`, `plusYears()`, `minusWeeks()`, `minusSeconds()`, and so on, are available as methods in `LocalDateTime` and `ZonedDateTime`. You'll also find a variety of adjustments like `withHour()` and `withYear()`, which you can use to create a new datetime object from an existing one, but with a different hour or year. Each of these methods creates a new adjusted datetime from an existing one.

`ZonedDateTimes` are subject to `ZoneRules` when you adjust them. So, if you, say, add a month to an existing `ZonedDateTime`, the `ZoneRules` will be used to determine if the new `ZonedDateTime` is GMT-7 or GMT-8, for instance, (depending on daylight savings time). If you want to create a datetime with a zone offset from GMT that does not use the `ZoneRules`, then you can use an `OffsetDateTime`. An `OffsetDateTime` is a fixed datetime and offset that doesn't change even if the `ZoneRules` change.

Periods, Durations, and Instants

So far, we've looked at how to create specific dates and times. The `java.time.*` package also includes ways to represent a period of time, whether that's a period of days, months, or years (a `Period`), a short period of minutes or hours (a `Duration`), or an instant in time (an `Instant`).

Periods   You're looking forward to the next eclipse on April 8, 2024, which you're going to watch in Austin, Texas, and you want to set a reminder for yourself one month in advance, so you don't forget. You could just say, well, I'll remind myself on March 8, 2024, but what fun would that be? Let's compute one month before the eclipse in code:

```
// Totality begins in Austin, TX in 2024 at 1:35pm and 56 seconds;
// Specify year, month, dayOfMonth, hour, minute, second, nano, zone
ZonedDateTime totalityAustin =
    ZonedDateTime.of(2024, 4, 8, 13, 35, 56, 0, ZoneId.of("US/Central"));
System.out.println("Next total eclipse in the US, date/time in Austin, TX: " +
    totalityAustin);
```

To create the reminder, we first create a `ZonedDateTime` for when totality begins in Austin. We use the `ZonedDateTIme.of()` static method to create the datetime with the arguments year, month, day, hours, minutes, seconds, nanoseconds, and zone id. We have no idea what the nanoseconds are for the totality beginning, so we just put 0. Notice we used 13 to specify 1 PM. Austin is in the U.S. Central time zone, so we get the `zoneId` using that name (which we got earlier when we displayed all the U.S. time-zone names). When we print this `ZonedDateTime`, we see

```
Next total eclipse in the US, date/time in Austin, TX:
2024-04-08T13:35:56-05:00[US/Central]
```

Now let's create the reminder for one month before this date and time by creating a `Period` that represents one month and subtract it from the date and time for the eclipse:

```
// Reminder for a month before
Period period = Period.ofMonths(1);
System.out.println("Period is " + period);
ZonedDateTime reminder = totalityAustin.minus(period);
System.out.println("DateTime of 1 month reminder: " + reminder);
```

Here's the output:

```
Period is P1M
DateTime of 1 month reminder: 2024-03-08T13:35:56-06:00[US/Central]
```

Notice how the period is displayed, with "P" meaning period and "1M" meaning month.

While we're here, let's see how to create a `LocalDateTime` from the `ZonedDateTime` for people who are in Austin:

```
System.out.println("Local DateTime (Austin, TX) of reminder: " +
    reminder.toLocalDateTime());
```

Notice the difference in the `LocalDateTime`—there's no time zone:

```
Local DateTime (Austin, TX) of reminder: 2024-03-08T13:35:56
```

And finally, let's figure out when we'll see the reminder in Madras, Oregon:

```
System.out.println("Zoned DateTime (Madras, OR) of reminder: " +
    reminder.withZoneSameInstant(ZoneId.of("US/Pacific")));
```

We'll see the reminder at 11 AM, two hours earlier than the reminder in Austin, because Madras is two hours behind.

```
Zoned DateTime (Madras, OR) of reminder: 2024-03-08T11:35:56-08:00[US/Pacific]
```

One more thing to notice about this code. The eclipse is happening in April 2024. April happens to be in summer time, or daylight savings time, so notice that during daylight savings, U.S. Central time is five hours behind GMT:

```
Next total eclipse in the US, date/time in Austin, TX:
2024-04-08T13:35:56-05:00[US/Central]
```

When we subtracted the one-month period from this date and time to get the date and time for our reminder, we compute that the reminder is on March 8, which is in winter time, or standard time:

```
DateTime of 1 month reminder: 2024-03-08T13:35:56-06:00[US/Central]
```

So, on March 8, 2024, Austin will be six hours behind GMT. Nice for us that Java correctly computed the time using `ZoneRules` behind the scenes.

Durations   How many minutes from the time the eclipse begins to the time totality begins? We can compute the time in a couple of ways; we're going to do it using `ChronoUnit` and `Duration`. `ChronoUnit` is an enum in `java.time` `.temporal` that provides a set of predefined units of time periods. For instance, `ChronoUnit.MINUTES` represents the concept of a minute. `ChronoUnit` also supplies a method `between()` that we can use to compute a `ChronoUnit` time period between two times. Once we have the number of minutes between two times, we can use that to create a `Duration`. `Duration`s have all kinds of handy methods for computing things, like adding and subtracting hours and minutes and seconds, or converting a `Duration` into a number of seconds or milliseconds, and so on. Think of `ChronoUnit` as a unit of time and `Duration` as specifying a period of time (like a `Period`, only for period lengths less than a day).

First, let's create two `LocalTime`s to represent the start of the eclipse (when the moon first starts to cross the sun) and the time of totality (when the moon completely obscures the sun):

```
// Eclipse begins in Austin, TX
LocalTime begins = LocalTime.of(12, 17, 32);    // 12:17:32
// Totality in Austin, TX
LocalTime totality = LocalTime.of(13, 35, 56);  // 13:35:56
System.out.println("Eclipse begins at " + begins +
   " and totality is at " + totality);
```

Notice we're just using `LocalTime` here, not `ZonedDateTime`, so we don't have to specify a time zone. The output looks like this:

```
Eclipse begins at 12:17:32 and totality is at 13:35:56
```

Now, let's use a `ChronoUnit` to compute the number of minutes between begins and `totality`:

```
// How many minutes between when the eclipse begins and totality?
long betweenMins = ChronoUnit.MINUTES.between(begins, totality);
System.out.println("Minutes between begin and totality: " + betweenMins);
```

The minutes returned by the `between()` method is a `long`. When we look at the output, we see we have 78 minutes between the beginning of the eclipse and the beginning of totality. Notice that we lost the number of seconds in this computation because we asked for the number of minutes between the two times.

Let's turn this into a `Duration`. As you might expect, we can turn the number of minutes into a `Duration` using `Duration.ofMinutes()`:

```
Duration betweenDuration = Duration.ofMinutes(betweenMins);
System.out.println("Duration: " + betweenDuration);
```

Looking at the output we see:

```
Duration: PT1H18M
```

PT means "period of time," meaning `Duration` (rather than `Period`), and then `1H18M` means "1 hour and 18 minutes" corresponding to our 78 minutes.

Just to double-check ourselves, let's take the `begin` `LocalTime` we created before and add back our `Duration` using the `LocalTime.plus()` method. We could also do this with our `betweenMins` value, using `LocalTime.plusMinutes()`. The `plus()` method takes a `TemporalAmount` (like a `Duration` or a `Period`), whereas `plusMinutes()` takes `minutes` as a `long`. Either way will work.

```
LocalTime totalityBegins = begins.plus(betweenDuration);
System.out.println("Totality begins, computed: " + totalityBegins);
```

The result is

```
Totality begins, computed: 13:35:32
```

This time is slightly different than our original `begins` time of 13:35:56 because we lost the seconds when we created the `Duration` from the minutes between begins and `totality`.

Instants   An `Instant` represents an instant in time. Makes sense, right? But how is it different from a `DateTime`? If you're used to timestamps, then you'll probably recognize an `Instant` as the number of seconds (and nanoseconds) since January 1, 1970—the standard Java epoch. `Instant`s can't be represented as just one `long`, like you might be used to, because an `Instant` includes nanoseconds, so the seconds plus the nanoseconds is too big for a `long`. However, once you've created an `Instant`, you can always get the number of seconds as a `long` value from the `Instant`.

`ZonedDateTimes` can be converted to `Instants` using the `toInstant()` method:

```
ZonedDateTime totalityAustin =
    ZonedDateTime.of(2024, 4, 8, 13, 35, 56, 0, ZoneId.of("US/Central"));
Instant totalityInstant = totalityAustin.toInstant();
System.out.println("Austin's eclipse instant is: " + totalityInstant);
```

Looking at the output we see

```
Austin's eclipse instant is: 2024-04-08T18:35:56Z
```

Even though we created a `ZonedDateTime` for Austin at 1:35 PM, in the `US/Central` time zone, the instant displays as 6:35 PM and shows a `Z` at the end. That datetime represents 6:35 PM GMT. The `Z` is how you know the time displayed is for the GMT zone, rather than the U.S. Central zone. This format is the `ISO_INSTANT` format of displaying a datetime.

Note that if you want to call the `toInstant()` method on a `LocalDateTime`, you'll need to supply a `ZoneOffset` as an argument. To create a unique instant in time that works globally, a time zone is required when the `Instant` is created. If we don't include a time zone, then *your* instant and *our* instant may mean two different things.

Let's once again compute the number of minutes between two times using `ChronoUnit.MINUTES`. This time we'll compute the minutes between now and the Austin eclipse as represented by `Instants` and then use that to create a `Duration`. We'll use the `totalityInstant` we created above for the instant of the totality, and we'll use the `Instant.now()` method to create an instant representing right now:

```
Instant nowInstant = Instant.now();  // represents now
Instant totalityInstant = totalityAustin.toInstant;  // same as above
long minsBetween =
    ChronoUnit.MINUTES.between(nowInstant, totalityInstant);
Duration durationBetweenInstants = Duration.ofMinutes(minsBetween);
System.out.println("Minutes between " + minsBetween +
    ", is duration " + durationBetweenInstants);
```

The output is

```
Minutes between 3405250, is duration PT56754H10M
```

As you can see (reading the `Duration`), between now and the next eclipse in Austin, we have only 56,754 hours and 10 minutes to wait. That eclipse will be here in no time.

Lastly, if you want to get the number of seconds since January 1, 1970, from an `Instant`, use the method `getEpochSecond()`:

```
Instant now = Instant.now();
System.out.println("Seconds since epoch: " + now.getEpochSecond());
```

The number of seconds is

```
Seconds since epoch: 1508286832
```

A Few Other Handy Methods and Examples

Let's add another reminder before the next eclipse, say, for three days before the eclipse, and then let's figure out what day of the week this reminder will occur:

```
// Another reminder 3 days before
System.out.println("DateTime of 3 day reminder: " +
    totalityAustin.minus(Period.ofDays(3)));
// What day of the week is that?
System.out.println("Day of week for 3 day reminder: " +
    totalityAustin.minus(Period.ofDays(3)).getDayOfWeek());
```

We see that the three-day reminder is on April 5, which is a Friday:

```
DateTime of 3 day reminder: 2024-04-05T13:35:56-05:00[US/Central]
Day of week for 3 day reminder: FRIDAY
```

And we really should call our sister in Paris a couple of hours after the next eclipse to tell her how it was:

```
ZonedDateTime localParis =
    totalityAustin.withZoneSameInstant(ZoneId.of("Europe/Paris"));
System.out.println("Eclipse happens at " + localParis + " Paris time");
System.out.println("Phone sister at 2 hours after totality: " +
    totalityAustin.plusHours(2) + ", " +
    localParis.plusHours(2) + " Paris time");
```

From the output, we can see that the eclipse happens at 8:35 Paris time, and when we call our sister two hours after the eclipse, it will be 3:35 PM Austin time and 10:35 PM Paris time:

```
Eclipse happens at 2024-04-08T20:35:56+02:00[Europe/Paris] Paris time
Phone sister at 2 hours after totality:
2024-04-08T15:35:56-05:00[US/Central],
2024-04-08T22:35:56+02:00[Europe/Paris] Paris time
```

If you tend to lose track of time, but you really, really don't want to miss the eclipse, you can check to make sure the eclipse is still in the future with this code:

```
// compare two ZonedDateTimes (must be the same type!)
System.out.println("Is the 2024 eclipse still in the future? " +
    ZonedDateTime.now().isBefore(totalityAustin));
```

Since we're writing this in 2017, the 2024 eclipse is still far in the future, so we see

```
Is the 2024 eclipse still in the future? true
```

And finally, we'd better do one more check about 2024. How about checking to see if 2024 is a leap year? You definitely don't want to miss the eclipse by a day:

```
System.out.println("Is 2024 a leap year? " + totalityAustin.isLeapYear());
```

Try this code and you'll get a compile-time error:

```
The method isLeapYear() is undefined for the type ZonedDateTime
```

Hmm. It turns out `isLeapYear()` is defined only for `LocalDate`, not for `LocalDateTime` or `ZonedDateTime`. We can fix the code by converting `totalityAustin` to a `LocalDate`:

```
System.out.println("Is 2024 a leap year? " +
    totalityAustin.toLocalDate().isLeapYear());
```

Another way to check for a leap year is

```
System.out.println("Is 2024 a leap year? " + Year.of(2024).isLeap());
```

The output from both lines of code shows that 2024 is, indeed, a leap year.

Formatting Output with DateTimeFormatter

Earlier we used `DateTimeFormatter` to specify a pattern when parsing a date string. We can also use `DateTimeFormatter` when we display a datetime as a string.

You might know that in the United States, we tend to write month/day/year, and in the European Union, they tend to write day/month/year. (Yes, that can get a bit confusing at times!)

Let's format and display the datetime of the eclipse in Austin using the European-preferred format. There are a couple of different ways we can do that. First, we can specify exactly the format we want using letters and symbols, as we described earlier:

```
System.out.println("Totality date/time written for sister in Europe: " +
    totalityAustin.format(
        DateTimeFormatter.ofPattern("dd/MM/yyyy hh:mm")));
```

Here, we're using the `format()` method of the `ZonedDateTime`, `totalityAustin`, and passing in a formatter. The formatter specifies a format to use for formatting the datetime, using allowed letters and symbols (see the `DateTimeFormatter` documentation for all the options). When we look at the output, we see

```
Totality date/time written for sister in Europe: 08/04/2024 01:35
```

Alternatively, we could specify a format style and a locale:

```
System.out.println("Totality date/time in UK Locale: " +
    totalityAustin.format(
      DateTimeFormatter.ofLocalizedDateTime(
        FormatStyle.SHORT)
        .withLocale(Locale.UK)));
```

Now when we look at the output, we see

```
Totality date/time in UK Locale: 08/04/24 13:35
```

You'll learn more about `Locales` shortly; essentially, `Locales` are designed to tailor data for a specific region. Here, we're creating a `DateTimeFormatter` by specifying a built-in style and then using that to create a new formatter for a specific locale, the UK locale. Creating a formatter with a specific locale means the formatter is adjusted appropriately for that locale. We see that the UK locale uses the day/month/year format for the date and the 24-hour format for the time. As you can see, there is a lot to the `java.time.*` package. There's no way you can memorize everything in the package for the exam, so we recommend you focus on the classes, properties, and methods in Tables 4-1 and 4-2 (later in the chapter) and familiarize yourself with the rest of the package by looking over the documentation to get a sense of what's there (see https://docs.oracle.com/javase/8/docs/api/java/time/package-summary.html).

You've probably noticed a pattern in the method names used in the `java.time.*` package. For instance, `of()` methods create a new date from, typically, a sequence of numbers specifying the year, month, day, and so on. `parse()` methods create a new date by parsing a string that's either in a standard ISO format already or by using a formatter. `with()` methods allow you to adjust a date with a `TemporalAdjuster` to make a new date. `plusX()` and `minusX()` methods create a new datetime object from an existing one by adding and subtracting `TemporalUnits` or longs representing weeks, minutes, and so on. Study the `LocalDateTime` and `ZonedDateTime` methods enough to get the hang of this pattern so you can recognize the methods on the exam (without having to memorize them all).

Using Dates and Times with Locales

The Locale class is your ticket to understanding how to internationalize your code. Both the DateTimeFormatter class and the NumberFormat class can use an instance of Locale to customize formatted output for a specific locale (and you just got a taste of this with DateTimeFormatter in the previous section).

You might ask how Java defines a locale. The API says a locale is "a specific geographical, political, or cultural region." The two Locale constructors you'll need to understand for the exam are

```
Locale(String language)
Locale(String language, String country)
```

The language argument represents an ISO 639 Language code, so, for instance, if you want to format your dates or numbers in Walloon (the language sometimes used in southern Belgium), you'd use "wa" as your language string. There are over 500 ISO Language codes, including one for Klingon ("tlh"), although, unfortunately, Java doesn't yet support the Klingon locale. We thought about telling you that you'd have to memorize all these codes for the exam...but we didn't want to cause any heart attacks. So rest assured, you will *not* have to memorize any ISO Language codes or ISO Country codes (of which there are about 240) for the exam.

Let's get back to how you might use these codes. If you want to represent basic Italian in your application, all you need is the Language code. If, on the other hand, you want to represent the Italian used in Switzerland, you'd want to indicate that the country is Switzerland (yes, the Country code for Switzerland is "CH"), but that the language is Italian:

```
Locale locIT = new Locale("it");        // Italian
Locale locCH = new Locale("it", "CH");  // Switzerland
```

Using these two locales on a date could give us output like this:

```
sabato 1 ottobre 2005
sabato, 1. ottobre 2005
```

Now let's put this all together in some code that creates a ZonedDateTime object and sets its date. We'll then take that datetime object and print it using locales from around the world:

```
Locale myLocale = Locale.getDefault();
System.out.println("My locale: " + myLocale);
LocalDateTime aDateTime = LocalDateTime.of(2024, 4, 8, 13, 35, 56);
System.out.println("The date and time: " +
    aDateTime.format(DateTimeFormatter.ofLocalizedDateTime(
                        FormatStyle.MEDIUM)));
ZonedDateTime zDateTime = ZonedDateTime.of(
                            aDateTime, ZoneId.of(
                            "US/Pacific"));
```

```
Locale locIT = new Locale("it", "IT");      // Italy
Locale locPT = new Locale("pt");            // Portugal
Locale locBR = new Locale("pt", "BR");      // Brazil
Locale locIN = new Locale("hi", "IN");      // India
Locale locJA = new Locale("ja");            // Japan
Locale locDK = new Locale("da", "DK");      // Denmark
System.out.println("Italy (Long) " +
    zDateTime.format(
        DateTimeFormatter.ofLocalizedDateTime(FormatStyle.LONG)
    .withLocale(Locale.ITALY)));
System.out.println("Italy (Short) " +
    aDateTime.format(
        DateTimeFormatter.ofLocalizedDateTime(FormatStyle.SHORT)
    .withLocale(locIT)));

System.out.println("Japan (Long) " +
    zDateTime.format(
        DateTimeFormatter.ofLocalizedDateTime(FormatStyle.LONG)
    .withLocale(Locale.JAPAN)));

System.out.println("Portugal (Long) " +
    zDateTime.format(
        DateTimeFormatter.ofLocalizedDateTime(FormatStyle.LONG)
    .withLocale(locPT)));

System.out.println("India (Long) " +
    zDateTime.format(
        DateTimeFormatter.ofLocalizedDateTime(FormatStyle.LONG)
    .withLocale(locIN)));

System.out.println("Denmark (Medium) " +
    zDateTime.format(
        DateTimeFormatter.ofLocalizedDateTime(FormatStyle.MEDIUM)
    .withLocale(locDK)));
```

This code, on our JVM, produces the output:

```
My locale: en_US
The date and time: Apr 8, 2024 1:35:56 PM
Italy (Long) 8 aprile 2024 13.35.56 PDT
Italy (Short) 08/04/24 13.35
Japan (Long) 2024/04/08 13:35:56 PDT
Portugal (Long) 8 de Abril de 2024 13:35:56 PDT
India (Long) 8 अप्रैल, 2024 1:35:56 अपराह्न PDT
Denmark (Medium) 08-04-2024 13:35:56
```

So you can see how a single `ZonedDateTime` object can be formatted to work for many locales and varying amounts of detail. (Note that you'll need Eclipse in UTF-8 format to see the Indian output properly.)

There are a couple more methods in `Locale` (`getDisplayCountry()` and `getDisplayLanguage()`) that you need to know for the exam. These methods let you create strings that represent a given locale's country and language in terms of both the default locale and any other locale:

```
Locale locBR = new Locale("pt", "BR");  // Brazil
Locale locDK = new Locale("da", "DK");  // Denmark
Locale locIT = new Locale("it", "IT");  // Italy

System.out.println("Denmark, country: " + locDK.getDisplayCountry());
System.out.println("Denmark, country, local: " +
    locDK.getDisplayCountry(locDK));
System.out.println("Denmark, language: " + locDK.getDisplayLanguage());
System.out.println("Denmark, language, local: " +
    locDK.getDisplayLanguage(locDK));

System.out.println("Brazil, country: " + locBR.getDisplayCountry());
System.out.println("Brazil, country, local: " +
    locBR.getDisplayCountry(locBR));
System.out.println("Brazil, language: " + locBR.getDisplayLanguage());
System.out.println("Brazil, language, local: " +
    locBR.getDisplayLanguage(locBR));
System.out.println("Italy, Danish language is: " +
    locDK.getDisplayLanguage(locIT));
```

This code, on our JVM, produces the output:

```
Denmark, country: Denmark
Denmark, country, local: Danmark
Denmark, language: Danish
Denmark, language, local: Dansk
Brazil, country: Brazil
Brazil, country, local: Brasil
Brazil, language: Portuguese
Brazil, language, local: português
Italy, Danish language is: danese
```

Our JVM's locale (the default for us, which we saw displayed earlier) is en_US, and when we display the country name for Brazil, in our locale, we get Brazil. In Brazil, however, the country is Brasil. Same with the language; for us the language of Brazil is Portuguese; for people in Brasil, it's português. Likewise, for Denmark, you can see how we have different names for the country and the language than the Danish do.

Finally, just for fun, we discovered that in Italy, the Danish language is called danese.

Orchestrating Date- and Time-Related Classes

When you work with dates and times, you'll often use several classes together. It's important to understand how the classes described earlier relate to each other and when to use which classes in combination. For instance, you need to know that if you're creating a new `ZonedDateTime` from an existing `LocalDate` and `LocalTime`, you need a `ZoneId` too; if you want to do date formatting for a specific locale, you need to create your `Locale` object before your `DateTimeFormatter` object because you'll need your `Locale` object as an argument to your `DateTimeFormatter` method; and so on. Tables 4-1 and 4-2 provide a quick overview and summary of common date- and time-related use cases: how to create datetime objects and how to adjust them. We are by no means

TABLE 4-1   Instance Creation for `java.time` Classes

java.time Class	Key Instance Creation Options

LocalDate	`LocalDate.now();`
	`LocalDate.of(2017, 8, 21);`
	`LocalDate.parse("2017-08-21");`

LocalTime	`LocalTime.now();`
	`LocalTime.of(10, 19, 36);`
	`LocalTime.parse("10:19:36");`

LocalDateTime	`LocalDateTime.now();`
	`LocalDateTime.of(aDate, aTime);`
	`LocalDateTime.parse("2017-04-08T10:19:36");`
	`LocalDateTime.parse(aDateTime, aFormatter);`
	`LocalDateTime.parse("2017-08-21T10:19,`
	`                aformatter);`

ZonedDateTime	`ZonedDateTime.now();`
	`ZonedDateTime.of(aDateTime, ZoneId.of(aZoneString));`
	`ZonedDateTime.parse("2017-04-08T10:19:36-05:00");`

OffsetDateTime	`OffsetDateTime.now();`
	`OffsetDateTime.of(aDateTime,`
	`                ZoneOffset.of("-05:00"));`
	`OffsetDateTime.parse("2017-04-08T10:19:36-05:00");`

format.
DateTimeFormatter
	`DateTimeFormatter.ofPattern("yyyy-MM-dd HH:mm");`
	`DateTimeFormatter.ofLocalizedDateTime(`
	`   FormatStyle.SHORT).withLocale(aLocale);`

Instant	`Instant.now();`
	`zonedDateTime.toInstant();`
	`aDateTime.toInstant(ZoneOffset.of("+5"));`

Duration	`Duration.between(aTime1, aTime2);` `Duration.ofMinutes(5);`
Period	`Period.between(aDate1, aDate2);` `Period.ofDays(3);`

util.Locale	`Locale.getDefault();`
	`new Locale(String language);`
	`new Locale(String language, String country);`

TABLE 4-2	Adjustment Options for `java.time` Classes

Class	Key Adjustment Options and Examples (all methods create a new datetime object)

LocalDate	`aDate.minusDays(3);`
	`aDate.plusWeeks(1);`
	`aDate.withYear(2018);`

LocalTime	`aTime.minus(3, ChronoUnit.MINUTES);`
	`aTime.plusMinutes(3);`
	`aTime.withHour(12);`

LocalDateTime	`aDateTime.minusDays(3);`
	`aDateTime.plusMinutes(10);`
	`aDateTime.plus(Duration.ofMinutes(5));`
	`aDateTime.withMonth(2);`

ZonedDateTime	`zonedDateTime.withZoneSameInstant(ZoneId.of("US/Pacific"));`

including all of the many available methods to work with dates and times, however, so make sure you peruse the documentation too (see https://docs.oracle.com/javase/8/docs/api/java/time/package-summary.html).

Properties Files (OCP Objective 12.2)

12.2 Create and read a Properties file.

Property files are typically used to externally store configuration settings and operating parameters for your applications. In the Java world, there are at least three variations on property files:

1. There is a system-level properties file that holds system information like hardware info, software versions, classpaths, and so on. The `java.lang.System` class has methods that allow you to update this file and view its contents. This property file is not on the exam.

2. There is a class called `java.util.Properties` that makes it easy for a programmer to create and maintain property files for whatever applications the programmer chooses. We'll talk about the `java.util.Properties`

class in this section. In this section, when we say "property" files, we're referring to files that are compliant with the `java.util.Properties` class.

3. There is a class called `java.util.ResourceBundle` that *can—* optionally—use `java.util.Properties` files to make it easier for a programmer to add localization and/or internationalization features to applications. After we discuss `java.util.Properties`, we'll discuss `java.util.ResourceBundle`.

The `java.util.Properties` class is used to create and/or maintain human-readable text files. It's also possible to create well-formed, `Properties`-compliant text files using a text editor. If you're using a `Properties` file for applications other than to support resource bundles, you can give them whatever legal filenames you want. Typically their names end in ".`properties`," e.g., "`MyApp.properties`." Other suffixes like ".`props`" are also common. The basic structure of a `Properties` file is a set of comments (usually comment lines begin with "#") at the top of the file, followed by a number of rows of text data, each row representing a key/value pair, with the key and value usually separated with an "=".

Almost everyone uses # for comments and = to separate key/value pairs. There are alternative syntax choices, though, which you should understand if you come across them.

Property files can use two styles of commenting:

```
! comment
```

or

```
# comment
```

Property files can define key/value pairs in any of the following formats:

```
key=value
key:value
key value
```

Let's refresh what we've learned about property files and take a closer look. Aside from comments, a property file contains key/value pairs:

```
# this file contains a single key/value
hello=Hello Java
```

A *key* is the first string on a line. Keys and values are usually separated by an equal sign. If you want to break up a single line into multiple lines, you use a backslash. Given an entry in a property file:

```
hello1 = Hello \
   World!
```

the code and output would be

```
System.out.println(rb.getString("hello1"));
Hello World!
```

If you actually want a line break, you use the standard Java \n escape sequence. Given an entry in a property file:

```
hello2 = Hello \nWorld  !
```

The code and output would be

```
System.out.println(rb.getString("hello2"));
Hello
World  !
```

You can mix and match these to your heart's content. Java helpfully ignores any whitespace before subsequent lines of a multiline property, so you can use indentation for clarity:

```
hello3 =     123\
    45
```

Given the above entry in a properties file, the code and output would be

```
System.out.println(rb.getString("hello3"));
12345
```

As we mentioned earlier, java.lang.System provides access to a property file. Although this file isn't on the exam, the following code

```
import java.util.*;
public class SysProps {
  public static void main(String[] args) {
    Properties p = System.getProperties();   // open system properties file
    p.setProperty("myProp", "myValue");      // add an entry
    p.list(System.out);                      // list the file's contents
  }
}
```

will produce output that contains entries like these:

```
myProp=myValue
java.version=1.8.0_45
os.name=Mac OS X
os.version=10.12.6
..
..
```

Again, what we're seeing here is a list of key/value pairs.

Let's move on to creating and working with our own property file. Here's some code that creates a new `Properties` object, adds a few properties, and then stores the contents of the `Properties` object to a file on disk:

```
import java.util.*;
import java.io.*;
class Props1 {
  public static void main(String[] args) {
    Properties p = new Properties();
    p.setProperty("k1", "v1");
    p.setProperty("k2", "v2");
    p.list(System.out);                    // what's in the object
    try {
      // creates or replaces file
      FileOutputStream out = new FileOutputStream("myProps1.props");
      p.store(out, "test-comment");        // adds header comment
      out.close();
    } catch (IOException e) {
      System.out.println("exc 1");
    }
  }
}
```

which produces the following output:

```
-- listing properties --
k2=v2
k1=v1
```

and a file named `myProps1.props`, which contains

```
#test-comment
#Fri Feb 02 14:53:30 PST 2018
k2=v2
k1=v1
```

Note that there are a couple of comments at the top of the file. Now let's run a second program that opens up the file we just created, adds a new key/value pair, then saves the result to a second file on disk:

```
import java.util.*;
import java.io.*;
class Props2 {
  public static void main(String[] args) {
    Properties p2 = new Properties();
    try {
      FileInputStream in = new FileInputStream("myProps1.props");
      p2.load(in);
      p2.list(System.out);
```

```
        p2.setProperty("newProp", "newData");
        p2.list(System.out);
        FileOutputStream out = new FileOutputStream("myProps2.props");
        p2.store(out, "myUpdate");
        in.close();
        out.close();
      } catch (IOException e) {
        System.out.println("exc 2");
      }
    }
  }
```

which produces

```
-- listing properties --
newProp=newData
k2=v2
k1=v1
```

and a file named myProps2.props, which contains

```
#myUpdate
#Fri Feb 02 14:53:58 PST 2018
newProp=newData
k2=v2
k1=v1
```

It's important to know that java.util.Properties inherits from java.util.Hashtable. Technically, when mucking around with property files, you could use methods from Hashtable like put() and get(), but Oracle encourages you to stick with the methods provided in the Properties class since those methods will force you to use arguments of type String. For the exam you should know the following methods from the Properties class:

```
String getProperty(String key)

void list(PrintStream out)

void load(InputStream inStream)

Object setProperty(String key, String value)

void store(OutputStream out, String headerComment)
```

Next, let's move on to the resource bundles to see how they work and how you can (if you want to) use property files to support your resource bundles.

Resource Bundles (OCP Objectives 12.1, 12.2, and 12.3)

12.1   Read and set the locale by using the Locale object.
12.2   Create and read a Properties file.
12.3   Build a resource bundle for each locale and load a resource bundle in an application.

Earlier, we used the `Locale` class to display dates for basic localization. For full-fledged localization, we also need to provide language- and country-specific strings for display. There are only two parts to building an application with resource bundles:

- `Locale`   You can use the same `Locale` we used for `DateFormat` and `NumberFormat` to identify which resource bundle to choose.
- `ResourceBundle`   Think of a `ResourceBundle` as a map. You can use property files or Java classes to specify the mappings.

Let's build a simple application to be used in Canada. Since Canada has two official languages, we want to let the user choose her favorite language. Designing our application, we decided to have it just output "Hello Java" to show off how cool it is. We can always add more text later.

We are going to externalize everything language specific to special property files. They're just property files that contain keys and string values to display, but they follow very specific, `ResourceBundle`-required naming conventions. Here are two simple resource bundle files:

A file named `Labels_en.properties` that contains a single line of data:

```
hello=Hello Java!
```

A second file named `Labels_fr.properties` that contains a single line of data:

```
hello=Bonjour Java!
```

It's critical to understand that when you use `Properties` files to support `ResourceBundle` objects, the naming of the files MUST follow two rules:

1. These files must end in ".`properties`."
2. The end of the name before the .`properties` suffix must be a string that starts with an underscore and then declares the Locale the file represents (e.g., `MyApp_en.properties` or `MyApp_fr.properties` or `MyApp_fr_CA.properties`). `ResourceBundle` only knows how to find the appropriate file via the filename. There is no requirement for the data in the file to contain locale information.

Using a resource bundle requires three steps: obtaining the `Locale`, getting the `ResourceBundle`, and looking up a value from the resource bundle. First, we create a `Locale` object. To review, this means one of the following:

```
new Locale("en")          // language - English
new Locale("en", "CA")    // language and country - Canadian English
Locale.CANADA             // constant for common locales - Canadian English
```

Next, we need to create the resource bundle. We need to know the bundle name of the resource bundle and the locale. The bundle name of the resource bundle is that part of the filename up to (but not including) the underscore that is the start of the locale info. For example, if a `Properties` file is named `MyApp_en.properties`, then the bundle name is "MyApp." Then we pass those values to a factory, which creates the resource bundle. The `getBundle()` method looks in the classpath for bundles that match the bundle name (in the code below, the bundle name is "`Labels`") and the provided `locale`.

```
ResourceBundle rb = ResourceBundle.getBundle("Labels", locale);
```

Finally, we use the resource bundle like a map and get a value based on the key:

```
rb.getString("hello");
```

So, back to our example, we have two files: `Labels_en.properties` and `Labels_fr.properties`. The following code takes a `locale` argument and builds a `ResourceBundle` object that's tied to the `Properties` file containing data for that `Locale` and read from the "resource bundle":

```
import java.util.Locale;
import java.util.ResourceBundle;

public class WhichLanguage {
  public static void main(String[] args) {
```

```
        Locale locale = new Locale(args[0]);
        ResourceBundle rb = ResourceBundle.getBundle("Labels", locale);
        System.out.println(rb.getString("hello"));
    }
}
```

Running the code twice, we get

```
> java WhichLanguage en
Hello Java!
> java WhichLanguage fr
Bonjour Java!
```

exam

w a t c h

The Java API for `java` `.util.ResourceBundle` *lists three good reasons to use resource bundles. Using resource bundles "allows you to write programs that can*

■ *Be easily localized, or translated, into different languages*

■ *Handle multiple locales at once*
■ *Be easily modified later to support even more locales"*

If you encounter any questions on the exam that ask about the advantages of using resource bundles, this quote from the API will serve you well.

on the job

The most common use of localization in Java is web applications. You can get the user's locale from information passed in the request rather than hard-coding it.

Java Resource Bundles

When we need to move beyond simple property file key to string value mappings, we can use resource bundles that are Java classes. We write Java classes that extend `ListResourceBundle`. The class name is similar to the one for property files. Only the extension is different.

```
import java.util.ListResourceBundle;
public class Labels_en_CA extends ListResourceBundle {
  protected Object[][] getContents() {
    return new Object[][] {
        { "hello", new StringBuilder("from Java") }
      };
  }
}
```

We implement `ListResourceBundle`'s one required method that returns an array of arrays. The inner array is key/value pairs. The outer array accumulates such pairs. Notice that now we aren't limited to `String` values. We can call `getObject()` to get a non-`String` value:

```
Locale locale = new Locale("en", "CA");
ResourceBundle rb = ResourceBundle.getBundle("Labels", locale);
System.out.println(rb.getObject("hello"));
```

which prints `"from Java"`.

Default Locale

What do you think happens if we call `ResourceBundle.getBundle("Labels")` without any locale? It depends. Java will pick the resource bundle that matches the locale the JVM is using. Typically, this matches the locale of the machine running the program, but it doesn't have to. You can even change the default locale at runtime, which might be useful if you are working with people in different locales so you can get the same behavior on all machines.

Let's explore the API to get and set the default locale:

```
// store locale so can put it back at end
Locale initial  = Locale.getDefault();
System.out.println(initial);

// set locale to Germany
Locale.setDefault(Locale.GERMANY);
System.out.println(Locale.getDefault());

// put original locale back
Locale.setDefault(initial);
System.out.println(Locale.getDefault());
```

which on our computer prints:

```
en_US
de_DE
en_US
```

For the first and last line, you may get different output depending on where you live. The key is that the middle of the program executes as if it were in Germany, regardless of where it is actually being run. It is good practice to restore the default unless your program is ending right away. That way, the rest of your code works normally—it probably doesn't expect to be in Germany.

Choosing the Right Resource Bundle

There are two main ways to get a resource bundle:

```
ResourceBundle.getBundle(baseName)
ResourceBundle.getBundle(baseName, locale)
```

Luckily, `ResourceBundle.getBundle(baseName)` is just shorthand for
`ResourceBundle.getBundle(baseName, Locale.getDefault())`, and you
only have to remember one set of rules. There are a few other overloaded signatures
for `getBundle()`, such as taking a `ClassLoader`. But don't worry—these aren't on
the exam.

Now on to the rules. How does Java choose the right resource bundle to use?
In a nutshell, Java chooses the most specific resource bundle it can while giving
preference to Java `ListResourceBundle`.

Going back to our Canadian application, we decide to request the Canadian
French resource bundle:

```
Locale locale = new Locale("fr", "CA");
ResourceBundle rb = ResourceBundle.getBundle("RB", locale);
```

Java will look for the following files in the classpath in this order:

```
RB_fr_CA.java         // exactly what we asked for
RB_fr_CA.properties

RB_fr.java            // couldn't find exactly what we asked for
RB_fr.properties      // now trying just requested language
RB_en_US.java         // couldn't find French
RB_en_US.properties   // now trying default Locale
RB_en.java            // couldn't find full default Locale country
RB_en.properties      // now trying default Locale language
RB.java               // couldn't find anything any matching Locale,
RB.properties         // now trying default bundle
```

If none of these files exist, Java gives up and throws a `MissingResourceException`.
Although this is a lot of things for Java to try, it is pretty easy to remember. Start
with the full `Locale` requested. Then fall back to just language. Then fall back to
the default `Locale`. Then fall back to the default bundle. Then cry.

Make sure you understand this because it is about to get more complicated.

You don't have to specify all the keys in all the property files. They can inherit
from each other. This is a good thing, as it reduces duplication.

```
RB_en.properties
  ride.in=Take a ride in the

RB_en_US.properties
  elevator=elevator
```

```
RB_en_UK.properties
  elevator=lift

Locale locale = new Locale("en", "UK");
ResourceBundle rb = ResourceBundle.getBundle("RB", locale);
System.out.println(rb.getString("ride.in") + " " +
                   rb.getString("elevator"));
```

Outputs:

```
Take a ride in the lift
```

The common "`ride.in`" property comes from the parent noncountry-specific bundle "`RB_en.properties`." The "`elevator`" property is different by country and comes from the UK version that we specifically requested.

The parent hierarchy is more specific than the search order. A bundle's parent always has a shorter name than the child bundle. If a parent is missing, Java just skips along that hierarchy. `ListResourceBundles` and `PropertyResourcesBundles` do not share a hierarchy. Similarly, the default locale's resource bundles do not share a hierarchy with the requested locale's resource bundles. Table 4-3 shows examples of bundles that do share a hierarchy.

Remember that searching for a property file uses a linear list. However, once a matching resource bundle is found, keys can only come from that resource bundle's hierarchy.

One more example to make this clear. Think about which resource bundles will be used from the previous code if we use the following code to request a resource bundle:

```
Locale locale = new Locale("fr", "FR");
ResourceBundle  rb = ResourceBundle.getBundle("RB", locale);
```

TABLE 4-3		
	Name of Resource Bundle	**Hierarchy**

Resource Bundle Lookups	`RB_fr_CA.java`	`RB.java`
		`RB_fr.java`
		`RB_fr_CA.java`

	`RB_fr_CA.properties`	`RB.properties`
		`RB_fr.properties`
		`RB_fr_CA.properties`

	`RB_en_US.java`	`RB.java`
		`RB_en.java`
		`RB_en_US.java`

	`RB_en_US.properties`	`RB.properties`
		`RB_en.properties`
		`RB_en_US.properties`

First, Java looks for `RB_fr_FR.java` and `RB_fr_FR.properties`. Because neither is found, Java falls back to using `RB_fr.java`. Then as we request keys from `rb`, Java starts looking in `RB_fr.java` and additionally looks in `RB.java`. Java started out looking for a matching file and then switched to searching the hierarchy of that file.

CERTIFICATION SUMMARY

Dates and Times   The `Date` and `Calendar` classes, as well as `DateFormat`, have all been replaced by classes in the `java.time` package, so pay close attention if you're transitioning from the old classes to the new. The key datetime classes to know from `java.time` are `LocalDate`, `LocalTime`, `LocalDateTime`, and `ZonedDateTime`. Each has a variety of methods to create and adjust datetime objects. You also need to know about `TemporalAdjusters` (like `TemporalAdjuster.firstDayOfMonth()`) and `TemporalUnits` (like `ChronoUnit.DAYS`), both from the `java.time.temporal` package, and `Instants`, `Periods`, and `Durations`, in the `java.time` package. `DataFormat` has been replaced with `DateTimeFormatter` in the `java.time.format` package, which is used to parse, format, and print datetime objects. The `Locale` class is used with `DateTimeFormatter` to generate a variety of output styles that are language and/or country specific.

Make sure you are clear on how to work with time zones and daylight savings time. Fortunately, the `ZonedDateTime` and related classes handle most of the hard work for you, but pay close attention to the format of the datetimes when they are represented as strings so you can recognize a local datetime from a zoned datetime and so you know how to create a `ZonedDateTime` using a `ZoneId`.

Locales, Properties Files, and Resource Bundles   Resource bundles allow you to move locale-specific information (usually strings) out of your code and into external files where they can easily be amended. This provides an easy way for you to localize your applications across many locales. Properties files allow you to create text files formatted as key/value pairs to store application customization parameters and such external to your application. The `ResourceBundle` class provides convenient ways to use files that are `Properties` class–compatible to store internationalization and localization values.

TWO-MINUTE DRILL

Here are some of the key points from the certification objectives in this chapter.

Dates and Times (OCP Objectives 7.1, 7.2, and 7.3)

☐ The classes you need to understand are those in `java.time`, `java.time.temporal`, and `java.time.format`, as well as `java.util.Locale`.

☐ `Date` and `Calendar` are no longer used, and most of the `Date` class's methods have been deprecated.

☐ A `LocalDate` is a date, and a `LocalTime` is a time. Combine the two to make a `LocalDateTime`. None of these types have a time zone associated with them.

☐ A `ZonedDateTime` is a datetime object with a time zone. All zoned datetimes are relative to Greenwich Mean Time (GMT). You may sometimes see GMT written as UTC.

☐ A `ZoneId` can be created from a string representing a time zone (e.g. `"US/Pacific"`).

☐ When you adjust `ZonedDateTimes`, daylight savings time will be automatically handled using the `ZoneRules`.

☐ If you want a datetime object with a time zone that is independent of zone rules, use an `OffsetDateTime`.

☐ A `Period` is a period of time that is a day or longer.

☐ A `Duration` is a period of time that is shorter than a day.

☐ An `Instant` is an instant in time and represents the number of seconds and nanoseconds since January 1, 1970. You can get the number of seconds as a `long` value from an `Instant` and convert any `ZonedDateTime` object into an `Instant`.

☐ There are several format "styles" available in the `java.format` class. You can use format styles such as `FormatStyle.SHORT` with `DateTimeFormatter` to format datetime objects.

☐ The `DateTimeFormatter` class is used to parse and create strings containing properly formatted dates.

- ☐ The `Locale` class is used in conjunction with `DateFormat` and `NumberFormat`.
- ☐ A `DateTimeFormatter` object can be constructed with a specific, immutable `Locale`.
- ☐ For the exam, you should understand creating `Locales` using either language or a combination of language and country.

Locales, Properties Files, and Resource Bundles (OCP 12.1, 12.2, and 12.3)

- ☐ The `java.util.Properties` class gives you a convenient way to create and maintain text files that are external to your applications and can hold configuration values.
- ☐ A file that is `java.util.Properties`–compliant and has a name that ends with a locale and a suffix of `.properties` can be used by `ResourceBundle.getBundle()`.
- ☐ A `ListResourceBundle` comes from Java classes, and a `PropertyResourceBundle` comes from `.properties` files.
- ☐ `ResourceBundle.getBundle(name)` uses the default `Locale`.
- ☐ `Locale.getDefault()` returns the JVM's default `Locale`. `Locale.setDefault(locale)` can change the JVM's locale.
- ☐ Java searches for resource bundles in this order: requested language/country, requested language, default locale language/country, default locale language, default bundle. Within each item, Java `ListResourceBundle` is favored over `PropertyResourceBundle`.
- ☐ Once a `ResourceBundle` is found, only parents of that bundle can be used to look up keys.

SELF TEST

1. Given the code fragment:

   ```
   ZonedDateTime zd = ZonedDateTime.parse("2020-05-04T08:05:00");
   System.out.println(zd.getMonth() + " " + zd.getDayOfMonth());
   ```

   What is the result? (Choose all that apply.)
   A. MAY 4
   B. APRIL 5
   C. MAY 4 2020
   D. APRIL 5 2020
   E. Compilation fails
   F. Runtime exception

2. Given the code fragment:

   ```
   LocalTime t1 = LocalTime.of(9, 0);
   LocalTime t2 = LocalTime.of(10, 5);
   ```

   Which of the following code fragment(s) will produce a new LocalTime t3 that represents the same time as t2? (Choose all that apply.)
   A. LocalTime t3 = t1.plus(65, ChronoUnit.MINUTES)
   B. LocalTime t3 = t1.plusMinutes(65);
   C. LocalTime t3 = t1.plusHours(1);
   D. LocalTime t3 = t1.plusDays(1);
   E. LocalTime t3 = t1.plus(Duration.ofMinutes(65));

3. Given the code fragment:

   ```
   1. LocalDate d1 = LocalDate.of(2018, 1, 1);
   2. LocalDate d2 = LocalDate.of(2018, 6, 15);
   3. _____ r = _____.between(d1, d2);
   4. System.out.println("Months and days: " + r.getMonths() + ", " + r.getDays());
   ```

   What are the correct types to fill in the blanks on line 3?
   A. Duration, Duration
   B. Instant, Period
   C. Period, Instant
   D. Period, ChronoUnit
   E. Period, Period
   F. Duration, LocalDate

4. How would you use `nowzdt` from the code fragment below to compute the equivalent time in Berlin, Germany? (Choose all that apply.)

```
ZonedDateTime nowzdt =
    ZonedDateTime.of(LocalDateTime.now(), ZoneId.of("US/Pacific"));
```

A.
```
ZonedDateTime berlinZdt = ZonedDateTime.from(nowzdt, ZoneId.of("Europe/Berlin"));
```

B.
```
ZonedDateTime berlinZdt = nowzdt.withZoneSameInstant(ZoneId.of("Europe/Berlin"));
```

C.
```
ZonedDateTime berlinZdt =
    ZonedDateTime.ofInstant(nowzdt.toInstant(), ZoneId.of("Europe/Berlin"));
```

D.
```
ZonedDateTime berlinZdt =
    nowzdt.withZoneId("Europe/Berlin"));
```

E.
```
ZonedDateTime berlinZdt = nowzdt.now(ZoneId.of("Europe/Berlin"));
```

5. The next total solar eclipse visible in South America is on July 2, 2019, at 16:55 UTC. Which code fragment will correctly compute and display the time in San Juan, Argentina, for this solar eclipse?

A.
```
ZonedDateTime totalityUTC = ZonedDateTime.of(
    LocalDateTime.of(2019, 7, 2, 16, 55));
ZonedDateTime totalitySanJuan =
    totalityUTC.withZoneSameInstant(ZoneId.of("America/Argentina/San_Juan"));
System.out.println(totalitySanJuan);
```

B.
```
ZonedDateTime totalityUTC = ZonedDateTime.of(
    LocalDateTime.of(2019, 7, 2, 4, 55, "PM") , ZoneId.of("Z"));
ZonedDateTime totalitySanJuan =
    totalityUTC.withZoneSameInstant(ZoneId.of("America/Argentina/San_Juan"));
System.out.println(totalitySanJuan);
```

C.
```
ZonedDateTime totalityUTC = ZonedDateTime.of(
    LocalDateTime.of(2019, 7, 2, 16, 55), ZoneId.of("Z"));
ZonedDateTime totalitySanJuan =
    totalityUTC.withZoneSameInstant(ZoneId.of("America/Argentina/San_Juan"));
System.out.println(totalitySanJuan);
```

D.

```
ZonedDateTime totalityUTC = ZonedDateTime.of(
    LocalDateTime.of(2019, 7, 2, 16, 55),
    ZoneId.of("America/Argentina/San_Juan"));
ZonedDateTime totalitySanJuan =
    totalityUTC.withZoneSameInstant(ZoneId.of("America/Argentina/San_Juan"));
System.out.println(totalitySanJuan);
```

E.

```
ZonedDateTime totalityUTC = ZonedDateTime.of(
    LocalDateTime.of(2019, 7, 2, 16, 55), ZoneId.of("Z "));
LocalDateTime totalitySanJuan =
    totalityUTC.withZoneSameInstant(ZoneId.of("America/Argentina/San_Juan"));
System.out.println(totalitySanJuan);
```

6. Given:

```
public class Canada {
  public static void main(String[] args) {
    ResourceBundle rb = ResourceBundle.getBundle("Flag",
      new Locale("en", "CA"));
    System.out.println(rb.getString("key"));
  }
}
```

Assume the default Locale is Italian. If each of the following is the only resource bundle on the classpath and contains key=value, which will be used? (Choose all that apply.)

A. `Flag.java`

B. `Flag_CA.properties`

C. `Flag_en.java`

D. `Flag_en.properties`

E. `Flag_en_CA.properties`

F. `Flag_fr_CA.properties`

7. Given three resource bundles and a Java class:

```
Train_en_US.properties: train=subway
Train_en_UK.properties: train=underground
Train_en.properties: ride = ride

1: public class ChooChoo {
2:   public static void main(String[] args) {
3:     Locale.setDefault(new Locale("en", "US"));
4:     ResourceBundle rb = ResourceBundle.getBundle("Train",
5:       new Locale("en", "US"));
6:     System.out.print(rb.getString("ride")
         + " " + rb.getString("train"));
7:   }
8: }
```

Which of the following, when made independently, will change the output to "ride underground"? (Choose all that apply.)

A. Add `train=underground` to `Train_en.properties`
B. Change line 3 to `Locale.setDefault(new Locale("en", "UK"));`
C. Change line 5 to `Locale.ENGLISH);`
D. Change line 5 to `new Locale("en", "UK"));`
E. Delete file `Train_en_US.properties`

8. Let's say you want to print the day of the week and the date of Halloween (October 31) 2018, at 5 PM in German, using the LONG style. Complete the code below using the following fragments. Note: You can use each fragment either zero or more times, and you might not need to fill all of the slots. You probably won't encounter a fill-in-the-blank question on the exam, but just in case, we put a few in the book, like this one.

Code:

```
import java._____
import java._____
import java._____

public class DateHalloween {
    public static void main(String[] args) {
        ZonedDateTime d = _____
        Locale locDE = new Locale("de");
        DayOfWeek day = _____
        String df = _____
        System.out.println(day + " " + df);
    }
}
```

Fragments:

```
io.*;
nio.*;
util.*;
time.*;
date.*;
time.format.*;
new ZonedDateTime(2018, 10, 31, 17, 0);
new LocalDate(2018, 10, 31, 17, 0);
ZonedDateTime.of(2018, 10, 31, 17, 0, 0, ZoneId.of("Europe/Berlin"));
ZonedDateTime.of(2018, 10, 31, 17, 0, 0, 0,
                ZoneId.of("Europe/Berlin"));
d.getDayOfWeek();
d.getDay();
DateTimeFormatter.of(FormatStyle.LONG).withLocale(locDE);
d.format(DateTimeFormatter.ofLocalizedDateTime(FormatStyle.LONG)
                    .withLocale(locDE));
```

9. Given two files:

```
package rb;
public class Bundle extends java.util.ListResourceBundle {
  protected Object[][] getContents() {
    return new Object[][] { { "123", 456 } };
  }
}
```

```
package rb;
import java.util.*;
public class KeyValue {
  public static void main(String[] args) {
    ResourceBundle rb = ResourceBundle.getBundle("rb.Bundle",
      Locale.getDefault());
    // insert code here
  }
}
```

Which, inserted independently, will compile? (Choose all that apply.)

A. `Object obj = rb.getInteger("123");`

B. `Object obj = rb.getInteger(123);`

C. `Object obj = rb.getObject("123");`

D. `Object obj = rb.getObject(123);`

E. `Object obj = rb.getString("123");`

F. `Object obj = rb.getString(123);`

10. Given the following code fragment:

```
LocalDateTime now = LocalDateTime.of(2017,10,27,14,22,54,0);
DateTimeFormatter formatter =
    DateTimeFormatter.ofPattern("_____");   // L1
String formattedDateTime = now.format(formatter);
System.out.println("Formatted DateTime: " + formattedDateTime);
```

Which `String` inserted as an argument to `DateTimeFormatter.ofPattern()` at `// L1` will produce the output? (Choose all that apply.)

```
Formatted DateTime: 2017-10-27 14:22:54
```

A. `"yyyy-MM-dd hh:mm:ss a"`

B. `"yyyy-MM-dd hh:mm:ss"`

C. `"yyyy-mm-dd HH:MM:ss"`

D. `"yyyy-MM-dd HH:mm:ss"`

E. `"yyyy-MM-dd HH:mm:ss Z"`

11. Given the following code fragment:

```
LocalDate d1 = LocalDate.of(2017, Month.NOVEMBER, 28);
System.out.print(d1 + ", ");
LocalDate d2 = d1.with(TemporalAdjusters.lastDayOfYear());
System.out.print(d2 + ", ");
LocalDate d3 = d1.plusDays(3).with(TemporalAdjusters.firstDayOfNextMonth());
System.out.print(d3 + ", ");
LocalDate d4 = d1.minusMonths(11).with(TemporalAdjusters.firstDayOfNextYear());
System.out.print(d4 + ", ");
LocalDate d5 = LocalDate.ofEpochDay(d1.plusDays(27).toEpochDay());
System.out.print(d5 + ", ");
LocalDate d6 = d1.minus(Period.ofDays(5));
System.out.println(d6);
```

What output will you see?

A. 2017-11-28, 2017-12-31, 2017-12-01, 2017-01-01, 2017-12-25, 2017-11-23

B. 2017-11-28T00:00, 2017-12-31T00:00, 2017-12-01T00:00, 2017-01-01T00:00, 2017-12-25T00:00, 2017-11-23T00:00

C. 2017-11-28, 2017-12-31, 2018-01-01, 2017-01-01, 2017-12-25, 2017-11-23

D. 2017-11-28T00:00, 2017-12-31T00:00, 2018-01-01T00:00, 2017-01-01T00:00, 2017-12-25T00:00, 2017-11-23T00:00

E. 2017-11-28, 2017-12-31, 2018-01-01, 2018-01-01, 2017-12-25, 2017-11-23

12. If it is 19:12:53 on October 27, 2017, in the US/Pacific Zone (which is GMT-8:00, summer time), then what does the following code fragment produce? (Choose all that apply.)

```
ZoneId zid = ZoneId.of("US/Eastern"); // GMT-5:00
Instant i = Instant.now();
ZonedDateTime zdt = i.atZone(zid);
System.out.println(zdt.format(
    DateTimeFormatter.ofLocalizedTime(FormatStyle.MEDIUM)));
```

A. 10:12:53 PM

B. 20:12:53

C. 19:12:53

D. 7:12:53 PM

E. 2017-10-27 10:12:53 PM

SELF TEST ANSWERS

1. ☑ **F** is correct. The string we are parsing has no time zone, so the parse will fail at runtime.
    ☒ **A, B, C, D,** and **E** are incorrect based on the above. (OCP Objective 7.2)

2. ☑ **A, B,** and **E** are correct. Each adds 1 hour and 5 minutes to `t1` to make a new `LocalTime` `t3`, which represents 10:05, the same time as `t2`. The `plus()` method takes an amount to add as a `long`, and a unit (**A**) or a `TemporalAmount` (**E**).
    ☒ **C** and **D** are incorrect. **C** adds only 1 hour to make 10 AM instead of 10:05 AM. **D** generated a compile error because `LocalTime` does not have a `plusDays()` method. (OCP Objective 7.1 and 7.3)

3. ☑ **E** is correct. Period is the correct type to measure a period of time in days.
    ☒ **A, B, C, D,** and **F** are incorrect based on the above. (OCP Objective 7.1 and 7.3)

4. ☑ **B** and **C** are correct. In both cases, we're creating an `Instant` from `nowzdt` and then creating a new `ZonedDateTime` from that `Instant`, representing the same time as `nowzdt`, in Berlin.
    ☒ **A, D,** and **E** are incorrect. **A** is incorrect because, although you can create a new `ZonedDateTime` from an existing `ZonedDateTime` with `from()`, you can't change the zone when you do. **D** is incorrect because `withZoneId()` is not a valid method. **E** is almost correct, except that it is not precisely the same time as `nowzdt` because you're calling the `now()` method again, though it may only be slightly different (perhaps only a few nanoseconds). (OCP Objective 7.2)

5. ☑ **C** is correct. We first create a `ZonedDateTime` for the UTC time with zone `"z"` (corresponding to GMT zone) and then create the equivalent `ZonedDateTime` for the San Juan, Argentina, zone.
    ☒ **A, B, D,** and **E** are incorrect. **A** is missing the time zone on the UTC time. **B** includes incorrect arguments to the `LocalDateTime.of()` method. **D** has the incorrect time zone on the UTC time. **E** has the incorrect type for `totalitySanJuan`. (OCP Objective 7.2)

6. ☑ **A, C, D,** and **E** are correct. The default `Locale` is irrelevant here since none of the choices use Italian. **A** is the default resource bundle. **C** and **D** use the language but not the country from the requested locale. **E** uses the exact match of the requested locale.
    ☒ **B** is incorrect because the language code of `CA` does not match `en`. And `CA` isn't a valid language code. **F** is incorrect because the language code `"fr"` does not match `en`. Even though the country code of `CA` does match, the language code is more important. (OCP Objectives 12.2 and 12.3)

7. ☑ **D** is correct. As is, the code finds resource bundle `Train_en_US.properties`, which uses `Train_en.properties` as a parent. Choice **D** finds resource bundle `Train_en_UK.properties`, which uses `Train_en.properties` as a parent.

☒ **A, B, C, E,** and **F** are incorrect. **A** is incorrect because both the parent and child have the same property. In this scenario, the more specific one (child) gets used. **B** is incorrect because the default locale only gets used if the requested resource bundle can't be found. **C** is incorrect because it finds the resource bundle `Train_en.properties`, which does not have any "train" key. **E** is incorrect because there is no "ride" key once we delete the parent. **F** is incorrect based on the above. (OCP Objectives 12.2 and 12.3)

8. Answer:

```
import java.util.*;
import java.time.*;
import java.time.format.*;
public class DateHalloween {
    public static void main(String[] args) {
        ZonedDateTime d = ZonedDateTime.of(2018, 10, 31, 17, 0, 0, 0,
                          ZoneId.of("Europe/Berlin"));
        Locale locDE = new Locale("de");
        DayOfWeek day = d.getDayOfWeek();
        String df = d.format(DateTimeFormatter
                .ofLocalizedDateTime(FormatStyle.LONG).withLocale(locDE));
        System.out.println(day + " " + df);
    }
}
```

Reminders: To create a `ZonedDateTime` with the `of()` method, you must include all portions of the date and time (including nanoseconds) and a zone. `DateTimeFormatter`
`.ofLocalizedDateTime()` returns a locale-specific date-time formatter, and `withLocale()` returns a copy of this formatter with a new locale. (OCP Objectives 7.2 and 12.1)

9. ☑ **C** and **E** are correct. When getting a key from a resource bundle, the key must be a string. The returned result must be a string or an object. While that object may happen to be an integer, the API is still `getObject()`. **E** will throw a ClassCastException since 456 is not a string, but it will compile.

☒ **A, B, D,** and **F** are incorrect because of the above. (OCP Objectives 12.2 and 12.3)

10. ☑ **D** is correct; this string corresponds to the format shown in the output.

☒ **A, B, C,** and **E** are incorrect. **A** uses hh for the hour, which will show 02 instead 14 (that is, a 12-hour format instead of a 24-hour format), and displays the AM/PM at the end, which is great if we're using 12-hour format, but that's not what we're looking for. **B** results in 12-hour format instead of 24-hour format. **C** switches months and minutes. **E** requires a

`ZonedDateTime` instead of a `LocalDateTime`, and using this `String` will throw a runtime exception when we try to format now with this formatter. (OCP Objectives 7.1 and 7.2)

11. ☑ **C** is correct because of the below.

   ☒ **A, B, D,** and **E** are incorrect. **B** and **D** show the time, and we are displaying `LocalDate` values that have no time associated with them. **A** has the incorrect value for d3, and **E** has the wrong value for d4. (OCP Objectives 7.1 and 7.3)

12. ☑ **A** is correct. We first get the `zoneId` for "US/Eastern" time, which is GMT-5:00, and the locale to US. We then create an `Instant` for "now," which is 19:12:53 on October 27, 2017 (7:12:53 PM PDT, which is 10:12:53 PM EDT). We then create a `ZonedDateTime` from the `Instant`, using the `zoneId` for "US/Eastern" and format it using `DateTimeFormatter` `.ofLocalizedTime()`, which turns the `ZonedDateTime` into a `LocalTime` (dropping the date and zone information) and display it in the `MEDIUM` format style for the US locale, resulting in `10:12:53 PM`. Format styles depend on local configuration, but we know this answer is correct because **B, C,** and **D** show the incorrect times, and **E** shows the date.

   ☒ **B, C, D,** and **E** are incorrect. **B, C,** and **D** show the incorrect times, and **E** shows the date, which we dropped when we formatted `zdt` to a localized time. (OCP Objectives 7.2)

5

I/O and NIO

- Read and Write Data from the Console

- Use BufferedReader, BufferedWriter, File, FileReader, FileWriter, FileInputStream, FileOutputStream, ObjectOutputStream, ObjectInputStream, and PrintWriter in the java.io Package

- Use Path Interface to Operate on File and Directory Paths

- Use Files Class to Check, Read, Delete, Copy, Move, Manage Metadata of a File or Directory

- Use Stream API with NIO.2

✓ Two-Minute Drill

Q&A Self Test

I/O (input/output) has been around since the beginning of Java. You could read and write files along with some other common operations. Then with Java 1.4, Java added more I/O functionality and cleverly named it NIO. That stands for "new I/O." Don't worry—you won't be asked about those Java 1.4 additions on the exam.

The APIs prior to Java 7 still had a few limitations when you had to write applications that focused heavily on files and file manipulation. Trying to write a little routine listing all the files created in the past day within a directory tree would have given you some headaches. There was no support for navigating directory trees, and just reading attributes of a file was also quite hard. As of Java 7, this whole routine is fewer than 15 lines of code!

Now what to name yet another I/O API? The name "new I/O" was taken, and "new new I/O" would just sound silly. Since the Java 7 functionality was added to package names that began with `java.nio`, the new name was NIO.2. For the purposes of this chapter and the exam, NIO is shorthand for NIO.2.

Since NIO (or NIO.2 if you like) builds on the original I/O, some of those concepts are still tested on the exam in addition to the new parts. Fortunately, you won't have to become a total I/O or NIO guru to do well on the exam. The intention of the exam team was to include just the basic aspects of these technologies, and in this chapter, we cover *more* than you'll need to get through these objectives on the exam.

CERTIFICATION OBJECTIVE

File Navigation and I/O (OCP Objectives 8.1 and 8.2)

8.1   *Read and write data from the console.*
8.2   *Use BufferedReader, BufferedWriter, File, FileReader, FileWriter, FileInputStream, FileOutputStream, ObjectOutputStream, ObjectInputStream, and PrintWriter in the java.io package.*

I/O has had a strange history with the OCP certification. It was included in all the versions of the exam, up to and including 1.2, then removed from the 1.4 exam, reintroduced for Java 5, extended for Java 6, and extended still more for Java 7 and 8.

I/O is a huge topic in general, and the Java APIs that deal with I/O in one fashion or another are correspondingly huge. A general discussion of I/O could include topics such as file I/O, console I/O, thread I/O, high-performance I/O, byte-oriented I/O, character-oriented I/O, I/O filtering and wrapping, serialization, and more. Luckily for us, the I/O topics included in the Java 8 exam are fairly well restricted to file I/O for characters and serialization.

Here's a summary of the I/O classes you'll need to understand for the exam:

- **File** The API says that the `File` class is "an abstract representation of file and directory pathnames." The `File` class isn't used to actually read or write data; it's used to work at a higher level, making new empty files, searching for files, deleting files, making directories, and working with paths.

- **FileReader** This class is used to read character files. Its `read()` methods are fairly low-level, allowing you to read single characters, the whole stream of characters, or a fixed number of characters. `FileReaders` are usually *wrapped* by higher-level objects such as `BufferedReaders`, which improve performance and provide more convenient ways to work with the data.

- **BufferedReader** This class is used to make lower-level `Reader` classes like `FileReader` more efficient and easier to use. Compared to `FileReaders`, `BufferedReaders` read relatively large chunks of data from a file at once and keep this data in a buffer. When you ask for the next character or line of data, it is retrieved from the buffer, which minimizes the number of times that time-intensive file-read operations are performed. In addition, `BufferedReader` provides more convenient methods, such as `readLine()`, that allow you to get the next line of characters from a file.

- **FileWriter** This class is used to write to character files. Its `write()` methods allow you to write character(s) or strings to a file. `FileWriters` are usually *wrapped* by higher-level `Writer` objects, such as `BufferedWriters` or `PrintWriters`, which provide better performance and higher-level, more flexible methods to write data.

- **BufferedWriter** This class is used to make lower-level classes like `FileWriters` more efficient and easier to use. Compared to `FileWriters`, `BufferedWriters` write relatively large chunks of data to a file at once, minimizing the number of times that slow file-writing operations are performed. The `BufferedWriter` class also provides a `newLine()` method to create platform-specific line separators automatically.

- **PrintWriter** This class has been enhanced significantly in Java 5. Because of newly created methods and constructors (like building a PrintWriter with a File or a String), you might find that you can use PrintWriter in places where you previously needed a Writer to be wrapped with a FileWriter and/or a BufferedWriter. New methods like format(), printf(), and append() make PrintWriters quite flexible and powerful.

- **FileInputStream** This class is used to read bytes from files and can be used for binary as well as text. Like FileReader, the read() methods are low-level, allowing you to read single bytes, a stream of bytes, or a fixed number of bytes. We typically use FileInputStream with higher-level objects such as ObjectInputStream.

- **FileOutputStream** This class is used to write bytes to files. We typically use FileOutputStream with higher-level objects such as ObjectOutputStream.

- **ObjectInputStream** This class is used to read an input stream and deserialize objects. We use ObjectInputStream with lower-level classes like FileInputStream to read from a file. ObjectInputStream works at a higher level so that you can read objects rather than characters or bytes. This process is called *deserialization.*

- **ObjectOutputStream** This class is used to write objects to an output stream and is used with classes like FileOutputStream to write to a file. This is called *serialization.* Like ObjectInputStream, ObjectOutputStream works at a higher level to write objects, rather than characters or bytes.

- **Console** This Java 6 convenience class provides methods to read input from the console and write formatted output to the console.

Creating Files Using the File Class

Objects of type File are used to represent the actual files (but not the data in the files) or directories that exist on a computer's physical disk. Just to make sure we're clear, when we talk about an object of type File, we'll say File, with a capital *F.*

When we're talking about what exists on a hard drive, we'll call it a file with a lowercase *f* (unless it's a variable name in some code). Let's start with a few basic examples of creating files, writing to them, and reading from them. First, let's create a new file and write a few lines of data to it:

```
import java.io.*;                           // The section 8 objectives
                                            // focus on classes from
                                            // java.io
class Writer1 {
  public static void main(String [] args) {
    File file = new File("fileWrite1.txt");   // There's no
                                            // file yet!
  }
}
```

If you compile and run this program, when you look at the contents of your current directory, you'll discover absolutely no indication of a file called `fileWrite1.txt`. When you make a new instance of the class `File`, *you're not yet making an actual file; you're just creating a filename.* Once you have a `File` *object,* there are several ways to make an actual file. Let's see what we can do with the `File` object we just made:

```
import java.io.*;

class Writer1 {
 public static void main(String [] args) {
   try {                                    // warning: exceptions possible
     boolean newFile = false;
     File file = new File               // it's only an object
                     ("fileWrite1.txt");
     System.out.println(file.exists());   // look for a real file
     newFile = file.createNewFile();       // maybe create a file!
     System.out.println(newFile);          // already there?
     System.out.println(file.exists());   // look again
   } catch(IOException e) { }
 }
}
```

This produces the output

```
false
true
true
```

And also produces an empty file in your current directory. If you run the code a *second* time, you get the output

```
true
false
true
```

Let's examine these sets of output:

■ **First execution** The first call to `exists()` returned `false`, which we expected…remember, `new File()` doesn't create a file on the disk! The `createNewFile()` method created an actual file and returned `true`, indicating that a new file was created and that one didn't already exist. Finally, we called `exists()` again, and this time it returned `true`, indicating the file existed on the disk.

■ **Second execution** The first call to `exists()` returns `true` because we built the file during the first run. Then the call to `createNewFile()` returns `false` since the method didn't create a file this time through. Of course, the last call to `exists()` returns `true`.

A couple of other new things happened in this code. First, notice that we had to put our file creation code in a try/catch. This is true for almost all of the file I/O code you'll ever write. I/O is one of those inherently risky things. We're keeping it simple for now and ignoring the exceptions, but we still need to follow

---

exam **Watch** *Remember, the exam creators are trying to jam as much code as they can into a small space, so in the previous example, instead of these three lines of code:*

```
boolean newFile = false;
...
newFile = file.createNewFile();
System.out.println(newFile);
```

you might see something like the following single line of code, which is a bit harder to read, but accomplishes the same thing:

```
System.out.println(file.createNewFile());
```

the handle-or-declare rule, since most I/O methods declare checked exceptions. We'll talk more about I/O exceptions later. We used a couple of `File`'s methods in this code:

- **`boolean exists()`**   This method returns `true` if it can find the actual file.
- **`boolean createNewFile()`**   This method creates a new file if it doesn't already exist.

Using FileWriter and FileReader

In practice, you probably won't use the `FileWriter` and `FileReader` classes without wrapping them (more about "wrapping" very soon). That said, let's go ahead and do a little "naked" file I/O:

```
import java.io.*;
class Writer2 {
  public static void main(String [] args) {
    char[] in = new char[50];              // to store input
    int size = 0;
    try {
      File file = new File(                // just an object
                "fileWrite2.txt");
      FileWriter fw =
                new FileWriter(file);  // create an actual file
                                       // & a FileWriter obj
      fw.write("howdy\nfolks\n");      // write characters to
                                       // the file
      fw.flush();                      // flush before closing
      fw.close();                      // close file when done
      FileReader fr =
                new FileReader(file);  // create a FileReader
                                       // object
      size = fr.read(in);              // read the whole file!
      System.out.print(size + " ");    // how many characters read
      for(char c : in)                 // print the array
        System.out.print(c);
      fr.close();                      // again, always close
    } catch(IOException e) { }
  }
}
```

which produces the output:

```
12 howdy
folks
```

Here's what just happened:

1. `FileWriter fw = new FileWriter(file)` did three things:
   a. It created a `FileWriter` reference variable, `fw`.
   b. It created a `FileWriter` object and assigned it to `fw`.
   c. It created an actual empty file out on the disk (and you can prove it).
2. We wrote 12 characters to the file with the `write()` method, and we did a `flush()` and a `close()`.
3. We made a new `FileReader` object, which also opened the file on disk for reading.
4. The `read()` method read the whole file, a character at a time, and put it into the `char[]` `in`.
5. We printed out the number of characters we read in `size`, and we looped through the `in` array, printing out each character we read, and then we closed the file.

Before we go any further, let's talk about `flush()` and `close()`. When you write data out to a stream, some amount of buffering will occur, and you never know for sure exactly when the last of the data will actually be sent. You might perform many write operations on a stream before closing it, and invoking the `flush()` method guarantees that the last of the data you thought you had already written actually gets out to the file. Whenever you're done using a file, either reading it or writing to it, you should invoke the `close()` method. When you are doing file I/O, you're using expensive and limited operating system resources, and so when you're done, invoking `close()` will free up those resources.

Now, back to our last example. This program certainly works, but it's painful in a couple of different ways:

1. When we were writing data to the file, we manually inserted line separators (in this case \n) into our data.
2. When we were reading data back in, we put it into a character array. It being an array and all, we had to declare its size beforehand, so we'd have been in trouble if we hadn't made it big enough! We could have read the data in one character at a time, looking for the end of the file after each `read()`, but that's pretty painful too.

Because of these limitations, we'll typically want to use higher-level I/O classes like `BufferedWriter` or `BufferedReader` in combination with `FileWriter` or `FileReader`.

Using FileInputStream and FileOutputStream

Using `FileInputStream` and `FileOutputStream` is similar to using `FileReader` and `FileWriter`, except you're working with byte data instead of character data. That means you can use `FileInputStream` and `FileOutputStream` to read and write binary data as well as text data.

We've rewritten the previous example to use `FileInputStream` and `FileOutputStream`; the code does exactly the same thing, but because we're working with bytes instead of characters, we made a few small modifications, which we'll point out:

```java
import java.io.*;
class Writer3 {
    public static void main(String [] args) {
        byte[] in = new byte[50];                   // bytes, not chars!
        int size = 0;
        FileOutputStream fos = null;
        FileInputStream fis = null;
        File file = new File("fileWrite3.txt");
        try {
            fos = new FileOutputStream(file);       // create a FileOutputStream
            String s = "howdy\nfolks\n";
            fos.write(s.getBytes("UTF-8"));         // write characters (bytes)
                                                    // to the file
            fos.flush();                            // flush before closing
            fos.close();                            // close file when done

            fis = new FileInputStream(file);        // create a FileInputStream
            size = fis.read(in);                    // read the file into in
            System.out.print(size + " ");           // how many bytes read
            for(byte b : in) {                      // print the array
                System.out.print((char)b);
            }
            fis.close();                            // again, always close
        } catch(IOException e) {
            e.printStackTrace();
        }
    }
}
```

As you can see, this example is almost exactly like the previous one, except we're using bytes rather than chars. That means we convert the `String` we write to the file to bytes for the `write()` method, and when we read, we read into an array of `bytes`, rather than an array of `chars`, and convert each `byte` to a `char` before we print it.

And like the previous example, this one is painful in the same ways. You'll typically find you use higher-level I/O classes like `ObjectInputStream` and `ObjectOutputStream`, rather than `FileInputStream` and `FileOutputStream`, unless you really need to read binary data byte by byte. We talk about `ObjectInputStream` and `ObjectOutputStream` in the section on serialization later in the chapter.

Combining I/O Classes

Java's entire I/O system was designed around the idea of using several classes in combination. Combining I/O classes is sometimes called *wrapping* and sometimes called *chaining*. The `java.io` package contains about 50 classes, 10 interfaces, and 15 exceptions. Each class in the package has a specific purpose (i.e., highly specialized), and the classes are designed to be combined with each other in countless ways to handle a wide variety of situations.

When it's time to do some I/O in real life, you'll undoubtedly find yourself poring over the `java.io` API, trying to figure out which classes you'll need and how to hook them together. For the exam, you'll need to do the same thing, but Oracle artificially reduced the API (phew!). In terms of studying for Exam Objective 8.2, we can imagine that the entire `java.io` package—consisting of the classes listed in Exam Objective 8.2 and summarized in Table 5-1—is our mini I/O API.

Now let's say we want to find a less painful way to write data to a file and read the file's contents back into memory. Starting with the task of writing data to a file, here's a process for determining what classes we'll need and how we'll hook them together:

1. We know that ultimately we want to hook to a `File` object. So whatever other class or classes we use, one of them must have a constructor that takes an object of type `File`.

2. Find a method that sounds like the most powerful, easiest way to accomplish the task. When we look at Table 5-1 we can see that `BufferedWriter` has a `newLine()` method. That sounds a little better than having to manually embed a separator after each line, but if we look further, we see that `PrintWriter` has a method called `println()`. That sounds like the easiest approach of all, so we'll go with it.

TABLE 5-1   `java.io` Mini API

java.io Class	Extends From	Key Constructor(s) Arguments	Key Methods

`File`	`Object`	`File, String`
		`String`
		`String, String`
			`createNewFile()`
			`delete()`
			`exists()`
			`isDirectory()`
			`isFile()`
			`list()`
			`mkdir()`
			`renameTo()`

`FileWriter`	`Writer`	`File`
		`String`
			`close()`
			`flush()`
			`write()`

`BufferedWriter`	`Writer`	`Writer`	`close()`
			`flush()`
			`newLine()`
			`write()`

`PrintWriter`	`Writer`	`File` (as of Java 5)
		`String` (as of Java 5)
		`OutputStream`
		`Writer`
			`close()`
			`flush()`
			`format()`, `printf()`
			`print()`, `println()`
			`write()`

`FileOutputStream`	`OutputStream`	`File` `String`	`close()` `write()`
`FileReader`	`Reader`	`File` `String`	`read()`
`BufferedReader`	`Reader`	`Reader`	`read()` `readLine()`
`FileInputStream`	`InputStream`	`File` `String`	`read()` `close()`

3. When we look at `PrintWriter`'s constructors, we see that we can build a `PrintWriter` object if we have an object of type `File`, so all we need to do to create a `PrintWriter` object is the following:

```
File file = new File("fileWrite2.txt");   // create a File
PrintWriter pw = new PrintWriter(file);   // pass file to
                                          // the PrintWriter
                                          // constructor
```

Okay, time for a pop quiz. Prior to Java 5, `PrintWriter` did not have constructors that took either a `String` or a `File`. If you were writing some I/O code in Java 1.4, how would you get a `PrintWriter` to write data to a file? Hint: You can figure this out by studying the mini I/O API in Table 5-1.

Here's one way to go about solving this puzzle: First, we know that we'll create a `File` object on one end of the chain and that we want a `PrintWriter` object on the other end. We can see in Table 5-1 that a `PrintWriter` can also be built using a `Writer` object. Although `Writer` isn't a *class* we see in the table, we can see that several other classes extend `Writer`, which, for our purposes, is just as good; any class that extends `Writer` is a candidate. Looking further, we can see that `FileWriter` has the two attributes we're looking for:

- It can be constructed using a `File`.
- It extends `Writer`.

Given all of this information, we can put together the following code (remember, this is a Java 1.4 example):

```
File file = new File("fileWrite2.txt");    // create a File object
FileWriter fw = new FileWriter(file);      // create a FileWriter
                                           // that will send its
                                           // output to a File

PrintWriter pw = new PrintWriter(fw);      // create a PrintWriter
                                           // that will send its
                                           // output to a Writer

pw.println("howdy");                       // write the data
pw.println("folks");
```

At this point, it should be fairly easy to put together the code to more easily read data from the file back into memory. Again, looking through the table, we see a method called `readLine()` that sounds like a much better way to read data. Going through a similar process, we get the following code:

```
File file =
      new File("fileWrite2.txt");    // create a File object AND
                                     // open "fileWrite2.txt"
FileReader fr =
        new FileReader(file);        // create a FileReader to get
                                     // data from 'file'
BufferedReader br =
        new BufferedReader(fr);      // create a BufferReader to
                                     // get its data from a Reader
String data = br.readLine();         // read some data
```

Working with Files and Directories

Earlier, we touched on the fact that the `File` class is used to create files and directories. In addition, `File`'s methods can be used to delete files, rename files, determine whether files exist, create temporary files, change a file's attributes, and differentiate between files and directories. A point that is often confusing is that an object of type `File` is used to represent *either a file or a directory.* We'll talk about both cases next.

We saw earlier that the statement

```
File file = new File("foo");
```

always creates a `File` object and then does one of two things:

1. If `"foo"` does NOT exist, no actual file is created.

2. If `"foo"` *does* exist, the new `File` object refers to the existing file.

Notice that `File file = new File("foo");` NEVER creates an actual file. There are two ways to create a file:

1. Invoke the `createNewFile()` method on a `File` object. For example:

   ```
   File file = new File("foo");    // no file yet
   file.createNewFile();           // make a file, "foo" which
                                   // is assigned to 'file'
   ```

2. Create a `Writer` or a `Stream`. Specifically, create a `FileWriter`, a `PrintWriter`, or a `FileOutputStream`. Whenever you create an instance of one of these classes, you automatically create a file, unless one already exists, for instance:

   ```
   File file = new File("foo");    // no file yet
   PrintWriter pw =
           new PrintWriter(file);  // make a PrintWriter object AND
                                   // make a file, "foo" to which
                                   // 'file' is assigned, AND assign
                                   // 'pw' to the PrintWriter
   ```

Creating a directory is similar to creating a file. Again, we'll use the convention of referring to an object of type `File` that represents an actual directory as a `Directory` object, with a capital *D* (even though it's of type `File`). We'll call an actual directory on a computer a directory, with a small *d*. Phew! As with creating a file, creating a directory is a two-step process; first we create a `Directory` (`File`) object; then we create an actual directory using the following `mkdir()` method:

```
File myDir = new File("mydir");    // create an object
myDir.mkdir();                     // create an actual directory
```

Once you've got a directory, you put files into it and work with those files:

```
File myFile = new File(myDir, "myFile.txt");
myFile.createNewFile();
```

This code is making a new file in a subdirectory. Since you provide the subdirectory to the constructor, from then on, you just refer to the file by its reference variable. In this case, here's a way that you could write some data to the file `myFile`:

```
PrintWriter pw = new PrintWriter(myFile);
pw.println("new stuff");
pw.flush();
pw.close();
```

Be careful when you're creating new directories! As we've seen, constructing a `Writer` or a `Stream` will often create a file for you automatically if one doesn't exist, but that's not true for a directory.

```
File myDir = new File("mydir");
// myDir.mkdir();                          // call to mkdir() omitted!
File myFile = new File(
            myDir, "myFile.txt");
myFile.createNewFile();                    // exception if no mkdir!
```

This will generate an exception that looks something like

```
java.io.IOException: No such file or directory
```

You can refer a `File` object to an existing file or directory. For example, assume we already have a subdirectory called `existingDir` in which an existing file `existingDirFile.txt` resides. This file contains several lines of text. When we run the following code:

```
File existingDir = new File("existingDir");    // assign a dir
System.out.println(existingDir.isDirectory());

File existingDirFile = new File(
        existingDir, "existingDirFile.txt");  // assign a file
System.out.println (existingDirFile.isFile());
```

```
FileReader fr = new FileReader(existingDirFile);
BufferedReader br = new BufferedReader(fr);      // make a Reader

String s;
while( (s = br.readLine()) != null)              // read data
  System.out.println(s);

br.close();
```

the following output will be generated:

```
true
true
existing sub-dir data
line 2 of text
line 3 of text
```

Take special note of what the `readLine()` method returns. When there is no more data to read, `readLine()` returns a `null`—this is our signal to stop reading the file. Also, notice that we didn't invoke a `flush()` method. When reading a file, no flushing is required, so you won't even find a `flush()` method in a `Reader` kind of class.

In addition to creating files, the `File` class lets you do things like renaming and deleting files. The following code demonstrates a few of the most common ins and outs of deleting files and directories (via `delete()`) and renaming files and directories (via `renameTo()`):

```
File delDir = new File("deldir");        // make a directory
delDir.mkdir();

File delFile1 = new File(
        delDir, "delFile1.txt");         // add file to directory
delFile1.createNewFile();

File delFile2 = new File(
        delDir, "delFile2.txt");         // add file to directory
delFile2.createNewFile();
delFile1.delete();                       // delete a file
System.out.println("delDir is "
                + delDir.delete());      // attempt to delete
                                         // the directory
File newName = new File(
        delDir, "newName.txt");          // a new object
delFile2.renameTo(newName);              // rename file

File newDir = new File("newDir");        // rename directory
delDir.renameTo(newDir);
```

This outputs

```
delDir is false
```

and leaves us with a directory called `newDir` that contains a file called `newName`
`.txt`. Here are some rules that we can deduce from this result:

- **delete()** You can't delete a directory if it's not empty, which is why
  the invocation `delDir.delete()` failed.
- **renameTo()** You must give the existing `File` object a valid new `File`
  object with the new name that you want. (If `newName` had been `null`,
  we would have gotten a `NullPointerException`.)
- **renameTo()** It's okay to rename a directory, even if it isn't empty.

There's a lot more to learn about using the `java.io` package, but as far as the
exam goes, we only have one more thing to discuss, and that is how to search for
a file. Assuming we have a directory named `searchThis` that we want to search
through, the following code uses the `File.list()` method to create a `String`
array of files and directories. We then use the enhanced `for` loop to iterate through
and print.

```
String[] files = new String[100];
File search = new File("searchThis");
files = search.list();                      // create the list

for(String fn : files)                      // iterate through it
  System.out.println("found " + fn);
```

On our system, we got the following output:

```
found dir1
found dir2
found dir3
found file1.txt
found file2.txt
```

Your results will almost certainly be different!

In this section, we've scratched the surface of what's available in the `java.io`
package. Entire books have been written about this package, so we're obviously
covering only a very small (but frequently used) portion of the API. On the other
hand, if you understand everything we've covered in this section, you will be in
great shape to handle any `java.io` questions you encounter on the exam, except
for the `Console` class, which we'll cover next.

The java.io.Console Class

Java 6 added the `java.io.Console` class. In this context, the *console* is the physical device with a keyboard and a display (like your Mac or PC). If you're running Java SE 6 from the command line, you'll typically have access to a console object, to which you can get a reference by invoking `System.console()`. Keep in mind that it's possible for your Java program to be running in an environment that doesn't have access to a console object, so be sure that your invocation of `System.console()` actually returns a valid console reference and not null.

The `Console` class makes it easy to accept input from the command line, both echoed and nonechoed (such as a password), and makes it easy to write formatted output to the command line. It's a handy way to write test engines for unit testing or if you want to support a simple but secure user interaction and you don't need a GUI.

On the input side, the methods you'll have to understand are `readLine` and `readPassword`. The `readLine` method returns a string containing whatever the user keyed in—that's pretty intuitive. However, the `readPassword` method doesn't return a string; it returns a character array. Here's the reason for this: Once you've got the password, you can verify it and then absolutely remove it from memory. If a string was returned, it could exist in a pool somewhere in memory, and perhaps some nefarious hacker could find it.

Let's take a look at a small program that uses a console to support testing another class:

```
import java.io.Console;

public class NewConsole {
  public static void main(String[] args) {
    String name = "";
    Console c = System.console();            // #1: get a Console
    char[] pw;
    pw = c.readPassword("%s", "pw: ");        // #2: return a char[]
    for(char ch: pw)
      c.format("%c ", ch);                    // #3: format output
    c.format("\n");

    MyUtility mu = new MyUtility();
    while(true) {
      name = c.readLine("%s", "input?: ");    // #4: return a String

      c.format("output: %s \n", mu.doStuff(name));
    }
  }
}
```

```
class MyUtility {                           // #5: class to test
  String doStuff(String arg1) {
    // stub code
    return "result is " + arg1;
  }
}
```

Let's review this code:

■ At line 1, we get a new `Console` object. Remember that we can't say this:

```
Console c = new Console();
```

■ At line 2, we invoke `readPassword`, which returns a `char[]`, not a string. You'll notice when you test this code that the password you enter isn't echoed on the screen.

■ At line 3, we're just manually displaying the password you keyed in, separating each character with a space. Later on in this chapter, you'll read about the `format()` method, so stay tuned.

■ At line 4, we invoke `readLine`, which returns a string.

■ At line 5 is the class that we want to test. We recommend that you use something like `NewConsole` to test the concepts that you're learning.

The `Console` class has more capabilities than are covered here, but if you understand everything discussed so far, you'll be in good shape for the exam.

CERTIFICATION OBJECTIVE

Files, Path, and Paths (OCP Objectives 9.1 and 9.2)

9.1   Use Path interface to operate on file and directory paths.
9.2   Use Files class to check, read, delete, copy, move, manage metadata of a file or directory.

The OCP 8 exam has two sections devoted to I/O. The previous section Oracle refers to as "Java I/O Fundamentals" (which we've referred to as the 8.*x* objectives), and it was focused on the `java.io` package. Now we're going to look at the set of objectives Oracle calls "Java File I/O (NIO.2)," whose specific objectives we'll refer to as *9.x*. The term *NIO.2* is a bit loosely defined, but most people (and the exam creators) define NIO.2 as being the key new features introduced in Java 7 that reside in two packages:

- `java.nio.file`
- `java.nio.file.attribute`

We'll start by looking at the important classes and interfaces in the `java.nio .file` package, and then we'll move to the `java.nio.file.attribute` package later in the chapter.

As you read earlier in the chapter, the `File` class represents a file or directory at a high level. NIO.2 adds three new central classes that you'll need to understand well for the exam:

- **Path**   This interface replaces `File` as the representation of a file or a directory when working in NIO.2. It is a lot more powerful than a `File`.
- **Paths**   This class contains static methods that create `Path` objects.
- **Files**   This class contains static methods that work with `Path` objects. You'll find basic operations in here like copying or deleting files.

The interface `java.nio.file.Path` is one of the key classes of file-based I/O under NIO.2. Just like the good old `java.io.File`, a `Path` represents only a location in the file system, like `C:\java\workspace\ocpjp7` (a Windows directory) or `/home/nblack/docs` (the `docs` directory of user `nblack` on UNIX). When you create a `Path` to a new file, that file does not exist until you actually create the file using `Files.createFile(Path target)`. The `Files` utility class will be covered in depth in the next section.

Let's take a look at these relationships another way. The `Paths` class is used to create a class implementing the `Path` interface. The `Files` class uses `Path` objects as parameters. All three of these were introduced in Java 7. Then there is the `File` class. It's been around since the beginning. `File` and `Path` objects know how to convert to the other. This lets any older code interact with the new APIs in `Files`. But notice what is missing. In the figure, there is no line between `File` and `Files`. Despite the similarity in name, these two classes do not know about each other.

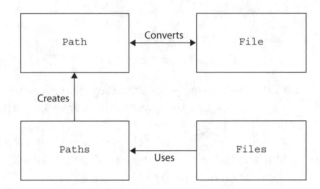

To make sure you know the difference between these key classes backward and forward, make sure you can fill in the four rightmost columns in Table 5-2.

Creating a Path

A `Path` object can be easily created by using the `get` methods from the `Paths` helper class. Remember you are calling `Paths.get()` and not `Path.get()`. If you don't remember why, study the last section some more. It's important to have this down cold.

Taking a look at two simple examples, we have:

```
Path p1 = Paths.get("/tmp/file1.txt");   // on UNIX
Path p2 = Paths.get("c:\\temp\\test");   // On Windows
```

TABLE 5-2		File	Files	Path	Paths
Comparing the Core Classes	Existed in Java 6?	Yes	No	No	No
	Concrete class or interface?	Concrete class	Concrete class	Interface	Concrete class
	Create using "new"	Yes	No	No	No
	Contains only static methods	No	Yes	No	Yes

The actual method we just called is `Paths.get(String first, String... more)`. This means we can write it out by separating the parts of the path.

```
Path p3 = Paths.get("/tmp", "file1.txt");   // same as p1
Path p4 = Paths.get("c:", "temp", "test");  // same as p2
Path p5 = Paths.get("c:\\temp", "test") ;   // also same as p2
```

As you can see, you can separate out folder and filenames as much or as little as you want when calling `Paths.get()`. For Windows, that is particularly cool because you can make the code easier to read by getting rid of the backslash and escape character.

Be careful when creating paths. The previous examples are absolute paths since they begin with the root (/ on UNIX or c: on Windows). When you don't begin with the root, the `Path` is considered a relative path, which means Java looks from the current directory. Which `file1.txt` do you think p6 has in mind?

```
Path p6 = Paths.get("tmp", "file1.txt");  // relative path - NOT same as p1
/ (root)
    |-- tmp
            | - file1.txt
            | - tmp
                    | - file1.txt
```

It depends. If the program is run from the root, it is the one in `/tmp/file1.txt`. If the program is run from `/tmp`, it is the one in `/tmp/tmp/file1.txt`. If the program is run from anywhere else, p6 refers to a file that does not exist.

One more thing to watch for. If you are on Windows, you might deal with a URL that looks like `file:///c:/temp`. The `file://` is a protocol just like `http://` is. This syntax allows you to browse to a folder in Internet Explorer. Your program might have to deal with such a `String` that a user copied/pasted from the browser. No problem, right? We learned to code:

```
Path p = Paths.get("file:///c:/temp/test");
```

Unfortunately, this doesn't work, and you get an exception about the colon being invalid that looks something like this:

```
Exception in thread "main" java.nio.file.InvalidPathException:
Illegal char <:>
at index 4: file:///c:/temp
```

`Paths` provides another method that solves this problem. `Paths.get(URI uri)` lets you (indirectly) convert the `String` to a `URI` (Uniform Resource Identifier) before trying to create a `Path`:

```
Path p = Paths.get(URI.create("file:///C:/temp"));
```

The last thing you should know is that the `Paths.get()` method we've been discussing is really a shortcut. You won't need to code the longer version, but it is good to understand what is going on under the hood. First, Java finds out what the default file system is. For example, it might be `WindowsFileSystemProvider`. Then Java gets the path using custom logic for that file system. Luckily, this all goes on without us having to write any special code or even think about it.

```
Path short = Paths.get("c:", "temp");
Path longer = FileSystems.getDefault()          // get default file system
    .getPath("c:", "temp");                      // then get the Path
```

Now that you know how to create a `Path` instance, you can manipulate it in various ways. We'll get back to that in a bit.

As far as the exam is concerned, `Paths.get()` is how to create a `Path` initially. There is another way that is useful when working with code that was written before Java 7:

```
Path  convertedPath = file.toPath();
File  convertedFile = path.toFile();
```

If you are updating older code that uses `File`, you can convert it to a `Path` and start calling the new classes. And if your newer code needs to call older code, it can convert back to a `File`.

Creating Files and Directories

With I/O, we saw that a file doesn't exist just because you have a `File` object. You have to call `createNewFile()` to bring the file into existence and `exists()` to check if it exists. Rewriting the example from earlier in the chapter to use NIO.2 methods, we now have:

```
Path path = Paths.get("fileWrite1.txt");        // it's only an object
System.out.println(Files.exists(path));          // look for a real file
Files.createFile(path);                          // create a file!
System.out.println(Files.exists(path));          // look again
```

NIO.2 has equivalent methods with two differences:

- You call static methods on `Files` rather than instance methods on `File`.
- Method names are slightly different.

See Table 5-3 for the mapping between old class/method names and new ones. You can still continue to use the older I/O approach if you happen to be dealing with `File` objects.

TABLE 5-3	I/O vs. NIO.2	

Description	I/O Approach	NIO.2 Approach
Create an empty file	`File file = new File("test");` `file.createNewFile():`	`Path path = Paths.get("test");` `Files.createFile(path);`
Create an empty directory	`File file = new File("dir");` `file.mkdir()`	`Path path = Paths.get("dir");` `Files.createDirectory(path);`
Create a directory, including any missing parent directories	`File file = new File("/a/b/c");` `file.mkdirs():`	`Path path = Paths.get("/a/b/c");` `Files.createDirectories(path);`
Check if a file or directory exists	`File file = new File("test");` `file.exists();`	`Path path = Paths.get("test");` `Files.exists(path);`

on the Job

The method `Files.notExists()` *supplements* `Files.exists()`. *In some incredibly rare situations, Java won't have enough permissions to know whether the file exists. When this happens, both methods return false.*

You can also create directories in Java. Suppose we have a directory named `/java` and we want to create the file `/java/source/directory/Program .java`. We could do this one at a time:

```
Path path1 = Paths.get("/java/source");
Path path2 = Paths.get("/java/source/directory");
Path file = Paths.get("/java/source/directory/Program.java");
Files.createDirectory(path1);    // create first level of directory
Files.createDirectory(path2);    // create second level of directory
Files.createFile(file);          // create file
```

Or we could create all the directories in one go:

```
Files.createDirectories(path2);  // create all levels of directories
Files.createFile(file);          // create file
```

Although both work, the second is clearly better if you have a lot of directories to create. And remember that the directory needs to exist by the time the file is created.

Copying, Moving, and Deleting Files

We often copy, move, or delete files when working with the file system. Up until Java 7, this was hard to do. Now, however, each is one line. Let's look at some examples:

```
Path source = Paths.get("/temp/test1.txt");   // exists
Path target = Paths.get("/temp/test2.txt");   // doesn't yet exist
Files.copy(source, target);                   // now two copies of the file
Files.delete(target);                         // back to one copy
Files.move(source, target);                   // still one copy
```

This is all pretty self-explanatory. We copy a file, delete the copy, and then move the file. Now, let's try another example:

```
Path one = Paths.get("/temp/test1.txt");     // exists
Path two = Paths.get("/temp/test2.txt");     // exists
Path targ = Paths.get("/temp/test23.txt");   // doesn't yet exist
Files.copy(one, targ);                       // now two copies of the file
Files.copy(two, targ);                       // oops,
                                             // FileAlreadyExistsException
```

Java sees it is about to overwrite a file that already exists. Java doesn't want us to lose the file, so it "asks" if we are sure by throwing an exception. `copy()` and `move()` actually take an optional third parameter—zero or more `CopyOptions`. The most useful option you can pass is `StandardCopyOption.REPLACE_EXISTING`.

```
Files.copy(two,  target,                      // ok. You know what
   StandardCopyOption.REPLACE_EXISTING);      // you are doing
```

We have to think about whether a file exists when deleting the file too. Let's say we wrote this test code:

```
Path path = Paths.get("/java/out.txt");
try {
   methodUnderTest();         // might throw an exception
   Files.createFile(path);    // file only gets created
                              // if methodUnderTest() succeeds
} finally {
   Files.delete(path);        // NoSuchFileException if no file
}
```

We don't know whether `methodUnderTest` works properly yet. If it does, the code works fine. If it throws an exception, we never create the file and `Files.delete()` throws a `NoSuchFileException`. This is a problem, as we only

| TABLE 5-4 | Files Methods |

Method	Description
`Path copy(Path source, Path target, CopyOption... options)`	Copy the file from source to target and return target
`Path move(Path source, Path target, CopyOption... options)`	Move the file from source to target and return target
`void delete(Path path)`	Delete the file and throw an exception if it does not exist
`boolean deleteIfExists(Path path)`	Delete the file if it exists and return whether file was deleted
`boolean exists(Path path, LinkOption... options)`	Return true if file exists
`boolean notExists(Path path, LinkOption... options)`	Return true if file does not exist

want to delete the file if it was created so we aren't leaving stray files around. There is an alternative. `Files.deleteIfExists(path)` returns true and deletes the file only if it exists. If not, it just quietly returns false. Most of the time, you can ignore this return value. You just want the file to not be there. If it never existed, mission accomplished.

on the

If you have to work on pre-Java 7 code, you can use the `FileUtils` class in Apache Commons IO (http://commons.apache.org/io). It has methods similar to many of the copy, move, and delete methods that are now built into Java.

To review, Table 5-4 lists the methods on `Files` that you are likely to come across on the exam. Luckily, the exam doesn't expect you to know all 30 methods in the API. The important thing to remember is to check the `Files` JavaDoc when you find yourself dealing with files.

Retrieving Information about a Path

The `Path` interface defines a bunch of methods that return useful information about the path that you're dealing with. In the following code listing, a `Path` is created referring to a directory and then we output information about the `Path` instance:

```
Path path = Paths.get("C:/home/java/workspace");
System.out.println("getFileName: " + path.getFileName());
System.out.println("getName(1): " +  path.getName(1));
System.out.println("getNameCount: "  + path.getNameCount());
```

```
System.out.println("getParent: " +  path.getParent());
System.out.println("getRoot: " +  path.getRoot());
System.out.println("subpath(0, 2): " + path.subpath(0, 2));
System.out.println("toString: " +  path.toString());
```

When you execute this code snippet on Windows, the following output is printed:

```
getFileName: workspace
getName(1): java
getNameCount: 3
getParent: C:\home\java
getRoot: C:\
subpath(0, 2): home\java
toString: C:\home\java\workspace
```

Based on this output, it is fairly simple to describe what each method does. Table 5-5 does just that.

Here is yet another interesting fact about the `Path` interface: It extends from `Iterable<Path>`. At first sight, this seems anything but interesting. But every class that (correctly) implements the `Iterable<?>` interface can be used as an expression in the enhanced `for` loop. You know you can iterate through an array or a `List`, but you can iterate through a `Path` as well. That's pretty cool!

TABLE 5-5	Method	Description
Path Methods	`String getFileName()`	Returns the filename or the last element of the sequence of name elements.
	`Path getName(int index)`	Returns the path element corresponding to the specified index. The 0th element is the one closest to the root. (On Windows, the root is usually C:\ and on UNIX, the root is /.)
	`int getNameCount()`	Returns the number of elements in this path, excluding the root.
	`Path getParent()`	Returns the parent path, or `null` if this path does not have a parent.
	`Path getRoot()`	Returns the root of this path, or `null` if this path does not have a root.
	`Path subpath(int beginIndex, int endIndex)`	Returns a subsequence of this path (not including a root element) as specified by the beginning (included) and ending (not included) indexes.
	`String toString()`	Returns the string representation of this path.

Using this functionality, it's easy to print the hierarchical tree structure of a file (or directory), as the following example shows:

```
int spaces = 1;
Path myPath = Paths.get("tmp", "dir1", "dir2", "dir3", "file.txt");
for (Path subPath : myPath) {
  System.out.format("%" + spaces + "s%s%n", "", subPath);
  spaces += 2; }
```

When you run this example, a (simplistic) tree is printed. Thanks to the variable `spaces` (which is increased with each iteration by 2), the different subpaths are printed like a directory tree.

```
tmp
  dir1
    dir2
      dir3
        file.txt
```

Normalizing a Path

Normally (no pun intended), when you create a `Path`, you create it in a direct way. However, all three of these return the same logical `Path`:

```
Path p1 = Paths.get("myDirectory");
Path p2 = Paths.get("./myDirectory");            // one dot means
                                                 // current directory
Path p3 = Paths.get("anotherDirectory", "..",    // two dots means go up
                    "myDirectory");              // one directory
```

p1 is probably what you would type if you were coding. p2 is just plain redundant. p3 is more interesting. The two directories—`anotherDirectory` and `myDirectory`—are on the same level, but we have to go up one level to get there:

```
/ (root)
   |-- anotherDirectory
   |-- myDirectory
```

You might be wondering why on earth we wouldn't just type `myDirectory` in the first place. And you would if you could. Sometimes, that doesn't work out. Let's look at a real example of why this might be.

```
/ (root)
   |-- Build_Project
       |-- scripts
           |-- buildScript.sh
   |-- My_Project
       |-- source
           |-- MyClass.java
```

If you wanted to compile `MyClass`, you would `cd` to `/My_Project/source` and run `javac MyClass.java`. Once your program gets bigger, it could be thousands of classes and have hundreds of jar files. You don't want to type in all of those just to compile, so someone writes a script to build your program. `buildScript.sh` now finds everything that is needed to compile and runs the `javac` command for you. The problem is that the current directory is now `/Build_Project/scripts`, not `/My_Project/source`. The build script helpfully builds a path for you by doing something like this:

```
String buildProject                          // build scripts to express
    = "/Build_Project/scripts";              // paths in relation to themselves

String upTwoDirectories = "../..";           // remember what .. means?

String myProject = "/My_Project/source";
Path path = Paths.get(buildProject,
            upTwoDirectories, myProject);     // build path from variables
System.out.println("Original: " + path);
System.out.println("Normalized: " + path.normalize());
```

which outputs:

```
Original:/Build_Project/scripts/../../My_Project/source
Normalized:/My_Project/source
```

Whew. The second one is much easier to read. The `normalize()` method knows that a single dot can be ignored. It also knows that any directory followed by two dots can be removed from a path.

Be careful when using this `normalize()`! It just looks at the `String` equivalent of the path and doesn't check the file system to see whether the directories or files actually exist.

Let's practice and see what `normalize` returns for these paths. This time, we aren't providing a directory structure to show that the directories and files don't need to be present on the computer. What do you think the following prints out?

```
System.out.println(Paths.get("/a/./b/./c").normalize());
System.out.println(Paths.get(".classpath").normalize());
System.out.println(Paths.get("/a/b/c/..").normalize());
System.out.println(Paths.get("../a/b/c").normalize());
```

The output is

```
/a/b/c
.classpath
/a/b
../a/b/c
```

The first one removes all the single dots since they just point to the current directory. The second doesn't change anything since the dot is part of a filename and not a directory. The third sees one set of double dots, so it only goes up one directory. The last one is a little tricky. The two dots do say to go up one directory. But since there isn't a directory before it, Path can't simplify it.

To review, normalize() removes unneeded parts of the Path, making it more like you'd normally type it. (That's not where the word "normalize" comes from, but it is a nice way to remember it.)

Resolving a Path

So far, you have an overview of all methods that can be invoked on a single Path object, but what if you need to combine two paths? You might want to do this if you have one Path representing your home directory and another containing the Path within that directory.

```
Path dir = Paths.get("/home/java");
Path file = Paths.get("models/Model.pdf");
Path result = dir.resolve(file);
System.out.println("result = " + result);
```

This produces the absolute path by merging the two paths:

```
result = /home/java/models/Model.pdf
```

path1.resolve(path2) should be read as "resolve path2 within path1's directory." In this example, we resolved the path of the file within the directory provided by dir.

Keeping this definition in mind, let's look at some more complex examples:

```
Path absolute = Paths.get("/home/java");
Path relative = Paths.get("dir");
Path file = Paths.get("Model.pdf");
System.out.println("1: " + absolute.resolve(relative));
System.out.println("2: " + absolute.resolve(file));
System.out.println("3: " + relative.resolve(file));
System.out.println("4: " + relative.resolve(absolute));   // BAD
System.out.println("5: " + file.resolve(absolute));        // BAD
System.out.println("6: " + file.resolve(relative));        // BAD
```

The output is

```
1:   /home/java/dir
2:   /home/java/Model.pdf
3:   dir/Model.pdf
4:   /home/java
5:   /home/java
6:   Model.pdf/dir
```

The first three do what you'd expect. They add the parameter to resolve to the provided path object. The fourth and fifth ones try to resolve an absolute path within the context of something else. The problem is that an absolute path doesn't depend on other directories. It is absolute. Therefore, `resolve()` just returns that absolute path. The output of the sixth one looks a little bit weird, but Java does the only right thing to do here. For all it knows the `Path` referred to by `Model.pdf` may be a directory and the `Path` referred to by `dir` may be a file!

Just like `normalize()`, keep in mind that `resolve()` will not check that the directory or file actually exists. To review, `resolve()` tells you how to resolve one path within another.

Relativizing a Path

Now suppose we want to do the opposite of resolve. We have the absolute path of our home directory and the absolute path of the music file in our home directory. We want to know just the music file directory and name.

```
Path dir = Paths.get("/home/java");
Path music = Paths.get("/home/java/country/Swift.mp3");
Path mp3 = dir.relativize(music);
System.out.println(mp3);
```

The output is

```
country/Swift.mp3.
```

Java recognized that the /home/java part is the same and returned a path of just the remainder.

path1.relativize(path2) should be read as "give me a path that shows how to get from path1 to path2." In this example, we determined that music is a file in a directory named country within dir.

Keeping this definition in mind, let's look at some more complex examples:

```
Path absolute1 = Paths.get("/home/java");
Path absolute2 = Paths.get("/usr/local");
Path absolute3 = Paths.get("/home/java/temp/music.mp3");
Path relative1 = Paths.get("temp");
Path relative2 = Paths.get("temp/music.pdf");
System.out.println("1: " + absolute1.relativize(absolute3));
System.out.println("2: " + absolute3.relativize(absolute1));
System.out.println("3: " + absolute1.relativize(absolute2));
System.out.println("4: " + relative1.relativize(relative2));
System.out.println("5: " + absolute1.relativize(relative1));//BAD
```

The output is

```
1: temp/music.mp3
2: ../..
3: ../../usr/local
4: music.pdf
Exception in thread "main" java.lang.IllegalArgumentException: 'other'
is different type of Path
```

Before you scratch your head, let's look at the logical directory structure here. Keep in mind the directory doesn't actually need to exist; this is just to visualize it.

```
/root
  | - usr
          | - local
  | - home
          | -- java
          | - temp
                  | - music.mp3
```

Now we can trace it through. The first example is straightforward. It tells us how to get to absolute3 from absolute1 by going down two directories. The second is similar. We get to absolute1 from absolute3 by doing the opposite—going up two directories. Remember from normalize() that a double dot means to go up a directory.

The third output statement says that we have to go up two directories and then down two directories to get from `absolute1` to `absolute2`. Java knows this because we provided absolute paths. The worst possible case is to have to go all the way up to the root like we did here.

The fourth output statement is okay. Even though they are both relative paths, there is enough in common for Java to tell what the difference in the path is.

The fifth example throws an exception. Java can't figure out how to make a relative path out of one absolute path and one relative path.

Remember, `relativize()` and `resolve()` are opposites. And just like `resolve()`, `relativize()` does not check that the path actually exists. To review, `relativize()` tells you how to get a relative path between two paths.

CERTIFICATION OBJECTIVE

File and Directory Attributes (OCP Objective 9.2)

9.2   Use Files class to check, read, delete, copy, move, manage metadata of a file or directory.

Metadata is data about data. For a file, you can think of the stuff that's in the file as the data, and the attributes of the file, like the date the file	*was created, as the metadata; that is, the data about the data that's in the file. When you see "metadata" in this objective, think "attributes" of files and directories.*

Reading and Writing Attributes the Easy Way

In this section, we'll add classes and interfaces from the `java.nio.file.attribute` package to the discussion. Prior to NIO.2, you could read and write just a handful of attributes. Just like we saw when creating files, there is a new way to do this using `Files` instead of `File`. Oracle also took the opportunity to clean up the method signatures a bit. The following example creates a file, changes the last modified date, prints it out, and deletes the file using both the old and new method names. We might do this if we want to make a file look as if it were created in the past. (As you can see, there is a lesson about not relying on file timestamps here!)

```
ZonedDateTime janFirstDateTime =
    ZonedDateTime.of(                              // create a date
        LocalDate.of(2017, 1, 1),
        LocalTime.of(10, 0), ZoneId.of("US/Pacific"));
Instant januaryFirst = janFirstDateTime.toInstant();

// old way
File file = new File("c:/temp/file");
file.createNewFile();                              // create the file
file.setLastModified(
    januaryFirst.getEpochSecond()*1000);           // set time
System.out.println(file.lastModified());           // get time
file.delete();                                     // delete the file

// new way
Path path = Paths.get("c:/temp/file2");
Files.createFile(path);                             // create another file
FileTime fileTime =                                // convert to the new
    FileTime.fromMillis(                           // FileTime object
        januaryFirst.getEpochSecond()*1000);
Files.setLastModifiedTime(path, fileTime);         // set time
System.out.println(Files.getLastModifiedTime(path)); // get time
Files.delete(path);
```

As you can see from the output, the only change in functionality is that the new `Files.getLastModifiedTime()` uses a human-friendly date format.

```
1483293600000
2017-01-01T18:00:00Z
```

The other common type of attribute you can set are file permissions. Both Windows and UNIX have the concept of three types of permissions. Here's what they mean:

- **Read** You can open the file or list what is in that directory.
- **Write** You can make a change to the file or add a file to that directory.
- **Execute** You can run the file if it is a runnable program or go into that directory.

TABLE 5-6	I/O vs. NIO.2 Permissions

Description	I/O Approach	NIO.2 Approach
Get the last modified date/time	`File file = new File("test");` `file.lastModified();`	`Path path = Paths.get("test");` `Files.getLastModifiedTime(path);`
Is read permission set	`File file = new File("test");` `file.canRead();`	`Path path = Paths.get("test");` `Files.isReadable(path);`
Is write permission set	`File file = new File("test");` `file.canWrite();`	`Path path = Paths.get("test");` `Files.isWritable(path);`
Is executable permission set	`File file = new File("test");` `file.canExecute();`	`Path path = Paths.get("test");` `Files.isExecutable(path);`

Set the last modified date/time (Note: `timeInMillis` is an appropriate `long`.)	`File file = new File("test");`
	`file.setLastModified(timeInMillis);`
		`Path path = Paths.get("test");`
		`FileTime fileTime = FileTime.`
		`fromMillis(timeInMillis);`
		`Files.setLastModifiedTime(path,`
		`fileTime);`

Printing out the file permissions is easy. Note that these permissions are just for the user who is running the program—you! There are other types of permissions as well, but these can't be set in one line.

```
System.out.println(Files.isExecutable(path));
System.out.println(Files.isReadable(path));
System.out.println(Files.isWritable(path));
```

Table 5-6 shows how to get and set these attributes that can be set in one line, both using the older I/O way and the new `Files` class. You may have noticed that setting file permissions isn't in the table. That's more code, so we will talk about it later.

Types of Attribute Interfaces

The attributes you set by calling methods on `Files` are the most straightforward ones. Beyond that, Java NIO.2 added attribute interfaces so you could read attributes that might not be on every operating system.

■ **BasicFileAttributes** In the JavaDoc, Oracle says these are "attributes common to many file systems." What they mean is that you can rely on these attributes being available to you unless you are writing Java code for some funky new operating system. Basic attributes include things like creation date.

- **PosixFileAttributes**   POSIX stands for Portable Operating System Interface. This interface is implemented by both UNIX- and Linux-based operating systems. You can remember this because POSIX ends in "x," as do UNIX and Linux.

- **DosFileAttributes**   DOS stands for Disk Operating System. It is part of all Windows operating systems. Even Windows 8 and 10 have a DOS prompt available.

There are also separate interfaces for setting or updating attributes. While the details aren't in scope for the exam, you should be familiar with the purpose of each one.

- **BasicFileAttributeView**   Used to set the last updated, last accessed, and creation dates.

- **PosixFileAttributeView**   Used to set the groups or permissions on UNIX/Linux systems. There is an easier way to set these permissions though, so you won't be using the attribute view.

- **DosFileAttributeView**   Used to set file permissions on DOS/Windows systems. Again, there is an easier way to set these, so you won't be using the attribute view.

- **FileOwnerAttributeView**   Used to set the primary owner of a file or directory.

- **AclFileAttributeView**   Sets more advanced permissions on a file or directory.

Working with BasicFileAttributes

The `BasicFileAttributes` interface provides methods to get information about a file or directory.

```
BasicFileAttributes basic = Files.readAttributes(path,  // assume a valid path
    BasicFileAttributes.class);
System.out.println("create: " + basic.creationTime());
System.out.println("access: " + basic.lastAccessTime());
System.out.println("modify: " + basic.lastModifiedTime());
System.out.println("directory: " + basic.isDirectory());
```

The sample output shows that all three date/time values can be different. A file is created once. It can be modified many times. And it can be last accessed for reading after that. The `isDirectory` method is the same as `Files.isDirectory(path)`. It is just an alternative way of getting the same information.

```
create: 2017-03-21T23:14:36Z
access: 2017-09-25T02:01:11Z
modify: 2017-04-12T17:38:51Z
directory: false
```

There are some more attributes on `BasicFileAttributes`, but they aren't on the exam and you aren't likely to need them when coding. Just remember to check the JavaDoc if you need more information about a file.

So far, you've noticed that all the attributes are read only. That's because Java provides a different interface for updating attributes. Let's write code to update the last accessed time:

```
BasicFileAttributes basic = Files.readAttributes(
    path, BasicFileAttributes.class);               // attributes
FileTime lastUpdated = basic.lastModifiedTime();    // get current
FileTime created = basic.creationTime();            // values
FileTime now = FileTime.fromMillis(System.currentTimeMillis());
BasicFileAttributeView basicView = Files.getFileAttributeView(
    path, BasicFileAttributeView.class);            // "view" this time
basicView.setTimes(lastUpdated, now, created);      // set all three
```

In this example, we demonstrated getting all three times. In practice, when calling `setTimes()`, you should pass null values for any of the times you don't want to change, and only pass `FileTimes` for the times you want to change.

The key takeaways here are that the "`XxxFileAttributes`" classes are read only and the "`XxxFileAttributeView`" classes allow updates.

e x a m

ⓦ a t c h   *The `BasicFileAttributes` and `BasicFileAttributeView` interfaces are a bit confusing. They have similar names but different functionality, and you get them in different ways. Try to remember these three things:*

- *`BasicFileAttributeView` is singular, but `BasicFileAttributes` is not.*

- *You get `BasicFileAttributeView` using `Files.getFileAttributeView`, and you get `BasicFileAttributes` using `Files.readAttributes`.*

- *You can ONLY update attributes in `BasicFileAttributeView`, not in `BasicFileAttributes`. Remember that the view is for updating.*

`PosixFileAttributes` and `DosFileAttributes` inherit from `BasicFileAttributes`. This means you can call Basic methods on a POSIX or DOS subinterface.

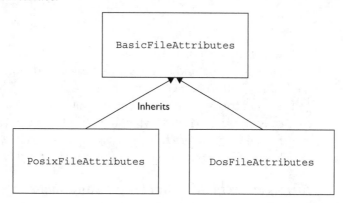

Try to use the more general type if you can. For example, if you are only going to use basic attributes, just get `BasicFileAttributes`. This lets your code remain operating system independent. If you are using a mix of basic and POSIX attributes, you can use `PosixFileAttributes` directly rather than calling `readAttributes()` twice to get two different ones.

Working with DosFileAttributes

`DosFileAttributes` adds four more attributes to the basics. We'll look at the most common ones here—hidden files and read-only files. Hidden files typically begin with a dot and don't show up when you type **dir** to list the contents of a directory. Read-only files are what they sound like—files that can't be updated. (The other two attributes are "archive" and "system," which you are quite unlikely to ever use.)

```
Path path= Paths.get("C:/test");
Files.createFile(path);                             // create file
Files.setAttribute(path, "dos:hidden", true);      // set attribute
Files.setAttribute(path, "dos:readonly", true);    // another one
DosFileAttributes dos = Files.readAttributes(path,
        DosFileAttributes.class);                   // dos attributes
System.out.println(dos.isHidden());
System.out.println(dos.isReadOnly());
Files.setAttribute(path, "dos:hidden", false);
Files.setAttribute(path, "dos:readonly", false);
dos = Files.readAttributes(path,
        DosFileAttributes.class);                   // get attributes again
System.out.println(dos.isHidden());
System.out.println(dos.isReadOnly());
Files.delete(path);
```

The output is

```
true
true
false
false
```

The first tricky thing in this code is that the String "readonly" is lowercase even though the method name is mixed case. If you forget and use the String "readOnly," an IllegalArgumentException will be thrown at runtime.

The other tricky thing is that you cannot delete a read-only file. That's why the code calls setAttribute a second time with false as a parameter, to make it no longer "read only" so the code can clean up after itself. And you can see that we had to call readAttributes again to see those updated values.

on the job

There is an alternative way to set these attributes so you don't have to worry about the String values. However, the exam wants you to know how to use Files. It is good to know both ways, though.

```
DosFileAttributeView view = Files.getFileAttributeView(path,
                                DosFileAttributeView.class);

view.setHidden(true);
view.setReadOnly(true);
```

Working with PosixFileAttributes

PosixFileAttributes adds two more attributes to the basics—groups and permissions. On UNIX, every file or directory has both an owner and group name.

UNIX permissions are also more elaborate than the basic ones. Each file or directory has nine permissions set in a String. A sample is "rwxrw-r--." Breaking this into groups of three, we have "rwx", "rw-," and "r--." These sets of permissions correspond to who gets them. In this example, the "user" (owner) of the file has read, write, and execute permissions. The "group" only has read and write permissions. UNIX calls everyone who is not the owner or in the group "other." "Other" only has read access in this example.

Now let's look at some code to set the permissions and output them in human-readable form:

```
Path path = Paths.get("/tmp/file2");
Files.createFile(path);
PosixFileAttributes posix = Files.readAttributes(path,
PosixFileAttributes.class);                          // get the Posix type
Set<PosixFilePermission> perms =
    PosixFilePermissions.fromString("rw-r--r--");    // UNIX style
Files.setPosixFilePermissions(path, perms);          // set permissions
System.out.println(posix.permissions());             // get permissions
```

The output looks like this:

```
[OWNER_WRITE, GROUP_READ, OTHERS_READ, OWNER_READ]
```

It's not symmetric. We gave Java the permissions in cryptic UNIX format and got them back in plain English. You can also output the group name:

```
System.out.println(posix.group());              // get group
```

which outputs something like this:

```
horse
```

Reviewing Attributes

Let's review the most common attributes information in Table 5-7.

TABLE 5-7	Common Attributes

Type	Read and Write an Attribute

Basic	```// read```
	
	```BasicFileAttributes basic = Files.readAttributes(path,```
	``` BasicFileAttributes.class);```
	```FileTime lastUpdated = basic.lastModifiedTime();```
	```FileTime created = basic.creationTime();```
	```FileTime now = FileTime.fromMillis(System.currentTimeMillis());```
	
	```// write```
	```BasicFileAttributeView basicView =```
	```Files.getFileAttributeView(path,```
	```BasicFileAttributeView.class);```
	```basicView.setTimes(lastUpdated, now, created);```

Posix (UNIX/Linux)	```PosixFileAttributes posix = Files.readAttributes(path,```
	```PosixFileAttributes.class);```
	```Set<PosixFilePermission> perms = PosixFilePermissions.```
	```fromString("rw-r--r--");```
	```Files.setPosixFilePermissions(path, perms);```
	```System.out.println(posix.group());```
	```System.out.println(posix.permissions());```

Dos (Windows)	```DosFileAttributes dos = Files.readAttributes(path,```
	``` DosFileAttributes.class);```
	```System.out.println(dos.isHidden());```
	```System.out.println(dos.isReadOnly());```
	```Files.setAttribute(path, "dos:hidden", false);```
	```Files.setAttribute(path, "dos:readonly", false);```

CERTIFICATION OBJECTIVE

DirectoryStream (OCP Objectives 9.2 and 9.3)

9.2 Use Files class to check, read, delete, copy, move, manage metadata of a file or directory.
9.3 Use Stream API with NIO.2.

Now let's return to more NIO.2 capabilities that you'll find in the `java.nio` `.file` package... You might need to loop through a directory. Let's say you were asked to list out all the users with a home directory on this computer.

```
/home
  | - users
          | - vafi
          | - eyra
```

```
Path dir = Paths.get("/home/users");
try (DirectoryStream<Path> stream =            // use try-with-resources
     Files.newDirectoryStream(dir)) {          // so we don't have close()
  for (Path path : stream)                      // loop through the stream
     System.out.println(path.getFileName());
}
```

As expected, this outputs

```
vafi
eyra
```

The `DirectoryStream` interface lets you iterate through a directory. But this is just the tip of the iceberg. Let's say we have hundreds of users and each day we want to only report on a few of them. The first day, we only want the home directories of users whose names begin with either the letter *v* or the letter *w*.

```
Path dir = Paths.get("/home/users");
try (DirectoryStream<Path> stream = Files.newDirectoryStream(
  dir, "[vw]*")) {                             // "v" or "w" followed by anything
for (Path path : stream)
     System.out.println(path.getFileName());
}
```

This time, the output is

```
vafi
```

Let's examine the expression `[vw] *`. `[vw]` means either of the characters v or w. The `*` is a wildcard that means zero or more of any character. Notice this is not a regular expression. (If it were, the syntax would be `[vw] .*`—see the dot in there.) `DirectoryStream` uses something called a *glob*. We will see more on globs later in the chapter.

There is one limitation with `DirectoryStream`. It can only look at one directory. One way to remember this is that it works like the `dir` command in DOS or the `ls` command in UNIX. Or you can remember that `DirectoryStream` streams one directory.

FileVisitor

Luckily, there is another class that does, in fact, look at subdirectories. Let's say you want to get rid of all the .class files before zipping up and submitting your assignment. You could go through each directory manually, but that would get tedious really fast. You could write a complicated command in Windows and another in UNIX, but then you'd have two programs that do the same thing. Luckily, you can use Java and only write the code once.

Java provides a `SimpleFileVisitor`. You extend it and override one or more methods. Then you can call `Files.walkFileTree`, which knows how to recursively look through a directory structure and call methods on a visitor subclass. Let's try our example:

```
/home
  | - src
          | - Test.java
          | - Test.class
          | - dir
                  | - AnotherTest.java
                  | - AnotherTest.class

public class RemoveClassFiles
      extends SimpleFileVisitor<Path> {          // need to extend visitor
      public FileVisitResult visitFile(          // called "automatically"
         Path file, BasicFileAttributes attrs)
              throws IOException {
          if ( file.getFileName().toString().endsWith(".class"))
            Files.delete(file);                  // delete the file
          return FileVisitResult.CONTINUE;       // go on to next file
      }
```

```
public static void main(String[] args) throws Exception {
    RemoveClassFiles dirs = new RemoveClassFiles();
    Files.walkFileTree(                        // kick off recursive check
            Paths.get("/home/src"),            // starting point
            dirs);                             // the visitor
}
}
```

This is a simple file visitor. It only implements one method: visitFile. This method is called for every file in the directory structure. It checks the extension of the file and deletes it if appropriate. In our case, two .class files are deleted.

There are two parameters to visitFile(). The first one is the Path object representing the current file. The other is a BasicFileAttributes interface. Do you remember what this does? That's right—it lets you find out if the current file is a directory, when it was created, and many other similar pieces of data.

Finally, visitFile() returns FileVisitResult.*CONTINUE*. This tells walkFileTree() that it should keep looking through the directory structure for more files.

Now that we have a feel for the power of this class, let's take a look at all the methods available to us with another example:

```
/home
  | - a.txt
  | - emptyChild
  | - child
          | - b.txt
          | - grandchild
                 | - c.txt

public class PrintDirs extends SimpleFileVisitor<Path> {
  public FileVisitResult preVisitDirectory(Path dir, BasicFileAttributes attrs)
{
    System.out.println("pre: " + dir);
    return FileVisitResult.CONTINUE; }
  public FileVisitResult visitFile(Path file, BasicFileAttributes attrs) {
    System.out.println("file: " + file);
    return FileVisitResult.CONTINUE; }
  public FileVisitResult visitFileFailed(Path file, IOException exc) {
    return FileVisitResult.CONTINUE; }
  public FileVisitResult postVisitDirectory(Path dir, IOException exc) {
    System.out.println("post: " + dir);
    return FileVisitResult.CONTINUE; }
  public static void main(String[] args) throws Exception {
    PrintDirs dirs = new PrintDirs();
    Files.walkFileTree(Paths.get("/home"), dirs); } }
```

You might get the following output:

```
pre:  /home
file: /home/a.txt
pre:  /home/child
file: /home/child/b.txt
pre:  /home/child/grandchild
file: /home/child/grandchild/c.txt
post: /home/child/grandchild
post: /home/child
pre:  /home/emptyChild
post: /home/emptyChild
post: /home
```

Note that Java goes down as deep as it can before returning back up the tree. This is called a *depth-first search*. We said "might" because files and directories at the same level can get visited in either order.

You can override as few or as many of the four methods as you'd like. Note that the second half of the methods have IOException as a parameter. This allows those methods to handle problems that came earlier when walking through the tree. Table 5-8 summarizes the methods.

You actually do have some control, though, through those FileVisitResult constants. Suppose we changed the preVisitDirectory method to the following:

```
public FileVisitResult preVisitDirectory(
  Path dir, BasicFileAttributes attrs) {
  System.out.println("pre: " + dir);
  String name = dir.getFileName().toString();
  if (name.equals("child"))
    return FileVisitResult.SKIP_SUBTREE;
  return FileVisitResult.CONTINUE;
}
```

TABLE 5-8

FileVisitor
Methods

Method	Description	IOException Parameter?
preVisitDirectory	Called before drilling down into the directory	No
visitFile	Called once for each file (but not for directories)	No
visitFileFailed	Called only if there was an error accessing a file, usually a permissions issue	Yes
postVisitDirectory	Called when finished with the directory on the way back up	Yes

Now the output is

```
pre:  /home
file: /home/a.txt
pre:  /home/child
pre:  /home/emptyChild
post: /home/emptyChild
post: /home
```

Since we instructed the program to skip the entire `child` subtree—i.e., we don't see the file: `b.txt`, or the subdirectory: `grandchild`—we also don't see the post visit call.

Now what do you think would happen if we changed `FileVisitResult.SKIP_SUBTREE` to `FileVisitResult.TERMINATE`? The output might be:

```
pre:  /home
file: /home/a.txt
pre:  /home/child
```

We see that as soon as the "child" directory came up, the program stopped walking the tree. And again, we are using "might" in terms of the output. It's also possible for `emptyChild` to come up first, in which case, the last line of the output would be `/home/emptyChild`.

There's one more result type. What do you think would happen if we changed `FileVisitResult.TERMINATE` to `FileVisitResult.SKIP_SIBLINGS`? The output happens to be the same as the previous example:

```
pre:  /home
file: /home/a.txt
pre:  /home/child
```

`SKIP_SIBLINGS` is a combination of `SKIP_SUBTREE` and "don't look in any folders at the same level." This means we skip everything under `child` and also skip `emptyChild`.

One more example to make sure you really understand what is going on. What do you think gets output if we use this method?

```
public FileVisitResult preVisitDirectory(Path dir,
  BasicFileAttributes attrs) {
  System.out.println("pre: " + dir);
  String name = dir.getFileName().toString();
  if (name.equals("grandchild"))
    return FileVisitResult.SKIP_SUBTREE;
  if ( name.equals("emptyChild"))
    return FileVisitResult.SKIP_SIBLINGS;
  return FileVisitResult.CONTINUE;
}
```

Assuming `child` is encountered before `emptyChild`, the output is

```
pre: /home
file: /home/a.txt
pre: /home/child
file: /home/child/b.txt
pre: /home/child/grandchild
post: /home/child
pre: /home/emptyChild
post: /home
```

We don't see `file: c.txt` or `post: /home/child/grandchild` because we skip `grandchild` the subtree. We don't see `post: /home/emptyChild` because we skip siblings of `emptyChild`. But wait. Isn't `/home/child` a sibling? It is. But the visitor goes in order. Since `child` was seen before `emptyChild`, it is too late to skip it. Just like when you print a document, it is too late to prevent pages from printing that have already printed. File visitor can only skip subtrees that it has not encountered yet.

PathMatcher

`DirectoryStream` and `FileVisitor` allowed us to go through the files that exist. Things can get complicated fast, though. Imagine you had a requirement to print out the names of all text files in any subdirectory of "password." You might be wondering why anyone would want to do this. Maybe a teammate foolishly stored passwords for everyone to see and you want to make sure nobody else did that. You could write logic to keep track of the directory structure, but that makes the code harder to read and understand. By the end of this section, you'll know a better way.

Let's start out with a simpler example to see what a `PathMatcher` can do:

```
Path path1 = Paths.get("/home/One.txt");
Path path2 = Paths.get("One.txt");
PathMatcher matcher = FileSystems.getDefault()  // get the PathMatcher
        .getPathMatcher(                          // for the right file system
        "glob:*.txt");                            // wait. What's a glob?
System.out.println(matcher.matches(path1));
System.out.println(matcher.matches(path2));
```

which outputs:

```
false
true
```

We can see that the code checks if a `Path` consists of any characters followed by ".txt." To get a `PathMatcher`, you have to call `FileSystems` `.getDefault().getPathMatcher` because matching works differently on different operating systems. `PathMatchers` use a new type that you probably haven't seen before called a glob. Globs are not regular expressions, although they might look similar at first. Let's look at some more examples of globs using a common method so we don't have to keep reading the same "boilerplate" code. (Boilerplate code is the part of the code that is always the same.)

```
public void matches(Path path, String glob) {
  PathMatcher matcher = FileSystems.getDefault().getPathMatcher(glob);
  System.out.println(matcher.matches(path));
}
```

In the world of globs, one asterisk means "match any character except for a directory boundary." Two asterisks means "match any character, including a directory boundary."

```
Path path = Paths.get("/com/java/One.java");
matches(path, "glob:*.java");      // false
matches(path, "glob:**/*.java");   // true
matches(path, "glob:*");           // false
matches(path, "glob:**");          // true
```

Remember that we are using a file system–specific `PathMatcher`. This means slashes and backslashes can be treated differently, depending on what operating system you happen to be running. The previous example does print the same output on both Windows and UNIX because it uses forward slashes. However, if you change just one line of code, the output changes:

```
Path path = Paths.get("com\\java\\One.java");
```

Now Windows still prints:

```
false
true
false
true
```

However, UNIX prints:

```
true
false
true
true
```

Why? Because UNIX doesn't see the backslash as a directory boundary. The lesson here is to use / instead of \ \ so your code behaves more predictably across operating systems.

Now let's match files with a four-character extension. A question mark matches any character. A character could be a letter or a number or anything else.

```
Path path1 = Paths.get("One.java");
Path path2 = Paths.get("One.ja^a");
matches(path1, "glob:*.????");      // true
matches(path1, "glob:*.???");       // false
matches(path2, "glob:*.????");      // true
matches(path2, "glob:*.???");       // false
```

Globs also provide a nice way to match multiple patterns. Suppose we want to match anything that begins with the names Kathy or Bert:

```
Path path1 = Paths.get("Bert-book");
Path path2 = Paths.get("Kathy-horse");
matches(path1, "glob:{Bert*,Kathy*}");    // true
matches(path2, "glob:{Bert,Kathy}*");     // true
matches(path1, "glob:{Bert,Kathy}");      // false
```

The first glob shows we can put wildcards inside braces to have multiple glob expressions. The second glob shows that we can put common wildcards outside the braces to share them. The third glob shows that without the wildcard, we will only match the literal strings "Bert" and "Kathy."

You can also use sets of characters like `[a-z]` or `[#$%]` in globs just like in regular expressions. You can also escape special characters with a backslash. Let's put this all together with a tricky example:

```
Path path1 = Paths.get("0*b/test/1");
Path path2 = Paths.get("9\\*b/test/1");
Path path3 = Paths.get("01b/test/1");
Path path4 = Paths.get("0*b/1");
String glob = "glob:[0-9]\\*{A*,b}/**/1";
matches(path1, glob);                      // true
matches(path2, glob);                      // false
matches(path3, glob);                      // false
matches(path4, glob);                      // false
```

Spelling out what the glob does, we have the following:

- **[0-9]**   One single digit. Can also be read as any one character from 0 to 9.
- *****   The literal character asterisk rather than the asterisk that means to match anything. A single backslash before * escapes it. However, Java won't let you type a single backslash, so you have to escape the backslash itself with another backslash.
- **{A*,b}**   Either a capital *A* followed by anything or the single character *b*.
- **/**/**   One or more directories with any name.
- **1**   The single character 1.

TABLE 5-9

Glob vs. Regular
Expression

What to Match	In a Glob	In a Regular Expression
Zero or more of any character, including a directory boundary	`**`	`.*`
Zero or more of any character, not including a directory boundary	`*`	N/A – no special syntax
Exactly one character	`?`	`.`
Any digit	`[0-9]`	`[0-9]`
Begins with cat or dog	`{cat, dog}*`	`(cat|dog).*`

The second path doesn't match because it has the literal backslash followed by the literal asterisk. The glob was looking for the literal asterisk by itself. The third path also doesn't match because there is no literal asterisk. The fourth path doesn't match because there is no directory between "b" and "1" for the `**` to match. Luckily, nobody would write such a crazy, meaningless glob. But if you can understand this one, you are all set. Globs tend to be simple expressions like `{*.txt,*.html}` when used for real.

Since globs are just similar enough to regular expressions to be tricky, Table 5-9 reviews the similarities and differences in common expressions. Regular expressions are more powerful, but globs focus on what you are likely to need when matching filenames.

By now, you've probably noticed that we are dealing with `Path` objects, which means they don't actually need to exist on the file system. But we wanted to print out all the text files that actually exist in a subdirectory of password. Luckily, we can combine the power of `PathMatchers` with what we already know about walking the file tree to accomplish this.

```
public class MyPathMatcher extends SimpleFileVisitor<Path> {
  private PathMatcher matcher =
    FileSystems.getDefault().getPathMatcher(
    "glob:**/password/**.txt");                    // ** means any subdirectory
  public FileVisitResult visitFile(Path file, BasicFileAttributes attrs)
    throws IOException {
    if (matcher.matches(file)) {
      System.out.println(file);
    }
    return FileVisitResult.CONTINUE;
  }
}
```

```
public static void main(String[] args) throws Exception {
  MyPathMatcher dirs = new MyPathMatcher();
  Files.walkFileTree(Paths.get("/"),  dirs);  // start with root
}
}
```

The code looks similar, regardless of what you want to do. You just change the glob pattern to what you actually want to match.

WatchService

The last thing you need to know about in NIO.2 is WatchService. Suppose you are writing an installer program. You check that the directory you are about to install into is empty. If not, you want to wait until the user manually deletes that directory before continuing. Luckily, you won't have to write this code from scratch, but you should be familiar with the concepts. Here's the directory tree:

```
/dir
  | - directoryToDelete
  | - other
```

Here's the code snippet:

```
Path dir = Paths.get("/dir");                         // get directory containing
                                                      // file/directory we care
                                                      // about
WatchService watcher = FileSystems.getDefault()       // file system-specific code
      .newWatchService();                             // create empty WatchService
dir.register(watcher, ENTRY_DELETE);                  // needs a static import!
                                                      // start watching for
                                                      // deletions
while (true) {                                        // loop until say to stop
  WatchKey key;
  try {
    key = watcher.take();                             // wait for a deletion
  } catch (InterruptedException x) {
      return;                                         // give up if something goes
                                                      // wrong
  }
  for (WatchEvent<?> event : key.pollEvents()) {
    WatchEvent.Kind<?> kind = event.kind();
    System.out.println(kind.name());                  // create/delete/modify
    System.out.println(kind.type());                  // always a Path for us
    System.out.println(event.context());              // name of the file
    String name = event.context().toString();
    if (name.equals("directoryToDelete")) {           // only delete right directory
      System.out.format("Directory deleted, now we can proceed");
```

```
        return;                                 // end program, we found what
                                                // we were waiting for
    }
  }
  key.reset();                                  // keep looking for events
}
```

Supposing we delete directory "`other`" followed by directory `directoryToDelete`, this outputs:

```
ENTRY_DELETE
interface java.nio.file.Path
other
ENTRY_DELETE
interface java.nio.file.Path
directoryToDelete
Directory deleted, now we can proceed
```

Notice that we had to watch the directory that contains the files or directories we are interested in. This is why we watched `/dir` instead of `/dir/directoryToDelete`. This is also why we had to check the context to make sure the directory we were actually interested in is the one that was deleted.

The basic flow of `WatchService` stays the same, regardless of what you want to do:

1. Create a new `WatchService`.
2. Register it on a `Path` listening to one or more event types.
3. Loop until you are no longer interested in these events.
4. Get a `WatchKey` from the `WatchService`.
5. Call `key.pollEvents` and do something with the events.
6. Call `key.reset` to look for more events.

Let's look at some of these in more detail. You register the `WatchService` on a `Path` using statements like the following:

```
dir1.register(watcher, ENTRY_DELETE);
dir2.register(watcher, ENTRY_DELETE, ENTRY_CREATE);
dir3.register(watcher, ENTRY_DELETE, ENTRY_CREATE, ENTRY_MODIFY);
```

(Note: These ENTRY_XXX constants can be found in the `StandardWatchEventKinds` class. Here and in later code, you'll probably want to create static imports for these constants.) You can register one, two, or three of the event types. ENTRY_DELETE means you want your program to be informed when a file or directory has been deleted. Similarly, ENTRY_CREATE means a new file or directory has been created. ENTRY_MODIFY means a file has been edited in the directory. These changes can be made manually by a human or by another program on the computer.

Renaming a file or directory is interesting, as it does not show up as ENTRY_ MODIFY. From Java's point of view, a rename is equivalent to creating a new file and deleting the original. This means that two events will trigger for a rename— both ENTRY_CREATE and ENTRY_DELETE. Actually editing a file will show up as ENTRY_MODIFY.

To loop through the events, we use while(true). It might seem a little odd to write a loop that never ends. Normally, there is a break or return statement in the loop so you stop looping once whatever event you were waiting for has occurred. It's also possible you want the program to run until you kill or terminate it at the command line.

Within the loop, you need to get a WatchKey. There are two ways to do this. The most common is to call take(), which waits until an event is available. It throws an InterruptedException if it gets interrupted without finding a key. This allows you to end the program. The other way is to call poll(), which returns null if an event is not available. You can provide optional timeout parameters to wait up to a specific period of time for an event to show up.

```
watcher.take();                          // wait "forever" for an event
watcher.poll();                          // get event if present right NOW
watcher.poll(10, TimeUnit.SECONDS);      // wait up to 10 seconds for an event
watcher.poll(1, TimeUnit.MINUTES);       // wait up to 1 minute for an event
```

Next, you loop through any events on that key. In the case of rename, you'll get one key with two events—the EVENT_CREATE and EVENT_DELETE. Remember that you get all the events that happened since the last time you called poll() or take(). This means you can get multiple seemingly unrelated events out of the same key. They can be from different files but are for the same WatchService.

```
for (WatchEvent<?> event : key.pollEvents()) {
```

Finally, you call key.reset(). This is very important. If you forget to call reset, the program will work for the first event, but then you will not be notified of any other events.

There are a few limitations you should be aware of with `WatchService`. *To begin with, it is slow. You could easily wait five seconds for the event to register. It also isn't 100 percent reliable. You can add code to check whether* `kind == OVERFLOW`, *but that just tells you something went wrong. You don't know what events you lost. In practice, you are unlikely to use* `WatchService`.

`WatchService` only watches the files and directories immediately beneath it. What if we want to watch to see if either p.txt or c.txt is modified?

```
/dir
  | - parent
        | - p.txt
        | - child
              | - c.txt
```

One way is to register both directories:

```
WatchService watcher =
  FileSystems.getDefault().newWatchService();
Path dir = Paths.get("/dir/parent");
dir.register(watcher, ENTRY_MODIFY);
Path child = Paths.get("dir/parent/child");
child.register(watcher, ENTRY_MODIFY);
```

This works. You can type in all the directories you want to watch. If we had a lot of child directories, this would quickly get to be too much work. Instead, we can have Java do it for us:

```
Path myDir = Paths.get("/dir/parent");
final WatchService watcher =                    // final so visitor can use it
  FileSystems.getDefault().newWatchService();
Files.walkFileTree(myDir, new SimpleFileVisitor<Path>() {
  public FileVisitResult preVisitDirectory(Path dir,
      BasicFileAttributes attrs) throws IOException {
      dir.register(watcher, ENTRY_MODIFY);     // watch each directory
      return FileVisitResult.CONTINUE;
  }
});
```

This code goes through the file tree recursively registering each directory with the watcher. The NIO.2 classes are designed to work together. For example, we could add `PathMatcher` to the previous example to only watch directories that have a specific pattern in their path.

CERTIFICATION OBJECTIVE

Serialization (Objective 8.2)

8.2   Use BufferedReader, BufferedWriter, File, FileReader, FileWriter, FileInputStream, FileOutputStream, ObjectOutputStream, ObjectInputStream, and PrintWriter in the java.io package.

Imagine you want to save the state of one or more objects. If Java didn't have serialization (as the earliest version did not), you'd have to use one of the I/O classes to write out the state of the instance variables of all the objects you want to save. The worst part would be trying to reconstruct new objects that were virtually identical to the objects you were trying to save. You'd need your own protocol for the way in which you wrote and restored the state of each object, or you could end up setting variables with the wrong values. For example, imagine you stored an object that has instance variables for height and weight. At the time you save the state of the object, you could write out the height and weight as two `ints` in a file, but the order in which you write them is crucial. It would be all too easy to re-create the object but mix up the height and weight values—using the saved height as the value for the new object's weight and vice versa.

Serialization lets you simply say "save this object and all of its instance variables." Actually, it is a little more interesting than that because you can add, "...unless I've explicitly marked a variable as `transient`, which means, don't include the transient variable's value as part of the object's serialized state."

Working with ObjectOutputStream and ObjectInputStream

The magic of basic serialization happens with just two methods: one to serialize objects and write them to a stream, and a second to read the stream and deserialize objects.

```
ObjectOutputStream.writeObject()    // serialize and write

ObjectInputStream.readObject()      // read and deserialize
```

The `java.io.ObjectOutputStream` and `java.io.ObjectInputStream` classes are considered to be *higher*-level classes in the java.io package, and as we learned earlier, that means you'll wrap them around *lower*-level classes, such as `java.io.FileOutputStream` and `java.io.FileInputStream`. Here's a small program that creates a `Cat` object, serializes it, and then deserializes it:

```
import java.io.*;

class Cat implements Serializable { }        // 1

public class SerializeCat {
  public static void main(String[] args) {
    Cat c = new Cat();                          // 2
    try {
      FileOutputStream fs = new FileOutputStream("testSer.ser");
      ObjectOutputStream os = new ObjectOutputStream(fs);
      os.writeObject(c);                        // 3
      os.close();
    } catch (Exception e) { e.printStackTrace(); }

    try {
      FileInputStream fis = new FileInputStream("testSer.ser");
      ObjectInputStream ois = new ObjectInputStream(fis);
      c = (Cat) ois.readObject();               // 4
      ois.close();
    } catch (Exception e) { e.printStackTrace(); }
  }
}
```

Let's take a look at the key points in this example:

1. We declare that the `Cat` class implements the `Serializable` interface. `Serializable` is a marker interface; it has no methods to implement. (In the next several sections, we'll cover various rules about when you need to declare classes `Serializable`.)

2. We make a new `Cat` object, which as we know is serializable.

3. We serialize the `Cat` object c by invoking the `writeObject()` method. It took a fair amount of preparation before we could actually serialize our `Cat`. First, we had to put all of our I/O-related code in a try/catch block. Next, we had to create a `FileOutputStream` to write the object to. Then, we wrapped the `FileOutputStream` in an `ObjectOutputStream`, which is the class that has the magic serialization method that we need. Remember that the invocation of `writeObject()` performs two tasks: it serializes the object, and then it writes the serialized object to a file.

4. We de-serialize the `Cat` object by invoking the `readObject()` method. The `readObject()` method returns an `Object`, so we have to cast the deserialized object back to a `Cat`. Again, we had to go through the typical I/O hoops to set this up.

This is a bare-bones example of serialization in action. Over the next few pages, we'll look at some of the more complex issues that are associated with serialization.

Object Graphs

What does it really mean to save an object? If the instance variables are all primitive types, it's pretty straightforward. But what if the instance variables are themselves references to *objects*? What gets saved? Clearly in Java it wouldn't make any sense to save the actual value of a reference variable, because the value of a Java reference has meaning only within the context of a single instance of a JVM. In other words, if you tried to restore the object in another instance of the JVM, even running on the same computer on which the object was originally serialized, the reference would be useless.

But what about the object that the reference refers to? Look at this class:

```
class Dog {
   private Collar theCollar;
   private int dogSize;
   public Dog(Collar collar, int size) {
     theCollar = collar;
     dogSize = size;
   }
   public Collar getCollar() { return theCollar; }
}
class Collar {
   private int collarSize;
   public Collar(int size) { collarSize = size; }
   public int getCollarSize() { return collarSize; }
}
```

Now make a dog... First, you make a `Collar` for the `Dog`:

```
Collar c = new Collar(3);
```

Then make a new `Dog`, passing it the `Collar`:

```
Dog d = new Dog(c, 8);
```

Now what happens if you save the `Dog`? If the goal is to save and then restore a `Dog`, and the restored `Dog` is an exact duplicate of the `Dog` that was saved, then the `Dog` needs a `Collar` that is an exact duplicate of the `Dog`'s `Collar` at the time the `Dog` was saved. That means both the `Dog` and the `Collar` should be saved.

And what if the `Collar` itself had references to other objects—perhaps a `Color` object? This gets quite complicated very quickly. If it were up to the programmer to know the internal structure of each object the `Dog` referred to, so that the programmer could be sure to save all the state of all those objects...whew. That would be a nightmare with even the simplest of objects.

Fortunately, the Java serialization mechanism takes care of all of this. When you serialize an object, Java serialization takes care of saving that object's entire "object graph." That means a deep copy of everything the saved object needs to be restored. For example, if you serialize a `Dog` object, the `Collar` will be serialized automatically. And if the `Collar` class contained a reference to another object, *that* object would also be serialized, and so on. And the only object you have to worry about saving and restoring is the `Dog`. The other objects required to fully reconstruct that `Dog` are saved (and restored) automatically through serialization.

Remember, you do have to make a conscious choice to create objects that are serializable by implementing the `Serializable` interface. If we want to save `Dog` objects, for example, we'll have to modify the `Dog` class as follows:

```
class Dog implements Serializable {
   // the rest of the code as before
   // Serializable has no methods to implement
}
```

And now we can save the `Dog` with the following code:

```
import java.io.*;
public class SerializeDog {
  public static void main(String[] args) {
    Collar c = new Collar(3);
    Dog d = new Dog(c, 8);
    try {
      FileOutputStream fs = new FileOutputStream("testSer.ser");
      ObjectOutputStream os = new ObjectOutputStream(fs);
      os.writeObject(d);
      os.close();
    } catch (Exception e) { e.printStackTrace(); }
  }
}
```

But when we run this code we get a runtime exception, something like this

```
java.io.NotSerializableException: Collar
```

What did we forget? The `Collar` class must *also* be `Serializable`. If we modify the `Collar` class and make it serializable, then there's no problem:

```
class Collar implements Serializable {
  // same
}
```

Here's the complete listing:

```java
import java.io.*;
public class SerializeDog {
  public static void main(String[] args) {
    Collar c = new Collar(3);
    Dog d = new Dog(c, 5);
    System.out.println("before: collar size is "
                       + d.getCollar().getCollarSize());
    try {
      FileOutputStream fs = new FileOutputStream("testSer.ser");
      ObjectOutputStream os = new ObjectOutputStream(fs);
      os.writeObject(d);
      os.close();
    } catch (Exception e) { e.printStackTrace(); }
    try {
      FileInputStream fis = new FileInputStream("testSer.ser");
      ObjectInputStream ois = new ObjectInputStream(fis);
      d = (Dog) ois.readObject();
      ois.close();
    } catch (Exception e) { e.printStackTrace(); }

    System.out.println("after:  collar size is "
                       + d.getCollar().getCollarSize());
  }
}
class Dog implements Serializable {
  private Collar theCollar;
  private int dogSize;
  public Dog(Collar collar, int size) {
    theCollar = collar;
    dogSize = size;
  }
  public Collar getCollar() { return theCollar; }
}
class Collar implements Serializable {
  private int collarSize;
  public Collar(int size) { collarSize = size; }
  public int getCollarSize() { return collarSize; }
}
```

This produces the output:

```
before: collar size is 3
after:  collar size is 3
```

But what would happen if we didn't have access to the `Collar` class source code? In other words, what if making the `Collar` class serializable was not an option? Are we stuck with a non-serializable `Dog`?

Obviously, we could subclass the `Collar` class, mark the subclass as `Serializable`, and then use the `Collar` subclass instead of the `Collar` class. But that's not always an option either for several potential reasons:

1. The `Collar` class might be final, preventing subclassing.

   OR

2. The `Collar` class might itself refer to other non-serializable objects, and without knowing the internal structure of `Collar`, you aren't able to make all these fixes (assuming you even wanted to *try* to go down that road).

   OR

3. Subclassing is not an option for other reasons related to your design.

So...*then* what do you do if you want to save a Dog?

That's where the `transient` modifier comes in. If you mark the Dog's `Collar` instance variable with `transient`, then serialization will simply skip the `Collar` during serialization:

```
class Dog implements Serializable {
    private transient Collar theCollar;   // add transient
    // the rest of the class as before
}

class Collar {                   // no longer Serializable
    // same code
}
```

Now we have a `Serializable Dog`, with a non-`Serializable Collar`, but the `Dog` has marked the `Collar transient`; the output is

```
before: collar size is 3
Exception in thread "main" java.lang.NullPointerException
```

So now what can we do?

Using writeObject and readObject

Consider the problem: we have a `Dog` object we want to save. The `Dog` has a `Collar`, and the `Collar` has state that should also be saved as part of the Dog's state. But...the `Collar` is not `Serializable`, so we must mark it `transient`. That means when the `Dog` is deserialized, it comes back with a null `Collar`. What can we do to somehow make sure that when the `Dog` is deserialized, it gets a new `Collar` that matches the one the `Dog` had when the `Dog` was saved?

Java serialization has a special mechanism just for this—a set of private methods you can implement in your class that, if present, will be invoked automatically during serialization and deserialization. It's almost as if the methods were defined in the `Serializable` interface, except they aren't. They are part of a special callback contract the serialization system offers you that basically says, "If you (the programmer) have a pair of methods matching this exact signature (you'll see them in a moment), these methods will be called during the serialization/deserialization process.

These methods let you step into the middle of serialization and deserialization. So they're perfect for letting you solve the `Dog`/`Collar` problem: when a `Dog` is being saved, you can step into the middle of serialization and say, "By the way, I'd like to add the state of the `Collar`'s variable (an `int`) to the stream when the `Dog` is serialized." You've manually added the state of the `Collar` to the `Dog`'s serialized representation, even though the `Collar` itself is not saved.

Of course, you'll need to restore the `Collar` during deserialization by stepping into the middle and saying, "I'll read that extra `int` I saved to the `Dog` stream, and use it to create a new `Collar`, and then assign that new `Collar` to the `Dog` that's being deserialized." The two special methods you define must have signatures that look *exactly* like this:

```
private void writeObject(ObjectOutputStream os) {
  // your code for saving the Collar variables
}


private void readObject(ObjectInputStream is) {
  // your code to read the Collar state, create a new Collar,
  // and assign it to the Dog
}
```

Yes, we're going to write methods that have the same name as the ones we've been calling! Where do these methods go? Let's change the `Dog` class:

```
class Dog implements Serializable {
  transient private Collar theCollar; // we can't serialize this
  private int dogSize;
  public Dog(Collar collar, int size) {
    theCollar = collar;
    dogSize = size;
  }
  public Collar getCollar() { return theCollar; }
  private void writeObject(ObjectOutputStream os) {
    //  throws IOException {                              // 1
    try {
    os.defaultWriteObject();                              // 2
```

```
            os.writeInt(theCollar.getCollarSize());              // 3
         } catch (Exception e) { e.printStackTrace(); }
      }
      private void readObject(ObjectInputStream is) {
         //   throws IOException, ClassNotFoundException {   // 4
         try {
         is.defaultReadObject();                              // 5
         theCollar = new Collar(is.readInt());                // 6
         } catch (Exception e) { e.printStackTrace(); }
      }
   }
```

In our scenario we've agreed that, for whatever real-world reason, we can't serialize a `Collar` object, but we want to serialize a `Dog`. To do this we're going to implement `writeObject()` and `readObject()`. By implementing these two methods you're saying to the compiler: "If anyone invokes `writeObject()` or `readObject()` concerning a `Dog` object, use this code as part of the read and write."

Let's take a look at the preceding code.

1. Like most I/O-related methods `writeObject()` can throw exceptions. You can declare them or handle them, but we recommend handling them.

2. When you invoke `defaultWriteObject()` from within `writeObject()`, you're telling the JVM to do the normal serialization process for this object. When implementing `writeObject()`, you will typically request the normal serialization process *and* do some custom writing and reading, too.

3. In this case, we decided to write an extra `int` (the collar size) to the stream that's creating the serialized `Dog`. You can write extra stuff before and/or after you invoke `defaultWriteObject()`. But...when you read it back in, you have to read the extra stuff in the same order you wrote it.

4. Again, we chose to handle rather than declare the exceptions.

5. When it's time to deserialize, `defaultReadObject()` handles the normal deserialization you'd get if you didn't implement a `readObject()` method.

6. Finally, we build a new `Collar` object for the `Dog` using the collar size that we manually serialized. (We had to invoke `readInt()` *after* we invoked `defaultReadObject()` or the streamed data would be out of sync!)

Remember, the most common reason to implement `writeObject()` and `readObject()` is when you have to save some part of an object's state manually. If you choose, you can write and read *all* of the state yourself, but that's very rare.

So, when you want to do only a *part* of the serialization/deserialization yourself, you *must* invoke the `defaultReadObject()` and `defaultWriteObject()` methods to do the rest.

Which brings up another question—why wouldn't *all* Java classes be serializable? Why isn't class `Object` serializable? There are some things in Java that simply cannot be serialized because they are runtime specific. Things like streams, threads, runtime, etc., and even some GUI classes (which are connected to the underlying OS) cannot be serialized. What is and is not serializable in the Java API is *not* part of the exam, but you'll need to keep them in mind if you're serializing complex objects.

How Inheritance Affects Serialization

Serialization is very cool, but in order to apply it effectively you're going to have to understand how your class's superclasses affect serialization.

e x a m

ⓦ a t c h

If a superclass is `Serializable`, *then, according to normal Java interface rules, all subclasses of that class automatically implement* `Serializable` *implicitly. In other words, a subclass of a class marked* `Serializable` *passes the IS-A test for* `Serializable` *and thus can be saved without having to explicitly mark the subclass as* `Serializable`. *You simply cannot tell whether a class is or is not* `Serializable` *unless you can see the class inheritance tree to see whether any other superclasses implement* `Serializable`. *If the class does not explicitly extend any other class and does not implement* `Serializable`, *then you know for certain that the class is not* `Serializable`, *because class* `Object` *does not implement* `Serializable`.

That brings up another key issue with serialization...what happens if a superclass is not marked `Serializable`, but the subclass is? Can the subclass still be serialized even if its superclass does not implement `Serializable`? Imagine this:

```
class Animal { }
class Dog extends Animal implements Serializable {
    // the rest of the Dog code
}
```

Now you have a `Serializable` `Dog` class with a non-`Serializable` superclass. This works! But there are potentially serious implications. To fully understand those implications, let's step back and look at the difference between an object that comes from deserialization versus an object created using new. Remember, when an object is constructed using new (as opposed to being deserialized), the following things happen (in this order):

1. All instance variables are assigned default values.

2. The constructor is invoked, which immediately invokes the superclass constructor (or another overloaded constructor, until one of the overloaded constructors invokes the superclass constructor).

3. All superclass constructors complete.

4. Instance variables that are initialized as part of their declaration are assigned their initial value (as opposed to the default values they're given prior to the superclass constructors completing).

5. The constructor completes.

But these things do not happen when an object is deserialized. When an instance of a serializable class is deserialized, the constructor does not run and instance variables are not given their initially assigned values! Think about it—if the constructor were invoked and/or instance variables were assigned the values given in their declarations, the object you're trying to restore would revert back to its original state, rather than coming back reflecting the changes in its state that happened sometime after it was created. For example, imagine you have a class that declares an instance variable and assigns it the int value 3 and includes a method that changes the instance variable value to 10:

```
class Foo implements Serializable {
    int num = 3;
    void changeNum() {  num = 10;    }
}
```

Obviously, if you serialize a Foo instance *after* the changeNum() method runs, the value of the num variable should be 10. When the Foo instance is deserialized, you want the num variable to still be 10! You obviously don't want the initialization (in this case, the assignment of the value 3 to the variable num) to happen. Think of constructors and instance variable assignments together as part of one complete object initialization process (and, in fact, they do become one initialization method in the bytecode). The point is, when an object is deserialized we do not want any of the normal initialization to happen. We don't want the constructor to run, and we don't want the explicitly declared values to be assigned. We want only the values saved as part of the serialized state of the object to be reassigned.

Of course, if you have variables marked `transient`, they will not be restored to their original state (unless you implement `readObject()`), but will instead be given the default value for that data type. In other words, even if you say

```
class Bar implements Serializable {
    transient int x = 42;
}
```

when the `Bar` instance is deserialized, the variable x will be set to a value of 0. Object references marked `transient` will always be reset to `null`, regardless of whether they were initialized at the time of declaration in the class.

So, that's what happens when the object is deserialized, and the class of the serialized object directly extends `Object`, or has only serializable classes in its inheritance tree. It gets a little trickier when the serializable class has one or more non-serializable superclasses.

Getting back to our non-serializable `Animal` class with a serializable `Dog` subclass example:

```
class Animal {
    public String name;
}
class Dog extends Animal implements Serializable {
    // the rest of the Dog code
}
```

Because `Animal` is not serializable, any state maintained in the `Animal` class, even though the state variable is inherited by the `Dog`, isn't going to be restored with the `Dog` when it's deserialized! The reason is, the (unserialized) `Animal` part of the `Dog` is going to be reinitialized, just as it would be if you were making a new `Dog` (as opposed to deserializing one). That means all the things that happen to an object during construction will happen—but only to the `Animal` parts of a `Dog`. In other words, the instance variables from the `Dog`'s class will be serialized and deserialized correctly, but the inherited variables from the non-serializable `Animal` superclass will come back with their default/initially assigned values rather than the values they had at the time of serialization.

If you are a serializable class but your superclass is *not* serializable, then any instance variables you inherit from that superclass will be reset to the values they were given during the original construction of the object. This is because the non-serializable class constructor *will* run!

In fact, every constructor above the first non-serializable class constructor will also run, no matter what, because once the first super constructor is invoked (during deserialization), it, of course, invokes its super constructor and so on, up the inheritance tree.

For the exam, you'll need to be able to recognize which variables will and will not be restored with the appropriate values when an object is deserialized, so be sure to study the following code example and the output:

```
import java.io.*;
class SuperNotSerial {
  public static void main(String [] args) {

    Dog d = new Dog(35, "Fido");
    System.out.println("before: " + d.name + " "
                        + d.weight);
    try {
      FileOutputStream fs = new FileOutputStream("testSer.ser");
      ObjectOutputStream os = new ObjectOutputStream(fs);
      os.writeObject(d);
      os.close();
    } catch (Exception e) { e.printStackTrace(); }
    try {
      FileInputStream fis = new FileInputStream("testSer.ser");
      ObjectInputStream ois = new ObjectInputStream(fis);
      d = (Dog) ois.readObject();
      ois.close();
    } catch (Exception e) { e.printStackTrace(); }

    System.out.println("after:  " + d.name + " "
                        + d.weight);
  }
}
class Dog extends Animal implements Serializable {
  String name;
  Dog(int w, String n) {
    weight = w;          // inherited
    name = n;            // not inherited
  }
}
class Animal {            // not serializable !
  int weight = 42;
}
```

which produces the output:

```
before: Fido 35
after:  Fido 42
```

The key here is that because Animal is not serializable, when the Dog was deserialized, the Animal constructor ran and reset the Dog's inherited weight variable.

watch *If you serialize a collection or an array, every element must be serializable! A single non-serializable element will cause serialization to fail. Note*

also that although the collection interfaces are not serializable, the concrete collection classes in the Java API are.

Serialization Is Not for Statics

Finally, you might have noticed that we've talked only about instance variables, not static variables. Should static variables be saved as part of the object's state? Isn't the state of a static variable at the time an object was serialized important? Yes and no. It might be important, but it isn't part of the instance's state at all. Remember, you should think of static variables purely as *class* variables. They have nothing to do with individual instances. But serialization applies only to *objects*. And what happens if you deserialize three different Dog instances, all of which were serialized at different times and all of which were saved when the value of a static variable in class Dog was different? Which instance would "win"? Which instance's static value would be used to replace the one currently in the one and only Dog class that's currently loaded? See the problem?

Static variables are *never* saved as part of the object's state...because they do not belong to the object!

on the job *As simple as serialization code is to write, versioning problems can occur in the real world. If you save a Dog object using one version of the class, but attempt to deserialize it using a newer different version of the class, deserialization might fail. See the Java API for details about versioning issues and solutions.*

CERTIFICATION SUMMARY

File I/O Remember that objects of type File can represent either files or directories, but that until you call createNewFile() or mkdir(), you haven't actually created anything on your hard drive. Classes in the java.io package are designed to be chained together. You will rarely use a FileReader or a FileWriter without "wrapping" them with a BufferedReader or BufferedWriter object, which gives you access to more powerful, higher-level methods. As of Java 5, the `PrintWriter` class has been enhanced with advanced `append()`, `format()`, and `printf()` methods, and when you couple that with new constructors that allow you to create `PrintWriters` directly from a `String` name or a `File` object, you may use `BufferedWriters` a lot less. The `Console` class allows you to read nonechoed input (returned in a `char[?]`) and is instantiated using `System.console()`.

NIO.2 objects of type `Path` can be files or directories and are a replacement of type `File`. `Paths` are created with `Paths.get()`. Utility methods in `Files` allow you to create, delete, move, copy, or check information about a `Path`. In addition, `BasicFileAttributes`, `DosFileAttributes` (Windows), and `PosixFileAttributes` (UNIX/Linux/Mac) allow you to check more advanced information about a `Path`. `BasicFileAttributeView`, `DosFileAttributeView`, and `PosixFileAttributeView` allow you to update advanced `Path` attributes.

Using a `DirectoryStream` allows you to iterate through a directory. Extending `SimpleFileVisitor` lets you walk a directory tree recursively looking at files and/or directories. With a `PathMatcher`, you can search directories for files using regex-esqu expressions called globs.

Finally, registering a `WatchService` provides notifications for new/changed/removed files or directories.

Serialization   Serialization lets you save, ship, and restore everything you need to know about a *live* object. And when your object points to other objects, they get saved too. The `java.io.ObjectOutputStream` and `java.io.ObjectInputStream` classes are used to serialize and deserialize objects. Typically, you wrap them around instances of `FileOutputStream` and `FileInputStream`, respectively.

The key method you invoke to serialize an object is `writeObject()`, and to deserialize an object invoke `readObject()`. In order to serialize an object, it must implement the `Serializable` interface. Mark instance variables `transient` if you don't want their state to be part of the serialization process. You can augment the serialization process for your class by implementing `writeObject()` and `readObject()`. If you do that, an embedded call to `defaultReadObject()` and `defaultWriteObject()` will handle the normal serialization tasks, and you can augment those invocations with manual *reading from* and *writing to* the stream.

If a superclass implements `Serializable` then all of its subclasses do too. If a superclass doesn't implement `Serializable`, then when a subclass object is deserialized, the unserializable superclass's constructor runs—be careful! Finally, remember that serialization is about instances, so static variables aren't serialized.

TWO-MINUTE DRILL

Here are some of the key points from the certification objectives in this chapter.

File I/O (OCP Objectives 8.1 and 8.2)

☐ The classes you need to understand in `java.io` are `File`, `FileReader`, `BufferedReader`, `FileWriter`, `BufferedWriter`, `PrintWriter`, and `Console`.

☐ A new `File` object doesn't mean there's a new file on your hard drive.

☐ `File` objects can represent either a file or a directory.

☐ The `File` class lets you manage (add, rename, and delete) files and directories.

☐ The methods `createNewFile()` and `mkdir()` add entries to your file system.

☐ `FileWriter` and `FileReader` are low-level I/O classes. You can use them to write and read files, but they should usually be wrapped.

☐ `FileOutputStream` and `FileInputStream` are low-level I/O classes. You can use them to write and read bytes to and from files, but they should usually be wrapped.

☐ Classes in `java.io` are designed to be "chained" or "wrapped." (This is a common use of the decorator design pattern.)

☐ It's very common to "wrap" a `BufferedReader` around a `FileReader` or a `BufferedWriter` around a `FileWriter` to get access to higher-level (more convenient) methods.

☐ `PrintWriters` can be used to wrap other `Writers`, but as of Java 5, they can be built directly from `Files` or `Strings`.

☐ As of Java 5, `PrintWriters` have `append()`, `format()`, and `printf()` methods.

☐ `Console` objects can read nonechoed input and are instantiated using `System.console()`.

Path, Paths, File, and Files (OCP Objectives 9.1 and 9.2)

☐ NIO.2 was introduced in Java 7.

☐ `Path` replaces `File` for a representation of a file or directory.

- ☐ `Paths.get()` lets you create a `Path` object.
- ☐ Static methods in `Files` let you work with `Path` objects.
- ☐ A `Path` object doesn't mean the file or directory exists on your hard drive.
- ☐ The methods `Files.createFile()` and `Files.createDirectory()` add entries to your file system.
- ☐ The `Files` class provides methods to move, copy, and delete `Path` objects.
- ☐ `Files.delete()` throws an exception and `Files.deleteIfExists()` returns false if the file does not exist.
- ☐ On `Path`, `normalize()` simplifies the path representation.
- ☐ On `Path`, `resolve()` and `relativize()` work with the relationship between two path objects.

File Attributes (OCP Objective 9.2)

- ☐ The `Files` class provides methods for common attributes, such as whether the file is executable and when it was last modified.
- ☐ For less common attributes the classes `BasicFileAttributes`, `DosFileAttributes`, and `PosixFileAttributes` read the attributes.
- ☐ `DosFileAttributes` works on Windows operating systems.
- ☐ `PosixFileAttributes` works on UNIX, Linux, and Mac operating systems.
- ☐ Attributes that can't be updated via the `Files` class are set using these classes: `BasicFileAttributeView`, `DosFileAttributeView`, `PosixFileAttributeView`, `FileOwnerAttributeView`, and `AclFileAttributeView`.

Directory Trees, Matching, and Watching for Changes (OCP Objective 9.2)

- ☐ `DirectoryStream` iterates through immediate children of a directory using glob patterns.
- ☐ `FileVisitor` walks recursively through a directory tree.
- ☐ You can override one or all of the methods of `SimpleFileVisitor`— `preVisitDirectory`, `visitFile`, `visitFileFailed`, and `postVisitDirectory`.

☐ You can change the flow of a file visitor by returning one of the `FileVisitResult` constants: CONTINUE, SKIP_SUBTREE, SKIP_SIBLINGS, or TERMINATE.

☐ `PathMatcher` checks if a path matches a glob pattern.

☐ Know what the following expressions mean for globs: `*`, `**`, `?`, and `{a,b}`.

☐ Directories register with `WatchService` to be notified about creation, deletion, and modification of files or immediate subdirectories.

☐ `PathMatcher` and `WatchService` use `FileSystems`-specific implementations.

Serialization (Objective 8.2)

☐ The classes you need to understand are all in the `java.io` package; they include `ObjectOutputStream` and `ObjectInputStream`, primarily, and `FileOutputStream` and `FileInputStream` because you will use them to create the low-level streams that the `ObjectXxxStream` classes will use.

☐ A class must implement `Serializable` before its objects can be serialized.

☐ The `ObjectOutputStream.writeObject()` method serializes objects, and the `ObjectInputStream.readObject()` method deserializes objects.

☐ If you mark an instance variable `transient`, it will not be serialized even though the rest of the object's state will be.

☐ You can supplement a class's automatic serialization process by implementing the `writeObject()` and `readObject()` methods. If you do this, embedding calls to `defaultWriteObject()` and `defaultReadObject()`, respectively, will handle the part of serialization that happens normally.

☐ If a superclass implements `Serializable`, then its subclasses do automatically.

☐ If a superclass doesn't implement `Serializable`, then, when a subclass object is deserialized, the superclass constructor will be invoked along with its superconstructor(s).

SELF TEST

The following questions will help you measure your understanding of the material presented in this chapter. Read all of the choices carefully, as there may be more than one correct answer. Choose all correct answers for each question. Stay focused.

1. Note: The use of "drag-and-drop" questions has come and gone over the years. In case Oracle brings them back into fashion, we threw a couple of them in the book.

   Using the fewest fragments possible (and filling the fewest slots possible), complete the following code so that the class builds a directory named "dir3" and creates a file named "file3" inside "dir3." Note you can use each fragment either zero or one times.

   Code:

```
import java.io._____

class Maker {
  public static void main(String[] args) {

      _____  _____  _____

      _____  _____  _____

      _____  _____  _____

      _____  _____  _____

      _____  _____  _____

      _____  _____  _____

      _____  _____  _____
} }
```

   Fragments:

```
File;         FileDescriptor;      FileWriter;      Directory;
try {         .createNewDir();     File dir         File
{ }           (Exception x)        ("dir3");        file
file          .createNewFile();    = new File       = new File
dir           (dir, "file3");      (dir, file);     .createFile();
} catch       ("dir3", "file3");   .mkdir();        File file
```

2. Given:

```
import java.io.*;

class Directories {
  static String [] dirs = {"dir1", "dir2"};
  public static void main(String [] args) {
    for (String d : dirs) {

      // insert code 1 here

      File file = new File(path, args[0]);

      // insert code 2 here
    }
  }
}
```

and that the invocation

```
java Directories file2.txt
```

is issued from a directory that has two subdirectories, "dir1" and "dir2," and that "dir1" has a file "file1.txt" and "dir2" has a file "file2.txt," and the output is "false true," which set(s) of code fragments must be inserted? (Choose all that apply.)

A. ```
String path = d;
   System.out.print(file.exists() + " ");
```

B. ```
String path = d;
   System.out.print(file.isFile() + " ");
```

C. ```
String path = File.separator + d;
   System.out.print(file.exists() + " ");
```

D. ```
String path = File.separator + d;
   System.out.print(file.isFile() + " ");
```

3. Given:

```
import java.io.*;
public class ReadingFor {
 public static void main(String[] args) {
   String s;
   try {
     FileReader fr = new FileReader("myfile.txt");
     BufferedReader br = new BufferedReader(fr);
     while((s = br.readLine()) != null)
       System.out.println(s);
     br.flush();
   } catch (IOException e) { System.out.println("io error"); }
 }
}
```

And given that `myfile.txt` contains the following two lines of data:

```
ab
cd
```

What is the result?

A. ab

B. abcd

C. ab

   cd

D. a

   b

   c

   d

E. Compilation fails

4. Given:

```
1. import java.io.*;
2. public class Talker {
3.  public static void main(String[] args) {
4.     Console c = System.console();
5.     String u = c.readLine("%s", "username: ");
6.     System.out.println("hello " + u);
7.     String pw;
8.     if(c != null && (pw = c.readPassword("%s", "password: ")) != null)
9.        // check for valid password
10.  }
11. }
```

If line 4 creates a valid `Console` object and if the user enters *fred* as a username and *1234* as a password, what is the result? (Choose all that apply.)

A. username:

    password:

B. username: fred

    password:

C. username: fred

    password: 1234

D. Compilation fails

E. An exception is thrown at runtime

5. Given:

```
3. import java.io.*;
4. class Vehicle { }
5. class Wheels { }
6. class Car extends Vehicle implements Serializable {  }
7. class Ford extends Car { }
8. class Dodge extends Car {
9.  Wheels w = new Wheels();
10. }
```

Instances of which class(es) can be serialized? (Choose all that apply.)

A. Car

B. Ford

C. Dodge

D. Wheels

E. Vehicle

6. Which of the following creates a `Path` object pointing to `c:/temp/exam`? (Choose all that apply.)

A. `new Path("c:/temp/exam")`

B. `new Path("c:/temp", "exam")`

C. `Files.get("c:/temp/exam")`

D. `Files.get("c:/temp", "exam")`

E. `Paths.get("c:/temp/exam")`

F. `Paths.get("c:/temp", "exam")`

7. Given a directory tree at the root of the C: drive and the fact that no other files exist:

```
dir x - |
..........| - dir y
..........| - file a
```

and these two paths:

```
Path one = Paths.get("c:/x");
Path two = Paths.get("c:/x/y/a");
```

Which of the following statements prints out: `y/a`?

A. `System.out.println(one.relativize(two));`

B. `System.out.println(two.relativize(one));`

C. `System.out.println(one.resolve(two));`

D. `System.out.println(two.resolve(one));`

E. `System.out.println(two.resolve(two));`

F. None of the above

8. Given the following statements:

     I.   A nonempty directory can usually be deleted using `Files.delete`

     II. A nonempty directory can usually be moved using `Files.move`

     III. A nonempty directory can usually be copied using `Files.copy`

 Which of the following is true?

 A. I only

 B. II only

 C. III only

 D. I and II only

 E. II and III only

 F. I and III only

 G. I, II, and III

9. Given:

```
new File("c:/temp/test.txt").delete();
```

 How would you write this line of code using Java 7 APIs?

 A. `Files.delete(Paths.get("c:/temp/test.txt"));`

 B. `Files.deleteIfExists(Paths.get("c:/temp/test.txt"));`

 C. `Files.deleteOnExit(Paths.get("c:/temp/test.txt"));`

 D. `Paths.get("c:/temp/test.txt").delete();`

 E. `Paths.get("c:/temp/test.txt").deleteIfExists();`

 F. `Paths.get("c:/temp/test.txt").deleteOnExit();`

10. Given:

```
public void read(Path dir) throws IOException {
  // CODE HERE
    System.out.println(attr.creationTime());
  }
```

 Which code inserted at `// CODE HERE` will compile and run without error on Windows? (Choose all that apply.)

 A. `BasicFileAttributes attr = Files.readAttributes(dir,`
 `BasicFileAttributes.class);`

 B. `BasicFileAttributes attr = Files.readAttributes(dir,`
 `DosFileAttributes.class);`

C. `DosFileAttributes attr = Files.readAttributes(dir,`
   `BasicFileAttributes.class);`

D. `DosFileAttributes attr = Files.readAttributes(dir,`
   `DosFileAttributes.class);`

E. `PosixFileAttributes attr = Files.readAttributes(dir,`
   `PosixFileAttributes.class);`

F. `BasicFileAttributes attr = new BasicFileAttributes(dir);`

G. `BasicFileAttributes attr =dir.getBasicFileAttributes();`

11. Which of the following are true? (Choose all that apply.)

A. The class `AbstractFileAttributes` applies to all operating systems

B. The class `BasicFileAttributes` applies to all operating systems

C. The class `DosFileAttributes` applies to Windows-based operating systems

D. The class `WindowsFileAttributes` applies to Windows-based operating systems

E. The class `PosixFileAttributes` applies to all Linux/UNIX-based operating systems

F. The class `UnixFileAttributes` applies to all Linux/UNIX-based operating systems

12. Given a partial directory tree:

```
dir x - |
.........| - dir y
.........| - file a
```

In what order can the following methods be called if walking the directory tree from x? (Choose all that apply.)

   I: preVisitDirectory x
   II: preVisitDirectory x/y
   III: postVisitDirectory x/y
   IV: postVisitDirectory x
   V: visitFile x/a

A. I, II, III, IV, V

B. I, II, III, V, IV

C. I, V, II, III, IV

D. I, V, II, IV, III

E. V, I, II, III, IV

F. V, I, II, IV, III

13. Given:

```
public class MyFileVisitor extends SimpleFileVisitor<Path> {
  // more code here
  public FileVisitResult visitFile(Path file, BasicFileAttributes attrs)
    throws IOException {
    System.out.println("File " + file);
    if ( file.getFileName().endsWith("Test.java")) {
      // CODE HERE
    }
    return FileVisitResult.CONTINUE;
  }
  // more code here
}
```

Which code inserted at // CODE HERE would cause the FileVisitor to stop visiting files
after it sees the file Test.java?

A. **return** FileVisitResult.CONTINUE;

B. **return** FileVisitResult.END;

C. **return** FileVisitResult.SKIP_SIBLINGS;

D. **return** FileVisitResult.SKIP_SUBTREE;

E. **return** FileVisitResult.TERMINATE;

F. **return** null;

14. Assume all the files referenced by these paths exist:

```
Path a = Paths.get("c:/temp/dir/a.txt");
Path b = Paths.get("c:/temp/dir/subdir/b.txt");
```

What is the correct string to pass to PathMatcher to match both these files?

A. "glob:*/*.txt"

B. "glob:**.txt"

C. "glob:*.txt"

D. "glob:/*/*.txt"

E. "glob:/**.txt"

F. "glob:/*.txt"

G. None of the above

15. Given a partial directory tree at the root of the drive:

```
dir x - |
.........| - file a.txt
.........| - dir y
...................| - file b.txt
..................| - dir y
...........................| - file c.txt
```

And the following snippet:

```
Path dir = Paths.get("c:/x");
try (DirectoryStream<Path> stream = Files.newDirectoryStream(dir, "**/*.txt")) {
for (Path path : stream) {
  System.out.println(path);
} }
```

What is the result?

A. `c:/x/a.txt`

B. `c:/x/a.txt`
   `c:/x/y/b.txt`
   `c:/x/y/z/c.txt`

C. Code compiles but does not output anything

D. Does not compile because `DirectoryStream` comes from `FileSystems`, not `Files`

E. Does not compile for another reason

16. Given a partial directory tree:

```
dir x - |
.........| - dir y
.........| -file a
```

and given that a valid `Path` object, `dir`, points to `x`, and given this snippet:

```
WatchKey key = dir.register(watcher, ENTRY_CREATE);
```

If a `WatchService` is set using the given `WatchKey`, what would be the result if a file is added to `dir y`?

A. No notice is given

B. A notice related to `dir x` is issued

C. A notice related to `dir y` is issued

D. Notices for both `dir x` and `dir y` are given

E. An exception is thrown

F. The behavior depends on the underlying operating system

17. Given:

```
import java.io.*;
class Player {
  Player() { System.out.print("p"); }
}
class CardPlayer extends Player implements Serializable {
  CardPlayer() { System.out.print("c"); }
  public static void main(String[] args) {
    CardPlayer c1 = new CardPlayer();
    try {
```

```
        FileOutputStream fos = new FileOutputStream("play.txt");
        ObjectOutputStream os = new ObjectOutputStream(fos);
        os.writeObject(c1);
        os.close();
        FileInputStream fis = new FileInputStream("play.txt");
        ObjectInputStream is = new ObjectInputStream(fis);
        CardPlayer c2 = (CardPlayer) is.readObject();
        is.close();
    } catch (Exception x ) { }
  }
}
```

What is the result?

A. pc

B. pcc

C. pcp

D. pcpc

E. Compilation fails

F. An exception is thrown at runtime

18. Given:

```
import java.io.*;

class Keyboard { }
public class Computer implements Serializable {
  private Keyboard k = new Keyboard();
  public static void main(String[] args) {
    Computer c = new Computer();
    c.storeIt(c);
  }
  void storeIt(Computer c) {
    try {
      ObjectOutputStream os = new ObjectOutputStream(
        new FileOutputStream("myFile"));
      os.writeObject(c);
      os.close();
      System.out.println("done");
    } catch (Exception x) {System.out.println("exc"); }
  }
}
```

What is the result? (Choose all that apply.)

A. exc

B. done

C. Compilation fails

D. Exactly one object is serialized

E. Exactly two objects are serialized

19. Given:

```
import java.io.*;

public class TestSer {
  public static void main(String[] args) {
    SpecialSerial s = new SpecialSerial();
    try {
      ObjectOutputStream os = new ObjectOutputStream(
        new FileOutputStream("myFile"));
      os.writeObject(s);  os.close();
      System.out.print(++s.z + " ");

      ObjectInputStream is = new ObjectInputStream(
        new FileInputStream("myFile"));
      SpecialSerial s2 = (SpecialSerial)is.readObject();
      is.close();
      System.out.println(s2.y + " " + s2.z);
    } catch (Exception x) {System.out.println("exc"); }
  }
}
class SpecialSerial implements Serializable {
  transient int y = 7;
  static int z = 9;
}
```

Which are true? (Choose all that apply.)

A. Compilation fails

B. The output is 10 0 9

C. The output is 10 0 10

D. The output is 10 7 9

E. The output is 10 7 10

F. In order to alter the standard deserialization process, you would implement the readObject() method in SpecialSerial

G. In order to alter the standard deserialization process, you would implement the defaultReadObject() method in SpecialSerial

SELF TEST ANSWERS

1. ☑ **Answer:**

```
import java.io.File;
class Maker {
  public static void main(String[] args) {
    try {
      File dir = new File("dir3");
      dir.mkdir();
      File file = new File(dir, "file3");
      file.createNewFile();
    } catch (Exception x) { }
  } }
```

Notes: The new File statements don't make actual files or directories, just objects. You need the mkdir() and createNewFile() methods to actually create the directory and the file. While drag-and-drop questions are no longer on the exam, it is still good to be able to complete them. (OCP Objective 8.2)

2. ☑ **A** and **B** are correct. Because you are invoking the program from the directory whose direct subdirectories are to be searched, you don't start your path with a File.separator character. The exists() method tests for either files or directories; the isFile() method tests only for files. Since we're looking for a file, both methods work.
   ☒ **C** and **D** are incorrect based on the above. (OCP Objective 8.2)

3. ☑ **E** is correct. You need to call flush() only when you're writing data. Readers don't have flush() methods. If not for the call to flush(), answer **C** would be correct.
   ☒ **A, B, C,** and **D** are incorrect based on the above. (OCP Objective 8.2)

4. ☑ **D** is correct. The readPassword() method returns a char[]. If a char[] were used, answer **B** would be correct.
   ☒ **A, B, C,** and **E** are incorrect based on the above. (OCP Objective 8.1)

5. ☑ **A** and **B** are correct. Dodge instances cannot be serialized because they "have" an instance of Wheels, which is not serializable. Vehicle instances cannot be serialized even though the subclass Car can be.
   ☒ **C, D,** and **E** are incorrect based on the above. (Pre-OCPJP 7 only)

6. ☑ **E** and **F** are correct since Paths must be created using the Paths.get() method. This method takes a varargs String parameter, so you can pass as many path segments to it as you like.
   ☒ **A** and **B** are incorrect because you cannot construct a Path directly. **C** and **D** are incorrect because the Files class works with Path objects but does not create them from Strings. (Objective 9.1)

7.   ☑   **A** is correct because it prints the path to get to `two` from `one`.
     ☒   **B** is incorrect because it prints out `../..`, which is the path to navigate to `one` from `two`. This is the reverse of what we want. **C, D,** and **E** are incorrect because it does not make sense to call `resolve` with absolute paths. They **might** print out `c:/x/c:/x/y/a`, `c:/x/y/a/c:/x`, and `c:/x/y/a/c:/x/y/a`, respectively. **F** is incorrect because of the above. Note that the directory structure provided is redundant. Neither `relativize()` nor `resolve()` requires either path to actually exist. (OCP Objective 9.1)

8.   ☑   **E** is correct because a directory containing files or subdirectories is copied or moved in its entirety. Directories can only be deleted if they are empty. Trying to delete a nonempty directory will throw a `DirectoryNotEmptyException`. The question says "usually" because copy and move success depends on file permissions. Think about the most common cases when encountering words such as "usually" on the exam.
     ☒   **A, B, C, D, F,** and **G** are incorrect because of the above. (OCP Objective 9.2)

9.   ☑   **B** is correct because, like the Java 7 code, it returns `false` if the file does not exist.
     ☒   **A** is incorrect because this code throws an exception if the file does not exist. **C, D, E,** and **F** are incorrect because they do not compile. There is no `deleteOnExit()` method, and file operations such as delete occur using the `Files` class rather than the path object directly. (OCP Objective 9.2)

10. ☑   **A, B,** and **D** are correct. Creation time is a basic attribute, which means you can read `BasicFileAttributes` or any of its subclasses to read it. `DosFileAttributes` is one such subclass.
     ☒   **C** is incorrect because you cannot cast a more general type to a more specific type. **E** is incorrect because this example specifies it is being run on Windows. Although it would work on UNIX, it throws an `UnsupportedOperationException` on Windows due to requesting the `WindowsFileSystemProvider` to get a POSIX class. **F** and **G** are incorrect because those methods do not exist. You must use the `Files` class to get the attributes. (OCP Objective 9.2)

11. ☑   **B, C,** and **E** are correct. `BasicFileAttributes` is the general superclass. `DosFileAttributes` subclasses `BasicFileAttributes` for Windows operating systems. `PosixFileAttributes` subclasses `BasicFileAttributes` for UNIX/Linux/Mac operating systems.
     ☒   **A, D,** and **F** are incorrect because no such classes exist. (OCP Objective 9.2)

12. ☑   **B** and **C** are correct because file visitor does a depth-first search. When files and directories are at the same level of the file tree, they can be visited in either order. Therefore, "y" and "a" could be reversed. All of the subdirectories and files are visited before `postVisit` is called on the directory.
     ☒   **A, D, E,** and **F** are incorrect because of the above. (OCP Objective 9.2)

13. ☑ **E** is correct because it is the correct constant to end the `FileVisitor`.
☒ **B** is incorrect because END is not defined as a result constant. **A, C,** and **D** are incorrect. Although they are valid constants, they do not end file visiting. CONTINUE proceeds as if nothing special has happened. SKIP_SUBTREE skips the subdirectory, which doesn't even make sense for a Java file. SKIP_SIBLINGS would skip any files in the same directory. Since we weren't told what the file structure is, we can't assume there weren't other directories or subdirectories. Therefore, we have to choose the most general answer of TERMINATE. **F** is incorrect because file visitor throws a `NullPointerException` if null is returned as the result. (OCP Objective 9.2)

14. ☑ **B** is correct. ** matches zero or more characters, including multiple directories.
☒ **A** is incorrect because */ only matches one directory. It will match "temp" but not "c:/temp," let alone "c:/temp/dir." **C** is incorrect because *.txt only matches filenames and not directory paths. **D, E,** and **F** are incorrect because the paths we want to match do not begin with a slash. **G** is incorrect because of the above. (OCP Objective 9.2)

15. ☑ **C** is correct because `DirectoryStream` only looks at files in the immediate directory. **/*.txt means zero or more directories followed by a slash, followed by zero or more characters followed by .txt. Since the slash is in there, it is required to match, which makes it mean one or more directories. However, this is impossible because `DirectoryStream` only looks at one directory. If the expression were simply *.txt, answer **A** would be correct.
☒ **A, B, D,** and **E** are incorrect because of the above. (OCP Objective 9.2).

16. ☑ **A** is correct because `WatchService` only looks at a single directory. If you want to look at subdirectories, you need to set recursive watch keys. This is usually done using a `FileVisitor`.
☒ **B, C, D, E,** and **F** are incorrect because of the above. (OCP Objective 9.2).

17. ☑ **C** is correct. It's okay for a class to implement `Serializable` even if its superclass doesn't. However, when you deserialize such an object, the non-serializable superclass must run its constructor. Remember, constructors don't run on deserialized classes that implement `Serializable`.
☒ **A, B, D, E,** and **F** are incorrect based on the above. (OCP Objective 8.2)

18. ☑ **A** is correct. An instance of type `Computer` Has-a `Keyboard`. Because `Keyboard` doesn't implement `Serializable`, any attempt to serialize an instance of `Computer` will cause an exception to be thrown.
☒ **B, C, D,** and **E** are incorrect based on the above. If `Keyboard` did implement `Serializable`, then two objects would have been serialized. (OCP Objective 8.2)

19. ☑ **C** and **F** are correct. **C** is correct because `static` and `transient` variables are not serialized when an object is serialized. **F** is a valid statement.
☒ **A, B, D,** and **E** are incorrect based on the above. **G** is incorrect because you don't implement the `defaultReadObject()` method; you call it from within the `readObject()` method, along with any custom read operations your class needs. (OCP Objective 8.2)

6
Generics and Collections

G enerics were the most talked about feature of Java 5. Some people love 'em, some people hate 'em, but they're here to stay. At their simplest, they can help make code easier to write and more robust. At their most complex, they can be very, very hard to create and maintain. Luckily, the exam creators stuck to the simple end of generics, covering the most common and useful features and leaving out most of the especially tricky bits. We'll also spend time looking at Java's rich set of classes that allow you to create collections of objects— you know, lists, sets, maps, and queues. It's safe to say that the care and feeding of collections of data is one of the most common programming activities that programmers perform, and the Java API provides a rich and powerful set of classes dedicated to collections.

CERTIFICATION OBJECTIVE

Override hashCode(), equals(), and toString() (OCP Objective 1.4)

1.4   Override hashCode, equals, and toString methods from Object class.

It might not be immediately obvious, but understanding `hashCode()` and `equals()` is essential to working with Java collections, especially when using Maps and when searching and sorting in general.

You're an object. Get used to it. You have state, you have behavior, you have a job. (Or at least your chances of getting one will go up after passing the exam.) If you exclude primitives, everything in Java is an object. Not just an *object*, but an Object with a capital O. Every exception, every event, every array extends from `java.lang.Object`. For the exam, you don't need to know every method in class `Object`, but you will need to know about the methods listed in Table 6-1.

Chapter 10 covers `wait()`, `notify()`, and `notifyAll()`. The `finalize()` method was covered in Chapter 3 of the *OCA Java SE 8 Programmer 1 Exam Guide* (McGraw-Hill Education, 2017). In this section, we'll look at the `hashCode()` and `equals()` methods because they are so often critical when using collections. Oh, that leaves `toString()`, doesn't it? Okay, we'll cover that right now because it takes two seconds.

TABLE 6-1	Methods of Class Object Covered on the Exam

Method	Description
`boolean equals (Object obj)`	Decides whether two objects are meaningfully equivalent
`void finalize()`	Called by the garbage collector when the garbage collector sees that the object cannot be referenced (rarely used, and deprecated in Java 9)
`int hashCode()`	Returns a hashcode int value for an object so that the object can be used in Collection classes that use hashing, including `Hashtable`, `HashMap`, and `HashSet`
`final void notify()`	Wakes up a thread that is waiting for this object's lock
`final void notifyAll()`	Wakes up *all* threads that are waiting for this object's lock
`final void wait()`	Causes the current thread to wait until another thread calls `notify()` or `notifyAll()` on this object
`String toString()`	Returns a "text representation" of the object

The toString() Method

Override `toString()` when you want a mere mortal to be able to read something meaningful about the objects of your class. Code can call `toString()` on your object when it wants to read useful details about your object. When you pass an object reference to the `System.out.println()` method, for example, the object's `toString()` method is called, and the return of `toString()` is shown in the following example:

```
public class HardToRead {
  public static void main (String [] args) {
    HardToRead h = new HardToRead();
    System.out.println(h);
  }
}
```

Running the `HardToRead` class gives us the lovely and meaningful

```
% java HardToRead
HardToRead@a47e0
```

The preceding output is what you get when you don't override the `toString()` method of class `Object`. It gives you the class name (at least that's meaningful) followed by the @ symbol, followed by the unsigned hexadecimal representation of the object's hashcode.

Trying to read this output might motivate you to override the `toString()` method in your classes, for example:

```
public class BobTest {
  public static void main (String[] args) {
    Bob f = new Bob("GoBobGo", 19);
    System.out.println(f);
  }
}
class Bob {
  int shoeSize;
  String nickName;
  Bob(String nickName, int shoeSize) {
    this.shoeSize = shoeSize;
    this.nickName = nickName;
  }
  public String toString() {
    return ("I am a Bob, but you can call me " + nickName +
            ". My shoe size is " + shoeSize);
  }
}
```

This ought to be a bit more readable:

```
% java BobTest
I am a Bob, but you can call me GoBobGo. My shoe size is 19
```

Some people affectionately refer to `toString()` as the "spill-your-guts method" because the most common implementations of `toString()` simply spit out the object's state (in other words, the current values of the important instance variables). That's it for `toString()`. Now we'll tackle `equals()` and `hashCode()`.

Overriding equals()

As we mentioned earlier, you might be wondering why we decided to talk about `Object.equals()` near the beginning of the chapter on collections. We'll be spending a lot of time answering that question over the next pages, but for now, it's enough to know that whenever you need to sort or search through a collection of objects, the `equals()` and `hashCode()` methods are essential. But before we go there, let's look at the more common uses of the `equals()` method.

You learned a bit about the `equals()` method in Chapter 4 of the *OCA Java SE 8 Programmer 1 Exam Guide* (McGraw-Hill Education, 2017). We discussed how comparing two object references using the `==` operator evaluates to `true` only when both references refer to the same object because `==` simply looks at the bits in the variable, and they're either identical or they're not. You saw that the `String` class has overridden the `equals()` method (inherited from the class `Object`), so you could compare two different `String` objects to see if their contents are meaningfully equivalent. Later in this chapter, we'll be discussing the so-called wrapper classes when it's time to put primitive values into collections. For now, remember that there is a wrapper class for every kind of primitive. The folks who created the `Integer` class (to support `int` primitives) decided that if two different `Integer` instances both hold the `int` value 5, as far as you're concerned, they are equal. The fact that the value 5 lives in two separate objects doesn't matter.

When you really need to know if two references are identical, use `==`. But when you need to know if the objects themselves (not the references) are equal, use the `equals()` method. For each class you write, you must decide if it makes sense to consider two different instances equal. For some classes, you might decide that two objects can never be equal. For example, imagine a `class Car` that has instance variables for things like make, model, year, configuration—you certainly don't want your car suddenly to be treated as the very same car as someone with a car that has identical attributes. Your car is your car and you don't want your neighbor Billy driving off in it just because "hey, it's really the same car; the `equals()` method said so." So no two cars should ever be considered exactly equal. If two references refer to one car, then you know that both are talking about one car, not two cars that have the same attributes. In the case of `class Car` you might not ever need, or want, to override the `equals()` method. Of course, you know that isn't the end of the story.

What It Means If You Don't Override equals()

There's a potential limitation lurking here: if you don't override a class's `equals()` method, you won't be able to use those objects as a key in a hashtable and you probably won't get accurate Sets such that there are no conceptual duplicates.

The `equals()` method in class `Object` uses only the `==` operator for comparisons, so unless you override `equals()`, two objects are considered equal only if the two references refer to the same object.

Let's look at what it means to not be able to use an object as a hashtable key. Imagine you have a car, a very specific car (say, John's red Subaru Outback as opposed to Mary's purple Mini) that you want to put in a `HashMap` (a type of hashtable we'll look at later in this chapter) so that you can search on a particular car and retrieve the corresponding `Person` object that represents the owner. So you add the car instance as the key to the `HashMap` (along with a corresponding `Person` object as the value). But now what happens when you want to do a search?

You want to say to the `HashMap` collection, "Here's the car; now give me the `Person` object that goes with this car." But now you're in trouble unless you still have a reference to the exact object you used as the key when you added it to the Collection. *In other words, you can't make an identical `Car` object and use it for the search.*

The bottom line is this: If you want objects of your class to be used as keys for a hashtable (or as elements in any data structure that uses equivalency for searching for—and/or retrieving—an object), then you must override `equals()` so that two different instances can be considered the same. So how would we fix the car? You might override the `equals()` method so it compares the unique VIN (Vehicle Identification Number) as the basis of comparison. That way, you can use one instance when you add it to a Collection and essentially re-create an identical instance when you want to perform a search based on that object as the key. Of course, overriding the `equals()` method for `Car` also allows the potential for more than one object representing a single unique car to exist, which might not be safe in your design. Fortunately, the `String` and wrapper classes work well as keys in hashtables—they override the `equals()` method. So rather than using the actual car instance as the key into the car/owner pair, you could simply use a `String` that represents the unique identifier for the car. That way, you'll never have more than one instance representing a specific car, but you can still use the car—or rather, one of the car's attributes—as the search key.

Implementing an equals() Method

Let's say you decide to override `equals()` in your class. It might look like this:

```
public class EqualsTest {
  public static void main (String [] args) {
    Moof one = new Moof(8);
    Moof two = new Moof(8);
    if (one.equals(two)) {
      System.out.println("one and two are equal");
    }
  }
}
class Moof {
  private int moofValue;
  Moof(int val) {
    moofValue = val;
  }
  public int getMoofValue() {
    return moofValue;
  }
```

```
public boolean equals(Object o) {
  if ((o instanceof Moof) && (((Moof)o).getMoofValue()
      == this.moofValue)) {
    return true;
  } else {
    return false;
  }
 }
}
```

Let's look at this code in detail. In the main() method of EqualsTest, we create two Moof instances, passing the same value 8 to the Moof constructor. Now look at the Moof class and let's see what it does with that constructor argument—it assigns the value to the moofValue instance variable. Now imagine that you've decided two Moof objects are the same if their moofValue is identical. So you override the equals() method and compare the two moofValues. It is that simple. But let's break down what's happening in the equals() method:

```
1. public boolean equals(Object o) {
2.   if ((o instanceof Moof) && (((Moof)o).getMoofValue()
          == this.moofValue)) {
3.      return true;
4.    } else {
5.      return false;
6.    }
7.  }
```

First of all, you must observe all the rules of overriding, and in line 1 we are, indeed, declaring a valid override of the equals() method we inherited from Object.

Line 2 is where all the action is. Logically, we have to do two things in order to make a valid equality comparison.

First, be sure that the object being tested is of the correct type! It comes in polymorphically as type Object, so you need to do an instanceof test on it. Having two objects of different class types be considered equal is usually not a good idea, but that's a design issue we won't go into here. Besides, you'd still have to do the instanceof test just to be sure you could cast the object argument to the correct type so you can access its methods or variables in order to actually do the comparison. Remember, if the object doesn't pass the instanceof test, then you'll get a runtime ClassCastException. For example:

```
public boolean equals(Object o) {
  if (((Moof)o).getMoofValue() == this.moofValue){
    // the preceding line compiles, but it's BAD!
    return true;
```

```
    } else {
      return false;
    }
  }
```

The `(Moof)o` cast will fail if `o` doesn't refer to something that IS-A `Moof`.

Second, compare the attributes we care about (in this case, just `moofValue`). Only the developer can decide what makes two instances equal. (For best performance, you're going to want to check the fewest number of attributes.)

In case you were a little surprised by the whole `((Moof)o).getMoofValue()` syntax, we're simply casting the object reference, `o`, Just-In-Time as we try to call a method that's in the `Moof` class but not in `Object`. Remember, without the cast, you can't compile because the compiler would see the object referenced by `o` as simply, well, an `Object`. And since the `Object` class doesn't have a `getMoofValue()` method, the compiler would squawk (technical term). But then, as we said earlier, even with the cast, the code fails at runtime if the object referenced by `o` isn't something that's castable to a `Moof`. So don't ever forget to use the `instanceof` test first. Here's another reason to appreciate the short-circuit `&&` operator—if the `instanceof` test fails, we'll never get to the code that does the cast, so we're always safe at runtime with the following:

```
if ((o instanceof Moof) && (((Moof)o).getMoofValue()
        == this.moofValue)) {
    return true;
} else {
    return false;
}
```

So that takes care of `equals()`...

Whoa...not so fast. If you look at the `Object` class in the Java API spec, you'll find what we call a contract specified in the `equals()` method. A Java contract is a set of rules that should be followed, or rather must be followed, if you want to provide a "correct" implementation as others will expect it to be. Or to put it another way: If you don't follow the contract, your code may still compile and run, but your code (or someone else's) may break at runtime in some unexpected way.

Remember that the `equals()`, `hashCode()`, *and* `toString()` *methods are all* `public`. *The following would not be a valid override of the* `equals()` *method, although it might appear to be if you don't look closely enough during the exam:*

```
class Foo { boolean equals(Object o) { } }
```

And watch out for the argument types as well. The following method is an overload, but not an override of the `equals()` *method:*

```
class Boo { public boolean equals(Boo b) { } }
```

Be sure you're very comfortable with the rules of overriding so that you can identify whether a method from `Object` *is being overridden, overloaded, or illegally redeclared in a class. The* `equals()` *method in class* `Boo` *changes the argument from* `Object` *to* `Boo`, *so it becomes an overloaded method and won't be called unless it's from your own code that knows about this new, different method that happens to also be named* `equals()`.

The equals() Contract

Pulled straight from the Java docs, the `equals()` contract says

- It is **reflexive**. For any reference value x, x.equals(x) should return true.
- It is **symmetric**. For any reference values x and y, x.equals(y) should return true if and only if y.equals(x) returns true.
- It is **transitive**. For any reference values x, y, and z, if x.equals(y) returns true and y.equals(z) returns true, then x.equals(z) must return true.
- It is **consistent**. For any reference values x and y, multiple invocations of x.equals(y) consistently return true or consistently return false, provided no information used in equals() comparisons on the object is modified.
- For any non-null reference value x, x.equals(null) should return false.

And you're so not off the hook yet. We haven't looked at the `hashCode()` method, but `equals()` and `hashCode()` are bound together by a joint contract that specifies if two objects are considered equal using the `equals()` method, then they must have identical hashcode values. So to be truly safe, your rule of thumb should be if you override `equals()`, override `hashCode()` as well. So let's switch over to `hashCode()` and see how that method ties in to `equals()`.

Overriding hashCode()

Hashcodes are typically used to increase the performance of large collections of data. The hashcode value of an object is used by some collection classes (we'll look at the collections later in this chapter). Although you can think of it as kind of an object ID number, it isn't necessarily unique. Collections such as `HashMap` and `HashSet` use the hashcode value of an object to determine how the object should be *stored* in the collection, and the hashcode is used again to help *locate* the object in the collection. For the exam, you do not need to understand the deep implementation details of how the collection classes use hashing, but you do need to know which collections use them (but, um, they all have "hash" in the name, so you should be good there). You must also be able to recognize an appropriate or correct implementation of `hashCode()`. This does not mean legal and does not even mean efficient. It's perfectly legal to have a terribly inefficient hashcode method in your class, as long as it doesn't violate the contract specified in the `Object` class documentation (we'll look at that contract in a moment). So for the exam, if you're asked to pick out an appropriate or correct use of hashcode, don't mistake appropriate for legal or efficient.

Understanding Hashcodes

In order to understand what's appropriate and correct, we have to look at how some of the collections use hashcodes.

Imagine a set of buckets lined up on the floor. Someone hands you a piece of paper with a name on it. You take the name and calculate an integer code from it by using A is 1, B is 2, and so on, adding the numeric values of all the letters in the name together. A given name will always result in the same code; see Figure 6-1.

We don't introduce anything random; we simply have an algorithm that will always run the same way given a specific input, so the output will always be identical for any two identical inputs. So far, so good? Now the way you use that code (and we'll call it a hashcode now) is to determine which bucket to place the piece of paper into (imagine that each bucket represents a different code number you might get). Now imagine that someone comes up and shows you a name and

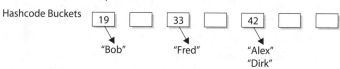

FIGURE 6-1

A simplified
hashcode
example

Key	Hashcode Algorithm	Hashcode
Alex	A(1) + L(12) + E(5) + X(24)	= 42
Bob	B(2) + O(15) + B(2)	= 19
Dirk	D(4) + I(9) + R(18) + K(11)	= 42
Fred	F(6) + R(18) + E(5) + D(4)	= 33

HashMap Collection

Hashcode Buckets

| 19 | | | 33 | | | 42 | | | |

"Bob"   "Fred"   "Alex"
                               "Dirk"

says, "Please retrieve the piece of paper that matches this name." So you look at the name they show you and run the same hashcode-generating algorithm. The hashcode tells you which bucket you should look in to find the name.

You might have noticed a little flaw in our system, though. Two different names might result in the same value. For example, the names Amy and May have the same letters, so the hashcode will be identical for both names. That's acceptable, but it does mean that when someone asks you (the bucket clerk) for the Amy piece of paper, you'll still have to search through the target bucket, reading each name until we find Amy rather than May. The hashcode tells you only which bucket to go into and not how to locate the name once we're in that bucket.

So, for efficiency, your goal is to have the papers distributed as evenly as possible across all buckets. Ideally, you might have just one name per bucket so that when someone asked for a paper, you could simply calculate the hashcode and just grab the one paper from the correct bucket, without having to flip through different papers in that bucket until you locate the exact one you're looking for. The least efficient (but still functional) hashcode generator would return the same hashcode (say, 42), regardless of the name, so that all the papers landed in the same bucket while the others stood empty. The bucket clerk would have to keep going to that one bucket and flipping painfully through each one of the names in the bucket until the right one was found. And if that's how it works, they might as well not use the hashcodes at all, but just go to the one big bucket and start from one end and look through each paper until they find the one they want.

This distributed-across-the-buckets example is similar to the way hashcodes are used in collections. When you put an object in a collection that uses hashcodes, the collection uses the hashcode of the object to decide in which bucket/slot the object should land. Then when you want to fetch that object (or, for a hashtable, retrieve the associated value for that object), you have to give the collection a reference to an object, which it then compares to the objects it holds in the collection. As long as the object stored in the collection, like a paper in the bucket, you're trying to search for has the same hashcode as the object you're using for the search (the name you show to the person working the buckets), then the object will be found. But—and this is a Big One—imagine what would happen if, going back to our name example, you showed the bucket worker a name and they calculated the code based on only half the letters in the name instead of all of them. They'd never find the name in the bucket because they wouldn't be looking in the correct bucket!

Now can you see why if two objects are considered equal, their hashcodes must also be equal? Otherwise, you'd never be able to find the object, since the default hashcode method in class `Object` virtually always comes up with a unique number for each object, even if the `equals()` method is overridden in such a way that two or more objects are considered equal. It doesn't matter how equal the objects are if their hashcodes don't reflect that. So one more time: If two objects are equal, their hashcodes must be equal as well.

Implementing hashCode()

What the heck does a real hashcode algorithm look like? People get their PhDs on hashing algorithms, so from a computer science viewpoint, it's beyond the scope of the exam. The part we care about here is the issue of whether you follow the contract. And to follow the contract, think about what you do in the `equals()` method. You compare attributes because that comparison almost always involves instance variable values (remember when we looked at two `Moof` objects and considered them equal if their `int moofValues` were the same?). Your `hashCode()` implementation should use the same instance variables. Here's an example:

```
class HasHash {
  public int x;
  HasHash(int xVal) { x = xVal; }

  public boolean equals(Object o) {
    HasHash h = (HasHash) o;          // Don't try at home without
                                      // instanceof test
    if (h.x == this.x) {
      return true;
```

```
    } else {
      return false;
    }
  }
  public int hashCode() { return (x * 17); }
}
```

This `equals()` method says two objects are equal if they have the same x value, so objects with the same x value will have to return identical hashcodes.

e x a m
w a t c h
A `hashCode()` that returns the same value for all instances, whether they're equal or not, is still a legal—even appropriate—`hashCode()` method! For example:

```
public int hashCode() { return 1492; }
```

This does not violate the contract. Two objects with an x value of 8 will have the same hashcode. But then again, so will two unequal objects, one with an x value of 12 and the other with a value of -920. This `hashCode()` method is horribly inefficient, remember, because it makes all objects land in the same bucket. Even so, the object can still be found as the collection cranks through the one and only bucket—using `equals()`—trying desperately to finally, painstakingly, locate the correct object. In other words, the hashcode was really no help at all in speeding up the search, even though improving search speed is hashcode's intended purpose! Nonetheless, this one-hash-fits-all method would be considered appropriate and even correct because it doesn't violate the contract. Once more, correct does not necessarily mean good.

Typically, you'll see `hashCode()` methods that do some combination of ^-ing (XOR-ing) a class's instance variables (in other words, twiddling their bits), along with perhaps multiplying them by a prime number. In any case, while the goal is to get a wide and random distribution of objects across buckets, the contract (and whether or not an object can be found) requires only that two equal objects have equal hashcodes. The exam does not expect you to rate the efficiency of a `hashCode()` method, but you must be able to recognize which ones will and will not work ("work" meaning "will cause the object to be found in the collection").

Now that we know that two equal objects must have identical hashcodes, is the reverse true? Do two objects with identical hashcodes have to be considered equal? Think about it—you might have lots of objects land in the same bucket because their hashcodes are identical, but unless they also pass the `equals()` test, they won't come up as a match in a search through the collection. This is exactly what you'd get with our very inefficient everybody-gets-the-same-hashcode method. It's legal and correct, just slooooow.

So in order for an object to be located, the search object and the object in the collection must both have identical hashcode values and return `true` for the `equals()` method. There's just no way out of overriding both methods to be absolutely certain that your objects can be used in Collections that use hashing.

The hashCode() Contract

Now coming to you straight from the fabulous Java API documentation for class `Object`, may we present (drumroll) the `hashCode()` contract:

- Whenever it is invoked on the same object more than once during an execution of a Java application, the `hashCode()` method must consistently return the same integer, provided that no information used in `equals()` comparisons on the object is modified. This integer need not remain consistent from one execution of an application to another execution of the same application.

- If two objects are equal according to the `equals(Object)` method, then calling the `hashCode()` method on each of the two objects must produce the same integer result.

- It is NOT required that if two objects are unequal according to the `equals(java.lang.Object)` method, then calling the `hashCode()` method on each of the two objects must produce distinct integer results. However, the programmer should be aware that producing distinct integer results for unequal objects may improve the performance of hashtables.

And what this means to you is...

Condition	Required	Not Required (But Allowed)
`x.equals(y) == true`	`x.hashCode() == y.hashCode()`	
`x.hashCode() == y.hashCode()`		`x.equals(y) == true`
`x.equals(y) == false`		No `hashCode()` requirements
`x.hashCode() != y.hashCode()`	`x.equals(y) == false`	

So let's look at what else might cause a hashCode() method to fail. What happens if you include a transient variable in your hashCode() method? Although that's legal (the compiler won't complain), under some circumstances, an object you put in a collection won't be found. As you might know, serialization saves an object so it can be reanimated later by deserializing it back to full objectness. But danger, Will Robinson—**transient variables are not saved when an object is serialized**. A bad scenario might look like this:

```
class SaveMe implements Serializable{
  transient int x;
  int y;
   SaveMe(int xVal, int yVal) {
     x = xVal;
     y = yVal;
   }
  public int hashCode() {
     return (x ^ y);                        // Legal, but not correct to
                                            // use a transient variable
  }
  public boolean equals(Object o) {
     SaveMe test = (SaveMe)o;
     if (test.y == y && test.x == x) {  // Legal, not correct
       return true;
     } else {
       return false;
     }
  }
}
```

Here's what could happen using code like the preceding example:

1. Give an object some state (assign values to its instance variables).
2. Put the object in a HashMap, using the object as a key.
3. Save the object to a file using serialization without altering any of its state.
4. Retrieve the object from the file through deserialization.
5. Use the deserialized (brought back to life on the heap) object to get the object out of the HashMap.

Oops. The object in the collection and the supposedly same object brought back to life are no longer identical. The object's transient variable will come back with a default value rather than the value the variable had at the time it was saved (or put into the HashMap). So using the preceding SaveMe code, if the value of x is 9 when the instance is put in the HashMap, then since x is used in the calculation of the hashcode, when the value of x changes, the hashcode changes too. And when that same instance of SaveMe is brought back from deserialization, x == 0, regardless of the value of x at the time the object was serialized. So the new hashcode calculation will give a different hashcode and the equals() method fails as well since x is used to determine object equality.

Bottom line: transient variables can really mess with your equals() and hashCode() implementations. Keep variables non-transient or, if they must be marked transient, don't use them to determine hashcodes or equality.

CERTIFICATION OBJECTIVE

Collections Overview (OCP Objective 3.2)

3.2   Create and use ArrayList, TreeSet, TreeMap, and ArrayDeque objects.

In this section, we're going to present a relatively high-level discussion of the major categories of collections covered on the exam. We'll be looking at their characteristics and uses from an abstract level. In the section after this one, we'll dive into each category of collection and show concrete examples of using each.

Can you imagine trying to write object-oriented applications without using data structures like hashtables or linked lists? What would you do when you needed to maintain a sorted list of, say, all the members in your *Simpsons* fan club? Obviously, you can do it yourself; there must be thousands of algorithm books you can buy. But with the kind of schedules programmers are under today, it's almost too painful to consider.

The Collections Framework in Java, which took shape with the release of JDK 1.2 and was expanded in 1.4 and again in Java 5 and yet again in Java 6, 7, and 8, gives you lists, sets, maps, and queues to satisfy most of your coding needs. They've been tried, tested, and tweaked. Pick the best one for your job, and you'll get good performance. And when you need something a little more custom, the Collections Framework in the java.util package is loaded with interfaces and utilities.

So What Do You Do with a Collection?

There are a few basic operations you'll normally use with collections:

- Add objects to the collection.
- Remove objects from the collection.

- Find out if an object (or group of objects) is in the collection.
- Retrieve an object from the collection without removing it.
- Iterate through the collection, looking at each element (object) one after another.

Key Interfaces and Classes of the Collections Framework

The Collections API begins with a group of interfaces, but also gives you a truckload of concrete classes. The core interfaces you need to know for the exam (and for life in general) are the following nine:

Collection	Set	SortedSet
List	Map	SortedMap
Queue	NavigableSet	NavigableMap

In Chapter 11, which deals with concurrency, we will discuss several classes related to the Deque interface. Other than those, there are 14 concrete implementation classes you need to know for the exam (there are others, but the exam doesn't specifically cover them).

Maps	Sets	Lists	Queues	Utilities
HashMap	HashSet	ArrayList	PriorityQueue	Collections
Hashtable	LinkedHashSet	Vector	ArrayDeque	Arrays
TreeMap	TreeSet	LinkedList		
LinkedHashMap				

Note: In the table above, we listed more classes than are officially mentioned in the Oracle objectives. Oracle's objectives can be on the terse side! The classes we'll talk about fall into three categories:

- **Definitely on the exam:** ArrayList, ArrayDeque, TreeMap, TreeSet, and Arrays
- **Somewhat likely to be on the exam:** Collections, HashMap, Hashtable, and PriorityQueue
- **Unlikely to be on the exam:** HashSet, LinkedHashMap, LinkedHashSet, LinkedList, and Vector

We've included the "unlikelies" because understanding them will give you a better overview of how the key interfaces work. Not all collections in the

FIGURE 6-2   The interface and class hierarchy for collections

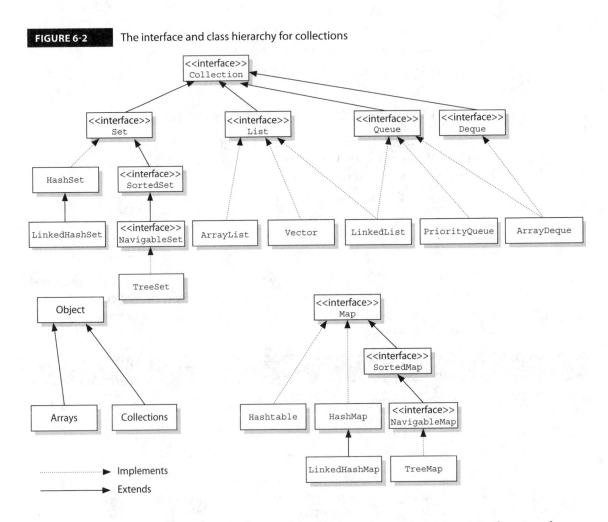

Collections Framework actually implement the `Collection` interface. In other words, not all collections pass the IS-A test for `Collection`. Specifically, none of the `Map`-related classes and interfaces extend from `Collection`. So while `SortedMap`, `Hashtable`, `HashMap`, `TreeMap`, and `LinkedHashMap` are all thought of as collections, none are actually extended from `Collection`-with-a-capital-C (see Figure 6-2). To make things a little more confusing, there are really three overloaded uses of the word "collection":

■ collection (lowercase *c*), which represents any of the data structures in which objects are stored and iterated over.

- Collection (capital *C*), which is actually the `java.util.Collection` interface from which `Set`, `List`, and `Queue` extend. (That's right, extend, not implement. There are no direct implementations of `Collection`.)
- Collections (capital *C* and ends with *s*) is the `java.util.Collections` class that holds a pile of `static` utility methods for use with collections.

You can easily mistake "Collections" for "Collection"—be careful. Keep in mind that Collections is a class, with static utility methods, whereas Collection **is an interface with declarations of the methods common to most collections, including** `add()`, `remove()`, `contains()`, `size()`, **and** `iterator()`.

Collections come in four basic flavors:

- **Lists**   *Lists* of things (classes that implement `List`)
- **Sets**   *Unique* things (classes that implement `Set`)
- **Maps**   Things with a *unique* ID (classes that implement `Map`)
- **Queues**   Things arranged in the order in which they are to be processed

Figure 6-3 illustrates the relative structures of a `List`, a `Set`, and a `Map`.
But there are subflavors within those four flavors of collections:

Sorted	Unsorted	Ordered	Unordered

An implementation class can be unsorted and unordered, ordered but unsorted, or both ordered and sorted. But an implementation can never be sorted but unordered, because sorting is a specific type of ordering, as you'll see in a moment. For example, a `HashSet` is an unordered, unsorted set, whereas a `LinkedHashSet` is an ordered (but not sorted) set that maintains the order in which objects were inserted.

Maybe we should be explicit about the difference between sorted and ordered, but first we have to discuss the idea of iteration. When you think of iteration, you may think of iterating over an array using, say, a `for` loop to access each element in the array in order ([0], [1], [2], and so on). Iterating through a collection usually means walking through the elements one after another, starting from the

FIGURE 6-3

Examples of a
`List`, a `Set`, and
a `Map`

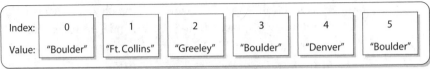

List: The salesman's itinerary (Duplicates allowed)

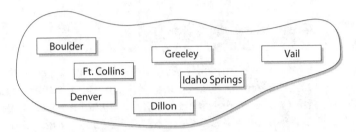

Set: The salesman's territory (No duplicates allowed)

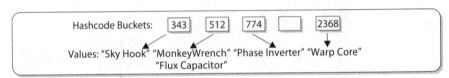

HashMap: The salesman's products (Keys generated from product IDs)

first element. Sometimes, though, even the concept of *first* is a little strange—in a `Hashtable`, there really isn't a notion of first, second, third, and so on. In a `Hashtable`, the elements are placed in a (seemingly) chaotic order based on the hashcode of the key. But something has to go first when you iterate; thus, when you iterate over a `Hashtable`, there will indeed be an order. But as far as you can tell, it's completely arbitrary and can change in apparently random ways as the collection changes.

Ordered   When a collection is ordered, it means you can iterate through the collection in a specific (not random) order. A `Hashtable` collection is not ordered. Although the `Hashtable` itself has internal logic to determine the order (based on hashcodes and the implementation of the collection itself), you won't find any order when you iterate through the `Hashtable`. An `ArrayList`, however, keeps the order established by the elements' index position (just like an array). `LinkedHashSet` keeps the order established by insertion, so the last element inserted is the last element in the `LinkedHashSet` (as opposed to an `ArrayList`, where you can insert an element at a specific index position). Finally, there are some collections that keep an order referred to as the natural order of the elements, and those collections are then not just ordered, but also sorted. Let's look at how natural order works for sorted collections.

Sorted   A sorted collection means that the order in the collection is determined according to some rule or rules, known as the "sort order." A sort order has nothing to do with when an object was added to the collection or when it was last accessed or at what "position" it was added. Sorting is done based on properties of the objects themselves. You put objects into the collection, and the collection will figure out what order to put them in, based on the sort order. A collection that keeps an order (such as any `List`, which uses insertion order) is not really considered sorted unless it sorts using some kind of sort order. Most commonly, the sort order used is something called the "natural order." What does that mean?

You know how to sort alphabetically—*A* comes before *B*, *F* comes before *G*, and so on. For a collection of `String` objects, then, the natural order is alphabetical. For `Integer` objects, the natural order is by numeric value—1 before 2, and so on. And for `Foo` objects, the natural order is...um...we don't know. There is no natural order for `Foo` unless or until the `Foo` developer provides one through an interface (*Comparable*) that defines how instances of a class can be compared to one another (does instance a come before b, or does instance b come before a?). If the developer decides that `Foo` objects should be compared using the value of some instance variable (let's say there's one called `bar`), then a sorted collection will order the `Foo` objects according to the rules in the `Foo` class for how to use the `bar` instance variable to determine the order. Of course, the `Foo` class might also inherit a natural order from a superclass rather than define its own order in some cases.

Aside from natural order as specified by the `Comparable` interface, it's also possible to define other different sort orders using another interface: *Comparator*. We will discuss how to use both `Comparable` and `Comparator` to define sort orders later in this chapter. But for now, just keep in mind that sort order (including natural order) is not the same as ordering by insertion, access, or index.

Now that we know about ordering and sorting, we'll look at each of the four interfaces, and we'll dive into the concrete implementations of those interfaces.

List Interface

A `List` cares about the index. The one thing that `List` has that nonlists don't is a set of methods related to the index. Those key methods include things like `get(int index)`, `indexOf(Object o)`, `add(int index, Object obj)`, and so on. All three `List` implementations are ordered by index position—a position that you determine either by setting an object at a specific index or by adding it without specifying position, in which case the object is added to the end. The three `List` implementations are described in the following sections.

ArrayList   Think of this as a growable array. It gives you fast iteration and fast random access. To state the obvious: It is an ordered collection (by index), but not sorted. `ArrayList` implements the `RandomAccess` interface—a marker interface (meaning it has no methods) that says, "This list supports fast (generally constant time) random access." Choose this over a `LinkedList` when you need fast iteration but aren't as likely to be doing a lot of insertion and deletion.

Vector (Unlikely to Be on the Exam)   `Vector` is a holdover from the earliest days of Java; `Vector` and `Hashtable` were two of the original collections—the rest were added with later versions of Java. A `Vector` is basically the same as an `ArrayList`, but `Vector` methods are synchronized for thread safety. You'll normally want to use `ArrayList` instead of `Vector` because the synchronized methods add a performance hit you might not need. And if you do need thread safety, there are utility methods in class `Collections` that can help. Of the classes discussed here, only `Vector` and `ArrayList` implement `RandomAccess`.

LinkedList (Unlikely to Be on the Exam)   A `LinkedList` is ordered by index position, like `ArrayList`, except that the elements are doubly linked to one another. This linkage gives you new methods (beyond what you get from the `List` interface) for adding and removing from the beginning or end, which makes it an easy choice for implementing a stack or queue. Keep in mind that a `LinkedList` may iterate more slowly than an `ArrayList`, but it's a good choice when you need fast insertion and deletion. As of Java 5, the `LinkedList` class has been enhanced to implement the `java.util.Queue` interface. As such, it now supports the common queue methods `peek()`, `poll()`, and `offer()`.

Set Interface

A `Set` cares about uniqueness—it doesn't allow duplicates. Your good friend the `equals()` method determines whether two objects are identical (in which case, only one can be in the set). The three `Set` implementations are described in the following sections.

HashSet (Unlikely to Be on the Exam)   A `HashSet` is an unsorted, unordered `Set`. It uses the hashcode of the object being inserted, so the more efficient your `hashCode()` implementation, the better access performance you'll get. Use this class when you want a collection with no duplicates and you don't care about order when you iterate through it.

LinkedHashSet (Unlikely to Be on the Exam)   A `LinkedHashSet` is an ordered version of `HashSet` that maintains a doubly linked `List` across all elements. Use this class instead of `HashSet` when you care about the iteration order. When you iterate through a `HashSet`, the order is unpredictable, whereas a `LinkedHashSet` lets you iterate through the elements in the order in which they were inserted.

TreeSet   The `TreeSet` is one of two sorted collections (the other being `TreeMap`). It uses a Red-Black tree structure (but you knew that) and guarantees that the elements will be in ascending order, according to natural order. Optionally, you can construct a `TreeSet` with a constructor that lets you give the collection your own rules for what the order should be (rather than relying on the ordering defined by the elements' class) by using a `Comparator`. As of Java 6, `TreeSet` implements `NavigableSet`.

Map Interface

A `Map` cares about unique identifiers. You map a unique key (the ID) to a specific value, where both the key and the value are, of course, objects. You're probably quite familiar with `Maps` since many languages support data structures that use a key/value or name/value pair. The `Map` implementations let you do things like search for a value based on the key, ask for a collection of just the values, or ask for a collection of just the keys. Like `Sets`, `Maps` rely on the `equals()` method to determine whether two keys are the same or different.

HashMap (Somewhat Likely to Be on the Exam) The HashMap gives you an unsorted, unordered Map. When you need a Map and you don't care about the order when you iterate through it, then HashMap is the way to go; the other maps add a little more overhead. Where the keys land in the Map is based on the key's hashcode, so, like HashSet, the more efficient your hashCode() implementation, the better access performance you'll get. HashMap allows one null key and multiple null values in a collection.

Hashtable (Somewhat Likely to Be on the Exam) Like Vector, Hashtable has existed from prehistoric Java times. For fun, don't forget to note the naming inconsistency: HashMap vs. Hashtable. Where's the capitalization of *t*? Oh well, you won't be expected to spell it. Anyway, just as Vector is a synchronized counterpart to the sleeker, more modern ArrayList, Hashtable is the synchronized counterpart to HashMap. Remember that you don't synchronize a class, so when we say that Vector and Hashtable are synchronized, we just mean that the key methods of the class are synchronized. Another difference, though, is that although HashMap lets you have null values as well as one null key, a Hashtable doesn't let you have anything that's null.

LinkedHashMap (Unlikely to Be on the Exam) Like its Set counterpart, LinkedHashSet, the LinkedHashMap collection maintains insertion order (or, optionally, access order). Although it will be somewhat slower than HashMap for adding and removing elements, you can expect faster iteration with a LinkedHashMap.

TreeMap You can probably guess by now that a TreeMap is a sorted Map. And you already know that, by default, this means "sorted by the natural order of the elements." Like TreeSet, TreeMap lets you define a custom sort order (via a Comparator) when you construct a TreeMap that specifies how the elements should be compared to one another when they're being ordered. As of Java 6, TreeMap implements NavigableMap.

Queue Interface

A Queue is designed to hold a list of "to-dos," or things to be processed in some way. Although other orders are possible, queues are typically thought of as FIFO (first-in, first-out). Queues support all of the standard Collection methods and they also have methods to add and subtract elements and review queue elements.

PriorityQueue (Somewhat Likely to Be on the Exam)   Since the LinkedList class has been enhanced to implement the Queue interface, basic queues can be handled with a LinkedList. The purpose of a PriorityQueue is to create a "priority-in, priority-out" queue as opposed to a typical FIFO queue. A PriorityQueue's elements are ordered either by natural ordering (in which case the elements that are sorted first will be accessed first) or according to a Comparator. In either case, the elements' ordering represents their relative priority.

ArrayDeque   The Deque interface was added in Java 6. Deque (pronounced "deck") is a double-ended queue, meaning you can add and remove items from both ends of the queue. ArrayDeque is one of the Collections that implements this interface, and it is a good choice for implementing either a queue or a stack because it is resizable with no capacity restrictions and it is designed to be high performance (but not thread safe).

e x a m
ⓦatch
You can easily eliminate some answers right away if you recognize that, for example, a Map can't be the class to choose when you need a name/value pair collection, since Map is an interface and not a concrete implementation class.

The wording on the exam is explicit when it matters, so if you're asked to choose an interface, choose an interface rather than a class that implements that interface. The reverse is also true—if you're asked to choose a class, don't choose an interface type.

Table 6-2 summarizes 12 of the 14 concrete collection-oriented classes you'll need to understand for the exam. Even though not all of these classes are listed in the Section 3 objectives, you may encounter them on the exam so it's a good idea to familarize yourself with the classes in this table. (Arrays and Collections are coming right up!)

TABLE 6-2   Collection Interface Concrete Implementation Classes

Class	Map	Set	List	Ordered	Sorted
HashMap	X			No	No
Hashtable	X			No	No
TreeMap	X			Sorted	By *natural order* or custom comparison rules
LinkedHashMap	X			By insertion order or last access order	No
HashSet		X		No	No
TreeSet		X		Sorted	By *natural order* or custom comparison rules
LinkedHashSet		X		By insertion order	No
ArrayList			X	By index	No
Vector			X	By index	No
LinkedList			X	By index	No
PriorityQueue				Sorted	By to-do order
ArrayDeque				By position	No

e x a m

ⓦ a t c h   *Be sure you know how to interpret Table 6-2 in a practical way. For the exam, you might be expected to choose a collection based on a particular requirement, where that need is expressed as a scenario. For example, which collection would you use if you needed to maintain and search on a list of parts identified by their unique alphanumeric serial number where the part would be of type `Part`? Would you change your answer at all if we modified the requirement such that you also need to be able to print out the parts in order by their serial number? For the first question, you can see that since you have a `Part` class but need to search for the objects based on a serial number, you need a `Map`. The key will be the serial number as a `String`, and the value will be the `Part` instance. The default choice should be `HashMap`, the quickest `Map` for access. But now when we amend the requirement to include getting the parts in order of their serial number, then we need a `TreeMap`—which maintains the natural order of the keys. Since the key is a `String`, the natural order for a `String` will be a standard alphabetical sort. If the requirement had been to keep track of which part was last accessed, then we'd probably need a `LinkedHashMap`. But since a `LinkedHashMap` loses the natural order (replacing it with last-accessed order), if we need to list the parts by serial number, we'll have to explicitly sort the collection using a utility method.*

Using Collections (OCP Objectives 2.6, 3.2, and 3.3)

2.6   *Create and use Lambda expressions.*
3.2   *Create and use ArrayList, TreeSet, TreeMap, and ArrayDeque objects.*
3.3   *Use java.util.Comparator and java.lang.Comparable interfaces.*
3.X   *Sort and search arrays and lists.*

We've taken a high-level theoretical look at the key interfaces and classes in the Collections Framework; now let's see how they work in practice.

ArrayList Basics

Let's start with a quick review of what you learned about `ArrayList`s from the previous book, *OCA Java SE 8 Programmer 1 Exam Guide* (McGraw-Hill Education, 2017). The `java.util.ArrayList` class is one of the most commonly used classes in the Collections Framework. It's like an array on vitamins. Some of the advantages `ArrayList` has over arrays are

- It can grow dynamically.
- It provides more powerful insertion and search mechanisms than arrays.

Let's take a look at using an `ArrayList` that contains strings. A key design goal of the Collections Framework was to provide rich functionality at the level of the main interfaces: `List`, `Set`, and `Map`. In practice, you'll typically want to instantiate an `ArrayList` polymorphically, like this:

```
List myList = new ArrayList();
```

Then as of Java 5 (yes, you might still encounter pre–Java 5 code out in the wild), you'd want to say

```
List<String> myList = new ArrayList<String>();
```

This kind of declaration follows the object-oriented programming principle of "coding to an interface," and it makes use of generics. We'll say lots more about generics later in this chapter, but for now, just know that, starting with Java 5, the `<String>` syntax is the way that you declare a collection's type. (Prior to Java 5, there was no way to specify the type of a collection, and when we cover generics, we'll talk about the implications of mixing Java 5 [typed] and pre–Java 5 [untyped] collections.)

In many ways, `ArrayList<String>` is similar to a `String[]` in that it declares a container that can hold only strings, but it's more powerful than a `String[]`. Let's look at some of the capabilities that an `ArrayList` has:

```
List<String> test = new ArrayList<String>();    // declare the ArrayList
String s = "hi";
test.add("string");                             // add some strings
test.add(s);
test.add(s+s);
System.out.println(test.size());                // use ArrayList methods
System.out.println(test.contains(42));
System.out.println(test.contains("hihi"));
test.remove("hi");
System.out.println(test.size());
```

which produces

```
3
false
true
2
```

There's a lot going on in this small program. Notice that when we declared the `ArrayList`, we didn't give it a size. Then we were able to ask the `ArrayList` for its size; we were able to ask whether it contained specific objects; we removed an object right out from the middle of it; and then we rechecked its size.

Autoboxing with Collections

In general, collections can hold objects but not primitives. Prior to Java 5, a common use for the so-called wrapper classes (e.g., `Integer`, `Float`, `Boolean`, and so on) was to provide a way to get primitives into and out of collections. Prior to Java 5, you had to "wrap" a primitive manually before you could put it into a collection. Starting with Java 5, primitives still have to be wrapped, but autoboxing takes care of it for you.

```
List myInts = new ArrayList();    // pre Java 5 declaration
myInts.add(new Integer(42));      // Use Integer to "wrap" an int
```

In the previous example, we create an instance of class `Integer` with a value of 42. We've created an entire object to "wrap around" a primitive value. As of Java 5, we can say:

```
myInts.add(42);                   // autoboxing handles it!
```

In this last example, we are still adding an `Integer` object to `myInts` (not an `int` primitive); it's just that autoboxing handles the wrapping for us. There are some sneaky implications when we need to use wrapper objects; let's take a closer look...

In the old, pre–Java 5 days, if you wanted to make a wrapper, unwrap it, use it, and then rewrap it, you might do something like this:

```
Integer y = new Integer(567);     // make it
int x = y.intValue();             // unwrap it
x++;                              // use it
y = new Integer(x);               // rewrap it
System.out.println("y = " + y);   // print it
```

As of Java 5, you can say

```
Integer y = new Integer(567);     // make it
y++;                              // unwrap it, increment it,
                                 // rewrap it
System.out.println("y = " + y);   // print it
```

Both examples produce the following output:

```
y = 568
```

And yes, you read that correctly. The code appears to be using the postincrement operator on an object reference variable! But it's simply a convenience. Behind the scenes, the compiler does the unboxing and reassignment for you. Earlier, we mentioned that wrapper objects are immutable...this example appears to contradict that statement. It sure looks like y's value changed from 567 to 568. What actually happened, however, is that a second wrapper object was created and its value was set to 568. If only we could access that first wrapper object, we could prove it...

Let's try this:

```
Integer y = 567;                      // make a wrapper
Integer x = y;                        // assign a second ref
                                      // var to THE wrapper

System.out.println(y==x);             // verify that they refer
                                      // to the same object
y++;                                  // unwrap, use, "rewrap"
System.out.println(x + " " + y);      // print values

System.out.println(y==x);             // verify that they refer
                                      // to different objects
```

which produces the output:

```
true
567 568
false
```

So, under the covers, when the compiler got to the line y++; it had to substitute something like this:

```
int x2 = y.intValue();                // unwrap it
x2++;                                 // use it
y = new Integer(x2);                  // rewrap it
```

Just as we suspected, there's gotta be a call to new in there somewhere.

Boxing, ==, and equals()

We just used == to do a little exploration of wrappers. Let's take a more thorough look at how wrappers work with ==, !=, and equals(). The API developers decided that for all the wrapper classes, two objects are equal if they are of the same type and have the same value. It shouldn't be surprising that

```
Integer i1 = 1000;
Integer i2 = 1000;
if(i1 != i2) System.out.println("different objects");
if(i1.equals(i2)) System.out.println("meaningfully equal");
```

produces the output

```
different objects
meaningfully equal
```

It's just two wrapper objects that happen to have the same value. Because they have the same `int` value, the `equals()` method considers them to be "meaningfully equivalent" and, therefore, returns `true`. How about this one?

```
Integer i3 = 10;
Integer i4 = 10;
if(i3 == i4) System.out.println("same object");
if(i3.equals(i4)) System.out.println("meaningfully equal");
```

This example produces the output:

```
same object
meaningfully equal
```

Yikes! The `equals()` method seems to be working, but what happened with `==` and `!=`? Why is `!=` telling us that `i1` and `i2` are different objects, when `==` is saying that `i3` and `i4` are the same object? In order to save memory, two instances of the following wrapper objects (created through boxing) will always be `==` when their primitive values are the same:

- Boolean
- Byte
- Character from \u0000 to \u007f (7f is 127 in decimal)
- Short and Integer from −128 to 127

When == is used to compare a primitive to a wrapper, the wrapper will be unwrapped and the comparison will be primitive to primitive.

Where Boxing Can Be Used

As we discussed earlier, it's common to use wrappers in conjunction with collections. Any time you want your collection to hold objects and primitives, you'll want to use wrappers to make those primitives collection-compatible. The general rule is that boxing and unboxing work wherever you can normally use a primitive or a wrapped object. The following code demonstrates some legal ways to use boxing:

```
class UseBoxing {
  public static void main(String [] args) {
    UseBoxing u = new UseBoxing();
    u.go(5);
  }
```

```
boolean go(Integer i) {        // boxes the int it was passed
  Boolean ifSo = true;         // boxes the literal
  Short s = 300;               // boxes the primitive
  if(ifSo) {                   // unboxing
    System.out.println(++s);   // unboxes, increments, reboxes
  }
  return !ifSo;                // unboxes, returns the inverse
}
}
```

e x a m

ⓦ **a t c h**   *Remember, wrapper reference variables can be null. That means you have to watch out for code that appears to be doing safe primitive operations but that could throw a* `NullPointerException`*:*

```
class Boxing2 {
  static Integer x;
  public static void main(String [] args) {
    doStuff(x);
  }
  static void doStuff(int z) {
    int z2 = 5;
    System.out.println(z2 + z);
} }
```

This code compiles fine, but the JVM throws a `NullPointerException` *when it attempts to invoke* `doStuff(x)` *because* x *doesn't refer to an* `Integer` *object, so there's no value to unbox.*

The Java 7 "Diamond" Syntax

In the OCA book (*OCA Java SE 8 Programmer 1 Exam Guide* [McGraw-Hill Education, 2017]), we discussed several small additions/improvements to the language that were added under the name "Project Coin." The last Project Coin improvement we'll discuss in this book is the "diamond syntax." We've already seen several examples of declaring type-safe collections, and as we go deeper into collections, we'll see lots more like this:

```
ArrayList<String> stuff = new ArrayList<String>();
List<Dog> myDogs = new ArrayList<Dog>();
Map<String, Dog> dogMap = new HashMap<String, Dog>();
```

Notice that the type parameters are duplicated in these declarations. As of Java 7, these declarations could be simplified to

```
ArrayList<String> stuff = new ArrayList<>();
List<Dog> myDogs = new ArrayList<>();
Map<String, Dog> dogMap = new HashMap<>();
```

Notice that in the simpler Java 7 declarations, the right side of the declaration included the two characters "<>," which together make a diamond shape—doh!

You cannot swap these; for example, the following declaration is NOT legal:

```
List<> stuff = new ArrayList<String>();     // NOT a legal diamond syntax
```

For the purposes of the exam, that's all you'll need to know about the diamond operator. For the remainder of the book, we'll use the pre-diamond syntax and the Java 7 diamond syntax somewhat randomly—just like the real world!

Sorting Collections and Arrays

Both collections and arrays can be sorted and searched using methods in the API.

Sorting Collections

Let's start with something simple, like sorting an `ArrayList` of strings alphabetically. What could be easier? There are a couple of ways to sort an `ArrayList`; for now we'll use the `java.util.Collections` class to sort, and return later to the `ArrayList`'s `sort()` method.

```
import java.util.*;
class TestSort1 {
  public static void main(String[] args) {
    ArrayList<String> stuff = new ArrayList<String>(); // #1
    stuff.add("Denver");
    stuff.add("Boulder");
    stuff.add("Vail");
    stuff.add("Aspen");
    stuff.add("Telluride");
    System.out.println("unsorted " + stuff);
    Collections.sort(stuff);                           // #2
    System.out.println("sorted   " + stuff);
  }
}
```

This produces something like this:

```
unsorted [Denver, Boulder, Vail, Aspen, Telluride]
sorted   [Aspen, Boulder, Denver, Telluride, Vail]
```

Line 1 is declaring an `ArrayList` of `Strings`, and line 2 is sorting the `ArrayList` alphabetically. We'll talk more about the `Collections` class, along with the `Arrays` class, in a later section; for now, let's keep sorting stuff.

Let's imagine we're building the ultimate home-automation application. Today we're focused on the home entertainment center and, more specifically, the DVD control center. We've already got the file I/O software in place to read and write data between the `dvdInfo.txt` file and instances of class `DVDInfo`. Here are the key aspects of the class:

```
class DVDInfo {
  String title;
  String genre;
  String leadActor;
  DVDInfo(String t, String g, String a) {
    title = t;  genre = g;  leadActor = a;
  }
  public String toString() {
    return title + " " + genre + " " + leadActor + "\n";
  }
  // getters and setter go here
}
```

Here's the DVD data that's in the `dvdinfo.txt` file:

```
Donnie Darko/sci-fi/Gyllenhall, Jake
Raiders of the Lost Ark/action/Ford, Harrison
2001/sci-fi/??
Caddyshack/comedy/Murray, Bill
Star Wars/sci-fi/Ford, Harrison
Lost in Translation/comedy/Murray, Bill
Patriot Games/action/Ford, Harrison
```

In our home-automation application, we want to create an instance of `DVDInfo` for each line of data we read in from the `dvdInfo.txt` file. For each instance, we will parse the line of data (remember `String.split()`?) and populate `DVDInfo`'s three instance variables. Finally, we want to put all of the `DVDInfo` instances into an `ArrayList`. Imagine that the `populateList()` method (shown next) does all of this. Here is a small piece of code from our application:

```
ArrayList<DVDInfo> dvdList = new ArrayList<DVDInfo>();
populateList();   // adds the file data to the ArrayList
System.out.println(dvdList);
```

You might get output like this:

```
[Donnie Darko sci-fi Gyllenhall, Jake
, Raiders of the Lost Ark action Ford, Harrison
, 2001 sci-fi ??
```

```
, Caddyshack comedy Murray, Bill
, Star Wars sci-fi Ford, Harrison
, Lost in Translation comedy Murray, Bill
, Patriot Games action Ford, Harrison
]
```

(Note: We overrode `DVDInfo`'s `toString()` method, so when we invoked `println()` on the `ArrayList`, it invoked `toString()` for each instance.)

Now that we've got a populated `ArrayList`, let's sort it:

```
Collections.sort(dvdlist);
```

Oops! You get something like this:

```
TestDVD.java:13: cannot find symbol
symbol  : method sort(java.util.ArrayList<DVDInfo>)
location: class java.util.Collections
    Collections.sort(dvdlist);
```

What's going on here? We know that the `Collections` class has a `sort()` method, yet this error implies that `Collections` does NOT have a `sort()` method that can take a `dvdlist`. That means there must be something wrong with the argument we're passing (`dvdlist`).

If you've already figured out the problem, our guess is that you did it without the help of the obscure error message shown earlier... How the heck do you sort instances of `DVDInfo`? Why were we able to sort instances of `String`? When you look up `Collections.sort()` in the API, your first reaction might be to panic. Hang tight—once again, the generics section will help you read that weird-looking method signature. If you read the description of the one-arg `sort()` method, you'll see that the `sort()` method takes a `List` argument and that the objects in the `List` must implement the `Comparable` interface. It turns out that `String` implements `Comparable`, and that's why we were able to sort a list of `Strings` using the `Collections.sort()` method.

The Comparable Interface

The `Comparable` interface is used by the `Collections.sort()` method and the `java.util.Arrays.sort()` method to sort `Lists` and arrays of objects, respectively. To implement `Comparable`, a class must implement a single method, `compareTo()`. Here's an invocation of `compareTo()`:

```
int x = thisObject.compareTo(anotherObject);
```

The `compareTo()` method returns an `int` with the following characteristics:

- **Negative** If `thisObject` < `anotherObject`
- **Zero** If `thisObject` == `anotherObject`
- **Positive** If `thisObject` > `anotherObject`

The `sort()` method uses `compareTo()` to determine how the `List` or object array should be sorted. Since you get to implement `compareTo()` for your own classes, you can use whatever weird criteria you prefer to sort instances of your classes. Returning to our earlier example for class `DVDInfo`, we can take the easy way out and use the `String` class's implementation of `compareTo()`:

```
class DVDInfo implements Comparable<DVDInfo> {    // #1
  // existing code
  public int compareTo(DVDInfo d) {
    return title.compareTo(d.getTitle());         // #2
} }
```

In line 1, we declare that class `DVDInfo` implements `Comparable` in such a way that `DVDInfo` objects can be compared to other `DVDInfo` objects. In line 2, we implement `compareTo()` by comparing the two `DVDInfo` object's titles. Because we know that the titles are strings and that `String` implements `Comparable`, this is an easy way to sort our `DVDInfo` objects by title. Before generics came along in Java 5, you would have had to implement `Comparable` using something like this:

```
class DVDInfo implements Comparable {
  // existing code
  public int compareTo(Object o) {    // takes an Object rather
                                      // than a specific type
    DVDInfo d = (DVDInfo)o;
    return title.compareTo(d.getTitle());
} }
```

This is still legal, but you can see that it's both painful and risky because you have to do a cast, and you need to verify that the cast will not fail before you try it.

exam
watch *It's important to remember that when you override `equals()`, you MUST take an argument of type `Object`,* *but that when you override `compareTo()`, you should take an argument of the type you're sorting.*

Putting it all together, our DVDInfo class should now look like this:

```
class DVDInfo implements Comparable<DVDInfo> {
  String title;
  String genre;
  String leadActor;
  DVDInfo(String t, String g, String a) {
    title = t;  genre = g;  leadActor = a;
  }
  public String toString() {
    return title + " " + genre + " " + leadActor + "\n";
  }
  public int compareTo(DVDInfo d) {
    return title.compareTo(d.getTitle());
  }
  public String getTitle() {
    return title;
  }
  // other getters and setters
}
```

Now, when we invoke Collections.sort(dvdList), we get

```
[2001 sci-fi ??
, Caddyshack comedy Murray, Bill
, Donnie Darko sci-fi Gyllenhall, Jake
, Lost in Translation comedy Murray, Bill
, Patriot Games action Ford, Harrison
, Raiders of the Lost Ark action Ford, Harrison
, Star Wars sci-fi Ford, Harrison
]
```

Hooray! Our ArrayList has been sorted by title. Of course, if we want our home-automation system to really rock, we'll probably want to sort DVD collections in lots of different ways. Since we sorted our ArrayList by implementing the compareTo() method, we seem to be stuck. We can only implement compareTo() once in a class, so how do we go about sorting our classes in an order different from what we specify in our compareTo() method? Good question. As luck would have it, the answer is coming up next.

Sorting with Comparator

While you were looking up the Collections.sort() method, you might have noticed that there is an overloaded version of sort() that takes both a List AND something called a *Comparator*. The Comparator interface gives you the capability to sort a given collection any number of different ways. The other handy thing about the `Comparator` interface is that you can use it to sort instances of any class—even classes you can't modify—unlike the `Comparable` interface, which forces you to change the class whose instances you want to sort. The `Comparator` interface is also very easy to implement, having only one method, `compare()`. Here's a small class that can be used to sort a `List` of `DVDInfo` instances by genre:

```
import java.util.*;
class GenreSort implements Comparator<DVDInfo> {
  public int compare(DVDInfo one, DVDInfo two) {
    return one.getGenre().compareTo(two.getGenre());
  }
}
```

The `Comparator.compare()` method returns an `int` whose meaning is the same as the `Comparable.compareTo()` method's return value. In this case, we're taking advantage of that by asking `compareTo()` to do the actual comparison work for us. Here's a test program that lets us test both our `Comparable` code and our new `Comparator` code:

```
import java.util.*;
import java.io.*;                       // populateList() needs this
public class TestDVD {
  ArrayList<DVDInfo> dvdlist = new ArrayList<DVDInfo>();
  public static void main(String[] args) {
    new TestDVD().go();
  }
  public void go() {
    populateList();
    System.out.println(dvdlist);        // output as read from file
    Collections.sort(dvdlist);
    System.out.println(dvdlist);        // output sorted by title

    GenreSort gs = new GenreSort();
    Collections.sort(dvdlist, gs);
    System.out.println(dvdlist);        // output sorted by genre
  }
  public void populateList() {
    // read the file, create DVDInfo instances, and
    // populate the ArrayList dvdlist with these instances
  }
}
```

You've already seen the first two output lists; here's the third:

```
[Patriot Games action Ford, Harrison
, Raiders of the Lost Ark action Ford, Harrison
, Caddyshack comedy Murray, Bill
```

```
, Lost in Translation comedy Murray, Bill
, 2001 sci-fi ??
, Donnie Darko sci-fi Gyllenhall, Jake
, Star Wars sci-fi Ford, Harrison
]
```

Because the `Comparable` and `Comparator` interfaces are so similar, expect the exam to try to confuse you. For instance, you might be asked to implement the `compareTo()` method in the `Comparator` interface. Study Table 6-3 to burn into your mind the differences between these two interfaces.

TABLE 6-3	java.lang.Comparable	java.util.Comparator
Comparing Comparable to Comparator	`int objOne.compareTo(objTwo)`	`int compare(objOne, objTwo)`
	Returns **negative** if `objOne < objTwo` **zero** if `objOne == objTwo` **positive** if `objOne > objTwo`	Same as `Comparable`
	You must modify the class whose instances you want to sort.	You build a class separate from the class whose instances you want to sort.
	Only **one** sort sequence can be created.	**Many** sort sequences can be created.
	Implemented frequently in the API by: `String`, wrapper classes, `LocalDate`, `LocalTime`...	Meant to be implemented to sort instances of third-party classes.

Creating a Comparator with a Lambda Expression

To sort the `dvdlist` using a `Comparator`, we created a class, `GenreSort`, that implemented the `Comparator` interface. This interface has just one abstract method, `compare()`, as we said earlier, and because of this, `Comparator` is what we call a "functional interface." You'll learn a whole lot more about functional interfaces in Chapter 8, but for now, just know that a functional interface is an interface with one and only one abstract method. Because it's abstract, you must implement it when you implement the `Comparator` interface, like you do with the `GenreSort` `Comparator`.

You might remember from the section "Using Simple Lambdas" in Chapter 6 of the *OCA Java SE 8 Programmer 1 Exam Guide* (McGraw-Hill Education, 2017), that we used the `java.util.function.Predicate` interface to create a lambda expression. A `Predicate` is also an example of a functional interface:

an interface with one abstract method. This is one of the things you need to know about lambda expressions; a lambda expression is an instance of a functional interface. That means whenever you're dealing with a class implementing a functional interface, like `Comparator`, you have an opportunity to use a lambda expression instead. Using lambda expressions certainly isn't required, but the nifty thing about using them is they can make your code more concise. Let's take another look at the `GenreSort` class:

```
class GenreSort implements Comparator<DVDInfo> {
    public int compare(DVDInfo one, DVDInfo two) {
        return one.getGenre().compareTo(two.getGenre());
    }
}
```

As it must, the class implements the `compare()` method. To use it to sort our DVDs by genre, we passed an instance of this class to `Collections.sort()` as the second argument, the `Comparator` argument:

```
GenreSort gs = new GenreSort();
Collections.sort(dvdlist, gs);
```

Because `GenreSort` is implementing a functional interface, we can actually replace the entire class with a lambda expression. This lambda expression will look a bit different from the `Predicate` lambda we used in Chapter 6 of *OCA Java SE 8 Programmer 1 Exam Guide*; this lambda needs to look like the `compare()` method of the `GenreSort` `Comparator`. To turn that `Comparator` into a lambda expression, here's what we do:

1. First we get the two parameters from the `compare()` method; those become the parameters for the lambda:

   ```
   (one, two)
   ```

   Because there are two parameters, we need to put them in parentheses.

2. Then, we write an arrow:

   ```
   (one, two) ->
   ```

3. Then we write the body of the lambda expression. What should the body be? Almost exactly what the body of the `compare()` method in `GenreSort` is:

   ```
   (one, two) -> one.getGenre().compareTo(two.getGenre())
   ```

We don't need to use the curly braces and a `return` because there's only one statement in the body of `compare()`, so we can just copy the expression part after the `return`, and the lambda will automatically return the value for us.

Now we have a lambda expression for the `Comparator`, so how do we use it? All we have to do is replace the `GenreSort` instance in our code with the lambda:

```
Collections.sort(dvdlist,
  (one, two) -> one.getGenre().compareTo(two.getGenre()));
```

Now, we can rewrite the test program and completely eliminate the need for a separate `GenreSort` class:

```
public class TestDVD {
    ArrayList<DVDInfo> dvdlist = new ArrayList<DVDInfo>();
    public static void main(String[] args) {
        new TestDVD().go();
    }
    public void go() {
        populateList();
        System.out.println(dvdlist);      // output as read from file
        Collections.sort(dvdlist);
        System.out.println(dvdlist);      // output sorted by title
        GenreSort gs = new GenreSort();
        Collections.sort(dvdlist, gs);
        System.out.println(dvdlist);      // output sorted by genre
        // Use a lambda expression as a Comparator
        Collections.sort(dvdlist,
            (one, two) ->
                one.getGenre().compareTo(two.getGenre()));
        System.out.println("--- sorted by genre, using Comparator lambda ---");
        System.out.println(dvdlist);
    }
}
```

If we want to delete the old code and delete the `GenreSort` class, we can because now we don't need that class at all to sort the `dvdlist`; we're using the lambda expression as the `Comparator` and writing the `Comparator` inline, where we need it when we call the `Collections.sort()` method.

You've seen the first three output lists; now here's a fourth:

```
--- sorted by genre, using Comparator lambda ---
[Patriot Games / action / Ford, Harrison
, Raiders of the Lost Ark / action / Ford, Harrison
, Caddyshack / comedy / Murray, Bill
, Lost in Translation / comedy / Murray, Bill
, 2001 / sci-fi / ??
, Donnie Darko / sci-fi / Gyllenhall, Jake
, Star Wars / sci-fi / Ford, Harrison
]
```

This is exactly the same output as we got using `GenreSort`, but now using a lambda expression instead. Just as you learned in Chapter 6 of *OCA Java SE 8*

Programmer 1 Exam Guide, a lambda expression passes code as an argument.
This time, the code is a Comparator method. You probably have a boatload of
questions about lambda expressions at this point, but hang on just a bit longer. We'll
cover all this in a lot more detail in Chapter 8. The thing to know about lambdas at
this stage is that they make convenient shortcuts for Comparators. Comparator
is a functional interface, so the entire class implementing the interface and the
compare() method can be replaced by a lambda.

Sorting ArrayLists Using the sort() Method

We've been using the java.util.Collections class to sort collections using
the class method sort(), passing in the collection to sort, in this instance, the
dvdlist ArrayList. ArrayLists can also be sorted directly by calling
the sort() method on the list. And just like Collections.sort(), the
ArrayList sort() method takes a Comparator. So we can pass in an instance
of a class that implements Comparator, like we did for our GenreSort class:

```
GenreSort gs = new GenreSort();
dvdlist.sort(gs);              // sort using GenreSort comparator
```

Or we can pass in a Comparator made from a lambda expression:

```
// sort by genre, using a lambda comparator
dvdlist.sort((one, two) -> one.getGenre().compareTo(two.getGenre()));
```

Either way we get the same results.

Sorting with the Arrays Class

Now let's look at using the java.util.Arrays class to sort arrays. The good
news is that sorting arrays of objects is just like sorting collections of objects. The
Arrays.sort() method is overloaded in the same way the Collections
.sort() method is:

- ■ `Arrays.sort(arrayToSort)`
- ■ `Arrays.sort(arrayToSort, Comparator)`

In addition, the Arrays.sort() method (the one-argument version) is
overloaded about a million times to provide a couple of sort methods for every type
of primitive. The Arrays.sort(myArray) methods that sort primitives always
sort based on natural order. Don't be fooled by an exam question that tries to sort a
primitive array using a Comparator.

Finally, remember that the `sort()` methods for both the `Collections` class and the `Arrays` class are `static` methods, and that they alter the objects they are sorting instead of returning a different sorted object.

---

e x a m

ⓦa t c h
We've talked a lot about sorting by natural order and using `Comparators` *to sort. The last rule you'll need to burn into your mind is that whenever you want to sort an array or a collection, the elements inside must all be mutually comparable. In other words, if* *you have an* `Object[]` *and you put* `Cat` *and* `Dog` *objects into it, you won't be able to sort it. In general, objects of different types should be considered NOT mutually comparable unless specifically stated otherwise.*

Searching Arrays and Collections

The `Collections` class and the `Arrays` class both provide methods that allow you to search for a specific element. When searching through collections or arrays, the following rules apply:

- Searches are performed using the `binarySearch()` method.
- Successful searches return the `int` index of the element being searched.
- Unsuccessful searches return an `int` index that represents the *insertion point*. The insertion point is the place in the collection/array where the element would be inserted to keep the collection/array properly sorted. Because positive return values and 0 indicate successful searches, the `binarySearch()` method uses negative numbers to indicate insertion points. Since 0 is a valid result for a successful search, the first available insertion point is -1. Therefore, the actual insertion point is represented as (-(insertion point) -1). For instance, if the insertion point of a search is at element 2, the actual insertion point returned will be -3.
- The collection/array being searched must be sorted before you can search it.
- If you attempt to search an array or collection that has not already been sorted, the results of the search will not be predictable.

■ If the collection/array you want to search was sorted in natural order, it *must* be searched in natural order. (Usually, this is accomplished by NOT sending a `Comparator` as an argument to the `binarySearch()` method.)

■ If the collection/array you want to search was sorted using a `Comparator`, it *must* be searched using the same `Comparator`, which is passed as the third argument to the `binarySearch()` method. Remember that `Comparators` cannot be used when searching arrays of primitives.

Let's take a look at a code sample that exercises the `binarySearch()` method:

```java
import java.util.*;
class SearchObjArray {
  public static void main(String [] args) {
    String [] sa = {"one", "two", "three", "four"};

    Arrays.sort(sa);                                      // #1
    for(String s : sa)
      System.out.print(s + " ");
    System.out.println("\none = "
                       + Arrays.binarySearch(sa,"one"));  // #2

    System.out.println("now reverse sort");
    ReSortComparator rs = new ReSortComparator();         // #3
    Arrays.sort(sa,rs);
    for(String s : sa)
      System.out.print(s + " ");
    System.out.println("\none = "
                       + Arrays.binarySearch(sa,"one"));  // #4
    System.out.println("one = "
                       + Arrays.binarySearch(sa,"one",rs)); // #5
  }
  static class ReSortComparator
               implements Comparator<String> {           // #6
    public int compare(String a, String b) {
      return b.compareTo(a);                              // #7
    }
  }
}
```

which produces something like this:

```
four one three two
one = 1
now reverse sort
two three one four
one = -1
one = 2
```

Here's what happened:

- ■ **#1** Sort the `sa` array alphabetically (the natural order).
- ■ **#2** Search for the location of element `"one"`, which is 1.
- ■ **#3** Make a `Comparator` instance. On the next line, we re-sort the array using the `Comparator`.
- ■ **#4** Attempt to search the array. We didn't pass the `binarySearch()` method the `Comparator` we used to sort the array, so we got an incorrect (undefined) answer.

e x a m

ⓦ a t c h *When solving, searching, and sorting questions, two big gotchas are*

1. *Searching an array or collection that hasn't been sorted.*
2. *Using a `Comparator` in either the sort or the search, but not both.*

- ■ **#5** Search again, passing the `Comparator` to `binarySearch()`. This time, we get the correct answer, 2.
- ■ **#6** We define the `Comparator`; it's okay for this to be an inner class. (We'll be discussing inner classes in Chapter 7.)
- ■ **#7** By switching the use of the arguments in the invocation of `compareTo()`, we get an inverted sort.

Converting Arrays to Lists to Arrays

A couple of methods allow you to convert arrays to `List`s and `List`s to arrays. The `List` and `Set` classes have `toArray()` methods, and the `Arrays` class has a method called `asList()`.

The `Arrays.asList()` method copies an array into a `List`. The API says, "Returns a fixed-size list backed by the specified array. (Changes to the returned list 'write through' to the array.)" When you use the `asList()` method, the array and the `List` become joined at the hip. When you update one of them, the other is updated automatically. Let's take a look:

```
String[] sa = {"one", "two", "three", "four"};
List sList = Arrays.asList(sa);                    // make a List
System.out.println("size " + sList.size());
System.out.println("idx2 " + sList.get(2));
```

```
sList.set(3,"six");                        // change List
sa[1] = "five";                            // change array
for(String s : sa)
  System.out.print(s + " ");
System.out.println("\nsl[1] " + sList.get(1));
```

This produces

```
size 4
idx2 three
one five three six
sl[1] five
```

Notice that when we print the final state of the array and the List, they have both been updated with each other's changes. Wouldn't something like this behavior make a great exam question?

Now let's take a look at the toArray() method. There's nothing too fancy going on with the toArray() method; it comes in two flavors: one that returns a new Object array, and one that uses the array you send it as the destination array:

```
List<Integer> iL = new ArrayList<Integer>();
for(int x=0; x<3; x++)
  iL.add(x);
Object[] oa = iL.toArray();                // create an Object array
Integer[] ia2 = new Integer[3];
ia2 = iL.toArray(ia2);                      // create an Integer array
```

Using Lists

Remember that Lists are usually used to keep things in some kind of order. You can use a LinkedList to create a first-in, first-out queue. You can use an ArrayList to keep track of what locations were visited and in what order. Notice that in both of these examples, it's perfectly reasonable to assume that duplicates might occur. In addition, Lists allow you to manually override the ordering of elements by adding or removing elements via the element's index. Before Java 5 and the enhanced for loop, the most common way to examine a List "element by element" was through the use of an Iterator. You'll still find Iterators in use in the Java code you encounter, and you might just find an Iterator or two on the exam. An Iterator is an object that's associated with a specific collection. It lets you loop through the collection step by step. The two Iterator methods you need to understand for the exam are

- **boolean hasNext()**   Returns true if there is at least one more element in the collection being traversed. Invoking hasNext() does NOT move you to the next element of the collection.

- **Object next()**   This method returns the next object in the collection AND moves you forward to the element after the element just returned.

Let's look at a little code that uses a List and an Iterator:

```
import java.util.*;
class Dog {
  public String name;
  Dog(String n) { name = n; }
}
class ItTest {
  public static void main(String[] args) {
    List<Dog> d = new ArrayList<Dog>();
    Dog dog = new Dog("aiko");
    d.add(dog);
    d.add(new Dog("clover"));
    d.add(new Dog("magnolia"));
    Iterator<Dog> i3 = d.iterator();   // make an iterator
    while (i3.hasNext()) {
      Dog d2 = i3.next();                    // cast not required
      System.out.println(d2.name);
    }
    System.out.println("size " + d.size());
    System.out.println("get1 " + d.get(1).name);
    System.out.println("aiko " + d.indexOf(dog));
    d.remove(2);
    Object[] oa = d.toArray();
    for(Object o : oa) {
      Dog d2 = (Dog)o;
      System.out.println("oa " + d2.name);
    }
  }
}
```

This produces

```
aiko
clover
magnolia
```

```
size 3
get1 clover
aiko 0
oa aiko
oa clover
```

First off, we used generics syntax to create the `Iterator` (an `Iterator` of type Dog). Because of this, when we used the `next()` method, we didn't have to cast the `Object` returned by `next()` to a `Dog`. We could have declared the `Iterator` like this:

```
Iterator i3 = d.iterator();  // make an iterator
```

But then we would have had to cast the returned value:

```
Dog d2 = (Dog)i3.next();
```

The rest of the code demonstrates using the `size()`, `get()`, `indexOf()`, and `toArray()` methods. There shouldn't be any surprises with these methods. Later in the chapter, Table 6-7 will list all of the `List`, `Set`, and `Map` methods you should be familiar with for the exam. As a last warning, remember that `List` is an interface!

Using Sets

Remember that `Set`s are used when you don't want any duplicates in your collection. If you attempt to add an element to a set that already exists in the set, the duplicate element will not be added, and the `add()` method will return `false`. Remember, `HashSet`s tend to be very fast because, as we discussed earlier, they use hashcodes.

You can also create a `TreeSet`, which is a `Set` whose elements are sorted. You must use caution when using a `TreeSet` (we're about to explain why):

```
import java.util.*;
class SetTest {
  public static void main(String[] args) {
    boolean[] ba = new boolean[5];
    // insert code here

    ba[0] = s.add("a");
    ba[1] = s.add(new Integer(42));
    ba[2] = s.add("b");
    ba[3] = s.add("a");
    ba[4] = s.add(new Object());
    for(int x=0; x<ba.length; x++)
      System.out.print(ba[x] + " ");
    System.out.println();
    for(Object o : s)
```

```
        System.out.print(o + " ");
    }
}
```

If you insert the following line of code, you'll get output that looks something like this:

```
Set s = new HashSet();          // insert this code
```

```
true true true false true
a java.lang.Object@e09713 42 b
```

It's important to know that the order of objects printed in the second `for` loop is not predictable: `HashSets` do not guarantee any ordering. Also, notice that the fourth invocation of `add()` failed because it attempted to insert a duplicate entry (a `String` with the value a) into the `Set`.

If you insert this line of code, you'll get something like this:

```
Set s = new TreeSet();          // insert this code
```

```
Exception in thread "main" java.lang.ClassCastException: java.lang.String
        at java.lang.Integer.compareTo(Integer.java:35)
        at java.util.TreeMap.compare(TreeMap.java:1093)
        at java.util.TreeMap.put(TreeMap.java:465)
        at java.util.TreeSet.add(TreeSet.java:210)
```

The issue is that whenever you want a collection to be sorted, its elements must be mutually comparable. Remember that unless otherwise specified, objects of different types are not mutually comparable.

Using Maps

Remember that when you use a class that implements `Map`, any classes that you use as a part of the keys for that map must override the `hashCode()` and `equals()` methods. (Well, you only have to override them if you're interested in retrieving stuff from your `Map`. Seriously, it's legal to use a class that doesn't override `equals()` and `hashCode()` as a key in a `Map`; your code will compile and run, you just won't find your stuff.) Here's some crude code demonstrating the use of a `HashMap`:

```
import java.util.*;
class Dog {
  public Dog(String n) { name = n; }
  public String name;
  public boolean equals(Object o) {
    if((o instanceof Dog) &&
       (((Dog)o).name == name)) {
```

```
            return true;
        } else {
            return false;
        }
    }
    public int hashCode() {return name.length(); }
}
class Cat { }

enum Pets {DOG, CAT, HORSE }

class MapTest {
    public static void main(String[] args) {
        Map<Object, Object> m = new HashMap<Object, Object>();

        m.put("k1", new Dog("aiko"));     // add some key/value pairs
        m.put("k2", Pets.DOG);
        m.put(Pets.CAT, "CAT key");
        Dog d1 = new Dog("clover");       // let's keep this reference
        m.put(d1, "Dog key");
        m.put(new Cat(), "Cat key");

        System.out.println(m.get("k1"));           // #1
        String k2 = "k2";
        System.out.println(m.get(k2));             // #2
        Pets p = Pets.CAT;
        System.out.println(m.get(p));              // #3
        System.out.println(m.get(d1));             // #4
        System.out.println(m.get(new Cat()));      // #5
        System.out.println(m.size());              // #6
    }
}
```

which produces something like this:

```
Dog@1c
DOG
CAT key
Dog key
null
5
```

Let's review the output. The first value retrieved is a Dog object (your value will vary). The second value retrieved is an enum value (DOG). The third value retrieved is a String; note that the key was an enum value. Pop quiz: what's the implication of the fact that we were able to successfully use an enum as a key?

The implication is that enums override equals() and hashCode(). And, if you look at the java.lang.Enum class in the API, you will see that, in fact, these methods have been overridden.

The fourth output is a `String`. The important point about this output is that the key used to retrieve the `String` was made of a `Dog` object. The fifth output is `null`. The important point here is that the `get()` method failed to find the `Cat` object that was inserted earlier. (The last line of output confirms that, indeed, 5 key/value pairs exist in the `Map`.) Why didn't we find the `Cat` key String? Why did it work to use an instance of `Dog` as a key, when using an instance of `Cat` as a key failed?

It's easy to see that `Dog` overrode `equals()` and `hashCode()` while `Cat` didn't.

Let's take a quick look at hashcodes. We used an incredibly simplistic hashcode formula in the `Dog` class—the hashcode of a `Dog` object is the length of the instance's name. So, in this example, the hashcode = 6. Let's compare the following two `hashCode()` methods:

```
public int hashCode() {return name.length(); }   // #1
public int hashCode() {return 4; }                // #2
```

Time for another pop quiz: Are the preceding two hashcodes legal? Will they successfully retrieve objects from a `Map`? Which will be faster?

The answer to the first two questions is Yes and Yes. Neither of these hashcodes will be very efficient (in fact, they would both be incredibly inefficient), but they are both legal, and they will both work. The answer to the last question is that the first hashcode will be a little bit faster than the second hashcode. In general, the more *unique* hashcodes a formula creates, the faster the retrieval will be. The first hashcode formula will generate a different code for each `name` length (for instance, the name `Robert` will generate one hashcode and the name `Benchley` will generate a different hashcode). The second hashcode formula will always produce the same result, 4, so it will be slower than the first.

Our last `Map` topic is: What happens when an object used as a key has its values changed? If we add two lines of code to the end of the earlier `MapTest.main()`,

```
d1.name = "magnolia";
System.out.println(m.get(d1));
```

we get something like this:

```
Dog@4
DOG
CAT key
Dog key
null
5
null
```

The Dog that was previously found now cannot be found. Because the Dog.name variable is used to create the hashcode, changing the name changed the value of the hashcode. As a final quiz for hashcodes, determine the output for the following lines of code if they're added to the end of MapTest.main():

```
d1.name = "magnolia";
System.out.println(m.get(d1));                    // #1
d1.name = "clover";
System.out.println(m.get(new Dog("clover")));     // #2
d1.name = "arthur";
System.out.println(m.get(new Dog("clover")));     // #3
```

Remember that the hashcode is equal to the length of the name variable. When you study a problem like this, it can be useful to think of the two stages of retrieval:

1. Use the hashCode() method to find the correct bucket.

2. Use the equals() method to find the object in the bucket.

In the first call to get(), the hashcode is 8 (magnolia) and it should be 6 (clover), so the retrieval fails at step 1, and we get null. In the second call to get(), the hashcodes are both 6, so step 1 succeeds. Once in the correct bucket (the "length of name = 6" bucket), the equals() method is invoked, and because Dog's equals() method compares names, equals() succeeds, and the output is Dog key. In the third invocation of get(), the hashcode test succeeds, but the equals() test fails because arthur is NOT equal to clover.

Navigating (Searching) TreeSets and TreeMaps

Note: This section and the next are fairly complex, and there is a good chance that you won't get any questions on these topics. But again, Oracle's objectives are somewhat terse, and we'd rather be on the safe side.

We've talked about searching lists and arrays. Let's turn our attention to searching TreeSets and TreeMaps. Java 6 introduced (among other things) two interfaces: java.util.NavigableSet and java.util.NavigableMap. For the purposes of the exam, you're interested in how TreeSet and TreeMap implement these interfaces.

Imagine that the Santa Cruz–Monterey ferry has an irregular schedule. Let's say that we have the daily Santa Cruz departure times stored in military time in a TreeSet. Let's look at some code that determines two things:

1. The last ferry that leaves before 4 PM (1600 hours)

2. The first ferry that leaves after 8 PM (2000 hours)

```
import java.util.*;
public class Ferry {
  public static void main(String[] args) {
    TreeSet<Integer> times = new TreeSet<Integer>();
    times.add(1205);    // add some departure times
    times.add(1505);
    times.add(1545);
    times.add(1830);
    times.add(2010);
    times.add(2100);

    // Java 5 version

    TreeSet<Integer> subset = new TreeSet<Integer>();
    subset = (TreeSet)times.headSet(1600);
    System.out.println("J5 - last before 4pm is: " + subset.last());

    TreeSet<Integer> sub2 = new TreeSet<Integer>();
    sub2 = (TreeSet)times.tailSet(2000);
    System.out.println("J5 - first after 8pm is: " + sub2.first());

    // Java 6 version using the new lower() and higher() methods

    System.out.println("J6 - last before 4pm is: " + times.lower(1600));
    System.out.println("J6 - first after 8pm is: " + times.higher(2000));
  }
}
```

This should produce the following:

```
J5 - last before 4pm is: 1545
J5 - first after 8pm is: 2010
J6 - last before 4pm is: 1545
J6 - first after 8pm is: 2010
```

As you can see in the preceding code, before the addition of the NavigableSet interface, zeroing in on an arbitrary spot in a Set—using the methods available in Java 5—was a compute-expensive and clunky proposition. On the other hand, using the Java 6 methods lower() and higher(), the code became a lot cleaner.

For the purpose of the exam, the NavigableSet methods related to this type of navigation are lower(), floor(), higher(), and ceiling(), and the mostly parallel NavigableMap methods are lowerKey(), floorKey(), ceilingKey(), and higherKey(). The difference between lower() and floor() is that lower() returns the element less than the given element, and floor() returns the element less than *or equal to* the given element. Similarly, higher() returns the element greater than the given element, and ceiling() returns the element greater than *or equal to* the given element. Table 6-4 summarizes the methods you should know for the exam.

TABLE 6-4	**Method**	**Description**
Important "Navigation"-Related Methods	`TreeSet.ceiling(e)`	Returns the lowest element >= e
	`TreeMap.ceilingKey(key)`	Returns the lowest key >= key
	`TreeSet.higher(e)`	Returns the lowest element > e
	`TreeMap.higherKey(key)`	Returns the lowest key > key
	`TreeSet.floor(e)`	Returns the highest element <= e
	`TreeMap.floorKey(key)`	Returns the highest key <= key
	`TreeSet.lower(e)`	Returns the highest element < e
	`TreeMap.lowerKey(key)`	Returns the highest key < key
	`TreeSet.pollFirst()`	Returns and removes the first entry
	`TreeMap.pollFirstEntry()`	Returns and removes the first key/value pair
	`TreeSet.pollLast()`	Returns and removes the last entry
	`TreeMap.pollLastEntry()`	Returns and removes the last key/value pair
	`TreeSet.descendingSet()`	Returns a `NavigableSet` in reverse order
	`TreeMap.descendingMap()`	Returns a `NavigableMap` in reverse order

Other Navigation Methods

In addition to the methods we just discussed, there were a few more methods new to Java 6 that could be considered "navigation" methods. (Okay, it's a little bit of a stretch to call these "navigation" methods, but just play along.)

Polling

The idea of polling is that we want both to retrieve and remove an element from either the beginning or the end of a collection. In the case of `TreeSet`, `pollFirst()` returns and removes the first entry in the set, and `pollLast()` returns and removes the last. Similarly, `TreeMap` now provides `pollFirstEntry()` and `pollLastEntry()` to retrieve and remove key/value pairs.

Descending Order

Also added in Java 6 for `TreeSet` and `TreeMap` were methods that returned a collection in the reverse order of the collection on which the method was invoked. The important methods for the exam are `TreeSet.descendingSet()` and `TreeMap.descendingMap()`.

Table 6-4 summarizes the "navigation" methods you'll need to know for the exam.

Backed Collections

Some of the classes in the `java.util` package support the concept of "backed collections." We'll use a little code to help explain the idea:

```
TreeMap<String, String> map = new TreeMap<String, String>();
map.put("a", "ant"); map.put("d", "dog"); map.put("h", "horse");

SortedMap<String, String> submap;
submap = map.subMap("b", "g");          // #1 create a backed collection

System.out.println(map + " " + submap);   // #2 show contents

map.put("b", "bat");                    // #3 add to original
submap.put("f", "fish");                // #4 add to copy

map.put("r", "raccoon");                // #5 add to original - out of range
// submap.put("p", "pig");              // #6 add to copy - out of range

System.out.println(map + " " + submap);   // #7 show final contents
```

This should produce something like this:

```
{a=ant, d=dog, h=horse} {d=dog}
{a=ant, b=bat, d=dog, f=fish, h=horse, r=raccoon} {b=bat, d=dog, f=fish}
```

The important method in this code is the `TreeMap.subMap()` method. It's easy to guess (and it's correct) that the `subMap()` method is making a copy of a portion of the `TreeMap` named `map`. The first line of output verifies the conclusions we've just drawn.

What happens next is powerful and a little bit unexpected (now we're getting to why they're called *backed* collections). When we add key/value pairs to either the original `TreeMap` or the partial-copy `SortedMap`, the new entries were automatically added to the other collection—sometimes. When `submap` was created, we provided a value range for the new collection. This range defines not only what should be included when the partial copy is created, but also defines the range of values that can be added to the copy. As we can verify by looking at the second line of output, we can add new entries to either collection within the range of the copy, and the new entries will show up in both collections. In addition, we can add a new entry to the original collection, even if it's outside the range of the copy. In this case, the new entry will show up only in the original—it won't be added to the copy because it's outside the copy's range. Notice that we commented out line 6. If you attempt to add an out-of-range entry to the copied collection, an exception will be thrown.

For the exam, you'll need to understand the basics just explained, plus a few more details about three methods from `TreeSet`—`headSet()`, `subSet()`, and `tailSet()`—and three methods from `TreeMap`—`headMap()`, `subMap()`, and `tailMap()`. As with the navigation-oriented methods we just discussed, we can see a lot of parallels between the `TreeSet` and the `TreeMap` methods. The `headSet()`/`headMap()` methods create a subset that starts at the beginning of the original collection and ends at the point specified by the method's argument. The `tailSet()`/`tailMap()` methods create a subset that starts at the point specified by the method's argument and goes to the end of the original collection. Finally, the `subSet()`/`subMap()` methods allow you to specify both the start and end points for the subset collection you're creating.

As you might expect, the question of whether the subsetted collection's end points are inclusive or exclusive is a little tricky. The good news is that for the exam you have to remember only that when these methods are invoked with end point *and* boolean arguments, the boolean always means "is inclusive." A little more good news is that all you have to know for the exam is that, unless specifically indicated by a boolean argument, a subset's starting point will always be inclusive. Finally, you'll notice when you study the API that all of the methods we've been discussing here have an overloaded version that was added in Java 6. The older methods return either a `SortedSet` or a `SortedMap`; the Java 6 and later methods return either a `NavigableSet` or a `NavigableMap`. Table 6-5 summarizes these methods.

TABLE 6-5	Important "Backed Collection" Methods for `TreeSet` and `TreeMap`

Method	Description
`headSet(e, b*)`	Returns a subset ending at element e and *exclusive* of e
`headMap(k, b*)`	Returns a submap ending at key k and *exclusive* of key k
`tailSet(e, b*)`	Returns a subset starting at and *inclusive* of element e
`tailMap(k, b*)`	Returns a submap starting at and *inclusive* of key k
`subSet(s, b*, e, b*)`	Returns a subset starting at element s and ending just before element e
`subMap(s, b*, e, b*)`	Returns a submap starting at key s and ending just before key e

* Note: These boolean arguments are optional. If they exist, it's a Java 6 method that lets you specify whether the start point and/or end point are exclusive, and these methods return a `NavigableXxx`. If the boolean argument(s) don't exist, the method returns either a `SortedSet` or a `SortedMap`.

exam
ⓦatch

Let's say that you've created a backed collection using either a `tailXxx()` *or* `subXxx()` *method. Typically, in these cases, the original and copy collections have different "first" elements. For the exam, it's important that you remember that the* `pollFirstXxx()` *methods will always remove the first*

entry from the collection on which they're invoked, but they will remove an element from the other collection only if it has the same value. So it's most likely that invoking `pollFirstXxx()` *on the copy will remove an entry from both collections, but invoking* `pollFirstXxx()` *on the original will remove only the entry from the original.*

Using the PriorityQueue Class and the Deque Interface

For the exam, you need to understand several of the classes that implement the `Deque` interface. These classes will be discussed in more detail in Chapter 11, the concurrency chapter.

Other than those concurrency-related classes, the last two collection classes you need to understand for the exam are `PriorityQueue` and `ArrayDeque`.

PriorityQueue

Unlike basic queue structures that are first-in, first-out by default, a `PriorityQueue` orders its elements using a user-defined priority. The priority can be as simple as natural ordering (in which, for instance, an entry of 1 would be a higher priority than an entry of 2). In addition, a `PriorityQueue` can be ordered using a `Comparator`, which lets you define any ordering you want. Queues have a few methods not found in other collection interfaces: `peek()`, `poll()`, and `offer()`.

```
import java.util.*;
class PQ {
  static class PQsort
        implements Comparator<Integer> {   // inverse sort
    public int compare(Integer one, Integer two) {
      return two - one;                     // unboxing
    }
  }
  public static void main(String[] args) {
    int[] ia = {1,5,3,7,6,9,8 };            // unordered data
    PriorityQueue<Integer> pq1 =
      new PriorityQueue<Integer>();         // use natural order
```

```
    for(int x : ia)                        // load queue
      pq1.offer(x);
    for(int x : ia)                        // review queue
      System.out.print(pq1.poll() + " ");
    System.out.println("");

    PQsort pqs = new PQsort();             // get a Comparator
    PriorityQueue<Integer> pq2 =
      new PriorityQueue<Integer>(10,pqs);  // use Comparator

    for(int x : ia)                        // load queue
      pq2.offer(x);
    System.out.println("size " + pq2.size());
    System.out.println("peek " + pq2.peek());
    System.out.println("size " + pq2.size());
    System.out.println("poll " + pq2.poll());
    System.out.println("size " + pq2.size());
    for(int x : ia)                        // review queue
      System.out.print(pq2.poll() + " ");
  }
}
```

This code produces something like this:

```
1 3 5 6 7 8 9
size 7
peek 9
size 7
poll 9
size 6
8 7 6 5 3 1 null
```

Let's look at this in detail. The first `for` loop iterates through the `ia` array and uses the `offer()` method to add elements to the `PriorityQueue` named `pq1`. The second `for` loop iterates through `pq1` using the `poll()` method, which returns the highest-priority entry in `pq1` AND removes the entry from the queue. Notice that the elements are returned in priority order (in this case, natural order). Next, we create a `Comparator`—in this case, a `Comparator` that orders elements in the opposite of natural order. We use this `Comparator` to build a second `PriorityQueue`, `pq2`, and we load it with the same array we used earlier. Finally, we check the size of `pq2` before and after calls to `peek()` and `poll()`. This confirms that `peek()` returns the highest-priority element in the queue without removing it, and `poll()` returns the highest-priority element AND removes it from the queue. Finally, we review the remaining elements in the queue.

ArrayDeque

ArrayDeque is a Collection class that implements the Deque interface. As we described earlier, Deque is an interface for double-ended queues, with methods for adding and removing elements to and from the queue at either end. Whereas the Deque interface allows for capacity-limited implementations, ArrayDeque has no capacity restrictions so adding elements will not fail.

The main advantage of ArrayDeque over, say, a List (like ArrayList or LinkedList) is performance. There are plenty of methods in the Deque interface to allow easy access to elements in the collection, and so ArrayDeque is a great choice if you're implementing a stack or queue. Unlike PriorityQueue, there is no natural ordering in ArrayDeque; it is simply a collection of elements that are stored in the order in which you add them. You'll also notice that many of the methods in ArrayDeque have similar names to PriorityQueue, primarily because both constructs are designed to implement queues. ArrayDeque implements both the Queue interface and the Deque interface, so there are several methods with different names that do the same thing.

Here's an example to demonstrate how the various methods in the ArrayDeque interface add and access elements and remove elements from the collection:

```
List<Integer> nums = Arrays.asList(10, 9, 8, 7, 6, 5);// Create several
ArrayDeques, each with space for 2 items

ArrayDeque<Integer> a = new ArrayDeque<>(2);
ArrayDeque<Integer> b = new ArrayDeque<>(2);
ArrayDeque<Integer> c = new ArrayDeque<>(2);
ArrayDeque<Integer> d = new ArrayDeque<>(2);
ArrayDeque<Integer> e = new ArrayDeque<>(2);

// add 6 items to each Deque, each using different methods
for (Integer n : nums) {
    a.offer(n);         // add on the end
    b.offerFirst(n);    // add on the front
    c.push(n);          // add on the front
    d.add(n);           // add on the end
    e.addFirst(n);      // add on the front
}

// display the deques
System.out.println("a: " + a);
System.out.println("b: " + b);
System.out.println("c: " + c);
System.out.println("d: " + d);
System.out.println("e: " + e);
```

In this example, we first create several empty `ArrayDeques` (a through e), each using the `ArrayDeque` constructor specifying the number of spaces to allocate, in this case, two. However, remember that `ArrayDeque` is not size constrained, so in the `for` loop, where we iterate through the `List` of numbers and add six numbers to each of the `ArrayDeques`, no exceptions are thrown and no errors are created.

As you can see in the output:

```
a: [10, 9, 8, 7, 6, 5]
b: [5, 6, 7, 8, 9, 10]
c: [5, 6, 7, 8, 9, 10]
d: [10, 9, 8, 7, 6, 5]
e: [5, 6, 7, 8, 9, 10]
```

the methods we're using to add elements to the deques result in different orderings of the deques depending on whether the method adds an element to the front of the deque or the end of the deque. The methods `offerFirst()`, `push()`, and `addFirst()` add elements to the front of the deque, so we see the numbers in reverse order of the `List`. The methods `offer()` and `add()` add elements to the end of the deque, so we see the numbers in the same order as they appeared in the `List`.

Next, let's do some experiments accessing the elements in deque e. First, we `peek()`, which returns the first element (sometimes called the *head* of the queue) without removing it from the deque:

```
System.out.println("First element of e: " + e.peek());
System.out.println("e hasn't changed: " + e);
```

This code produces the output:

```
First element of e: 5
e hasn't changed: [5, 6, 7, 8, 9, 10]
```

Then we `poll()`, which removes the first element from the deque and returns it:

```
System.out.println("First element of e: " + e.poll());
System.out.println("e has been modified: " + e);
```

We see the output:

```
First element of e: 5
e has been modified: [6, 7, 8, 9, 10]
```

Then we `pop()`, which also removes the first element from the deque and returns it:

```
System.out.println("First element of e: " + e.pop());
System.out.println("e has been modified: " + e);
```

So we get the output:

```
First element of e: 6
e has been modified: [7, 8, 9, 10]
```

Then we `pollLast()`, which removes the last element from the deque (sometimes called the *tail* of the queue) and returns it:

```
System.out.println("Last element of e: " + e.pollLast());
System.out.println("e has been modified: " + e);
```

This code produces:

```
Last element of e: 10
e has been modified: [7, 8, 9]
```

Then we call `removeLast()` three times to remove the three remaining elements from the end of the deque, returning each one, so we see the elements in reverse order from the end of the deque:

```
System.out.println("Remove all remaining elements of e: " +
    e.removeLast() + " " + e.removeLast() + " " + e.removeLast());
System.out.println("e has been modified: " + e);
```

The output is

```
Remove all remaining elements of e: 9 8 7
e has been modified: []
```

Now, e is empty.

Next, let's test to see what happens if we use various methods to try to remove another item from the deque. If we `pop()` or `remove()`, we get a `java.util` `.NoSuchElementException` error:

```
// calling pop() throws a java.util.NoSuchElementException
System.out.println("Try to pop one more item: " + e.pop());

// calling remove() throws a java.util.NoSuchElementException
System.out.println("Try to remove one more item: " + e.remove());
```

But if we `poll()`, we get `null`:

```
// There's nothing left, so calling poll() returns null
System.out.println("Try to poll one more item: " + e.poll());
```

So we see the output:

```
Try to poll one more item: null
```

Remember that, unlike many of the Deque classes we'll look at in Chapter 11, ArrayDeque is not thread safe, so you have to synchronize on classes that access a shared ArrayDeque in a multithreaded environment.

Method Overview for Arrays and Collections

For these two classes, we've already covered the trickier methods you might encounter on the exam. Table 6-6 lists a summary of the methods you should be aware of. (Note: The T[] syntax will be explained later in this chapter; for now, think of it as meaning "any array that's NOT an array of primitives.")

| TABLE 6-6 | Key Methods in Arrays and Collections |

Key Methods in java.util.Arrays	Descriptions
`static List asList(T[])`	Convert an array to a List (and bind them).
`static int binarySearch(Object[], key)` `static int binarySearch(primitive[], key)`	Search a sorted array for a given value; return an index or insertion point.
`static int binarySearch(T[], key, Comparator)`	Search a Comparator-sorted array for a value.
`static boolean equals(Object[], Object[])` `static boolean equals(primitive[], primitive[])`	Compare two arrays to determine if their contents are equal.
`static void sort(Object[ ] )` `static void sort(primitive[ ] )`	Sort the elements of an array by natural order.
`static void sort(T[], Comparator)`	Sort the elements of an array using a Comparator.
`static String toString(Object[])` `static String toString(primitive[])`	Create a String containing the contents of an array.
Key Methods in java.util.Collections	**Descriptions**
`static int binarySearch(List, key)` `static int binarySearch(List, key, Comparator)`	Search a "sorted" List for a given value; return an index or insertion point.
`static void reverse(List)`	Reverse the order of elements in a List.
`static Comparator reverseOrder()` `static Comparator reverseOrder(Comparator)`	Return a Comparator that sorts the reverse of the collection's current sort sequence.
`static void sort(List)` `static void sort(List, Comparator)`	Sort a List either by natural order or by a Comparator.

Method Overview for List, Set, Map, and Queue

For these four interfaces, we've already covered the trickier methods you might encounter on the exam. Table 6-7 lists a summary of the List, Set, and Map methods you should be aware of.

For the exam, the PriorityQueue methods that are important to understand are offer() (which is similar to add()), peek() (which retrieves the element at the head of the queue but doesn't delete it), and poll() (which retrieves the head element and removes it from the queue).

The corresponding ArrayDeque methods do the same things. We also talked about the ArrayDeque methods pop(), pollLast(), remove(), and

TABLE 6-7   Key Methods in List, Set, and Map

Key Interface Methods	List	Set	Map	Descriptions
boolean **add**(element) boolean **add**(index, element)	X X	X		Add an element. For Lists, optionally add the element at an index point.
boolean **contains**(object) boolean **containsKey**(object key) boolean **containsValue**(object value)	X	X	X X	Search a collection for an object (or, optionally for Maps, a key); return the result as a boolean.
object get(index) object get(key)	X		X	Get an object from a collection via an index or a key.
int indexOf(object)	X			Get the location of an object in a List.
Iterator iterator()	X	X		Get an Iterator for a List or a Set.
Set keySet()			X	Return a Set containing a Map's keys.
put(key, value)			X	Add a key/value pair to a Map.
element remove(index) element remove(object) element remove(key)	X X	X	X	Remove an element via an index, or via the element's value, or via a key.
int size()	X	X	X	Return the number of elements in a collection.
Object[] toArray() T[] toArray(T[])	X	X		Return an array containing the elements of the collection.

removeLast().pop() and remove() remove the first element from the deque, and pollLast() and removeLast() remove the last element from the deque. Just remember that elements in the ArrayDeque are simply ordered by their position in the deque.

exam

watch *It's important to know some of the details of natural ordering. The following code will help you understand the relative positions of uppercase characters, lowercase characters, and spaces in a natural ordering:*

```
String[] sa = {">ff<", "> f<", ">f <", ">FF<" }; // ordered?
PriorityQueue<String> pq3 = new PriorityQueue<String>();
for(String s : sa)
  pq3.offer(s);
for(String s : sa)
  System.out.print(pq3.poll() + " ");
```

This produces

```
> f< >FF< >f < >ff<
```

If you remember that spaces sort before characters and that uppercase letters sort before lowercase characters, you should be good to go for the exam.

CERTIFICATION OBJECTIVE

Generic Types (OCP Objective 3.1)

3.1   Create and use a generic class.

Now would be a great time to take a break. This innocent-sounding objective unpacks into a world of complexity. When you're well rested, come on back and strap yourself in—the next several pages might get bumpy.

Arrays in Java have always been type-safe—an array declared as type String (String []) *can't accept* Integers (or ints), Dogs, *or anything other than*

`Strings`. But remember that before Java 5 there was no syntax for declaring a type-safe collection. To make an `ArrayList` of `Strings`, you said,

```
ArrayList myList = new ArrayList();
```

or the polymorphic equivalent

```
List myList = new ArrayList();
```

There was no syntax that let you specify that `myList` will take `Strings` and only `Strings`. And with no way to specify a type for the `ArrayList`, the compiler couldn't enforce that you put only things of the specified type into the list. As of Java 5, we can use generics, and while they aren't only for making type-safe collections, that's just about all most developers use generics for. So, although generics aren't just for collections, think of collections as the overwhelming reason and motivation for adding generics to the language.

And it was not an easy decision, nor has it been an entirely welcome addition. Because along with all the nice, happy type-safety, generics come with a lot of baggage—most of which you'll never see or care about—but there are some gotchas that come up surprisingly quickly. We'll cover the ones most likely to show up in your own code, and those are also the issues that you'll need to know for the exam.

The biggest challenge for the Java engineers in adding generics to the language (and the main reason it took them so long) was how to deal with legacy code built without generics. The Java engineers obviously didn't want to break everyone's existing Java code, so they had to find a way for Java classes with both type-safe (generic) and nontype-safe (nongeneric/pre–Java 5) collections to still work together. Their solution isn't the friendliest, but it does let you use older nongeneric code, as well as use generic code that plays with nongeneric code. But notice we said "plays" and not "plays WELL."

While you can integrate Java 5 and later generic code with legacy, nongeneric code, the consequences can be disastrous, and unfortunately, most of the disasters happen at runtime, not compile time. Fortunately, though, most compilers will generate warnings to tell you when you're using unsafe (meaning nongeneric) collections.

The Java 7 exam covered both pre–Java 5 (nongeneric) and generic-style collections. You may still see questions on the Java 8 exam that expect you to understand the tricky problems that can come from mixing nongeneric and generic code together, although it is less likely. And like some of the other topics in this book, you could fill an entire book if you really wanted to cover every detail about generics.

The Legacy Way to Do Collections

Here's a review of a pre–Java 5 `ArrayList` intended to hold `Strings`. (We say "intended" because that's about all you had—good intentions—to make sure that the `ArrayList` would hold only `Strings`.)

```
List myList = new ArrayList();   // can't declare a type

myList.add("Fred");              // OK, it will hold Strings

myList.add(new Dog());           // and it will hold Dogs too

myList.add(new Integer(42));     // and Integers...
```

A nongeneric collection can hold any kind of object! A nongeneric collection is quite happy to hold anything that is NOT a primitive.

This meant it was entirely up to the programmer to be...careful. Having no way to guarantee collection type wasn't very programmer friendly for such a strongly typed language. We're so used to the compiler stopping us from, say, assigning an `int` to a `boolean` or a `String` to a `Dog` reference, but with collections, it was, "Come on in! The door is always open! All objects are welcome here any time!"

And since a collection could hold anything, the methods that get objects out of the collection could have only one kind of return type—`java.lang.Object`. That meant getting a `String` back out of our only-`Strings`-intended list required a cast:

```
String s = (String) myList.get(0);
```

And since you couldn't guarantee that what was coming out really was a `String` (since you were allowed to put anything in the list), the cast could fail at runtime.

So generics takes care of both ends (the putting in and getting out) by enforcing the type of your collections. Let's update the `String` list:

```
List<String> myList = new ArrayList<String>();
myList.add("Fred");          // OK, it will hold Strings
myList.add(new Dog());       // compiler error!!
```

Perfect. That's exactly what we want. By using generics syntax—which means putting the type in angle brackets `<String>`—we're telling the compiler that this collection can hold only `String` objects. The type in angle brackets is referred to as the "parameterized type," "type parameter," or, of course, just old-fashioned "type." In this chapter, we'll refer to it both ways.

So now that what you put IN is guaranteed, you can also guarantee what comes OUT, and that means you can get rid of the cast when you get something from the collection. Instead of

```
String s = (String)myList.get(0);  // pre-generics, when a
                                   // String wasn't guaranteed
```

we can now just say

```
String s = myList.get(0);
```

The compiler already knows that `myList` contains only things that can be assigned to a `String` reference, so now there's no need for a cast. So far, it seems pretty simple. And with the new `for` loop, you can, of course, iterate over the guaranteed-to-be-`String` list:

```
for (String s : myList) {
  int x = s.length();
  // no need for a cast before calling a String method! The
  // compiler already knew "s" was a String coming from myList
}
```

And, of course, you can declare a type parameter for a method argument, which then makes the argument a type-safe reference:

```
void takeListOfStrings(List<String> strings) {
  strings.add("foo");  // no problem adding a String
}
```

The previous method would NOT compile if we changed it to

```
void takeListOfStrings(List<String> strings) {
  strings.add(new Integer(42)); // NO!! strings is type safe
}
```

Return types can obviously be declared type-safe as well:

```
public List<Dog> getDogList() {
  List<Dog> dogs = new ArrayList<Dog>();
  // more code to insert dogs
  return dogs;
}
```

The compiler will stop you from returning anything not compatible with a `List<Dog>` (although what is and is not compatible is going to get very interesting in a minute). And since the compiler guarantees that only a type-safe

`Dog List` is returned, those calling the method won't need a cast to take `Dogs` from the `List`:

```
Dog d = getDogList().get(0);  // we KNOW a Dog is coming out
```

With pre–Java 5 nongeneric code, the `getDogList()` method would be

```
public List getDogList() {
  List dogs = new ArrayList();
  // code to add only Dogs... fingers crossed...
  return dogs; // a List of ANYTHING will work here
}
```

and the caller would need a cast:

```
Dog d = (Dog) getDogList().get(0);
```

(The cast in this example applies to what comes from the `List`'s `get()` method; we aren't casting what is returned from the `getDogList()` method, which is a `List`.)

But what about the benefit of a completely heterogeneous collection? In other words, what if you liked the fact that before generics you could make an `ArrayList` that could hold any kind of object?

```
List myList = new ArrayList();  // old-style, non-generic
```

is almost identical to

```
List<Object> myList = new
              ArrayList<Object>(); // holds ANY object type
```

Declaring a `List` with a type parameter of `<Object>` makes a collection that works in almost the same way as the original pre–Java 5 nongeneric collection—you can put ANY object type into the collection. You'll see a little later that nongeneric collections and collections of type `<Object>` aren't entirely the same, but most of the time, the differences do not matter.

Oh, if only this were the end of the story...but there are still a few tricky issues with methods, arguments, polymorphism, and integrating generic and nongeneric code, so we're just getting warmed up here.

Generics and Legacy Code

The easiest thing about generics you'll need to know for the exam is how to update nongeneric code to make it generic. You just add a type in angle brackets (`<>`) immediately following the collection type in BOTH the variable declaration and the constructor call (or you use the Java 7 diamond syntax), including any place you declare a variable (so that means arguments and return types, too). A pre–Java 5 `List` meant to hold only Integers:

```
List myList = new ArrayList();
```

becomes

```
List<Integer> myList = new ArrayList<Integer>();  // (or the J7 diamond!)
```

and a list meant to hold only `Strings` goes from

```
public List changeStrings(ArrayList s) { }
```

to this:

```
public List<String> changeStrings(ArrayList<String> s) { }
```

Easy. And if there's code that used the earlier nongeneric version and performed a cast to get things out, that won't break anyone's code:

```
Integer i = (Integer) list.get(0); // cast no longer needed,
                                   // but it won't hurt
```

Mixing Generic and Nongeneric Collections

Now here's where it starts to get interesting... Imagine we have an `ArrayList` of type `Integer` and we're passing it into a method from a class whose source code we don't have access to. Will this work?

```
// a Java 5 or later class using a generic collection
import java.util.*;
public class TestLegacy {
  public static void main(String[] args) {
    List<Integer> myList = new ArrayList<Integer>();
                              // type safe collection
    myList.add(4);
    myList.add(6);
    Adder adder = new Adder();
    int total = adder.addAll(myList);
                              // pass it to an untyped argument
    System.out.println(total);
  }
}
```

The older nongenerics class we want to use:

```
import java.util.*;
class Adder {
  int addAll(List list) {
    // method with a non-generic List argument,
    // but assumes (with no guarantee) that it will be Integers
    Iterator it = list.iterator();
    int total = 0;
    while (it.hasNext()) {
      int i = ((Integer)it.next()).intValue();
      total += i;
    }
    return total;
  }
}
```

Yes, this works just fine. You can mix correct generic code with older nongeneric code, and everyone is happy.

In the previous example, the addAll() legacy method assumed (trusted? hoped?) that the list passed in was, indeed, restricted to Integers, even though when the code was written, there was no guarantee. It was up to the programmers to be careful.

Since the addAll() method wasn't doing anything except getting the Integer (using a cast) from the list and accessing its value, there were no problems. In that example, there was no risk to the caller's code, but the legacy method might have blown up if the list passed in contained anything but Integers (which would cause a ClassCastException).

But now imagine that you call a legacy method that doesn't just *read* a value, but *adds* something to the ArrayList. Will this work?

```
import java.util.*;
public class TestBadLegacy {
  public static void main(String[] args) {
    List<Integer> myList = new ArrayList<Integer>();
    myList.add(4);
    myList.add(6);
    Inserter in  = new Inserter();
    in.insert(myList);            // pass List<Integer> to legacy code
  }
}
class Inserter {
  // method with a non-generic List argument
  void insert(List list) {
    list.add(new Integer(42));  // adds to the incoming list
  }
}
```

Sure, this code works. It compiles, and it runs. The `insert()` method puts an `Integer` into the list that was originally typed as `<Integer>`, so no problem. But...what if we modify the `insert()` method like this:

```
void insert(List list) {
  list.add(new String("42"));   // put a String in the list
                                // passed in
}
```

Will that work? Yes, sadly, it does! It both compiles and runs. No runtime exception. Yet, someone just stuffed a `String` into a *supposedly* type-safe `ArrayList` of type `<Integer>`. How can that be?

Remember, the older legacy code was allowed to put anything at all (except primitives) into a collection. And in order to support legacy code, Java 5 and later allowed your newer type-safe code to make use of older code (it would have been a nightmare to ask several million Java developers to modify all their existing code).

So, the Java 5 or later compiler (from now on "the Java 5 compiler") was *forced* into letting you compile your new type-safe code even though your code invokes a method of an older class that takes a nontype-safe argument and does who knows what with it.

However, just because **the Java 5 compiler** (remember this means Java 5 and later), allows this code to compile doesn't mean it has to be HAPPY about it. In fact, the compiler will warn you that you're taking a big, big risk sending your nice protected `ArrayList<Integer>` into a dangerous method that can have its way with your list and put in `Floats`, `Strings`, or even `Dogs`.

When you called the `addAll()` method in the earlier example, it didn't insert anything to the list (it simply added up the values within the collection), so there was no risk to the caller that his list would be modified in some horrible way. It compiled and ran just fine. But in the second version, with the legacy `insert()` method that adds a `String`, the compiler generated a warning:

```
javac TestBadLegacy.java
Note: TestBadLegacy.java uses unchecked or unsafe operations.
Note: Recompile with -Xlint:unchecked for details.
```

Remember that *compiler warnings are NOT considered a compiler failure.* The compiler generated a perfectly valid class file from the compilation, but it was kind enough to tell you by saying, in so many words, "I seriously hope you know what you are doing because this old code has NO respect (or even knowledge) of your `<Integer>` typing and can do whatever the heck it wants to your precious `ArrayList<Integer>`."

Be sure you know the difference between "compilation fails" and "compiles without error" and "compiles without warnings" and "compiles with warnings." In most questions on the exam, *you care only about compiles versus compilation fails—compiler warnings don't matter for most of the exam. But when you are using generics and mixing both typed and untyped code, warnings matter.*

Back to our example with the legacy code that does an insert. Keep in mind that for BOTH versions of the insert() method (one that adds an Integer and one that adds a String), the compiler issues warnings. The compiler does NOT know whether the insert() method is adding the right thing (Integer) or the wrong thing (String). The reason the compiler produces a warning is because the method is ADDING something to the collection! In other words, the compiler knows there's a chance the method might add the wrong thing to a collection the caller thinks is type-safe.

For the purposes of the exam, unless the question includes an answer that mentions warnings, even if you know the compilation will produce warnings, that is still a successful compile! Compiling with warnings is NEVER considered a compilation failure.
One more time—if you see code that you know will compile with warnings, you *must NOT choose "Compilation fails" as an answer. The bottom line is this: Code that compiles with warnings is still a successful compile. If the exam question wants to test your knowledge of whether code will produce a warning (or what you can do to the code to ELIMINATE warnings), the question (or answer) will explicitly include the word "warnings."*

So far, we've looked at how the compiler will generate warnings if it sees that there's a chance your type-safe collection could be harmed by older nontype-safe code. But one of the questions developers often ask is, "Okay, sure, it compiles, but why does it RUN? Why does the code that inserts the wrong thing into my list work at runtime?" In other words, why does the JVM let old code stuff a String into your ArrayList<Integer> without any problems at all? No exceptions, nothing.

Just a quiet, behind-the-scenes, total violation of your type safety that you might not discover until the worst possible moment.

There's one Big Truth you need to know to understand why it runs without problems—the JVM has no idea that your `ArrayList` was supposed to hold only `Integers`. The typing information does not exist at runtime! All your generic code is strictly for the compiler. Through a process called "type erasure," the compiler does all of its verifications on your generic code and then strips the type information out of the class bytecode. At runtime, ALL collection code— both legacy and Java 5 and later code you write using generics—looks exactly like the pregeneric version of collections. None of your typing information exists at runtime. In other words, even though you WROTE

```
List<Integer> myList = new ArrayList<Integer>();
```

by the time the compiler is done with it, the JVM sees what it always saw before Java 5 and generics:

```
List myList = new ArrayList();
```

The compiler even inserts the casts for you—the casts you had to do to get things out of a pre–Java 5 collection.

Think of generics as strictly a compile-time protection. The compiler uses generic type information (the `<type>` in the angle brackets) to make sure that your code doesn't put the wrong things into a collection and that you do not assign what you get from a collection to the wrong reference type. But NONE of this protection exists at runtime.

This is a little different from arrays, which give you BOTH compile-time protection and runtime protection. Why did they do generics this way? Why is there no type information at runtime? To support legacy code. At runtime, collections are collections just like the old days. What you gain from using generics is compile-time protection that guarantees you won't put the wrong thing into a typed collection, and it also eliminates the need for a cast when you get something out, since the compiler already knows that only an `Integer` is coming out of an `Integer` list.

The fact is, you don't NEED runtime protection...until you start mixing up generic and nongeneric code, as we did in the previous example. Then you can have disasters at runtime. The only advice we have is to pay very close attention to those compiler warnings:

```
javac TestBadLegacy.java
Note: TestBadLegacy.java uses unchecked or unsafe operations.
Note: Recompile with -Xlint:unchecked for details.
```

This compiler warning isn't very descriptive, but the second note suggests that you recompile with -Xlint:unchecked. If you do, you'll get something like this:

```
javac -Xlint:unchecked TestBadLegacy.java
TestBadLegacy.java:17: warning: [unchecked] unchecked call to add(E)
as a member of the raw type java.util.List
        list.add(new String("42"));
             ^
1 warning
```

When you compile with the -Xlint:unchecked flag, the compiler shows you exactly which method(s) might be doing something dangerous. In this example, since the list argument was not declared with a type, the compiler treats it as legacy code and assumes no risk for what the method puts into the "raw" list.

On the exam, you must be able to recognize when you are compiling code that will produce warnings but still compile. And any code that compiles (even with warnings) will run! No type violations will be caught at runtime by the JVM, *until* those type violations mess with your code in some other way. In other words, the act of adding a String to an <Integer> list won't fail at runtime *until* you try to treat that String-you-think-is-an-Integer as an Integer.

For example, imagine you want your code to pull something out of your *supposedly* type-safe ArrayList<Integer> that older code put a String into. It compiles (with warnings). It runs...or at least the code that actually adds the String to the list runs. But when you take the String that wasn't supposed to be there out of the list and try to assign it to an Integer reference or invoke an Integer method, you're dead.

Keep in mind, then, that the problem of putting the wrong thing into a typed (generic) collection does not show up at the time you actually do the add() to the collection. It only shows up later, when you try to use something in the list and it doesn't match what you were expecting. In the old (pre–Java 5) days, you always assumed that you might get the wrong thing out of a collection (since they were all nontype-safe), so you took appropriate defensive steps in your code. The problem with mixing generic and nongeneric code is that you won't be expecting those problems if you have been lulled into a false sense of security by having written type-safe code. Just remember that the moment you turn that type-safe collection over to older nontype-safe code, your protection vanishes.

Again, pay very close attention to compiler warnings and be prepared to see issues like this come up on the exam.

exam
watch

When using legacy (nontype-safe) collections, watch out for unboxing problems! If you declare a nongeneric collection, the `get()` method ALWAYS returns a reference of type `java.lang.Object`. Remember that unboxing can't convert a plain-old `Object` to a primitive, even if that `Object` reference refers to an `Integer` (or some other wrapped primitive) on the heap. Unboxing converts only from a wrapper class reference (like an `Integer` or a `Long`) to a primitive.
Unboxing gotcha, continued:

```
List test = new ArrayList();
test.add(43);
int x = (Integer)test.get(0);      // you must cast !!

List<Integer> test2 = new ArrayList<Integer>();
test2.add(343);
int x2 = test2.get(0);             // cast not necessary
```

Watch out for missing casts associated with pre–Java 5 nongeneric collections.

Polymorphism and Generics

Generic collections give you the same benefits of type safety that you've always had with arrays, but there are some crucial differences that can bite you if you aren't prepared. Most of these have to do with polymorphism.

You've already seen that polymorphism applies to the "base" type of the collection:

```
List<Integer> myList = new ArrayList<Integer>();
```

In other words, we were able to assign an `ArrayList` to a `List` reference because `List` is a supertype of `ArrayList`. Nothing special there—this polymorphic assignment works the way it always works in Java, regardless of the generic typing.

But what about this?

```
class Parent { }
class Child extends Parent { }
List<Parent> myList = new ArrayList<Child>();
```

Think about it for a minute.
Keep thinking…

No, it doesn't work. There's a very simple rule here—the type of the variable declaration must match the type you pass to the actual object type. If you declare `List<Foo> foo`, then whatever you assign to the foo reference MUST be of the generic type `<Foo>`. Not a subtype of `<Foo>`. Not a supertype of `<Foo>`. Just `<Foo>`.

These are wrong:

```
List<Object> myList = new ArrayList<JButton>();       // NO!
List<Number> numbers = new ArrayList<Integer>();      // NO!
// remember that Integer is a subtype of Number
```

But these are fine:

```
List<JButton> bList = new ArrayList<JButton>(); // yes
List<Object> oList = new ArrayList<Object>();   // yes
List<Integer> iList = new ArrayList<Integer>(); // yes
```

So far, so good. Just keep the generic type of the reference and the generic type of the object to which it refers identical. In other words, polymorphism applies here to only the "base" type. And by "base," we mean the type of the collection class itself—the class that can be customized with a type. In this code,

```
List<JButton> myList = new ArrayList<JButton>();
```

`List` and `ArrayList` are the *base* type and `JButton` is the *generic* type. So an `ArrayList` can be assigned to a `List`, but a collection of `<JButton>` cannot be assigned to a reference of `<Object>`, even though `JButton` is a subtype of `Object`.

The part that feels wrong for most developers is that this is NOT how it works with arrays, where you *are* allowed to do this:

```
import java.util.*;
class Parent { }
class Child extends Parent { }
public class TestPoly {
  public static void main(String[] args) {
    Parent[] myArray = new Child[3];            // yes
  }
}
```

which means you're also allowed to do this:

```
Object[] myArray = new JButton[3];                  // yes
```

but not this:

```
List<Object> list = new ArrayList<JButton>();    // NO!
```

Why are the rules for typing of arrays different from the rules for generic typing? We'll get to that in a minute. For now, just burn it into your brain that polymorphism does not work the same way for generics as it does with arrays.

Generic Methods

If you weren't already familiar with generics, you might be feeling very uncomfortable with the implications of the previous no-polymorphic-assignment-for-generic-types thing. And why shouldn't you be uncomfortable? One of the biggest benefits of polymorphism is that you can declare, say, a method argument of a particular type and at runtime be able to have that argument refer to any subtype—including those you'd never known about at the time you wrote the method with the supertype argument.

For example, imagine a classic (simplified) polymorphism example of a veterinarian (`AnimalDoctor`) class with a method `checkup()`. And right now, you have three `Animal` subtypes—`Dog`, `Cat`, and `Bird`—each implementing the `abstract checkup()` method from `Animal`:

```
abstract class Animal {
  public abstract void checkup();
}
class Dog extends Animal {
  public void checkup() {    // implement Dog-specific code
    System.out.println("Dog checkup");
  }
}
class Cat extends Animal {
  public void checkup() {    // implement Cat-specific code
    System.out.println("Cat checkup");
  }
}
class Bird extends Animal {
  public void checkup() {    // implement Bird-specific code
    System.out.println("Bird checkup");
} }
```

Forgetting collections/arrays for a moment, just imagine what the `AnimalDoctor` class needs to look like in order to have code that takes any kind of `Animal` and invokes the `Animal checkup()` method. Trying to overload the `AnimalDoctor` class with `checkup()` methods for every possible kind of animal is ridiculous and obviously not extensible. You'd have to change the `AnimalDoctor` class every time someone added a new subtype of `Animal`.

So in the `AnimalDoctor` class, you'd probably have a polymorphic method:

```
public void checkAnimal(Animal a) {
  a.checkup(); // does not matter which animal subtype each
             // Animal's overridden checkup() method runs
}
```

And, of course, we do want the `AnimalDoctor` to also have code that can take arrays of `Dogs`, `Cats`, or `Birds` for when the vet comes to the dog, cat, or bird kennel. Again, we don't want overloaded methods with arrays for each potential `Animal` subtype, so we use polymorphism in the `AnimalDoctor` class:

```
public void checkAnimals(Animal[] animals) {
  for(Animal a : animals) {
    a.checkup();
    }
  }
```

Here is the entire example, complete with a test of the array polymorphism that takes any type of animal array (`Dog[]`, `Cat[]`, `Bird[]`):

```
import java.util.*;
abstract class Animal {
  public abstract void checkup();
}
class Dog extends Animal {
  public void checkup() {    // implement Dog-specific code
    System.out.println("Dog checkup");
  }
}
class Cat extends Animal {
  public void checkup() {    // implement Cat-specific code
    System.out.println("Cat checkup");
  }
}
class Bird extends Animal {
  public void checkup() {     // implement Bird-specific code
    System.out.println("Bird checkup");
  }
}
public class AnimalDoctor {
  // method takes an array of any animal subtype
  public void checkAnimals(Animal[] animals) {
    for(Animal a : animals) {
      a.checkup();
    }
  }
  public static void main(String[] args) {
      // test it
```

```
        Dog[] dogs = {new Dog(), new Dog()};
        Cat[] cats = {new Cat(), new Cat(), new Cat()};
        Bird[] birds = {new Bird()};

        AnimalDoctor doc = new AnimalDoctor();
        doc.checkAnimals(dogs);   // pass the Dog[]
        doc.checkAnimals(cats);   // pass the Cat[]
        doc.checkAnimals(birds);  // pass the Bird[]
    }
}
```

This works fine, of course (we know, we know, this is old news). But here's why we brought this up as a refresher—this approach does NOT work the same way with type-safe collections!

In other words, a method that takes, say, an `ArrayList<Animal>` will NOT be able to accept a collection of any `Animal` subtype! That means `ArrayList<Dog>` cannot be passed into a method with an argument of `ArrayList<Animal>`, even though we already know that this works just fine with plain-old arrays.

Obviously, this difference between arrays and `ArrayList` is consistent with the polymorphism assignment rules we already looked at—the fact that you cannot assign an object of type `ArrayList<JButton>` to a `List<Object>`. But this is where you really start to feel the pain of the distinction between typed arrays and typed collections.

We know it won't work correctly, but let's try changing the `AnimalDoctor` code to use generics instead of arrays:

```
public class AnimalDoctorGeneric  {
  // change the argument from Animal[] to ArrayList<Animal>
  public void checkAnimals(ArrayList<Animal> animals) {
    for(Animal a : animals) {
      a.checkup();
    }
  }
  public static void main(String[] args) {
    // make ArrayLists instead of arrays for Dog, Cat, Bird
    List<Dog> dogs = new ArrayList<Dog>();
    dogs.add(new Dog());
    dogs.add(new Dog());
    List<Cat> cats = new ArrayList<Cat>();
    cats.add(new Cat());
    cats.add(new Cat());
    List<Bird> birds = new ArrayList<Bird>();
    birds.add(new Bird());
    // this code is the same as the Array version
    AnimalDoctorGeneric doc = new AnimalDoctorGeneric();
    // this worked when we used arrays instead of ArrayLists
```

```
doc.checkAnimals(dogs);  // send a List<Dog>
doc.checkAnimals(cats);  // send a List<Cat>
doc.checkAnimals(birds); // send a List<Bird>
  }
}
```

So what does happen?

```
javac AnimalDoctorGeneric.java
AnimalDoctorGeneric.java:51: checkAnimals(java.util.ArrayList<Animal>)
in AnimalDoctorGeneric cannot be applied to (java.util.List<Dog>)
      doc.checkAnimals(dogs);
          ^
AnimalDoctorGeneric.java:52: checkAnimals(java.util.ArrayList<Animal>)
in AnimalDoctorGeneric cannot be applied to (java.util.List<Cat>)
      doc.checkAnimals(cats);
          ^
AnimalDoctorGeneric.java:53: checkAnimals(java.util.ArrayList<Animal>)
in AnimalDoctorGeneric cannot be applied to (java.util.List<Bird>)
      doc.checkAnimals(birds);
          ^

3 errors
```

The compiler stops us with errors, not warnings. You simply CANNOT assign the individual `ArrayList`s of `Animal` subtypes (`<Dog>`, `<Cat>`, or `<Bird>`) to an `ArrayList` of the supertype `<Animal>`, which is the declared type of the argument.

This is one of the biggest gotchas for Java programmers who are so familiar with using polymorphism with arrays, where the same scenario (`Animal []` can refer to `Dog []`, `Cat []`, or `Bird []`) works as you would expect. We have two real issues:

1. Why doesn't this work?

2. How do you get around it?

You'd hate us and all of the Java engineers if we told you that there wasn't a way around it—that you had to accept it and write horribly inflexible code that tried to anticipate and code overloaded methods for each specific `<type>`. Fortunately, there is a way around it.

But first, why can't you do it if it works for arrays? Why can't you pass an `ArrayList<Dog>` into a method with an argument of `ArrayList<Animal>`?

We'll get there, but first, let's step way back for a minute and consider this perfectly legal scenario:

```
Animal[] animals = new Animal[3];
animals[0] = new Cat();
animals[1] = new Dog();
```

Part of the benefit of declaring an array using a more abstract supertype is that the array itself can hold objects of multiple subtypes of the supertype, and then you can manipulate the array, assuming everything in it can respond to the `Animal` interface (in other words, everything in the array can respond to method calls defined in the `Animal` class). So here, we're using polymorphism, not for the object that the array reference points to, but rather what the array can actually HOLD—in this case, any subtype of `Animal`. You can do the same thing with generics:

```
List<Animal> animals = new ArrayList<Animal>();
animals.add(new Cat());  // OK
animals.add(new Dog());  // OK
```

So this part works with both arrays and generic collections—we can add an instance of a subtype into an array or collection declared with a supertype. You can add `Dog`s and `Cat`s to an `Animal` array (`Animal[]`) or an `Animal` collection (`ArrayList<Animal>`).

And with arrays, this applies to what happens within a method:

```
public void addAnimal(Animal[] animals) {
  animals[0] = new Dog();  // no problem, any Animal works
                           // in Animal[]
}
```

If this is true and you can put `Dog`s into an `ArrayList<Animal>`, then why can't you use that same kind of method scenario? Why can't you do this?

```
public void addAnimal(ArrayList<Animal> animals) {
  animals.add(new Dog()); // sometimes allowed...
}
```

Actually, you CAN do this under certain conditions. The previous code WILL compile just fine IF what you pass into the method is also an `ArrayList<Animal>`. This is the part where it differs from arrays, because in the array version, you COULD pass a `Dog[]` into the method that takes an `Animal[]`.

The ONLY thing you can pass to a method argument of `ArrayList<Animal>` is an `ArrayList<Animal>`! (Assuming you aren't trying to pass a subtype of `ArrayList`, since, remember, the "base" type can be polymorphic.)

The question is still out there—why is this bad? And why is it bad for `ArrayList` but not arrays? Why can't you pass an `ArrayList<Dog>` to an argument of `ArrayList<Animal>`? Actually, the problem IS just as dangerous whether you're using arrays or a generic collection. It's just that the compiler and JVM behave differently for arrays versus generic collections.

The reason it is dangerous to pass a collection (array or `ArrayList`) of a subtype into a method that takes a collection of a supertype is because you might add something. And that means you might add the WRONG thing! This is probably really obvious, but just in case (and to reinforce), let's walk through some scenarios. The first one is simple:

```
public void foo() {
  Dog[] dogs = {new Dog(), new Dog()};
  addAnimal(dogs);            // no problem, send the Dog[] to the method
}
public void addAnimal(Animal[] animals) {
  animals[0] = new Dog();    // ok, any Animal subtype works
}
```

This is no problem. We passed a `Dog[]` into the method and added a `Dog` to the array (which was allowed since the method parameter was type `Animal[]`, which can hold any `Animal` subtype). But what if we changed the calling code to

```
public void foo() {
  Cat[] cats = {new Cat(), new Cat()};
  addAnimal(cats);            // no problem, send the Cat[] to the method
}
```

and the original method stays the same:

```
public void addAnimal(Animal[] animals) {
  animals[0] = new Dog();  // Eeek! We just put a Dog
                           // in a Cat array!

}
```

The compiler thinks it is perfectly fine to add a `Dog` to an `Animal[]` array, since a `Dog` can be assigned to an `Animal` reference. The problem is that if you passed in an array of an `Animal` subtype (`Cat`, `Dog`, or `Bird`), the compiler does not know. The compiler does not realize that out on the heap somewhere is an array of type `Cat[]`, not `Animal[]`, and you're about to try to add a `Dog` to it. To the compiler, you have passed in an array of type `Animal`, so it has no way to recognize the problem.

THIS is the scenario we're trying to prevent, regardless of whether it's an array or an `ArrayList`. The difference is that the compiler lets you get away with it for arrays, but not for generic collections.

The reason the compiler won't let you pass an `ArrayList<Dog>` into a method that takes an `ArrayList<Animal>` is because within the method, that parameter is of type `ArrayList<Animal>`, and that means you could put *any* kind of `Animal` into it. There would be no way for the compiler to stop you from putting a `Dog` into a `List` that was originally declared as `<Cat>` but is now referenced from the `<Animal>` parameter.

We still have two questions... How do you get around it? And why the heck does the compiler allow you to take that risk for arrays but not for `ArrayList` (or any other generic collection)?

The reason you can get away with compiling this for arrays is that there is a runtime exception (`ArrayStoreException`) that will prevent you from putting the wrong type of object into an array. If you send a `Dog` array into the method that takes an `Animal` array and you add only `Dog`s (including `Dog` subtypes, of course) into the array now referenced by `Animal`, no problem. But if you DO try to add a `Cat` to the object that is actually a `Dog` array, you'll get the exception.

But there IS no equivalent exception for generics because of type erasure! In other words, at runtime, the JVM KNOWS the type of arrays, but does NOT know the type of a collection. All the generic type information is removed during compilation, so by the time it gets to the JVM, there is simply no way to recognize the disaster of putting a `Cat` into an `ArrayList<Dog>`, and vice versa (and it becomes exactly like the problems you have when you use legacy, nontype-safe code).

So this actually IS legal code:

```
public void addAnimal(List<Animal> animals) {
   animals.add(new Dog());   // this is always legal,
                             // since Dog can
                             // be assigned to an Animal
                             // reference
  }
  public static void main(String[] args) {
    List<Animal> animals = new ArrayList<Animal>();
    animals.add(new Dog());
    animals.add(new Dog());
    AnimalDoctorGeneric doc = new AnimalDoctorGeneric();
    doc.addAnimal(animals); // OK, since animals matches
                            // the method arg
  }
```

As long as the only thing you pass to the `addAnimals(List<Animal>)` is an `ArrayList<Animal>`, the compiler is pleased—knowing that any `Animal` subtype you add will be valid (you can always add a `Dog` to an `Animal` collection, yada, yada, yada). But if you try to invoke `addAnimal()` with an argument of any OTHER `ArrayList` type, the compiler will stop you, since at runtime the JVM would have no way to stop you from adding a `Dog` to what was created as a `Cat` collection.

For example, this code that changes the generic type to `<Dog>` without changing the `addAnimal()` method will NOT compile:

```
public void addAnimal(List<Animal> animals) {
   animals.add(new Dog());  // still OK as always
}
public static void main(String[] args) {
  List<Dog> animals = new ArrayList<Dog>();
  animals.add(new Dog());
  animals.add(new Dog());
  AnimalDoctorGeneric doc = new AnimalDoctorGeneric();
  doc.addAnimal(animals); // THIS is where it breaks!
}
```

The compiler says something like:

```
javac AnimalDoctorGeneric.java
AnimalDoctorGeneric.java:49: addAnimal(java.util.List<Animal>) in
AnimalDoctorGeneric cannot be applied to (java.util.List<Dog>)
        doc.addAnimal(animals);
        ^
1 error
```

Notice that this message is virtually the same one you'd get trying to invoke any method with the wrong argument. It's saying that you simply cannot invoke `addAnimal(List<Animal>)` using something whose reference was declared as `List<Dog>`. (It's the reference type, not the actual object type, that matters—but remember: The generic type of an object is ALWAYS the same as the generic type declared on the reference. `List<Dog>` can refer ONLY to collections that are subtypes of `List` but which were instantiated as generic type `<Dog>`.)

Once again, remember that once inside the `addAnimals()` method, all that matters is the type of the parameter—in this case, `List<Animal>`. (We changed it from `ArrayList` to `List` to keep our "base" type polymorphism cleaner.)

Back to the key question—how do we get around this? If the problem is related only to the danger of adding the wrong thing to the collection, what about the `checkup()` method that used the collection passed in as read-only? In other words, what about methods that invoke `Animal` methods on each thing in the collection, which will work regardless of which kind of `ArrayList` subtype is passed in?

And that's a clue! It's the `add()` method that is the problem, so what we need is a way to tell the compiler, "Hey, I'm using the collection passed in just to invoke methods on the elements—and I promise not to ADD anything into the collection." And there IS a mechanism to tell the compiler that you can take any generic subtype of the declared argument type because you won't be putting anything in the collection. And that mechanism is the wildcard `<?>`.

The method signature would change from

```
public void addAnimal(List<Animal> animals)
```

to

```
public void addAnimal(List<? extends Animal> animals)
```

By saying `<? extends Animal>`, we're saying, "I can be assigned a collection that is a subtype of `List` and typed for `<Animal>` or anything that *extends* `Animal`. And, oh yes, I SWEAR that I will not ADD anything into the collection." (There's a little more to the story, but we'll get there.)

So, of course, the `addAnimal()` method shown previously won't actually compile, even with the wildcard notation, because that method DOES add something.

```
public void addAnimal(List<? extends Animal> animals) {
   animals.add(new Dog());  // NO! Can't add if we
                            // use <? extends Animal>
}
```

You'll get a very strange error that might look something like this:

```
javac AnimalDoctorGeneric.java
AnimalDoctorGeneric.java:38: cannot find symbol
symbol   : method add(Dog)
location: interface java.util.List<capture of ? extends Animal>
       animals.add(new Dog());
                  ^
1 error
```

which basically says, "You can't add a `Dog` here." If we change the method so that it doesn't add anything, it works.

But wait—there's more. (And by the way, everything we've covered in this generics section is likely to be tested for on the exam, with the exception of "type erasure," which you aren't required to know any details of.)

First, the `<? extends Animal>` means that you can take any subtype of `Animal`; however, that subtype can be EITHER a subclass of a class (abstract or concrete) OR a type that implements the interface after the word `extends`. In other words, the keyword `extends` in the context of a wildcard represents BOTH subclasses and interface implementations. There is no `<? implements Serializable>` syntax. If you want to declare a method that takes anything that is of a type that implements `Serializable`, you'd still use `extends` like this:

```
void foo(List<? extends Serializable> list) // odd, but correct
                                            // to use "extends"
```

This looks strange since you would never say this in a class declaration because `Serializable` is an interface, not a class. But that's the syntax, so burn it in your brain!

One more time—there is only ONE wildcard keyword that represents *both* interface implementations and subclasses. And that keyword is `extends`. But when you see it, think "IS-A," as in something that passes the `instanceof` test.

However, there is another scenario where you can use a wildcard AND still add to the collection, but in a safe way—the keyword `super`.

Imagine, for example, that you declared the method this way:

```
public void addAnimal(List<? super Dog> animals) {
    animals.add(new Dog());      // adding is sometimes OK with super
}
public static void main(String[] args) {
    List<Animal> animals = new ArrayList<Animal>();
    animals.add(new Dog());
    animals.add(new Dog());
    AnimalDoctorGeneric doc = new AnimalDoctorGeneric();
    doc.addAnimal(animals);      // passing an Animal List
}
```

Now what you've said in this line

```
public void addAnimal(List<? super Dog> animals)
```

is essentially, "Hey, compiler, please accept any `List` with a generic type that is of type `Dog` or a supertype of `Dog`. Nothing lower in the inheritance tree can come in, but anything higher than `Dog` is okay."

You probably already recognize why this works. If you pass in a list of type `Animal`, then it's perfectly fine to add a `Dog` to it. If you pass in a list of type `Dog`, it's perfectly fine to add a `Dog` to it. And if you pass in a list of type `Object`, it's STILL fine to add a `Dog` to it. When you use the `<? super ...>` syntax, you are telling the compiler that you can accept the type on the right side of `super` or any of its supertypes, since—and this is the key part that makes it work—a collection declared as any supertype of `Dog` will be able to accept a `Dog` as an element. `List<Object>` can take a `Dog`. `List<Animal>` can take a `Dog`. And `List<Dog>` can take a `Dog`. So passing any of those in will work. So the super keyword in wildcard notation lets you have a restricted, but still possible, way to add to a collection.

The wildcard gives you polymorphic assignments, but with certain restrictions that you don't have for arrays. Quick question: Are these two identical?

```
public void foo(List<?> list) { }
public void foo(List<Object> list) { }
```

If there IS a difference (and we're not yet saying there is), what is it?

There IS a huge difference. List<?>, which is the wildcard <?> without the keywords extends or super, simply means "any type." So that means any type of List can be assigned to the argument. That could be a List of <Dog>, <Integer>, <JButton>, <Socket>, whatever. And using the wildcard alone, without the keyword super (followed by a type), means that you cannot ADD anything to the list referred to as List<?>.

List<Object> is completely different from List<?>. List<Object> means that the method can take ONLY a List<Object>. Not a List<Dog> or a List<Cat>. It does, however, mean you can add to the list because the compiler has already made certain that you're passing only a valid List<Object> into the method.

Based on the previous explanations, figure out if the following will work:

```
import java.util.*;
public class TestWildcards {
  public static void main(String[] args) {
    List<Integer> myList = new ArrayList<Integer>();
    Bar bar = new Bar();
    bar.doInsert(myList);
  }
}
class Bar {
  void doInsert(List<?> list) {
    list.add(new Dog());
  }
}
```

If not, where is the problem?

The problem is in the list.add() method within doInsert(). The <?> wildcard allows a list of ANY type to be passed to the method, but the add() method is not valid, for the reasons we explored earlier (that you could put the wrong kind of thing into the collection). So this time, the TestWildcards class is fine, but the Bar class won't compile because it does an add() in a method that

---

uses a wildcard (without `super`). What if we change the `doInsert()` method to this:

```
import java.util.*;
public class TestWildcards {
  public static void main(String[] args) {
    List<Integer> myList = new ArrayList<Integer>();
    Bar bar = new Bar();
    bar.doInsert(myList);
  }
}
class Bar {
  void doInsert(List<Object> list) {
    list.add(new Dog());
  }
}
```

Now will it work? If not, why not?

This time, class `Bar`, with the `doInsert()` method, compiles just fine. The problem is that the `TestWildcards` code is trying to pass a `List<Integer>` into a method that can take ONLY a `List<Object>`. And *nothing* else can be substituted for `<Object>`.

By the way, `List<? extends Object>` and `List<?>` are absolutely identical! They both say, "I can refer to any type of object." But as you can see, neither of them is the same as `List<Object>`. One way to remember this is that if you see the wildcard notation (a question mark ?), this means "many possibilities." If you do NOT see the question mark, then it means the `<type>` in the brackets and absolutely NOTHING ELSE. `List<Dog>` means `List<Dog>` and not `List<Beagle>`, `List<Poodle>`, or any other subtype of `Dog`. But `List<? extends Dog>` could mean `List<Beagle>`, `List<Poodle>`, and so on. Of course, `List<?>` could be...anything at all.

Keep in mind that the wildcards can be used only for reference declarations (including arguments, variables, return types, and so on). They can't be used as the type parameter when you create a new typed collection. Think about that—while a reference can be abstract and polymorphic, the actual object created must be of a specific type. You have to lock down the type when you make the object using `new`.

As a little review before we move on with generics, look at the following statements and figure out which will compile:

```
1) List<?> list = new ArrayList<Dog>();
2) List<? extends Animal> aList = new ArrayList<Dog>();
3) List<?> foo = new ArrayList<? extends Animal>();
4) List<? extends Dog> cList = new ArrayList<Integer>();
5) List<? super Dog> bList = new ArrayList<Animal>();
6) List<? super Animal> dList = new ArrayList<Dog>();
```

The correct answers (the statements that compile) are 1, 2, and 5. The three that won't compile are

- **Statement**   (3) `List<?> foo = new ArrayList<? extends Animal>();`
- **Problem**   You cannot use wildcard notation in the object creation. So the `new ArrayList<? extends Animal>()` will not compile.
- **Statement**   (4) `List<? extends Dog> cList = new ArrayList<Integer>();`
- **Problem**   You cannot assign an `Integer` list to a reference that takes only a `Dog` (including any subtypes of `Dog`, of course).
- **Statement**   (6) `List<? super Animal> dList = new ArrayList<Dog>();`
- **Problem**   You cannot assign a `Dog` to `<? super Animal>`. The `Dog` is too "low" in the class hierarchy. Only `<Animal>` or `<Object>` would have been legal.

Generic Declarations

Until now, we've talked about how to create type-safe collections and how to declare reference variables, including arguments and return types, using generic syntax. But here are a few questions: How do we even know that we're allowed/ supposed to specify a type for these collection classes? And does generic typing work with any other classes in the API? And finally, can we declare our own classes as generic types? In other words, can we make a class that requires that someone pass a type in when they declare it and instantiate it?

First, the one you obviously know the answer to—the API tells you when a parameterized type is expected. For example, this is the API declaration for the `java.util.List` interface:

```
public interface List<E>
```

The `<E>` is a placeholder for the type you pass in. The `List` interface is behaving as a generic "template" (sort of like C++ templates), and when you write your code, you change it from a generic `List` to a `List<Dog>` or `List<Integer>`, and so on.

The E, by the way, is only a convention. Any valid Java identifier would work here, but E stands for "Element," and it's used when the template is a collection.

The other main convention is T (stands for "type"), used for, well, things that are NOT collections.

Now that you've seen the interface declaration for List, what do you think the add() method looks like?

```
boolean add(E o)
```

In other words, whatever E is when you declare the List, *that's what you can add to it.* So imagine this code:

```
List<Animal> list = new ArrayList<Animal>();
```

The E in the List API suddenly has its waveform collapsed and goes from the abstract <your type goes here> to a List of Animals. And if it's a List of Animals, then the add() method of List must obviously behave like this:

```
boolean add(Animal a)
```

When you look at an API for a generics class or interface, pick a type parameter (Dog, JButton, even Object) and do a mental find and replace on each instance of E (or whatever identifier is used as the placeholder for the type parameter).

Making Your Own Generic Class

Let's try making our own generic class to get a feel for how it works, and then we'll look at a few remaining generics syntax details. Imagine someone created a class Rental that manages a pool of rentable items:

```
public class Rental {
  private List rentalPool;
  private int maxNum;
  public Rental(int maxNum, List rentalPool) {
    this.maxNum = maxNum;
    this.rentalPool = rentalPool;
  }
  public Object getRental() {
    // blocks until there's something available
    return rentalPool.get(0);
  }
  public void returnRental(Object o) {
    rentalPool.add(o);
  }
}
```

Now imagine you wanted to make a subclass of Rental that was just for renting cars. You might start with something like this:

```
import java.util.*;
public class CarRental extends Rental {
```

```
public CarRental(int maxNum, List<Car> rentalPool) {
  super(maxNum, rentalPool);
}
public Car getRental() {
  return (Car) super.getRental();
}
public void returnRental(Car c) {
  super.returnRental(c);
}
public void returnRental(Object o) {
  if (o instanceof Car) {
    super.returnRental(o);
  } else {
    System.out.println("Cannot add a non-Car");
    // probably throw an exception
} } }
```

But then, the more you look at it, the more you realize

1. You are doing your own type checking in the `returnRental()` method. You can't change the argument type of `returnRental()` to take a `Car`, since it's an override (not an overload) of the method from class `Rental`. (Overloading would take away your polymorphic flexibility with `Rental`.)

2. You really don't want to make separate subclasses for every possible kind of rentable thing (cars, computers, bowling shoes, children, and so on).

But given your natural brilliance (heightened by this contrived scenario), you quickly realize that you can make the `Rental` class a generic type—a template for any kind of `Rentable` thing—and you're good to go.

(We did say contrived...since in reality, you might very well want to have different behaviors for different kinds of rentable things, but even that could be solved cleanly through some kind of behavior composition as opposed to inheritance (using the Strategy design pattern, for example). And no, the Strategy design pattern isn't on the exam, but we still think you should read our design patterns book. Think of the kittens.) So here's your new and improved generic `Rental` class:

```
import java.util.*;
public class RentalGeneric<T> {            // "T" is for the type
                                           // parameter
  private List<T> rentalPool;              // Use the class type for the
                                           // List type
  private int maxNum;
  public RentalGeneric(
    int maxNum, List<T> rentalPool) {      // constructor takes a
                                           // List of the class type
```

```
      this.maxNum = maxNum;
      this.rentalPool = rentalPool;
    }
    public T getRental() {                        // we rent out a T
      // blocks until there's something available
      return rentalPool.get(0);
    }
    public void returnRental(T returnedThing) { // and the renter
                                                //  returns a T
      rentalPool.add(returnedThing);
    }
  }
```

Let's put it to the test:

```
class TestRental {
  public static void main (String[] args) {
    //make some Cars for the pool
    Car c1 = new Car();
    Car c2 = new Car();
    List<Car> carList = new ArrayList<Car>();
    carList.add(c1);
    carList.add(c2);
    RentalGeneric<Car> carRental = new
                      RentalGeneric<Car>(2, carList);
    // now get a car out, and it won't need a cast
    Car carToRent = carRental.getRental();
    carRental.returnRental(carToRent);
    // can we stick something else in the original carList?
    carList.add(new Cat("Fluffy"));
  }
}
```

We get one error:

```
kathy% javac1.5 RentalGeneric.java
RentalGeneric.java:38: cannot find symbol
symbol   : method add(Cat)
location: interface java.util.List<Car>
    carList.add(new Cat("Fluffy"));
               ^

1 error
```

Now we have a Rental class that can be *typed* to whatever the programmer chooses, and the compiler will enforce it. In other words, it works just as the Collections classes do. Let's look at more examples of generic syntax you might find in the API or source code. Here's another simple class that uses the parameterized type of the class in several ways:

```
public class TestGenerics<T> {    // as the class type
  T anInstance;                   // as an instance variable type
  T [] anArrayOfTs;               // as an array type
```

```
TestGenerics(T anInstance) {      // as an argument type
   this.anInstance = anInstance;
}
T getT() {                        // as a return type
   return anInstance;
}
}
```

Obviously, this is a ridiculous use of generics, and in fact, you'll see generics only rarely outside of collections. But you do need to understand the different kinds of generic syntax you might encounter, so we'll continue with these examples until we've covered them all.

You can use more than one parameterized type in a single class definition:

```
public class UseTwo<T, U> {
  T one;
  U two;
  UseTwo(T one, U two) {
    this.one = one;
    this.two = two;
  }
  T getT() { return one; }
  X getU() { return two; }

// test it by creating it with <String, Integer>

  public static void main (String[] args) {
    UseTwo<String, Integer> twos =
                 new UseTwo<String, Integer>("foo", 42);

    String theT = twos.getT(); // returns a String
    int theU = twos.getU();    // returns Integer, unboxes to int
  }
}
```

And you can use a form of wildcard notation in a class definition to specify a range (called "bounds") for the type that can be used for the type parameter:

```
public class AnimalHolder<T extends Animal> {           // use "T" instead
                                                        // of "?"
 T animal;
 public static void main(String[] args) {
   AnimalHolder<Dog> dogHolder = new AnimalHolder<Dog>(); // OK
   AnimalHolder<Integer> x = new AnimalHolder<Integer>(); // NO!
 }
}
```

Creating Generic Methods

Until now, every example we've seen uses the class parameter type—the type declared with the class name. For example, in the `UseTwo<T,X>` declaration, we used the `T` and `X` placeholders throughout the code. But it's possible to define a parameterized type at a more granular level—a method.

Imagine you want to create a method that takes an instance of any type, instantiates an `ArrayList` of that type, and adds the instance to the `ArrayList`. The class itself doesn't need to be generic; basically, we just want a utility method that we can pass a type to and that can use that type to construct a type-safe collection. Using a generic method, we can declare the method without a specific type and then get the type information based on the type of the object passed to the method. For example:

```
import java.util.*;
public class CreateAnArrayList {
  public <T> void makeArrayList(T t) {   // take an object of an
                                         // unknown type and use a
                                         // "T" to represent the type

    List<T> list = new ArrayList<T>();   // now we can create the
                                         // list using "T"

    list.add(t);
    }
}
```

In the preceding code, if you invoke the `makeArrayList()` method with a `Dog` instance, the method will behave as though it looked like this all along:

```
public void makeArrayList(Dog t) {
  List<Dog> list = new ArrayList<Dog>();
  list.add(t);
}
```

And, of course, if you invoke the method with an `Integer`, then the `T` is replaced by `Integer` (not in the bytecode, remember—we're describing how it appears to behave, not how it actually gets it done).

The strangest thing about generic methods is that you must declare the type variable BEFORE the return type of the method:

```
public <T> void makeArrayList(T t)
```

The `<T>` before `void` simply defines what `T` is before you use it as a type in the argument. You MUST declare the type like that unless the type is specified for the class. In `CreateAnArrayList`, the class is not generic, so there's no type parameter placeholder we can use.

You're also free to put boundaries on the type you declare. For example, if you want to restrict the `makeArrayList()` method to only `Number` or its subtypes (`Integer`, `Float`, and so on), you would say

```
public <T extends Number> void makeArrayList(T t)
```

e x a m

ⓦ **a t c h**   *It's tempting to forget that the method argument is NOT where you declare the type parameter variable T. In order to use a type variable like T, you must have declared it either as the class parameter type or in the method before the return type. The following might look right:*

```
public void makeList(T t) { }
```

But the only way for this to be legal is if there is actually a class named T, in which case the argument is like any other type declaration for a variable. And what about constructor arguments? They, too, can be declared with a generic type, but then it looks even stranger, since constructors have no return type at all:

```
public class Radio {
  public <T> Radio(T t) { }  // legal constructor
}
```

e x a m

ⓦ **a t c h**   *If you REALLY want to get ridiculous (or fired), you can declare a class with a name that is the same as the type parameter placeholder:*

```
class X { public <X> X(X x) { } }
```

Yes, this works. The X that is the constructor name has no relationship to the <X> type declaration, which has no relationship to the constructor argument identifier, which is also, of course, X. The compiler is able to parse this and treat each of the different uses of X independently. So there is no naming conflict between class names, type parameter placeholders, and variable identifiers.

a t c h

One of the most common mistakes programmers make when creating generic classes or methods is to use a `<?>` in the wildcard syntax rather than a type variable `<T>`, `<E>`, and so on. This code might look right, but isn't:

```
public class NumberHolder<? extends Number> { }
```

While the question mark works when declaring a reference for a variable, it does NOT work for generic class and method declarations. This code is not legal:

```
public class NumberHolder<?> { ? aNum; }      // NO!
```

But if you replace the `<?>` with a legal identifier, you're good:

```
public class NumberHolder<T> { T aNum; }      // Yes
```

In practice, **98 percent** of what you're likely to do with generics is simply declare and use type-safe collections, including using (and passing) them as arguments. But now you know much more (but by no means everything) about the way generics work.

If this was clear and easy for you, that's excellent. If it was…painful…just know that adding generics to the Java language very nearly caused a revolt among some of the most experienced Java developers. Most of the outspoken critics are simply unhappy with the complexity, or aren't convinced that gaining type-safe collections is worth the ten-million little rules you have to learn now. It's true that with Java 5, learning Java got harder. But trust us…we've never seen it take more than two days to "get" generics. That's 48 consecutive hours.

CERTIFICATION SUMMARY

We began with a quick review of the `toString()` method. The `toString()` method is automatically called when you ask `System.out.println()` to print an object—you override it to return a `String` of meaningful data about your objects.

Next, we reviewed the purpose of `==` (to see if two reference variables refer to the same object) and the `equals()` method (to see if two objects are meaningfully equivalent). You learned the downside of not overriding `equals()`—you may not be able to find the object in a collection. We discussed a little bit about how to write a good `equals()` method—don't forget to use `instanceof` and refer to the object's significant attributes. We reviewed the contracts for overriding `equals()` and `hashCode()`. We learned about the theory behind hashcodes, the difference between legal, appropriate, and efficient hashcoding. We also saw that even though wildly inefficient, it's legal for a `hashCode()` method to always return the same value.

Next, we turned to collections, where we learned about `Lists`, `Sets`, and `Maps` and the difference between ordered and sorted collections. We learned the key attributes of the common collection classes and when to use which. Along the way, we introduced the "diamond" syntax, and we talked about autoboxing primitives into and out of wrapper class objects.

We covered the ins and outs of the `Collections` and `Arrays` classes: how to sort and how to search. We learned about converting arrays to `Lists` and back again.

Finally, we tackled generics. Generics let you enforce compile-time type-safety on collections or other classes. Generics help assure you that when you get an item from a collection, it will be of the type you expect, with no casting required. You can mix legacy code with generics code, but this can cause exceptions. The rules for polymorphism change when you use generics, although by using wildcards you can still create polymorphic collections. Some generics declarations allow reading of a collection, but allow very limited updating of the collection.

All in all, one fascinating chapter.

TWO-MINUTE DRILL

Here are some of the key points from this chapter.

Overriding hashCode() and equals() (OCP Objectives 1.4, 3.3, and 3.X)

- ☐ `equals()`, `hashCode()`, and `toString()` are `public`.
- ☐ Override `toString()` so that `System.out.println()` or other methods can see something useful, like your object's state.
- ☐ Use `==` to determine if two reference variables refer to the same object.
- ☐ Use `equals()` to determine if two objects are meaningfully equivalent.
- ☐ If you don't override `equals()`, your objects won't be useful hashing keys.
- ☐ If you don't override `equals()`, different objects can't be considered equal.
- ☐ Strings and wrappers override `equals()` and make good hashing keys.
- ☐ When overriding `equals()`, use the `instanceof` operator to be sure you're evaluating an appropriate class.
- ☐ When overriding `equals()`, compare the objects' significant attributes.
- ☐ Highlights of the `equals()` contract:
    - ☐ **Reflexive** `x.equals(x)` is true.
    - ☐ **Symmetric** If `x.equals(y)` is true, then `y.equals(x)` must be true.
    - ☐ **Transitive** If `x.equals(y)` is true, and `y.equals(z)` is true, then `z.equals(x)` is true.
    - ☐ **Consistent** Multiple calls to `x.equals(y)` will return the same result.
    - ☐ **Null** If `x` is not `null`, then `x.equals(null)` is false.
- ☐ If `x.equals(y)` is true, then `x.hashCode() == y.hashCode()` is true.
- ☐ If you override `equals()`, override `hashCode()`.
- ☐ `HashMap`, `HashSet`, `Hashtable`, `LinkedHashMap`, and `LinkedHashSet` use hashing.
- ☐ An appropriate `hashCode()` override sticks to the `hashCode()` contract.
- ☐ An efficient `hashCode()` override distributes keys evenly across its buckets.

- [ ] An overridden `equals()` must be at least as precise as its `hashCode()` mate.
- [ ] To reiterate: if two objects are equal, their hashcodes must be equal.
- [ ] It's legal for a `hashCode()` method to return the same value for all instances (although in practice it's very inefficient).
- [ ] Highlights of the `hashCode()` contract:
    - [ ] Consistent: Multiple calls to `x.hashCode()` return the same integer.
    - [ ] If `x.equals(y)` is `true`, `x.hashCode() == y.hashCode()` is `true`.
    - [ ] If `x.equals(y)` is `false`, then `x.hashCode() == y.hashCode()` can be either `true` or `false`, but `false` will tend to create better efficiency.
- [ ] Transient variables aren't appropriate for `equals()` and `hashCode()`.

Collections (OCP Objective 3.2)

- [ ] Common collection activities include adding objects, removing objects, verifying object inclusion, retrieving objects, and iterating.
- [ ] Three meanings for "collection":
    - [ ] **collection**   Represents the data structure in which objects are stored
    - [ ] **Collection**   `java.util` interface from which `Set` and `List` extend
    - [ ] **Collections**   A class that holds static collection utility methods
- [ ] Four basic flavors of collections include `Lists`, `Sets`, `Maps`, and `Queues`:
    - [ ] **Lists of things**   Ordered, duplicates allowed, with an index.
    - [ ] **Sets of things**   May or may not be ordered and/or sorted; duplicates not allowed.
    - [ ] **Maps of things with keys**   May or may not be ordered and/or sorted; duplicate keys are not allowed.
    - [ ] **Queues of things to process**   Ordered by FIFO or by priority.
- [ ] Four basic subflavors of collections: Sorted, Unsorted, Ordered, and Unordered:
    - [ ] **Ordered**   Iterating through a collection in a specific, nonrandom order
    - [ ] **Sorted**   Iterating through a collection in a sorted order
- [ ] Sorting can be alphabetic, numeric, or programmer-defined.

Key Attributes of Common Collection Classes (OCP Objective 3.2)

- [ ] **ArrayList**   Fast iteration and fast random access.
- [ ] **Vector**   It's like a slower `ArrayList`, but it has synchronized methods.
- [ ] **LinkedList**   Good for adding elements to the ends, i.e., stacks and queues.
- [ ] **HashSet**   Fast access, assures no duplicates, provides no ordering.
- [ ] **LinkedHashSet**   No duplicates, iterates by insertion order.
- [ ] **TreeSet**   No duplicates, iterates in sorted order.
- [ ] **HashMap**   Fastest updates (key/values); allows one `null` key, many `null` values.
- [ ] **Hashtable**   Like a slower `HashMap` (as with `Vector`, due to its synchronized methods). No `null` values or `null` keys allowed.
- [ ] **LinkedHashMap**   Faster iterations; iterates by insertion order or last accessed; allows one `null` key, many `null` values.
- [ ] **TreeMap**   A sorted map.
- [ ] **PriorityQueue**   A to-do list ordered by the elements' priority.
- [ ] **ArrayDeque**   Like an `ArrayList` only better performance; ordered only by index. Good for stacks and queues.

Using Collection Classes (OCP Objectives 3.2 and 3.3)

- [ ] Collections hold only objects, but primitives can be autoboxed.
- [ ] Java 7 and later allows "diamond" syntax: `List<Dog> d = new ArrayList<>();`.
- [ ] Iterate with the enhanced `for` or with an `Iterator` via `hasNext()` and `next()`.
- [ ] `hasNext()` determines if more elements exist; the `Iterator` does NOT move.
- [ ] `next()` returns the next element AND moves the `Iterator` forward.
- [ ] To work correctly, a `Map`'s keys must override `equals()` and `hashCode()`.
- [ ] Queues and Deques use `offer()` to add an element, `poll()` to remove the head of the queue, and `peek()` to look at the head of a queue.
- [ ] TreeSets and TreeMaps have navigation methods like `floor()` and `higher()`.
- [ ] You can create/extend "backed" subcopies of `TreeSets` and `TreeMaps`.

Sorting and Searching Arrays and Lists (OCP Objectives 2.6 and 3.3)

☐ Sorting can be in natural order or via a `Comparable` or many `Comparators`.

☐ Implement `Comparable` using `compareTo()`; provides only one sort order.

☐ Create many `Comparators` to sort a class many ways; implement `compare()`.

☐ Use a lambda expression as a shorthand to create a `Comparator`.

☐ To be sorted and searched, an array's or `List`'s elements must be *comparable*.

☐ To be searched, an array or `List` must first be sorted.

Utility Classes: Collections and Arrays (OCP Objectives 3.2 and 3.3)

☐ These `java.util` classes provide

    ☐ A `sort()` method. Sort using a `Comparator` or sort using natural order.

    ☐ A `binarySearch()` method. Search a presorted array or `List`.

    ☐ `Arrays.asList()` creates a `List` from an array and links them together.

    ☐ `Collections.reverse()` reverses the order of elements in a `List`.

    ☐ `Collections.reverseOrder()` returns a `Comparator` that sorts in reverse.

    ☐ `Lists` and `Sets` have a `toArray()` method to create arrays.

Generics (OCP Objective 3.1)

☐ Generics let you enforce compile-time type-safety on Collections (or other classes and methods declared using generic type parameters).

☐ An `ArrayList<Animal>` can accept references of type `Dog`, `Cat`, or any other subtype of `Animal` (subclass, or if `Animal` is an interface, implementation).

☐ When using generic collections, a cast is not needed to get (declared type) elements out of the collection. With nongeneric collections, a cast is required:

```
List<String> gList = new ArrayList<String>();
List list = new ArrayList();
// more code
String s = gList.get(0);           // no cast needed
String s = (String)list.get(0);    // cast required
```

☐ You can pass a generic collection into a method that takes a nongeneric collection, but the results may be disastrous. The compiler can't stop the method from inserting the wrong type into the previously type-safe collection.

☐ If the compiler can recognize that nontype-safe code is potentially endangering something you originally declared as type-safe, you will get a compiler warning. For instance, if you pass a `List<String>` into a method declared as

```
void foo(List aList) { aList.add(anInteger); }
```

you'll get a warning because `add()` is potentially "unsafe."

☐ "Compiles without error" is not the same as "compiles without warnings." A compilation *warning* is not considered a compilation *error* or *failure*.

☐ Generic type information does not exist at runtime—it is for compile-time safety only. Mixing generics with legacy code can create compiled code that may throw an exception at runtime.

☐ Polymorphic assignments apply only to the base type, not the generic type parameter. You can say

```
List<Animal> aList = new ArrayList<Animal>();   // yes
```

You can't say

```
List<Animal> aList = new ArrayList<Dog>();      // no
```

☐ The polymorphic assignment rule applies everywhere an assignment can be made. The following are NOT allowed:

```
void foo(List<Animal> aList) { }  // cannot take a List<Dog>
List<Animal> bar() { }            // cannot return a List<Dog>
```

☐ Wildcard syntax allows a generic method to accept subtypes (or supertypes) of the declared type of the method argument:

```
void addD(List<Dog> d) {}           // can take only <Dog>
void addD(List<? extends Dog>) {}  // take a <Dog> or <Beagle>
```

☐ The wildcard keyword `extends` is used to mean either "extends" or "implements." So in `<? extends Dog>`, Dog can be a class or an interface.

☐ When using a wildcard `List<? extends Dog>`, the collection can be accessed but not modified.

☐ When using a wildcard `List<?>`, any generic type can be assigned to the reference, but for access only—no modifications.

☐ `List<Object>` refers only to a `List<Object>`, whereas `List<?>` or `List<? extends Object>` can hold any type of object, but for access only.

- [ ] Declaration conventions for generics use `T` for type and `E` for element:

```
public interface List<E>   // API declaration for List
boolean add(E o)           // List.add() declaration
```

- [ ] The generics type identifier can be used in class, method, and variable declarations:

```
class Foo<t> { }           // a class
T anInstance;              // an instance variable
Foo(T aRef) {}             // a constructor argument
void bar(T aRef) {}        // a method argument
T baz() {}                 // a return type
```

The compiler will substitute the actual type.

- [ ] You can use more than one parameterized type in a declaration:

```
public class UseTwo<T, X> { }
```

- [ ] You can declare a generic method using a type not defined in the class:

```
public <T> void makeList(T t) { }
```

This is NOT using `T` as the return type. This method has a `void` return type, but to use `T` within the argument, you must declare the `<T>`, which happens before the return type.

SELF TEST

The following questions will help you measure your understanding of the material presented in this chapter. Read all of the choices carefully, as there may be more than one correct answer. Choose all correct answers for each question. Stay focused.

1. Given:

```
public static void main(String[] args) {

    // INSERT DECLARATION HERE
    for (int i = 0; i <= 10; i++) {
      List<Integer> row = new ArrayList<Integer>();
      for (int j = 0; j <= 10; j++)
        row.add(i * j);
      table.add(row);
    }
    for (List<Integer> row : table)
      System.out.println(row);
    }
```

Which statements could be inserted at // INSERT DECLARATION HERE to allow this code to compile and run? (Choose all that apply.)

A. List<List<Integer>> table = new List<List<Integer>>();
B. List<List<Integer>> table = new ArrayList<List<Integer>>();
C. List<List<Integer>> table = new ArrayList<ArrayList<Integer>>();
D. List<List, Integer> table = new List<List, Integer>();
E. List<List, Integer> table = new ArrayList<List, Integer>();
F. List<List, Integer> table = new ArrayList<ArrayList, Integer>();
G. None of the above

2. Which statements are true about comparing two instances of the same class, given that the equals() and hashCode() methods have been properly overridden? (Choose all that apply.)

A. If the equals() method returns true, the hashCode() comparison == might return false

B. If the equals() method returns false, the hashCode() comparison == might return true

C. If the hashCode() comparison == returns true, the equals() method must return true

D. If the hashCode() comparison == returns true, the equals() method might return true

E. If the hashCode() comparison != returns true, the equals() method might return true

3. Given:

```
public static void before() {
  Set set = new TreeSet();
  set.add("2");
  set.add(3);
  set.add("1");
  Iterator it = set.iterator();
    while (it.hasNext())
  System.out.print(it.next() + " ");
}
```

Which statements are true?

A. The before() method will print 1 2

B. The before() method will print 1 2 3

C. The before() method will print three numbers, but the order cannot be determined

D. The before() method will not compile

E. The before() method will throw an exception at runtime

4. Given:

```
import java.util.*;
class MapEQ {
  public static void main(String[] args) {
    Map<ToDos, String> m = new HashMap<ToDos, String>();
    ToDos t1 = new ToDos("Monday");
    ToDos t2 = new ToDos("Monday");
    ToDos t3 = new ToDos("Tuesday");
    m.put(t1, "doLaundry");
    m.put(t2, "payBills");
    m.put(t3, "cleanAttic");
    System.out.println(m.size());
  }
}
class ToDos{
  String day;
  ToDos(String d) { day = d; }
  public boolean equals(Object o) {
    return ((ToDos)o).day.equals(this.day);
  }
  // public int hashCode() { return 9; }
}
```

Which is correct? (Choose all that apply.)

A. As the code stands, it will not compile

B. As the code stands, the output will be 2

C. As the code stands, the output will be 3

D. If the `hashCode()` method is uncommented, the output will be 2

E. If the `hashCode()` method is uncommented, the output will be 3

F. If the `hashCode()` method is uncommented, the code will not compile

5. Given:

```
12. public class AccountManager {
13.    private Map accountTotals = new HashMap();
14.    private int retirementFund;
15.
16.    public int getBalance(String accountName) {
17.      Integer total = (Integer) accountTotals.get(accountName);
18.      if (total == null)
19.        total = Integer.valueOf(0);
20.      return total.intValue();
21.    }
23.    public void setBalance(String accountName, int amount) {
24.      accountTotals.put(accountName, Integer.valueOf(amount));
25.    }
26. }
```

This class is going to be updated to make use of appropriate generic types, with no changes in behavior (for better or worse). Which of these steps could be performed? (Choose three.)

A. Replace line 13 with

```
private Map<String, int> accountTotals = new HashMap<String, int>();
```

B. Replace line 13 with

```
private Map<String, Integer> accountTotals = new HashMap<String, Integer>();
```

C. Replace line 13 with

```
private Map<String<Integer>> accountTotals = new HashMap<String<Integer>>();
```

D. Replace lines 17–20 with

```
int total = accountTotals.get(accountName);
    if (total == null)
        total = 0;
    return total;
```

E. Replace lines 17–20 with

```
Integer total = accountTotals.get(accountName);
    if (total == null)
        total = 0;
    return total;
```

F. Replace lines 17–20 with

```
return accountTotals.get(accountName);
```

G. Replace line 24 with

```
accountTotals.put(accountName, amount);
```

H. Replace line 24 with

```
accountTotals.put(accountName, amount.intValue());
```

6. Given:

```
interface Hungry<E> { void munch(E x); }
interface Carnivore<E extends Animal> extends Hungry<E> {}
interface Herbivore<E extends Plant> extends Hungry<E> {}
abstract class Plant {}
class Grass extends Plant {}
abstract class Animal {}
class Sheep extends Animal implements Herbivore<Sheep> {
  public void munch(Sheep x) {}
}
class Wolf extends Animal implements Carnivore<Sheep> {
  public void munch(Sheep x) {}
}
```

Which of the following changes (taken separately) would allow this code to compile?
(Choose all that apply.)

A. Change the `Carnivore` interface to

```
interface Carnivore<E extends Plant> extends Hungry<E> {}
```

B. Change the `Herbivore` interface to

```
interface Herbivore<E extends Animal> extends Hungry<E> {}
```

C. Change the `Sheep` class to

```
class Sheep extends Animal implements Herbivore<Plant> {
  public void munch(Grass x) {}
}
```

D. Change the `Sheep` class to

```
class Sheep extends Plant implements Carnivore<Wolf> {
    public void munch(Wolf x) {}
}
```

E. Change the `Wolf` class to

```
class Wolf extends Animal implements Herbivore<Grass> {
  public void munch(Grass x) {}
}
```

F. No changes are necessary

7. Which collection class(es) allows you to grow or shrink its size and provides indexed access to its elements, but whose methods are not synchronized? (Choose all that apply.)

   A. `java.util.HashSet`

   B. `java.util.LinkedHashSet`

   C. `java.util.List`

   D. `java.util.ArrayList`

   E. `java.util.Vector`

   F. `java.util.PriorityQueue`

   G. `java.util.ArrayDeque`

8. Given a method declared as

   ```
   public static <E extends Number> List<E> process(List<E> nums)
   ```

   A programmer wants to use this method like this:

   ```
   // INSERT DECLARATIONS HERE

   output = process(input);
   ```

   Which pairs of declarations could be placed at `// INSERT DECLARATIONS HERE` to allow the code to compile? (Choose all that apply.)

   A. `ArrayList<Integer> input = null;`
      `ArrayList<Integer> output = null;`

   B. `ArrayList<Integer> input = null;`
      `List<Integer> output = null;`

   C. `ArrayList<Integer> input = null;`
      `List<Number> output = null;`

   D. `List<Number> input = null;`
      `ArrayList<Integer> output = null;`

   E. `List<Number> input = null;`
      `List<Number> output = null;`

   F. `List<Integer> input = null;`
      `List<Integer> output = null;`

   G. None of the above

9. Given the proper import statement(s) and

   ```
   13.  PriorityQueue<String> pq = new PriorityQueue<String>();
   14.  pq.add("2");
   15.  pq.add("4");
   16.  System.out.print(pq.peek() + " ");
   17.  pq.offer("1");
   ```

```
18.    pq.add("3");
19.    pq.remove("1");
20.    System.out.print(pq.poll() + " ");
21.    if(pq.remove("2")) System.out.print(pq.poll() + " ");
22.    System.out.println(pq.poll() + " " + pq.peek());
```

What is the result?

A. 2 2 3 3

B. 2 2 3 4

C. 4 3 3 4

D. 2 2 3 3 3

E. 4 3 3 3 3

F. 2 2 3 3 4

G. Compilation fails

H. An exception is thrown at runtime

10.   Given the proper import statement(s) and

```
ArrayDeque<String> ad = new ArrayDeque<>();
ad.add("2");
ad.add("4");
System.out.print(ad.peek() + " ");
ad.offer("1");
ad.add("3");
ad.remove();
System.out.print(ad.poll() + " ");
if (ad.peek().equals("2")) System.out.print(ad.poll() + " ");
System.out.println(ad.poll() + " " + ad.peek());
```

What is the result?

A. 2 2 3 3

B. 2 2 3 4

C. 4 3 3 4

D. 2 2 4 3

E. 2 4 1 3

F. 2 2 3 3 4

G. Compilation fails

H. An exception is thrown at runtime

11. Given:

```
3. import java.util.*;
4. public class Mixup {
5.   public static void main(String[] args) {
6.     Object o = new Object();
7.     // insert code here
8.     s.add("o");
9.     s.add(o);
10.  }
11. }
```

And these three fragments:

```
I.   Set s = new HashSet();
II.  TreeSet s = new TreeSet();
III. LinkedHashSet s = new LinkedHashSet();
```

When fragments I, II, or III are inserted independently at line 7, which are true? (Choose all that apply.)

A. Fragment I compiles

B. Fragment II compiles

C. Fragment III compiles

D. Fragment I executes without exception

E. Fragment II executes without exception

F. Fragment III executes without exception

12. Given:

```
3. import java.util.*;
4. class Turtle {
5.   int size;
6.   public Turtle(int s) { size = s; }
7.   public boolean equals(Object o) { return (this.size == ((Turtle)o).size); }
8.   // insert code here
9. }
10. public class TurtleTest {
11.   public static void main(String[] args) {
12.     LinkedHashSet<Turtle> t = new LinkedHashSet<Turtle>();
13.     t.add(new Turtle(1));   t.add(new Turtle(2));   t.add(new Turtle(1));
14.     System.out.println(t.size());
15.   }
16. }
```

And these two fragments:

```
I.   public int hashCode() { return size/5; }
II.  // no hashCode method declared
```

If fragment I or II is inserted independently at line 8, which are true? (Choose all that apply.)

A. If fragment I is inserted, the output is 2

B. If fragment I is inserted, the output is 3

C. If fragment II is inserted, the output is 2

D. If fragment II is inserted, the output is 3

E. If fragment I is inserted, compilation fails

F. If fragment II is inserted, compilation fails

13. (OCJPJ 6 only) Given the proper import statement(s) and

```
13.   TreeSet<String> s = new TreeSet<String>();
14.   TreeSet<String> subs = new TreeSet<String>();
15.   s.add("a"); s.add("b"); s.add("c"); s.add("d"); s.add("e");
16.
17.   subs = (TreeSet)s.subSet("b", true, "d", true);
18.   s.add("g");
19.   s.pollFirst();
20.   s.pollFirst();
21.   s.add("c2");
22.   System.out.println(s.size() +" "+ subs.size());
```

Which are true? (Choose all that apply.)

A. The size of s is 4

B. The size of s is 5

C. The size of s is 7

D. The size of subs is 1

E. The size of subs is 2

F. The size of subs is 3

G. The size of subs is 4

H. An exception is thrown at runtime

14. (Note: Some of the classes used in this question are very unlikely to be on the real exam. Feel free to skip this question.)

Given:

```
3. import java.util.*;
4. public class Magellan {
5.   public static void main(String[] args) {
6.     TreeMap<String, String> myMap = new TreeMap<String, String>();
7.     myMap.put("a", "apple"); myMap.put("d", "date");
8.     myMap.put("f", "fig"); myMap.put("p", "pear");
9.     System.out.println("1st after mango: " +   // sop 1
10.       myMap.higherKey("f"));
11.     System.out.println("1st after mango: " +   // sop 2
```

```
12.         myMap.ceilingKey("f"));
13.      System.out.println("1st after mango: " +    // sop 3
14.        myMap.floorKey("f"));
15.      SortedMap<String, String> sub = new TreeMap<String, String>();
16.      sub = myMap.tailMap("f");
17.      System.out.println("1st after mango: " +    // sop 4
18.        sub.firstKey());
19.    }
20. }
```

Which of the `System.out.println` statements will produce the output `1st after mango: p`? (Choose all that apply.)

A. sop 1

B. sop 2

C. sop 3

D. sop 4

E. None; compilation fails

F. None; an exception is thrown at runtime

15. Given:

```
3. import java.util.*;
4. class Business { }
5. class Hotel extends Business { }
6. class Inn extends Hotel { }
7. public class Travel {
8.   ArrayList<Hotel> go() {
9.      // insert code here
10.   }
11. }
```

Which statement inserted independently at line 9 will compile? (Choose all that apply.)

A. `return new ArrayList<Inn>();`

B. `return new ArrayList<Hotel>();`

C. `return new ArrayList<Object>();`

D. `return new ArrayList<Business>();`

16. Given:

```
3. import java.util.*;
4. class Dog { int size; Dog(int s) { size = s; } }
5. public class FirstGrade {
6.   public static void main(String[] args) {
7.     TreeSet<Integer> i = new TreeSet<Integer>();
8.     TreeSet<Dog> d = new TreeSet<Dog>();
```

```
9.
10.        d.add(new Dog(1));  d.add(new Dog(2));  d.add(new Dog(1));
11.        i.add(1);  i.add(2);  i.add(1);
12.        System.out.println(d.size() + " " + i.size());
13.      }
14.    }
```

What is the result?

A. 1 2

B. 2 2

C. 2 3

D. 3 2

E. 3 3

F. Compilation fails

G. An exception is thrown at runtime

17. Given:

```
3.  import java.util.*;
4.  public class GeoCache {
5.    public static void main(String[] args) {
6.      String[] s = {"map", "pen", "marble", "key"};
7.      Othello o = new Othello();
8.      Arrays.sort(s,o);
9.      for(String s2: s) System.out.print(s2 + " ");
10.     System.out.println(Arrays.binarySearch(s, "map"));
11.   }
12.   static class Othello implements Comparator<String> {
13.     public int compare(String a, String b) { return b.compareTo(a); }
14.   }
15. }
```

Which are true? (Choose all that apply.)

A. Compilation fails

B. The output will contain a 1

C. The output will contain a 2

D. The output will contain a -1

E. An exception is thrown at runtime

F. The output will contain "key map marble pen"

G. The output will contain "pen marble map key"

18. Given:

```
class DogSort implements Comparator<Dog> {
   public int compare(Dog one, Dog two) {
      return one.getName().compareTo(two.getName());
   }
}
Dog boi = new Dog("boi", 30, 6);
Dog clover = new Dog("clover", 35, 12);
Dog zooey = new Dog("zooey", 45, 8);
ArrayList<Dog> dogs = new ArrayList<>(Arrays.asList(zooey, clover, boi));
```

Which of the following code fragments sorts the dogs in ascending order by name? (Choose all that apply.)

A. ```
    DogSort dogSorter = new DogSort();
    dogs.sort(dogSorter);
    ```

B.  `dogs.sort((d1, d2) -> d1.getName().compareTo(d2.getName()));`

C.  `dogs.sort(DogSort);`

D.  ```
    dogs.sort(int compare(d1, d2) ->
                    d1.getName().compareTo(d2.getName()));
    ```

E. `dogs.sort((d1, d2) -> d2.getName().compareTo(d1.getName()));`

SELF TEST ANSWERS

1. ☑ **B** is correct.
   ☒ **A** is incorrect because `List` is an interface, so you can't say `new List()`, regardless of any generic types. **D, E,** and **F** are incorrect because `List` only takes one type parameter (a `Map` would take two, not a `List`). **C** is tempting, but incorrect. The type argument `<List<Integer>>` must be the same for both sides of the assignment, even though the constructor `new ArrayList()` on the right side is a subtype of the declared type `List` on the left. (OCP Objective 3.2)

2. ☑ **B** and **D** are correct. **B** is true because often two dissimilar objects can return the same hashcode value. **D** is true because if the `hashCode()` comparison returns `==`, the two objects might or might not be equal.
   ☒ **A, C,** and **E** are incorrect. **C** is incorrect because the `hashCode()` method is very flexible in its return values, and often two dissimilar objects can return the same hashcode value. **A** and **E** are a negation of the `hashCode()` and `equals()` contract. (OCP Objectives 1.4 and 3.3)

3. ☑ **E** is correct. You can't put both `Strings` and `ints` into the same `TreeSet`. Without generics, the compiler has no way of knowing what type is appropriate for this `TreeSet`, so it allows everything to compile. At runtime, the `TreeSet` will try to sort the elements as they're added, and when it tries to compare an `Integer` with a `String`, it will throw a `ClassCastException`. Note that although the `before()` method does not use generics, it does use autoboxing. Watch out for code that uses some new features and some old features mixed together.
   ☒ **A, B, C,** and **D** are incorrect based on the above. (OCP Objective 3.1)

4. ☑ **C** and **D** are correct. If `hashCode()` is not overridden, then every entry will go into its own bucket, and the overridden `equals()` method will have no effect on determining equivalency. If `hashCode()` is overridden, then the overridden `equals()` method will view `t1` and `t2` as duplicates.
   ☒ **A, B, E,** and **F** are incorrect based on the above. (OCP Objectives 1.4, 3.3)

5. ☑ **B, E,** and **G** are correct.
   ☒ **A** is incorrect because you can't use a primitive type as a type parameter. **C** is incorrect because a `Map` takes two type parameters separated by a comma. **D** is incorrect because an `int` can't autobox to a `null`, and **F** is incorrect because a `null` can't unbox to `0`. **H** is incorrect because you can't autobox a primitive just by trying to invoke a method with it. (OCP Objectives 3.2)

6. ☑ **B** is correct. The problem with the original code is that `Sheep` tries to implement `Herbivore<Sheep>` and `Herbivore` declares that its type parameter `E` can be any type that extends `Plant`.

☒ Since a `Sheep` is not a `Plant`, `Herbivore<Sheep>` makes no sense—the type `Sheep` is outside the allowed range of `Herbivore`'s parameter `E`. Only solutions that either alter the definition of a `Sheep` or alter the definition of `Herbivore` will be able to fix this. So **A, E,** and **F** are eliminated. **B** works—changing the definition of an `Herbivore` to allow it to eat `Sheep` solves the problem. **C** doesn't work because an `Herbivore<Plant>` must have a `munch(Plant)` method, not `munch(Grass)`. And **D** doesn't work, because in **D** we made `Sheep` extend `Plant`—now the `Wolf` class breaks because its `munch(Sheep)` method no longer fulfills the contract of `Carnivore`. (OCP Objective 3.1)

7. ☑ **D** is correct. All of the collection classes allow you to grow or shrink the size of your collection. `ArrayList` provides an index to its elements. The newer collection classes tend not to have synchronized methods. `Vector` is an older implementation of `ArrayList` functionality and has synchronized methods; it is slower than `ArrayList`.

☒ **A, B, C, E,** and **F** are incorrect based on the logic described earlier. **C**, `List`, is an interface, and **F** and **G**, `PriorityQueue` and `ArrayDeque`, do not offer access by index. (OCP Objective 3.2)

8. ☑ **B, E,** and **F** are correct.

☒ The return type of process is definitely declared as a `List`, not an `ArrayList`, so **A** and **D** are incorrect. **C** is incorrect because the return type evaluates to `List<Integer>` and that can't be assigned to a variable of type `List<Number>`. Of course, all these would probably cause a `NullPointerException` since the variables are still null—but the question only asked us to get the code to compile. (OCP Objective 3.1)

9. ☑ **B** is correct. For the sake of the exam, `add()` and `offer()` both add to (in this case) naturally sorted queues. The calls to `poll()` both return and then remove the first item from the queue, so the test fails.

☒ **A, C, D, E, F, G,** and **H** are incorrect based on the above. (OCP Objective 3.2)

10. ☑ **E** is correct. `add()` and `offer()` both add to the end of the deque. The calls to `poll()` and `remove()` both return and then remove the first item from the queue. The calls to `peek()` return the first item in the queue without removing it. The test fails because the first item is not `"2"`" (it's been removed).

☒ **A, B, C, D, F, G,** and **H** are incorrect based on the above. (OCP Objective 3.2)

11. ☑ **A, B, C, D,** and **F** are all correct.

☒ Only **E** is incorrect. Elements of a `TreeSet` must in some way implement `Comparable`. (OCP Objective 3.3)

12. ☑ **A** and **D** are correct. While fragment II wouldn't fulfill the `hashCode()` contract (as you can see by the results), it is legal Java. For the purpose of the exam, if you don't override `hashCode()`, every object will have a unique hashcode.

☒ **B, C, E,** and **F** are incorrect based on the above. (OCP Objectives 1.4, 3.3)

13. ☑ **B** and **F** are correct. After `"g"` is added, `TreeSet` s contains six elements and `TreeSet` subs contains three (b, c, d), because `"g"` is out of the range of subs. The first `pollFirst()` finds and removes only the `"a"`. The second `pollFirst()` finds and removes the `"b"` from *both* `TreeSet`s (remember they are backed). The final `add()` is in range of both `TreeSet`s. The final contents are `[c,c2,d,e,g]` and `[c,c2,d]`.

☒ **A, C, D, E, G,** and **H** are incorrect based on the above. (OCP Objective 3.2)

14. ☑ **A** is correct. The `ceilingKey()` method's argument is inclusive. The `floorKey()` method would be used to find keys before the specified key. The `firstKey()` method's argument is also inclusive.

☒ **B, C, D, E,** and **F** are incorrect based on the above. (OCP Objective 3.2)

15. ☑ **B** is correct.

☒ **A** is incorrect because polymorphic assignments don't apply to generic type parameters. **C** and **D** are incorrect because they don't follow basic polymorphism rules. (OCP Objective 3.1)

16. ☑ **G** is correct. Class Dog needs to implement `Comparable` in order for a `TreeSet` (which keeps its elements sorted) to be able to contain Dog objects.

☒ **A, B, C, D, E,** and **F** are incorrect based on the above. (OCP Objectives 3.2 and 3.3)

17. ☑ **D** and **G** are correct. First, the `compareTo()` method will reverse the normal sort. Second, the `sort()` is valid. Third, the `binarySearch()` gives –1 because it needs to be invoked using the same `Comparator` (o) as was used to sort the array. Note that when the `binarySearch()` returns an "undefined result," it doesn't officially have to be a –1, but it usually is, so if you selected only **G**, you get full credit!

☒ **A, B, C, E,** and **F** are incorrect based on the above. (OCP Objective 3.3)

18. ☑ **A** and **B** are correct. **A** uses the `dogSorter` comparator made from the `DogSort` `Comparator` class, and **B** uses the lambda expression equivalent of `dogSorter`.

☒ **C, D,** and **E** are incorrect. The argument to **C** is the class name for the `Comparator` rather than an instance. **D** uses the incorrect syntax for a lambda expression. **E** is almost right, but it sorts the dogs in the wrong order. (OCP Objective 2.6).

7
Inner Classes

Inner classes (including static nested classes) appear throughout the exam. The code used to represent questions on virtually *any* topic on the exam can involve inner (aka nested) classes. Unless you deeply understand the rules and syntax for inner classes, you're likely to miss questions you'd otherwise be able to answer. *As if the exam weren't already tough enough*.

This chapter looks at the ins and outs (inners and outers?) of inner classes and exposes you to the kinds of (often strange-looking) syntax examples you'll see scattered throughout the entire exam. So you've really got two goals for this chapter—to learn what you'll need to answer questions testing your inner-class knowledge and to learn how to read and understand inner-class code so you can handle questions testing your knowledge of *other* topics.

What's all the hoopla about inner classes? Before we get into it, we have to warn you (if you don't already know) that inner classes have inspired passionate love 'em or hate 'em debates since first introduced in version 1.1 of the language. For once, we're going to try to keep our opinions to ourselves here and just present the facts as you'll need to know them for the exam. It's up to you to decide how—and to what extent—you should use inner classes in your own development. We mean it. We believe they have some powerful, efficient uses in very specific situations, including code that's easier to read and maintain, but they can also be abused and lead to code that's as clear as a cornfield maze and to the syndrome known as "reuseless": *code that's useless over and over again*.

Inner classes let you define one class within another. They provide a type of scoping for your classes because you can make one class *a member of another class*. Just as classes have member *variables* and *methods*, a class can also have member *classes*. They come in several flavors, depending on how and where you define the inner class, including a special kind of inner class known as a "top-level nested class" (an inner class marked `static`), which technically isn't really an inner class. Because a static nested class is still a class defined within the scope of another class, we'll cover them in this chapter on inner classes. We'll also take another brief look at lambda expressions, which are often used as an alternative syntax (shorthand) for inner classes, so this is a good time to get more familiar with lambda expression syntax before we do a deep dive in the next chapter.

Many of the questions on the exam that make use of inner classes are focused on other certification topics and only use inner classes along the way. So in this chapter, we'll discuss the following four inner-class *topics*:

- Inner classes ("nested class" in the objective)
- Method-local inner classes ("local class" in the objective)

- Anonymous inner classes
- Static nested classes ("static inner class" in the objective)

The one certification objective directly related to inner classes is OCP Objective 2.3:

- Create inner classes including static inner class, local class, nested class, and anonymous inner class

which captures all the topics above in one objective.

CERTIFICATION OBJECTIVE

Nested Classes (OCP Objective 2.3)

2.3   Create inner classes including static inner class, local class, nested class, and anonymous inner class.

Note: As we've mentioned, mapping Objective 2.3 to this chapter is somewhat accurate, but it's also a bit misleading. You'll find inner classes used for many different exam topics. For that reason, we're not going to keep saying that this chapter is for Objective 2.3.

Inner Classes

You're an OO programmer, so you know that for reuse and flexibility/extensibility, you need to keep your classes specialized. In other words, a class should have code *only* for the things an object of that particular type needs to do; any *other* behavior should be part of another class better suited for *that* job. Sometimes, though, you find yourself designing a class where you discover you need behavior that not only belongs in a separate specialized class, but also needs to be intimately tied to the class you're designing.

Event handlers are perhaps the best example of this (and are, in fact, one of the main reasons inner classes were added to the language in the first place). If you have a GUI class that performs some job, like, say, a chat client, you might want the chat-client-specific methods (accept input, read new messages from server, send user input back to server, and so on) to be in the class. But how do those methods get invoked in the first place? A user clicks a button. Or types some text in the input field. Or a separate thread doing the I/O work of getting messages from the server has messages that need to be displayed in the GUI. So you have chat-client-specific methods, but you also need methods for handling the "events" (button presses, keyboard typing, I/O available, and so on) that drive the calls on those chat-client methods. The ideal scenario—from an OO perspective—is to keep the chat-client-specific methods in the ChatClient class and put the event-handling *code* in a separate event-handling *class.*

Nothing unusual about that so far; after all, that's how you're supposed to design OO classes. As *specialists.* But here's the problem with the chat-client scenario: The event-handling code is intimately tied to the chat-client-specific code! Think about it: When users click a Send button (indicating that they want their typed-in message to be sent to the chat server), the chat-client code that sends the message needs to read from a *particular* text field. In other words, if the user clicks Button A, the program is supposed to extract the text from the TextField B *of a particular ChatClient instance.* Not from some *other* text field from some *other* object, but specifically the text field that a specific instance of the ChatClient class has a reference to. So the event-handling code needs access to the members of the ChatClient object to be useful as a "helper" to a particular ChatClient instance.

And what if the ChatClient class needs to inherit from one class, but the event-handling code is better off inheriting from some *other* class? You can't make a class extend more than one class, so putting all the code (the chat-client-specific code and the event-handling code) in one class won't work in that case. So what you'd really like to have is the benefit of putting your event code in a separate class (better OO, encapsulation, and the ability to extend a class other than the class the ChatClient extends), but still allow the event-handling code to have easy access to the members of the ChatClient (so the event-handling code can, for example, update the ChatClient's private instance variables). You *could* manage it by making the members of the ChatClient accessible to the event-handling class by, for example, marking them public. But that's not a good solution either.

You already know where this is going—one of the key benefits of an inner class is the "special relationship" an *inner class instance* shares with *an instance of the outer class.* That "special relationship" gives code in the inner class access to members of the enclosing (outer) class, *as if the inner class were part of the outer class.* In fact, that's exactly what it means: The inner class *is* a part of the outer class. Not just a "part," but a full-fledged, card-carrying *member* of the outer class. Yes, an inner class instance has access to all members of the outer class, *even those marked private.* (Relax, that's the whole point, remember? We want this separate inner class instance to have an intimate relationship with the outer class instance, but we still want to keep everyone *else* out. And besides, if you wrote the outer class, then you also wrote the inner class! So you're not violating encapsulation; you *designed* it this way.)

Coding a "Regular" Inner Class

We use the term *regular* here to represent inner classes that are not

- Static
- Method-local
- Anonymous

For the rest of this section, though, we'll just use the term "inner class" and drop the "regular." (When we switch to one of the other three types in the preceding list, you'll know it.) You define an inner class within the curly braces of the outer class:

```
class MyOuter {
    class MyInner { }
}
```

Piece of cake. And if you compile it:

```
%javac MyOuter.java
```

you'll end up with *two* class files:

```
MyOuter.class
MyOuter$MyInner.class
```

The inner class is still, in the end, a separate class, so a separate class file is generated for it. But the inner class file isn't accessible to you in the usual way. You can't say

```
%java MyOuter$MyInner
```

in hopes of running the main() method of the inner class **because a regular inner class cannot have static declarations of any kind.** *The only way you can access the inner class is through a live instance of the outer class!* In other words, only at runtime, when there's already an instance of the outer class to tie the inner class instance to. You'll see all this in a moment. First, let's beef up the classes a little:

```
class MyOuter {
    private int x = 7;

    // inner class definition
    class MyInner {
```

```
    public void seeOuter() {
        System.out.println("Outer x is " + x);
    }
} // close inner class definition

} // close outer class
```

The preceding code is perfectly legal. Notice that the inner class is, indeed, accessing a private member of the outer class. That's fine, because the inner class is also a member of the outer class. So just as any member of the outer class (say, an instance method) can access any other member of the outer class, `private` or not, the inner class—also a member—can do the same.

Okay, so now that we know how to write the code giving an inner class access to members of the outer class, how do you actually use it?

Instantiating an Inner Class

To create an instance of an inner class, *you must have an instance of the outer class* to tie to the inner class. There are no exceptions to this rule: an inner class instance can never stand alone without a direct relationship to an instance of the outer class.

Instantiating an Inner Class from Within the Outer Class   Most often, it is the outer class that creates instances of the inner class, since it is usually the outer class wanting to use the inner instance as a helper for its own personal use. We'll modify the `MyOuter` class to create an instance of `MyInner`:

```
class MyOuter {
  private int x = 7;
  public void makeInner() {
    MyInner in = new MyInner();   // make an inner instance
    in.seeOuter();
  }

  class MyInner {
    public void seeOuter() {
      System.out.println("Outer x is " + x);
    }
  }
}
```

You can see in the preceding code that the `MyOuter` code treats `MyInner` just as though `MyInner` were any other accessible class—it instantiates it using the class name (`new MyInner()`) and then invokes a method on the reference variable (`in.seeOuter()`). But the only reason this syntax works is because the outer class instance method code is doing the instantiating. In other words, *there's already an instance of the outer class—the instance running the* `makeInner()` *method.* So how do you instantiate a `MyInner` object from somewhere outside the `MyOuter` class? Is it even possible? (Well, since we're going to all the trouble of making a whole new subhead for it, as you'll see next, there's no big mystery here.)

Creating an Inner Class Object from Outside the Outer Class Instance Code Whew. Long subhead there, but it does explain what we're trying to do. If we want to create an instance of the inner class, we must have an instance of the outer class. You already know that, but think about the implications...it means that without a reference to an instance of the outer class, you can't instantiate the inner class from a `static` method of the outer class (because, don't forget, in static code, *there is no* `this` *reference*), or from any other code in any other class. Inner class instances are always handed an implicit reference to the outer class. The compiler takes care of it, so you'll never see anything but the end result—the ability of the inner class to access members of the outer class. The code to make an instance from anywhere outside nonstatic code of the outer class is simple, but you must memorize this for the exam!

```
public static void main(String[] args) {
  MyOuter mo = new MyOuter();     // gotta get an instance!
  MyOuter.MyInner inner = mo.new MyInner();
  inner.seeOuter();
}
```

The preceding code is the same, regardless of whether the `main()` method is within the `MyOuter` class or some *other* class (assuming the other class has access to `MyOuter`, and since `MyOuter` has default access, that means the code must be in a class within the same package as `MyOuter`).

If you're into one-liners, you can do it like this:

```
public static void main(String[] args) {
  MyOuter.MyInner inner = new MyOuter().new MyInner();
  inner.seeOuter();
}
```

You can think of this as though you're invoking a method on the outer instance, but the method happens to be a special inner class instantiation method, and it's invoked using the keyword new. Instantiating an inner class is the *only* scenario in which you'll invoke new *on* an instance as opposed to invoking new to *construct* an instance.

Here's a quick summary of the differences between inner class instantiation code that's *within* the outer class (but not `static`) and inner class instantiation code that's *outside* the outer class:

- From *inside* the outer class instance code, use the inner class name in the normal way:

```
MyInner mi = new MyInner();
```

- From *outside* the outer class instance code, the inner class name must now include the outer class's name:

```
MyOuter.MyInner
```

To instantiate it, you must use a reference to the outer class:

```
new MyOuter().new MyInner();
```

or

```
outerObjRef.new MyInner();
```

if you already have an instance of the outer class.

Referencing the Inner or Outer Instance from Within the Inner Class

How does an object refer to itself normally? By using the `this` reference. Here is a quick review of `this`:

- The keyword `this` can be used only from within instance code. In other words, not within static code.
- The `this` reference is a reference to the currently executing object. In other words, the object whose reference was used to invoke the currently running method.
- The `this` reference is the way an object can pass a reference to itself to some other code as a method argument:

```
public void myMethod() {
  MyClass mc = new MyClass();
  mc.doStuff(this);  // pass a ref to object running myMethod
}
```

Within the inner class code, the `this` reference refers to the instance of the inner class, as you'd probably expect, since `this` always refers to the currently executing object. But what if the inner class code wants an explicit reference to the outer class instance that the inner instance is tied to? In other words, *how do you reference the "outer `this`"*? Although normally, the inner class code doesn't need a reference to the outer class, since it already has an implicit one it's using to access the members of the outer class, it would need a reference to the outer class if it needed to pass that reference to some other code, as follows:

```
class MyInner {
  public void seeOuter() {
    System.out.println("Outer x is " + x);
    System.out.println("Inner class ref is " + this);
    System.out.println("Outer class ref is " + MyOuter.this);
  }
}
```

If we run the complete code as follows:

```
class MyOuter {
  private int x = 7;
  public void makeInner() {
    MyInner in = new MyInner();
    in.seeOuter();
  }
  class MyInner {
    public void seeOuter() {
      System.out.println("Outer x is " + x);
      System.out.println("Inner class ref is " + this);
      System.out.println("Outer class ref is " + MyOuter.this);
    }
  }
  public static void main (String[] args) {
    MyOuter.MyInner inner = new MyOuter().new MyInner();
    inner.seeOuter();
  }
}
```

the output is something like this:

```
Outer x is 7
Inner class ref is MyOuter$MyInner@113708
Outer class ref is MyOuter@33f1d7
```

So the rules for an inner class referencing itself or the outer instance are as follows:

■ To reference the inner class instance itself from *within* the inner class code, use this.

■ To reference the "*outer this*" (the outer class instance) from within the inner class code, use NameOfOuterClass.this (example, MyOuter.this).

Member Modifiers Applied to Inner Classes

A regular inner class is a member of the outer class just as instance variables and methods are, so the following modifiers can be applied to an inner class:

- final
- abstract
- public
- private
- protected
- static—*but static turns it into a static nested class, not an inner class*
- strictfp

Method-Local Inner Classes

A regular inner class is scoped inside another class's curly braces, but outside any method code (in other words, at the same level that an instance variable is declared). But you can also define an inner class within a method:

```
class MyOuter2 {
  private String x = "Outer2";

  void doStuff() {
    class MyInner {
      public void seeOuter() {
        System.out.println("Outer x is " + x);
      } // close inner class method
    }   // close inner class definition
  }     // close outer class method doStuff()

}       // close outer class
```

The preceding code declares a class, MyOuter2, with one method, doStuff(). But *inside* doStuff(), another class, MyInner, is declared, and it has a method of its own, seeOuter(). The previous code is completely useless, however, because *it never instantiates the inner class!* Just because you *declared* the class doesn't mean you created an *instance* of it. So to *use* the inner class, you must make an instance of it somewhere *within the method but below the inner class definition* (or the compiler won't be able to find the inner class). The following legal code shows how to instantiate and use a method-local inner class:

```
class MyOuter2 {
  private String x = "Outer2";
  void doStuff() {
```

```
class MyInner {
  public void seeOuter() {
    System.out.println("Outer x is " + x);
  }  // close inner class method
}    // close inner class definition

MyInner mi = new MyInner();  // This line must come
                             // after the class
mi.seeOuter();
}  // close outer class method doStuff()
}    // close outer class
```

What a Method-Local Inner Object Can and Can't Do

A method-local inner class can be instantiated only within the method where the inner class is defined. In other words, no other code running in any other method—inside or outside the outer class—can ever instantiate the method-local inner class. Like regular inner class objects, the method-local inner class object shares a special relationship with the enclosing (outer) class object and can access its `private` (or any other) members. However, *the inner class object cannot use the local variables of the method the inner class is in.* Why not?

Think about it. The local variables of the method live on the stack and exist only for the lifetime of the method. You already know that the scope of a local variable is limited to the method the variable is declared in. When the method ends, the stack frame is blown away and the variable is history. But even after the method completes, the inner class object created within it might still be alive on the heap if, for example, a reference to it was passed into some other code and then stored in an instance variable. Because the local variables aren't guaranteed to be alive as long as the method-local inner class object is, the inner class object can't use them. *Unless the local variables are marked `final` or are effectively final!* The following code attempts to access a local variable from within a method-local inner class:

```
class MyOuter2 {
  private String x = "Outer2";
  void doStuff() {
    String z = "local variable";
    class MyInner {
      public void seeOuter() {
        System.out.println("Outer x is " + x);
        System.out.println("Local var z is " + z);
        z = "changing the local variable";   // Won't compile!
      }  // close inner class method
    }      // close inner class
    x = "Changing Outer2";
    MyInner mi = new MyInner();
```

```
                mi.seeOuter();
        }            // close outer class doStuff() method
        public static void main(String args[]) {
            MyOuter2 mo2 = new MyOuter2();
            mo2.doStuff();
        }
}               // close outer class
```

Compiling the preceding code *really* upsets the compiler:

```
Local variable z defined in an enclosing scope must be final or effectively
final
```

Removing the line that changes z fixes the problem, and marking the local variable z as final, although optional, is a good reminder that we can't change it if we want to be able to use z in seeOuter():

```
class MyOuter2 {
    private String x = "Outer2";
        void doStuff() {
            final String z = "local variable";    // now MyInner can use z!
            class MyInner {
                public void seeOuter() {
                    System.out.println("Outer x is " + x);
                    System.out.println("Local var z is " + z);
                    // we removed the line that changed z
                }  // close inner class method
            }       // close inner class
            x = "Changing Outer2";
            MyInner mi = new MyInner();
            mi.seeOuter();
        }           // close outer class doStuff() method
    }               // close outer class doStuff() method
    public static void main(String args[]) {
        MyOuter2 mo2 = new MyOuter2();
        mo2.doStuff();
    }
}
```

Notice that even though x is not final, or effectively final, and we also use x in the seeOuter() method of MyInner, that's fine because x is a field of MyOuter2, not a local variable of the method doStuff().

Just a reminder about modifiers within a method: The same rules apply to method-local inner classes as to local variable declarations. You can't, for example, mark a method-local inner class public, private, protected, static, transient, and the like. For the purpose of the exam, the only modifiers you *can* apply to a method-local inner class are abstract and final, but, as always, never both at the same time.

e x a m

ⓦatch **Remember that a local class declared in a** `static` **method has access to only** `static` **members of the enclosing class, since there is no associated instance of the enclosing class. If you're in a** `static`

method, there is no `this`**, so an inner class in a** `static` **method is subject to the same restrictions as the** `static` **method. In other words, no access to instance variables.**

Anonymous Inner Classes

So far, we've looked at defining a class within an enclosing class (a regular inner class) and within a method (a method-local inner class). We're now going to look at the most unusual syntax you might ever see in Java: inner classes declared without any class name at all (hence, the word *anonymous*). And if that's not weird enough, you can define these classes, not just within a method, but even within an *argument* to a method. We'll look first at the *plain-old* (as if there is such a thing as a plain-old anonymous inner class) version (actually, even the plain-old version comes in two flavors), then at the argument-declared anonymous inner class, and finally at anonymous inner classes expressed with lambdas.

Perhaps your most important job here is to *learn to not be thrown when you see the syntax.* The exam is littered with anonymous inner class code—you might see it on questions about threads, wrappers, overriding, garbage collection, and...well, you get the idea.

Plain-Old Anonymous Inner Classes, Flavor One

Check out the following legal-but-strange-the-first-time-you-see-it code:

```
class Popcorn {
  public void pop() {
    System.out.println("popcorn");
  }
}
class Food {
  Popcorn p = new Popcorn() {
    public void pop() {
      System.out.println("anonymous popcorn");
    }
  };
}
```

Let's look at what's in the preceding code:

- We define two classes: Popcorn and Food.
- Popcorn has one method: pop().
- Food has one instance variable, declared as type Popcorn. That's it for Food. Food has *no* methods.

And here's the big thing to get: the Popcorn reference variable refers, *not* to an instance of Popcorn, but to *an instance of an anonymous (unnamed) subclass of Popcorn.*

Let's look at just the anonymous class code:

```
2. Popcorn p = new Popcorn() {
3.    public void pop() {
4.       System.out.println("anonymous popcorn");
5.    }
6. };
```

Line 2 Line 2 starts out as an instance variable declaration of type Popcorn. But instead of looking like this:

```
Popcorn p = new Popcorn(); // notice the semicolon at the end
```

there's a curly brace at the end of line 2, where a semicolon would normally be.

```
Popcorn p = new Popcorn() { // a curly brace, not a semicolon
```

You can read line 2 as saying,

Declare a reference variable, p, of type Popcorn. Then declare a new class that has no name but that is a *subclass* of Popcorn. And here's the curly brace that opens the class definition...

Line 3 Line 3, then, is actually the first statement within the new class definition. And what is it doing? Overriding the pop() method of the superclass Popcorn. This is the whole point of making an anonymous inner class—to *override one or more methods of the superclass!* (Or to implement methods of an interface, but we'll save that for a little later.)

Line 4 Line 4 is the first (and, in this case, *only*) statement within the overriding pop() method. Nothing special there.

Line 5 Line 5 is the closing curly brace of the pop() method. Nothing special.

Line 6 Here's where you have to pay attention: Line 6 includes a *curly brace closing off the anonymous class definition* (it's the companion brace to the one on line 2), but there's more! Line 6 also has *the semicolon that ends the statement started on line 2*—the statement where it all began—the statement declaring and initializing the Popcorn reference variable. And what you're left with is a Popcorn reference to a brand-new *instance* of a brand-new, Just-In-Time, anonymous (no name) *subclass* of Popcorn.

---

e x a m
watch

The closing semicolon is hard to spot. Watch for code like this:

```
2. Popcorn p = new Popcorn() {
3.    public void pop() {
4.       System.out.println("anonymous popcorn");
5.    }
6. }                    //  Missing the semicolon needed to end
                         //  the statement started on 2!
7. Foo f = new Foo();
```

You'll need to be especially careful about the syntax when inner classes are involved, because the code on line 6 looks perfectly natural. It's rare to see semicolons following curly braces.

Polymorphism is in play when anonymous inner classes are involved. Remember that, as in the preceding Popcorn example, we're using a superclass reference variable type to refer to a subclass object. What are the implications? You can only call methods on an anonymous inner class reference that are defined in the reference variable type! This is no different from any other polymorphic references—for example,

```
class Horse extends Animal {
  void buck() { }
}
class Animal {
  void eat() { }
}
class Test {
  public static void main (String[] args) {
    Animal h = new Horse();
    h.eat();   // Legal, class Animal has an eat() method
    h.buck();  // Not legal! Class Animal doesn't have buck()
  }
}
```

So on the exam, you must be able to spot an anonymous inner class that—rather than overriding a method of the superclass—defines its own new method. The method definition isn't the problem, though; the real issue is, how do you invoke that new method? The reference variable type (the superclass) won't know anything about that new method (defined in the anonymous subclass), so the compiler will complain if you try to invoke any method on an anonymous inner class reference that is not in the superclass class definition.

Check out the following **illegal** code:

```
class Popcorn {
  public void pop() {
    System.out.println("popcorn");
  }
}

class Food {
  Popcorn p = new Popcorn() {
    public void sizzle() {
      System.out.println("anonymous sizzling popcorn");
    }
    public void pop() {
      System.out.println("anonymous popcorn");
    }
  };

  public void popIt() {
    p.pop();     // OK, Popcorn has a pop() method
    p.sizzle();  // Not Legal! Popcorn does not have sizzle()
  }
}
```

Compiling the preceding code gives us something like this:

```
Anon.java:19: cannot resolve symbol
symbol  : method sizzle  ()
location: class Popcorn
      p.sizzle();
       ^
```

which is the compiler's way of saying, "I can't find method `sizzle()` in class Popcorn," followed by, "Get a clue."

Plain-Old Anonymous Inner Classes, Flavor Two

The only difference between flavor one and flavor two is that flavor one creates an anonymous *subclass* of the specified *class* type, whereas flavor two creates an anonymous *implementer* of the specified *interface* type. In the previous examples, we defined a new anonymous subclass of type Popcorn as follows:

```
Popcorn p = new Popcorn() {
```

But if `Popcorn` were an *interface* type instead of a *class* type, then the new anonymous class would be an *implementer* of the *interface* rather than a *subclass* of the *class*. Look at the following example:

```
interface Cookable {
  public void cook();
}
class Food {
  Cookable c = new Cookable() {
    public void cook() {
      System.out.println("anonymous cookable implementer");
    }
  };
}
```

The preceding code, like the Popcorn example, still creates an instance of an anonymous inner class, but this time, the new Just-In-Time class is an implementer of the `Cookable` interface. And note that this is the only time you will ever see the syntax:

```
new Cookable()
```

where `Cookable` is an *interface* rather than a non-`abstract` class type. Think about it: *You can't instantiate an interface,* yet that's what the code *looks* like it's doing. But, of course, it's not instantiating a `Cookable` object—it's creating an instance of a new anonymous implementer of `Cookable`. You can read this line:

```
Cookable c = new Cookable() {
```

as "Declare a reference variable of type `Cookable` that, obviously, will refer to an object from a class that implements the `Cookable` interface. But, oh yes, we don't yet *have* a class that implements `Cookable`, so we're going to make one right here, right now. We don't need a name for the class, but it will be a class that implements `Cookable`, and this curly brace starts the definition of the new implementing class."

One more thing to keep in mind about anonymous interface implementers—*they can implement only one interface.* There simply isn't any mechanism to say that your anonymous inner class is going to implement multiple interfaces. In fact, an anonymous inner class can't even extend a class and implement an interface at the same time. The inner class has to choose either to be a subclass of a named class—and not directly implement any interfaces at all—*or* to implement a single interface. By directly, we mean actually using the keyword `implements` as part of the class declaration. If the anonymous inner class is a subclass of a class type, it automatically becomes an implementer of any interfaces implemented by the superclass.

Don't be fooled by any attempts to instantiate an interface except in the case of an anonymous inner class. The following is not legal:

```
Runnable r = new Runnable();   // can't instantiate interface
```

whereas the following is legal, because it's instantiating an `implementer` *of the* `Runnable` *interface (an anonymous implementation class):*

```
Runnable r = new Runnable() {  // curly brace, not semicolon
  public void run() { }
};
```

Argument-Defined Anonymous Inner Classes

If you understood what we've covered so far in this chapter, then this last part will be simple. If you *are* still a little fuzzy on anonymous classes, however, then you should reread the previous sections. If they're not completely clear, we'd like to take full responsibility for the confusion. But we'll be happy to share.

Okay, if you've made it to this sentence, then we're all going to assume you understood the preceding section, and now we're just going to add one new twist. Imagine the following scenario. You're typing along, creating the Perfect Class, when you write code calling a method on a `Bar` object and that method takes an object of type `Foo` (an interface).

```
class MyWonderfulClass {
  void go() {
    Bar b = new Bar();
    b.doStuff(ackWeDoNotHaveAFoo!); // Don't try to compile this at home
  }
}
interface Foo {
  void foof();
}
class Bar {
  void doStuff(Foo f) { }
}
```

No problemo, except that you don't *have* an object from a class that implements Foo, and you can't instantiate one, either, because *you don't even have a class that implements Foo*, let alone an instance of one. So you first need a class that implements Foo, and then you need an instance of that class to pass to the `Bar` class's `doStuff()`

method. Savvy Java programmer that you are, you simply define an anonymous inner class *right inside the argument.* That's right, just where you least expect to find a class. And here's what it looks like:

```
1. public class MyWonderfulClass {
2.     void go() {
3.         Bar b = new Bar();
4.         b.doStuff(new Foo() {
5.             public void foof() {
6.                 System.out.println("foofy");
7.             }  // end foof() method
8.         });    // end inner class def, arg, and b.doStuff stmt.
9.     }          // end go()
10. }              // end class
11.
12. interface Foo {
13.     void foof();
14. }
15. class Bar {
16.     void doStuff(Foo f) {
17.         f.foof();
18.     };
19. }
```

All the action starts on line 4. We're calling doStuff() on a Bar object, but the method takes an instance that IS-A Foo, where Foo is an interface. So we must make both an *implementation* class and an *instance* of that class, all right here in the argument to doStuff(). So that's what we do. We write

```
new Foo() {
```

to start the new class definition for the anonymous class that implements the Foo interface. Foo has a single method to implement, foof(), so on lines 5, 6, and 7, we implement the foof() method. Then on line 8—whoa!—more strange syntax appears. The first curly brace closes off the new anonymous class definition. But don't forget that this all happened as part of a method argument, so the closing parenthesis,), finishes off the method invocation, and then we must still end the statement that began on line 4, so we end with a semicolon. Study this syntax! You will see anonymous inner classes on the exam, and you'll have to be very, very picky about the way they're closed. If they're *argument local,* they end like this:

```
});
```

but if they're just plain-old anonymous classes, then they end like this:

```
};
```

Regardless, be careful. Any question from any part of the exam might involve anonymous inner classes as part of the code.

To run this code, simply create a new `MyWonderfulClass` and call its `go()` method:

```
MyWonderfulClass c = new MyWonderfulClass();

c.go();
```

and you will see the output:

```
foofy
```

We'll come back to `MyWonderfulClass` at the very end of the chapter to see how we can write the anonymous inner class as a lambda expression. But before we do that, one more variation on inner classes.

Static Nested Classes

We saved the easiest variation on inner classes for last, as a kind of treat!

You'll sometimes hear static nested classes referred to as *static inner classes* (and that's the way they are referred to in OCP Objective 2.3), but they really aren't inner classes at all based on the standard definition of an inner class. Whereas an inner class (regardless of the flavor) enjoys that *special relationship* with the outer class (or rather, the *instances* of the two classes share a relationship), a static nested class does not. It is simply a non-inner (also called "top-level") class scoped within another. So with static classes, it's really more about name-space resolution than about an implicit relationship between the two classes.

A static nested class is simply a class that's a static member of the enclosing class:

```
class BigOuter {
  static class Nested { }
}
```

The class itself isn't really "static"; there's no such thing as a static class. The `static` modifier in this case says that the nested class is *a static member of the outer class.* That means it can be accessed, as with other static members, *without having an instance of the outer class.*

Instantiating and Using Static Nested Classes

You use standard syntax to access a static nested class from its enclosing class. The syntax for instantiating a static nested class from a nonenclosing class is a little different from a normal inner class and looks like this:

```
class BigOuter {
  static class Nest {void go() { System.out.println("hi"); } }
}
```

```
class Broom {
  static class B2 {void goB2() { System.out.println("hi 2"); } }
  public static void main(String[] args) {
    BigOuter.Nest n = new BigOuter.Nest();    // both class names
    n.go();
    B2 b2 = new B2();                          // access the enclosed class
    b2.goB2();
  }
}
```

which produces

```
hi
hi 2
```

e x a m

ⓦ a t c h   *Just as a static method does   instance variables and nonstatic methods of*
not have access to the instance variables   the outer class. Look for static nested classes
and nonstatic methods of the class, a static   with code that behaves like a nonstatic
nested class does not have access to the   (regular inner) class.

CERTIFICATION OBJECTIVE

Lambda Expressions as Inner Classes (OCP Objective 2.6)

2.6 Create and use Lambda expressions.

Inner classes are often used for short, quick implementations of a class. Flavor two of anonymous inner classes showed you how to implement an interface with an anonymous class, either as a separate statement (as in the `Cookable` example) or as an argument (as in the `MyWonderfulClass` example).

When implementing an interface with an anonymous inner class, you'll often have opportunities to use lambda expressions to make your code more concise. In fact, some say lambdas are another way of writing anonymous inner classes. As you'll see, they certainly seem perfect for this job.

Let's take another look at MyWonderfulClass as a first example:

```
public class MyWonderfulClass {
    public static void main(String[] args) {
        MyWonderfulClass c = new MyWonderfulClass();
        c.go();
    }
    void go() {
        Bar b = new Bar();
        b.doStuff(new Foo() {
            public void foof() {
                System.out.println("foofy");
            }  // end foof() method
        });    // end inner class def, arg, and bo.doStuff stmt
    }          // end go()
}              // end class
interface Foo {
    void foof();
}
class Bar {
    void doStuff(Foo f) {
        f.foof();
    };
}
```

Foo is an interface, and we need an instance of a class that implements that interface to pass to the doStuff() method of Bar, so we use an anonymous inner class. Notice one important thing about Foo: it's an interface with *one abstract method*. Does that sound familiar (from the previous chapter)? Yes, Foo is a *functional interface*.

That means we can replace the entire inner class with a lambda expression. Let's go through the same process we did in the previous chapter (with GenreSort) to see how we can convert the Foo anonymous inner class into a lambda expression.

1. First we get any parameters from the abstract method in Foo, foof(); those become the parameters for the lambda. In this case we don't have any parameters, so we write:

   ```
   ()
   ```

2. Then, we add an arrow:

   ```
   () ->
   ```

3. Then we write the body of the lambda expression. What should the body be? Exactly the same as the body of the foof() method in the Foo instance we're passing to doStuff(). That is:

   ```
   () -> System.out.println("foofy")
   ```

We don't need to use any curly braces (or a return) because there's only one statement in the body of `foof()`, so we can just copy the expression as is. `foof()` is `void` (no return value), so in this case, the lambda expression will not automatically return a value (Java knows that `foof()` is `void` because it says so in `Foo`, so it's smart enough to know not to generate a return). Notice that we don't need a semicolon on the expression on the right either; however, as you'll see shortly, when we write a lambda expression as part of a statement, we still need to end the statement it's part of with a semicolon.

Now, let's see how to use this lambda expression:

```
1. public class MyWonderfulClass {
2.     void go() {
3.         Bar b = new Bar();
4.         b.doStuff(() -> System.out.println("foofy"));   // lambda magic!
5.     }
6. }
7. interface Foo {
8.     void foof();
9. }
10. class Bar {
11.     void doStuff(Foo f) {
12.         f.foof();
13.     };
14. }
```

Wow, that's a lot easier to read, isn't it? And definitely more concise. It might take you a while to get the hang of reading lambda expressions, but once you do, you'll find getting rid of the extra stuff that goes along with an inner class is a good way to make your code more concise and readable.

The important line to look at is line 4. Compare it to the code using the anonymous inner class. This lambda expression is "standing in" for the `foof()` function in the instance of the class implementing `Foo`.

But wait! There's no instance here. There's only a lambda expression that looks a lot more like a function than an object. And `doStuff()` is expecting an instance. So what gives?

Because `Foo` is a functional interface and has only one abstract method, Java knows that the function you're supplying as the lambda expression must be the function that implements that abstract method, `foof()`. It knows that the argument to `doStuff()` must be an instance of a class that implements the `Foo` interface, but the only really important part of that instance is the implementation of that one abstract method. So we shortcut by eliminating all the extra fluff of creating that class and instantiating the object and just provide the method, in the form of a lambda expression.

We can make the instance object—the instance of a class that implements the `Foo` interface—a bit more explicit by creating it separately and then passing the instance to `doStuff()`:

```
void go() {
    Bar b = new Bar();
    b.doStuff(() -> System.out.println("foofy"));
    // more explicitly obvious version below
    Foo f = () -> System.out.println("foofy 2"); // create the lambda
    b.doStuff(f);                                 // pass to doStuff
}
```

You'll see lambda expressions written this way on the exam, so get lots of practice reading and writing them this way. The syntax of lambda expressions takes some getting used to because it hides a whole bunch of stuff going on behind the scenes. The trick is to remember that the type of a lambda expression is a functional interface. And when used to simplify inner classes, the important thing to know for the exam is that you can substitute a lambda expression for an anonymous inner class whenever that class is implementing a functional interface.

Comparator Is a Functional Interface

Let's take one more look at the DVD example from the previous chapter to help inner classes and lambda expressions sink in just a bit more.

In that example we created a class `GenreSort` that implemented `Comparator`, which we could use with the `Collections.sort()` method or with the `sort()` method of our `dvdlist ArrayList`, both of which take a comparator as an argument.

That `GenreSort` class looked like this:

```
class GenreSort implements Comparator<DVDInfo> {
    public int compare(DVDInfo dvd1, DVDInfo dvd2) {
        return dvd1.getGenre().compareTo(dvd2.getGenre());
    }
}
```

First, let's turn this into an anonymous inner class. Here's the revised `go()` method from the `TestDVD` class:

```
public void go() {
  populateList();
  // Now the GenreSort comparator is made using an
  // anonymous inner class
  Comparator<DVDInfo> genreSort = new Comparator<DVDInfo>() {
```

```
      public int compare(DVDInfo dvd1, DVDInfo dvd2) {
        return dvd1.getGenre().compareTo(dvd2.getGenre());
      } };
    dvdlist.sort(genreSort);         // use the comparator to sort
}
```

This is an example of flavor two of anonymous inner classes: that is, we're creating an instance of a class that implements the `Comparator` interface. We store this instance in the variable `genreSort`. Just like before, we pass that instance to the `sort()` method, which uses it to sort the items in the `dvdlist ArrayList` by calling the `compare()` method we implemented in the comparator.

Take a careful look at the code to see how we translated the `GenreSort` class from an outer class into an anonymous inner class.

`Comparator` is a functional interface, meaning it has one abstract method that we must implement to make an instance of a class that implements the `Comparator` interface. So, we can scrap that inner class entirely and use a lambda expression instead:

```
dvdlist.sort((dvd1, dvd2) ->
    dvd1.getGenre().compareTo(dvd2.getGenre()));
```

This code is no different from what you saw in the previous chapter, only now instead of replacing the outer class `GenreSort`, we're replacing the anonymous inner class. It's exactly the same idea.

Note that we could also write the code like this:

```
Comparator<DVDInfo> genreSort = (dvd1, dvd2) ->
    dvd1.getGenre().compareTo(dvd2.getGenre());
dvdlist.sort(genreSort);
```

On the exam, you'll see lambdas used both ways: passed directly as arguments and assigned to variables. Assigning the lambda to a variable first makes the type of the lambda more explicit, but the type can always be inferred from the type signature of the method you're passing the lambda into.

For the exam, remember that you'll still see plenty of inner classes, because not all inner classes can be replaced by lambda expressions. Lambda expressions stand in for methods in classes that implement a functional interface. Don't be tricked by interfaces that might look functional but aren't. We'll cover all the rules that determine exactly what constitutes a functional interface in the next chapter.

CERTIFICATION SUMMARY

Inner classes will show up throughout the exam, in any topic, and these are some of the exam's hardest questions. You should be comfortable with the sometimes bizarre syntax and know how to spot legal and illegal inner class definitions.

We looked first at "regular" inner classes, where one class is a member of another. You learned that coding an inner class means putting the class definition of the inner class inside the curly braces of the enclosing (outer) class, but outside of any method or other code block. You learned that an inner class *instance* shares a special relationship with a specific *instance* of the outer class and that this special relationship lets the inner class access all members of the outer class, including those marked `private`. You learned that to instantiate an inner class, you *must* have a reference to an instance of the outer class.

Next, we looked at method-local inner classes—classes defined *inside* a method. The code for a method-local inner class looks virtually the same as the code for any other class definition, except that you can't apply an access modifier the way you can with a regular inner class. You learned why method-local inner classes must use `final` or effectively final local variables declared within the method—the inner class instance may outlive the stack frame, so the local variable might vanish while the inner class object is still alive. You saw that to *use* the inner class you need to instantiate it and that the instantiation must come *after* the class declaration in the method.

We also explored the strangest inner class type of all—the *anonymous* inner class. You learned that they come in two forms: normal and argument-defined. Normal, ho-hum, anonymous inner classes are created as part of a variable assignment, whereas argument-defined inner classes are actually declared, defined, and automatically instantiated *all within the argument to a method!* We covered the way anonymous inner classes can be either a subclass of the named class type or an *implementer* of the named interface. Finally, we looked at how polymorphism applies to anonymous inner classes: You can invoke on the new instance only those methods defined in the named class or interface type. In other words, even if the anonymous inner class defines its own new method, no code from anywhere outside the inner class will be able to invoke that method.

As if we weren't already having enough fun for one day, we pushed on to static nested classes, which really aren't inner classes at all. Known as `static` nested classes, a nested class marked with the `static` modifier is quite similar to any other non-inner class, except that to access it, the code must have access to both the nested and enclosing class. We saw that because the class is `static`, no instance of the enclosing class is needed, and thus the static nested class *does not share a special relationship with any instance of the enclosing class.* Remember, static inner classes can't access instance methods or variables of the enclosing class.

And finally, just to seal the fate of inner classes entirely, we showed how you can replace an anonymous inner class that's implementing a functional interface with a lambda expression. Using lambda expressions as shorthand for anonymous inner classes usually makes your code a lot more concise because you no longer have to write out the instance of the class that's implementing an interface; instead, you just supply the method that's standing in for the instance. Get ready for a lot more on this topic in the next chapter, but before we get there, practice what you've learned in this chapter with the two-minute drill and self test.

TWO-MINUTE DRILL

Here are some of the key points from this chapter. Most are related to OCP Objective 2.3.

Regular Inner Classes (OCP Objective 2.3)

☐ A "regular" inner class is declared *inside* the curly braces of another class, but *outside* any method or other code block.

☐ An inner class is a full-fledged member of the enclosing (outer) class, so it can be marked with an access modifier as well as the abstract or final modifiers. (Never both abstract and final together—remember that abstract *must* be subclassed, whereas final *cannot* be subclassed.)

☐ An inner class instance shares a special relationship with an instance of the enclosing class. This relationship gives the inner class access to *all* of the outer class's members, including those marked private.

☐ To instantiate an inner class, you must have a reference to an instance of the outer class.

☐ From code within the enclosing class, you can instantiate the inner class using only the name of the inner class, as follows:

```
MyInner mi = new MyInner();
```

☐ From code outside the enclosing class's instance methods, you can instantiate the inner class only by using both the inner and outer class names and a reference to the outer class, as follows:

```
MyOuter mo = new MyOuter();
MyOuter.MyInner inner = mo.new MyInner();
```

☐ From code within the inner class, the keyword this holds a reference to the inner class instance. To reference the *outer* this (in other words, the instance of the outer class that this inner instance is tied to), precede the keyword this with the outer class name, as follows: MyOuter.this;

Method-Local Inner Classes (OCP Objective 2.3)

☐ A method-local inner class is defined within a method of the enclosing class.

☐ For the inner class to be used, you must instantiate it, and that instantiation must happen within the same method, but *after* the class definition code.

❑ A method-local inner class cannot use variables declared within the method (including parameters) unless those variables are marked `final` or are effectively final.

❑ The only modifiers you can apply to a method-local inner class are `abstract` and `final`. (Never both at the same time, though.)

Anonymous Inner Classes (OCP Objective 2.3)

❑ Anonymous inner classes have no name, and their type must be either a subclass of the named type or an implementer of the named interface.

❑ An anonymous inner class is always created as part of a statement; don't forget to close the statement after the class definition with a curly brace. This is a rare case in Java, a curly brace followed by a semicolon.

❑ Because of polymorphism, the only methods you can call on an anonymous inner class reference are those defined in the reference variable class (or interface), even though the anonymous class is really a subclass or implementer of the reference variable type.

❑ An anonymous inner class can extend one subclass *or* implement one interface. Unlike nonanonymous classes (inner or otherwise), an anonymous inner class cannot do both. In other words, it cannot both extend a class *and* implement an interface, nor can it implement more than one interface.

❑ An argument-defined inner class is declared, defined, and automatically instantiated as part of a method invocation. The key to remember is that the class is being defined within a method argument, so the syntax will end the class definition with a curly brace, followed by a closing parenthesis to end the method call, followed by a semicolon to end the statement: `});`

Static Nested Classes (OCP Objective 2.3)

❑ Static nested classes are inner classes marked with the `static` modifier.

❑ A `static` nested class is *not* an inner class; it's a top-level nested class.

❑ Because the nested class is `static`, it does not share any special relationship with an instance of the outer class. In fact, you don't need an instance of the outer class to instantiate a `static` nested class.

❑ For the purposes of the exam, instantiating a `static` nested class requires using both the outer and nested class names as follows:

```
BigOuter.Nested n = new BigOuter.Nested();
```

☐ A static nested class cannot access non-static members of the outer class because it does not have any implicit reference to the outer instance (in other words, the nested class instance does not get an *outer* this reference).

Replacing Inner Classes with Lambda Expressions (OCP Objective 2.6)

☐ Lambda expressions are a good way to write anonymous inner classes that implement functional interfaces.

☐ Instead of writing out an instance of the class using an anonymous inner class like this:

```
b.doStuff(new Foo() {
    public void foof() { System.out.println("foofy"); }
});
```

we can replace the anonymous inner class with a lambda expression, like this:

```
b.doStuff(() -> System.out.println("foofy"));
```

☐ You can replace anonymous inner classes with lambda expressions *only* if the inner class implements a functional interface. Be careful on the exam; make sure the interface is really functional.

SELF TEST

The following questions will help you measure your understanding of the dynamic and life-altering material presented in this chapter. Read all of the choices carefully. Take your time. Breathe.

1. Which are true about a `static` nested class? (Choose all that apply.)

A. You must have a reference to an instance of the enclosing class in order to instantiate it

B. It does not have access to nonstatic members of the enclosing class

C. Its variables and methods must be `static`

D. If the outer class is named `MyOuter` and the nested class is named `MyInner`, it can be instantiated using new `MyOuter.MyInner();`

E. It must extend the enclosing class

2. Given:

```
class Boo {
    Boo(String s) { }
    Boo() { }
}
class Bar extends Boo {
    Bar() { }
    Bar(String s) {super(s);}
    void zoo() {
    // insert code here
    }
}
```

Which statements create an anonymous inner class from within class `Bar`? (Choose all that apply.)

A. `Boo f = new Boo(24) { };`

B. `Boo f = new Bar() { };`

C. `Boo f = new Boo() {String s; };`

D. `Bar f = new Boo(String s) { };`

E. `Boo f = new Boo.Bar(String s) { };`

3. Which are true about a method-local inner class? (Choose all that apply.)

A. It must be marked `final`

B. It can be marked `abstract`

C. It can be marked `public`

D. It can be marked `static`

E. It can access private members of the enclosing class

4. Given:

```
1. public class TestObj {
2.    public static void main(String[] args) {
3.      Object o = new Object() {
4.        public boolean equals(Object obj) {
5.           return true;
6.        }
7.      }
8.      System.out.println(o.equals("Fred"));
9.    }
10. }
```

What is the result?

A. An exception occurs at runtime

B. `true`

C. `Fred`

D. Compilation fails because of an error on line 3

E. Compilation fails because of an error on line 4

F. Compilation fails because of an error on line 8

G. Compilation fails because of an error on a line other than 3, 4, or 8

5. Given:

```
1. public class HorseTest {
2.    public static void main(String[] args) {
3.      class Horse {
4.        public String name;
5.        public Horse(String s) {
6.           name = s;
7.        }
8.      }
9.      Object obj = new Horse("Zippo");
10.     System.out.println(obj.name);
11.   }
12. }
```

What is the result?

A. An exception occurs at runtime at line 10

B. `Zippo`

C. Compilation fails because of an error on line 3

D. Compilation fails because of an error on line 9

E. Compilation fails because of an error on line 10

6. Given:

```
public abstract class AbstractTest {
  public int getNum() {
    return 45;
  }
  public abstract class Bar {
    public int getNum() {
      return 38;
    }
  }
  public static void main(String[] args) {
    AbstractTest t = new AbstractTest() {
      public int getNum() {
        return 22;
      }
    };
    AbstractTest.Bar f = t.new Bar() {
       public int getNum() {
         return 57;
       }
    };
    System.out.println(f.getNum() + " " + t.getNum());
  }
}
```

What is the result?

A. 57 22

B. 45 38

C. 45 57

D. An exception occurs at runtime

E. Compilation fails

7. Given:

```
3. public class Tour {
4.   public static void main(String[] args) {
5.     Cathedral c = new Cathedral();
6.     // insert code here
7.     s.go();
8.   }
9. }
10. class Cathedral {
11.   class Sanctum {
12.     void go() { System.out.println("spooky"); }
13.   }
14. }
```

Which, inserted independently at line 6, compiles and produces the output "spooky"? (Choose all that apply.)

A. `Sanctum s = c.new Sanctum();`

B. `c.Sanctum s = c.new Sanctum();`

C. `c.Sanctum s = Cathedral.new Sanctum();`

D. `Cathedral.Sanctum s = c.new Sanctum();`

E. `Cathedral.Sanctum s = Cathedral.new Sanctum();`

8. Given:

```
5. class A { void m() { System.out.println("outer"); } }
6.
7. public class TestInners {
8.    public static void main(String[] args) {
9.       new TestInners().go();
10.   }
11.   void go() {
12.      new A().m();
13.      class A { void m() { System.out.println("inner"); } }
14.   }
15.   class A { void m() { System.out.println("middle"); } }
16. }
```

What is the result?

A. `inner`

B. `outer`

C. `middle`

D. Compilation fails

E. An exception is thrown at runtime

9. Given:

```
3. public class Car {
4.    class Engine {
5.       // insert code here
6.    }
7.    public static void main(String[] args) {
8.       new Car().go();
9.    }
10.   void go() {
11.      new Engine();
12.   }
13.   void drive() { System.out.println("hi"); }
14. }
```

Which, inserted independently at line 5, produces the output "hi"? (Choose all that apply.)

A. `{ Car.drive(); }`

B. `{ this.drive(); }`

C. `{ Car.this.drive(); }`

D. `{ this.Car.this.drive(); }`

E. `Engine() { Car.drive(); }`

F. `Engine() { this.drive(); }`

G. `Engine() { Car.this.drive(); }`

10. Given:

```
3. public class City {
4.    class Manhattan {
5.      void doStuff() throws Exception { System.out.print("x "); }
6.    }
7.    class TimesSquare extends Manhattan {
8.      void doStuff() throws Exception { }
9.    }
10.   public static void main(String[] args) throws Exception {
11.     new City().go();
12.   }
13.   void go() throws Exception { new TimesSquare().doStuff(); }
14. }
```

What is the result?

A. x

B. x x

C. No output is produced

D. Compilation fails due to multiple errors

E. Compilation fails due only to an error on line 4

F. Compilation fails due only to an error on line 7

G. Compilation fails due only to an error on line 10

H. Compilation fails due only to an error on line 13

11. Given:

```
3. public class Navel {
4.    private int size = 7;
5.    private static int length = 3;
6.    public static void main(String[] args) {
7.      new Navel().go();
8.    }
9.    void go() {
10.     int size = 5;
```

```
11.        System.out.println(new Gazer().adder());
12.    }
13.    class Gazer {
14.      int adder() { return size * length; }
15.    }
16. }
```

What is the result?

A. 15

B. 21

C. An exception is thrown at runtime

D. Compilation fails due to multiple errors

E. Compilation fails due only to an error on line 4

F. Compilation fails due only to an error on line 5

12. Given:

```
3. import java.util.*;
4. public class Pockets {
5.    public static void main(String[] args) {
6.        String[] sa = {"nickel", "button", "key", "lint"};
7.        Sorter s = new Sorter();
8.        for(String s2: sa) System.out.print(s2 + " ");
9.        Arrays.sort(sa,s);
10.       System.out.println();
11.       for(String s2: sa) System.out.print(s2 + " ");
12.    }
13.    class Sorter implements Comparator<String> {
14.      public int compare(String a, String b) {
15.         return b.compareTo(a);
16.      }
17.    }
18. }
```

What is the result?

A. Compilation fails

B. button key lint nickel
       nickel lint key button

C. nickel button key lint
       button key lint nickel

D. nickel button key lint
       nickel button key lint

E. nickel button key lint
       nickel lint key button

F. An exception is thrown at runtime

13. Given:

```
import java.util.*;
public class Pockets2 {
   public static void main(String[] args) {
      String[] sa = {"nickel", "button", "key", "lint"};
      for (String s2: sa) System.out.print(s2 + " ");
      Arrays.sort(sa, (a, b) -> a.compareTo(b));
      System.out.println();
      for (String s2: sa) System.out.print(s2 + " ");
   }
}
```

What is the result?

A. Compilation fails

B. button key lint nickel
       nickel lint key button

C. nickel button key lint
       button key lint nickel

D. nickel button key lint
       nickel button key lint

E. nickel button key lint
       nickel lint key button

F. An exception is thrown at runtime

SELF TEST ANSWERS

Note: Most of the questions in this chapter relate to OCP Objective 2.3. We've talked about the actual mapping of inner class ideas to the exam, so we will NOT be citing Objective numbers in the answers to the questions in this chapter, except for the last question, which relates to Objective 2.6.

1. ☑ **B** and **D** are correct. **B** is correct because a static nested class is not tied to an instance of the enclosing class, and thus can't access the nonstatic members of the class (just as a `static` method can't access nonstatic members of a class). **D** uses the correct syntax for instantiating a static nested class.

   ☒ **A** is incorrect because static nested classes do not need (and can't use) a reference to an instance of the enclosing class. **C** is incorrect because static nested classes can declare and define nonstatic members. **E** is wrong because...it just is. There's no rule that says an inner or nested class has to extend anything.

2. ☑ **B** and **C** are correct. **B** is correct because anonymous inner classes are no different from any other class when it comes to polymorphism. That means you are always allowed to declare a reference variable of the superclass type and have that reference variable refer to an instance of a subclass type, which, in this case, is an anonymous subclass of `Bar`. Since `Bar` is a subclass of `Boo`, it all works. **C** uses correct syntax for creating an instance of `Boo`.

   ☒ **A** is incorrect because it passes an `int` to the `Boo` constructor, and there is no matching constructor in the `Boo` class. **D** is incorrect because it violates the rules of polymorphism; you cannot refer to a superclass type using a reference variable declared as the subclass type. The superclass doesn't have everything the subclass has. **E** uses incorrect syntax.

3. ☑ **B** and **E** are correct. **B** is correct because a method-local inner class can be `abstract`, although it means a subclass of the inner class must be created if the `abstract` class is to be used (so an `abstract` method-local inner class is probably not useful). **E** is correct because a method-local inner class works like any other inner class—it has a special relationship to an instance of the enclosing class, thus it can access all members of the enclosing class.

   ☒ **A** is incorrect because a method-local inner class does not have to be declared `final` (although it is legal to do so). **C** and **D** are incorrect because a method-local inner class cannot be made `public` (remember—local variables can't be `public`) or `static`.

4. ☑ **G** is correct. This code would be legal if line 7 ended with a semicolon. Remember that line 3 is a statement that doesn't end until line 7, and a statement needs a closing semicolon!

   ☒ **A, B, C, D, E,** and **F** are incorrect based on the program logic just described. If the semicolon were added at line 7, then answer **B** would be correct—the program would print `true`, the return from the `equals()` method overridden by the anonymous subclass of `Object`.

5. ☑ **E** is correct. If you use a reference variable of type `Object`, you can access only those members defined in class `Object`.
☒ **A, B, C,** and **D** are incorrect based on the program logic just described.

6. ☑ **A** is correct. You can define an inner class as `abstract`, which means you can instantiate only concrete subclasses of the `abstract` inner class. The object referenced by the variable `t` is an instance of an anonymous subclass of `AbstractTest`, and the anonymous class overrides the `getNum()` method to return `22`. The object referenced by variable `f` is an instance of an anonymous subclass of `Bar`, and the anonymous `Bar` subclass also overrides the `getNum()` method to return `57`. Remember that to create a `Bar` instance, we need an instance of the enclosing `AbstractTest` class to tie to the new `Bar` inner class instance. `AbstractTest` can't be instantiated because it's `abstract`, so we created an anonymous subclass (non-`abstract`) and then used the instance of that anonymous subclass to tie to the new `Bar` subclass instance.
☒ **B, C, D,** and **E** are incorrect based on the program logic just described.

7. ☑ **D** is correct. It is the only code that uses the correct inner class instantiation syntax.
☒ **A, B, C,** and **E** are incorrect based on the above text.

8. ☑ **C** is correct. The `"inner"` version of `class A` isn't used because its declaration comes after the instance of `class A` is created in the `go()` method.
☒ **A, B, D,** and **E** are incorrect based on the above text.

9. ☑ **C** and **G** are correct. **C** is the correct syntax to access an inner class's outer instance method from an initialization block, and **G** is the correct syntax to access it from a constructor.
☒ **A, B, D, E,** and **F** are incorrect based on the above text.

10. ☑ **C** is correct. The inner classes are valid, and all the methods (including `main()`), correctly throw an exception, given that `doStuff()` throws an exception. The `doStuff()` in class `TimesSquare` overrides class `Manhattan`'s `doStuff()` and produces no output.
☒ **A, B, D, E, F, G,** and **H** are incorrect based on the above text.

11. ☑ **B** is correct. The inner class `Gazer` has access to `Navel`'s `private static` and private instance variables.
☒ **A, C, D, E,** and **F** are incorrect based on the above text.

12. ☑ **A** is correct. The inner class `Sorter` must be declared `static` to be called from the `static` method `main()`. If `Sorter` had been `static`, answer **E** would be correct.
☒ **B, C, D, E,** and **F** are incorrect based on the above text.

13. ☑ **C** is correct. We're using a lambda expression to stand in for the `Comparator` we pass to `Arrays.sort()`. There is no inner (or outer) class we need to supply; the JDK knows we are supplying a lambda expression that implements the `compareTo()` method for `Comparator` because of the type signature of `Arrays.sort()`. In this case, we are sorting the list in ascending order.

☒ **A, B, D, E,** and **F** are incorrect based on the above text. (Objective 2.6)

8

Lambda Expressions and Functional Interfaces

O ne of the big new language features added in Java 8 is the lambda expression. We've already talked a bit about lambdas, introducing the basic syntax and the idea of functional interfaces. You've seen how to use a lambda expression to replace an inner class (e.g., a `Comparator`) and you've also seen how to pass a lambda expression—really, just a block of code—to methods that expect Comparators, like `Collections.sort()`. Those earlier tastes of lambda expressions probably left you with more questions than answers, and this chapter is where we dive into all those details. As with inner classes, you'll need to know the syntax of lambda expressions and when you can use them like the back of your hand. You'll also need to get familiar with a variety of functional interfaces so you can recognize them easily. Do that and you'll sail through the lambda expressions part of the exam.

CERTIFICATION OBJECTIVE

Lambda Expression Syntax (OCP Objective 2.6)

2.6   Create and use Lambda expressions.

You already know (a little) how lambda expressions can make your code more concise. Concise code is good, but only if it makes sense. And, let's face it, lambda expression syntax can take some getting used to. Let's take another look at the syntax and talk about the varieties of lambda expression syntax you might expect to see in the real world and on the exam.

Imagine you've got a super simple interface, `DogQuerier`, with one abstract method, `test()` (remember that all interface methods are abstract unless they are declared default or static):

```
interface DogQuerier {
    public boolean test(Dog d);
}
```

We say that `DogQuerier` is a "functional interface": it's an interface with one abstract method.

Later, you use an inner class to define an instance of a class that implements this interface:

```
DogQuerier dq = new DogQuerier() {
    public boolean test(Dog d) { return d.getAge() > 9; }
};
```

Wait, scrap that—we can make the code much more concise by replacing that inner class with a lambda expression:

```
DogQuerier dq = (d) -> d.getAge() > 9;
```

You use that lambda expression just like you'd use the instance of the inner class:

```
System.out.println("Is Boi older than 9? " + dq.test(boi));
```

(assuming boi is a Dog with a getAge() method, of course).

Think of a lambda expression as a shorthand way of writing an instance of a class that implements a functional interface. It looks a lot like a method (in fact, some call lambda expressions "anonymous methods"), but it's a bit more than that; it's more like an instance with everything but the method stripped away. The important part of the instance is the method (the rest can be inferred from the interface definition), so the lambda expression is the syntax of the instance that's been boiled down to the bare essentials.

To make the lambda expression, we copy the parameter of the test() method from the inner class, then write an arrow, and then copy the expression in the body of the test method, leaving out the return and the semicolon:

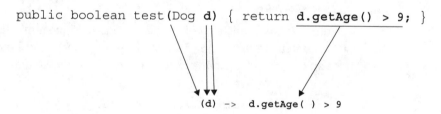

The type of the lambda expression is DogQuerier. That's the same as the type of the interface and the same as the type of the instance being created by the inner class.

```
DogQuerier dq = (d) -> d.getAge() > 9;
```

And, of course, when we write the statement assigning the lambda to the instance variable, we end that statement with a semicolon. Now let's look at some variations. Because the test() method has only one parameter, it's perfectly legal to leave off the parentheses around the parameter and write the lambda like this instead:

```
DogQuerier dq = d -> d.getAge() > 9;
```

If you have more than one parameter, however, you *must* use the parentheses.

You might be wondering: how does the lambda "know" what d's type is supposed to be? That can be inferred from the `DogQuerier` interface definition. However, there may be times when the type can't be inferred and you will need to write it in. And, in this example, you can supply the type if you want to, but if you do, you'll have to use the parentheses around the parameter:

```
DogQuerier dq = (Dog d) -> d.getAge() > 9;
```

What about the return value's type? That, too, can be inferred from the `DogQuerier` interface definition. And wait a sec, where'd that `return` go to anyway?

The rule is, if there is only one expression in the lambda, then the value of that expression gets returned by default, and you don't need a return. In fact, if you try to write

```
DogQuerier dq = d -> return d.getAge() > 9;  // does not compile
```

you'll get a compile-time error:

```
Syntax error on token "->", { expected after this token.
```

If you want to write `return`, then you'll have to write the lambda like this:

```
DogQuerier dq = d -> { return d.getAge() > 9; };
```

In other words, if the body of your lambda is anything more than an expression—that is, a statement or multiple statements—you'll need to use the curly braces. Here's an example of a lambda expression with multiple statements:

```
DogQuerier dq = d -> {
    System.out.println("Testing " + d.getName());
    return d.getAge() > 9;
};
```

To summarize, we can write the original `DogQuerier` instance as a lambda expression in the following ways, all of which are equivalent:

```
DogQuerier dq = (d) -> d.getAge() > 9;
DogQuerier dq = d -> d.getAge() > 9;
DogQuerier dq = (Dog d) -> d.getAge() > 9;
DogQuerier dq = d -> { return d.getAge() > 9; };
```

Here's the full code so you can test the `DogQuerier` lambda expression:

```
// Our trusty Dog class
public class Dog {
    private String name;
    private int weight;
    private int age;
    public Dog(String name, int weight, int age) {
```

```
            this.name = name;
            this.weight = weight;
            this.age = age;
        }
        public String getName() { return this.name; }
        public int getWeight() { return this.weight; }
        public int getAge() { return this.age; }
        public String toString() { return this.name; }
    }
    // Our functional interface to test dogs
    interface DogQuerier {
        public boolean test(Dog d);
    }

    public class TestDogs {
        public static void main(String[] args) {
            Dog boi = new Dog("boi", 30, 6);
            Dog clover = new Dog("clover", 35, 12);
            // We don't need this inner class anymore; replace with a lambda
    // DogQuerier dq = new DogQuerier() {
    //     public boolean test(Dog d) { return d.getAge() > 9; }
    // };
    DogQuerier dq = d -> d.getAge() > 9;  // replaces the inner class
    System.out.println("Is Boi older than 9? " + dq.test(boi));
    System.out.println("Is Clover older than 9? " + dq.test(clover));
        }
    }
```

The output is

```
Is Boi older than 9? false
Is Clover older than 9? true
```

Here are a few examples of invalid lambda expression syntax to watch out for:

```
Sheep s -> s.color.equals(color);
```

Needs parentheses around the argument.

```
(Sheep s) -> if (s.color.equals(color)) return true; else return false;
```

Needs {} around body of lambda and an ending ;

```
SheepQuerier testSheep = s, n -> s.age > n;
```

Needs parentheses around the arguments.

Passing Lambda Expressions to Methods

Lambda expressions are easy to pass to methods. It's a bit like passing a block of code to a method. To demonstrate, let's add a class to our `Dogs` example:

```
class DogsPlay {
   DogQuerier dogQuerier;
   public DogsPlay(DogQuerier dogQuerier) {
      this.dogQuerier = dogQuerier;
   }
   public boolean doQuery(Dog d) {
      return dogQuerier.test(d);
   }
}
```

The constructor for the `DogsPlay` class takes a `DogQuerier` instance. We can pass the `dq` instance we created with a lambda expression to `DogsPlay` like this:

```
DogsPlay dp = new DogsPlay(dq);
```

Or we can pass a lambda expression directly:

```
DogsPlay dp = new DogsPlay(d -> d.getAge() > 9);
```

When we call `dp.doQuery()` and pass in a dog, the `test()` method of the `DogQuerier` gets called:

```
System.out.println("Is Boi older than 9? " + dp.doQuery(boi));
```

And we see the output:

```
Is Boi older than 9? false
```

The lambda expression we're passing to `DogsPlay` is simple; it has one `Dog` parameter and simply tests that dog's age and returns true or false.

Accessing Variables from Lambda Expressions

What do you think happens if a lambda has a reference to another variable? While you can declare and use variables within the lambda expression, just like you would in the body of a method, the lambda is essentially just creating a nested block, so you can't use the same variable name as you've used in the enclosing scope. So this is fine:

```
int numCats = 3;
DogQuerier dqWithCats = d -> {
   int numBalls = 1;          // completely new variable local to lambda
```

```
    numBalls++;                // can modify numBalls
    System.out.println("Number of balls: " + numBalls);  // can access numBalls
    System.out.println("Number of cats: " + numCats);    // can access numCats
    return d.getAge() > 9;
};
```

But this is not:

```
int numCats = 3;
int numBalls = 1;               // now we have numBalls in enclosing scope
DogQuerier dqWithCats = d -> {
    int numBalls = 5;           // won't compile! Trying to redeclare numBalls
    System.out.println("Number of balls: " + numBalls);
    System.out.println("Number of cats: " + numCats);
    return d.getAge() > 9;
};
```

A lambda expression "captures" variables from the enclosing scope, so you can access those variables in the body of the lambda, but those variables must be final or effectively final. An effectively final variable is a variable or parameter whose value isn't changed after it is initialized. Let's see what happens if we try to modify the number of cats in the lambda expression:

```
int numCats = 3;
DogQuerier dqWithCats = d -> {
    int numBalls = 1;
    numBalls++;
    numCats++;                  // Won't compile! Can't change numCats
    System.out.println("Number of balls: " + numBalls);
    System.out.println("Number of cats: " + numCats);
    return d.getAge() > 9;
};
```

If we try to change the value either in the lambda itself or elsewhere in the enclosing scope, we will get an error. We can *use* the value of numCats, but we can't *change* it. So this will work:

```
int numCats = 3;               // numCats is effectively final
DogQuerier dqWithCats = d -> {
    int numBalls = 1;
    numBalls++;
    System.out.println("Number of balls: " + numBalls);
    System.out.println("Number of cats: " + numCats);  // Okay to use numCats
    return d.getAge() > 9;
};
```

The value of the variable numCats is captured by the lambda so it can be used later when we invoke the lambda (by calling its test() method).

Let's see what happens when we pass a lambda with captured values to the `DogsPlay` constructor:

```
System.out.println("--- use DogsPlay ---");
DogsPlay dp = new DogsPlay(dqWithCats);
System.out.println("Is Clover older than 9? " + dp.doQuery(clover));
```

This works fine; the captured value for `numCats` is sent along with the lambda to `DogsPlay` and used when the lambda is invoked later when we call `doQuery()`. Here is the output:

```
--- use DogsPlay ---
Number of balls: 2
Number of cats: 3
Is Clover older than 9? True
```

CERTIFICATION OBJECTIVE

Functional Interfaces (OCP Objectives 3.5, 4.1, 4.2, 4.3, and 4.4)

3.5 Iterate using forEach methods of Streams and List.
4.1 Use the built-in interfaces included in the java.util.function package such as Predicate, Consumer, Function, and Supplier.
4.2 Develop code that uses primitive versions of functional interfaces.
4.3 Develop code that uses binary versions of functional interfaces.
4.4 Develop code that uses the UnaryOperator interface.

Lambda expressions work by standing in for instances of classes that implement interfaces with one abstract method, so there is no confusion about which method the lambda is defining. As we've said before, we call these interfaces with one and only one abstract method "functional interfaces." There's nothing particularly special about them, except their relationship to lambda expressions. We can explicitly identify a functional interface using the `@FunctionalInterface` annotation, like this:

```
@FunctionalInterface
interface DogQuerier {
    public boolean test(Dog d);
}
```

This annotation is not required but can be helpful when you want to ensure you don't inadvertently add methods to a functional interface that will then break other code. If you use the DogQuerier type to define a lambda expression and then later add another abstract method to this interface, without the @FunctionalInterface annotation, you'll get a compiler error, "The target type of this expression must be a functional interface." Yikes!

By using the @FunctionalInterface, the compiler will warn you that adding an extra method won't work and you can avoid the error. Seeing that annotation, you'll be reminded that you created a functional interface for a reason, so you'll know not to change it. You may not see @FunctionalInterface used on the exam, but you'll definitely be expected to identify functional interfaces with or without this annotation.

Built-in Functional Interfaces

Functional interfaces turn out to be useful in all sorts of scenarios, some of which we'll get into here and some in the next chapter. You've already seen one useful functional interface: the Comparator. In addition, with Java 8 we get a big collection of functional interfaces in the java.util.function package, where you'll find Predicate, which you've also seen before, along with a variety of others. You will need to be familiar with them all.

Looking at the list, you might be wondering why you need all these different kinds of functional interfaces? Well, you probably won't ever need them all, but it's nice to have them available to use when you need a functional interface and don't want to define your own. As you'll see, there are many more uses for these interfaces than you might think, and having those interfaces already defined can save you time and code when you just want a quick lambda expression and don't want to bother with creating your own functional interface.

What Makes an Interface Functional?

We already said that a functional interface is an interface with one and only one abstract method. Let's delve into this just a little more because it can get a bit tricky.

Take a look at the Java 8 API documentation (https://docs.oracle.com/javase/8/docs/api/java/util/function/Predicate.html) for java.util.function.Predicate, and you'll find it has five methods: and(), isEqual(), negate(), or(), and test(). Every method except test() is declared as static or default, so it's pretty easy to determine that test() is the single abstract method in this functional interface. And, indeed, if you look under "Abstract Methods" for this interface, you'll see one method there, `test()`. Clearly, `Predicate` is a functional interface.

Now, take a look at the documentation for `java.util.Comparator`. This has quite a few default and static methods, so click on "Abstract Methods" to narrow down your search for its one and only one abstract method. What do you see? Two methods: `compare()` and `equals()`. But we said this is a functional interface, so why are two abstract methods listed here? `equals()` is inherited from `Object`, and inherited public methods are not counted when you're determining whether an interface is a functional interface. So even though `equals()` is abstract in `Comparator`, because it's inherited, it doesn't count. Tricky! Be ready to spot this on the exam.

To sum up, here is the rule for functional interfaces: A functional interface is an interface that has one abstract method. Default methods don't count; static methods don't count; and methods inherited from Object don't count.

Oh, and just so you know, the single abstract method in a functional interface is called the "functional method."

Categories of Functional Interfaces

You'll find 43 functional interfaces in `java.util.function`, and they all fall into one of four categories: suppliers, consumers, predicates, or functions. Each functional interface has a single abstract method (the functional method) and sometimes static and default methods.

The basic types of functional interfaces are `Supplier`, `Consumer`, `Predicate`, and `Function`.

Suppliers   Suppliers supply results. `java.util.function.Supplier`'s functional method, `get()`, never takes an argument, and it always returns something.

Consumers   Consumers consume values. `java.util.function.Consumer`'s functional method, `accept()`, always takes an argument and never returns anything.

Predicates   Predicates test things (and do logical operations). `java.util.function.Predicate`'s functional method, `test()`, takes a value, does a logical test, and returns true or false.

Functions   You can think of functions as the most generic of the functional interfaces. `java.util.function.Function`'s functional method, `apply()`, takes an argument and returns a value.

All of the functional interfaces in `java.util.function` are variations of suppliers, consumers, predicates, and functions. For example, `BooleanSupplier` is a supplier whose functional method supplies a boolean value. An `IntConsumer` is a consumer whose functional method takes an `int` value. And so on. Most of the variations are either to give you a way to provide more arguments (e.g., a `BiConsumer` that takes two arguments instead of one) or avoid autoboxing (e.g., `IntConsumer` and `BooleanSupplier`), which makes them more efficient. We'll give a lot of examples in the next few sections, so you get a sense of how these work.

When you first start working with functional interfaces, they can seem rather abstract. That's because, on their own, they don't really mean anything. What on earth is the point of having a `Function` interface with a method that takes a value and returns a value? That seems like the most generic thing in the world and rather pointless.

Seeing these interfaces in use and using them yourself will help make them seem less abstract and more useful. One good way to see functional interfaces in use is to look at the Oracle API documentation for one of the interfaces and click on "USE" in the top navigation bar. This shows you how that functional interface is used in the rest of the JDK.

Working with Suppliers

Let's begin with a super simple supplier:

```
Supplier<Integer> answerSupplier = () -> 42;
System.out.println("Answer to everything: " + answerSupplier.get());
```

And in the output we see

```
Answer to everything: 42
```

We've made a `Supplier` whose functional method, `get()` returns an `Integer` object, `42`.

Looking at the definition of `java.util.function.Supplier`, we can see that it's defined like this:

```
@FunctionalInterface
public interface Supplier<T>
```

And its functional method is `get()`, which returns a value of type `T`. So here `T` is a type parameter indicating the type of what's returned from the functional method. We like the method detail from the documentation page where it describes what the `get()` method returns: "A result." About as generic as you can get, right? This is why functional interfaces can feel so abstract when you first start working with them.

Just to cement how the lambda expression is being used for `answerSupplier` in the code above, let's take a look at how we might create a `Supplier` without using a lambda expression, so you can see one more time how we get to the lambda from, say, an inner class. Remember, `Supplier` is just an interface! So we can make an instance of a class implementing that interface the old-fashioned way, with an inner class, like this:

```
Supplier<Integer> answerSupplierInnerClass = new Supplier<Integer>() {
    public Integer get() {
        return 42;
    }
};
```

As you can see, using a lambda expression to stand in for this inner class is a whole lot shorter and easier. Hopefully by this point, you've got the hang of reading lambda expressions. From here on out, we'll primarily use lambda expressions when implementing functional interfaces. That said, remember you might see a full-blown implementation of a functional interface on the exam.

Okay, so a supplier that supplies `42` every time isn't that interesting; let's try another one:

```
Supplier<String> userSupplier = () -> {
    Map<String, String> env = System.getenv();  // get the system environment map
    return env.get("USER");                      // get the value with the key
                                                 // "USER" from the map and
                                                 // return it (Note: on Windows,
                                                 // this key is "USERNAME")
};
System.out.println("User is: " + userSupplier.get());
```

Here we've got a supplier with multiple statements, so we're using a slightly longer form of the lambda expression with curly braces to define a block of code and including a `return` statement to return the `String` that this supplier expects. In this case the `String` that's returned is the system username.

The key thing to note about both of these suppliers is they take no arguments and return an object. That's what suppliers do.

IntSupplier   Looking at `java.util.function`, we can see that there are some variations on supplier, including `IntSupplier`, `DoubleSupplier`, and `LongSupplier`. As you can guess, these supply an `int`, a `double`, and a `long`, respectively. These are there primarily to avoid autoboxing in case you want a primitive, rather than an object, back from the supplier. The functional method names of each of these is different and is not `get()`, so you'll need to remember that for the exam. For example, the functional method of `IntSupplier` is `getAsInt()`, so we can use the following code to make a supplier that returns a new random `int` when you call the `getAsInt()` method:

```
Random random = new Random();
IntSupplier randomIntSupplier = () -> random.nextInt(50);
int myRandom = randomIntSupplier.getAsInt();
System.out.println("Random number: " + myRandom);
```

Notice that `IntSupplier` doesn't use a type parameter, because the functional method returns a primitive. This avoids the autoboxing to `Integer` that we get with `Supplier<Integer>` (as in our `answerSupplier` above), which saves just a tiny bit of computation time (woo hoo!).

What's the Point of Supplier?   At this stage, you might be asking yourself, What is the point of a supplier? After all we could just as easily write `42`, or `random.nextInt(50)`, or put the block of code into a regular method, instead of creating a lambda expression and then calling its functional method.

Looking at how `Suppliers` are used in the JDK can give you a hint as to where and why they are useful. As an example we'll take a look at the `java.util.logging.Logger` class, which has been augmented with several methods that take `Supplier` as an argument. `Logger` is used to log messages for a system or application component, and you can set the logging level to determine what kinds of messages and how many messages to log. We can use the `log()` method to log a string if the log level is set, like this:

```
Logger logger = Logger.getLogger("Status Logger");
logger.setLevel(Level.SEVERE);

// Later...
String currentStatus = "Everything's okay";
logger.log(Level.INFO, currrentStatus);
```

In this example, we do *not* see the current status string logged because the log level is set to `SEVERE` and our call to the `log()` method says only log the message if the level is set to INFO or below (logging levels are ordered with SEVERE at the highest level, and INFO is a couple of levels below that). If we write this instead

```
String currentStatus = "Something's horribly wrong!";
logger.log(Level.SEVERE, currentStatus);
```

then we will see the message.

Now what if we need to do some expensive call to check the status of the system? Here we've hard-coded the status to a String but it's more likely that the status is actually determined by, say, making a network call to see if a system is up or down. If we go ahead and compute the status before sending a string to the log() method, then we've potentially wasted time checking the status if the log level is not set high enough that we'll actually log the status string. This is where Supplier comes in handy.

A new log() method in Logger takes a level and a Supplier<String> rather than a String. Let's see how we might use this. We'll write some code that will determine the status of a system by sending a network request to a host to check to see if it's up and running. Imagine this is part of a bigger program that does something useful with the data from the host (in this case, javaranch.com); perhaps it alerts you every time someone posts a new message.

We want to log the status—that is, whether the host is up—when things are fine, but only if the logging level is set to INFO or below. We don't want to bother checking the status and logging anything if the logging level is set to SEVERE. In that case, we only want to log messages that indicate things are really bad!

And we want to log the status if things go wrong, pretty much no matter what the logging level is, so we'll log the status if the level is set to SEVERE or below (and since SEVERE is the highest level, then we'll *always* log the status if things go wrong).

Here's the code:

```
String host = "coderanch.com";
int port = 80;
// set up logging
Logger logger = Logger.getLogger("Status Logger");
logger.setLevel(Level.SEVERE);              // line 5

// in case we need to check the status
Supplier<String> status = () -> {
    int timeout = 1000;
    try (Socket socket = new Socket()) {
        socket.connect(new InetSocketAddress(host, port), timeout);
        return "up";
    } catch (IOException e) {
```

```
            return "down";                  // Error; can't reach the system!
        }
    };

    try {
        logger.log(Level.INFO, status);     // only calls the get() method of the
                                             // status Supplier if level is INFO
                                             // or below
        // do stuff with coderanch.com
        // ...
    } catch (Exception e) {
        logger.log(Level.SEVERE, status);   // calls the get() method of the status
                                             // Supplier if level is SEVERE or below
    }
```

The logger's `log()` method takes the status `Supplier` and checks the log level. Because we've set the log level to `SEVERE` on line 5, in the `try` block, where we call the `log()` method with `Level.INFO`, the `log()` method won't bother calling the `get()` method of the status `Supplier`, and so we avoid making that expensive network call. And, of course, in the `catch` block, we're passing `Level.SEVERE` with the status `Supplier`, so if we end up in this `catch` block, we'll always use the `Supplier`: the `log()` method will call the status `Supplier`'s `get()` method, get the status (a `String`—look at the type parameter on the `Supplier`), and log it.

Imagine if you were to always check the status to get the string to pass to `log()` instead. In that case, you'd be checking the status unnecessarily in the case where everything's fine and the logging level is set to `SEVERE`.

So using a `Supplier` here avoids that expensive operation when it's unnecessary. We're passing a block of code (the `Supplier`) that gets executed only if a certain condition applies. We don't have to check that condition ourselves; `Logger` does it for us and then can call the `get()` method on the `Supplier` only if it needs to. (You can test the log status yourself by adding a

```
throw new IOException();
```

in the `try` block if you want).

It's no different than if you created your own `Supplier` interface with a `get()` method that could be called whenever a value is needed, but having these built-in functional interfaces that other parts of the JDK can use in situations like this makes life just a bit easier for you. And using lambda expressions to eliminate one more step (actually instantiating a class that implements that interface) reduces your work, helps make your code more concise, and (once you're used to reading lambda expressions) easier to read.

Working with Consumers

You can think of consumers as the opposite of suppliers (like matter and antimatter, it helps keeps the universe balanced). Consumers accept one or more arguments and don't return anything. So this lambda expression

```
Consumer<String> redOrBlue = pill -> {
    if (pill.equals("red")) {
        System.out.println("Down the rabbit hole");
    } else if (pill.equals("blue")) {
        System.out.println("Stay in lala land");
    }
};
```

implements the `java.util.function.Consumer` interface, which is defined like this:

```
@FunctionalInterface
public interface Consumer<T>
```

The `Consumer`'s functional method is `accept()`, which takes an object of type `T` and returns nothing, so we use the `redOrBlue` consumer like this:

```
redOrBlue.accept("red");
```

and see the output:

```
Down the rabbit hole
```

As with suppliers, there are variations on consumers in the `java.util` `.function` package. `IntConsumer`, `DoubleConsumer`, and `LongConsumer` do what you'd expect: their `accept()` methods take one primitive argument and avoid the autoboxing you get with `Consumer`.

In addition to these, there's `ObjIntConsumer`, `ObjDoubleConsumer`, and `ObjLongConsumer`, whose `accept()` methods take an object (type `T`) and an int, a double, or a long.

And finally we have `BiConsumer`, which is similar, except that its `accept()` method takes two objects (types `T` and `U`, meaning the two objects don't have to be of the same type). So the `BiConsumer` interface looks like this:

```
@FunctionalInterface
public interface BiConsumer<T,U>
```

with one function method, `accept()`:

```
void accept(T t, U u)
```

Here's a good use for a `BiConsumer`:

```
Map<String, String> env = System.getenv();
BiConsumer<String, String> printEnv = (key, value) -> {
   System.out.println(key + ": " + value);
};
printEnv.accept("USER", env.get("USER"));
```

The `printEnv BiConsumer` is a lambda expression with two arguments that we are using to display a key and value from a `Map`. To use the `printEnv` consumer, we call its `accept()` method, passing in two strings, and see the result displayed in the console.

ForEach   Now is a good time to talk about the `forEach()` method that's been added to the Java 8 `Iterable` interface. Why? Because `forEach()` expects a consumer. You'll end up using `forEach()` a lot, as it's a handy way to iterate through collections.

Here's how you use `forEach()` with a `Consumer` to iterate through a `List` and display each item in the list:

```
List<String> dogNames = Arrays.asList("boi", "clover", "zooey");
Consumer<String> printName = name -> System.out.println(name);
dogNames.forEach(printName);      // pass the printName consumer to
                                  // forEach()
```

We could, of course, combine the last two of these lines, like this:

```
dogNames.forEach(name -> System.out.println(name));
```

This consumer takes a `String` and just prints it.

The kind of consumer `forEach()` expects depends on the type of collection you're using. For example, when you iterate through `List`, you're accessing one object at a time, so the consumer you'll use is `Consumer` (that is, a consumer whose `accept()` method expects one argument, an object). And for `Map`, the consumer you'll use is a `BiConsumer` (that is, a consumer whose `accept()` method expects two arguments, both objects). Let's use the `BiConsumer` we created earlier, `printEnv`, with the `Map`'s `forEach()` method to display every key/value pair in the map:

```
Map<String, String> env = System.getenv();
BiConsumer<String, String> printEnv = (key, value) -> {
   System.out.println(key + ": " + value);
};

env.forEach(printEnv);      // the forEach() method of Map expects a BiConsumer
```

This displays every key/value pair in the `Map` that you get from `System.getenv()`.

Side Effects from Within Lambdas   You already know that there are restrictions on modifying the value of variables from within lambda expressions. For instance, if you define a variable in the enclosing scope of a lambda expression, you can't modify that variable from within the lambda:

```
String username;
BiConsumer<String, String> findUsername = (key, value) -> {
    if (key.equals("USER")) username = value;  // compile error!
                                               // username must be
                                               // effectively final
};
env.forEach(findUsername);
```

This code will not compile because we're trying to change the value of username from within the lambda expression. Remember that variables declared outside a lambda expression must be final or effectively final to be used within a lambda expression.

However, we can cheat. Although we can't modify a variable from within a lambda expression, we *can* modify a field of an object. If we want to use forEach() to iterate through a collection of objects to, say, find a value, we can't return the value we find (because forEach() takes a consumer and the accept() method of a consumer is void), but we can change the field of an object from within the lambda to do effectively the same thing:

```
public class Consumers {
    public static void main(String[] args) {
        Map<String, String> env = System.getenv();
        User user = new User();
        BiConsumer<String, String> findUsername = (key, value) -> {
            if (key.equals("USER")) user.setUsername(value);
        };
        env.forEach(findUsername);
        System.out.println("Username from env: " + user.getUsername());
    }
}
class User {
    String username;
    public void setUsername(String username) {
        this.username = username;
    }
    public String getUsername() {
        return this.username;
    }
}
```

Note that this code will be less efficient than using a `for` loop iteration and breaking out of the iteration once the value is found. You might not ever need to do this, but now you know you can, just in case. In the next chapter on Streams, you'll learn a better way to extract and collect values that doesn't rely on side effects, as we're doing here.

andThen...   andThen the murders began... Oh wait, no. This isn't a crime thriller; it's a Java book.

`andThen()` is actually a default method of the `Consumer` interface that you can use to chain consumers together. Let's imagine you have a `Dog` that can bark:

```
public class Dog {
    private String name;
    private int age;
    private int weight;

    public Dog(String name, int weight, int age) {
        this.name = name;
        this.weight = weight;
        this.age = age;
    }
    // getters and setters here...
    public String toString() { return this.name; }
    public void bark() { System.out.println("Woof!"); }
}
```

Now let's make some dogs and display them with `forEach()`:

```
public class ConsumerDogs {
    public static void main(String[] args) {
        List<Dog> dogs = new ArrayList<>();
        Dog boi = new Dog("boi", 30, 6);
        Dog clover = new Dog("clover", 35, 12);
        Dog zooey = new Dog("zooey", 45, 8);
        dogs.add(boi); dogs.add(clover); dogs.add(zooey);

        Consumer<Dog> displayName = d -> System.out.print(d + " ");
        dogs.forEach(displayName);      // line 10
    }
}
```

When you run this, you'll see

```
boi clover zooey
```

Now let's say we want to display the dog's name *andThen* we want to have the dog bark. Can we do it with consumers? Yes! Here's how:

```
dogs.forEach(displayName.andThen(d -> d.bark()));
```

Replace line 10 with this line and now you'll see

```
boi Woof!
clover Woof!
zooey Woof!
```

So how does this work? We're passing a "composed `Consumer`" to the `forEach()` method of the dogs `ArrayList`. Let's step through this.

First, note that the `forEach()` method is calling the `accept()` method of the `Consumer` you're passing in behind the scenes. So for each dog d in the list, `forEach()` is essentially doing this:

```
displayName.accept(d)
```

When the `andThen()` method of the `Consumer` is called, it says, okay, now use that same dog object, d, that we just used in the first `Consumer` for the `accept()` method of the second `Consumer`. Note that we've written the second `Consumer` as an inline lambda (rather than as a separate declaration like we did for `displayName`)—but, of course, it works the same way. So the dog d whose name we just displayed is used in the second `Consumer`, and we call that dog's `bark()` method, which simply displays `Woof!` in the console. And so the result we see is the dog's name followed by `Woof!` for each of the dogs in the list.

You might think that you could write both lambdas inline, like this:

```
dogs.forEach((d -> System.out.print(d + " ")).andThen(d -> d.bark()));
```

But you can't. You'll get a compile error. You can, however, use named consumers for both:

```
Consumer<Dog> displayName = d -> System.out.print(d + " ");
Consumer<Dog> doBark = d -> d.bark();
dogs.forEach(displayName.andThen(doBark));
```

Most (but not all!) of the consumers in `java.util.function` have an `andThen()` method, and notice that the type of the consumer you pass to the `andThen()` method must match the type of the consumer used as the first operation. So you can chain a `Consumer` with a `Consumer` and a `BiConsumer` with a `BiConsumer`, but not a `Consumer` with a `BiConsumer`.

Working with Predicates

Remember earlier in this chapter we created a `DogQuerier` interface and used that interface to create an inner class and then a lambda expression.

Our interface looked like this:

```
interface DogQuerier {
    public boolean test(Dog d);
}
```

This interface is a functional interface, with a functional method `test()`, so although we could create an instance using an inner class:

```
DogQuerier dq = new DogQuerier() {
    public boolean test(Dog d) { return d.getAge() > 9; }
};
```

we realized we could create an instance much more concisely using a lambda expression like this:

```
DogQuerier dq = d -> d.getAge() > 9;  // replaces inner class!
```

Well, take a look at `java.util.function.Predicate`, and the interface might look familiar:

```
@FunctionalInterface
public interface Predicate<T> {
    boolean test(T t);
    // default and static methods here.
}
```

`Predicate` is a functional interface, with a functional method, `test()`, which returns a `boolean`, just like our `DogQuerier`. That means we can use the built-in `Predicate` interface in place of the `DogQuerier` interface (and get rid of the `DogQuerier` interface definition completely). Let's do that:

```
Dog boi = new Dog("boi", 30, 6);
Dog clover = new Dog("clover", 35, 12);

Predicate<Dog> p = d -> d.getAge() > 9;
System.out.println("Is Boi older than 9? " + p.test(boi));
System.out.println("Is Clover older than 9? " + p.test(clover));
```

Boi is 6, and Clover is 12, so we see `false` and `true` for the results, just like we did before with `DogQuerier`.

Notice that one thing we must do to use `Predicate` in place of `DogQuerier` is add a type parameter to `Predicate`. Whereas we created `DogQuerier` to be specific to dogs, `Predicate` is a generic functional interface, so we have to provide a bit more information. The `T` argument defined in the `test()` method means we can pass any object to `Predicate`, so by adding a type parameter to `Predicate`, the predicate will know what type of argument to expect.

Let's expand the example just a bit so we can experiment more with predicates.

```java
public class Dog {
    private String name;
    private int age;
    private int weight;

    public Dog(String name, int weight, int age) {
        this.name = name;
        this.weight = weight;
        this.age = age;
    }
    // getters and setters here
    // add a better description of the dog:
    public String toString() {
        return this.name + " is " + this.age + " years old and weighs " +
this.weight + " pounds";
    }
    public void bark() { System.out.println("Woof!"); }
}


public class TestDogPredicates {
    public static void main(String[] args) {
        ArrayList<Dog> dogs = new ArrayList<>();
        Dog boi = new Dog("boi", 30, 6);
        Dog clover = new Dog("clover", 35, 12);
        Dog aiko = new Dog("aiko", 50, 10);
        Dog zooey = new Dog("zooey", 45, 8);
        Dog charis = new Dog("charis", 120, 7);
        dogs.add(boi); dogs.add(clover); dogs.add(aiko);
        dogs.add(zooey); dogs.add(charis);

        System.out.println("--- All dogs ---");
        dogs.forEach(d -> System.out.println(d));

        System.out.println("--- Dogs younger than 9 ---");
        printDogIf(dogs, (d) -> d.getAge() < 9);

        System.out.println("--- Dogs 9 or older ---");
        printDogIf(dogs, (d) -> d.getAge() >= 9);
    }

    public static void printDogIf(ArrayList<Dog> dogs, Predicate<Dog> p) {
        for (Dog d : dogs) {
            if (p.test(d)) {
                System.out.println(d);
            }
        }
    }
}
```

What we've done here is create a method `printDogIf()` that takes a list of dogs and a `Predicate`, and tests each dog in the list against the predicate to see if the dog should be displayed. We can then use this method to display all the dogs younger than 9 with one predicate and display all the dogs 9 or older with another.

Running this code, we get the following output:

```
--- All dogs ---
boi is 6 years old and weighs 30 pounds
clover is 12 years old and weighs 35 pounds
aiko is 10 years old and weighs 50 pounds
zooey is 8 years old and weighs 45 pounds
charis is 7 years old and weighs 120 pounds
--- Dogs younger than 9 ---
boi is 6 years old and weighs 30 pounds
zooey is 8 years old and weighs 45 pounds
charis is 7 years old and weighs 120 pounds
--- Dogs 9 or older ---
clover is 12 years old and weighs 35 pounds
aiko is 10 years old and weighs 50 pounds
```

Now let's check out how `Predicates` are used in the JDK. One example is the `removeIf()` method of `ArrayList`, which takes a `Predicate` and removes an item from the `ArrayList` if the predicate's `test()` method returns true for that item. So, we can remove all dogs whose names begin with "c" (sorry Charis and Clover!) like this:

```
Predicate<Dog> findCs = d -> d.getName().startsWith("c");
dogs.removeIf(findCs);
System.out.println("---- After removing dogs whose names begin with c ---");
dogs.forEach(d -> System.out.println(d));
```

And see that, indeed, Charis and Clover have been removed from the output:

```
---- After removing dogs whose names begin with c ---
boi is 6 years old and weighs 30 pounds
aiko is 10 years old and weighs 50 pounds
zooey is 8 years old and weighs 45 pounds
```

Predicate's Default and Static Methods   If you look at the `Predicate` interface in the `java.util.function` package, you'll probably notice that `Predicate` has a few default methods and one static method. The default methods, `and()`, `or()`, and `negate()`, are there so you can chain predicates together, much like we did with consumers and the `andThen()` method. This can save you time creating new predicates that are logical combinations of predicates you already have. So, for instance, if we have a `Predicate` that tests to see if a dog's age is 6, we can easily test for a dog not being age 6 with the `negate()` method:

```
Predicate<Dog> age = d -> d.getAge() == 6;
System.out.println("Is boi NOT 6? " + age.negate().test(boi));
```

And we get the result false because Boi is, indeed, 6 years old:

```
Is boi NOT 6? false
```

The `or()` and `and()` methods both take other predicates, so to chain them together you need two predicates. Let's create predicates to see if a dog's name is "boi" and the dog's age is 6 and a third predicate that chains the first two together with `and()`:

```
Predicate<Dog> name = d -> d.getName().equals("boi");
Predicate<Dog> age = d -> d.getAge() == 6;
Predicate<Dog> nameAndAge = d -> name.and(age).test(d);
System.out.println("--- Test name and age of boi ---");
System.out.println("Is boi named 'boi' and age 6? " + nameAndAge.test(boi));
boi.setAge(7);
System.out.println("Is boi named 'boi' and age 6? " + nameAndAge.test(boi));
```

First, we test to see if Boi is named "boi" and is age 6, then we set Boi's age to 7, and test again. We get the output:

```
--- Test name and age of boi ---
Is boi named 'boi' and age 6? true
Is boi named 'boi' and age 6? false
```

We can simplify the nameAndAge `Predicate` even further by writing

```
Predicate<Dog> nameAndAge = name.and(age);
```

This works! Remember, what this does is create a new `Predicate` that is the composition of two `Predicates`, name and age. So the result of calling the `and()` method on the name predicate with the argument age is a new `Predicate<Dog>` that ands the result of calling `name.test()` on a dog and `age.test()` on that same dog.

The syntax for chaining can take a bit getting used to. Try writing a few of your own predicates, combining them with `and()`, `or()`, and `negate()`, to get the hang of it.

The static method in `Predicate`, `isEqual()`, just gives you a way to test if one object equals another, using the same test as `equals()` uses when comparing two objects (that is, are they the same object?).

```
Predicate<Dog> p = Predicate.isEqual(zooey);
System.out.println("Is aiko the same object as zooey? " + p.test(aiko));
System.out.println("Is zooey the same object as zooey? " + p.test(zooey));
```

One thing to note about `isEqual()` is this method is defined only on the predicates that take objects as arguments.

Along with `Predicate`, you'll find `BiPredicate`, `DoublePredicate`, `IntPredicate`, and `LongPredicate` in `java.util.function`. You can probably guess what these do. Yep, `BiPredicate`'s `test()` method takes two arguments, whereas `DoublePredicate`, `IntPredicate`, and `LongPredicate` each take one argument of a primitive type (to avoid autoboxing).

Here's a quick `IntPredicate` to demonstrate:

```
IntPredicate universeAnswer = i -> i == 42;
System.out.println("Is the answer 42? " + universeAnswer.test(42));
```

`IntPredicate` is better than `Predicate<Integer>` for this example because the argument `i` doesn't have to be converted from `Integer` to `int` before it's tested. It's a similar idea with `DoublePredicate` and `LongPredicate`.

BiPredicate `BiPredicate` is just a variation on `Predicate` that allows you to pass in two objects for testing instead of one. Let's say we have an `ArrayList` of books and we want to create a set of predicates that will determine if we should buy a book based on its name, its price, or its name *and* price together. Here's how we might do that with `BiPredicate`:

```
List<Book> books = new ArrayList<>();
// fill the books list with books here...
BiPredicate<String, Double> javaBuy = (name, price) -> name.contains("Java");
BiPredicate<String, Double> priceBuy = (name, price) -> price < 55.00;
BiPredicate<String, Double> definitelyBuy = javaBuy.and(priceBuy);
books.forEach(book -> {
    if (definitelyBuy.test(book.getName(), book.getPrice())) {
        System.out.println("You should definitely buy " + book.getName()
                        + "(" + book.getPrice() + ")");
    }
});
```

If we load up our books `ArrayList` with the following books:

```
"Your Brain is Better with Java", 58.99
"OCP8 Java Certification Study Guide", 53.39
"Is Java Coffee or Programming?", 39.86
"While you were out Java happened", 12.99
```

then what we'll see in the output when we run this code is

```
You should definitely buy "OCP8 Java Certification Study Guide"(53.39)
You should definitely buy "Is Java Coffee or Programming?"(39.86)
You should definitely buy "While you were out Java happened"(12.99)
```

These are the books with Java in the title and a price less than $55.00.

Caveat Time Of course, you don't *need* BiPredicate lambda expressions to write this code; you could just write the test (does the name contain "Java" and is the price less than 55.00) in the forEach lambda expression. Likewise, we haven't exactly needed many of the lambda expressions we've written in the simple examples throughout this chapter so far.

The main reason to use lambda expressions is if you'll end up using them in other ways too, and if having the code packaged up into lambdas will help make your code more concise and get you some code reuse (same reasons why you might use an inner class or even an external class). And, of course, if a method of a Java class, like the Logger log() example, requires a functional interface, like a Supplier, then that's a great reason to use a lambda expression (although, again, you don't *have* to—they are a convenience).

A big caveat here is that although we're showing lots of examples of building lambda expressions using the built-in functional interfaces so you get practice for the exam, once you're back in the real world, think about whether you really need a lambda expression before you write one.

Working with Functions

We saved the most abstract of the functional interfaces from java.util.function for last. Aren't you lucky? Of course, by now, we hope you're feeling pretty solid about using functional interfaces.

The purpose of the apply() functional method in the Function interface is to take one value and turn it into another. The two values don't have to be the same type, so in the Function interface definition, we have two different type parameters, T (the type of the argument to apply()) and R (the type of the return value):

```
@FunctionalInterface
public interface Function<T,R> {
    R apply(T t);
}
```

We can create an instance of Function to turn an Integer into a String:

```
Function<Integer, String> answer = a -> {
   if (a == 42) return "forty-two";
   else return "No answer for you!";
};
System.out.println(answer.apply(42));
System.out.println(answer.apply(64));
```

If you run this code, you'll see the output:

```
forty-two
No answer for you!
```

A `BiFunction` is similar except the `apply()` method takes two arguments and returns a value:

```
BiFunction<String, String, String> firstLast =
    (first, last) -> first + " " + last;
System.out.println("First and Last name: " + firstLast.apply("Joe", "Smith"));
```

In this example, the `BiFunction` `apply()` method takes two `Strings` and returns a `String`, but you could pass two arguments of different types and return a value of a third type. What we see, of course, is

```
First and Last name: Joe Smith
```

Functions in the JDK   Let's use both a `Function` and a `BiFunction` in an example using the `Map` methods `computeIfAbsent()` and `replaceAll()`. These are two examples from the JDK where you'll find `Function` and `BiFunction` used.

```
public class Functions {
    public static void main(String[] args) {
        Map<String, String> aprilWinner = new TreeMap<>();
        aprilWinner.put("April 2017", "Bob");
        aprilWinner.put("April 2016", "Annette");
        aprilWinner.put("April 2015", "Lamar");

        System.out.println("--- List, before checking April 2014 ---");
        aprilWinner.forEach((k, v) -> System.out.println(k + ": " + v));

        // no key for April 2014, so John Doe gets added to the map
        aprilWinner.computeIfAbsent("April 2014", (k) -> "John Doe");

        // key April 2014 now has a value, so Jane won't be added
        aprilWinner.computeIfAbsent("April 2014", (k) -> "Jane Doe");

        System.out.println("--- List, after checking April 2014 ---");
        aprilWinner.forEach((k, v) -> System.out.println(k + ": " + v));

        // use a BiFunction to replace all values in the map with
        // uppercase values
        aprilWinner.replaceAll((key, oldValue) -> oldValue.toUpperCase());
        System.out.println("--- List, after replacing values with
uppercase ---");
```

```
        aprilWinner.forEach((k, v) -> System.out.println(k + ": " + v));

    }
}
```

The output is as follows:

```
--- List, before checking April 2014 ---
April 2015: Lamar
April 2016: Annette
April 2017: Bob
--- List, after checking April 2014 ---
April 2014: John Doe
April 2015: Lamar
April 2016: Annette
April 2017: Bob
--- List, after replacing values with uppercase ---
April 2014: JOHN DOE
April 2015: LAMAR
April 2016: ANNETTE
April 2017: BOB
```

We first use `computeIfAbsent()` to add a key and value to our `Map` of April winners if that key/value pair doesn't yet exist in the `Map`.

`computeIfAbsent()` takes a key and a `Function`. The `Function` provides a value to store in the `Map` for the key if a value for that key doesn't yet exist. The argument in the `Function` lambda expression is the key, so you could create a value based on the key, but in this example, we're keeping it super simple and just returning a `String`.

Then we use the `replaceAll()` method to replace every value in the `Map` with the uppercase version of the old value. So where we have stored `Bob`, we'll now be storing `BOB`.

`replaceAll()` takes a `BiFunction`. The lambda expression we pass to `replaceAll()` has two arguments, a key, and the current value in the `Map`, and returns a new value to store in the `Map` for that key. In this example, we're just returning the previous value in uppercase.

More Functions `Function` has a couple of default methods and a static method in addition to its functional method, `apply()`: `andThen()`, `compose()`, and `identity()`. `andThen()` is similar to the `Consumer`'s `andThen()` method, applying `Function`s in sequence. `compose()` is the same except it applies the `Function`s in reverse order.

And the static method in `Function` is `identity()`, which just returns its input argument:

```
Function<Integer, Integer> id = Function.identity();
System.out.println(id.apply(42));
```

Answer: 42. (Of course.)

What on earth is an identity function used for? Imagine a scenario where you have defined a method that takes a `Function` as an argument that changes a value in a data structure. But in some cases, you don't want that value to change. In those cases, pass the identity `Function` as an easy "do nothing" operation.

Along with `Function` and `BiFunction`, as you might expect, you'll also find `DoubleFunction` (`apply()` takes a `double` as an argument and returns an object), `IntFunction` (`apply()` takes an `int` as an argument and returns an object), and `LongFunction` (`apply()` takes a `long` as an argument and returns an object).

Ah, but wait, there's more! We also have `DoubleToIntFunction`, `DoubleToLongFunction`, `IntToDoubleFunction`, `IntToLongFunction`, `LongToDoubleFunction`, `LongToIntFunction`, `ToDoubleFunction`, `ToIntFunction`, `ToLongFunction`, `ToDoubleBiFunction`, `ToIntBiFunction`, and last but definitely not least, `ToLongBiFunction`.

Oh, my goodness—the variations the JDK authors thought of when creating the functional interfaces. (It's a wonder they didn't think of 100 more.) We are pretty sure you can make a good guess at what these do. The main trick with these is that the functional method is not `apply()`; it's a slight variation on `apply()`, so just keep that in the back of your mind.

For instance, how about `IntToDoubleFunction`? The functional method is `applyAsDouble()`, and yes, it takes an `int` and returns a `double`, avoiding all that inefficient autoboxing. How about `ToIntFunction`? The `applyAsInt()` method takes an object and returns an `int`.

Okay, we are sure you get the hang of it at this point, and we'll leave you to the Java docs to find out more if you're interested. For the exam, focus on `Function` and `BiFunction`, but be aware that these other variations exist and remember that there are variations in the functional method names that go with them.

Working with Operators

Finally (yes, really!), we have the operator variations on the functional interfaces. All the operators are, in fact, slightly modified versions of other functional interfaces.

Let's pick the one operator you should be familiar with for the exam, UnaryOperator, to look at, and you can explore the rest on your own.

UnaryOperator extends the Function interface, so its functional method is also apply(). However, unlike Function, it requires that the type of the argument to apply() be the same as the type of the return value, so UnaryOperator is defined like this:

```
@FunctionalInterface
public interface UnaryOperator<T>
extends Function<T,T>
```

The T, T in the Function type parameters is what tips you off that the type of the argument and return value must be the same. That's why you only have to specify one type parameter for UnaryOperator:

```
UnaryOperator<Double> log2 = v -> Math.log(v) / Math.log(2);
System.out.println(log2.apply(8.0));
```

In this example, we're defining a log2 UnaryOperator that computes the log base 2 of a value. Log base 2 of 8.0 is 3.0 because 2 * 2 * 2 (3 times) is 8.

Notice that you could, of course, use Function<Double, Double> instead... that's essentially the same thing. UnaryOperator saves a little typing and makes it a bit clearer that you're defining an operator that takes a value that is the same type as the return value...but that's about it. It's just a slightly restricted version of Function. And the same applies to the other operators in the package.

Time to pat yourself on the back, take a break, and eat some cookies, because you made it through all of the functional interfaces in java.util.function. As long as you have a good sense of how to use them to create lambda expressions and how to use the core interfaces that we've covered here, you'll be in solid shape.

CERTIFICATION OBJECTIVE

Method References (OCP Objective 3.8)

3.8   Use method references with Streams.

You already know that a lambda expression is a shorthand way of writing an instance of a class that implements a functional interface. Believe it or not, there are a few circumstances when you can make your code even *more* concise by writing a shorthand for the lambda expression (yes, it's a shorthand for the shorthand).

Sometimes, the only thing a lambda expression does is call another method, for instance:

```
List<String> trees = Arrays.asList("fir", "cedar", "pine");
trees.forEach(t -> System.out.println(t));
```

Here we're using a lambda expression to take a tree name, t, and pass it to `System.out.println()`. This code is already pretty short; can we shorten it even more? Yes! Apparently, the Java 8 authors like finding ways to avoid typing, so they invented the "method reference":

```
List<String> trees = Arrays.asList("fir", "cedar", "pine");
trees.forEach(System.out::println);
```

This method reference is a shorthand way of writing the lambda expression. But wait, where did the argument t go and don't we need that? We know that `forEach()` takes a `Consumer`, and we know what it's consuming is tree names, which are `Strings`. And we know that `System.out.println()` takes a `String`. A lot can be inferred from this shorthand for the lambda expression. Here what's inferred is that we want to call the `println()` method of `System.out`, passing in the `String` object that we have at hand via the `forEach()`. Of course, keep in mind, we can't do anything fancy with how we print the tree name because we're not specifying anything but the method to call on the tree name argument that the `Consumer` (the method reference) is getting behind the scenes.

Kinds of Method References

The `System.out::println` method reference is an example of a "method reference," meaning we're calling a method, `println()`, of `System.out`. You can create method references for your own methods, too:

```
public class MethodRefs {
  public static void main(String[] args) {
    List<String> trees = Arrays.asList("fir", "cedar", "pine");

    trees.forEach(t -> System.out.println(t));  // print with lambda
    trees.forEach(System.out::println);         // print with a
                                                 // method reference

    trees.forEach(MethodRefs::printTreeStatic); // print with our own
                                                 // static method reference
  }

  public static void printTreeStatic(String t) {
    System.out.println("Tree name: " + t);
  }
}
```

For this code, we'll see this output:

```
fir
cedar
pine
fir
cedar
pine
Tree name: fir
Tree name: cedar
Tree name: pine
```

First, the tree names are printed using a lambda expression; then the tree names are printed using an *instance method reference* to `System.out.println()` and finally a longer string using a *static method reference* to our own static method, `printTreeStatic()`. A "static method reference" is a method reference to a static method. The method reference to `System.out.println()` is an "instance method reference"—that is, a reference to the `println()` instance method of `System.out`.

Writing `::` instead of `.` in the method reference takes a little getting used to; you'll find yourself typing a `.` instead of a `::` and then going back to fix it (at least we do!). What the method reference does here is make a `Consumer` that calls the method on the implicit argument that's getting passed to that lambda behind the scenes.

In addition to instance and static method references, there are a couple of other types of method references: method references for arbitrary objects and constructor method references. We'll see some more examples of method references in the next chapter when we talk about streams.

Write Your Own Functional Interface

Guess what, you already wrote your own functional interface. Remember `DogQuerier`? Yep, that's the one:

```
@FunctionalInterface
interface DogQuerier {
    public boolean test(Dog d);
}
```

Of course, `DogQuerier` is all about `Dog`s. You then saw that `DogQuerier` is really just a `Dog` version of `Predicate`, which works on any type of object.

You might want to write a functional interface that works on any type of object, too. Imagine, for instance, that you want an interface with a `test()` method that takes three objects and returns a `boolean`—a `TriPredicate` if you will. There is no `TriPredicate` in `java.util.function` (only `Predicate` and `BiPredicate`), so how about writing your own?

```
@FunctionalInterface
interface TriPredicate<T, U, V> {
    boolean test(T t, U u, V v);
}
```

We're specifying an interface with three type parameters: `T`, `U`, and `V`. The `test()` method takes three types of objects to test, and they can all be of differing types or all the same. Now let's write a lambda expression of this type and test it out:

```
public void triPredicate() {
    TriPredicate<String, Integer, Integer> theTest =
        (s, n, w) -> {
            if (s.equals("There is no spoon") && n > 2 && w < n) {
                return true;
            } else {
                return false;
            }
        };
    System.out.println("Pass the test? " +
                        theTest.test("Follow the White Rabbit", 2, 3));
    System.out.println("Pass the test? " +
                        theTest.test("There is no spoon", 101, 3));
}
```

We see this output:

```
Pass the test? false
Pass the test? true
```

The trick to writing your own generic functional interfaces is having a good handle on generics. As long as you understand what a functional interface is and how to use generics to specify parameter and return types, you're good to go.

Functional Interface Overview

As we've said, the `java.util.function` package has 43 different functional interfaces. You need to make sure you are familiar with the core interfaces: `Supplier`, `Consumer`, `Predicate`, and `Function`. In addition, you should understand the variations on these core interfaces—the primitive interfaces designed to avoid autoboxing, and the `Bi`-versions that allow you to pass two parameters to the functional methods rather than one. You don't need to memorize all 43 interfaces, but you need to understand the patterns of the variations and their functional method names. We've listed the core interfaces, plus several variations, and their functional methods in Table 8-1. In addition to the functional methods, you should be familiar with the default and static methods in the interfaces, such as `andThen()`, `and()`, `negate()`, `or()`, and so on. We don't list those in Table 8-1, so look at the online documentation for details beyond what we've covered in this chapter.

Note: You should review all the functional interfaces in `java.util.function` for variations on the functional interfaces covered in Table 8-1 and for details of the default and static methods of interfaces.

e x a m
ⓦ a t c h
You know that functional interfaces are just interfaces with one abstract method—the functional method. The interfaces in Table 8-1 have been added to the JDK to make it easier for you to write code, but as you know, there's nothing particularly special about functional interfaces beyond their use in the JDK (as we saw with `Logger`*).*

There are a few functional interfaces already in the JDK, not listed in `java.util`
`.function`*. You've already seen one of these—*`Comparator`*—with its functional method,* `compare()`*. Another is* `Comparable`*, which is implemented by various types (like* `String`*,* `LocalDateTime`*, and so on) for sorting.*

A third example is `Runnable`*, which has a functional method,* `run()`*. So where you might have implemented a* `Runnable` *as an inner class before:*

```
Runnable r = new Runnable() {
   @Override
   public void run() {
      System.out.println("Do this");
   }
};
```

you can now use a lambda expression instead:

```
Runnable r = () -> System.out.println("Do this");
```

TABLE 8-1	Functional Interfaces Covered on the Exam	

Interface	Functional Method	Description
`Supplier<T>`	`T get()`	Suppliers supply results. The `Supplier`'s functional method `get()` takes no arguments and supplies a generic object result (`T`).
`Consumer<T>`	`void accept(T t)`	Consumers consume values. The `Consumer`'s functional method `accept()` takes a generic object argument (`T`) and returns no value.
`Predicate<T>`	`boolean test(T t)`	Predicates test things (and do logical operations). The `Predicate`'s functional method `test()` takes a generic object argument (`T`) and returns a `boolean`.
`Function<T,R>`	`R apply(T t)`	Functions are generic functional interfaces. The functional method `apply()` takes a generic object argument (`T`) and returns a generic object (`R`).
`IntSupplier`	`int getAsInt()`	Supplies `int` values (to avoid autoboxing). Note the difference in the functional method name (`getAsInt()` rather than `get()`, as for `Supplier`). This pattern is used across the various primitive versions of the functional interfaces.
`IntConsumer`	`void accept(int value)`	Consumes `int` values.
`IntPredicate`	`boolean test(int value)`	Tests `int` values.
`IntFunction<R>`	`R apply(int value)`	The `IntFunction`'s functional method `apply()` takes an `int` argument and returns a generic object result (`R`).
`BiConsumer<T,U>`	`void accept(T t, U u)`	Consumes two values.
`BiPredicate<T,U>`	`boolean test(T t, U u)`	The `BiPredicate`'s functional method `test()` takes two generic arguments (`T, U`).
`BiFunction<T,U,R>`	`R apply(T t, U u)`	The `BiFunction`'s functional method `apply()` takes two generic arguments (`T, U`) and returns a generic object result (`R`).
`UnaryOperator<T>`	`T apply(T t)`	The `UnaryOperator`'s functional method `apply()` takes one generic operator (`T`) and returns a value of the same type (`T`).

CERTIFICATION SUMMARY

We began this chapter by looking at what lambda expressions are, how to write lambda expressions, and when to write them. Lambdas are syntax shorthands for writing a class to implement a functional interface and then instantiating that class. With lambdas, you focus on the method that's implementing the abstract method of the interface (remember, there's only one, because the functional interfaces have only one abstract method) and eliminate the other syntax, so you end up with more concise code.

The lambda syntax can take a little getting used to, but there aren't too many rules to remember: you use an `->` symbol with parameters on the left and a method body on the right. One trick is that if a lambda expression is just one expression, you can even eliminate the { and } that usually go with a method body, like this:

```
() -> 42
```

We talked about how you can think of lambdas as chunks of code that you pass around. We can pass an object to a method, and we can pass a lambda expression to a method. Remembering that a lambda represents an instance of a class that implements an interface can help you see how this works.

When lambdas refer to variables from their enclosing scope, those variables are "captured" and so you can refer to them when applying a lambda later. The important key here, however, is that the variables must be final or effectively final.

Then we delved into functional interfaces. A functional interface is simply an interface that has one abstract method—the functional method. Lambda expressions are related to functional interfaces because the type of a lambda expression is always a functional interface. Why? Because the method the lambda expression defines is the one and only functional method in that interface, so there is no confusion in the lambda expression syntax about which method you're writing.

The tricky part of functional interfaces is learning about the new interfaces defined in `java.util.function`. Forty-three new interfaces are there to help you shortcut the process of writing functional interfaces and also to provide a way for other JDK methods to accept objects of a functional interface type. The core functional interfaces are `Consumer`, `Supplier`, `Predicate`, and `Function`, and all the other functional interfaces in `java.util.function` are variations on these. We talked about a few examples in which new JDK methods, like the `Logger`'s `log()` method, can now take objects of one of the types in this package.

As we covered the various functional interfaces, we looked at the functional methods defined for each one, like the `Predicate`'s `test()` method and the

`Supplier`'s `get()` method, and some of the static and default methods included in some of the functional interfaces, too, like the `Consumer`'s `andThen()` method.

We talked about operators, which are just slight variations on the other functional interfaces and have a restriction that the parameter type is the same as the return value type. So, if you define a `UnaryOperator` whose functional method takes an `Integer`, that operator method must return an `Integer` too.

A lambda expression is a syntax shorthand to make your code more concise, and a method reference is a shorthand that can make your code even more concise in certain situations, such as when you're just passing on an argument to another method. A common example for this is replacing a lambda expression that simply prints its argument:

```
Consumer<String> c = (s) -> System.out.println(s);
```

with a method reference:

```
Consumer<String> c = System.out::println;
```

Java can infer that you want to pass on the argument to the `Consumer` (which must have an argument; it's a `Consumer`!) to the `System.out.println()` method. Again, this syntax takes some getting used to. You'll see it again in the next chapter and get more practice with it.

TWO-MINUTE DRILL

Here are some of the key points from this chapter.

Create and Use Lambda Expressions (OCP Objective 2.6)

☐ A lambda expression is a shorthand syntax for an instance of a class that implements a functional interface.

☐ Use - > to define a lambda expression with the arguments on the left and the body on the right of the arrow.

☐ Typically, we leave off the types of a lambda's arguments because they can be inferred from the functional interface definition.

☐ If you have multiple parameters for a lambda, then you must surround them with parentheses.

☐ If you have no parameters for a lambda, then you must use empty parentheses, ().

☐ If you specify the type of a parameter of a lambda, you must use parentheses.

☐ If the body of a lambda expression has multiple statements, you must use curly braces.

☐ Lambda expressions are often used in place of an inner class.

☐ If the body of a lambda expression simply evaluates an expression and returns a value, you can leave off the `return` keyword.

☐ The type of the return value of a lambda expression is inferred from the functional interface definition.

☐ You can pass lambda expressions to methods, either by name or by writing them inline.

☐ Lambda expressions capture variables from the enclosing scope if they are used within the body of the lambda.

☐ All captured variables in a lambda expression must be final or effectively final.

Iterate Using forEach Methods of List (OCP Objective 3.5)

☐ The `forEach()` method in collection types, like `List`, takes a `Consumer` and allows you to easily iterate through the collection. The `Consumer`'s `accept()` method argument is the current object in the collection you are iterating over.

Use the Built-in Interfaces Included in the java.util.function Package such as Predicate, Consumer, Function, and Supplier (OCP Objective 4.1)

- ☐ A functional interface is an interface with one abstract method.
- ☐ The single abstract method in a functional interface is called the functional method.
- ☐ Functional interfaces can include any number of default and static methods in addition to the functional method.
- ☐ Functional interfaces can redefine public methods from `Object`.
- ☐ Use `@FunctionalInterface` to annotate functional interfaces.
- ☐ If you add a second abstract method to a functional interface annotated with `@FunctionalInterface`, you will get a compiler error: "Invalid '@ FunctionalInterface' annotation; [interface name] is not a functional interface."

Core Functional Interfaces (OCP Objectives 4.1, 4.2, 4.3, 4.4)

- ☐ The JDK provides several built-in functional interfaces in `java.util .function`.
- ☐ All of these functional interfaces fall into one of four categories: suppliers, consumers, predicates, or functions.
- ☐ The basic functional interfaces from this package are `Supplier`, `Consumer`, `Predicate`, and `Function`.
  - ☐ The functional method of `Supplier` is `get()`. It returns a value.
  - ☐ The functional method of `Consumer` is `accept()`. It takes an argument and returns no value.
  - ☐ The functional method of `Predicate` is `test()`. It takes an argument and returns a boolean.
  - ☐ The functional method of `Function` is `apply()`. It takes an argument and returns a value.

Using Functional Interfaces (OCP Objectives 4.1, 4.2, 4.3, 4.4)

- ☐ You can compose consumers with the `andThen()` default method.
- ☐ Use the same type of consumer when composing two consumers together.
- ☐ Perform logical tests with predicates using the default predicate methods `and()`, `or()`, and `negate()`.

- ☐ A `Predicate`'s static `isEqual()` method returns a `Predicate` that tests to see if two objects are equal. Note that this method is only available in the `Predicate` interface, not the predicate variations in `java.util.function`.
- ☐ Compose `Function`s together with the methods `andThen()` and `compose()`.
- ☐ Check carefully to see which functional interfaces support which default and static methods.
- ☐ The `forEach()` method in collection types, like `List`, takes a `Consumer` and allows you to easily iterate through the collection. The `Consumer`'s `accept()` method argument is the current object in the collection you are iterating over.
- ☐ The `replaceAll()` method in collection types, like `List`, takes a `UnaryOperator` and allows you to replace items in the `List` with different values, ones that could be based on the current values or completely new values.
- ☐ The built-in functional interfaces are conveniences so you don't have to create your own.
- ☐ The built-in functional interfaces are used in several ways in the Java 8 JDK, including with Streams (see Chapter 9).
- ☐ Creating your own functional interfaces is no different from creating any interface except you must make sure the interface has only one abstract method.
- ☐ Brush up on generics (Chapter 6) to make sure you know how to create a functional interface with generic types.

Develop Code That Uses Primitive Versions of Functional Interfaces (OCP Objective 4.2)

- ☐ Some variations of functional interfaces in the `java.util.package` are meant to handle primitive values to avoid autoboxing.
- ☐ `IntSupplier`'s functional method, `getAsInt()`, takes no arguments and returns an `int`. This is to avoid autoboxing the result as `Integer`, in case you need a primitive.
- ☐ Likewise, `DoubleSupplier`'s functional method, `getAsDouble()`, takes no arguments and returns a `double`.

- ☐ `IntConsumer`'s functional method, `accept()`, takes an `int` and does not return any value.
- ☐ `IntPredicate`'s functional method, `test()`, takes an `int` and returns a `boolean`.
- ☐ `IntFunction`'s functional method, `apply()`, takes an `int` and returns an object value.
- ☐ The functional method name in functional interfaces is not always the same (e.g., `IntSupplier` uses `getAsInt()` rather than `get()`, and `IntToLongFunction` uses `applyAsLong()` rather than `apply()`), so note the patterns of naming conventions for functional methods.

Develop Code That Uses Binary Versions of Functional Interfaces (OCP Objective 4.3)

- ☐ Some variations of functional interfaces in the `java.util.package` are meant to allow multiple arguments.
- ☐ `BiConsumer`'s functional method, `accept()`, takes two arguments and returns no value.
- ☐ `BiPredicate`'s functional method, `test()`, takes two arguments and returns a `boolean`.
- ☐ `BiFunction`'s functional method, `apply()`, takes two arguments and returns a value.
- ☐ The `forEach()` method in the `Map` collection type takes a `BiConsumer`, and the arguments of the `accept()` method are the key and value of the current `Map` entry.

Develop Code That Uses the UnaryOperator Interface (OCP Objective 4.4)

- ☐ The operator functional interfaces in `java.util.function` are variations on the function interfaces (such as `Function`).
- ☐ Whereas `Function` takes a value of a type and returns a value of perhaps a different type, the `UnaryOperator` takes a value of a type and returns a value of that same type.

SELF TEST

The following questions will help you measure your understanding of the material in this chapter. If you don't get them all, go back and review and try again.

1. Which of these are functional interfaces? (Choose all that apply.)

A.

```
interface Question {
    default int answer() {
        return 42;
    }
}
```

B.

```
interface Tree {
    void grow();
}
```

C.

```
interface Book {
    static void read() {
        System.out.println("Turn the page...");
    }
}
```

D.

```
interface Flower {
    boolean equals(Object f);
    default void bloom() {
        System.out.println("Petals are opening");
    }
    String pick();
}
```

2. Given the following interface:

```
@FunctionalInterface
interface FtoC {
    double convert(double f);
}
```

Which of the following expressions are legal? (Choose all that apply.)

A. `FtoC converter = (f) -> (f - 32.0) * 5/9;`
B. `FtoC converter = f -> (f - 32.0) * 5/9;`
C. `FtoC converter = f -> return ((f - 32.0) * 5/9);`

D. `double converter = f -> (f - 32.0) * 5/9;`

E. `FtoC converter = f -> { return (f - 32.0) * 5/9; };`

3. Which of the following compiles correctly?

A. `Predicate<String> p = (s) -> System.out.println(s);`

B. `Consumer<String> c = (s) -> System.out.println(s);`

C. `Supplier<String> s = (s) -> System.out.println(s);`

D. `Function<String> f = (s) -> System.out.println(s);`

4. Given the code fragment:

```
System.out.format("Total = %.2f", computeTax(10.00, (p) -> p * 0.05));
```

Which method would you use for `computeTax()` so the code fragment prints
`Total = 10.50`?

A.

```
double computeTax(double price, Function<Double> op) {
   return op.apply(price) + price;
}
```

B.

```
double computeTax(double price, UnaryOperator<Double> op) {
   return op.apply(price) + price;
}
```

C.

```
double computeTax(double price, double op) {
   return op.apply(price) + price;
}
```

D.

```
Function<Double, Double> computeTax(double price, UnaryOperator<Double> op) {
   return op.apply(price) + price;
}
```

5. Given:

```
class Reading {
   int year;
   int month;
   int day;
   double value;

   Reading(int year, int month, int day, double value) {
      this.year = year; this.month = month; this.day = day; this.value = value;
   }
}
```

and the code fragment:

```
List<Reading> readings = Arrays.asList(
            new Reading(2017, 1, 1, 405.91),
            new Reading(2017, 1, 8, 405.98),
            new Reading(2017, 1, 15, 406.14),
            new Reading(2017, 1, 22, 406.48),
            new Reading(2017, 1, 29, 406.20),
            new Reading(2017, 2, 5, 406.03));
```

Which code fragment will sort the readings in ascending order by value and print the value of each reading?

A.

```
readings.sort((r1, r2) -> r1.value < r2.value ? -1 : 1);
readings.forEach(System.out.println(r.value));
```

B.

```
readings.sort((r1, r2) -> r1.value < r2.value ? 1 : -1);
readings.forEach(System.out::println(r.value));
```

C.

```
readings.sort((r1, r2) -> r1.value < r2.value ? -1 : 1);
readings.forEach(System.out::println);
```

D.

```
readings.sort((r1, r2) -> r1.value < r2.value ? -1 : 1);
readings.forEach(r -> System.out.println(r.value));
```

6. Given the code fragments:

```
class Human {
    public Integer age;
    public String name;

    public Human(Integer age, String name) {
        this.age = age;
        this.name = name;
    }
    public Integer getAge() { return this.age; }
}
```

and

```
Supplier<Human> human = () -> new Human(34, "Joe");
Human joe = human.XXXX;
```

Which code fragment inserted at XXXX will cause a new Human object to be stored in the variable joe?

A. push()

B. get()

C. apply()

D. test()

E. accept()

7. Given:

```
class Human {
    public Integer age;
    public String name;

    public Human(Integer age, String name) {
        this.age = age;
        this.name = name;
    }
    public Integer getAge() { return this.age; }
}
```

and the code fragment:

```
Human jenny = new Human(18, "Jenny");
Human jeff = new Human(17, "Jeff");
Human jill = new Human(21, "Jill");
List<Human> people = new ArrayList<>(Arrays.asList(jenny, jeff, jill));
// L1
people.forEach(printAdults);
```

Which code fragment inserted at line // L1 will print the names of only adults (those humans whose age is older than 17)?

A.

```
Predicate<Human> printAdults = p -> { if (p.getAge() >= 18) {
    System.out.println(p.name);
}};
```

B.

```
Predicate<Human> adult = p -> p.getAge() >= 18;
Consumer<Human> printAdults = p -> { if (p.getAge(adult.test()) >= 18) {
    System.out.println(p.name);
}};
```

534 Chapter 8: Lambda Expressions and Functional Interfaces

C.

```
Predicate adult = p -> p.getAge() >= 18;
Consumer printAdults = p -> { if (adult.test(p)) {
    System.out.println(p.name);
}};
```

D.

```
Consumer printAdults(Human p) {
    if (p.getAge() >= 18) {
        System.out.println(p.name);
    }
}
```

8. Given:

```
List<String> birds =
        Arrays.asList("eagle", "seagull", "albatross", "buzzard", "goose");
int longest = 0;
birds.forEach(b -> {                    // L3
    if (b.length() > longest) {
        longest = b.length();           // L5
    }
});
System.out.println("Longest bird name is length: " + longest);
```

What is the result?

A. "Longest bird name is length: 9"

B. Compilation fails because of an error on line L5

C. Compilation fails because of an error on line L3

D. A runtime exception occurs on line L5

9. Given the following code fragment:

```
Supplier<List<Double>> readingsSupplier =
    Arrays.asList(405.91, 405.98, 406.14, 406.48, 406.20, 406.03);
for (Double r : readingsSupplier.get()) { System.out.print(r + " "); }
```

What is the result?

A. 405.91

B. 405.91 405.98 406.14 406.48 406.2 406.03

C. An exception is thrown at runtime

D. Compilation fails

10. Given the code fragment:

```
BiFunction<Integer, String, String> foo = (n, s) -> {
    String newString = "";
    for (int i = 0; i < n; i++) {
        newString = s + " " + newString;
    }
    return newString;
};
Function<String, String> bar = (s) -> s + "bar";
System.out.println(foo.andThen(bar).apply(3, "foo"));
```

What is the result?

A. foo foo foo bar bar bar

B. foo foo foo bar

C. foo foo foo

D. Compilation fails

11. Given the code fragment:

```
List<String> trees = Arrays.asList("FIR", "CEDAR", "PINE");
// L1
trees.replaceAll(convert);
trees.forEach(t -> System.out.print(t + " "));
```

Which fragment(s), inserted independently at // L1, produce the output? (Choose all that apply.)

```
fir cedar pine
```

A. UnaryOperator<String> convert = (t) -> t.toLowerCase();

B. UnaryOperator<String, String> convert = (t) -> t.toLowerCase();

C. Function<String, String> convert = (t) -> t.toLowerCase();

D. Supplier<String> convert = (t) -> t.toLowerCase();

12. Given the code fragment:

```
Map<String, String> todos = new HashMap<String, String>();
todos.put("monday", "wash dog");
todos.put("tuesday", "weed yard");
// L1
todos.forEach(printTodo);
```

Which fragment(s), inserted independently at // L1, produce the to-do items, both key and value, in the Map? (Choose all that apply.)

A.

```
Function<String, String> printTodo =
    (String k, String v) -> System.out.println("On " + k + " do: " + v);
```

B.

```
Consumer<String, String> printTodo =
    (String k, String v) -> System.out.println("On " + k + " do: " + v);
```

C.

```
Consumer<Map> printTodo =
    (Map m) -> System.out.println("On " + m.keySet() + "do: " + m.values());
```

D.

```
BiConsumer<String, String> printTodo =
    (String k, String v) -> System.out.println("On " + k + " do: " + v);
```

13. Given the code fragments:

```
class TodoList {
    public void checkTodoDay(Map<String, String> todos, Predicate<String> isDay) {
        todos.forEach((d, t) -> {
            if (isDay.test(d)) {
                System.out.println("You really should do this today! " + t);
            }
        });
    }
}
```

and

```
Map<String, String> todos = new HashMap<String, String>();
todos.put("monday", "wash dog");
todos.put("tuesday", "weed yard");
TodoList todoList = new TodoList();
// L1
```

Which fragment(s), inserted independently at // L1, display the output consisting of the to-do item for Tuesday? (Choose all that apply.)

A.

```
todoList.checkTodoDay(todos,
    (k) -> if (k.equals("tuesday")) return true; else return false; );
```

B.

```
todoList.checkTodoDay(todos, (k, v) -> {
    if (k.equals("tuesday")) {
```

```
        System.out.println("You really should do this today! " + v);
    }
});
```

C.

```
todoList.checkTodoDay(todos, (k) -> k.equals("tuesday"));
```

D.

```
todoList.checkTodoDay(todos, (k) -> k.test("tuesday"));
```

14. Given the code fragment:

```
DoubleSupplier d = () -> 42.0;
// L1
```

Which fragment(s), inserted independently at `// L1`, produce the output (Choose all that apply.)

```
The answer is: 42.0
```

A.

```
System.out.println("The answer is: " + d.get());
```

B.

```
double answer = d.getAsDouble();
System.out.println("The answer is: " + answer);
```

C.

```
System.out.println("The answer is: " + d.getAsDouble());
```

D.

```
double answer = d.get();
System.out.println("The answer is: " + answer);
```

SELF TEST ANSWERS

1. ☑ **B** and **D** are correct. For **B**, we just have one abstract method, so this is a functional interface. Although **D** includes the `equals()` method (implying that classes implementing this interface must implement an `equals()` method), this method doesn't count because it's inherited from `Object`. The default method `bloom()` is default and so doesn't count; the method `pick()` is the functional method.

   ☒ **A** is incorrect because the interface has no functional method (one abstract method). A default method is not a functional method. Likewise, **C** is incorrect because the interface has no functional method (one abstract method). A static method is not a functional method. (OCP Objective 4.1)

2. ☑ **A, B,** and **E** are correct variations on writing lambda expressions.

   ☒ **C** and **D** are incorrect. **C** is invalid syntax for lambda expressions, with a return statement that's not enclosed in { }. **D** is incorrect because it has the wrong type for the lambda expression. (OCP Objective 2.6)

3. ☑ **B** is correct. The lambda expression is a consumer, so only the type `Consumer` is correct for this lambda expression—the functional method takes an argument and returns nothing.

   ☒ **A, C,** and **D** are incorrect based on the above. (OCP Objective 4.1)

4. ☑ **B** is correct. `computeTax()` is a method that takes two arguments, a `double` and a `UnaryOperator`, and returns a `double` value. We know that the lambda expression is a `UnaryOperator` because the functional method takes a `Double` and returns a `Double` (with autoboxing and autounboxing).

   ☒ **A, C,** and **D** are incorrect. **A** could almost work because a `UnaryOperator` is a type of `Function`; however, a correct declaration of the `Function` would specify the type of both the argument and the return value, because unlike `UnaryOperator`, they are not necessarily the same type. (OCP Objective 4.4)

5. ☑ **D** is correct. The `sort()` method of the `List` requires a `Comparator`, which can be expressed as a lambda expression implementing the `compare()` functional method. This method must return a −1 or 1 (for items that are not equal) depending on the ordering; because we want ascending order, we test if object 1 is less than object 2 and return −1 if so; otherwise, 1 is returned to get ascending order. Because we are comparing the values of the `reading` objects, we use the `value` field of each `reading` object to make the comparison. In the `forEach`, we supply a `Consumer`, whose functional method takes a `reading` object and prints the `value` field of that `reading`. **D** properly supplies a `Consumer` to `forEach` that prints just the `values`.

    ☒   **A, B,** and **C** are incorrect. **A** is incorrect because we don't supply a `Consumer` for the `forEach`. **B** is incorrect because we are using invalid syntax for the method reference. Here we can't use a method reference because we are printing the `reading` values, not the whole `reading` object, and so must specify more details about the argument to the `Consumer`'s functional method than allowed with a method reference, which is why **C** is incorrect. **C** prints the entire `reading` object, rather than just the `value`. (OCP Objectives 3.3, 3.5, and 4.1)

6.   ☑   **B** is correct. `human` is a `Supplier`, so its functional method is `get()`. Calling `get()` returns a new `Human` with the name Joe and the age 34.
    ☒   **A, C, D,** and **E** are incorrect based on the above. (OCP Objective 4.1)

7.   ☑   **C** is correct. We know `printAdults` must be a `Consumer` that prints adults in the `people ArrayList`. The functional method of the `Consumer` will take a `Human` object. Then we must test that object to see if the `Human` is 18 or older, which we can do by defining a `Predicate` whose functional method returns true if the `Human`'s age is 18 or older. We use the `Predicate` by calling the function method, `test()`. If the `Human` passes the test, we print the `Human`'s name.
    ☒   **A, B,** and **D** are incorrect. **A** is incorrect because we haven't defined the `printAdults` as a `Consumer`. **B** is incorrect because, although we are defining the `printAdults Consumer` in the body of the `Consumer`'s functional method, we are using the `Predicate` wrong. **D** can initially be tempting, but if you look carefully, the syntax is incorrect. Either we must implement the `Consumer` interface with an inner class or with a lambda expression. (OCP Objective 4.1)

8.   ☑   **B** is correct. The code does not compile because the variable `longest` from the lambda's enclosing scope must be final or effectively final, and we are trying to change the value of `longest` within the lambda.
    ☒   **A, C,** and **D** are incorrect for the above reasons. (OCP Objective 2.6)

9.   ☑   **D** is correct. The code does not compile because `readingsSupplier` is not being assigned a `Supplier`; rather it is being assigned a `List`.
    ☒   **A, B,** and **C** are incorrect for the above reasons. (OCP Objective 4.1)

10.   ☑   **B** is correct. In the last line of the code, we are first calling the `apply()` method of the `foo BiFunction` and then calling the `apply()` method of the `bar Function`. Looking at the first line of code, we see that `foo`'s `apply()` method is implemented by the lambda expression and takes two arguments, an `integer n` and a `String`. The method concatenates the `String n` times (with a space between) and then returns it. So by calling `apply()` with the arguments 3 and `"foo"`, the `String "foo foo foo"` is returned. Then we call the `apply()` method of `bar`. The `andThen()` method of the `foo BiFunction` passes the value

returned from the first `BiFunction` to the `Function` whose `apply()` method is called, so `"foo foo foo"` gets passed to the `apply()` method of `bar`, which is implemented with a lambda expression and takes a `String`, concatenates `"bar"` to that `String`, and returns it, resulting in `"foo foo foo bar"`. (Note, too, this is an example of how you can combine a `BiFunction` with a `Function` using `andThen()`!)

☒ **A, C,** and **D** are incorrect for the above reasons. (OCP Objectives 4.1 and 4.3)

11. ☑ **A** is correct. The `List replaceAll()` method takes a `UnaryOperator`. In this case, the `UnaryOperator`'s functional method takes a `String` and returns the lowercase value of that `String`. Because it's a `UnaryOperator`, we need only specify one type parameter.

☒ **B, C,** and **D** are incorrect. **B** looks like it might be correct if you forget that `UnaryOperator` uses only one type parameter. **C** is tempting because a `UnaryOperator` is a type of `Function`, but `replaceAll()` specifies a `UnaryOperator` as an argument. **D** can't work because a `Supplier`'s functional method does not take an argument. (OCP Objective 4.4)

12. ☑ **D** is correct. To use `forEach()` with a `Map`, we need a `BiConsumer`, whose functional method takes two arguments, both `Strings`.

☒ **A, B,** and **C** are incorrect for the above reasons. (OCP Objective 4.3)

13. ☑ **C** is correct. To print the to-do item for Tuesday, we need to call the to-do list's `checkTodoDay()` method, passing the list of to-dos and a `Predicate`. We can see in the body of the `checkTodoDay()` method that we call the `Predicate`'s `test()` method on the map key, which is the day, a `String`, and if the test passes, we display the value in the map. So the `Predicate` should test to see if the day is equal to `"tuesday"` and return true if it is.

☒ **A, B,** and **D** are incorrect. **A** could work, but the syntax is incorrect (we should use `{ }` for statements in the body of the lambda) and will cause a compile error. **B** is incorrect because the `Predicate`'s `test()` method doesn't take two values; it takes only one, the key (day). **D** is incorrect because the `test()` method is not valid for a `String`; we need `equals()` instead. (OCP Objective 4.1)

14. ☑ **B** and **C** are correct. To get a `double` value from a `DoubleSupplier`, you must use the `getAsDouble()` functional method.

☒ **A** and **D** are incorrect. **A** and **D** are incorrectly using `get()` instead of `getAsDouble()`. (OCP Objective 4.2)

9
Streams

I n the previous chapter we looked at how we can use lambda expressions to represent instances of classes that implement functional interfaces and explored a few places in the JDK where functional interfaces are used, like with the Logger's `log()` method and with the new `Iterable.forEach()` method.

Well, get ready for more. In this chapter about streams, we'll use the functional interfaces you just learned about. The `java.util.stream` package's Stream interface has over 30 methods, and about three-quarters of those work with functional interfaces in some way.

Like lambdas and functional interfaces, streams are another new addition in Java 8. The syntax of streams will be new to you and will take some getting used to. As you go through the chapter, take time to practice writing examples and testing the code to get the hang of it. The concept of streams is something quite new, too; at first, you might think streams are just another way of organizing data, like a collection, but they are actually about processing data efficiently, sometimes in ways you might initially find unintuitive given how you're used to programming in Java.

Because streams are related to collections (you can make a stream from a `Collection` type to process the data in the collection) and to lambdas (we'll be using lambdas frequently to operate on streams); on the exam, you'll often see streams questions mixed in with questions that use collections and lambdas. The certification objectives related to streams are also mixed in with collections, functional interfaces, and lambdas, as you'll see throughout this chapter.

CERTIFICATION OBJECTIVE

What Is a Stream? (OCP Objective 3.4)

3.4   Collections Streams and Filters.

A *stream* is a sequence of elements (you can think of these elements as data) that can be processed with operations. That's plenty vague as a definition, so to get a better handle on what a stream is, let's make one:

```
Integer[] myNums = { 1, 2, 3 };
Stream<Integer> myStream = Arrays.stream(myNums);
```

Here, myNums is an array of three Integers. We're using the Arrays.stream() method to create a stream from that array. The resulting stream, myStream, is a stream of Integers. What does the stream look like?

```
System.out.println(myStream);
```

This results in the output:

```
java.util.stream.ReferencePipeline$Head@14ae5a5
```

Okay, so far this is clear as mud, right?!

Initially, you might think that a stream is a bit like a data structure, like a List or an array. After all, we're making a stream out an array of three integers:

```
Integer[] myNums = { 1, 2, 3 };
Stream<Integer> myStream = Arrays.stream(myNums);
```

But streams are not a data structure to organize data like a List is or an array is; rather, they are a way to process data that you can think of as flowing through the stream, much like water flows through a stream in the real world. An *array* is a way of describing how data is organized and gives you flexible ways to access that data. Now, think of a stream as a way to *operate* on data that's flowing from an array through the stream. We say that the array is the stream's source (like a spring is the source of water for a real stream).

So far, myStream is just a description of where we're sourcing data. In this example:

```
Integer[] myNums = { 1, 2, 3 };
Stream<Integer> myStream = Arrays.stream(myNums);
```

we're saying "the source of the data for myStream is myNums, an array of three integers, 1, 2, 3." That's why when we try to display the stream, we don't see any data; we just see a cryptic description of the object that's describing how to get at the data.

Okay, so let's add an operation and do something with the stream of elements:

```
Integer[] myNums = { 1, 2, 3 };   // create an array
Stream<Integer> myStream = Arrays.stream(myNums);   // stream the array
long numElements = myStream.count(); // get the number of elements in the stream
System.out.println("Number of elements in the stream: " + numElements);
```

The result is

```
Number of elements in the stream: 3
```

Here, we've added an operation count() to myStream. The count() method simply returns the count of elements in the stream as a long value. Getting a number from the stream, the count of elements, means that stream is done. That is, we can't perform any more operations on the stream because the stream's been turned into one number by the `count()` operation. We say that the `count()` operation is a "terminal operation" because the stream ends there: no more data flows through the stream after the `count()` is done.

The real power of streams comes from the "intermediate operations" you can perform between the source and the end of the stream. For instance, you could filter for even numbers (intermediate operation one), multiply each of those even numbers by 2 (intermediate operation two), and then display the results in the console (terminal operation). By specifying multiple operations on a stream, you are essentially defining a set of things you want to do in a particular order to the data in the source. You could write it all out using a `for` loop and multiple lines of code (possibly even using one or more temporary or new data structures), but with streams, you can be more concise.

You can string together as many of these intermediate operations as you like, but for now, we'll begin with just one:

```
Integer[] myNums = { 1, 2, 3 };
Stream<Integer> myStream = Arrays.stream(myNums);
long numElements =
  myStream
    .filter((i) -> i > 1) // add an intermediate operation to filter the stream
    .count();             // terminal operation, counts the elements in a
stream
System.out.println("Number of elements > 1: " + numElements);
```

The result we get with this code is

```
Number of elements > 1: 2
```

Now, rather than just counting the elements of the stream, we're first filtering the stream, looking for elements whose value is greater than 1. Notice that the `filter()` method takes a `Predicate`, and recall from the previous chapter that a `Predicate` is an interface with one abstract method, `test()`, that takes a value and returns a boolean. Here, we're representing the `Predicate` with a lambda expression; the value we take as an argument is one element from the stream of data; and we return true if the value of the element is greater than 1. You can read the code

```
myStream.filter((i) -> i > 1).count()
```

like this: "As the elements of `myStream` flow by, keep only those greater than 1, and count how many elements there are." The `filter()` method is calling the `test()`

method of the `Predicate` you pass to `filter()` behind the scenes, and if the value passes the test, that value gets passed on to `count()`.

Notice that the `filter()` method of `myStream` produces a stream. It's a slightly modified stream consisting only of elements whose values are greater than 1. We're now calling the `count()` method on that filtered stream, rather than on the original `myStream`. Intermediate operations always produce another stream—that's how we can chain multiple operations together to manipulate the data as it flows by in the stream. As long as we keep doing intermediate operations, we keep the stream of data flowing; it ends only when we perform a terminal operation like `count()`. That turns the stream into one thing—say, a number—and ends the stream. We'll look at streams with multiple intermediate operations shortly.

Now, let's try filtering for elements > 2 and count the results:

```
Integer[] myNums = { 1, 2, 3 };
Stream<Integer> myStream = Arrays.stream(myNums);
long numElements = myStream.filter((i) -> i > 1).count();
System.out.println("Number of elements > 1: " + numElements);
numElements = myStream.filter((i) -> i > 2).count(); // filter by > 2 instead
System.out.println("Number of elements > 2: " + numElements);
```

Run that code and you'll get an exception:

```
Exception in thread "main" java.lang.IllegalStateException: stream has
already been operated upon or closed
```

Hmm. What does it mean the "stream has already been operated upon or closed"?

Streams can be used only once. To turn again to our analogy: Imagine you're standing on the bank of the stream. Once the water in the stream has flowed by you, you can't see it again. That water is gone, and you can't get it back.

No problem, we can just create the stream again. In Java, streams are lightweight objects, so you can create multiple streams if you need to:

```
Integer[] myNums = { 1, 2, 3 };
Stream<Integer> myStream = Arrays.stream(myNums);
long numElements = myStream.filter((i) -> i > 1).count();
System.out.println("Number of elements > 1: " + numElements);
numElements =
  Arrays.stream(myNums)
    .filter((i) -> i > 2) // filter by > 2 on a whole new stream
    .count();
System.out.println("Number of elements > 2: " + numElements);
```

We can't reuse `myStream`, so here, we've created a new stream from the `myNums` array. We're filtering that stream using a `Predicate` that tests for an element greater than 2 and then counting the elements that pass that test. We do all three things: create the stream, filter the stream, and count the elements in one line of code.

In our example, we have only 1 element greater than 2, so we see this as the result:

```
Number of elements > 1: 2    // result of the 1st filter by > 1
Number of elements > 2: 1    // result of the 2nd filter by > 2
```

In Java, a stream is an object that gets its data from a source, but it doesn't store any data itself. The data flowing through the stream can be operated on, multiple times if we want, with intermediate operations, like `filter()`. The stream ends when we use a terminal operation, like `count()`, and once we've used a stream, we can't reuse it.

CERTIFICATION OBJECTIVE

How to Create a Stream (OCP Objectives 3.5 and 9.3)

3.5   *Iterate using forEach methods of Streams and List.*
9.3   *Use Stream API with NIO.2.*

There are a variety of ways you can create a stream. Given that streams are for data processing, you'll probably find you most often create streams from collections, arrays, and files. The collection, array, or file you use to create the stream is the "source" of the stream and provides the data that will flow through the stream. Remember that the stream itself does not contain any data; it operates on the data that is contained in the source, as that data flows through the stream operations.

Create a Stream from a Collection

Let's step through some examples of how to create a stream. First, here's how you can create a stream from a basic `List`, one of the collection types:

```
List<Double> tempsInPhoenix = Arrays.asList(123.6, 118.0, 113.0, 112.5,
    115.8, 117.0, 110.2, 110.1, 106.0, 106.4);
System.out.println("Number of days over 110 in 10 day period: " +
tempsInPhoenix
    .stream()                    // stream the List of Doubles
    .filter(t -> t > 110.0)      // filter the stream
    .count());                   // count the Doubles that pass the filter test
```

This code produces the output:

```
Number of days over 110 in 10 day period: 8
```

What we're doing in this code is first creating a List of Doubles; then we're using that List as a source for a stream that filters values, in this case temperatures greater than 110.0, and counts them. Notice that to create the stream, we're calling the stream() method of the tempsInPhoenix List. This method is a default method of the Collection interface and so is inherited by all classes that implement Collection. The stream() method's signature is

```
default Stream<E> stream()
```

You can see that stream() returns an object of type Stream, with a generic object type parameter, meaning the stream is a stream of any object type. If we were to split the line where we create the stream in the code above into two and store the stream in a variable, we'd write the code like this:

```
Stream<Double> tempStream = tempsInPhoenix.stream();
System.out.println("Number of days over 110 in 10 day period: " +
tempStream.filter(t -> t > 110.0).count());
```

using Double as the type parameter for the stream whose source is a List of Doubles.

Don't forget that a Map (HashMap, TreeMap, etc.) is not a collection inheriting from Collection. If you want to stream a Map, you must first use the entrySet() method to turn the Map into a Set, which *is* a Collection type:

```
Map<String, Integer> myMap = new HashMap<String, Integer>();
myMap.put("Boi", 6); myMap.put("Zooey", 3); myMap.put("Charis", 8);
System.out.println("Number of items in the map with value > 4: " +
myMap
    .entrySet()      // get a Set of Map.Entry objects
    .stream()        // stream the Set
    .filter(d -> d.getValue() > 4)    // filter the Map.Entry objects
    .count());       // count the objects
```

Here, we create a HashMap and add three items to the Map, each with a String and Integer value—a dog's name and age. Then we stream the dog data from the Map and count the number of dogs older than 4.

If we try to stream the Map directly, we'll get a compile-time error. Instead, we first call entrySet() on the Map and then call stream() on the resulting Set. We then call the filter() operation on this stream and get a Map.Entry object as the argument to the Predicate lambda we pass to the filter. We filter to get only dogs older than 4 and count the results (there are two).

Build a Stream with Stream.of()

`Stream.of()` is quite flexible; it works with any object values, so you can create a `Stream` of `Strings`, `Integers`, `Doubles`, etc. The method signature is

```
static <T> Stream<T> of(T... values)
```

meaning you can supply the `of()` method with any number of arguments, and you get back an ordered stream of those values.

We can use `Stream.of()` to create a stream from our array of Integers, myNums, like this:

```
Integer[] myNums = { 1, 2, 3 };
Stream<Integer> myStream = Stream.of(myNums);
```

Then we use myStream just like we did before to filter and count the items.

We can make that code even shorter by skipping declaring the array altogether and supply Integer values directly, like this:

```
Stream<Integer> myStream = Stream.of(1, 2, 3);
```

The source of the `Stream` here is a little fuzzy; you aren't actually storing the data values in a data structure first, like you are if you're streaming the myNums array. The source is there; it's just hidden behind the scenes.

Create a Stream from an Array

You've already seen how to use `Arrays.stream()` to stream an array; earlier we created an array of Integers and streamed it. Here's another example of streaming an array, this time, an array of Strings:

```
String[] dogs = { "Boi", "Zooey", "Charis" };          // make an array
Stream<String> dogStream = Arrays.stream(dogs);        // stream it
System.out.println("Number of dogs in array: " + dogStream.count()); // count it
```

And we see 3 as the result for the number of dogs in the array. (Of course, this code is completely contrived as you'd never stream an array to count the number of items, but you get the point, we hope).

Another way to create a stream from an array is to use the `Stream.of()` method. For our example with the Strings of dog names, we could rewrite the line to create the stream like this:

```
Stream<String> dogStream = Stream.of(dogs);
```

Create a Stream from a File

Using a stream to process data in a file is easy. You know you can use `Files` to read data from a file; the static `lines()` method of `Files` returns a `Stream`, so we can stream the data using the file as the source. Here is the signature of the `Files.lines()` method:

```
public static Stream<String> lines(Path path) throws IOException
```

So to create a stream from a file you write:

```
Stream<String> stream = Files.lines(Paths.get(filename)));
```

This sets up the stream, but how do you process the data from the stream? You can use the `Stream`'s `forEach()` method:

```
stream.forEach(line -> …do something with the line of data from the file…)
```

The `forEach()` method on a stream works much like the `forEach()` method on a collection. It takes a `Consumer`, which we can represent with a lambda expression, and processes each line from the file in the body of the lambda. The `File.lines()` method provides one line at a time from the file as each data element in the stream, which makes processing data from the file easy.

Here's an example to bring this together. We have a file, "dvdinfo.txt," containing the name, genre, and star of a movie, one per line:

```
Donnie Darko/sci-fi/Gyllenhall, Jake
Raiders of the Lost Ark/action/Ford, Harrison
2001/sci-fi/??
Caddyshack/comedy/Murray, Bill
Star Wars/sci-fi/Ford, Harrison
Lost in Translation/comedy/Murray, Bill
Patriot Games/action/Ford, Harrison
```

We want to read the lines of the file, creating a new `DVDInfo` object for each movie entry:

```java
class DVDInfo {
   String title;
   String genre;
   String leadActor;

   DVDInfo(String t, String g, String a) {
      title = t; genre = g; leadActor = a;
   }
   public String toString() {
      return title + " / " + genre + " / " + leadActor;
   }
   // getters and setters here
}
```

Here's how we can do that using the file as a source for a stream, and using the `forEach()` method to process each line from the file:

```java
public class DVDs {
public static void main(String[] args) {
  List<DVDInfo> dvds = loadDVDs("dvdinfo.txt"); // load the DVDs from a file
  dvds.forEach(System.out::println);            // just print the DVDs
}
public static List<DVDInfo> loadDVDs(String filename) {
  List<DVDInfo> dvds = new ArrayList<DVDInfo>();
  // stream a file, line by line
    try (Stream<String> stream = Files.lines(Paths.get(filename))) {
      stream.forEach(line -> {        // use forEach to display each line
        String[] dvdItems = line.split("/");
        DVDInfo dvd = new DVDInfo(dvdItems[0], dvdItems[1], dvdItems[2]);
        dvds.add(dvd);                // for now; there's a better way
      });
    } catch (IOException e) {
      System.out.println("Error reading DVDs");
      e.printStackTrace();
    }
    return dvds;
  }
}
```

We see the output from printing the DVDs:

```
Donnie Darko / sci-fi / Gyllenhall, Jake
Raiders of the Lost Ark / action / Ford, Harrison
2001 / sci-fi / ??
Caddyshack / comedy / Murray, Bill
Star Wars / sci-fi / Ford, Harrison
Lost in Translation / comedy / Murray, Bill
Patriot Games / action / Ford, Harrison
```

When processing data from a file using a stream with `forEach()` like we do here, remember that within the lambda expression we pass to `forEach()`, all variables must be final or effectively final, so we can't modify a variable directly (e.g., by changing its value to a value from the file). However, also remember that we *can* add to or modify the fields of an object from within the lambda expression, so that's how we can add each DVD to the `List` of `dvds`. The `dvds` `List` is effectively final (we don't try to create a new `List` object and assign it to the `dvds` property within the lambda), but the contents of the `List` can still be modified by adding new DVDs to it. As a result, once the stream terminates (i.e., the last line from the file is read), we have all the DVDs from the file stored in the `dvds` `List`. We must store the DVDs somewhere if we want to use them after the stream is complete because the stream itself doesn't hold any data! However, there's a better way to store the DVDs in the `dvds` `List`, which we'll see later on in the chapter, so put a bookmark here and we'll return to this example later. For more `Files` methods that create streams, check the Online Appendix.

The `forEach()` method of `Stream` is another example of a terminal operation (along with `count()`, which we saw earlier). It does not produce another stream; rather it takes each item flowing by in the stream and consumes it (with a `Consumer`). It doesn't produce anything (i.e., `forEach()` is void), so whatever you want to do with the data you're processing with `forEach()` must happen in the `Consumer` you pass to it.

Primitive Value Streams

As you might expect, there are also primitive streams designed to avoid autoboxing, for `doubles`, `ints`, and `longs`. These are `DoubleStream`, `IntStream`, and `LongStream`, respectively. So, you can create a `DoubleStream` like this:

```
DoubleStream s3 = DoubleStream.of(406.13, 406.42, 407.18, 409.01);
```

Notice there's no type parameter on the stream because this is a stream of `double` values and that's specified by the type itself, `DoubleStream`.

---

e x a m
ⓦatch

Keep in mind the difference between a `Stream<Double>` and `DoubleStream`. The first is a stream of `Double` objects; the second is a stream of `double` values. If you create a `List<Double>` and then stream it:

```
List<Double> co2Monthly = Arrays.asList(406.13, 406.42, 407.18, 409.01);
Stream<Double> s1 = co2Monthly.stream();
```

the stream is type `Stream<Double>`. Don't get fooled on the exam with this small distinction!

Summary of Methods to Create Streams

As you've just seen, there are a variety of ways to make streams—from collections, arrays, files, and values. Table 9-1 summarizes the methods you should be familiar with for the exam. And keep a close eye on those types; it can be easy to slip up and think you're creating a `DoubleStream` when you're creating a `Stream<Double>`! Note: This is not an exhaustive list of all the ways to create streams, so see each interface/class for more details and options.

| TABLE 9-1 | | Methods to Create Streams |

Interface/Class	Creates a...	With method...
`Collection`	`Stream<E>`	`stream()`
`Arrays`	`Stream<T>`	`stream(T[] array)` `stream(T[] array, int startInclusive, int endExclusive)`

`Arrays`	`IntStream,`
	`DoubleStream,`
	`LongStream`
		`stream(int[] array),`
		`stream(double[] array),`
		`stream(long[] array)`
		(and versions with start/end like `Stream`)

`Files`	`Stream<String>`	`lines(Path path),` `lines(Path path, Charset cs)`
`Stream`	`Stream<T>`	`of(T... values),` `of(T t)`
`DoubleStream`	`DoubleStream`	`of(double... values),` `of(double t)`
`IntStream`	`IntStream`	`of(int... values),` `of(int t)`
`LongStream`	`LongStream`	`of(long... values),` `of(long t)`

Why Streams?

You might be wondering why streams were added to Java. So far the examples you've seen are relatively simple, and you could easily accomplish the same thing using iteration over a `Collection`. The code might be a bit more concise, but it doesn't seem to really do anything fantastically different.

The main reason to use streams is when you start doing multiple intermediate operations. So far, we've been performing only one intermediate operation: a filter, using a variety of different `Predicates` to filter the data we get from the stream before we count it. However, when we use multiple intermediate operations, we start seeing the benefits of streams.

First, here's a quick example:

```
List<String> names =
    Arrays.asList("Boi", "Charis", "Zooey", "Bokeh", "Clover", "Aiko");
names.stream()                                // Create the stream
    .filter(   s -> s.startsWith("B")
            || s.startsWith("C"))             // Filter by first letter
```

```
.filter(s -> s.length() > 3)          // Filter by length
.forEach(System.out::println);        // print
```

Here, we've got a list of names. Let's say we want to see the names that begin with "B" or "C" and have a length > 3.

First, we stream the names from the source `List`, `names`. Then, we filter on the starting letter "B" or "C". The result is that only names that start with "B" or "C" get passed through to the next filter. The next filter checks the length of the string and only passes through strings whose length is greater than 3. Both of these filter operations are "intermediate operations" because the stream continues; the stream is slightly modified (some data elements are discarded if they don't pass the test in the filter), but any data elements left in the stream continue flowing through the stream.

Finally we have a "terminal operation" that ends the stream: the `forEach()` method, which just prints the names. And we see the output:

```
Charis
Bokeh
Clover
```

You're probably saying to yourself, what's the big deal? We could do the same thing using iteration, right?

The big deal is that streams use something called a "pipeline," which can, in some circumstances, dramatically improve the efficiency of data processing. To understand how the stream pipeline works, let's break the above code down a bit more and see what happens in each step.

CERTIFICATION OBJECTIVE

The Stream Pipeline (OCP Objective 3.6)

3.6   Describe Stream interface and Stream pipeline.

A stream pipeline consists of three parts: a source, zero or more intermediate operations, and a terminal operation. The *source* describes where the data is coming from; the *intermediate operations* operate on the stream and produce another, perhaps modified, stream; and the *terminal operation* ends the stream and typically produces a value or some output.

So the stream pipeline in our code above defines the names `List` as the source for the stream, contains two intermediate operations that filter the data, and then terminates with `forEach()`, which prints the data:

```
List<String> names =
     Arrays.asList("Boi", "Charis", "Zooey", "Bokeh", "Clover", "Aiko");
names.stream()                           // the source
    .filter(   s -> s.startsWith("B")    // intermediate op
               || s.startsWith("C"))
    .filter(s -> s.length() > 3)         // intermediate op
    .forEach(System.out::println);       // terminal op
```

One analogy often used at this point is an assembly line. When you stream the names `List`, the first data element of the list is streamed to the first filter operation. At that point the second filter and the `forEach()` are just waiting for a data element. Once the first filter is complete, that data element is possibly discarded, if it doesn't begin with a "B" or "C", in which case the second filter and the `forEach()` never see it. This makes the subsequent stream more efficient.

If the data element is not discarded, then it's passed along to the second filter, which starts working on that element. In the meantime, the second data element is streamed to the first filter. Just like the assembly line, we now have the first filter working on the second data element, while the second filter is still working on the first one.

If the second filter's `Predicate` test is passed on the first data element, that element is passed along to the `forEach()`, which starts working on it (by printing it out). In the meantime, the second data element is passed to the second filter, assuming it passes the `Predicate` test in the first filter. Then the third data element is streamed to the first filter.

As you can see, the assembly-line analogy works pretty well for the pipeline. Like an assembly line, we can get some efficiencies working with streams for two reasons: First, we can do multiple operations on data in one pass, and Java is optimized so it keeps minimal intermediate state during the operations part of the pipeline. Second, in some circumstances, we can parallelize streams to take advantage of the underlying architecture of the system and do parallel computations very easily. Not all streams can be parallelized, but some can. We'll talk more about parallel streams later in "A Taste of Parallel Streams."

There's one other thing you should know about streams: they are lazy! And, despite what you might think, lazy streams can be more efficient.

Streams Are Lazy

Look again at the code:

```
names.stream()                          // the source
    .filter(   s -> s.startsWith("B")   // intermediate op
           || s.startsWith("C"))
    .filter(s -> s.length() > 3)        // intermediate op
    .forEach(System.out::println);      // terminal op
```

What do you think happens if we write the following instead:

```
names.stream()                          // the source
    .filter(   s -> s.startsWith("B")   // intermediate op
           || s.startsWith("C"))
    .filter(s -> s.length() > 3);       // intermediate op
```

That is, we've written the pipeline without the `forEach()` terminal operation.

You know that what you get back from the second `filter()` is another stream. But has anything actually happened yet? Is any data flowing through the stream?

The answer is no. Nothing has happened. Going back to the assembly-line analogy, the worker at station 1 (filter one) is still sitting idle, as is the worker at station 2 (filter two). That's because no terminal operation has been executed yet. We've got everything set up, but nothing to kick-start the data processing.

Not until the `forEach()` is executed does anything happen. As soon as the terminal operation is executed, then the assembly line kicks into gear, and the data starts flowing from the source through the stream and into the operations.

It's important to note here that our analogies of the water stream and the assembly line break down when you remember that streams don't hold any data. Even though we talk about data elements as "flowing through the stream," the data is never "in" the stream (unlike water that really is in a real-life stream and items that really are in an assembly line). The operations you define on a stream are how you specify ways to manipulate the data that's in the source in a particular order. In that sense, of course, streams are lazy because no data is flowing, even though it helps us to think about streams that way.

This laziness makes streams more efficient because the JDK can perform optimizations to combine the operations efficiently, to operate on the data in a single pass, and to reduce operations on data whenever possible. If it's not necessary to run an operation on a piece of data (e.g., because we've already found the data element we're looking for, or because we've eliminated a data element in a prior intermediate operation, or because we've limited the number of data elements we want to operate on), then we can avoid even getting the data element from the source.

For most, if not all, of the simple examples we'll be working with in this book in preparation for the exam, the stream pipeline will not offer any tremendous advantage beyond thinking about data processing in a new way, and perhaps more concise code. However, once you get in the real world and start working with large amounts of data, you may realize the benefits of streams from an efficiency standpoint, especially if you can work with streams that can be parallelized (which we'll get to later, as we said before).

Operating on Streams (OCP Objectives 3.7 and 5.1)

3.7   Filter a collection by using lambda expressions.
5.1   Develop code to extract data from an object using peek() and map() methods including primitive versions of the map() method.

You may have heard the expression "map-filter-reduce": a general abstraction to describe functions that operate on a sequence of elements. It perfectly describes what we are often doing with streams: we might "map" an input to a slightly different output, then "filter" that output by some criteria, and finally "reduce" to a single value or to a printed output. When you map-filter-reduce, you are simply specifying a sequence of operations to be performed on the data in the stream's source that leads to a result. As we said earlier, instead of using a stream, you could create a `for` loop over the source data structure yourself, apply each of the operations in turn, accumulate the results into a new data structure, and you'd accomplish the same thing as a stream. The advantage of a stream is twofold: you can (often) write a sequence of operations to perform on the stream more concisely, and you can (sometimes) take advantage of some optimizations the JDK does under the covers to perform those operations more efficiently.

With streams, we take the map-filter-reduce abstraction and translate it into operations using the `map()`, `filter()`, and `reduce()` methods (and their variations) on a stream.

You've already seen the Java `Stream`'s `filter()` method. As we said earlier, `filter()` takes a `Predicate` and tests each element in the stream pipeline, producing a stream of elements that pass the test.

The Stream's map() method is another intermediate operation; however, unlike filter(), map() doesn't winnow down the elements of a stream; rather, map() transforms elements of a stream. For instance, map() might compute the square of a number, mapping a stream of numbers to a stream of their squares. Or map() might get the age of a Person so that the next step (say, a filter) can find ages greater than 21.

The map() method takes a Function. Remember from the previous chapter that the purpose of a Function is to transform a value. The Function's apply() method takes one value and produces another value (not necessarily of the same type), so the Function you pass to map() will "map" one value to another. The Function's functional method apply() that you pass into map() gets called by map() behind the scenes, and the value returned from apply() gets passed on to the next operation in the stream pipeline.

Reduce is both a general method, reduce(), as well as a specific method like count() and others you'll see shortly. All reductions are also terminal operations. Reduction operations are designed to combine multiple inputs into one summary result, which could be a single number, like the reduction operation count() produces, or a collection of values, which we'll see examples of later.

The Stream's reduce() method is a general method for reducing a stream to a value; the basic version of reduce() takes a BiFunction (a Function whose apply() method takes two arguments and produces one value) and applies it to pairs of elements from the stream, returning a value. You can think of reduce() as a way to "accumulate" a result, such as summing the values of a stream. Reductions like count(), sum(), and average() are defined as methods of streams; if you want a custom reduce function you can define it yourself using reduce().

(Notice how all those functional interfaces from the previous chapter are showing up here?)

As we work with map-filter-reduce, keep in mind that the stream pipeline specifies a sequence of operations to perform on the data in a source data structure, like an array. There is one stream of data that gets modified and winnowed (the *map-filter* part) as it passes through the pipeline, and eventually, the data elements in the stream are reduced (the *reduce* part) to a value (when the stream is no longer a stream again, but rather a single value or another data structure).

Let's take a look at a map-filter-reduce set of operations on a stream. We'll define a List of Integers, take the square of each Integer, test to see whether the square is greater than 20, and if it is, we'll add 1 to a count, result. Before we do, we'll look at how we might do this with Java 7, so we can compare it with how we compute this using streams.

Here's the Java 7 way:

```
List<Integer> nums = Arrays.asList(1, 2, 3, 4, 5, 6);
long result = 0;
for (Integer n : nums) {
   int square = n * n;
   if (square > 20) {
      result = result + 1;
      System.out.println("Square of " + n + " is: " + square);
   }
}
System.out.println("Result: " + result);
```

With the output:

```
Square of 5 is: 25
Square of 6 is: 36
Result: 2
```

We're simply creating a List, and using a for loop to iterate over the list, compute the square, print out the square if it is greater than 20, and print the number of squares > 20.

And here's the Java 8 way, with streams:

```
List<Integer> nums = Arrays.asList(1, 2, 3, 4, 5, 6);
long result = nums.stream()
     .map(n -> n * n)          // map values in stream to squares
                               //    (map intermediate op)
     .filter(n -> n > 20)      // keep only squares > 20
                               //    (filter intermediate op)
     .count()                  // count the squares > 20 (reduction op)

System.out.println("Result (stream): " + result);
```

With the output:

```
Result (stream): 2
```

Here, we're streaming the List of Integers, first mapping the number from the stream to its square, then filtering the squares so that we keep only those squares greater than 20, and then reducing using the count() operation to count the squares > 20.

Which code do you like better? You're very familiar with the for loop iteration; the stream pipeline with a map-filter-reduce sequence is likely new to you. They both accomplish the same thing. Using streams like this has the potential to be a bit more efficient (not so much with this particular example because it's so simple) and is more concise.

Notice that we can't print the number with its square using the streams way. Why? Because by the time we get to the `count()` reduction operation, the only elements we have access to in the stream are the squares of the numbers. The original numbers are stored only in the original `List`. And don't be tempted to try to somehow keep track of the index of the square; that won't work and doesn't fit the patterns of how we use stream pipelines.

We can create a "sort of" solution to the problem like this, however:

```
long result = nums.stream()
    .peek(n -> System.out.print("Number is: " + n + ", ")) // print the number
    .map(n -> n * n)
    .filter(n -> n > 20)
    .peek(n -> System.out.print("Square is: " + n + ", ")) // print the square
    .count();
```

And see the output:

```
Number is: 1, Number is: 2, Number is: 3, Number is: 4, Number is: 5,
Square is: 25, Number is: 6, Square is: 36, Result (stream): 2
```

The method `peek()` is an intermediate operation that allows you to "peek" into the stream as the elements flow by. It takes a `Consumer` and produces the same exact stream as it's called on, so it doesn't change the values or filter them in any way. Here we're using it to peek at the numbers in the original stream before we map those numbers to squares and then filter them. We see all the numbers in the original stream, rather than just the numbers that have squares greater than 20.

You might feel a bit limited by this, but remember that streams are designed for data processing, so typically we're looking for the result of a sequence of operations applied to a big set of data, and, other than when we're debugging, we're not going to be looking at the data as it flows by.

A more typical example of a map-filter-reduce operation might be to stream a data set of readings, map the stream to get a particular value from a reading, filter that stream to eliminate any outliers, and then find the average reading of that stream. We'll tackle this example next, and in the process, you'll see a new way to map values and learn about the concept of "optional" values.

Map-Filter-Reduce with average() and Optionals (OCP Objectives 5.3 and 5.4)

5.3 *Develop code that uses the Optional class.*
5.4 *Develop code that uses Stream data methods and calculation methods.*

Imagine you have a piece of equipment that's taking a reading once per week, and you want to find the average of the readings you've measured so far this year. You know that the readings should probably be between 406 and 407, so you decide to throw away readings that are less than 406 or greater than 407 because those may be errors.

You start by creating a class for the readings:

```
class Reading {
    int year;
    int month;
    int day;
    double value;

    Reading(int year, int month, int day, double value) {
        this.year = year; this.month = month;
        this.day = day; this.value = value;
    }
}
```

Each reading gets stored with its value, along with the year, month, and day, in a Reading object, and the Reading objects are stored in a List:

```
List<Reading> readings = Arrays.asList(
    new Reading(2017, 1, 1, 405.91),
    new Reading(2017, 1, 8, 405.98),
    new Reading(2017, 1, 15, 406.14),
    new Reading(2017, 1, 22, 406.48),
    new Reading(2017, 1, 29, 406.20),
    new Reading(2017, 2, 5, 407.12),
    new Reading(2017, 2, 12, 406.03));
```

Now let's use a stream to find the average of the readings that are between 406 and 407. The first thing we'll do is stream the readings:

```
readings.stream()
```

For this computation, we're interested only in the value portion of the readings because we're trying to get the average. We can map each reading to its value, essentially converting the reading to a single `double` value. But we can't use `map()` because `map()` takes a `Function` whose `apply()` method takes an object and returns an object. Here's the method signature of `map()`:

```
<R> Stream<R> map(Function<? super T,? extends R> mapper)
```

As we said earlier, `map()` takes a `Function` (called `mapper` in the signature above). `map()` applies that `Function` (by calling the `apply()` method) on each value in the stream. Recall that the `Function`'s `apply()` method takes an object and returns an object. So if we call `map()` on a `Stream` of objects, like we want to do here with our stream of `Reading` objects, what we get back is also a stream of objects. But `Reading.value` is a `double`, not a `Double`, so what we really want to get back is a stream of `doubles`.

Is there a solution? Yes, of course! The `Stream.mapToDouble()` method takes a `ToDoubleFunction`, whose `applyAsDouble()` method takes an object and returns a `double`:

```
double applyAsDouble(T value)
```

This is exactly what we need, so the next step in the stream pipeline is `mapToDouble()`:

```
readings.stream().mapToDouble(r -> r.value)
```

We use a lambda expression for the `ToDoubleFunction`, pass in a `Reading` object, `r`, to the `applyAsDouble()` method (which gets called by `mapToDouble()` behind the scenes), and get back the `double` value, `r.value`.

Keeping track of the type in these situations is tricky! Notice: what we get back from the `mapToDouble()` method of the `Stream` that we created with `readings.stream()` is a `DoubleStream`:

```
DoubleStream mapToDouble(ToDoubleFunction<? super T> mapper)
```

So by calling `mapToDouble()`, we've converted the initial `Stream` of `Reading` objects (`Stream<Reading>`) into a stream of `doubles`, and that stream has the type `DoubleStream`.

The capitalization on these types can be very confusing. Don't mix up a `DoubleStream` with a `Stream<Double>` here, or forget that `ToDoubleFunction`'s `applyAsDouble()` method returns a `double`. It's easy to get mixed up on this issue and think you're working with `Doubles` when you're actually working with `doubles` (or vice versa), and in this case, it matters a lot, as you'll see shortly.

After all that, where are we?

```
readings.stream().mapToDouble(r -> r.value)
```

We've mapped the stream of `Reading` objects into a stream of `doubles`, and next we want to filter the stream so we keep only the values greater than or equal to 406.0 and less than 407.0:

```
readings.stream()
    .mapToDouble(r -> r.value)
    .filter(v -> v >= 406.0 && v < 407.00)
```

We've changed the variable we're using in the lambda expression in `filter()` from `r` (for `Reading`) to `v` (for `value`) as a reminder that the stream we're filtering is a `DoubleStream`: that is, a stream of the `double` values from the `List` of `Readings`.

Note again that at this point in the computation, nothing has actually happened. The stream is lazy! No computation is going on until we get to the reduce part of the map-filter-reduce: the terminal operation. So far we have a source (the `List` of `Readings`), a stream, and two intermediate operations.

The reduction operation we are going to use is the `average()` method. But if you look for `average()` in the `Stream` interface, you will not find it. That's because `average()` is a method of the `DoubleStream` interface (and its primitive cousins, `IntStream` and `LongStream`). That makes sense because `average()` is designed to work with numbers, not objects. And it's convenient that we mapped the stream of `Readings` into a stream of `doubles` (we *do* plan ahead for these examples).

Here is the type signature for the `DoubleStream`'s `average()` method:

```
OptionalDouble average()
```

You probably expected `average()` to return a `double`, right? And what on earth is this `OptionalDouble` thing?

An `OptionalDouble` is one of several types of optionals that are new in Java 8, which represent values that may or may not be there. Strange! Why would the average of our readings not be there?

Well, think about it this way. What if the source is empty? That is, what if our `List` of `Readings` is empty? Or what if, when we filter the stream, the filter eliminates all the values from the stream, so the result of the filter is an empty stream? We don't know until we get to `average()` whether there's anything actually *in* the stream (remember, the stream is lazy). And, as you know, the average value of a set of values is computed by adding up all the values and then dividing by the number of values. If the number of values is 0, then you'd be dividing by 0, which, as we all know, is a *very bad thing to do*.

Whenever we compute the average of some collection of values, we always have to check to make sure there's at least one of them so we don't get ourselves into this situation. But if we forget to check to see whether our source is empty before we stream it, or, perhaps more likely, we're in the middle of a stream pipeline and we've created an empty stream by filtering out all the values, presto: we're in a situation where we're trying to compute the average of an empty stream and we're going to get ourselves into trouble. Optionals help prevent that trouble.

It doesn't make sense to return `null` in this situation because we're expecting a primitive `double`. And it doesn't make sense to return 0.0 because that could be a valid result for the average. Instead, we get back an `OptionalDouble`, which is a `double` value that might or might not be there. To finish off this line of code, we terminate the stream pipeline with a call to `average()` and store the result in an `OptionalDouble` variable, avg:

```
OptionalDouble avg =
    readings.stream()
        .mapToDouble(r -> r.value)
        .filter(v -> v >= 406.0 && v < 407.00)
        .average();
```

If you try to print the value of avg, like this:

```
System.out.println("Average of 406 readings: " + avg);
```

what you see is

```
Average of 406 readings: OptionalDouble[406.2125]
```

The correct result—that is, the average of the readings—is 406.2125, but we're seeing that result wrapped an `OptionalDouble`. How do you get a `double` value out of an `OptionalDouble`? You use the `getAsDouble()` method:

```
System.out.println("Average of 406 readings: " + avg.getAsDouble());
```

And now you'll see the result:

```
Average of 406 readings: 406.2125
```

The problem with this code, however, is if the `OptionalDouble` is empty, then you'll get a `NoSuchElementException`. Just because you get an `OptionalDouble` back from `average()` doesn't mean you completely abdicate responsibility for checking to make sure there's a value there before you try to use it!

If you do try to call `getAsDouble()` on an empty `OptionalDouble`, you'll see

```
Exception in thread "main" java.util.NoSuchElementException: No value present
```

meaning you're trying to get a `double` that isn't there. A better way to write this code is to first check to make sure there is a value *present* in the `OptionalDouble` with the `isPresent()` method:

```
if (avg.isPresent()) {
    System.out.println("Average of 406 readings: " + avg.getAsDouble());
} else {
    System.out.println("Empty optional!");
}
```

If there's a value, we print it; otherwise, we print a message saying the optional must have been empty. Now if you run the code on an empty `List`, or a `List` with no values in the 406–407 range, you won't get a runtime error and you'll see the message:

```
Empty optional!
```

Whew! We finally have our average value, 406.2125, for our `List` of `Readings` using a stream pipeline. That was a lot to take in. We introduced map-filter-reduce, talked about how map works in more detail and how map and filter differ, and introduced optionals, which we'll be returning to in more detail.

e x a m

ⓦ a t c h
There's ample room for confusion with `DoubleStream`, `Stream<Double>`, `getAsDouble()`, etc. Adding to the confusion is that sometimes a reduction will return an `OptionalDouble` and sometimes an `Optional<Double>` (and, likewise, for `long`/`Long` and `int`/`Integer`).
This is a good time to pay close attention to types, type parameters, and method
signatures. There will be times on the exam when you'll have to select the correct type as part of your answer, and knowing the difference between `DoubleStream` and `Stream<Double>` or `OptionalDouble` and `Optional<Double>` will be the key to choosing the correct answer.

Reduce

What we did with this example code is take a source, a List of Readings, stream it, map the readings (mapping a Reading to a double), filter the values (keeping only values between 406 and 407), and then reduce (by taking the average). Let's return to the reduce part of map-filter-reduce.

You've seen a couple of reductions so far: count() and average(). The count() method is defined for both Stream and the primitive versions of Stream: IntStream, LongStream, and DoubleStream, while average() is defined only for the primitive streams. Other handy methods defined on the primitive streams include min(), max(), and sum(), which result in the minimum value in a stream, the maximum value in a stream, and the sum of the values in a stream.

Like average(), min() and max() also return optional values. If you are looking for the max() reading in our List of Readings, you'd write:

```
OptionalDouble max =
    readings.stream()
        .mapToDouble(r -> r.value)
        .max();
if (max.isPresent()) {
    System.out.println("Max of all readings: " + max.getAsDouble());
} else {
    System.out.println("Empty optional!");
}
```

Looking at the type signature of sum(), however, you will probably notice that sum() does not return an optional value. Rather, DoubleStream.sum() returns a double. Why do average(), max(), and min() return optionals, but sum() does not?

As with average(), it makes no sense to take the max() or min() of an empty stream. Therefore, an optional value is returned, indicating that a value may not exist.

Taking the sum() of an empty list makes a little more sense if you assume the sum of an empty stream is 0.0. And, in fact, if you try to sum() an empty DoubleStream, that's exactly what you'll get:

```
List<Reading> readings2 = Arrays.asList();  // empty list for testing sum
double sum = readings2.stream().mapToDouble(r -> r.value).sum();
System.out.println("Sum of all readings: " + sum);
```

produces the output:

```
Sum of all readings: 0.0
```

By default, the sum of an empty stream is 0. Let's take a look at how you can write your own reduction methods with `reduce()` and have an opportunity to provide a default value in case you have an empty stream.

Using reduce()

The methods `count()`, `average()`, `min()`, `max()`, and `sum()` are all reduction methods already defined on streams. You can also define your own reductions using the `reduce()` method. We'll rewrite the code to sum the values in the (original, nonempty) `readings` list using `reduce()` rather than `sum()`.

What is `sum()` doing to "reduce" a `DoubleStream` of `double` values into one value? It's taking values as they flow from the stream and adding them up, so that's what we need to do in `reduce()` if we want to create our own sum reduction method.

If we look at the type signature of `DoubleStream.reduce()`, we see

```
OptionalDouble reduce(DoubleBinaryOperator op)
```

In the previous chapter, we looked only at `UnaryOperators`, but hopefully, if you studied the Java 8 Functional APIs a bit further, you ran across `BinaryOperators`, which are like `UnaryOperators` except their functional methods take two values as arguments, rather than one. And recall that operators are a special case of `Function` in that the arguments and the return value of the functional method must be the same type.

A `DoubleBinaryOperator` is an operator whose functional method, `applyAsDouble()`, takes two `double` values and returns a `double`.

To write our own method to sum all the values in the stream using `reduce()`, we pass a `DoubleBinaryOperator` to `reduce()`, which adds the two arguments together and returns the sum:

```
OptionalDouble sum =
    readings.stream()
        .mapToDouble(r -> r.value)
        .reduce((v1, v2) -> v1 + v2);
if (sum.isPresent()) {
    System.out.println("Sum of all readings: " + sum.getAsDouble());
}
```

And we see the output:

```
Sum of all readings: 2843.8600000000006
```

The `reduce()` method sums all the values in the stream, two at a time, to get a total sum. In other words, it computes the final result by "accumulating" the values coming in from the stream.

You might wonder, well, how does this work when we are streaming elements one at a time? If you're thinking of the assembly-line analogy, you might be thinking of `reduce()` as the last station on the assembly line and imagining `reduce()` getting one element at a time.

Again, think of reductions as *accumulators:* they accumulate values from the stream so they can compute one value. It's as if the final station in the assembly line is putting all the values from the stream into one big box in order to do the terminal operation on them.

e x a m
w a t c h

Don't forget: this analogy of the assembly line isn't quite correct. We think of elements flowing through a stream one at a time, like items on an assembly line, but in reality, it doesn't quite work that way. There is no data in a stream; we're simply defining operations on the stream's source (a data structure) that happen in a particular **sequence and then get a result by terminating with a reduction. Although it's helpful to think of it like a stream of water or an assembly line as a way to understand streams, how the JDK handles that computation internally is probably quite different: with optimizations and even parallelization, the reality is not like the analogy.**

Take another look at the code above and notice that when we switched from `sum()` to `reduce()`, we had to go back to using `OptionalDouble` for the result. That's because `reduce()` is a general reduction function that takes any `DoubleBinaryOperator`. We know that the `applyAsDouble()` method must produce a number, but in the situation where the stream is empty, that `applyAsDouble()` method will never get called, so we need a way to say there might not be a result at all. Again, that's what the `OptionalDouble` says.

There's another `reduce()` method in `DoubleStream` that takes an *identity* along with an accumulator function and returns a `double`:

```
double reduce(double identity, DoubleBinaryOperator op)
```

The identity argument serves two roles: it provides an initial value and a value to return if the stream is empty.

If you provide the identity value, you're providing an initial value for the result of applying the accumulator function, `op`. The sum is computed by adding values from the stream to this initial value, and when the stream is empty, the identity provides a default result for the sum. For a method that produces a sum, it makes sense for that identity value to be 0.0. Because we have a value to return when the stream is empty, we no longer have to use an `OptionalDouble` because we'll always get a value back:

```
double sum = readings.stream()
   .mapToDouble(r -> r.value)
   .reduce(0.0, (v1, v2) -> v1 + v2);              // provide an identity
value
System.out.println("Sum of all readings: " + sum); // print 0.0 if stream
                                                    // is empty
```

Associative Accumulations

We just showed you how to use `reduce()` to build your own function that sums up the values in a stream. So you might be thinking, hey I could try the same thing for average. You might even try writing the following code:

```
OptionalDouble avgWithReduce =
    readings.stream()                           // stream the readings
        .mapToDouble(r -> r.value)              // map to double values
        .filter(v -> v >= 406.0 && v < 407.00) // filter 406 values
        .reduce((v1, v2) -> (v1 + v2) / 2);    // take the average
if (avgWithReduce.isPresent()) {
    System.out.println("Average of 406 readings: " +
    avgWithReduce.getAsDouble());
} else {
    System.out.println("Empty optional!");
}
```

What you might see is

```
Average of 406 readings: 406.31125
```

Not only is that answer different from the one we got before (which was 406.2125), but you also might get a different answer from ours. What is going on here?

Let's take a look at how we replaced the call to `average()` with a call to `reduce()`:

```
reduce((v1, v2) -> (v1 + v2) / 2)
```

As we did with sum, we're passing a `DoubleBinaryOperator` to `reduce`, whose functional method takes two values. We're summing those two values and dividing by two. The idea is that `reduce()` operates on two values from the stream at a time, so we'll get an average for two values and then average that result with the next value that comes in from the stream. It sounds like it should work, but it clearly doesn't. Something's up.

The problem is that `average()`—unlike `sum()`, `max()`, and `min()`—is not *associative*. If you stretch your mind back to high-school algebra, you might (or might not) recall that an operator is associative if the following is true:

```
(A operator B) operator C = A operator (B operator C)
```

Addition is associative, thus,

```
(1 + 2) + 3 = 1 + (2 + 3)
```

The parentheses indicate which operators to apply first. So, on the left, we compute 1 + 2, get 3, and then add 3, to get 6. On the right, we compute 2 + 3, get 5, and then add 1, to get 6 again. We get the same result; therefore, addition (i.e., `sum()`) is associative.

Our problem with the code above that replaces the call to `average()` with a `reduce()`:

```
reduce((v1, v2) -> (v1 + v2) / 2)
```

is that average is *not* an associative operator. That might seem odd; it feels like it should be associative, but it's really not.

The average of 1, 2, and 3 is 2, right?

$1 + 2 + 3 = 6.\ 6 / 3 = 2$

Yep.

Okay, now try this:

The average of 1 and 2 = 1.5

The average of 1.5 and 3 = 2.25

And this:

The average of 2 and 3 = 2.5

The average of 2.5 and 1 = 1.75

Average is clearly *not* associative!

Reduction operations *must* be associative in order to work correctly with streams. That's why you can't define your own average function with `reduce()`; average is not associative. So to take the average of a stream, you must use the `average()` method.

What about `min()` and `max()`? They are both associative reductions. Try writing your own versions using `reduce()`. Convince yourself that these operators really are associative and then try writing the code to find the min and max of a stream of values.

map-filter-reduce Methods

With map, as with all things streams, there are a variety of options depending on the types you are working with. Review Table 9-2 to get a sense of the patterns of names used with streams and primitive streams. (Note: This is not an exhaustive list of all the ways to map, filter, and reduce, so see each interface for more details and options.)

TABLE 9-2   Methods to Map, Filter, and Reduce

Interface	Method	Returns...
`Stream`	`map(Function<? super T,` `    ? extends R> mapper`	`Stream<R>`

`Stream`	`mapToDouble(`
	`    ToDoubleFunction<? Super T>`
	`    mapper),`
	
	`mapToInt(`
	`    ToIntFunction<? Super T>`
	`    mapper),`
	
	`mapToLong(`
	`    ToLongFunction<? Super T>`
	`    mapper)`
		`DoubleStream,`
		
		`IntStream,`
		
		`LongStream`

`DoubleStream`	`map(`
	`    DoubleUnaryOperator`
	`        mapper),`
	`mapToInt(`
	`    DoubleToIntFunction`
	`        mapper),`
	
	`mapToLong(`
	`    DoubleToLongFunction`
	`        mapper),`
	
	`mapToObj(`
	`    DoubleFunction<? Extends U>`
	`        mapper)`
		`DoubleStream,`
		
		`IntStream,`
		
		`LongStream,`
		
		`Stream<U>`

TABLE 9-2   Methods to Map, Filter, and Reduce (*Continued*)

Interface	Method	Returns...
`IntStream`	Like `DoubleStream`, but for ints	
`LongStream`	Like `DoubleStream`, but for longs	
`Stream`	`filter(Predicate<? super T> predicate)`	`Stream<T>`
`DoubleStream`	`filter(DoublePredicate predicate)`	`DoubleStream`
`IntStream`	`filter(IntPredicate predicate)`	`IntStream`
`LongStream`	`filter(LongPredicate predicate)`	`LongStream`
`Stream`	`reduce(BinaryOperator<T> accumulator),` `reduce(T identity, BinaryOperator<T> Accumulator)`	`Optional<T>,` `T`
`DoubleStream`	`reduce(DoubleBinaryOperator op),` `reduce(double identity, DoubleBinaryOperator op)`	`OptionalDouble,` `double`
`IntStream`	`reduce(IntBinaryOperator op),` `reduce(int identity, IntBinaryOperator op)`	`OptionalInt,` `int`
`LongStream`	`reduce(LongBinaryOperator op),` `reduce(long identity, LongBinaryOperator op)`	`OptionalLong,` `long`
`Stream`	`count()`	`long`
`DoubleStream,` `IntStream,` `LongStream`	`count(),` `sum()`	`long,` `double, int, long`
`DoubleStream,` `IntStream,` `LongStream`	`average()`	`OptionalDouble`
`DoubleStream,` `IntStream,` `LongStream`	`max(), min()`	`OptionalDouble,` `OptionalInt,` `OptionalLong`

The key idea to remember with map-filter-reduce is the purpose of each: `map()` maps values to modify the type or create a new value from the existing value, but without changing the number of elements in the stream you're working with; `filter()` potentially winnows the values you're working with, depending on the result of the `Predicate` test; and `reduce()` (and its equivalents) changes the stream of values to one value (or a collection of values) as a terminal operation.

CERTIFICATION OBJECTIVE

Optionals (OCP Objective 5.3)

5.3 Develop code that uses the Optional class.

We've explored optionals a bit, and now it's time to dig in a bit more as optionals are an important part of working with streams and you'll encounter optionals on the exam. You'll need to make sure you know which stream operations return optionals and the correct type for those optionals. Table 9-3 summarizes the methods that result in optionals that we cover in this chapter.

TABLE 9-3   Stream Methods That Return Optionals

Interface	Method	Returns...
Stream	findAny()	Optional<T>
Stream	findFirst()	Optional<T>
Stream	max(Comparator<? super T> comparator)	Optional<T>
Stream	min(Comparator<? super T> comparator)	Optional<T>
Stream	reduce(BinaryOperator<T> accumulator)	Optional<T>
DoubleStream	average()	OptionalDouble
DoubleStream	findAny(), findFirst()	OptionalDouble
DoubleStream	max(), min()	OptionalDouble
DoubleStream	reduce(DoubleBinaryOperator op)	OptionalDouble
IntStream, LongStream	Similar methods to DoubleStream	OptionalInt, OptionalLong

What is an optional? It's a container that may or may not contain a value. You can think of an optional as a wrapper around a value and that wrapper provides various methods to determine whether a value is there and, if it is, to get that value.

Optionals show up a lot with streams, because, as you've seen, if a stream is empty at any part of the pipeline, then there's a chance that no value will be returned by the terminal operation of a stream pipeline. Optionals provide a way for the JDK to handle that situation without having to throw a runtime exception.

The types of optionals include Optional<T> (for objects) and three primitive optionals, OptionalDouble, OptionalInt, and OptionalLong.

You've seen how we used OptionalDouble with the average() operation; now let's take a look at how we might use Optional<Double> for comparison:

```
Stream<Double> doublesStream =
      Stream.of(1.0, 2.0, 3.0, 4.0);                 // stream of doubles
Optional<Double> aNum = doublesStream.findFirst(); // first the first double
if (aNum.isPresent()) {                            // check to see if aNum
                                                   // has a value
   System.out.println("First number from the doubles stream: " + aNum.get());
} else {
   System.out.println("Doubles stream is empty");
}
```

You should see the output:

```
First number from the doubles stream: 1.0
```

We're creating a stream of Double values, using Stream.of() (notice that the doubles are being autoboxed into Doubles to create the Stream<Double>), and then we're using the stream terminal operation method, findFirst(), to find the first element of the stream.

We'll get into findFirst() in more detail later, but what it does, as you might guess, is find the first element of the stream. Typically, you'll use findFirst() after filtering the stream, but here, we just want to return the first element of the original stream.

That element is a Double object, so the type we use for the return value from findFirst() is Optional<Double>. Note that OptionalDouble will not work here! Why? Because findFirst() is operating on a stream of Doubles, not a stream of doubles. Again, pay very close attention to the types here.

Just like before, now that we have an optional value, we need to first test to see whether it's present, with isPresent(), before trying to get that Double value from the Optional. Because we're working with a Double object rather than a primitive type, the method we use to get the value is get().

exam
ⓦatch

Recall that the method for `OptionalDouble` *is* `getAsDouble()`*, and note the patterns for the method names for optionals and primitive optionals:*

- **Get a value from an** `Optional<T>`: `get()`
- **Get a value from an** `OptionalDouble`: `getAsDouble()`
- **Get a value from an** `OptionalInt`: `getAsInt()`
- **Get a value from an** `OptionalLong`: `getAsLong()`

Another way to test to see whether an optional contains a value and, if it does, to then get that value, is the `ifPresent()` method. This method takes a `Consumer` and tests to see whether the optional value is present; if it is, then the unwrapped value is passed to the `Consumer`:

```
Stream<Double> doublesStream = Stream.of(1.0, 2.0, 3.0, 4.0);
Optional<Double> aNum = doublesStream.findFirst();
aNum.ifPresent(n ->
          System.out.println("First number from the doubles stream: " + n));
```

Note here that the type of n is `Double`, not `Optional<Double>`, so to print n, we just write n, not `n.get()`. You'll see the output:

```
First number from the doubles stream: 1.0
```

If your `doublesStream` is empty, then you will not see any output at all.

You can create your own optionals, too. For instance, here's how to create an `Optional<Dog>` (using our previous class for Dog):

```
Dog boi = new Dog("boi", 30, 6); // create a dog named "boi" with weight 30,
                                 // age 6
Optional<Dog> optionalBoi = Optional.of(boi);
optionalBoi.ifPresent(System.out::println);
```

This will give you the output:

```
boi is 6 years old and weighs 30 pounds
```

What happens if `boi` happens to be `null`? Try this:

```
boi = null;                                     // boi is null!
Optional<Dog> optionalBoi = Optional.of(boi);   // potential problem here
optionalBoi.ifPresent(System.out::println);
```

Run it and you'll see the error:

```
Exception in thread "main" java.lang.NullPointerException
```

If you are in a situation in which you might be creating an optional from a null object, then you have to take an extra precaution and use the `Optional.ofNullable()` method rather than `Optional.of()`. The `ofNullable()` method creates the optional if the object you pass in is not `null`; otherwise, it creates an empty optional:

```
boi = null;
Optional<Dog> optionalBoi = Optional.ofNullable(boi); // check for null
optionalBoi.ifPresent(System.out::println);
if (!optionalBoi.isPresent()) System.out.println("Boi must be null");
```

You should see the output:

```
Boi must be null
```

You can also create empty optionals directly. Assume we have a `List` of `Dog` objects. We can create an empty `Optional<Dog>` and then assign it a value later by streaming the `List` of `Dogs`, using `findFirst()` to find the first `Dog`:

```
Optional<Dog> emptyDog = Optional.empty(); // make an empty Dog optional
if (!emptyDog.isPresent()) {
    System.out.println("Empty dog must be empty");
}
emptyDog = dogs.stream().findFirst();       // find the first dog in
                                            // the list, assign it to emptyDog
emptyDog.ifPresent(d -> System.out.println("Empty dog is no longer empty"));
```

Run this code and you'll see

```
Empty dog must be empty
Empty dog is no longer empty
```

Another way to handle an empty optional is the `orElse()` method. With this method you get the value in the optional, or, if that optional is empty, you get the value you specify with the `orElse()` method:

```
Optional<Dog> emptyDog = Optional.empty();
Dog aDog = emptyDog.orElse(new Dog("Default Dog", 50, 10));
System.out.println("A Dog: " + aDog);
```

You will get the output:

```
A Dog: Default Dog is 10 years old and weighs 50 pounds
```

Try changing `emptyDog` to `optionalBoi`:

```
Dog boi = new Dog("boi", 30, 6);                    // create a dog named "boi"
                                                    // with weight 30, age 6
Optional<Dog> optionalBoi = Optional.of(boi);  // not an empty optional
```

```
Dog aDog =                                            // get boi, or if optionalBoi
                                                      // is empty, get Default Dog.
        optionalBoi.orElse(new Dog("Default Dog", 50, 10));
    System.out.println("A Dog: " + aDog);
```

And now you should see

```
A Dog: boi is 6 years old and weighs 30 pounds
```

because `optionalBoi` does, indeed, contain a Dog, `boi`.

Table 9-4 summarizes the `Optional` methods.

TABLE 9-4	Methods of the Optional Class	

Class	Method	Returns...
`Optional`	`empty()`	`Optional<T>`
`Optional`	`get()`	`T`
`Optional`	`ifPresent(Consumer<? super T> consumer)`	`void`
`Optional`	`isPresent()`	`boolean`
`Optional`	`of()`	`Optional<T>`
`Optional`	`ofNullable(T value)`	`Optional<T>`
`Optional`	`orElse(T other)`	`T`
`OptionalDouble, OptionalInt, OptionalLong`	Each has similar methods to the above methods that return primitive optionals or primitives for each type	`double, int, long`

CERTIFICATION OBJECTIVE

Searching and Sorting with Streams (OCP Objectives 5.2 and 5.5)

5.2 Search for data by using search methods of the Stream classes including findFirst, findAny, anyMatch, allMatch, noneMatch.
5.5 Sort a collection using Stream API.

The `Stream` interface provides several methods for searching for elements in streams: `allMatch`, `anyMatch`, `noneMatch`, `findFirst`, and `findAny`. All of these operations are terminal operations; that is, they all return a single value, not a stream.

In addition, all of these operations are *short-circuiting* operations: that is, as soon as the result is determined, then the operation stops. So, for instance, if you are using `allMatch()` to determine whether each element passes a matching test, as soon as an element that doesn't pass the test is found, the operation stops, and the boolean result, `false`, is returned. All these operations can also be parallelized, so all can operate on streams efficiently.

Searching to See Whether an Element Exists

The methods `allMatch()`, `anyMatch()`, and `noneMatch()` all take a `Predicate` to do a matching test and return a boolean. Let's go back to our trusty dogs, and try these methods on a stream of dogs. Here's the `Dog` class:

```
class Dog {
   private String name;
   private int age;
   private int weight;

   public Dog(String name, int weight, int age) {
      this.name = name; this.weight = weight; this.age = age;
   }
   // getters and setters here
   public String toString() {
      return this.name + " is " + this.age + " years old and weighs "
                      + this.weight + " pounds";
   }
}
```

And here's a `List` of dogs:

```
List<Dog> dogs = new ArrayList<>();
Dog boi = new Dog("boi", 30, 6);
Dog clover = new Dog("clover", 35, 12);
Dog aiko = new Dog("aiko", 50, 10);
Dog zooey = new Dog("zooey", 45, 8);
Dog charis = new Dog("charis", 120, 7);
dogs.add(boi); dogs.add(clover); dogs.add(aiko);
dogs.add(zooey); dogs.add(charis);
```

Now that we've got a `List` of dogs, we can stream it and perform stream pipeline operations on the dogs.

First, we'll look for dogs whose weight is greater than 50 pounds and whose names start with "c" using anyMatch(). The anyMatch() method will stop searching as soon as it's found at least one dog whose name starts with "c":

```
boolean cNames =
    dogs.stream()                                // stream the dogs
                                                 // keep dogs whose weight > 50
        .filter(d -> d.getWeight() > 50)
                                                 // do any dog names start with c?
        .anyMatch(d -> d.getName().startsWith("c"));
System.out.println(
    "Are there any dogs > 50 pounds whose name starts with 'c'? " + cNames);
```

You should see the output:

```
Are there any dogs > 50 pounds whose name starts with 'c'? true
```

The dog that matched must be "charis" because he weighs over 50 pounds.

Now let's use allMatch() to find whether all the dogs in the list have an age greater than 5. Here, we map the stream of dogs to a stream of their ages first and then use allMatch() to check each dog to make sure each has an age greater than 5. allMatch() will stop and return false as soon as it finds any dog that fails this test.

```
boolean isOlder =
    dogs.stream()
      .mapToInt(d -> d.getAge())     // map from Dog to the Dog's age (integer)
      .allMatch(a -> a > 5);         // do all dogs have an age > 5?
System.out.println("Are all the dogs age older than 5? " + isOlder);
```

All our dogs are older than 5, so you should see

```
Are all the dogs age older than 5? true
```

Finally, we'll use noneMatch() to make sure that none of the dogs in the stream are named "red". First, we map the stream of dogs to a stream of the dog names, and then we use noneMatch() to check the name:

```
boolean notRed =
    dogs.stream()
      .map(d -> d.getName())              // map from Dog to Dog's name (String)
      .noneMatch(n -> n.equals("red"));   // are any of the dogs named "red"?
System.out.println("None of the dogs are red: " + notRed);
```

Since none of our dogs have the name "red," you should see

```
None of the dogs are red: true
```

Searching to Find and Return an Object

All of these matching methods determine whether a match exists or not. If you want to actually get back a result of a match, then you can use findFirst() or findAny(). Neither of these methods takes an argument, so you need to filter first to narrow down the elements you might be searching for. Because filter() could potentially filter out all the elements of the stream, leaving you with an empty stream, you can guess that findFirst() and findAny() both return optionals in case they are called on empty streams; in which case, there is no valid result and the optional will be empty.

Let's use findAny() to find any Dog in our list of dogs that weighs more than 50 pounds and whose name begins with "c". You already know we have one of these dogs (we had a true result when we did the same test earlier with anyMatch()), but this time we want to actually get a Dog object back and use it.

```
Optional<Dog> c50 =
   dogs.stream()                                      // stream the dogs
      .filter(d -> d.getWeight() > 50)                // keep dogs with weight > 50
      .filter(d -> d.getName().startsWith("c"))       // keep dogs with name "c"
      .findAny();                                      // pick any dog from the
                                                       // stream
                                                       // and return it

c50.ifPresent(System.out::println);
```

The output is

```
charis is 7 years old and weighs 120 pounds
```

In this example, only one dog passed the tests in both filters; only "charis" weighs more than 50 pounds and has a name beginning with "c". So findAny() returns the one dog left in the stream when we call that operation.

But what if there's more than one dog in the stream when we call findAny()? For instance, if we look for any dog whose age is older than 5, all the dogs will pass that filter test, so all the dogs will still be in the stream when we call findAny():

```
Optional<Dog> d5 =
   dogs.stream()
      .filter(d -> d.getAge() > 5)
      .findAny();
d5.ifPresent(System.out::println);
```

You'll probably see the output:

```
boi is 6 years old and weighs 30 pounds
```

Of course, boi happens to be the first dog in the stream, but technically `findAny()` could return *any* of the dogs in the stream. There's no guarantee it will be the first one (particularly when you parallelize the stream, which we'll get to later on).

exam

Watch *Don't forget that all these matching and finding methods are short-circuiting. That means that as soon as `findAny()` finds a dog that matches, everything stops.*

Let's add a `peek()` at just the right spot to see what's happening in the stream when we run this code. Give this a try:

```
Optional<Dog> d5 =
    dogs.stream()
        .filter(d -> d.getAge() > 5).peek(System.out::println)
        .findAny();
d5.ifPresent(System.out::println);
```

Remember that `peek()` allows you to "peek" into the stream. It takes a `Consumer` and returns exactly the same stream as you call it on, so it makes no changes to anything. It's simply a window to what's flowing by on the stream.

Run this and you'll probably see

```
boi is 6 years old and weighs 30 pounds    // from the peek
boi is 6 years old and weighs 30 pounds    // from the final print
```

So if you're asked on the exam what output you'll see with a `peek()`, make sure you understand how this works. You might be tempted to choose an answer that shows all the dogs printed with the peek and then `boi` for the final print, but that wouldn't be correct.

Sorting

We often want to sort things stored in data structures, so it makes sense we might want to sort elements flowing through a stream pipeline, too. The `Stream` interface includes a `sorted()` method that you can use to sort a stream of elements by natural order or by providing a `Comparator` to determine the order.

Sorting by natural order is easy: just add the `sorted()` operator into the stream pipeline, like this:

```
Stream.of("Jerry", "George", "Kramer", "Elaine")
   .sorted()
   .forEach(System.out::println);
```

If you run this code, you'll see the output:

```
Elaine
George
Jerry
Kramer
```

What if you want to sort more complex objects, like Duck objects? Here's a Duck:

```
class Duck implements Comparable<Duck> {
   String name;
   String color;
   int age;

   public Duck(String name, String color, int age) {
      this.name = name; this.color = color; this.age = age;
   }
   // getters and setters here…
   public String toString() {
      return (getName() + " is " + getColor() + " and is "
            + getAge() + " years old.");
   }
   @Override                     // describe how to sort Ducks
   public int compareTo(Duck duck) {
      return this.getName().compareTo(duck.getName());
   }
}
```

We've gone ahead and made the Duck a Comparable and implemented the `compareTo()` method that sorts by name so we can sort these Ducks:

```
List<Duck> ducks = Arrays.asList(    // create a List of Ducks
   new Duck("Jerry", "yellow", 3),
   new Duck("George", "brown", 4),
   new Duck("Kramer", "mottled", 6),
   new Duck("Elaine", "white", 2)
);
ducks.stream()
     .sorted()                      // sort ducks by name
     .forEach(System.out::println);  // print them
```

Run this code and you should see

```
Elaine is white and is 2 years old.
George is brown and is 4 years old.
Jerry is yellow and is 3 years old.
Kramer is mottled and is 6 years old.
```

The `compareTo()` method we provided in the `Duck` class sorts the ducks by their names.

What if you want to change the sort when you stream the ducks? You can use `sorted()` with a `Comparator`:

```
ducks.stream()
    .sorted((d1, d2) -> d1.getAge() - d2.getAge())    // sort ducks by age
    .forEach(System.out::println);
```

Here, you're providing a `Comparator` to `sorted()` that it will use to sort the `Ducks` (instead of the `compareTo()` method in the `Duck` class). The result is

```
Elaine is white and is 2 years old.
Jerry is yellow and is 3 years old.
George is brown and is 4 years old.
Kramer is mottled and is 6 years old.
```

Now the ducks are sorted by age.

Comparators are handy because they can be defined separately from the class, like we did to sort the ducks by age rather than by name (which is the default sort order, defined by the `Comparable`).

Above, we passed the `Comparator` directly to the `sorted()` method using a lambda expression. If we wanted to, we could write out the `Comparator` separately, assign it to a variable, and then pass that variable to `sorted()`, like this:

```
Comparator<Duck> byAgeLambda = (d1, d2) -> d1.getAge() - d2.getAge();
ducks.stream()
    .sorted(byAgeLambda)             // pass the Comparator to sorted
    .forEach(System.out::println);
```

You've seen us use comparators like this before (in the previous chapter). `Comparator` also has some handy static methods that you're likely to see when defining comparators for use with streams: `comparing()`, `reversed()`, and `thenComparing()`.

Let's write three `Comparators` to sort ducks by their `color`, by their `name`, and by their `age`, using the `Comparator.comparing()` method. The `comparing()` method takes a `Function` whose functional method expects a property to sort by, like `Duck.age`, as an argument and returns a `Comparator` that compares objects by that property.

```
Comparator<Duck> byColor = Comparator.comparing(Duck::getColor);
Comparator<Duck> byName = Comparator.comparing(Duck::getName);
Comparator<Duck> byAge = Comparator.comparing(Duck::getAge);
```

Here, we're using a method reference to specify each `Function` that `comparing()` will use to get the properties of the `Duck` we want to compare by for each `Comparator`. Now that we have these comparators, we can use them to sort ducks in various combinations.

We can sort by age:

```
ducks.stream().sorted(byAge).forEach(System.out::println);
```

Or sort by age reversed:

```
ducks.stream().sorted(byAge.reversed()).forEach(System.out::println);
```

Note that `reversed()` is a method of the `Comparator`, that returns a new `Comparator` that has the reverse ordering.

We can also sort by one property and then by another property, using the `thenComparing()` method. `thenComparing()` returns a `Comparator` that compares first by the `Comparator` you call it on and then by the `Comparator` you pass in. To sort by name, and then by age, we'll write:

```
byName.thenComparing(byAge)
```

Before we do that, let's add a few more `Ducks`:

```
List<Duck> ducks = Arrays.asList(
    new Duck("Jerry", "yellow", 3),
    new Duck("George", "brown", 4),
    new Duck("Kramer", "mottled", 6),
    new Duck("Elaine", "white", 2),
    new Duck("Jerry", "mottled", 10),
    new Duck("George", "white", 12),
    new Duck("Kramer", "brown", 11),
    new Duck("Elaine", "brown", 13)
);
```

We have our original four ducks, as well as four new ducks with the same names but different colors and all much older. (Think of these as the "bizarro" ducks.)

Now let's sort the ducks, first by name and then by age:

```
ducks.stream()
    .sorted(byName.thenComparing(byAge))
    .forEach(System.out::println);
```

The result is:

```
Elaine is white and is 2 years old.
Elaine is brown and is 13 years old.
George is brown and is 4 years old.
George is white and is 12 years old.
Jerry is yellow and is 3 years old.
Jerry is mottled and is 10 years old.
Kramer is mottled and is 6 years old.
Kramer is brown and is 11 years old.
```

And, of course, we could sort by color and then by age:

```
ducks.stream()
    .sorted(byColor.thenComparing(byAge))
    .forEach(System.out::println);
```

Or a variety of other combinations.

Finally, another method of `Stream` that comes in handy when sorting streams is `distinct()`. This method returns a stream with distinct elements, so if an element is repeated in the stream, you'll end up with only one of them.

Let's say, for instance, that you want to see how many different colors your ducks are. You only need to see the color once, even if you have multiple ducks with the same color.

Here's a revised List of Ducks:

```
List<Duck> ducks = Arrays.asList(
    new Duck("Jerry", "yellow", 3),
    new Duck("George", "brown", 4),
    new Duck("Kramer", "mottled", 6),
    new Duck("Elaine", "white", 2),
    new Duck("Huey", "mottled", 2),
    new Duck("Louie", "white", 4),
    new Duck("Dewey", "brown", 6)
);
```

You can see that we have 1 yellow, 2 brown, 2 mottled, and 2 white ducks.

To get the list of distinct colors of ducks, we'll first map each `Duck` to its color, then use `distinct()` to make sure we get a stream of distinct color `Strings`, and then print those:

```
ducks.stream()
    .map(d -> d.getColor())      // get the duck colors
    .distinct()                  // make sure there are no repeats!
    .forEach(System.out::println); // print the colors
```

And we see

```
yellow
brown
mottled
white
```

e x a m
ⓦ a t c h

We slipped some method references into this section: `Duck::getColor`, `Duck::getName`, `Duck::getAge`, *and* `System.out::println`. *Recall from the previous chapter when we described how* `System.out::println` *is a method reference: a shorthand for a lambda expression. For example, we replaced a lambda expression like this:*

```
Stream.of("Elain","Jerry", "George", "Kramer")
    .forEach(n -> System.out.println(n));        // uses a lambda expression
```

with a method reference like this:

```
Stream.of("Elain","Jerry", "George", "Kramer")
    .forEach(System.out::println);               // uses a method reference
```

Method references simply replace lambda expressions that do nothing except call another function. For this instance method reference, `System.out` *is the class and* `println` *is the instance method. We use the* "`::`" *syntax to indicate the method reference.*

Take another look at `Duck::getColor`, `Duck::getName`, *and* `Duck::getAge`. *These, too, are method references to instance methods. They are a type of method reference that refers to a nonstatic method of an instance of a type. If we wrote those method references out as lambda expressions, they'd look like this:*

```
Comparator<Duck> byColor = Comparator.comparing(d -> d.getColor());
Comparator<Duck> byName = Comparator.comparing(d -> d.getName());
Comparator<Duck> byAge = Comparator.comparing(d -> d.getAge());
```

So, for instance, the lambda `d -> d.getColor()` *is a* `Function` *whose functional method takes an object of type* `Duck` *and returns an object of type* `String`, *mapping a* `Duck` *to his or her color.*

The code

```
Comparator<Duck> byColor = Comparator.comparing(Duck::getColor);
```

uses an instance method reference *to replace the lambda, where the instance we're using is an instance of* `Duck` *and the method is* `getColor()`. *Remember, method references are shorthand for lambdas that just turn around and call another method.*

Methods to Search and Sort Streams

The searching and sorting methods on streams are straightforward; the main thing is to get the types correct! Table 9-5 details these methods.

TABLE 9-5   Searching and Sorting on Streams

Interface	Method	Description
`Stream`	`allMatch(Predicate<? super T> predicate)`	Returns a `boolean`; true if all elements in the stream pass the `Predicate` test. Stops when any element fails the test.
`Stream`	`anyMatch(Predicate<? super T> predicate)`	Returns a `boolean`; true if any of the elements in the stream pass the `Predicate` test. Stops when any element passes the test.
`Stream`	`noneMatch(Predicate<? super T> predicate)`	Returns a `boolean`; true if none of the elements in the stream pass the `Predicate` test. Stops when any element passes the test.
`Stream`	`findFirst()`	Returns an `Optional<T>` with the first element from the stream or an empty optional if the stream is empty.
`Stream`	`findAny()`	Returns an `Optional<T>` with an element from the stream (no guarantees about which one!) or an empty optional if the stream is empty.

`DoubleStream, IntStream, LongStream`	`allMatch(DoublePredicate predicate),`
	
	`allMatch(IntPredicate predicate),`
	
	`allMatch(LongPredicate predicate)`
		Returns a `boolean`; true if all elements in the stream pass the `Predicate` test. Stops when any element fails the test.

`DoubleStream, IntStream, LongStream`	`anyMatch(DoublePredicate predicate),`
	
	`anyMatch(IntPredicate predicate),`
	
	`anyMatch(LongPredicate predicate)`
		Returns a `boolean`; true if any of the elements in the stream pass the `Predicate` test. Stops when any element passes the test.

TABLE 9-5	Searching and Sorting on Streams (*Continued*)	
Interface	**Method**	**Description**
DoubleStream, IntStream, LongStream	noneMatch(DoublePredicate predicate), noneMatch(IntPredicate predicate), noneMatch(LongPredicate predicate)	Returns a boolean; true if none of the elements in the stream pass the Predicate test. Stops when any element passes the test.
DoubleStream	findFirst()	Returns an OptionalDouble: the first element in the stream or an empty optional if the stream is empty.
IntStream	findFirst()	Returns an OptionalInt: the first element in the stream or an empty optional if the stream is empty.
LongStream	findFirst()	Returns an OptionalLong: the first element in the stream or an empty optional if the stream is empty.
DoubleStream	findAny()	Returns an OptionalDouble: an element in the stream or an empty optional if the stream is empty.
IntStream	findAny()	Returns an OptionalInt: an element in the stream or an empty optional if the stream is empty.
LongStream	findAny()	Returns an OptionalDouble: an element in the stream or an empty optional if the stream is empty.
Stream, DoubleStream, IntStream, LongStream	sorted()	Returns a Stream<T> (or primitive stream type). Sort elements of a stream by natural order
Stream	sorted(Comparator<? super T> comparator)	Returns a Stream<T>. Sort elements of a stream by the provided Comparator.
Stream, DoubleStream, IntStream, LongStream	distinct()	Returns a Stream<T> (or primitive stream type) with distinct elements. For Stream<T>, the Object.equals(Object) test is used.

Don't Modify the Source of a Stream

You might have heard that when you're using Java streams, you are programming in a "functional" style. Aside from being a more declarative way of writing code (thus the stream pipeline versus several statements to specify operations), the key tenet of functional programming is to avoid *side effects*—that is, changing state stored in variables and fields—during computation. Instead, you process data using operations that produce new values (rather than changing old ones). Functional programming style makes it easier to prove the correctness of your program and to replicate results, and avoiding state changes makes it easier to implement optimizations in the compiled code. Although Java is far from being a functional programming language, streams are a step toward a functional style of programming that encourages this idea of avoiding state changes on the original data structure being processed via a stream.

At this point in the chapter, we're going to share something really important about streams. That is, you should never, ever try to modify the source of a stream from within the stream pipeline.

You might be tempted at times, but don't. It just isn't done. Java won't give you a compile-time error if you try and may not even give you a runtime error, although your results will not be guaranteed. But just don't do it. Ever.

One reason you might be tempted, say, is if you're looking for elements that pass a test and you want to modify that element in the source, or perhaps even delete that element from the source. For example, you might want to remove all dogs who weigh less than 50 pounds from the list of dogs:

```
dogs.stream().filter(d -> {
    if (d.getWeight() < 50) {
        dogs.remove(d);
        return false;
    }
    return true;
}).forEach(System.out::println);
```

You might *think* that you'll see a list of the dogs whose weights are greater than or equal to 50, and you might *think* the dogs list will now contain only dogs whose weights are greater than or equal to 50, but what you'll probably get instead is something like this:

```
aiko is 10 years old and weighs 50 pounds
Exception in thread "main" java.lang.NullPointerException
```

So what do you do if you want to get a list of all dogs whose weight is greater than or equal to 50 after you've done the stream computation?

The best way to do this is to collect the dogs at the end of the stream pipeline into a new collection. And, of course, Java provides an easy way for you to do just that with the `Stream.collect()` method.

Let's collect all dogs who weigh 50 pounds or more. Remember, here are our dogs:

```
List<Dog> dogs = new ArrayList<>();
Dog boi = new Dog("boi", 30, 6);
Dog clover = new Dog("clover", 35, 12);
Dog aiko = new Dog("aiko", 50, 10);
Dog zooey = new Dog("zooey", 45, 8);
Dog charis = new Dog("charis", 120, 7);
dogs.add(boi); dogs.add(clover); dogs.add(aiko);
dogs.add(zooey); dogs.add(charis);
```

Looking at that list, we'd expect to end up with two dogs: Aiko who weighs 50 pounds and Charis who weighs 120 pounds (that's a big dog!).

Here's how we can use a stream pipeline to filter all dogs who weigh 50 pounds or more and collect them into a new `List`, heavyDogs:

```
List<Dog> heavyDogs =
    dogs.stream()                            // stream the dogs
        .filter(d -> d.getWeight() >= 50) // filter only dogs >= 50 pounds
        .collect(Collectors.toList());    // collect the dogs into a new List
```

We can then print this list:

```
heavyDogs.forEach(System.out::println);
```

And see the output:

```
aiko is 10 years old and weighs 50 pounds
charis is 7 years old and weighs 120 pounds
```

Collecting Values from Streams (OCP Objectives 3.8, 5.6, and 9.3)

3.8   Use method references with Streams.
5.6   Save results to a collection using the collect method and group/partition data using the Collectors class.
9.3   Use Stream API with NIO.2.

The `collect()` method is a reduction operation: it reduces a stream into a collection of objects or a value. The `Collector` you pass to the method specifies how to reduce the stream, say, into a `List` or a `Set`. The `Collectors` class provides implementations of `Collector` that each determine how you collect, everything from methods to make a simple list, like `toList()`, to methods that allow you to group items in your `Collection`, resulting in a map so values are organized by a key value.

As you collect, you can

- Group values together based on a `Function` (returns a `Map`)
- Partition values into true/false partitions based on a `Predicate` (returns a `Map`)
- Map values into other values using a `Function` (returns a `Collector`)
- Join values into a `String`
- Count values as you collect

Let's make a `Person` class and a nice collection of people with names and ages, so we have some data to work with. Then we'll stream the `Collection` of people and use the various `Collectors` to process the data in a few different ways.

Here's the `Person` class:

```
class Person {
    public String name;
    public Integer age;

    public Person(String name, Integer age) {
        this.name = name; this.age = age;
    }
    public String getName() { return this.name; }
    public Integer getAge() { return this.age; }
    public String toString() {
        return this.name + " is " + this.age + " years old";
    }
}
```

Now, we'll make a bunch of `Persons` and add them to a `List`:

```
Person beth = new Person("Beth", 30);
Person eric = new Person("Eric", 31);
Person deb = new Person("Deb", 31);
```

```
Person liz = new Person("Liz", 30);
Person wendi = new Person("Wendi", 34);
Person kathy = new Person("Kathy", 35);
Person bert = new Person("Bert", 32);
Person bill = new Person("Bill", 34);
Person robert = new Person("Robert", 38);

List<Person> people = new ArrayList<Person>();
people.add(beth); people.add(eric); people.add(deb);
people.add(liz); people.add(wendi); people.add(kathy);
people.add(bert); people.add(bill); people.add(robert);
```

Now that we have a great collection of people with names and ages, we can stream people and use `Collectors` to organize and process our collection. Let's begin with the simplest way to collect people: we'll collect everyone whose age is 34 into a `List`:

```
List<Person> peopleAge34 =
    people.stream()                        // stream the people
        .filter(p -> p.getAge() == 34)     // find people age 34
        .collect(Collectors.toList());     // collect 34s into a new List
System.out.println("People aged 34: "      // print 34s
            + peopleAge34);
```

Here, we're streaming the `List` of `Persons`, using `filter()` with a `Predicate` to test to see whether the `Person`'s age is 34, and collecting those `Persons` who pass that test into a new `List`.

When we print that `List`, we see

```
People aged 34: [Wendi is 34 years old, Bill is 34 years old]
```

There's no guarantee what kind of `List` you get using `Collectors.toList()`. If you specifically want an `ArrayList`, you can use the `toCollection()` method instead, like this:

```
List<Person> peopleAge34 =
    people.stream()                        // stream the people
        .filter(p -> p.getAge() == 34)     // find people age 34
        .collect(Collectors.toCollection(ArrayList::new));   // make an ArrayList
```

And get the same output.

exam
watch

Notice here that we're passing a method reference to the `Collectors` *.toCollection()* *method. Looking at the documentation for* `Collectors.toCollection()`, *we see that this method takes a* `Supplier` *whose functional method must return a new empty* `Collection` *of the "appropriate type." We could write the code like this:*

```
ArrayList<Dog> heavyDogs =
    dogs.stream()
      .filter(d -> d.getWeight() >= 50)
      .collect(Collectors.toCollection(() -> new ArrayList<Dog>()));
```

providing the `Supplier () -> new ArrayList<Dog>()` *as the argument to* `Collectors.toCollection()`. *Recall that a method reference is shorthand for a lambda expression that just turns around and calls another method. So by writing* `ArrayList::new` *instead of the lambda, we are saying the same thing as the lambda expression above: that is, just call the constructor (with new) of an* `ArrayList<Dog>` *to create a new* `ArrayList`. *This is a slightly different kind of method reference than you saw earlier in this chapter, when we used instance method references to refer to instance methods, like a* `Duck`'s `getColor()` *method with* `Duck::getColor`. *This form of method reference is the* **constructor method reference**, *and it's just a shorthand for a lambda that creates a new instance of a class.*

Using collect() with Files.lines()

Think back to how we handled getting DVDs from a file using `Files.lines()` earlier (in the section "Create a Stream from a File"). In that example, we streamed `String` data about DVDs from the file and added DVDs one at a time to a `List` in a `forEach()` consumer:

```
List<DVDInfo> dvds = new ArrayList<DVDInfo>();
try (Stream<String> stream = Files.lines(Paths.get(filename))) {
    stream.forEach(line -> {
        String[] dvdItems = line.split("/");
        DVDInfo dvd = new DVDInfo(dvdItems[0], dvdItems[1], dvdItems[2]);
        dvds.add(dvd);  // need a better way to do this!
    });
}
```

Now that you know how to use `collect()`, you can probably think of a better way to do this, right? While the solution above works, it's not the recommended way to collect items from a stream into a `List` because you are modifying an object that's defined outside the stream pipeline—in other words, your stream pipeline has a *side effect*. Using `collect()` is the preferred way to do this, and, as you'll see, along with avoiding an unnecessary side effect, it also makes your code clearer.

Here's another quick example of using `Files.lines()` to stream data from a file, and this time we'll add that data to a `List` using `collect()`. Imagine we have a file, "names.txt," with the following names in it:

```
Jerry
George
Kramer
Elaine
Huey
Louie
Dewey
```

Using `collect()`, we can easily add these names to a `List`, like this:

```
String filename = "names.txt";
try (Stream<String> stream = Files.lines(Paths.get(filename))) {
   List<String> data = stream.collect(Collectors.toList()); // collect names
   data.forEach(System.out::println);                       // print names
} catch(IOException e) {
   System.out.println(e);
}
```

EXERCISE 9-1

Collecting Items in a List

Try rewriting the earlier DVDs example to use `collect()` instead of adding DVDs manually to the `dvds` List in the `forEach()` loop. Just as with the simple names example, you can use `Collectors.toList()` to add DVDs to the `dvds` List. Here's a hint: you'll need to map the lines (`Strings`) you're streaming from the "dvdinfo.txt" file to `DVDInfo` objects before you collect them.

Using `collect()` is a much better, and preferred way, to collect streamed items into a `List`.

Grouping and Partitioning

Now what if we want to group people by age? We can use the `Collectors.groupingBy()` method. We specify *how* to group `Person` objects by passing a `Function` to the `groupingBy()` method, which returns a `Collector` that will collect data elements from the stream and group them in a `Map` by a key, according to that `Function`.

You can think of the `Function` as a "classification function." If we want to group people by age, then we need to pass a `Function` to `groupingBy()` that maps a `Person` to their age:

```
Map<Integer, List<Person>> peopleByAge =
    people.stream()
        .collect(Collectors.groupingBy(Person::getAge));
System.out.println("People by age: " + peopleByAge);
```

When we print the resulting `Map`, we see

```
People by age: {32=[Bert is 32 years old], 34=[Wendi is 34 years old, Bill
is 34 years old], 35=[Kathy is 35 years old], 38=[Robert is 38 years old],
30=[Beth is 30 years old, Liz is 30 years old], 31=[Eric is 31 years old, Deb
is 31 years old]}
```

Notice that the `Map` you get back uses an age (`Integer`) as a key and the value is a `List` of the same type of object in the stream; in this case, that's `Person`. Also notice that the way `System.out.println()` shows us a `Person` in the output is by using the `toString()` method, but the values in the `List` associated with each are not `Strings`; they are `Persons` (you can see from the type parameter on `List<Person>` that that is the case).

So now we have a map with `Integers` (ages) for keys and `List<Person>`s for values, and we can see that, for instance, Bert is 32 and Wendi and Bill are 34, and so on.

The `groupingBy()` method is heavily overloaded with a variety of options for grouping values in a `Collection`. For instance, you can use a version of `groupingBy()` that takes a classification `Function` as a first argument and a `Collector` as a second argument. That `Collector` argument allows you to reduce the values of the `Map` you get as the result of the `groupingBy()` method, thus reducing each value `List` into another value. Yeah, we know, that's tricky to understand, so let's look at an example.

Here, we're going to group people by age, but rather than create a `List` of the people associated with a certain age in a `Map`, as we did above, now we're going to count the number of people in the `List` associated with a given age and use that value in the resulting `Map` instead. So we have two reductions going on here: we have a `groupingBy()` reduction to group people by age and then we have a counting() reduction to count the people in the List associated with a particular age:

```
Map<Integer, Long> numPeopleWithAge =
    people.stream()
        .collect(Collectors.groupingBy(    // we're going to group by...
            Person::getAge,                 // ... age
            Collectors.counting()));        // and count rather than List
System.out.println("People by age: " + numPeopleWithAge);
```

The result of this code is

```
People by age: {32=1, 34=2, 35=1, 38=1, 30=2, 31=2}
```

So now we can see we have 2 people who are 30, 2 people who are 34, 2 people who are 31, and 1 of each other age. To count the people in each list, we use the Collectors.counting() method, which returns a Collector that simply counts the number of input elements. The result of calling collect() on this Collector is a Map from ages to the number of people of a given age.

What if we want to group people by age, but list only their name rather than the entire Person object in the Map? That is, we want a map of ages and names (Map<Integer, List<String>>) rather than a map of ages and Person objects (Map<Integer, List<Person>>)?

We can do that by passing a Collectors.mapping() Collector as that second argument to groupingBy():

```
Map<Integer, List<String>> namesByAge =
    people.stream()
        .collect(
            Collectors.groupingBy(
                Person::getAge,              // group by age
                Collectors.mapping(          // map from Person to...
                    Person::getName,         // .. name
                    Collectors.toList()      // collect names in a list
                )
            )
        );
System.out.println("People by age: " + namesByAge);
```

Here, we're streaming the people and calling the collect() method on the stream, passing in the groupingBy collector. This groupingBy() collector takes two arguments, the Function that determines how we're going to group (by age) and another Collector that tells us how to reduce the values in the Map associated with each age. Remember that for the simplest version of groupingBy(), each value is just a List of Persons who are that age. But now we're using the mapping() collector to further reduce or modify that List of Persons.

The mapping() method maps each Person to another value. What we'd like to do is map a Person to their name. Taking a look at the mapping() method, we see that its first argument is a Function whose functional method takes an object of the type we're mapping from (a Person) and returns another object, in this case, the Person's name, a String. The second argument to mapping() is a collector that tells us what to do with the potentially multiple values we're mapping. Remember that we can have multiple people of the same age, so we're mapping a List of Persons to a List of their names. That second argument specifies how we'd like to collect those names. We'll use toList() to keep it easy, but you could also choose toCollection() to create an ArrayList or some other collection for the names.

The output we see is

```
People by age: {32=[Bert], 34=[Wendi, Bill], 35=[Kathy], 38=[Robert],
30=[Beth, Liz], 31=[Eric, Deb]}
```

So now our Map maps age keys to Lists of String names.

Partitioning as you collect is essentially a more specialized kind of groupingBy(). The partitioningBy() method organizes the results into a Map like groupingBy() does, but partitioningBy() takes a Predicate rather than a Function, so the results are split into two groups (partitions) based on whether the items in the stream pass the test in the Predicate. Let's partition our results by the test: is the person older than 34?

```
Map<Boolean, List<Person>> peopleOlderThan34 =
    people.stream()
        .collect(
            Collectors.partitioningBy(p -> p.getAge() > 34));
System.out.println("People > 34: " + peopleOlderThan34);
```

As you might expect, the result is a Map that maps booleans to Persons, so all people 34 or younger will be mapped to the key false, and all people older than 34 will be mapped to the key true:

```
People > 34: {false=[Beth is 30 years old, Eric is 31 years old, Deb is 31
years old, Liz is 30 years old, Wendi is 34 years old, Bert is 32 years old,
Bill is 34 years old], true=[Kathy is 35 years old, Robert is 38 years old]}
```

Perhaps you can see how powerful streams and collectors are together? Although this code may not feel intuitive to you, it certainly is more concise than writing the equivalent code without using streams to create these Maps, and you avoid having to create some intermediate data structures yourself. The whole idea is that Java can optimize the code used to create the resulting Maps behind the scenes so these types of operations become a lot more efficient.

atch

We slipped another example of an instance method reference by you in this section: `Person::getAge`. *We did this to group people by age.* `groupingBy()` *takes a* `Function` *that maps a* `Person` *object to another value to use that value as the mapping key—in this case, telling* `groupingBy()` *to map people by age.*

The method reference `Person::getAge` *is an instance method reference that refers to a nonstatic method of an instance of a* `Person`. *If we wrote that method reference out as a lambda expression, it would look like this:*

```
(p) -> p.getAge()
```

So this lambda is a `Function` *whose functional method takes an object of type* `Person` *and returns an object of type* `Integer`, *mapping a* `Person` *to their age.*

Summing and Averaging

A couple of other useful collectors are `summingInt()` and `averagingInt()` (and their long and double counterparts). As you might guess, these need to work on numbers, so both take a `ToIntFunction` (that is a `Function` that maps an object to an `int`). To experiment with these, we'll need to add a few more people to our list of people. We're going to add people with the same names so we can group by name and then find the sum of ages and the average of ages. You'll see what we mean in just a moment. Let's first add three more people to our list:

```
Person bill2 = new Person("Bill", 40);
Person beth2 = new Person("Beth", 45);
Person bert2 = new Person("Bert", 38);
people.add(bill2); people.add(beth2); people.add(bert2);
```

Now we have two people named "Bert" in our list; the first Bert (from way back) is age 32, and the second Bert (bert2) is age 38. Likewise, for "Beth" and "Bill," we now have two people with the name "Beth" and two people with the name "Bill," each of different ages.

First, we want to sum the ages of the two Berts, the two Beths, and the two Bills, and group by name. Perhaps we're computing person-years of life experience of all people whose names begin with "B." (This scenario is completely contrived, of course, but if you were counting occurrences of Scrabble words, then this would make a lot more sense.)

Here's how we get the sum of the ages of people whose names begin with "B" and group by name:

```
Map<String, Integer> sumOfBAges =
    people.stream()                                    // stream people
        .filter(p -> p.getName().startsWith("B"))      // filter "B" names
        .collect(                                       // collect
            Collectors.groupingBy(                      // groupBy
            Person::getName,                            // … name
            Collectors.summingInt(Person::getAge)       // and sum of ages
        )
    );
System.out.println("People by sum of age: " + sumOfBAges);
```

The output of this code is

```
People by sum of age: {Bill=74, Beth=75, Bert=70}
```

The code took the ages of the two Bills and added them together. It does the same thing with the two Beths and the two Berts, and groups the results by name in a Map. So the total age of all the Bills is 74, all the Beths is 75, and all the Berts is 70.

What about the average age of the people whose names begin with "B"? Yep, that's what `averagingInt()` is for:

```
Map<String, Double> avgOfBAges =    // note we need Double not Integer
                                    // for the values!
    people.stream()
        .filter(p -> p.getName().startsWith("B"))
        .collect(
            Collectors.groupingBy(
                Person::getName,
                // now average ages instead of sum of ages
                Collectors.averagingInt(Person::getAge)
            )
    );
System.out.println("People by avg of age: " + avgOfBAges);
```

This code produces the output:

```
People by avg of age: {Bill=37.0, Beth=37.5, Bert=35.0}
```

Now, we've computed the average age of all the Bills, the average age of all the Beths, and the average age of all the Berts, grouped them by name, and collected the results in a Map.

It's important to note here that the `averagingInt()` Collector reduces the ages to a Double, so the type signature on this Map is Map<String, Double>

(compare with the type signature on the result of the `summingInt()` `Collector` example, which is `Map<String, Integer>`).

In both these examples, we are first collecting `Person` objects, grouping people by name, and then doing a second reduction on the `Person` objects that are the values of the first (implicit) `Map` created by the grouping. In the case of `summingInt()`, we are reducing with a `Collector` that sums the ages of all the `Person` objects associated with a given name; in the case of `averagingInt()`, we are reducing with a `Collector` that averages the ages of all the `Person` objects associated with a given name. Sometimes these second reductions on the value portions of the first reduction are called "downstream processing" because they work on the results of the first reduction on a stream.

Counting, joining, maxBy, and minBy

So far we've looked at collectors that, when used with the `collect()` method, reduce a stream to a `Collection` type, like a `List` or a `Map`. There are a few other collectors that work with `collect()` to reduce a stream to a single value, such as a `String`, instead.

We used the `Collectors.counting()` method above to create a `Collector` that counts elements being collected. A simple example of using `counting()` is

```
Long n = people.stream().collect(Collectors.counting());
System.out.println("Count: " + n);
```

This simply counts the items in the people stream. You already know how to do this with the `Stream` method `count()`, and there's no reason to create a `Collector` here to count elements in a stream, so we provide this example just to show how it works at the most basic level. More typically, you'll find `Collectors.counting()` used like we did above, as part of a `groupingBy()` operation.

The `Collectors.joining()` method returns a `Collector` that takes stream elements and concatenates them into a `String` by order in which they are encountered (which may or may not be the order of the original `Collection` you're streaming!).

For instance, we can get the name of every `Person` who's older than 34 and join those names together into one `String` like this:

```
String older34 =
    people.stream()                              // stream people
        .filter(p -> p.getAge() > 34)            // filter for older than 34
        .map(Person::getName)                    // map Person to name
        .collect(Collectors.joining(","));       // join names into one string
System.out.println("Names of people older than 34: " + older34);
```

Here, we're streaming the people `List` (the original list, without the duplicate names), filtering to get only people older than 34, mapping those people to their names (so at that point in the pipeline, we have a stream of `String` names), and then collecting those names into one `String`, with each name separated by a comma:

```
Names of people older than 34: Kathy,Robert
```

The `joining()` method requires as input an object that implements the `CharSequence` interface and includes `String`, which is what we're using here.

The methods `maxBy()` and `minBy()` do what you expect: they collect (reduce) to the max and min of the input elements, respectively. Let's use `maxBy()` to find the oldest person in the `people` stream:

```
Optional<Person> oldest =
  people.stream()
    .collect(Collectors.maxBy((p1, p2) -> p1.getAge() - p2.getAge()));
oldest.ifPresent(p -> System.out.println("Oldest person: " + p));
```

The `maxBy()` method takes a `Comparator` (as does `minBy()`) to compare the elements from the stream as they are being collected and returns a `Collector` that, when used with the `Stream.collect()` method, will reduce the stream to the "max" of the elements in the stream as measured by that `Comparator`.

Notice that `maxBy()` returns an `Optional<Person>`, not a `Person`, because when finding the max as you are collecting a stream, if that stream is empty, there will be no value. So we use the `ifPresent()` method of the `Optional` to make sure there is a value there before we try to print it out.

The advantage to finding the max of our `Person` stream using `collect()` with the `maxBy()` collector, rather than just using the `max()` terminal operation on the stream, like this:

```
people.stream().mapToInt(p -> p.getAge()).max();
```

is that our result is a `Person` object. Remember, `IntStream.max()` works only on numbers, so we when we mapped our `Person` stream to a stream of `Integers` in order to use `max()` to find the oldest person, we got a number back. By using `maxBy()` with `collect()`, we can find the `Person` object who has the highest age and get the whole `Person` back, not just their age. (We could also use the `Stream` `.max()` method and provide a comparator to do essentially the same thing.)

Stream Methods to Collect and Their Collectors

Using streams with collectors can get fairly complex, especially when you have multiple downstream operations. On the exam, you'll likely see only one or two levels of nesting when using collectors (e.g., a `groupingBy()` used with a mapping()) but be sure to get lots of practice using the `Stream` `collect()` method with collectors of various kinds.

Table 9-6 shows the variations on the `collect()` method. In this section we used only the first variation—the simplest method that takes a `Collector` created with one of the `Collectors` methods [e.g., `toList()`]—but be aware of the other variation where you need to supply supplier, accumulator, and combiner arguments to specify how the `collect()` method reduces elements in case it shows up on the exam. Most of the time, you'll typically use a `Collectors` method to create a `Collector` (which you can think of as an abstraction hiding the details

TABLE 9-6	Using Streams with Collectors	
Interface	**Method**	**Description**
`Stream`	`collect(Collector<? super T, A, R>` `collector)`	Reduces a stream to an instance of a mutable type, like a `Collection`. The `Collector` stands in for a constructor, an accumulator, and a combiner (see below).

`Stream`	`collect(Supplier<R> supplier,`
	    `BiConsumer(<R,? super T>`
	        `accumulator,`
	    `BiConsumer<R, R> combiner)`
		Reduces a stream to an instance of a mutable type. `Supplier` provides a new instance of the mutable type such as a `Collection`; accumulator adds each element of the stream to the collection; combiner specifies how to merge elements from one collection to another. A `Collector` can be used to capture all three components.

`DoubleStream,`
`IntStream,`
`LongStream`
	`collect(Supplier<R> supplier,`
	    `ObjDoubleConsumer(<R>`
	        `accumulator,`
	    `BiConsumer<R, R> combiner)`
	
	`collect(Supplier<R> supplier,`
	    `ObjIntConsumer(<R>`
	        `accumulator,`
	    `BiConsumer<R, R> combiner)`
	
	`collect(Supplier<R> supplier,`
	    `ObjLongConsumer(<R>`
	        `accumulator,`
	    `BiConsumer<R, R> combiner)`
		Reduces a stream to an instance of a mutable type.

of a supplier, accumulator, and combiner that actually determine how the collect reduction is done) and use that with collect(), as we did in this section.

Table 9-7 shows some of the Collectors methods you can use to create Collectors to collect elements; for more options and variations (which will likely not be on the exam), check out the Collectors class in the documentation. Remember that all the methods in the Collectors class are static methods that each produce a Collector—and don't get those two types mixed up!

TABLE 9-7	Collectors Methods

Method	Description
toList()	Returns a Collector that accumulates elements into a new List.
toMap(Function<? super T, ? extends K> keyMapper, Function<? super T, ? extends U> valueMapper)	Returns a Collector that accumulates elements into a new Map.
toSet()	Returns a Collector that accumulates elements into a new Set.
toCollection(Supplier<C> collectionFactory)	Returns a Collector that accumulates elements into a new Collection.
groupingBy(Function<? super T, ? extends K> classifier)	Returns a Collector that implements the group by operation, which groups elements by a classification Function, and returns the results in a Map. We used this to map Person objects by age.
groupingBy(Function<? super T, ? extends K> classifier, Collector<? super T, A, D> downstream)	Returns a Collector that groups elements according to a classification Function and then performs an additional reduction on the values associated with a given key in the resulting Map. We used this to count the number of people of a certain age and map the count to age.
partitioningBy(Predicate<? super T> predicate)	Returns a Collector that partitions elements according to the Predicate (into true and false partitions) and returns a Map. This is a more specific version of groupingBy.
mapping(Function<? super T, ? extends U> mapper, Collector<? super U, A, R> downstream)	Modifies a Collector that accepts elements of type U into a Collector that accepts elements of type T by applying the mapper Function to each element before it's accumulated in the Collector's reduction. We used this to map a Person object to a String (the person's name) before grouping by the person's age.

TABLE 9-7	Collectors Methods (*Continued*)
Method	**Description**
summingInt(ToIntFunction<? super T> mapper)	Returns a `Collector` that computes the sum of input elements. We used this to sum the ages (type `Integer`) of `Person` objects with the same name; we used the mapper to map a `Person` to their age. Similar methods are `summingDouble` and `summingLong` (producing a `Double` sum and a `Long` sum, respectively). If no elements are present, the result is 0.

averagingInt(
  ToIntFunction<? super T>
    mapper)
	Returns a `Collector` that computes the average of input elements. We used this to create a `Map` of `Person` names and their average age (type `Double`). Similar methods are `averagingDouble` and `averagingLong` (both of which produce `Double` values for the average). The mapper we used maps a `Person` to their age.

counting()	Returns a `Collector` that counts the number of elements and returns a `long`. If no elements are present, the result is 0.
joining()	Returns a `Collector` that concatenates elements into a `String`. We used this to concatenate `Person` names to associate a `String` of names with an age.
maxBy(Comparator<? super T> comparator)	Returns a `Collector` that returns the maximum element determined by the `Comparator`.
minBy(Comparator<? super T> comparator)	Returns a `Collector` that returns the minimum element determined by the `Comparator`.

CERTIFICATION OBJECTIVE

Streams of Streams (OCP Objective 5.7)

5.7   Use flatMap() methods in the Stream API.

Imagine you have a file containing space-separated words in multiple lines. Something like this:

```
rabbits dogs giraffes lions Java tigers
penguins Java deer birds Java Java monkeys
horses whales Java antelope bears Java
Java insects Java raccoons rats zebras
koalas snakes spiders cats hippopotamuses
```

You want to read the file and determine how many times the word "Java" appears in the file.

You already know you can create a stream from a file, so you do that to get started:

```
Stream<String> input = Files.lines(Paths.get("java.txt"));
```

So far so good.

Now, you know the input stream is going to stream one line at a time from the file "java.txt," and so to get words, rather than lines, you can split each line, like this:

```
input.map(line -> line.split(" "))
```

What does this produce? You know the split() method on String creates an array of Strings, and you know map() produces a stream, so what this line of code does is take the stream of lines coming from the file, splits each line into a String[], and generates a Stream of String arrays, which we write as Stream<String[]>:

```
Stream<String[]> inputStream = input.map(line -> line.split(" "));
```

So what do we do with a stream of String arrays? What we want is the individual strings in each array, so we can filter the words that are equal to "Java" and count them to see how many times "Java" appears in the file. So how do we turn the Stream<String[]> into a stream of Strings?

What if we stream each of the arrays in the stream? We know we can create a stream from an array with Arrays.stream() and that inputStream is a stream of String arrays. What about mapping each array to a stream, so each array becomes a stream of strings, and then process that? Let's try:

```
inputStream.map(array -> Arrays.stream(array)).forEach(System.out::println);
```

This is what you'll see:

```
java.util.stream.ReferencePipeline$Head@72ea2f77
java.util.stream.ReferencePipeline$Head@33c7353a
java.util.stream.ReferencePipeline$Head@681a9515
java.util.stream.ReferencePipeline$Head@3af49f1c
java.util.stream.ReferencePipeline$Head@19469ea2
```

Hmm, something's not quite right... We expected each word from the file to print, but instead we see what looks like streams. Why?

Well, what we're creating with

```
inputStream.map(array -> Arrays.stream(array))
```

is actually a stream of streams:

```
Stream<Stream<String>> ss =
    inputStream.map(array -> Arrays.stream(array));
```

So when we try to print this out:

```
ss.forEach(System.out::println);
```

each item we see displayed is a `Stream<String>`, rather than a `String`. When we streamed each array of `Strings` created by the split, each of those streams becomes an element in the main stream that is streaming the arrays. Thus, a stream of streams.

What can we do with a stream of streams? Well, it turns out there's a method just for this situation in the Stream API: `flatMap()`.

The `flatMap()` method is similar to `map()` in that it maps a stream of one type into a stream of another type, but it does something extra; `flatMap()` "flattens" out the streams, essentially concatenating them into one stream. It replaces each stream with its contents, creating one stream from many.

So instead of mapping each array to a stream, we're going to *flat map* each array to a stream. The stream that results from the `flatMap()` is one big flat stream, rather than a stream of streams. That's really hard to see without an example, so let's give this a try:

```
Stream<String> ss =
    inputStream.flatMap(array -> Arrays.stream(array));
ss.forEach(System.out::println);
```

Think of taking a two-dimensional array and flattening it to a one-dimensional array, like this:

```
[ [ 1, 2 ], [ 3, 4 ] ] -> [ 1, 2, 3, 4 ]  .
```

That's what `flatMap()` does with streams. The result of using `flatMap()` on the stream of arrays is a flat stream of all the contents of each array, which is the words in the file.

If you run that code, you'll see all the words in the file:

```
rabbits
dogs
giraffes
lions
Java
tigers
penguins
Java
deer
...
```

Great! We've made progress. Our goal is count the number of words equal to "Java." Hopefully that task is easier now; you just need to `filter()` and `count()`. Here's the whole code so you can run it yourself:

```
try {
  long n = Files.lines(Paths.get("java.txt")) // stream lines from the file
    .map(line -> line.split(" "))              // split each line into String[]
    .flatMap(array -> Arrays.stream(array))    // stream arrays, and flatten
    .filter(w -> w.equals("Java"))             // filter the words = "Java"
    .count();                                  // count "Java"
  System.out.println("Number of times 'Java' appears: " + n);
} catch (IOException e) {
  System.out.println("Oops, error! " + e.getMessage());
}
```

Run that and you should see that "Java" appears in the file eight times.

The `Stream` interface also includes `flatMapToDouble()`, `flatMapToInt()`, and `flatMapToLong()`, to flat map to a `DoubleStream`, an `IntStream`, and a `LongStream`, respectively, in case you need that. Each of the primitive stream types just mentioned also include their own `flatMap()` methods that take a `DoubleFunction`, an `IntFunction`, and a `LongFunction`, respectively.

What do you think? The final code is actually pretty concise, and it's fairly easy to process the data in the file. It's certainly a different way of thinking about processing data. Do you find the code easier or more difficult to read? It definitely takes some getting used to.

Keeping track of your streams—e.g., What is the type of your stream? Is it a stream of `Strings` or a stream of streams?—can get a bit tricky at times. Paying attention to exactly what each method produces so you know what type you're dealing with is important in all aspects of working with streams, as we hope you've discovered in this chapter.

CERTIFICATION OBJECTIVE

Generating Streams (OCP Objective 3.4)

3.4 Collections, Streams, and Filters.

What do you think will happen if you run the following code:

```
Stream.iterate(0, s -> s + 1);
```

Looking at the documentation for `Stream.iterate()`, it says `iterate()` returns an "infinite sequential order Stream." Oh my, did you get yourself an infinite loop here?

Actually no, you didn't. Remember that streams are lazy. `Stream.iterate()` returns a stream, and you know that nothing starts to happen until you tack a terminal operation, like `count()` or `forEach()` or `collect()`, onto the stream pipeline.

The `iterate()` operation creates an infinite sequential `Stream`, starting with the first argument (known as the "seed") followed by elements created by the `UnaryOperator` that you supply as the second argument. In our example above, the stream will generate whole numbers starting at 0, adding 1 to the seed first and then each subsequent number, forever.

Okay, so here's code you probably shouldn't try (okay, *definitely* shouldn't try):

```
Stream
    .iterate(0, s -> s + 1)        // create an infinite stream
    .forEach(System.out::println); // don't try this at home!
```

Here, the `forEach()` terminal operation will never end because the stream is infinite. Because `iterate()` creates an infinite stream, we need some way to limit how much we get from the stream so we don't get ourselves in trouble. We can do that with the `limit()` operation:

```
Stream
    .iterate(0, s -> s + 1)        // create an infinite stream...
    .limit(4)                      // but limit it to 4 things
    .forEach(System.out::println); // print the 4 things
```

Now it's safe to run this code, because we are limiting the stream to 4 numbers, starting with 0, so we see the output:

```
0
1
2
3
```

To work safely with infinite streams, you need a short-circuiting operation. That could be `limit()`, like we used above, or it can also be an operation like `findFirst()`, `findAny()`, or `anyMatch()`.

Let's say you've got a sensor that generates an infinite stream of data. We won't actually build one of those, but we'll simulate one, like this:

```
class Sensor {
    String value = "up";
    int i = 0;
    public Sensor() { }
```

```
        public String next() {
            i = i + 1;
            return i > 10 ? "down" : "up";
        }
    }
```

This sensor has a `next()` method that returns the status of the sensor. We return "up" values for the status until `i` is 10 and return "down" when `i` > 10. The value `i` is incremented each time we call `next()`, so the first 10 results will be "up" and all subsequent results will be "down." In a real sensor, we'd get data from the sensor and keep returning the latest status (use your imagination).

Now let's use this sensor with an infinite stream. For this example, we'll use the `Stream` method `generate()`, which takes a `Supplier`. The `generate()` method generates an infinite stream from elements supplied by the `Supplier`. Our `Supplier` is going to get values from the sensor to stream:

```
Sensor s = new Sensor();
Stream<String> sensorStream = Stream.generate(() -> s.next());
```

So `sensorStream` is an infinite stream of values we get by calling the sensor's `next()` method. That infinite stream contains 10 "up" elements and a potentially infinite number of "down" elements.

Now we can write code to look for the first "down" value in the infinite stream, like this:

```
Optional<String> result =
  sensorStream
    .filter(v -> v.equals("down"))   // filter to get all down values
    .findFirst();                    // find the first down value and stop
result.ifPresent(System.out::println);
```

The `findFirst()` method is a short-circuiting method, so as soon as we find a "down" value in the stream, everything stops. Whew! We averted another infinity problem. Of course, that assumes there is a "down" value somewhere in the stream; if there's not, then the stream will keep generating values and `findFirst()` will never complete.

Infinite streams are handy when you're dealing with a source of potentially infinite data, like a sensor. In practice, because we'd actually like to do something with the data we get from a sensor, we need to process the data into chunks, defined perhaps by a timestamp or by the number of results so far or by a particular value that indicates a change. Use caution when dealing with infinite streams because you need a way to specify a stopping point with a short-circuiting operation in order to perform the reduction and get a result.

Although `Stream.iterate()` is a good way to generate numbers up to a certain point, another way you can generate numbers is with `range()`. In practice, this might actually be more useful. This is a method on the primitive streams `IntStream` and `LongStream`:

```
IntStream numStream = IntStream.range(10, 15); // generate numbers 10...14
numStream.forEach(System.out::println);
```

This produces the output:

```
10
11
12
13
14
```

If you want a stream of numbers inclusive of the second argument, use `rangeClosed()`:

```
IntStream numStream =
    IntStream.rangeClosed(10, 15);    // generate numbers 10...15
numStream.forEach(System.out::println);
```

You'll get the output:

```
10
11
12
13
14
15
```

As you saw, the `limit()` method allows you to limit the number of elements in a stream, so you can, for instance, limit a stream to the first five even numbers in a stream:

```
IntStream evensBefore10 =
    IntStream                              // rangeClosed is static
        .rangeClosed(0, 20)                // generate numbers 0...20
        .filter(i -> i % 2 == 0)           // filter evens
        .limit(5);                         // limit to 5 results
evensBefore10.forEach(System.out::println);
```

And get the output:

```
0
2
4
6
8
```

What if you want to skip the first five items instead and print only the even numbers between 10 and 20? You can use `skip()`:

```
IntStream evensAfter10 =
    IntStream
        .rangeClosed(0, 20)          // generate numbers 0...20
        .filter(i -> i % 2 == 0)     // filter evens
        .skip(5);                    // skip first 5 results
evensAfter10.forEach(System.out::println);
```

And you see

```
10
12
14
16
18
20
```

Methods to Generate Streams

All the methods in Table 9-8 are static stream methods to generate streams, except `limit()` and `skip()`, which you'll use to control how many items and which items go into the stream. Be extra careful with `iterate()` and `generate()`; both methods create infinite streams so you need to use these with `limit()` or one of the short-circuiting methods discussed earlier.

Caveat Time Again

Streams are fun to play with, and they are cool because they are still kind of new. But just because it's new doesn't mean it's always better. We sold you pretty hard on streams being concise and potentially more efficient for data processing, but there are times when you may not want to use streams. For example, just doing a simple iteration over a `List` might be *slower* using a stream than a `for` loop. It's worth testing to find out for your particular use case. In addition, functional code with streams and lambdas isn't always easy to read, particularly if you're used to reading code written in a more imperative style. So our caveat is this: just because you *can* use streams doesn't mean they are always appropriate. Keep this in mind as you go beyond the exam and into the real world again.

Where streams can really shine is when you can parallelize them. We're going to briefly talk about parallel streams now and then talk about them more later in the book when we talk about concurrency in depth.

TABLE 9-8	Stream Methods to Generate Streams

Method	Description
`iterate(T seed, UnaryOperator<T> function)`	Applies a `function` to a `seed` and then to each subsequent value, and returns an infinite stream consisting of the resulting elements. For example, we created an infinite stream by starting with a `seed` of 0 and using a `function` that adds 1 to its input, resulting in a stream of `Integers`: 0, 1, 2, 3....
	Primitive streams `DoubleStream`, `IntStream`, and `LongStream` each have their own versions that use the primitive unary operators for the `function` (`DoubleUnaryOperator`, `IntUnaryOperator`, and `LongUnaryOperator`) and whose seeds are of type `double`, `int`, and `long`, respectively.
`generate(Supplier<T> s)`	Returns an infinite stream consisting of elements generated by the provided `Supplier`. We used this to generate a stream of "up" and "down" values.
	Primitive streams `DoubleStream`, `IntStream`, and `LongStream` have their own versions that use the primitive suppliers (`DoubleSupplier`, `IntSupplier`, and `LongSupplier`) and generate primitive streams, respectively.
`range(int startInclusive, int endExclusive)`, `range(long startInclusive, long endExclusive)`	Primitive streams `IntStream` and `LongStream` only: this method produces a sequential stream of elements, incrementing by 1 (e.g., 0, 1, 2, 3...), not including the `endExclusive` value.
`rangeClosed(int startInclusive, int endInclusive)`, `rangeClosed(long startInclusive, long endInclusive)`	Primitive streams `IntStream` and `LongStream` only: this method produces a sequential stream of elements, incrementing by 1 (e.g., 0, 1, 2, 3...), including the `endInclusive` value.
`limit(long maxSize)`	Returns a stream consisting of the elements of the stream on which it's called, limited to `maxSize` number of elements (for all stream types).
`skip(long n)`	Returns a stream consisting of the elements of the stream on which it's called, after n elements from the stream have been skipped (for all stream types).

CERTIFICATION OBJECTIVE

A Taste of Parallel Streams

10.6 Use parallel Streams including reduction, decomposition, merging processes, pipelines and performance.

We've mentioned a couple of times in this chapter that it's possible to process streams in parallel. So far, all the streams we've worked with have been serial streams: streams that process one data element at a time. *Parallel streams* can process elements in a stream concurrently. The way Java does this is to split a stream into substreams and then execute the operations defined in the stream pipeline on each of these substreams concurrently, meaning each substream is processed in a thread. If you have multiple cores, then Java will use multiple threads to process the stream and you might get some performance benefits. (We say "might" here because whether you get those benefits depends on your system as well as the data you're processing and how you're processing it. We won't go into an in-depth discussion on the performance tradeoffs of parallel streams, but if you're interested, it's well worth a deep dive into the literature about what makes for good use cases for parallel streams).

You're going to learn a whole lot more about threads and parallel streams in the upcoming chapter on threads, so for now, we're just going to give you a taste.

Let's say you have some numbers and you want to sum them.

```
List<Integer> nums = Arrays.asList(1, 2, 3, 4, 5, 6, 7, 8, 9, 10);
int sum = nums.stream()                    // stream the numbers
    .mapToInt(n -> n)                      // map Integer to int for sum
    .sum();                                // sum the ints
System.out.println("Sum is: " + sum);      // result is 55
```

This stream is a serial stream, so each number is added to the sum one at a time.

To make this a parallel stream, we simply call the method `parallel()` on the stream before we sum:

```
List<Integer> nums = Arrays.asList(1, 2, 3, 4, 5, 6, 7, 8, 9, 10);
int sum = nums.stream()
        .parallel()                        // make the stream parallel
        .mapToInt(n -> n)
        .sum();
System.out.println("Sum is: " + sum);      // result is still 55 (whew!)
```

Now, the stream is processed concurrently, meaning the stream is split into substreams, and (if you have enough cores) each substream is processed on a separate thread. Let's visualize how that works with some diagrams.

For a serial stream, we have one thread handling the entire sum operation:

```
1   2   3   4   5   6   7   8   9   10
    3   3   4   5   6   7   8   9   10
        6       4   5   6   7   8   9   10
            10      5   6   7   8   9   10
                15      6   7   8   9   10
                    21      7   8   9   10
                        28      8   9   10
                            36      9   10
                                45      10
                                    55
```

For a parallel stream, we have multiple threads handling the sum operation concurrently:

```
    Thread 1           Thread 2

1   2   3   4   5 | 6   7   8   9   10
    3   3   4   5 | 13      8   9   10
        6       4   5 |   21      9   10
            10      5 |       30      10
                15   |           40
                     
                    55
```

Because each thread can compute the sum simultaneously with the other threads, the whole operation should take less time to compute than if you're using a serial stream.

One thing to be careful of with parallel streams is performing an operation that relies on a specific ordering. If you use a parallel stream, you may get unexpected results. Let's compare using forEach() to display the items in a stream when the stream is serial and when the stream is parallel.

Here's the code using a serial stream:

```
Arrays.asList("boi", "charis", "zooey", "aiko")
    .stream()                       // stream the names
    .forEach(System.out::println);  // display them
```

The output you see is

```
boi
charis
zooey
aiko
```

In other words, you see the data in the same order as it appears in the source of the stream, the original List of names. That is because, by default, the stream is serial, and the elements in the stream are processed in order.

If you run the same code with a parallel stream instead:

```
Arrays.asList("boi", "charis", "zooey", "aiko")
    .stream()                        // stream the names
    .parallel()                      // ... in parallel
    .forEach(System.out::println);   // display them
```

You'll potentially get a different ordering in the output every time you run the code. For instance, when we ran this code, we saw

```
zooey
charis
boi
aiko
```

And if we run it again, we'll likely see a different ordering again. That's because the final result depends on the order in which the threads complete, not the order of the original collection. The ordering of the stream didn't matter when we were summing numbers (the sum is the same, independent of order), but the order matters a lot if you are expecting to see the content of the stream in the same order as the content in the original Collection.

That is just a small taste of parallel streams, and you'll learn a lot more about them a bit later on in Chapter 11, where we cover concurrency.

CERTIFICATION SUMMARY

A stream is a fairly abstract concept: it is a sequence of elements supporting operations. Knowing the difference between a stream and a data structure is key to understanding streams, and the analogies we used in this chapter—real-life streams and assembly lines—are meant to remind you that streams are for specifying a sequence of operations—the stream pipeline—to perform on a source. Streams never actually hold data like a data structure does. Once you wrap your head around that, then you'll have a much easier time getting the hang of the pipeline operations, of which there are many that you can perform on a stream.

You create a stream from a source, like a `List` or a `File`; specify the sequence of intermediate operations to perform; and finally, provide the terminal operation that terminates the stream and perhaps reduces the stream into a single value or displays the values from the stream in the console. But streams are lazy, so none of the intermediate operations in the pipeline actually do anything until that terminal operation is executed.

The main way you operate on streams is with mapping functions, filter functions, and reduction functions. Mapping functions map values to other values, perhaps changing the type along the way. Filter functions filter out some of the values (or none or all, depending on the filter), so you can eliminate values that don't pass a test. Finally, reduction functions provide the terminal operations on streams to reduce a stream to a single value or to a collection. This map-filter-reduce perspective on stream operations is a handy way to organize the many operations you'll encounter as you work with streams.

Streams can be sorted and searched, like data structures can—but remember you can't modify the source of a stream. When you, say, sort a stream, you need to collect the sorted values into a new data structure if you want to keep them around. Searching produces a value, but because a stream might be empty, you need a way to represent the concept of a value that may or may not be there. This is when you first encountered the optionals: values that are wrapped in the `Optional` type so you can work with empty streams without creating any problems. Of course, there are a variety of ways to get values back out of the `Optional` wrapper so you can work with the result as you normally do.

If you want to keep multiple values from a stream rather than reducing the stream to a single value, then you need a way to collect those values into a new data structure. This is what the `collect()` reduction method does. This method takes a `Collector`, which is an operation that accumulates the elements into a data structure like a `List` or a `Map`. As you're collecting elements, you can group them, partition them, count them, map them, reduce them, and more. Collectors are versatile, providing many different ways of collecting values from the stream into a result. We touched on some of the collection strategies in this chapter for the operations you'll apply on the exam, but you can take this topic a lot further if you want to explore on your own.

Generating streams is a way of pushing a (potentially) infinite number of values through the stream pipeline. However, in practice, you can't actually work with an infinite stream (at least not on today's computers!), so you need to limit it in some way, either by limiting how many items to use or by short-circuiting the stream pipeline with a searching method like `findAny()`.

At the end of the chapter, we took a sneak peek at parallel streams, which are streams that can be operated on concurrently. Parallel streams are where you are likely to see the main performance benefits of using streams in your code, and parallel streams are certainly one of the easiest ways to take advantage of concurrency in your code, as you'll see when we get to Chapter 11 (although, as with all things related to concurrency, there are some potential landmines you'll need to watch out for when you get there).

TWO-MINUTE DRILL

Here are some of the key points from this chapter.

What Is a Stream? (OCP Objective 3.4)

- ☐ A stream is a sequence of elements that can be processed with operations.
- ☐ A stream is not a data structure; it does not store any data.
- ☐ A stream pipeline consists of a source, an optional sequence of intermediate operations, and a terminal operation.
- ☐ The source of a stream can be a collection, an array, a file, or one or more values.
- ☐ You can create a stream of objects or a stream of primitive values.
- ☐ The type of a stream of objects is Stream<T>, and the primitive stream types are DoubleStream, IntStream, and LongStream.
- ☐ Pay close attention to the difference between Stream<Double> and DoubleStream and the operations allowed on each (and the same with other primitive type streams).
- ☐ Intermediate operations operate on a stream and return a stream.
- ☐ Terminal operations terminate the stream, returning a value other than a stream or void.
- ☐ filter() is an example of an intermediate operation. Pass filter() a Predicate and use filter() to filter values out of the stream that don't pass the Predicate test. For example, you can filter out elements that are less than 5 from a stream like this:

```
Stream.of(0, 1, 1, 2, 3, 5, 8, 13).filter(i -> i >= 5);
```

  The stream returned by this filter operation is a stream of numbers: 5, 8, 13.

- ☐ forEach() is a terminal operation on a stream. forEach() takes a Consumer and consumes each element of the stream on which it's called. We often use forEach() to display the values in the stream at the end of the stream pipeline, like this:

```
Stream.of("foo", "bar").forEach(System.out::println);
```

☐ count() is a terminal operation on a stream that counts the elements in the stream.

☐ Streams can only be used once. Streams are lightweight objects, so you can easily create another stream.

How to Create a Stream (OCP Objectives 3.5 and 9.3)

☐ Create a stream from a collection, like a List, using the stream() method.

☐ Create a stream from one or more values using Stream.of().

☐ Create an empty stream using Stream.empty().

☐ Create a stream from an array using Arrays.stream() or Stream.of() (and IntStream.of(), LongStream.of(), and DoubleStream.of()).

☐ Create a stream (Stream<String>) from a File using Files.lines().

☐ Streams have several benefits: you can define multiple intermediate operations on streams. The JDK can optimize the operations, so you may see a performance enhancement, especially when you can parallelize the stream.

The Stream Pipeline (OCP Objectives 3.6)

☐ A stream pipeline consists of a source, a sequence of intermediate operations, and a terminal operation.

☐ A common analogy to use for the stream pipeline is the assembly line. Each assembly-line station is analogous to an intermediate operation, so that a stream element visits each operation, where it is (usually) modified and passed on until it reaches the terminal operation or is discarded (via a filter).

☐ Streams are lazy, meaning until you define and execute a terminal operation on the stream, no processing happens.

Operating on Streams (OCP Objectives 3.7 and 5.1)

☐ Map-filter-reduce is a general abstraction to describe functions that operate on a sequence of elements.

☐ Stream operations map(), filter(), and reduce() implement mapping operations, filtering operations, and reduction operations (terminal operations), respectively.

☐ Mapping operations typically modify elements from the stream, transforming an element from one value to another or from one type to another.

- ☐ Filter operations typically winnow elements from the stream so that any element that doesn't pass a test is discarded from the stream.
- ☐ Reduction operations reduce the stream to a single value, or a collection.
- ☐ `map()` and `filter()`, and their variations, are intermediate operations.
- ☐ `reduce()` and its variations are terminal operations.
- ☐ `map()` takes a `Function`, which takes an input value and produces an output value.
- ☐ `filter()` takes a `Predicate`, which tests the input value and passes the stream element on to the next intermediate operation if the result of the test is true.
- ☐ The methods `average()`, `count()`, `sum()`, `max()`, and `min()` are predefined reductions on streams.
- ☐ `sum()` and `average()` are defined only on the primitive stream types.
- ☐ `max()` and `min()` are defined on all streams. On `Stream<T>`, `max()` and `min()` take a `Comparator` to determine which stream element is the maximum or minimum, respectively.
- ☐ `reduce()` takes an (optional) identity value and a `BinaryOperator` to reduce the stream to one value. If the identity value is provided, this is used as the result if the stream is empty; otherwise, the identity is used as the basis for the `BinaryOperator` accumulator. If no identity value is provided, `reduce()` returns an `Optional`.
- ☐ The `peek()` method is a way to "peek" into the values currently in the stream. The method makes no changes to the values in the stream and is often used with a `Consumer` that displays the values to the console for debugging purposes. `peek()` should not be used in production code.

Map-Filter-Reduce with average() and Optionals (OCP Objectives 5.3 and 5.4)

- ☐ Some stream methods produce `Optional` values.
- ☐ `Optional` is a wrapper around a value that may or may not be there.
- ☐ `average()` is an example of a reduction operation that produces an optional value, an `OptionalDouble`.
- ☐ The `reduce()` method used without an identity argument produces an optional because there may be no value if the stream is empty.

☐ If you supply an identity argument to reduce(), the method will produce a value (not an optional), and use the identity value if the stream is empty.

☐ The sum() method does not produce an optional because, by default, it uses 0 as the identity value.

☐ The average() method cannot be replaced with your own implementation using reduce() because average is not an associative operation. All reduce() operations must be associative operations, meaning you can accumulate the elements for the reduction in any order and get the same result. Sum is an example of an associative operation, so you could implement sum() yourself using reduce().

Optionals (OCP Objective 5.3)

☐ An optional is a container, or wrapper, that may or may not contain a value.

☐ Operations that produce no value if a stream is empty produce optionals. For example, findFirst(), findAny(), max(), min(), and average() all produce optionals.

☐ Before getting a value from an optional, first test to see if the optional contains a value with isPresent().

☐ The types of optionals are Optional<T> (for objects) and primitive optionals, OptionalDouble, OptionalInt, and OptionalLong.

☐ To get a value from a nonempty optional, use get(), getAsDouble(), getAsInt(), or getAsLong() for the different types of optionals.

☐ The ifPresent() method tests to see whether an optional is present and then passes the unwrapped value to the Consumer argument to ifPresent().

☐ Most of the time optionals are created by stream operations; however, you can create your own optional using Optional.of().

☐ The ofNullable() method creates an Optional value from an object, first testing to see whether the object is null. If the object is null, then an empty Optional is created.

☐ You can create your own empty Optional with Optional.empty().

☐ Use the orElse() method to get a value from an Optional and provide a default value to use if the Optional is empty.

Searching and Sorting with Streams (OCP Objectives 5.2 and 5.5)

- ☐ Searching operations on streams are short-circuiting, meaning the stream processing stops once the `Predicate` test passed to the search method is passed.

- ☐ The search methods on streams include `allMatch()`, `anyMatch()`, `noneMatch()`, `findFirst()`, and `findAny()`.

- ☐ The methods `allMatch()`, `anyMatch()`, and `noneMatch()` are terminal operations on a stream that return a boolean indicating if a match was found (or not).

- ☐ The methods `findFirst()` and `findAny()` are terminal operations that return an `Optional` value whose parameterized type depends on the type of the stream. In case no item is found, the value returned is an empty `Optional`.

- ☐ You can sort elements of a stream using the `sorted()` method. By default, the `sorted()` method uses natural ordering. If the objects in the source of the stream are `Comparable`, the sort will use that order. If the elements of a stream are primitive, the natural order for sorting is used for `double`, `int`, and `long`.

- ☐ You can pass a `Comparator` to the `sorted()` method to override the natural sort order and define your own sort order.

- ☐ `Comparator` is a functional interface with one functional method, `compare()`, so you can use a lambda expression to pass a `Comparator` to the `sorted()` method.

- ☐ You can use the `Comparator.comparing()` method with a `Function` to create a `Comparator` to use with `sorted()`.

- ☐ Use `thenComparing()` to combine comparators for sorting by one value then another.

- ☐ Instance method references refer to methods of an instance. Use the `::` syntax to create a method reference as a shorthand for a lambda that simply calls another method. For example, you can replace a lambda expression that calls the `getColor()` method of a `Duck` instance:

```
d -> d.getColor()
```

with an instance method reference:

```
Duck::getColor
```

☐ Streams are a functional style of programming in which you must be careful to avoid side effects. Stream patterns encourage you to avoid modifying the source of the stream in any stream pipeline operations, and in fact, modifying the source of a stream can lead to unexpected results.

Collecting Values from Streams (OCP Objectives 3.8 and 5.6)

☐ The source of a stream is often a Collection. Many reduction methods on streams, such as sum() and average(), turn stream elements into a single value. You can collect the elements in a stream into a new Collection using the stream method collect().

☐ The collect() stream method is a reduction (terminal) operation.

☐ A Collector is an operation that accumulates elements into a result. You can specify a Collector with four functions: a supplier, an accumulator, a combiner, and a finisher (optional). Or, you can use one of the methods in the Collectors class to create a Collector.

☐ The Collectors class has ready-made Collectors, such as a Collector to accumulate elements into a List.

☐ Use the Collectors.toList() method to create a Collector that accumulates stream elements into a List. Collectors.toMap() and Collectors.toSet() accumulate stream elements into a Map and Set, respectively.

☐ If you want a more specific Collection type, use the Collectors .toCollection() method, passing a Supplier that provides a new instance of the Collection type you want (such as ArrayList).

 ☐ The method reference ArrayList::new is a constructor method reference that is shorthand for a lambda expression () -> new ArrayList<T>() (where T is a valid type parameter, such as String, and depends on the type of the elements in the stream).

 ☐ You can use constructor method references as Suppliers for the Collectors.toCollection() method.

☐ Use the Collectors.groupingBy() method to group elements as you collect them. The Collectors.groupingBy() method returns a Collector that produces a Map.

☐ Use the Collectors.partitioningBy() method to group elements into two partitions as you collect them. The Collectors.partitioningBy() method returns a Collector that produces a Map with two keys, true and false.

- [ ] The `Collectors.groupingBy()` method can accept downstream collectors to further reduce results. For instance, instead of creating a `Map` that maps age keys to a `List` of `Person` objects that have that age, you can use the `Collectors.counting()` method to reduce the `List` of `Person` objects to their count, resulting in a `Map` from age keys to number of `Persons` with that age values.

- [ ] `Collectors.counting()` returns a `Collector` that counts the number of input elements and returns a `Long`.

- [ ] You can use `Collectors.mapping()` as a downstream `Collector` that maps values from one type to another before they are accumulated. For instance, we used `Collectors.mapping()` to create a `Collector` that maps `Person` objects to names and to collect them in a `List`.

- [ ] `Collectors.summingInt()` and `Collectors.averagingInt()`, and their `Double` and `Long` counterparts, produce `Collectors` that sum values and average values, respectively. These can be used as downstream collectors.

- [ ] `Collectors.joining()` produces a `Collector` that concatenates `String` elements (and any `CharSequence`-based types) to one `String`.

- [ ] `Collectors.counting()` produces a `Collector` that counts elements and returns a `Long`.

- [ ] `Collectors.maxBy()` and `Collectors.minBy()` produce a `Collector` that finds the maximum or minimum element in a stream when supplied with a `Comparator`.

Streams of Streams (OCP Objective 5.7)

- [ ] Sometimes the type of `Stream` in a pipeline is a `Stream` of `Streams`. For instance: `Stream<Stream<String>>` is a stream of string streams.

- [ ] You can use the `Stream` method `flatMap()` to flatten streams, essentially concatenating the values from each stream within the stream. For instance, to flatten a `Stream<Stream<String>>` sss that you created with code like this:

```
Stream<Stream<String>> sss =
    Stream.of(Stream.of("one", "two"),
            Stream.of("three", "four"),
            Stream.of("five", "six"));
```

you could write:

```
sss.flatMap(s -> s).forEach(System.out::println);
```

Generating Streams (OCP Objective 3.4)

- ☐ You can create infinite streams with the `Stream` methods `iterate()` and `generate()`.
- ☐ The `Stream` method `iterate()` method takes a seed (e.g., 0) and a `UnaryOperator` to generate a sequential ordered stream of values. The primitive streams have corresponding `iterate()` methods that generate streams of primitive values.
- ☐ The `Stream` method `generate()` method takes a `Supplier` that generates values for a `Stream`.
- ☐ Be careful when working with infinite streams. To do something useful with them, you need to limit the size of the stream with `limit()` or by using a short-circuiting method like `anyMatch()` or `findAny()`.
- ☐ You can generate `IntStreams` and `LongStreams` streams using the `range()` and `rangeClosed()` methods, which produce a sequence of numbers from a start value to an end value.

A Taste of Parallel Streams (OCP Objective 10.6)

- ☐ By default, streams are sequential, meaning the operations in the stream pipeline are processed sequentially on the source data.
- ☐ You can parallelize a stream using the `parallel()` method. But be careful how you use this method; not all stream pipelines can be parallelized!
- ☐ We'll take a more in-depth look at parallel streams in Chapter 11, which covers concurrency.

SELF TEST

The following questions will help you practice using stream operations, and build and measure your understanding of the material in this chapter.

1. Given the code fragment:

```
int[] nums = { 1, 2, 3, 4, 5, 6, 7, 8, 9, 10 };
int sum = Arrays.stream(nums)
    // L1
```

   Which code fragment inserted at line // L1 will compile correctly and sum the numbers in the array nums and store the value in the variable sum?

   A. `.reduce((n1, n2) -> n1 + n2);`

   B. `.reduce(0, (n1, n2) -> n1 + n2);`

   C. `.reduce(nums);`

   D. `.reduce(0, n1 + n2);`

2. Given the following code fragment:

```
try (Stream<String> stream = Files.lines(Paths.get("names.txt"))) {
    // L1
    System.out.println("Sorted names in the file: " + names);
} catch(IOException e) {
    System.out.println("Error reading names.txt");
    e.printStackTrace();
}
```

   and a file, "names.txt," with one name per line, which of the following code fragments inserted at line // L1 will produce a sorted List of names in the variable names?

   A.

```
List<String> names = stream.sorted().toList();
```

   B.

```
List<String> names = stream
    .comparing((n1, n2) -> n1.compareTo(n2))
    .collect(Collectors.toList());
```

   C.

```
List<String> names = stream.collect(Collectors.toList()).sorted();
```

   D.

```
List<String> names = stream.sorted().collect(Collectors.toList());
```

3. What are the correct types for variables `s1` and `s2` in the code fragment below?

    ```
    TYPE s1 = Stream.of(1, 2, 3, 4, 5, 6, 7, 8, 9, 10);
    TYPE s2 = s1.mapToInt(i -> i);
    ```

    A. `Stream<Integer>` and `Stream<Integer>`
    B. `IntStream` and `IntStream`
    C. `IntStream` and `Stream<Integer>`
    D. `Stream<Integer>` and `IntStream`
    E. `Stream<Integer>` and `List<Integer>`

4. Given the code fragments:

    ```
    class Duck implements Comparable<Duck> {
        String name;
        String color;
        int age;

        public Duck(String name, String color, int age) {
            this.name = name; this.color = color; this.age = age;
        }
        // getters and setters here
        public String toString() {
            return getName() + " is " + getColor() + " and is "
                            + getAge() + " years old.";
        }
        @Override
        public int compareTo(Duck duck) {
            return this.getName().compareTo(duck.getName());
        }
    }

    List<Duck> ducks = Arrays.asList(
        new Duck("Jerry", "yellow", 3),
        new Duck("George", "brown", 4),
        new Duck("Kramer", "mottled", 6),
        new Duck("Elaine", "white", 2),
        new Duck("Huey", "mottled", 2),
        new Duck("Louie", "white", 4),
        new Duck("Dewey", "brown", 6)
    );
    ```

    Which code fragment could you use for CODE in the call to `map()` in the following code fragment:

    ```
    System.out.print("Duck names: ");
    ducks.stream().map(CODE).forEach(d -> System.out.print(d + " "));
    System.out.println();
    ```

    to correctly print the string (choose all that apply):

    ```
    Duck names: Jerry George Kramer Elaine Huey Louie Dewey
    ```

A. `Duck::getName`

B. `d::d.getName()`

C. `d -> d.getName()`

D. `d.getName()`

5. Given the Duck class and ducks List:

```
class Duck implements Comparable<Duck> {
    String name;
    String color;
    int age;

    public Duck(String name, String color, int age) {
        this.name = name; this.color = color; this.age = age;
    }
    // getters and setters here
    public String toString() {
        return getName() + " is " + getColor() + " and is "
                        + getAge() + " years old.";
    }
    @Override
    public int compareTo(Duck duck) {
        return this.getName().compareTo(duck.getName());
    }
}

List<Duck> ducks = Arrays.asList(
    new Duck("Jerry", "yellow", 3),
    new Duck("George", "brown", 4),
    new Duck("Kramer", "mottled", 6),
    new Duck("Elaine", "white", 2),
    new Duck("Huey", "mottled", 2),
    new Duck("Louie", "white", 4),
    new Duck("Dewey", "brown", 6)
);
```

What output does the following code fragment produce?

```
ducks.stream()
    .filter(d -> d.getColor().equals("mottled"))
    .map(d -> d.getName())
    .forEach(d -> System.out.print(d + " "));
```

A. `Kramer Huey`

B. `Jerry George Kramer Elaine Huey Louie Dewey`

C. No output, the code does not compile

D. `Kramer is mottled and is 6 years old. Huey is mottled and is 2 years old.`

6. Given the `Duck` class and `ducks List`:

```
class Duck implements Comparable<Duck> {
    String name;
    String color;
    int age;

    public Duck(String name, String color, int age) {
        this.name = name; this.color = color; this.age = age;
    }
    // getters and setters here
    public String toString() {
        return getName() + " is " + getColor() + " and is "
                        + getAge() + " years old.";
    }
    @Override
    public int compareTo(Duck duck) {
        return this.getName().compareTo(duck.getName());
    }
}

List<Duck> ducks = Arrays.asList(
    new Duck("Jerry", "yellow", 3),
    new Duck("George", "brown", 4),
    new Duck("Kramer", "mottled", 6),
    new Duck("Elaine", "white", 2),
    new Duck("Huey", "mottled", 2),
    new Duck("Louie", "white", 4),
    new Duck("Dewey", "brown", 6)
);
```

Which code fragment would you use to compute the average age of the ducks as a whole number?

A.
```
double avgAge =
    ducks.stream().mapToInt(d -> d.getAge()).average();
```

B.
```
OptionalDouble avgAge =
    ducks.stream().mapToInt(d -> d.getAge()).average();
```

C.
```
Double avgAge =
    ducks.stream().mapToDouble(d -> d.getAge()).average();
```

D.
```
double avgAge =
    ducks.stream().map(d -> d.getAge()).average();
```

7. Given the Duck class and ducks List:

```
class Duck implements Comparable<Duck> {
    String name;
    String color;
    int age;

    public Duck(String name, String color, int age) {
        this.name = name; this.color = color; this.age = age;
    }
    // getters and setters here
    public String toString() {
        return getName() + " is " + getColor() + " and is "
                        + getAge() + " years old.";
    }
    @Override
    public int compareTo(Duck duck) {
        return this.getName().compareTo(duck.getName());
    }
}

List<Duck> ducks = Arrays.asList(
    new Duck("Jerry", "yellow", 3),
    new Duck("George", "brown", 4),
    new Duck("Kramer", "mottled", 6),
    new Duck("Elaine", "white", 2),
    new Duck("Huey", "mottled", 2),
    new Duck("Louie", "white", 4),
    new Duck("Dewey", "brown", 6)
);
```

Which code fragment would you use to count how many mottled ducks there are?

A.

```
long count = ducks.stream().filter(d -> d.getColor().equals("mottled")).count();
```

B.

```
int count = ducks.stream().filter(d -> d.getColor().equals("mottled")).count();
```

C.

```
long count = ducks.stream().filter(d -> d.equals("mottled")).count();
```

D.

```
long count = ducks.stream().filter(Duck::getColor().equals("mottled")).count();
```

8. Given the `Duck` class and `ducks List`:

```java
class Duck implements Comparable<Duck> {
    String name;
    String color;
    int age;

    public Duck(String name, String color, int age) {
        this.name = name; this.color = color; this.age = age;
    }
    // getters and setters here
    public String toString() {
        return getName() + " is " + getColor() + " and is "
                         + getAge() + " years old.";
    }
    @Override
    public int compareTo(Duck duck) {
        return this.getName().compareTo(duck.getName());
    }
}

List<Duck> ducks = Arrays.asList(
    new Duck("Jerry", "yellow", 3),
    new Duck("George", "brown", 4),
    new Duck("Kramer", "mottled", 6),
    new Duck("Elaine", "white", 2),
    new Duck("Huey", "mottled", 2),
    new Duck("Louie", "white", 4),
    new Duck("Dewey", "brown", 6)
);
```

And the following code fragment:

```java
ducks.stream()
    .collect(Collectors.groupingBy(d -> d.getColor()))
    .forEach((c, dl) -> {
        System.out.print("Ducks who are " + c + ": ");
        dl.forEach(d -> System.out.print(d.getName() + " "));
        System.out.println();
    });
```

What is the result?

A. Compilation fails

B. An exception is thrown at runtime

C.

```
{Ducks who are color:[Kramer Huey ], Ducks who are color:[Elaine Louie ], Ducks
who are color:[Jerry ], Ducks who are color:[George Dewey ]}
```

D.

```
Ducks who are mottled: Kramer Huey
Ducks who are white: Elaine Louie
Ducks who are yellow: Jerry
Ducks who are brown: George Dewey
```

9. Given the Duck class and ducks List:

```
class Duck implements Comparable<Duck> {
    String name;
    String color;
    int age;

    public Duck(String name, String color, int age) {
        this.name = name; this.color = color; this.age = age;
    }
    // getters and setters here
    public String toString() {
        return getName() + " is " + getColor() + " and is "
                        + getAge() + " years old.";
    }
    @Override
    public int compareTo(Duck duck) {
        return this.getName().compareTo(duck.getName());
    }
}

List<Duck> ducks = Arrays.asList(
    new Duck("Jerry", "yellow", 3),
    new Duck("George", "brown", 4),
    new Duck("Kramer", "mottled", 6),
    new Duck("Elaine", "white", 2),
    new Duck("Huey", "mottled", 2),
    new Duck("Louie", "white", 4),
    new Duck("Dewey", "brown", 6)
);
```

and the following code fragment:

```
TYPE duckMap =
    ducks.stream()
    .collect(Collectors.groupingBy(d -> d.getColor(), Collectors.toList()));
```

What is the correct type for `duckMap` in `TYPE`?

A. `Map<String, Duck>`

B. `List<Duck>`

C. `Map<String, List<Duck>>`

D. `Map<List<Duck>, String>`

10. Given the code fragment:

```
List<Integer> myInts = Arrays.asList(5, 10, 7, 2, 8);
TYPE minInteger = myInts.stream().mapToInt(i -> i).min();
```

What is the correct `TYPE` for `minInteger`?

A. `int`

B. `Integer`

C. `OptionalInt`

D. `Optional<Integer>`

E. `Stream<Integer>`

F. `IntStream`

11. Given the following code:

```
class Temperature {
    String location;
    Double temp;
    public Temperature(String location, Double temp) {
        this.location = location; this.temp = temp;
    }
    public String getLocation() { return this.location; }
    public Double getTemp() { return this.temp; }
    public String toString() {
        return "July average temp at " + location + " was " + temp;
    }
}
List<Temperature> julyAvgs = new ArrayList<Temperature>();
julyAvgs.add(new Temperature("Death Valley, CA", 107.4));
julyAvgs.add(new Temperature("Salt Lake City, UT", 85.3));
julyAvgs.add(new Temperature("Reno, NV", 80.5));
julyAvgs.add(new Temperature("Bishop, CA", 80.8));
julyAvgs.add(new Temperature("Phoenix, AZ", 106.0));
julyAvgs.add(new Temperature("Miami, FL", 85.7));
```

and the following code fragment:

```
Comparator<Temperature>
    tCompare = ((t1, t2) -> t1.getTemp().compareTo(t2.getTemp()));
TYPE max = julyAvgs.stream().max(tCompare);
```

What is the correct TYPE for max?

A. `Optional<Double>`

B. `Optional<Temperature>`

C. `OptionalDouble`

D. `Temperature`

E. `Double`

F. `double`

12. Given the `Temperature` class and `julyAvgs List`:

```
class Temperature {
    String location;
    Double temp;
    public Temperature(String location, Double temp) {
        this.location = location; this.temp = temp;
    }
    public String getLocation() { return this.location; }
    public Double getTemp() { return this.temp; }
    public String toString() {
        return "July average temp at " + location + " was " + temp;
    }
}
List<Temperature> julyAvgs = new ArrayList<Temperature>();
julyAvgs.add(new Temperature("Death Valley, CA", 107.4));
julyAvgs.add(new Temperature("Salt Lake City, UT", 85.3));
julyAvgs.add(new Temperature("Reno, NV", 80.5));
julyAvgs.add(new Temperature("Bishop, CA", 80.8));
julyAvgs.add(new Temperature("Phoenix, AZ", 106.0));
julyAvgs.add(new Temperature("Miami, FL", 85.7));
```

and the following code fragment:

```
TYPE maxT = julyAvgs.stream().mapToDouble(t -> t.getTemp()).max();
```

What is the correct TYPE for maxT?

A. `Optional<Double>`

B. `Optional<Temperature>`

C. `OptionalDouble`

D. `Temperature`

E. `Double`

F. `double`

13. Given the `Temperature` class and `julyAvgs` List:

```
class Temperature {
    String location;
    Double temp;
    public Temperature(String location, Double temp) {
        this.location = location; this.temp = temp;
    }
    public String getLocation() { return this.location; }
    public Double getTemp() { return this.temp; }
    public String toString() {
        return "July average temp at " + location + " was " + temp;
    }
}
List<Temperature> julyAvgs = new ArrayList<Temperature>();
julyAvgs.add(new Temperature("Death Valley, CA", 107.4));
julyAvgs.add(new Temperature("Salt Lake City, UT", 85.3));
julyAvgs.add(new Temperature("Reno, NV", 80.5));
julyAvgs.add(new Temperature("Bishop, CA", 80.8));
julyAvgs.add(new Temperature("Phoenix, AZ", 106.0));
julyAvgs.add(new Temperature("Miami, FL", 85.7));
```

and the following code fragment:

```
Comparator<Temperature> tCompare =
    ((t1, t2) -> t1.getTemp().compareTo(t2.getTemp()));
Optional<Temperature> min = julyAvgs.stream().min(tCompare);
min.ifPresent(m -> System.out.println("Min: " + m));
Optional<Temperature> coolerSpot =
    julyAvgs.stream().filter(t -> t.getTemp() < 100.0).findAny();
if (coolerSpot.isPresent()) {
    System.out.println("A cooler spot for July: " + coolerSpot.get());
} else {
    System.out.println("No place cool in July!");
}
```

Will the minimum temperature, `min`, be the same as `coolerSpot`?

A. Yes

B. No

C. Maybe

14. Given the `Temperature` class and `julyAvgs` List:

```
class Temperature {
    String location;
    Double temp;
    public Temperature(String location, Double temp) {
        this.location = location; this.temp = temp;
    }
    public String getLocation() { return this.location; }
```

```
   public Double getTemp() { return this.temp; }
   public String toString() {
      return "July average temp at " + location + " was " + temp;
   }
}
List<Temperature> julyAvgs = new ArrayList<Temperature>();
julyAvgs.add(new Temperature("Death Valley, CA", 107.4));
julyAvgs.add(new Temperature("Salt Lake City, UT", 85.3));
julyAvgs.add(new Temperature("Reno, NV", 80.5));
julyAvgs.add(new Temperature("Bishop, CA", 80.8));
julyAvgs.add(new Temperature("Phoenix, AZ", 106.0));
julyAvgs.add(new Temperature("Miami, FL", 85.7));
```

and the following code fragment:

```
Comparator<Temperature> tCompare =
   ((t1, t2) -> t1.getTemp().compareTo(t2.getTemp()));
List<Temperature> sortedTemps =
   julyAvgs.stream()
            // L1
sortedTemps.forEach(System.out::println);
```

Which fragment(s), inserted independently at // L1, cause the code to print the
Temperatures from high temp to low temp?

A.

```
.sorted().reversed().collect(Collectors.toList());
```

B.

```
.sorted(Comparator.comparing(t -> t.getTemp())).collect(Collectors.toList());
```

C.

```
.sorted(tCompare).collect(Collectors.toList());
```

D.

```
.sorted(tCompare.reversed()).collect(Collectors.toList());
```

15. Given the Temperature class and julyAvgs List:

```
class Temperature {
   String location;
   Double temp;
   public Temperature(String location, Double temp) {
      this.location = location; this.temp = temp;
   }
   public String getLocation() { return this.location; }
   public Double getTemp() { return this.temp; }
```

```
    public String toString() {
        return "July average temp at " + location + " was " + temp;
    }
}
List<Temperature> julyAvgs = new ArrayList<Temperature>();
julyAvgs.add(new Temperature("Death Valley, CA", 107.4));
julyAvgs.add(new Temperature("Salt Lake City, UT", 85.3));
julyAvgs.add(new Temperature("Reno, NV", 80.5));
julyAvgs.add(new Temperature("Bishop, CA", 80.8));
julyAvgs.add(new Temperature("Phoenix, AZ", 106.0));
julyAvgs.add(new Temperature("Miami, FL", 85.7));
```

and the following code fragment:

```
julyAvgs.stream()
    .mapToLong(t -> Math.round(t.getTemp()))
    .sorted()
    .distinct()
    .forEach(t -> System.out.print(t + " "));
```

What does this code display?

A. 80.5 80.8 85.3 85.7 106.0 107.4

B. 81 81 85 86 106 107

C. 81 85 86 106 107

D. 107 85 81 81 106 86

16. Given the Temperature class and julyAvgs List:

```
class Temperature {
    String location;
    Double temp;
    public Temperature(String location, Double temp) {
        this.location = location; this.temp = temp;
    }
    public String getLocation() { return this.location; }
    public Double getTemp() { return this.temp; }
    public String toString() {
        return "July average temp at " + location + " was " + temp;
    }
}
List<Temperature> julyAvgs = new ArrayList<Temperature>();
julyAvgs.add(new Temperature("Death Valley, CA", 107.4));
julyAvgs.add(new Temperature("Salt Lake City, UT", 85.3));
julyAvgs.add(new Temperature("Reno, NV", 80.5));
julyAvgs.add(new Temperature("Bishop, CA", 80.8));
julyAvgs.add(new Temperature("Phoenix, AZ", 106.0));
julyAvgs.add(new Temperature("Miami, FL", 85.7));
```

What does the following code fragment display?

```
Map<Boolean, List<String>> temp100 =
    julyAvgs.stream().collect(
        Collectors.partitioningBy(t -> t.getTemp() >= 100.0,
                            Collectors.mapping(t -> t.getLocation(),
                                    Collectors.toList())));
System.out.println(temp100);
```

A.

```
Salt Lake City, UT, Reno, NV, Bishop, CA, Miami, FL, Death Valley, CA, Phoenix, AZ
```

B.

```
{false=[Salt Lake City, UT, Reno, NV, Bishop, CA, Miami, FL], true=[Death Valley,
CA, Phoenix, AZ]}
```

C.

```
106 107
```

D.

```
Death Valley, CA, Phoenix, AZ
```

17. Given the Temperature class and julyAvgs List:

```
class Temperature {
    String location;
    Double temp;
    public Temperature(String location, Double temp) {
        this.location = location; this.temp = temp;
    }
    public String getLocation() { return this.location; }
    public Double getTemp() { return this.temp; }
    public String toString() {
        return "July average temp at " + location + " was " + temp;
    }
}
List<Temperature> julyAvgs = new ArrayList<Temperature>();
julyAvgs.add(new Temperature("Death Valley, CA", 107.4));
julyAvgs.add(new Temperature("Salt Lake City, UT", 85.3));
julyAvgs.add(new Temperature("Reno, NV", 80.5));
julyAvgs.add(new Temperature("Bishop, CA", 80.8));
julyAvgs.add(new Temperature("Phoenix, AZ", 106.0));
julyAvgs.add(new Temperature("Miami, FL", 85.7));
```

Which of the following fragments will print `Temperature` objects sorted by location?

A.

```
julyAvgs.stream()
    .map(t -> t.getLocation())
    .sorted()
    .forEach(System.out::println);
```

B.

```
julyAvgs.stream()
    .sorted(Temperature::getLocation)
    .forEach(System.out::println);
```

C.

```
julyAvgs.stream()
    .sorted((t1, t2) -> t1.getLocation().compareTo(t2.getLocation()))
    .forEach(System.out::println);
```

D.

```
julyAvgs.stream()
    .map(t -> t.getLocation())
    .sorted((l1, l2) -> l1.compareTo(l2))
    .forEach(System.out::println);
```

SELF TEST ANSWERS

1. ☑ **B** is correct. We provide an identity for reduce() so we get back an int, rather than an optional.
   ☒ **A** is incorrect because reduce() needs an identity or it creates an Optional. **C** and **D** are incorrect syntax for reduce(), and both result in compile errors. (OCP Objective 3.4)

2. ☑ **D** is correct. We call sorted() to sort the stream and collect() to collect the results in a List.
   ☒ **A, B,** and **C** are incorrect. For **A**, toList() is a method of Collectors, not Stream. For **B**, comparing() is a method of Comparator, not Stream [you pass a Comparator to sorted()]. For **C**, sorted() is an intermediate stream operation that should be called before the collect() reduction, a terminal operation. (OCP Objectives 3.4, 3.6, 5.5, 5.6, and 9.3)

3. ☑ **D** is correct. The ints in the call to Stream.of() get autoboxed to Integers. (If we'd used IntStream.of() instead, then we could use IntStream as the type for s1.) Given that s1 is a Stream<Integer>, when we call mapToInt() on elements of the stream (which maps objects to ints), we are converting the Integer objects to ints, so the type of s2 must be IntStream.
   ☒ **A, B, C,** and **E** are incorrect based on the above information. (OCP Objectives 3.4 and 5.1)

4. ☑ **A** and **C** are correct. **A** is a method reference shorthand for **C**.
   ☒ **B** and **D** are incorrect. **B** has incorrect syntax for a lambda expression and method reference. **D** is not a lambda expression and should be. (OCP Objective 4.4)

5. ☑ **A** is correct. Filter all ducks who have "mottled" color and map ducks to their name.
   ☒ **B, C,** and **D** are incorrect. **B** shows all the ducks instead of just "mottled" ducks. **D** shows the result if you print the full Duck [via toString()] but you are mapping a duck to its name before printing. (OCP Objectives 3.4, 3.5, 3.7, and 5.1)

6. ☑ **B** is correct. We stream the ducks and map each duck to its age (an int) and then reduce to the average of the ages. Note that we are using mapToInt() to map a duck to its age. average() returns an optional.
   ☒ **A, C, D,** and **E** are incorrect. **A, C,** and **D** don't compile. average() returns an OptionalDouble. In **D**, we have an additional problem with map() because the lambda maps a duck to its age (a primitive), but map() is used to map an object to an object. (OCP Objectives 3.4, 5.1, 5.3, and 5.4)

7. ☑ **A** is correct. We stream the ducks and filter for ducks whose color is "mottled." We call `count()` to reduce to the number of mottled ducks.
   ☒ **B, C,** and **D** are incorrect. **B** doesn't compile [`count()` returns a `long`]. In **C**, d in filter is a `Duck`, not a `String`, so it will not equal "mottled" and the `count` will be 0. **D** doesn't compile because of invalid syntax for the expected `Predicate` in `filter()`. (OCP Objectives 3.4, 3.7, and 5.4)

8. ☑ **D** is correct. We stream the ducks and group them by their color, creating a `Map`. We then use `forEach()` to take each map entry (ducks by their color) and display the `Map` key—the color—and the `Map` value, which is a list of `Ducks`. We further iterate through each list of ducks to display just the names.
   ☒ **A, B,** and **C** are incorrect. **A** and **B** are incorrect based on the above information. **C** is incorrect because it shows the `Duck` name printed as a `List` rather than as `Strings` and shows the word "color" rather than the `color` value of each duck (the `Map` key for the `Map` produced by `Collectors.groupingBy()`). (OCP Objectives 5.1 and 5.6)

9. ☑ **C** is correct. `Collectors.groupingBy()` creates a `Map` with `color Strings` as keys and `Lists` of `Ducks` as values.
   ☒ **A, B,** and **D** are incorrect based on the above information. (OCP Objectives 3.4 and 5.6)

10. ☑ **C** is correct. `min()` is a reduction method that produces an optional type. We start with a `Stream<Integer>`; `mapToInt()` creates an `IntStream`, so `min()` produces an `OptionalInt`.
    ☒ **A, B,** and **D** are incorrect based on the above information. (OCP Objectives 3.4, 5.1, and 5.4)

11. ☑ **B** is correct. `max()` takes a `Comparator`, which takes two `Temperature` objects and compares them using the `temp` field, producing the maximum `Temperature` object in the `List`.
    ☒ **A, C, D, E,** and **F** are incorrect based on the above information. (OCP Objectives 3.4, 5.3, and 5.4)

12. ☑ **C** is correct. We map each `Temperature` object to its (unboxed) `double temp` and take the `max()` of the stream of `doubles`, producing an `OptionalDouble`.
    ☒ **A, B, D, E,** and **F** are incorrect. (OCP Objectives 3.4, 5.1, 5.3, and 5.4)

13. ☑ **C** is correct. The minimum is 80.5 in Reno, Nevada. `findAny()` finds any `Temperature` from the filtered stream of `Temperatures` < 100; for a nonparallel stream, it's usually the first one, 85.3 in Salt Lake City, but there is no guarantee that `findAny()` will return the first `Temperature` in the filtered stream.
    ☒ **A** and **B** are incorrect based on the above information. (OCP Objectives 3.4, 3.7, 5.1, 5.2, 5.3, and 5.4)

14. ☑ **D** is correct. We stream the `Temperatures` using the `tCompare` `Comparator`, which sorts the `Temperatures` from low to high based on the `temp` value, so we then reverse that ordering with `reversed()`. Then we collect the results in a `List`.

    ☒ **A, B,** and **C** are incorrect. **A** has two problems: `Temperature` isn't `Comparable`, and `reversed()` is a method on `Comparators`, so this code will not compile. **B** and **C** work but print the temperatures from low to high instead of high to low. (OCP Objectives 3.4, 5.5, and 5.6)

15. ☑ **C** is correct. We stream the `Temperatures` and map each temperature to a long value by rounding the `Temperature`'s `temp` value. We then remove any duplicates by calling `distinct()` (eliminating the repeated 81 value) and then print them out.

    ☒ **A, B,** and **D** are incorrect. For **A,** notice in the code fragment that we are using `Math.round()` to cut off the decimal points (so we process `longs`, not `doubles`). We are using `distinct()` to eliminate duplicates, so we shouldn't see 81 twice as we do in **B**. **D** is sorted in the wrong order; natural order is ascending for `long` values. (OCP Objectives 3.4, 3.5, 3.6, 5.1, and 5.5)

16. ☑ **B** is correct. We are creating a partition, so we will get (and display) a `Map` with two keys, `true` and `false`, partitioned by whether the `temp` value of a `Temperature` is >= 100.0. Each `Temperature` is mapped (downstream) to its `location` and the locations for each partition are collected into a `List`. The locations are `Strings`, so we see a `List` of `String` locations for each partition.

    ☒ **A, C,** and **D** are incorrect based on the above information. (OCP Objectives 3.4 and 5.6)

17. ☑ **C** is correct. We sort the `Temperature` objects by location and print. `sorted()` takes a `Comparator`.

    ☒ **A, B,** and **D** are incorrect. **A** and **D** display only locations, not the whole `Temperature` object. **B** produces a compile error because `sorted()` requires a `Comparator`, and we've provided a `Function`. (OCP Objectives 3.4, 3.8, 5.1, and 5.5)

EXERCISE ANSWER

Exercise 9-1: Collecting Items in a List

Using `collect()` to collect DVDs into a `List` of `DVDInfo` objects as we read the dvds from a file, we can rewrite our `loadDVDs()` method as shown on the next page.

```
public static List<DVDInfo> loadDVDs(String filename) {
    List<DVDInfo> dvds = new ArrayList<DVDInfo>();
    try (Stream<String> stream = Files.lines(Paths.get(filename))) {
        dvds = stream.map(line -> {
                String[] dvdItems = line.split("/");
                DVDInfo dvd =
                    new DVDInfo(dvdItems[0], dvdItems[1], dvdItems[2]);
                return dvd;
            }).collect(Collectors.toList());
    } catch (IOException e) {
        System.out.println("Error reading DVDs");
        e.printStackTrace();
    }
    return dvds;
}
```

This solution has the benefit of being more clear and avoids the side effect of modifying an object that's defined outside the stream pipeline.

10
Threads

- Create Worker Threads Using Runnable, Callable, and Use an ExecutorService to Concurrently Execute Tasks

- Identify Potential Threading Problems among Deadlock, Starvation, Livelock, and Race Conditions

- Use Synchronized keyword and java.util .concurrent.atomic Package to Control the Order of Thread Execution

✓ Two-Minute Drill

Q&A Self Test

Defining, Instantiating, and Starting Threads (OCP Objective 10.1)

10.1 Create worker threads using Runnable, Callable, and use an ExecutorService to concurrently execute tasks.

Imagine a stockbroker application with a lot of complex capabilities. One of its functions is "download last stock option prices," another is "check prices for warnings," and a third time-consuming operation is "analyze historical data for company XYZ."

In a single-threaded runtime environment, these actions execute one after another. The next action can happen *only* when the previous one is finished. If a historical analysis takes half an hour, and the user selects to perform a download and check afterward, the warning may come too late to, say, buy or sell stock as a result.

We just imagined the sort of application that cries out for multithreading. Ideally, the download should happen in the background (that is, in another thread). That way, other processes could happen at the same time so that, for example, a warning could be communicated instantly. All the while, the user is interacting with other parts of the application. The analysis, too, could happen in a separate thread so the user can work in the rest of the application while the results are being calculated.

So what exactly is a thread? In Java, "thread" means two different things:

- An instance of class `java.lang.Thread`
- A thread of execution

An instance of `Thread` is just...an object. Like any other object in Java, it has variables and methods, and it lives and dies on the heap. But a *thread of execution* is an individual process (a "lightweight" process) that has its own call stack. In Java, there is *one thread per call stack*—or, to think of it in reverse, *one call stack per thread.* Even if you don't create any new threads in your program, threads are back there running.

The `main()` method, which starts the whole ball rolling, runs in one thread, called (surprisingly) the *main* thread. If you looked at the main call stack (and you can any time you get a stack trace from something that happens after main begins, but not within another thread), you'd see that `main()` is the first method on the stack—the method at the bottom. But as soon as you create a *new* thread, a new stack materializes and methods called from *that* thread run in a call stack that's separate from the `main()` call stack. That second new call stack is said to run concurrently with the main thread, but we'll refine that notion as we go through this chapter.

You might find it confusing that we're talking about code running *concurrently—* what gives? The JVM, which gets its turn at the CPU by whatever scheduling mechanism the underlying OS uses, operates like a mini-OS and schedules *its* own threads, regardless of the underlying operating system. In some JVMs, the Java threads are actually mapped to native OS threads, but we won't discuss that here; native threads are not on the exam. Nor is it required to understand how threads behave in different JVM environments. In fact, the most important concept to understand from this entire chapter is this:

When it comes to threads, very little is guaranteed.

So be very cautious about interpreting the behavior you see on *one* machine as "the way threads work." The exam expects you to know what is and is not guaranteed behavior so that you can design your program in such a way that it will work, regardless of the underlying JVM. *That's part of the whole point of Java.*

on the Job **Don't make the mistake of designing your program to be dependent on a particular implementation of the JVM. As you'll learn a little later, different JVMs can run threads in profoundly different ways. For example, one JVM might be sure that all threads get their turn, with a fairly even amount of time allocated for each thread in a nice, happy, round-robin fashion. But in other JVMs, a thread might start running and then just hog the whole show, never stepping out so others can have a turn. If you test your application on the "nice turn-taking" JVM and you don't know what is and is not guaranteed in Java, then you might be in for a big shock when you run it under a JVM with a different thread-scheduling mechanism.**

The thread questions are among the most difficult questions on the exam. In fact, for most people, they *are* the toughest questions on the exam, and with three objectives for threads, you'll be answering a *lot* of thread questions. If you're not already familiar with threads, you'll probably need to spend some time experimenting. Also, one final disclaimer: *This chapter makes almost no attempt to teach you how to design a good, safe multithreaded application. We only scratch the surface of that huge topic in this chapter!* You're here to learn the basics of threading and what you need to get through the thread questions on the exam. Before you can write decent multithreaded code, however, you really need to study more of the complexities and subtleties of multithreaded code.

Note: The topic of daemon threads is NOT on the exam. All of the threads discussed in this chapter are "user" threads. You and the operating system can create a second kind of thread called a daemon thread. The difference between these two types of threads (user and daemon) is that the JVM exits an application only when all user threads are complete—the JVM doesn't care about letting daemon threads complete, so once all user threads are complete, the JVM will shut down, regardless of the state of any daemon threads. Once again, this topic is NOT on the exam.

Making a Thread

A thread in Java begins as an instance of `java.lang.Thread`. You'll find methods in the `Thread` class for managing threads, including creating, starting, and pausing them. For the exam, you'll need to know, at a minimum, the following methods:

```
start()
yield()
sleep()
run()
```

The action happens in the `run()` method. Think of the code you want to execute in a separate thread as *the job to do.* In other words, you have some work that needs to be done—say, downloading stock prices in the background while other things are happening in the program—so what you really want is that *job* to be executed in its own thread. So, if the *work* you want done is the *job,* the one *doing* the work (actually executing the job code) is the *thread.* And the *job always starts from a* `run()` *method,* as follows:

```
public void run() {
  // your job code goes here
}
```

You always write the code that needs to be run in a separate thread in a `run()` method. The `run()` method will call other methods, of course, but the thread of execution—the new call stack—always begins by invoking `run()`. So where does the `run()` method go? In one of the two classes you can use to define your thread job.

You can define and instantiate a thread in one of two ways:

- Extend the `java.lang.Thread` class.
- Implement the `Runnable` interface.

You need to know about both for the exam, although in the real world, you're much more likely to implement `Runnable` than extend `Thread`. Extending the `Thread` class is the easiest, but it's usually not good OO practice. Why? Because subclassing should be reserved for specialized versions of more general superclasses. So the only time it really makes sense (from an OO perspective) to extend `Thread` is when you have a more specialized version of a `Thread` class. In other words, because *you have more specialized thread-specific behavior.* Chances are, though, that the thread work you want is really just a job to be done *by* a thread. In that case, you should design a class that implements the `Runnable` interface, which also leaves your class free to extend some *other* class.

Defining a Thread

To define a thread, you need a place to put your `run()` method, and as we just discussed, you can do that by extending the `Thread` class or by implementing the `Runnable` interface. We'll look at both in this section.

Extending java.lang.Thread

The simplest way to define code to run in a separate thread is to

- Extend the `java.lang.Thread` class.
- Override the `run()` method.

It looks like this:

```
class MyThread extends Thread {
  public void run() {
    System.out.println("Important job running in MyThread");
  }
}
```

The limitation with this approach (besides being a poor design choice in most cases) is that if you extend `Thread`, *you can't extend anything else.* And it's not as if you really need that inherited `Thread` class behavior; because in order to use a thread, you'll need to instantiate one anyway.

Keep in mind that you're free to overload the run() method in your Thread subclass:

```
class MyThread extends Thread {
  public void run() {
    System.out.println("Important job running in MyThread");
  }
  public void run(String s) {
    System.out.println("String in run is " + s);
  }
}
```

But know this: The overloaded run(String s) method will be ignored by the Thread class unless you call it yourself. The Thread class expects a run() method with no arguments, and it will execute this method for you in a separate call stack after the thread has been started. With a run(String s) method, the Thread class won't call the method for you, and even if you call the method directly yourself, execution won't happen in a new thread of execution with a separate call stack. It will just happen in the same call stack as the code that you made the call from, just like any other normal method call.

Implementing java.lang.Runnable

Implementing the Runnable interface gives you a way to extend any class you like but still define behavior that will be run by a separate thread. It looks like this:

```
class MyRunnable implements Runnable {
  public void run() {
    System.out.println("Important job running in MyRunnable");
  }
}
```

Notice that the Runnable interface is a functional interface, that is, an interface with one abstract method, run(). That means we can also write a Runnable like this:

```
Runnable r = () ->
    System.out.println("Important job running in a Runnable");
```

Regardless of which mechanism you choose, you've now got yourself some code that can be run by a thread of execution. Let's take a look at *instantiating* your thread-capable class, and then we'll figure out how to actually get the thing *running*.

Instantiating a Thread

Remember, every thread of execution begins as an instance of class `Thread`. Regardless of whether your `run()` method is in a `Thread` subclass or a `Runnable` implementation class, you still need a `Thread` object to do the work.

If you extended the `Thread` class, instantiation is dead simple (we'll look at some additional overloaded constructors in a moment):

```
MyThread t = new MyThread();
```

If you implement `Runnable`, instantiation is only slightly less simple. To have code run by a separate thread, *you still need a Thread instance.* But rather than combining both the *thread* and the *job* (the code in the `run()` method) into one class, you've split it into two classes—the `Thread` class for the *thread-specific* code and your `Runnable` implementation class for your *job-that-should-be-run-by-a-thread* code. (Another common way to think about this is that the `Thread` is the "worker," and the `Runnable` is the "job" to be done.)

First, you instantiate your `Runnable` class:

```
MyRunnable r = new MyRunnable();
```

Next, you get yourself an instance of `java.lang.Thread` (*somebody* has to run your job...), and you *give it your job!*

```
Thread t = new Thread(r);   // Pass your Runnable to the Thread
```

Or, if you want to use a lambda expression, you can eliminate `MyRunnable` and write:

```
Thread t = new Thread(
  () -> System.out.println("Important job running in a Runnable")
);
```

If you create a thread using the no-arg constructor, the thread will call its own `run()` method when it's time to start working. That's exactly what you want when you extend `Thread`, but when you use `Runnable`, you need to tell the new thread to use *your* `run()` method rather than its own. The `Runnable` you pass to the `Thread` constructor is called the *target* or the *target* `Runnable`.

You can pass a single `Runnable` instance to multiple `Thread` objects so that the same `Runnable` becomes the target of multiple threads, as follows:

```
public class TestThreads {
  public static void main (String [] args) {
    // MyRunnable r = new MyRunnable(); // OR get rid of MyRunnable and write:
    Runnable r = () ->
      System.out.println("Important job running in a Runnable");
```

```
        Thread foo = new Thread(r);
        Thread bar = new Thread(r);
        Thread bat = new Thread(r);
    }
}
```

Giving the same target to multiple threads means that several threads of execution will be running the very same job (and that the same job will be done multiple times).

The Thread *class itself implements* Runnable. *(After all, it has a* run() *method that we were overriding.) This means that you could pass a* Thread *to another* Thread's *constructor:*

```
Thread t = new Thread(new MyThread());
```

This is a bit silly, but it's legal. In this case, you really just need a Runnnable, *and creating a whole other* Thread *is overkill.*

Besides the no-arg constructor and the constructor that takes a Runnable (the target, i.e., the instance with the job to do), there are other overloaded constructors in class Thread. The constructors we care about are

- Thread()
- Thread(Runnable target)
- Thread(Runnable target, String name)
- Thread(String name)

You need to recognize all of them for the exam! A little later, we'll discuss some of the other constructors in the preceding list.

So now you've made yourself a Thread instance, and it knows which run() method to call. *But nothing is happening yet.* At this point, all we've got is a plain-old Java object of type Thread. *It is not yet a thread of execution.* To get an actual thread—a new call stack—we still have to *start* the thread.

When a thread has been instantiated but not started (in other words, the start() method has not been invoked on the Thread instance), the thread is said to be in the *new* state. At this stage, the thread is not yet considered *alive.* Once the `start()` method is called, the thread is considered *alive* (even though the `run()` method may not have actually started executing yet). A thread is considered *dead* (no longer *alive*) after the `run()` method completes. The `isAlive()` method is the best way to determine if a thread has been started but has not yet completed its `run()` method. (Note: The `getState()` method is very useful for debugging, but you don't have to know it for the exam.)

Starting a Thread

You've created a `Thread` object and it knows its target (either the passed-in `Runnable` or itself, if you extended class `Thread`). Now it's time to get the whole thread thing happening—to launch a new call stack. It's so simple; it hardly deserves its own subheading:

```
t.start();
```

Prior to calling `start()` on a `Thread` instance, the thread (when we use lowercase t, we're referring to the *thread of execution* rather than the `Thread` class) is said to be in the *new* state, as we said. The new state means you have a `Thread` *object* but you don't yet have a *true thread*. So what happens after you call `start()`? The good stuff:

- A new thread of execution starts (with a new call stack).
- The thread moves from the *new* state to the *runnable* state.
- When the thread gets a chance to execute, its target `run()` method will run.

Be *sure* you remember the following: You start a *Thread*, not a *Runnable*. You call `start()` on a `Thread` instance, not on a `Runnable` instance. The following example demonstrates what we've covered so far—defining, instantiating, and starting a thread:

```java
public class TestThreads {
  public static void main (String [] args) {
    Runnable r = () -> {
      for (int x = 1; x < 6; x++) {
        System.out.println("Runnable running " + x);
      }
    };
    Thread t = new Thread(r);
    t.start();
  }
}
```

Running the preceding code prints out exactly what you'd expect:

```
% java TestThreads
Runnable running 1
Runnable running 2
Runnable running 3
Runnable running 4
Runnable running 5
```

(If this isn't what you expected, go back and reread everything in this objective.)

There's nothing special about the run () *method as far as Java is concerned. Like* main (), *it just happens to be the name (and signature) of the method that the new thread knows to invoke. So if you see code that calls the* run () *method on a* Runnable *(or even on a* Thread *instance), that's perfectly legal. But it doesn't mean the* run () *method will run in a separate thread! Calling a* run () *method directly just means you're invoking a method from whatever thread is currently executing, and the* run () *method goes onto the current call stack rather than at the beginning of a new call stack. The following code does not start a new thread of execution:*

```
Thread t = new Thread();
t.run();           // Legal, but does not start a new thread
```

So what happens if we start multiple threads? We'll run a simple example in a moment, but first we need to know how to print out which thread is executing. We can use the getName() method of class Thread and have each Runnable print out the name of the thread executing that Runnable object's run() method. The following example instantiates a thread and gives it a name, and then the name is printed out from the run() method:

```
class NameRunnable implements Runnable {
  public void run() {
    System.out.println("NameRunnable running");
    System.out.println("Run by "
      + Thread.currentThread().getName());
  }
}
public class NameThread {
  public static void main (String [] args) {
    NameRunnable nr = new NameRunnable();
    Thread t = new Thread(nr);
```

```
    t.setName("Fred");
    t.start();
  }
}
```

Running this code produces the following extra-special output:

```
% java NameThread
NameRunnable running
Run by Fred
```

To get the name of a thread, you call—who would have guessed—getName() on the Thread instance. But the target Runnable instance doesn't even *have* a reference to the Thread instance, so we first invoked the static Thread .currentThread() method, which returns a reference to the currently executing thread, and then we invoked getName() on that returned reference.

Even if you don't explicitly name a thread, it still has a name. Let's look at the previous code, commenting out the statement that sets the thread's name:

```
public class NameThread {
  public static void main (String [] args) {
    NameRunnable nr = new NameRunnable();
    Thread t = new Thread(nr);
    // t.setName("Fred");
    t.start();
  }
}
```

Running the preceding code now gives us

```
% java NameThread
NameRunnable running
Run by Thread-0
```

And since we're getting the current thread by using the static Thread .*currentThread*() method, we can even get the name of the thread running our main code:

```
public class NameThreadTwo {
  public static void main (String [] args) {
    System.out.println("thread is "
      + Thread.currentThread().getName());
  }
}
```

which prints out

```
% java NameThreadTwo
thread is main
```

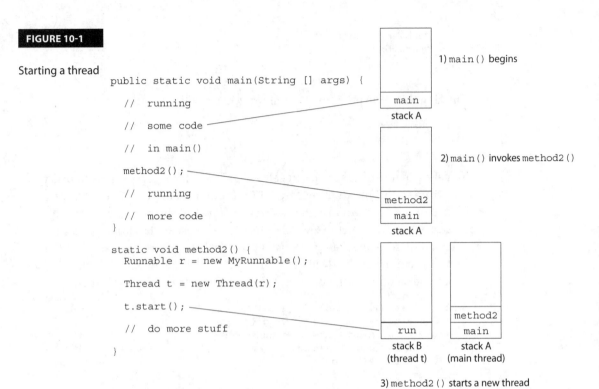

FIGURE 10-1

Starting a thread

```
public static void main(String [] args) {

    //  running

    //  some code

    //  in main()

    method2();

    //  running

    //  more code
}

static void method2() {
    Runnable r = new MyRunnable();

    Thread t = new Thread(r);

    t.start();

    //  do more stuff

}
```

1) `main()` begins

main
stack A

2) `main()` invokes `method2()`

method2
main
stack A

method2
main

run
stack B
(thread t)

method2
main
stack A
(main thread)

3) `method2()` starts a new thread

That's right, the main thread already has a name—*main*. (Once again, what are the odds?) Figure 10-1 shows the process of starting a thread.

Starting and Running Multiple Threads

Enough playing around here; let's actually get multiple threads going (more than two, that is). We already had two threads, because the `main()` method starts in a thread of its own, and then `t.start()` started a *second* thread. Now we'll do more. The following code creates a single `Runnable` instance and three `Thread` instances. All three `Thread` instances get the same `Runnable` instance, and each thread is given a unique name. Finally, all three threads are started by invoking `start()` on the `Thread` instances. And just to hammer in one more time how you can use a lambda expression in place of an explicit `Runnable` class, we'll eliminate `NameRunnable`, and replace it with a lambda.

```
// No need for NameRunnable if we use lambdas...
public class ManyNames {
    public static void main(String [] args) {
```

```
    // Make one Runnable
    Runnable nr = () -> {
      for (int x = 1; x <= 3; x++) {
        System.out.println("Run by " +
          Thread.currentThread().getName() + ", x is " + x);
      }
    };
    Thread one = new Thread(nr);
    Thread two = new Thread(nr);
    Thread three = new Thread(nr);

    one.setName("Fred");
    two.setName("Lucy");
    three.setName("Ricky");
    one.start();
    two.start();
    three.start();
  }
}
```

Running this code **might** produce the following:

```
% java ManyNames
Run by Fred, x is 1
Run by Fred, x is 2
Run by Fred, x is 3
Run by Lucy, x is 1
Run by Lucy, x is 2
Run by Lucy, x is 3
Run by Ricky, x is 1
Run by Ricky, x is 2
Run by Ricky, x is 3
```

Well, at least that's what it printed when we ran it—this time, on our machine. But the behavior you see here is not guaranteed. This is so crucial that you need to stop right now, take a deep breath, and repeat after me, "The behavior is not guaranteed." You need to know, for your future as a Java programmer as well as for the exam, that there is nothing in the Java specification that says threads will start running in the order in which they were started (in other words, the order in which start() was invoked on each thread). And there is no guarantee that once a thread starts executing, it will keep executing until it's done. Or that a loop will complete before another thread begins. No siree, Bob.

Nothing is guaranteed in the preceding code except this:

Each thread will start, and each thread will run to completion.

Within each thread, things will happen in a predictable order. But the actions of different threads can mix in unpredictable ways. If you run the program multiple times or on multiple machines, you may see different output. Even if you don't see different output, you need to realize that the behavior you see is not guaranteed. Sometimes a little change in the way the program is run will cause a difference to emerge. Just for fun we bumped up the loop code so that each `run()` method ran the `for` loop 400 times rather than 3, and eventually we did start to see some wobbling:

```
Runnable nr = () -> {
  for (int x = 1; x <= 400; x++) {
    System.out.println("Run by " +
      Thread.currentThread().getName() + ", x is " + x);
  }
};
```

Running the preceding code, with each thread executing its run loop 400 times, started out fine but then became nonlinear. Here's just a snippet from the command-line output of running that code. To make it easier to distinguish each thread, we put Fred's output in italics and Lucy's in bold and left Ricky's alone:

```
Run by Fred, x is 345
Run by Ricky, x is 313
Run by Lucy, x is 341
Run by Ricky, x is 314
Run by Lucy, x is 342
Run by Ricky, x is 315
Run by Fred, x is 346
Run by Lucy, x is 343
Run by Fred, x is 347
Run by Lucy, x is 344
```

...it continues on...

Notice that there's not really any clear pattern here. If we look at only the output from Fred, we see the numbers increasing one at a time, as expected:

```
Run by Fred, x is 345
Run by Fred, x is 346
Run by Fred, x is 347
```

And similarly, if we look only at the output from Lucy or Ricky—each one individually is behaving in a nice, orderly manner. But together—chaos! In the previous fragment we see Fred, then Lucy, then Ricky (in the same order we originally started the threads), but then Lucy butts in when it was Fred's turn. What nerve! And then Ricky and Lucy trade back and forth for a while until finally Fred gets another chance. They jump around like this for a while after this. Eventually (after the part shown earlier), Fred finishes, then Ricky, and finally Lucy finishes with a long sequence of output. So even though Ricky was started third, he actually completed second. And if we run it again, we'll get a different result. Why? Because it's up to the scheduler, and we don't control the scheduler! Which brings up another key point to remember: Just because a series of threads are started in a particular order doesn't mean they'll run in that order. For any group of started threads, order is not guaranteed by the scheduler. And duration is not guaranteed. You don't know, for example, if one thread will run to completion before the others have a chance to get in, or whether they'll all take turns nicely, or whether they'll do a combination of both. There is a way, however, to start a thread but tell it not to run until some other thread has finished. You can do this with the `join()` method, which we'll look at a little later.

A thread is done being a thread when its target `run()` method completes.

When a thread completes its `run()` method, the thread ceases to be a thread of execution. The stack for that thread dissolves, and the thread is considered dead. (Technically, the API calls a dead thread "terminated," but we'll use "dead" in this chapter.) Not dead and gone, however—just dead. It's still a `Thread` *object,* just not a *thread of execution.* So if you've got a reference to a `Thread` instance, then even when that `Thread` instance is no longer a thread of execution, you can still call methods on the `Thread` instance, just like any other Java object. What you can't do, though, is call `start()` again.

Once a thread has been started, it can never be started again.

If you have a reference to a `Thread` and you call `start()`, it's started. If you call `start()` a second time, it will cause an exception (an `IllegalThreadStateException`, which is a kind of `RuntimeException`, but you don't need to worry about the exact type). This happens whether or not the `run()` method has completed from the first `start()` call. Only a new thread can be started, and then only once. A runnable thread or a dead thread cannot be restarted.

So far, we've seen three thread states: *new, runnable,* and *dead.* We'll look at more thread states before we're done with this chapter.

The Thread Scheduler

The thread scheduler is the part of the JVM (although most JVMs map Java threads directly to native threads on the underlying OS) that decides which thread should run at any given moment and also takes threads *out* of the run state. Assuming a single processor machine, only one thread can actually *run* at a time. Only one stack can ever be executing at one time. And it's the thread scheduler that decides *which* thread—of all that are eligible—will actually *run*. When we say *eligible*, we really mean *in the runnable state*.

Any thread in the *runnable* state can be chosen by the scheduler to be the one and only running thread. If a thread is not in a runnable state, then it cannot be chosen to be the *currently running* thread. And just so we're clear about how little is guaranteed here:

> *The order in which runnable threads are chosen to run is not guaranteed.*

Although *queue* behavior is typical, it isn't guaranteed. Queue behavior means that when a thread has finished with its "turn," it moves to the end of the line of the runnable pool and waits until it eventually gets to the front of the line, where it can be chosen again. In fact, we call it a runnable *pool*, rather than a runnable *queue*, to help reinforce the fact that threads aren't all lined up in some guaranteed order.

Although we don't *control* the thread scheduler (we can't, for example, tell a specific thread to run), we can sometimes influence it. The following methods give us some tools for *influencing* the scheduler. Just don't ever mistake influence for control.

Methods from the java.lang.Thread Class   Some of the methods that can help us influence thread scheduling are as follows:

```
public static void sleep(long millis) throws InterruptedException
public static void yield()
public final void join() throws InterruptedException
public final void setPriority(int newPriority)
```

Note that both `sleep()` and `join()` have overloaded versions not shown here.

Methods from the java.lang.Object Class   Every class in Java inherits the following three thread-related methods:

```
public final void wait() throws InterruptedException
public final void notify()
public final void notifyAll()
```

The wait() method has three overloaded versions (including the one listed here).

We'll look at the behavior of each of these methods in this chapter. First, though, we're going to look at the different states a thread can be in.

Thread States and Transitions

We've already seen three thread states—*new, runnable,* and *dead*—but wait! There's more! The thread scheduler's job is to move threads in and out of the *running* state. While the thread scheduler can move a thread from the running state back to runnable, other factors can cause a thread to move out of running, but *not* back to runnable. One of these is when the thread's run() method completes, in which case, the thread moves from the running state directly to the dead state. Next, we'll look at some of the other ways in which a thread can leave the running state and where the thread goes.

Thread States

A thread can be only in one of five states (see Figure 10-2):

- **New**   This is the state the thread is in after the Thread instance has been created but the start() method has not been invoked on the thread. It is a live Thread object, but not yet a thread of execution. At this point, the thread is considered *not alive.*

- **Runnable**   This is the state a thread is in when it's eligible to run but the scheduler has not selected it to be the running thread. A thread first enters the runnable state when the start() method is invoked, but a thread can also return to the runnable state after either running or coming back from a blocked, waiting, or sleeping state. When the thread is in the runnable state, it is considered *alive.*

- **Running**   This is it. The "big time." Where the action is. This is the state a thread is in when the thread scheduler selects it from the runnable pool to be the currently executing process. A thread can transition out of a running state for several reasons, including because "the thread scheduler felt like it." We'll look at those other reasons shortly. Note that in Figure 10-2, there are several ways to get to the runnable state, but only *one* way to get to the running state: the scheduler chooses a thread from the runnable pool.

■ **Waiting/blocked/sleeping**   This is the state a thread is in when it's not eligible to run. Okay, so this is really three states combined into one, but they all have one thing in common: the thread is still alive but is currently not eligible to run. In other words, it is not *runnable,* but it might *return* to a runnable state later if a particular event occurs. A thread may be *blocked* because it's waiting for a resource (like I/O or an object's lock), in which case the event that sends it back to runnable is the availability of the resource— for example, if data comes in through the input stream the thread code is reading from or if the object's lock suddenly becomes available. A thread may be *sleeping* because the thread's run code *tells* it to sleep for some period of time, in which case, the event that sends it back to runnable causes it to wake up because its sleep time has expired. Or the thread may be *waiting* because the thread's run code *causes* it to wait. In that case, an event occurs, causing another thread to be sent a notifcation that it may no longer be necessary to wait. Then the waiting thread will become runnable again. The important point is that one thread does not *tell* another thread to block. Some methods may *look* like they tell another thread to block, but they don't. If you have a reference t to another thread, you can write something like this:

```
t.sleep();    or    t.yield();
```

But those are actually static methods of the Thread class—*they don't affect the instance* t; instead, they are defined to always affect the thread that's currently executing. (This is a good example of why it's a bad idea to use an instance variable to access a static method—it's misleading. There *is* a method, suspend(), in the Thread class that lets one thread tell another to suspend, but the suspend() method has been deprecated and won't be on the exam [nor will its counterpart resume()].) There is also a stop() method, but it, too, has been deprecated and we won't even go there. Both suspend() and stop() turned out to be very dangerous, so you shouldn't use them, and again, because they're deprecated, they won't appear on the exam. Don't study 'em; don't use 'em. Note also that a thread in a blocked state is still considered *alive*.

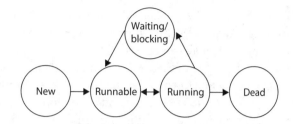

FIGURE 10-2

Transitioning
between thread
states

- **Dead** A thread is considered dead when its `run()` method completes. It may still be a viable `Thread` object, but it is no longer a separate thread of execution. Once a thread is dead, it can never be brought back to life! (The whole "I see dead threads" thing.) If you invoke `start()` on a dead `Thread` instance, you'll get an exception at runtime. And it probably doesn't take a rocket scientist to tell you that if a thread is dead, it is no longer considered *alive*.

Preventing Thread Execution

A thread that's been stopped usually means a thread that's moved to the dead state. But you also need to be able to recognize when a thread will get kicked out of running but *not* be sent back to either runnable or dead.

For the purpose of the exam, we aren't concerned with a thread blocking on I/O (say, waiting for something to arrive from an input stream from the server). We *are* concerned with the following:

- Sleeping
- Waiting
- Blocked because it needs an object's lock

Sleeping

The `sleep()` method is a `static` method of class `Thread`. You use it in your code to "slow a thread down" by forcing it to go into a sleep mode before coming back to runnable (where it still has to beg to be the currently running thread). When a thread sleeps, it drifts off somewhere and doesn't return to runnable until it wakes up.

So why would you want a thread to sleep? Well, you might think the thread is moving too quickly through its code. Or you might need to force your threads to take turns, since reasonable turn-taking isn't guaranteed in the Java specification. Or imagine a thread that runs in a loop, downloading the latest stock prices and analyzing them. Downloading prices one after another would be a waste of time, as most would be quite similar—and even more important, it would be an incredible waste of precious bandwidth. The simplest way to solve this is to cause a thread to pause (sleep) for five minutes after each download.

You do this by invoking the static `Thread.sleep()` method, giving it a time in milliseconds as follows:

```
try {
  Thread.sleep(5*60*1000);  // Sleep for 5 minutes
} catch (InterruptedException ex) { }
```

Notice that the `sleep()` method can throw a checked `InterruptedException` (you'll usually know if that is a possibility because another thread has to explicitly do the interrupting), so you must acknowledge the exception with a handle or declare. Typically, you wrap calls to `sleep()` in a `try/catch`, as in the preceding code.

Let's modify our Fred, Lucy, Ricky code by using `sleep()` to *try* to force the threads to alternate rather than letting one thread dominate for any period of time. Where do you think the call to the `sleep()` method should go?

```
class NameRunnable implements Runnable {
  public void run() {
    for (int x = 1; x < 4; x++) {
      System.out.println("Run by "
        + Thread.currentThread().getName());
      try {
        Thread.sleep(1000);
      } catch (InterruptedException ex) { }
    }
  }
}
public class ManyNames {
  public static void main (String [] args) {

    // Make one Runnable
    NameRunnable nr = new NameRunnable();

    Thread one = new Thread(nr);
    one.setName("Fred");
    Thread two = new Thread(nr);
    two.setName("Lucy");
    Thread three = new Thread(nr);
```

```
        three.setName("Ricky");

        one.start();
        two.start();
        three.start();
    }
}
```

Running this code shows Fred, Lucy, and Ricky alternating nicely:

```
% java ManyNames
Run by Fred
Run by Lucy
Run by Ricky
Run by Fred
Run by Lucy
Run by Ricky
Run by Fred
Run by Lucy
Run by Ricky
```

Just keep in mind that the behavior in the preceding output is still not guaranteed. You can't be certain how long a thread will actually run *before* it gets put to sleep, so you can't know with certainty that only one of the three threads will be in the runnable state when the running thread goes to sleep. In other words, if two threads are awake and in the runnable pool, you can't know with certainty that the least recently used thread will be the one selected to run. *Still, using sleep() is the best way to help all threads get a chance to run!* Or at least to guarantee that one thread doesn't get in and stay until it's done. When a thread encounters a sleep call, it *must* go to sleep for *at least* the specified number of milliseconds (unless it is interrupted before its wake-up time, in which case, it immediately throws the `InterruptedException`).

e x a m

ⓦatch   *Just because a thread's sleep() expires and it wakes up does not mean it will return to running! Remember, when a thread wakes up, it simply goes back to the runnable state. So the time specified in sleep() is the minimum duration in which the thread won't run, but it is not the exact duration in which the thread* won't run. So you can't, for example, rely on the sleep() method to give you a perfectly accurate timer. Although in many applications using sleep() as a timer is certainly good enough, you must know that a sleep() time is not a guarantee that the thread will start running again as soon as the time expires and the thread wakes.

Remember that `sleep()` is a static method, so don't be fooled into thinking that one thread can put another thread to sleep. You can put `sleep()` code anywhere since *all* code is being run by *some* thread. When the executing code (meaning the currently running thread's code) hits a `sleep()` call, it puts the currently running thread to sleep.

EXERCISE 10-1

Creating a Thread and Putting It to Sleep

In this exercise, we will create a simple counting thread. It will count to 100, pausing one second between each number. Also, in keeping with the counting theme, it will output a string every ten numbers.

1. Create a class and extend the `Thread` class. As an option, you can implement the `Runnable` interface.

2. Override the `run()` method of `Thread`. This is where the code will go that will output the numbers.

3. Create a `for` loop that will loop 100 times. Use the modulus operation to check whether there are any remainder numbers when divided by 10.

4. Use the static method `Thread.sleep()` to pause. (Remember, the one-arg version of `sleep()` specifies the amount of time of sleep in milliseconds.)

Thread Priorities and yield( )

To understand `yield()`, you must understand the concept of thread *priorities.* Threads always run with some priority, usually represented as a number between 1 and 10 (although in some cases, the range is less than 10). The scheduler in most JVMs uses preemptive, priority-based scheduling (which implies some sort of time slicing). *This does not mean that all JVMs use time slicing.* The JVM specification does not require a VM to implement a time-slicing scheduler, where each thread is allocated a fair amount of time and then sent back to runnable to give another thread a chance. Although many JVMs do use time slicing, some may use a scheduler that lets one thread stay running until the thread completes its `run()` method.

In most JVMs, however, the scheduler does use thread priorities in one important way: If a thread enters the runnable state and it has a higher priority than any of the threads in the pool and a higher priority than the currently running thread, *the lower-priority running thread usually will be bumped back to runnable and the highest-priority thread will be chosen to run.* In other words, at any given time, the currently running thread usually will not have a priority that is lower than any of the threads in the pool. *In most cases, the running thread will be of equal or greater priority than the highest-priority threads in the pool.* This is as close to a guarantee about scheduling as you'll get from the JVM specification, so you must never rely on thread priorities to guarantee the correct behavior of your program.

on the
job

Don't rely on thread priorities when designing your multithreaded application. Because thread-scheduling priority behavior is not guaranteed, it's better to avoid modifying thread priorities. Usually, default priority will be fine.

What is also *not* guaranteed is the behavior when threads in the pool are of equal priority or when the currently running thread has the same priority as threads in the pool. All priorities being equal, a JVM implementation of the scheduler is free to do just about anything it likes. That means a scheduler might do one of the following (among other things):

■ Pick a thread to run, and run it there until it blocks or completes.

■ Time-slice the threads in the pool to give everyone an equal opportunity to run.

Setting a Thread's Priority

A thread gets a default priority that is *the priority of the thread of execution that creates it.* For example, in the code

```
public class TestThreads {
  public static void main (String [] args) {
    MyThread t = new MyThread();
  }
}
```

the thread referenced by t will have the same priority as the *main* thread because the main thread is executing the code that creates the MyThread instance.

You can also set a thread's priority directly by calling the `setPriority()` method on a `Thread` instance, as follows:

```
FooRunnable r = new FooRunnable();
Thread t = new Thread(r);
t.setPriority(8);
t.start();
```

Priorities are set using a positive integer, usually between 1 and 10, and the JVM will never change a thread's priority. However, values 1 through 10 are not guaranteed. Some JVMs might not recognize 10 distinct values. Such a JVM might merge values from 1 to 10 down to maybe values from 1 to 5, so if you have, say, 10 threads, each with a different priority, and the current application is running in a JVM that allocates a range of only 5 priorities, then 2 or more threads might be mapped to one priority.

Although *the default priority is 5*, the `Thread` class has the three following constants (`static final` variables) that define the range of thread priorities:

```
Thread.MIN_PRIORITY   (1)
Thread.NORM_PRIORITY  (5)
Thread.MAX_PRIORITY   (10)
```

The yield( ) Method

So what does the `static Thread.yield()` have to do with all this? Not that much, in practice. What `yield()` is *supposed* to do is make the currently running thread head back to runnable to allow other threads of the same priority to get their turn. So the intention is to use `yield()` to promote graceful turn-taking among equal-priority threads. In reality, though, the `yield()` method isn't guaranteed to do what it claims, and even if `yield()` does cause a thread to step out of running and back to runnable, *there's no guarantee the yielding thread won't just be chosen again over all the others!* So while `yield()` might—and often does—make a running thread give up its slot to another runnable thread of the same priority, there's no guarantee.

A `yield()` won't ever cause a thread to go to the waiting/sleeping/blocking state. At most, a `yield()` will cause a thread to go from running to runnable, but again, it might have no effect at all.

The join( ) Method

The non-`static` `join()` method of class `Thread` lets one thread "join onto the end" of another thread. If you have a thread B that can't do its work until another thread A has completed *its* work, then you want thread B to "join" thread A.

This means that thread B will not become runnable until A has finished (and entered the dead state).

```
Thread t = new Thread();
t.start();
t.join();
```

The preceding code takes the currently running thread (if this were in the main() method, then that would be the main thread) and *joins* it to the end of the thread referenced by t. This blocks the current thread from becoming runnable until after the thread referenced by t is no longer alive. In other words, the code t.join() means "Join me (the current thread) to the end of t, so that t must finish before I (the current thread) can run again." You can also call one of the overloaded versions of join() that takes a timeout duration so that you're saying, "Wait until thread t is done, but if it takes longer than 5,000 milliseconds, then stop waiting and become runnable anyway." Figure 10-3 shows the effect of the join() method.

FIGURE 10-3		

The join() method

Output	Key Events in the Threads' Code	
A is running		
A is running		
A is running		
A is running		
A is running	Thread b = new Thread(aRunnable);	doStuff()
A is running ——	b.start();	
A is running		Stack A is running
B is running	// Threads bounce back and forth	
B is running		
A is running		
B is running		
A is running		doStuff() doOther()
A is running		
B is running		
B is running		
A is running		Stack A is Stack B is
B is running		running running
A is running ——	b.join(); // A joins to the end	
B is running	// of B	
B is running		
B is running		
B is running		
B is running		doOther()
B is running		
B is running ——	// Thread B completes !!	Stack B
A is running ——	// Thread A starts again !	
A is running		
A is running		
A is running		doStuff()
A is running		
A is running		Stack A
		Stack A joined to Stack B

So far, we've looked at three ways a running thread could leave the running state:

- **A call to `sleep()`**   Guaranteed to cause the current thread to stop executing for at least the specified sleep duration (although it might be *interrupted* before its specified time).
- **A call to `yield()`**   Not guaranteed to do much of anything, although typically, it will cause the currently running thread to move back to runnable so that a thread of the same priority can have a chance.
- **A call to `join()`**   Guaranteed to cause the current thread to stop executing until the thread it joins with (in other words, the thread it calls `join()` on) completes, or if the thread it's trying to join with is not alive, the current thread won't need to back out.

Besides those three, we also have the following scenarios in which a thread might leave the running state:

- The thread's `run()` method completes. Duh.
- A call to `wait()` on an object (we don't call `wait()` on a *thread*, as we'll see in a moment).
- A thread can't acquire the *lock* on the object whose method code it's attempting to run.
- The thread scheduler can decide to move the current thread from running to runnable in order to give another thread a chance to run. No reason is needed—the thread scheduler can trade threads in and out whenever it likes.

CERTIFICATION OBJECTIVE

Synchronizing Code, Thread Problems (OCP Objectives 10.2 and 10.3)

10.2   Identify potential threading problems among deadlock, starvation, livelock, and race conditions.
10.3   Use synchronized keyword and java.util.concurrent.atomic package to control the order of thread execution.

Can you imagine the havoc that can occur when two different threads have access to a single instance of a class, and both threads invoke methods on that object…and those methods modify the state of the object? In other words, what might happen if *two* different threads call, say, a setter method on a *single* object? A scenario like that might corrupt an object's state by changing its instance variable values in an inconsistent way, and if that object's state is data shared by other parts of the program, well, it's too scary to even visualize.

But just because we enjoy horror, let's look at an example of what might happen. The following code demonstrates what happens when two different threads are accessing the same account data. Imagine that two people each have a checkbook for a single checking account (or two people each have ATM cards, but both cards are linked to only one account).

In this example, we have a class called Account that represents a bank account. To keep the code short, this account starts with a balance of 50 and can be used only for withdrawals. The withdrawal will be accepted even if there isn't enough money in the account to cover it. The account simply reduces the balance by the amount you want to withdraw:

```
class Account {
  private int balance = 50;
  public int getBalance() {
    return balance;
  }
  public void withdraw(int amount) {
    balance = balance - amount;
  }
}
```

Now here's where it starts to get fun. Imagine a couple, Fred and Lucy, who both have access to the account and want to make withdrawals. But they don't want the account to ever be overdrawn, so just before one of them makes a withdrawal, he or she will first check the balance to be certain there's enough to cover the withdrawal. Also, withdrawals are always limited to an amount of 10, so there must be at least 10 in the account balance in order to make a withdrawal. Sounds reasonable. But that's a two-step process:

1. Check the balance.
2. If there's enough in the account (in this example, at least 10), make the withdrawal.

What happens if something separates step 1 from step 2? For example, imagine what would happen if Lucy checks the balance and sees there's just exactly enough in the account, 10. *But before she makes the withdrawal, Fred checks the balance and also sees that there's enough for his withdrawal.* Since Lucy has verified the balance but not yet made her withdrawal, Fred is seeing "bad data." He is seeing the account balance *before* Lucy actually debits the account, but at this point, that debit is certain to occur. Now both Lucy and Fred believe there's enough to make their withdrawals. Now imagine that Lucy makes *her* withdrawal, so there isn't enough in the account for Fred's withdrawal, but he thinks there is because when he checked, there was enough! Yikes. In a minute, we'll see the actual banking code, with Fred and Lucy, represented by two threads, each acting on the same `Runnable`, and that `Runnable` holds a reference to the one and only account instance—so, two threads, one account.

The logic in our code example is as follows:

1. The `Runnable` object holds a reference to a single account.

2. Two threads are started, representing Lucy and Fred, and each thread is given a reference to the same `Runnable` (which holds a reference to the actual account).

3. The initial balance on the account is 50, and each withdrawal is exactly 10.

4. In the `run()` method, we loop five times, and in each loop we

   ■ Make a withdrawal (if there's enough in the account).

   ■ Print a statement *if the account is overdrawn* (which it should never be since we check the balance *before* making a withdrawal).

5. The `makeWithdrawal()` method in the test class (representing the behavior of Fred or Lucy) will do the following:

   ■ Check the balance to see if there's enough for the withdrawal.

   ■ If there is enough, print out the name of the one making the withdrawal.

   ■ Go to sleep for 500 milliseconds—just long enough to give the other partner a chance to get in before you actually *make* the withdrawal.

   ■ Upon waking up, complete the withdrawal and print that fact.

   ■ If there wasn't enough in the first place, print a statement showing who you are and the fact that there wasn't enough.

So what we're really trying to discover is if the following is possible: for one partner to check the account and see that there's enough, but before making the actual withdrawal, the other partner checks the account and *also* sees that there's enough. When the account balance gets to 10, if both partners check it before making the withdrawal, both will think it's okay to withdraw, and the account will be overdrawn by 10!

Here's the code:

```
public class AccountDanger implements Runnable {
  private Account acct = new Account();
  public static void main (String [] args) {
    AccountDanger r = new AccountDanger();
    Thread one = new Thread(r);
    Thread two = new Thread(r);
    one.setName("Fred");
    two.setName("Lucy");
    one.start();
    two.start();
  }
  public void run() {
    for (int x = 0; x < 5; x++) {
      makeWithdrawal(10);
      if (acct.getBalance() < 0) {
        System.out.println("account is overdrawn!");
      }}}
  private void makeWithdrawal(int amt) {
    if (acct.getBalance() >= amt) {
      System.out.println(Thread.currentThread().getName()
                      + " is going to withdraw");
      try {
        Thread.sleep(500);
      } catch(InterruptedException ex) { }
      acct.withdraw(amt);
      System.out.println(Thread.currentThread().getName()
                      + " completes the withdrawal");
    } else {
      System.out.println("Not enough in account for "
                      + Thread.currentThread().getName()
                      + " to withdraw " + acct.getBalance());
    }}}
```

(Note: You might have to tweak this code a bit on your machine to the "account overdrawn" behavior. You might try much shorter sleep times; you might try adding a sleep to the run() method... In any case, experimenting will help you lock in the concepts.) So what happened? Is it possible that, say, Lucy checked the balance, fell asleep, Fred checked the balance, Lucy woke up and completed *her* withdrawal, then Fred completes *his* withdrawal, and in the end, they overdraw the account? Look at the (numbered) output:

```
% java AccountDanger
  1. Fred is going to withdraw
  2. Lucy is going to withdraw
  3. Fred completes the withdrawal
  4. Fred is going to withdraw
  5. Lucy completes the withdrawal
  6. Lucy is going to withdraw
```

```
 7. Fred completes the withdrawal
 8. Fred is going to withdraw
 9. Lucy completes the withdrawal
10. Lucy is going to withdraw
11. Fred completes the withdrawal
12. Not enough in account for Fred to withdraw 0
13. Not enough in account for Fred to withdraw 0
14. Lucy completes the withdrawal
15. account is overdrawn!
16. Not enough in account for Lucy to withdraw -10
17. account is overdrawn!
18. Not enough in account for Lucy to withdraw -10
19. account is overdrawn!
```

Although each time you run this code the output might be a little different, let's walk through this particular example using the numbered lines of output. For the first four attempts, everything is fine. Fred checks the balance on line 1 and finds it's okay. At line 2, Lucy checks the balance and finds it okay. At line 3, Fred makes his withdrawal. At this point, the balance Lucy checked for (and believes is still accurate) has actually changed since she last checked. And now Fred checks the balance *again,* before Lucy even completes her first withdrawal. By this point, even Fred is seeing a potentially inaccurate balance because we know Lucy is going to complete her withdrawal. It is possible, of course, that Fred will complete his before Lucy does, but that's not what happens here.

On line 5, Lucy completes her withdrawal and then, before Fred completes his, Lucy does another check on the account on line 6. And so it continues until we get to line 8, where Fred checks the balance and sees that it's 20. On line 9, Lucy completes a withdrawal that she had checked for earlier, and this takes the balance to 10. On line 10, Lucy checks again, sees that the balance is 10, so she knows she can do a withdrawal. *But she didn't know that Fred, too, has already checked the balance on line 8 so he thinks it's safe to do the withdrawal!* On line 11, Fred completes the withdrawal he approved on line 8. This takes the balance to 0. But Lucy still has a pending withdrawal that she got approval for on line 10! You know what's coming.

On lines 12 and 13, Fred checks the balance and finds that there's not enough in the account. But on line 14, Lucy completes her withdrawal and BOOM! The account is now overdrawn by 10—*something we thought we were preventing by doing a balance check prior to a withdrawal.*

Figure 10-4 shows the timeline of what can happen when two threads concurrently access the same object.

This problem is known as a "race condition," where multiple threads can access the same resource (typically an object's instance variables) and can produce

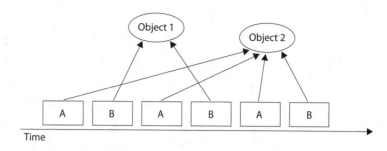

Thread A will access Object 2 only

Thread B will access Object 1, and then Object 2

corrupted data if one thread "races in" too quickly before an operation that should be "atomic" has completed.

Preventing the Account Overdraw

So what can be done? The solution is actually quite simple. We must guarantee that the two steps of the withdrawal—*checking* the balance and *making* the withdrawal—are never split apart. We need them to always be performed as one operation, even when the thread falls asleep in between step 1 and step 2! We call this an "atomic operation" (although the physics is a little outdated—in this case, "atomic" means "indivisible") because the operation, regardless of the number of actual statements (or underlying bytecode instructions), is completed *before* any other thread code that acts on the same data.

You can't guarantee that a single thread will stay running throughout the entire atomic operation. But you can guarantee that even if the thread running the atomic operation moves in and out of the running state, no other running thread will be able to act on the same data. In other words, if Lucy falls asleep after checking the balance, we can stop Fred from checking the balance until after Lucy wakes up and completes her withdrawal.

So how do you protect the data? You must do two things:

■ Mark the variables `private`.
■ Synchronize the code that modifies the variables.

Remember, you protect the variables in the normal way—using an access control modifier. It's the method code that you must protect so only one thread at a time can be executing that code. You do this with the `synchronized` keyword.

We can solve all of Fred and Lucy's problems by adding one word to the code. We mark the `makeWithdrawal()` method `synchronized` as follows:

```
private synchronized void makeWithdrawal(int amt) {
  if (acct.getBalance() >= amt) {
    System.out.println(Thread.currentThread().getName() +
                       " is going to withdraw");
    try {
      Thread.sleep(500);
    } catch(InterruptedException ex) { }
    acct.withdraw(amt);
    System.out.println(Thread.currentThread().getName() +
                           " completes the withdrawal");
  } else {
    System.out.println("Not enough in account for "
                  + Thread.currentThread().getName()
                  + " to withdraw " + acct.getBalance());
  }
}
```

Now we've guaranteed that once a thread (Lucy or Fred) starts the withdrawal process by invoking `makeWithdrawal()`, the other thread cannot enter that method until the first one completes the process by exiting the method. The new output shows the benefit of synchronizing the `makeWithdrawal()` method:

```
% java AccountDanger
Fred is going to withdraw
Fred completes the withdrawal
Lucy is going to withdraw
Lucy completes the withdrawal
Fred is going to withdraw
Fred completes the withdrawal
Lucy is going to withdraw
Lucy completes the withdrawal
Fred is going to withdraw
Fred completes the withdrawal
Not enough in account for Lucy to withdraw 0
Not enough in account for Fred to withdraw 0
Not enough in account for Lucy to withdraw 0
Not enough in account for Fred to withdraw 0
Not enough in account for Lucy to withdraw 0
```

Notice that now both threads, Lucy and Fred, always check the account balance *and* complete the withdrawal before the other thread can check the balance.

Synchronization and Locks

How does synchronization work? With locks. Every object in Java has a built-in lock that only comes into play when the object has synchronized method code. When we enter a synchronized non-`static` method, we automatically acquire the lock associated with the current instance of the class whose code we're executing (the `this` instance). Acquiring a lock for an object is also known as getting the lock, or locking the object, locking *on* the object, or synchronizing on the object. We may also use the term *monitor* to refer to the object whose lock we're acquiring. Technically, the lock and the monitor are two different things, but most people talk about the two interchangeably, and we will too.

Since there is only one lock per object, if one thread has picked up the lock, no other thread can pick up the lock until the first thread releases (or returns) the lock. This means no other thread can enter the synchronized code (which means it can't enter any `synchronized` method of that object) until the lock has been released. Typically, releasing a lock means the thread holding the lock (in other words, the thread currently in the `synchronized` method) exits the `synchronized` method. At that point, the lock is free until some other thread enters a `synchronized` method on that object. Remember the following key points about locking and synchronization:

- Only methods (or blocks) can be `synchronized`, not variables or classes.
- Each object has just one lock.
- Not all methods in a class need to be `synchronized`. A class can have both `synchronized` and non-`synchronized` methods.
- If two threads are about to execute a `synchronized` method in a class and both threads are using the same instance of the class to invoke the method, only one thread at a time will be able to execute the method. The other thread will need to wait until the first one finishes its method call. In other words, once a thread acquires the lock on an object, no other thread can enter any of the `synchronized` methods in that class (for that object).
- If a class has both `synchronized` and non-`synchronized` methods, multiple threads can still access the class's non-`synchronized` methods! If you have methods that don't access the data you're trying to protect, then you don't need to synchronize them. Synchronization can cause a hit in some cases (or even deadlock if used incorrectly), so you should be careful not to overuse it.
- If a thread goes to sleep, it holds any locks it has—it doesn't release them.
- A thread can acquire more than one lock. For example, a thread can enter a `synchronized` method, thus acquiring a lock, and then immediately invoke a `synchronized` method on a different object, thus acquiring that lock as well. As the stack unwinds, locks are released again. Also, if a thread acquires a lock and then attempts to call a `synchronized` method on

that same object, no problem. The JVM knows that this thread already has the lock for this object, so the thread is free to call other `synchronized` methods on the same object, using the lock the thread already has.

■ You can synchronize a block of code rather than a method.

Because synchronization does hurt concurrency, you don't want to synchronize any more code than is necessary to protect your data. So if the scope of a method is more than needed, you can reduce the scope of the synchronized part to something less than a full method—to just a block. We call this, strangely, a *synchronized block,* and it looks like this:

```
class SyncTest {
  public void doStuff() {
    System.out.println("not synchronized");
    synchronized(this) {
      System.out.println("synchronized");
    }
  }
}
```

When a thread is executing code from within a `synchronized` block, including any method code invoked from that `synchronized` block, the code is said to be executing in a synchronized context. The real question is, synchronized on what? Or, synchronized on which object's lock?

When you synchronize a method, the object used to invoke the method is the object whose lock must be acquired. But when you synchronize a block of code, you specify which object's lock you want to use as the lock, so you could, for example, use some third-party object as the lock for this piece of code. That gives you the ability to have more than one lock for code synchronization within a single object.

Or you can synchronize on the current instance (`this`) as in the previous code. Since that's the same instance that `synchronized` methods lock on, it means you could always replace a `synchronized` method with a non-synchronized method containing a `synchronized` block. In other words, this:

```
public synchronized void doStuff() {
  System.out.println("synchronized");
}
```

is equivalent to this:

```
public void doStuff() {
  synchronized(this) {
    System.out.println("synchronized");
  }
}
```

These methods both have the exact same effect—in practical terms. The compiled bytecodes may not be exactly the same for the two methods, but they *could* be—and any differences are not really important. The first form is shorter and more familiar to most people, but the second can be more flexible.

Can Static Methods Be Synchronized?

static methods can be synchronized. There is only one copy of the static data you're trying to protect, so you only need one lock per class to synchronize static methods—a lock for the whole class. There is such a lock; every class loaded in Java has a corresponding instance of java.lang.Class representing that class. It's that java.lang.Class instance whose lock is used to protect any synchronized static methods of the class. There's nothing special you have to do to synchronize a static method:

```
public static synchronized int getCount() {
  return count;
}
```

Again, this could be replaced with code that uses a synchronized block. If the method is defined in a class called MyClass, the equivalent code is as follows:

```
public static int getCount() {
  synchronized(MyClass.class) {
    return count;
  }
}
```

Wait—what's that MyClass.class thing? That's called a *class literal*. It's a special feature in the Java language that tells the compiler (who tells the JVM): Go and find me the instance of Class that represents the class called MyClass. You can also do this with the following code:

```
public static void classMethod() throws ClassNotFoundException {
  Class cl = Class.forName("MyClass");
  synchronized (cl) {
    // do stuff
  }
}
```

However, that's longer, ickier, and most importantly, *not on the OCP exam*. But it's quick and easy to use a class literal—just write the name of the class and add .class at the end. No quotation marks needed. Now you've got an expression for the Class object you need to synchronize on.

Synchronizing a Block of Code

In this exercise, we will attempt to synchronize a block of code. Within that block of code, we will get the lock on an object so that other threads cannot modify it while the block of code is executing. We will be creating three threads that will all attempt to manipulate the same object. Each thread will output a single letter 100 times and then increment that letter by one. The object we will be using is StringBuffer.

We could synchronize on a String object, but strings cannot be modified once they are created, so we would not be able to increment the letter without generating a new String object. The final output should have 100 *A*s, 100 *B*s, and 100 *C*s, all in unbroken lines.

1. Create a class and extend the Thread class.
2. Override the run() method of Thread. This is where the synchronized block of code will go.
3. For our three thread objects to share the same object, we will need to create a constructor that accepts a StringBuffer object in the argument.
4. The synchronized block of code will obtain a lock on the StringBuffer object from step 3.
5. Within the block, output the StringBuffer 100 times and then increment the letter in the StringBuffer.
6. Finally, in the main() method, create a single StringBuffer object using the letter *A*, then create three instances of our class and start all three of them.

What Happens If a Thread Can't Get the Lock?

If a thread tries to enter a synchronized method and the lock is already taken, the thread is said to be blocked on the object's lock. Essentially, the thread goes into a kind of pool for that particular object and has to sit there until the lock is released and the thread can again become runnable/running. Just because a lock is released doesn't mean any particular thread will get it. There might be three threads waiting for a single lock, for example, and there's no guarantee that the thread that has waited the longest will get the lock first.

When thinking about blocking, it's important to pay attention to which objects are being used for locking:

- Threads calling non-`static` `synchronized` methods in the same class will only block each other if they're invoked using the same instance. That's because they each lock on `this` instance, and if they're called using two different instances, they get two locks, which do not interfere with each other.

- Threads calling `static` `synchronized` methods in the same class will always block each other—they all lock on the same `Class` instance.

- A `static` `synchronized` method and a non-`static` `synchronized` method will not block each other, ever. The `static` method locks on a `Class` instance, while the non-`static` method locks on the `this` instance—these actions do not interfere with each other at all.

- For `synchronized` blocks, you have to look at exactly what object has been used for locking. (What's inside the parentheses after the word `synchronized`?) Threads that synchronize on the same object will block each other. Threads that synchronize on different objects will not.

Table 10-1 lists the thread-related methods and whether the thread gives up its lock as a result of the call.

So When Do I Need to Synchronize?

Synchronization can get pretty complicated, and you may be wondering why you would want to do this at all if you can help it. But remember the earlier "race conditions" example with Lucy and Fred making withdrawals from their account.

TABLE 10-1	Give Up Locks	Keep Locks	Class Defining the Method
Methods and Lock Status	`wait ()`	`notify()` (Although the thread will probably exit the synchronized code shortly after this call and thus give up its locks)	`java.lang.Object`
		`join()`	`java.lang.Thread`
		`sleep()`	`java.lang.Thread`
		`yield()`	`java.lang.Thread`

When we use threads, we usually need to use some synchronization somewhere to make sure our methods don't interrupt each other at the wrong time and mess up our data. Generally, any time more than one thread is accessing mutable (changeable) data, you synchronize to protect that data to make sure two threads aren't changing it at the same time (or that one isn't changing it at the same time the other is reading it, which is also confusing). You don't need to worry about local variables—each thread gets its own copy of a local variable. Two threads executing the same method at the same time will use different copies of the local variables, and they won't bother each other. However, you do need to worry about `static` and non-`static` fields if they contain data that can be changed.

For changeable data in a non-`static` field, you usually use a non-`static` method to access it. By synchronizing that method, you will ensure that any threads trying to run that method *using the same instance* will be prevented from simultaneous access. But a thread working with a *different* instance will not be affected because it's acquiring a lock on the other instance. That's what we want—threads working with the same data need to go one at a time, but threads working with different data can just ignore each other and run whenever they want to; it doesn't matter.

For changeable data in a `static` field, you usually use a `static` method to access it. And again, by synchronizing the method, you ensure that any two threads trying to access the data will be prevented from simultaneous access, because both threads will have to acquire locks on the `Class` object for the class the `static` method's defined in. Again, that's what we want.

However—what if you have a non-`static` method that accesses a `static` field? Or a `static` method that accesses a non-`static` field (using an instance)? In these cases, things start to get messy quickly, and there's a very good chance that things will not work the way you want. If you've got a `static` method accessing a non-`static` field and you synchronize the method, you acquire a lock on the Class object. But what if there's another method that also accesses the non-`static` field, this time using a non-`static` method? It probably synchronizes on the current instance (`this`) instead. Remember that a `static synchronized` method and a non-`static synchronized` method will not block each other—they can run at the same time. Similarly, if you access a `static` field using a non-`static` method, two threads might invoke that method using two different `this` instances. Which means they won't block each other because they use different locks. Which means two threads are simultaneously accessing the same `static` field—exactly the sort of thing we're trying to prevent.

It gets very confusing trying to imagine all the weird things that can happen here. To keep things simple, in order to make a class thread-safe, methods that access changeable fields need to be synchronized.

Access to static fields should be done using static synchronized methods. Access to non-static fields should be done using non-static synchronized methods, for example:

```
public class Thing {
  private static int staticField;
  private int nonstaticField;
  public static synchronized int getStaticField() {
    return staticField;
  }
  public static synchronized void setStaticField(
                                      int staticField) {
    Thing.staticField = staticField;
  }
  public synchronized int getNonstaticField() {
    return nonstaticField;
  }
  public synchronized void setNonstaticField(
                                      int nonstaticField) {
    this.nonstaticField = nonstaticField;
  }
}
```

What if you need to access both static and non-static fields in a method? Well, there are ways to do that, but it's beyond what you need for the exam. You will live a longer, happier life if you JUST DON'T DO IT. Really. Would we lie?

Thread-Safe Classes

When a class has been carefully synchronized to protect its data (using the rules just given or using more complicated alternatives), we say the class is "thread-safe." Many classes in the Java APIs already use synchronization internally in order to make the class "thread-safe." For example, StringBuffer and StringBuilder are nearly identical classes, except that all the methods in StringBuffer are synchronized when necessary, whereas those in StringBuilder are not. Generally, this makes StringBuffer safe to use in a multithreaded environment, whereas StringBuilder is not. (In return, StringBuilder is a little bit faster because it doesn't bother synchronizing.) However, even when a class is "thread-safe," it is often dangerous to rely on these classes to provide the thread protection you need. (C'mon, the repeated quotes used around "thread-safe" had to be a clue, right?)

You still need to think carefully about how you use these classes. As an example, consider the following class:

```
import java.util.*;
public class NameList {
  private List<String> names = Collections.synchronizedList(
                                     new LinkedList<>());

  public void add(String name) {
    names.add(name);
  }
  public String removeFirst() {
    if (names.size() > 0)
      return (String) names.remove(0);
    else
      return null;
  }
}
```

The method `Collections.synchronizedList()` returns a `List` whose methods are all `synchronized` and "thread-safe" according to the documentation (like a Vector—but since this is the 21st century, we're not going to use a Vector here). The question is, can the `NameList` class be used safely from multiple threads? It's tempting to think that yes, because the data in names is in a synchronized collection, the `NameList` class is "safe" too. However, that's not the case—the `removeFirst()` may sometimes throw an `IndexOutOfBoundsException`. What's the problem? Doesn't it correctly check the `size()` of names before removing anything to make sure there's something there? How could this code fail? Let's try to use `NameList` like this:

```
public static void main(String[] args) {
  final NameList nl = new NameList();
  nl.add("Ozymandias");
  class NameDropper extends Thread {
    public void run() {
      String name = nl.removeFirst();
      System.out.println(name);
    }
  }
  Thread t1 = new NameDropper();
  Thread t2 = new NameDropper();
  t1.start();
  t2.start();
}
```

What might happen here is that one of the threads will remove the one name and print it, and then the other will try to remove a name and get `null`. If we think just about the calls to names.size() and names.remove(0), they occur in this order:

Thread t1 executes names.size(), which returns 1.
Thread t1 executes names.remove(0), which returns Ozymandias.
Thread t2 executes names.size(), which returns 0.
Thread t2 does not call remove(0).

The output here is

```
Ozymandias
null
```

However, if we run the program again, something different might happen:

Thread t1 executes names.size(), which returns 1.
Thread t2 executes names.size(), which returns 1.
Thread t1 executes names.remove(0), which returns Ozymandias.
Thread t2 executes names.remove(0), which throws an exception because the list is now empty.

The thing to realize here is that in a "thread-safe" class like the one returned by synchronizedList(), each *individual* method is synchronized. So names.size() is synchronized, and names.remove(0) is synchronized. But nothing prevents another thread from doing something else to the list *in between* those two calls. And that's where problems can happen.

There's a solution here: Don't rely on Collections.synchronizedList(). Instead, synchronize the code yourself:

```
import java.util.*;
public class NameList {
  private List names = new LinkedList();
  public synchronized void add(String name) {
    names.add(name);
  }
  public synchronized String removeFirst() {
    if (names.size() > 0)
      return (String) names.remove(0);
    else
      return null;
  }
}
```

Now the entire removeFirst() method is synchronized, and once one thread starts it and calls names.size(), there's no way the other thread can cut in and steal the last name. The other thread will just have to wait until the first thread completes the removeFirst() method.

The moral here is that just because a class is described as "thread-safe" doesn't mean it is *always* thread-safe. If individual methods are synchronized, that may not be enough—you may be better off putting in synchronization at a higher level (i.e., put it in the block or method that *calls* the other methods). Once you do that, the original synchronization (in this case, the synchronization inside the object returned by `Collections.synchronizedList()`) may well become redundant.

Thread Deadlock

Perhaps the scariest thing that can happen to a Java program is deadlock. Deadlock occurs when two threads are blocked, with each waiting for the other's lock. Neither can run until the other gives up its lock, so they'll sit there forever.

This can happen, for example, when thread A hits `synchronized` code, acquires a lock B, and then enters another method (still within the `synchronized` code it has the lock on) that's also `synchronized`. But thread A can't get the lock to enter this `synchronized` code—block C—because another thread D has the lock already. So thread A goes off to the waiting-for-the-C-lock pool, hoping that thread D will hurry up and release the lock (by completing the `synchronized` method). But thread A will wait a very long time indeed, because while thread D picked up lock C, it then entered a method `synchronized` on lock B. Obviously, thread D can't get the lock B because thread A has it. And thread A won't release it until thread D releases lock C. But thread D won't release lock C until after it can get lock B and continue. And there they sit. The following example demonstrates deadlock:

```
1. public class DeadlockRisk {
2.   private static class Resource {
3.     public int value;
4.   }
5.   private Resource resourceA = new Resource();
6.   private Resource resourceB = new Resource();
7.   public int read() {
8.     synchronized(resourceA) { // May deadlock here
9.       synchronized(resourceB) {
10.         return resourceB.value + resourceA.value;
11.       }
12.     }
13.   }
14.
15.   public void write(int a, int b) {
16.     synchronized(resourceB) { // May deadlock here
```

```
17.        synchronized(resourceA) {
18.           resourceA.value = a;
19.           resourceB.value = b;
20.        }
21.     }
22.  }
23. }
```

Assume that `read()` is started by one thread and `write()` is started by another. If there are two different threads that may read and write independently, there is a risk of deadlock at line 8 or 16. The reader thread will have `resourceA`, the writer thread will have `resourceB`, and both will get stuck waiting for the other.

Code like this almost never results in deadlock because the CPU has to switch from the reader thread to the writer thread at a particular point in the code, and the chances of deadlock occurring are quite small. The application may work fine 99.9 percent of the time.

The preceding simple example is easy to fix; just swap the order of locking for either the reader or the writer at lines 16 and 17 (or lines 8 and 9). More complex deadlock situations can take a long time to figure out.

Regardless of how little chance there is for your code to deadlock, the bottom line is that if you deadlock, you're dead. There are design approaches that can help avoid deadlock, including strategies for always acquiring locks in a predetermined order.

But that's for you to study and is beyond the scope of this book. We're just trying to get you through the exam. If you learn everything in this chapter, though, you'll still know more about threads than most experienced Java programmers.

Thread Livelock

Livelock is almost as scary to a Java program as deadlock. Livelock is similar to deadlock, except that the threads aren't officially dead; they're just too busy to make progress.

Imagine you've got a program with two threads and two locks. Each thread must get both locks in order to proceed with the work it needs to do. Thread one successfully acquires lock 1 and then tries to get lock 1 and fails, because thread 2 has already gotten lock 2. Thread 1 then unlocks lock 1, giving thread 2 a chance to get it, waits a little while and then tries to get lock 1 and lock 2 again.

At the same time, thread 2 gets lock 2 and then attempts to get lock 1. Well, thread 1 already has lock 1, so lock 2 does a similar thing: it unlocks lock 2, giving thread 1 a chance to get it, waits a little while, and then tries to get lock 2 and lock 1 again.

Livelock occurs if thread 1 tries to get lock 2 when thread 2 has lock 2, and thread 2 tries to get lock 1 when thread 1 has lock 1; they both free up the locks they have, so then thread 1 and thread 2 are both waiting on the other thread to get the lock each wants and then both get their locks again and go back to trying to get the lock the other thread has…over and over and over again.

In this situation, the threads are not completely deadlocked, but they are making no progress. This is an extremely tricky problem to detect! The timing has to be just right, so you might find your code runs perfectly fine 99 percent of the time and livelocks 1 percent of the time. Fortunately, Java makes livelock hard to do; with ReentrantLock (more on this in Chapter 11 where we talk about concurrency) and careful ordering of how your threads attempt to access locks, you will be unlikely to encounter this problem.

Thread Starvation

Starvation is related to livelock. Starvation is when a thread is unable to make progress because it cannot get access to a shared resource that other threads are hogging. This could happen when another thread gets access to a synchronized resource and then goes into an infinite loop or takes a really long time to use the resource. It could also happen if one thread has higher priority than another thread so the first thread always gets a resource when both threads attempt to access that resource at the same time.

If you are not fiddling with thread priorities—and you are careful about how long a thread can keep access to a resource before yielding or timing out—then you should be able to avoid starvation. Good thread schedulers will help prevent starvation by allocating time fairly between threads behind the scenes.

Race Conditions

A race condition is another scenario that can crop up when working with multiple threads. To understand what a race condition is and how it can occur, let's revisit the singleton pattern from Chapter 2.

In that chapter, we mentioned that our singleton implementation is not thread-safe without some precautions. Let's take a look at how we might use the Show singleton from that chapter in a multithreaded program to see where things can go wrong. In the process, we'll create a race condition.

```
public class Show {
    private static Show INSTANCE;
    private Set<String> availableSeats;
```

```
    public static Show getInstance() {   // create a singleton instance
        if (INSTANCE == null) {
            INSTANCE = new Show();        // should be only one Show!
        }
        return INSTANCE;
    }
    private Show() {
        availableSeats = new HashSet<String>();
        availableSeats.add("1A");
        availableSeats.add("1B");
    }
    public boolean bookSeat(String seat) {
        return availableSeats.remove(seat);
    }
}

public class TestShow {
    public static void main(String[] args) {
        TestShow testThreads = new TestShow();
        testThreads.go();
    }
    public void go() {
        // create Thread 1, which will try to book seats 1A and 1B
        Thread getSeats1 = new Thread(() -> {
            ticketAgentBooks("1A");
            ticketAgentBooks("1B");
        });
        // create Thread 2, which will try to book seats 1A and 1B
        Thread getSeats2 = new Thread(() -> {
            ticketAgentBooks("1A");
            ticketAgentBooks("1B");
        });
        // start both threads
        getSeats1.start();
        getSeats2.start();
    }
    public void ticketAgentBooks(String seat) {
        // get the one instance of the Show Singleton
        Show show = Show.getInstance();
        // book a seat and print
        System.out.println(Thread.currentThread().getName() + ": "
            + show.bookSeat(seat));
    }
}
```

When we run the code, here's what we get:

```
Thread-1: true
Thread-1: true
Thread-0: true
Thread-0: false
```

Uh oh. It looks like we've sold seat 1A twice! That means two people will show up for the concert and expect to get the same seat.

This issue is caused by a *race condition*. A race condition is when two or more threads try to access and change a shared resource at the same time, and the result is dependent on the order in which the code is executed by the threads.

Let's step through the code and see how this happens. In TestShow, in go() (which we call from main()), we create two threads. Each thread tries to book seats 1A and 1B by calling ticketAgentBooks(). We start both threads.

Imagine a scenario where thread one calls ticketAgentBooks() with the argument "1A". Thread one calls Show.getInstance(). It executes the code:

```
if (INSTANCE == null)
```

and determines the value in INSTANCE is, indeed, null, and so is just about to execute the next line of code when BOOM! The thread is descheduled, and thread two begins executing.

Now, thread two calls ticketAgentBooks() with the argument "1A". Thread two calls Show.getInstance(). It executes the code:

```
if (INSTANCE == null)
```

and determines the value of INSTANCE is, indeed, null, and so executes the next line of code:

```
INSTANCE = new Show();
```

Thread two then gets descheduled and thread one begins executing again. It then executes the line:

```
INSTANCE = new Show();
```

Now we have two instances of Show. So when thread one then uses its instance of Show to book a seat by calling show.bookSeat() on "1A", it succeeds. Similarly, when thread two uses its instance of Show to book a seat, it too succeeds. We had two threads racing to get what should have been one shared resource, and because of timing, we end up with two instances of a resource and a failure in our program logic.

We can fix this race condition by making the getInstance() method synchronized and the INSTANCE variable volatile:

```
private static volatile Show INSTANCE;
public static synchronized Show getInstance() {
  if (INSTANCE == null) {
    INSTANCE = new Show();
  }
  return INSTANCE;
}
```

The volatile keyword makes sure that the variable INSTANCE is atomic; that is, a write to the variable happens all at once. Nothing can interrupt this process: it either happens completely, or it doesn't happen at all. So in getInstance(), where we create a new instance of Show() and assign it to INSTANCE, that entire operation must complete before the thread can be interrupted.

The *synchronized* keyword makes sure only one thread at a time can access the getInstance() method. That ensures we won't get a race condition: in other words, we can't check the value of INSTANCE in one thread, then stop, and do the same in another thread.

You can run this code, but you might find it still doesn't work! Why?

Take a look at the method bookSeat() in Show. When we book a seat by calling this method from the ticketAgentBooks() method, we are changing another shared resource, the availableSeats Set. However, the Set is not thread-safe! That means a thread could be interrupted in the middle of removing seat "1A" from the Set, and another thread could come along and access the Set. If the operations to remove the seat from the availableSeats Set get interleaved, we can still end up in a situation where two threads can book the same seat.

To solve this problem, we must synchronize the bookSeat() method, too:

```
public synchronized boolean bookSeat(String seat) {
   return availableSeats.remove(seat);
}
```

Now when we run the code, we should find that each seat can be booked by only one thread:

```
Thread-0: true
Thread-1: false
Thread-0: true
Thread-1: false
```

Notice that this does not mean that a thread will get both seats. Right? A thread can still be interrupted in between the two seat bookings:

```
Thread-1: false
Thread-1: true
Thread-0: true
Thread-0: false
```

If you want to make sure you sell both seats to the same thread, you have to do even more work. But that's enough for now (and enough about race conditions for the exam).

In a multithreaded environment, we need to make sure our code is designed so it's not dependent on the ordering of the threads. In situations where our code is dependent on ordering or dependent on certain operations not being interrupted, we can get race conditions. As you've seen, there are ways to fix race conditions, but like deadlock, livelock, and starvation, they can be tricky to detect.

You've seen an example where a race condition led to two threads both getting seat "1A". There are also race conditions in which neither thread gets seat "1A". It's far better for neither thread to end up with a seat than for two threads to end up with the same seat (while the venue operator might be unhappy having an empty, unsold seat, it's worse to have customers fighting over seats!). However, by fixing the race conditions in this code, we've enabled the seats to be sold to the threads properly, so only one thread gets any given seat.

CERTIFICATION OBJECTIVE

Thread Interaction (OCP Objectives 10.2 and 10.3)

10.2   Identify potential threading problems among deadlock, starvation, livelock, and race conditions.

10.3   Use synchronized keyword and java.util.concurrent.atomic package to control the order of thread execution.

The last thing we need to look at is how threads can interact with one another to communicate about—among other things—their locking status. The `Object` class has three methods, `wait()`, `notify()`, and `notifyAll()`, that help threads communicate the status of an event that the threads care about. For example, if one thread is a mail-delivery thread and one thread is a mail-processor thread, the mail-processor thread has to keep checking to see if there's any mail to process. Using the wait and notify mechanism, the mail-processor thread could check for mail, and if it doesn't find any, it can say, "Hey, I'm not going to waste my time checking for mail every two seconds. I'm going to go hang out, and when the mail deliverer puts something in the mailbox, have him notify me so I can go back to runnable and do some work." In other words, using `wait()` and `notify()` lets one thread put itself into a "waiting room" until some *other* thread notifies it that there's a reason to come back out.

One key point to remember (and keep in mind for the exam) about `wait()`/ `notify()` is this:

`wait()`, `notify()`, and `notifyAll()` must be called from within a synchronized context! A thread can't invoke a `wait()` or `notify()` method on an object unless it owns that object's lock.

Here we'll present an example of two threads that depend on each other to proceed with their execution, and we'll show how to use `wait()` and `notify()` to make them interact safely at the proper moment.

Think of a computer-controlled machine that cuts pieces of fabric into different shapes and an application that allows users to specify the shape to cut. The current version of the application has one thread, which loops, first asking the user for instructions, and then directs the hardware to cut the requested shape:

```
public void run(){
  while(true){
    // Get shape from user
    // Calculate machine steps from shape
    // Send steps to hardware
  }
}
```

This design is not optimal because the user can't do anything while the machine is busy and while there are other shapes to define. We need to improve the situation.

A simple solution is to separate the processes into two different threads, one of them interacting with the user and another managing the hardware. The user thread sends the instructions to the hardware thread and then goes back to interacting with the user immediately. The hardware thread receives the instructions from the user thread and starts directing the machine immediately. Both threads use a common object to communicate, which holds the current design being processed.

The following pseudocode shows this design:

```
public void userLoop(){
  while(true){
    // Get shape from user
    // Calculate machine steps from shape
    // Modify common object with new machine steps
  }
}

public void hardwareLoop(){
  while(true){
    // Get steps from common object
    // Send steps to hardware
  }
}
```

The problem now is to get the hardware thread to process the machine steps as soon as they are available. Also, the user thread should not modify them until they have all been sent to the hardware. The solution is to use `wait()` and `notify()` and also to synchronize some of the code.

The methods `wait()` and `notify()`, remember, are instance methods of `Object`. In the same way that every object has a lock, every object can have a list of threads that are waiting for a signal (a notification) from the object. A thread gets on this waiting list by executing the `wait()` method of the target object. From that moment, it doesn't execute any further instructions until the `notify()` method of the target object is called. If many threads are waiting on the same object, only one will be chosen (in no guaranteed order) to proceed with its execution. If there are no threads waiting, then no particular action is taken. Let's take a look at some real code that shows one object waiting for another object to notify it (take note, it is somewhat complex):

```
1. class ThreadA {
2.   public static void main(String [] args) {
3.     ThreadB b = new ThreadB();
4.     b.start();
5.
6.     synchronized(b) {
7.       try {
8.         System.out.println("Waiting for b to complete...");
9.         b.wait();
10.      } catch (InterruptedException e) {}
11.      System.out.println("Total is: " + b.total);
12.    }
13.  }
14. }
15.
16. class ThreadB extends Thread {
17.   int total;
18.
19.   public void run() {
20.     synchronized(this) {
21.       for(int i=0;i<100;i++) {
22.         total += i;
23.       }
24.       notify();
25.     }
26.   }
27. }
```

This program contains two objects with threads: `ThreadA` contains the main thread, and `ThreadB` has a thread that calculates the sum of all numbers from 0 through 99. As soon as line 4 calls the `start()` method, `ThreadA` will continue with the next line of code in its own class, which means it could get to line 11 before `ThreadB` has finished the calculation. To prevent this, we use the `wait()` method in line 9.

Notice in line 6 the code synchronizes itself with the object b—this is because in order to call wait() on the object, ThreadA must own a lock on b. For a thread to call wait() or notify(), the thread has to be the owner of the lock for that object. When the thread waits, it temporarily releases the lock for other threads to use, but it will need it again to continue execution. It's common to find code like this:

```
synchronized(anotherObject) { // this has the lock on anotherObject
  try {
    anotherObject.wait();
      // the thread releases the lock and waits
      // To continue, the thread needs the lock,
      // so it may be blocked until it gets it.
  } catch(InterruptedException e){}
}
```

The preceding code waits until notify() is called on anotherObject.

```
synchronized(this) { notify(); }
```

This code notifies a single thread currently waiting on the this object. The lock can be acquired much earlier in the code, such as in the calling method. Note that if the thread calling wait() does not own the lock, it will throw an IllegalMonitorStateException. This exception is not a checked exception, so you don't have to *catch* it explicitly. You should always be clear whether a thread has the lock of an object in any given block of code.

Notice in lines 7–10 there is a try/catch block around the wait() method. A waiting thread can be interrupted in the same way as a sleeping thread, so you have to take care of the exception:

```
try {
  wait();
} catch(InterruptedException e) {
  // Do something about it
}
```

In the next example, the way to use these methods is to have the hardware thread wait on the shape to be available and the user thread to notify after it has written the steps. The machine steps may comprise global steps, such as moving the required fabric to the cutting area, and a number of substeps, such as the direction and length of a cut. As an example, they could be

```
int fabricRoll;
int cuttingSpeed;
Point startingPoint;
float[] directions;
float[] lengths;
etc..
```

It is important that the user thread does not modify the machine steps while the hardware thread is using them, so this reading and writing should be synchronized. The resulting code would look like this:

```
class Operator extends Thread {
  public void run(){
    while(true){
        // Get shape from user
      synchronized(this){
          // Calculate new machine steps from shape
        notify();
      }
    }
  }
}
class Machine extends Thread {
  Operator operator; // assume this gets initialized
  public void run(){
    while(true){
      synchronized(operator){
        try {
          operator.wait();
        } catch(InterruptedException ie) {}
        // Send machine steps to hardware
      }
    }
  }
}
```

The machine thread, once started, will immediately go into the waiting state and will wait patiently until the operator sends the first notification. At that point, it is the operator thread that owns the lock for the object, so the hardware thread gets stuck for a while. It's only after the operator thread abandons the synchronized block that the hardware thread can really start processing the machine steps.

While one shape is being processed by the hardware, the user may interact with the system and specify another shape to be cut. When the user is finished with the shape and it is time to cut it, the operator thread attempts to enter the synchronized block, maybe blocking until the machine thread has finished with the previous machine steps. When the machine thread has finished, it repeats the loop, going again to the waiting state (and therefore releasing the lock). Only then can the operator thread enter the synchronized block and overwrite the machine steps with the new ones.

Having two threads is definitely an improvement over having one, although in this implementation, there is still a possibility of making the user wait. A further improvement would be to have many shapes in a queue, thereby reducing the possibility of requiring the user to wait for the hardware.

There is also a second form of wait() that accepts a number of milliseconds as a maximum time to wait. If the thread is not interrupted, it will continue normally whenever it is notified or the specified timeout has elapsed. This normal continuation consists of getting out of the waiting state, but to continue execution, it will have to get the lock for the object:

```
synchronized(a){   // The thread gets the lock on 'a'
    a.wait(2000);  // Thread releases the lock and waits for notify
                   // only for a maximum of two seconds, then goes back
                   // to Runnable
                   // The thread reacquires the lock
                   // More instructions here
}
```

e x a m

w a t c h

When the wait() *method is invoked on an object, the thread executing that code gives up its lock on the object immediately. However, when* notify() *is called, that doesn't mean the thread gives up its lock at that moment. If*

the thread is still completing synchronized code, the lock is not released until the thread moves out of synchronized code. So just because notify() *is called, this doesn't mean the lock becomes available at that moment.*

Using notifyAll( ) When Many Threads May Be Waiting

In most scenarios, it's preferable to notify *all* of the threads that are waiting on a particular object. If so, you can use notifyAll() on the object to let all the threads rush out of the waiting area and back to runnable. This is especially important if you have several threads waiting on one object, but for different reasons, and you want to be sure that the *right* thread (along with all of the others) is notified.

```
notifyAll(); // Will notify all waiting threads
```

All of the threads will be notified and start competing to get the lock. As the lock is used and released by each thread, all of them will get into action without a need for further notification.

As we said earlier, an object can have many threads waiting on it, and using notify() will affect only one of them. Which one, exactly, is not specified and depends on the JVM implementation, so you should never rely on a particular thread being notified in preference to another.

In cases in which there might be a lot more waiting, the best way to do this is by using notifyAll(). Let's take a look at this in some code. In this example, there is one class that performs a calculation and many readers that are waiting to receive the completed calculation. At any given moment, many readers may be waiting.

```
1. class Reader extends Thread {
2.    Calculator c;
3.
4.    public Reader(Calculator calc) {
5.       c = calc;
6.    }
7.
8.    public void run() {
9.       synchronized(c) {
10.          try {
11.            System.out.println("Waiting for calculation...");
12.              c.wait();
13.          } catch (InterruptedException e) {}
14.            System.out.println("Total is: " + c.total);
15.          }
16.       }
17.
18.    public static void main(String [] args) {
19.       Calculator calculator = new Calculator();
20.       new Reader(calculator).start();
21.       new Reader(calculator).start();
22.       new Reader(calculator).start();
23.       new Thread(calculator).start();
24.    }
25. }
26.
27. class Calculator implements Runnable {
28.    int total;
29.
30.    public void run() {
31.       synchronized(this) {
32.          for(int i = 0; i < 100; i++) {
33.             total += i;
34.          }
35.          notifyAll();
36.       }
37.    }
38. }
```

The program starts three threads that are all waiting to receive the finished calculation (lines 18–24) and then starts the calculator with its calculation. Note that if the run() method at line 30 used notify() instead of notifyAll(), only one reader would be notified instead of all the readers.

Using wait( ) in a Loop

Actually, both of the previous examples (Machine/Operator and Reader/Calculator) had a common problem. In each one, there was at least one thread calling `wait()` and another thread calling `notify()` or `notifyAll()`. This works well enough as long as the waiting threads have actually started waiting before the other thread executes the `notify()` or `notifyAll()`. But what happens if, for example, the `Calculator` runs first and calls `notify()` before the `Readers` have started waiting? This could happen since we can't guarantee the order in which the different parts of the thread will execute. Unfortunately, when the Readers run, they just start waiting right away. They don't do anything to see if the event they're waiting for has already happened. So if the `Calculator` has already called `notifyAll()`, it's not going to call `notifyAll()` again—and the waiting `Readers` will keep waiting forever. This is probably *not* what the programmer wanted to happen. Almost always, when you want to wait for something, you also need to be able to check if it has already happened. Generally, the best way to solve this is to put in some sort of loop that checks on some sort of conditional expressions and only waits if the thing you're waiting for has not yet happened. Here's a modified, safer version of the earlier fabric-cutting machine example:

```
class Operator extends Thread {
  Machine machine; // assume this gets initialized
  public void run() {
    while (true) {
      Shape shape = getShapeFromUser();
      MachineInstructions job =
                    calculateNewInstructionsFor(shape);
      machine.addJob(job);
    }
  }
}
```

The operator will still keep on looping forever, getting more shapes from users, calculating new instructions for those shapes, and sending them to the machine. But now the logic for `notify()` has been moved into the `addJob()` method in the `Machine` class:

```
class Machine extends Thread {
  List<MachineInstructions> jobs =
                    new ArrayList<MachineInstructions>();

  public void addJob(MachineInstructions job) {
    synchronized (jobs) {
      jobs.add(job);
      jobs.notify();
```

```
      }
    }
    public void run() {
      while (true) {
        synchronized (jobs) {
          // wait until at least one job is available
          while (jobs.isEmpty()) {
            try {
              jobs.wait();
            } catch (InterruptedException ie) { }
          }
          // If we get here, we know that jobs is not empty
          MachineInstructions instructions = jobs.remove(0);
          // Send machine steps to hardware
        }
      }
    }
  }
```

A machine keeps a list of the jobs it's scheduled to do. Whenever an operator adds a new job to the list, it calls the addJob() method and adds the new job to the list. Meanwhile, the run() method just keeps looping, looking for any jobs on the list. If there are no jobs, it will start waiting. If it's notified, it will stop waiting and then recheck the loop condition: Is the list still empty? In practice, this double-check is probably not necessary, as the only time a notify() is ever sent is when a new job has been added to the list. However, it's a good idea to require the thread to recheck the isEmpty() condition whenever it's been woken up because it's possible that a thread has accidentally sent an extra notify() that was not intended. There's also a possible situation called *spontaneous wakeup* that may exist in some situations—a thread may wake up even though no code has called notify() or notifyAll(). (At least, no code you know about has called these methods. Sometimes, the JVM may call notify() for reasons of its own, or code in some other class calls it for reasons you just don't know.) What this means is that when your thread wakes up from a wait(), you don't know for sure why it was awakened. By putting the wait() method in a while loop and rechecking the condition that represents what we were waiting for, we ensure that *whatever* the reason we woke up, we will re-enter the wait() if (and only if) the thing we were waiting for has not happened yet. In the Machine class, the thing we were waiting for is for the jobs list to not be empty. If it's empty, we wait, and if it's not, we don't.

Note also that both the run() method and the addJob() method synchronize on the same object—the jobs list. This is for two reasons. One is because we're calling wait() and notify() on this instance, so we need to synchronize in order to avoid an IllegalMonitorStateException. The other reason is that the data in the jobs list is changeable data stored in a field that is accessed by two different threads. We need to synchronize in order to access that changeable data safely. Fortunately, the same `synchronized` blocks that allow us to `wait()` and `notify()` also provide the required thread safety for our other access to changeable data. In fact, this is a main reason why synchronization is required to use `wait()` and `notify()` in the first place—you almost always need to share some mutable data between threads at the same time, and that means you need synchronization. Notice that the `synchronized` block in `addJob()` is big enough to also include the call to `jobs.add(job)`—which modifies shared data. And the `synchronized` block in `run()` is large enough to include the whole `while` loop—which includes the call to `jobs.isEmpty()`, which accesses shared data.

The moral here is that when you use `wait()` and `notify()` or `notifyAll()`, you should almost always also have a `while` loop around the `wait()` that checks a condition and forces continued waiting until the condition is met. And you should also make use of the required synchronization for the `wait()` and `notify()` calls to also protect whatever other data you're sharing between threads. If you see code that fails to do this, there's usually something wrong with the code—even if you have a hard time seeing what exactly the problem is.

TABLE 10-2	**Class Object**	**Class Thread**	**Interface Runnable**
Key Thread Methods	`wait()`	`start()`	`run()`
	`notify()`	*`yield()`*	
	`notifyAll()`	*`sleep()`*	
		`join()`	

CERTIFICATION SUMMARY

This chapter covered the required thread knowledge you'll need to apply on the certification exam. Threads can be created by either extending the `Thread` class or implementing the `Runnable` interface. The only method that must be implemented in the `Runnable` interface is the `run()` method, but the thread doesn't become a *thread of execution* until somebody calls the `Thread` object's `start()` method. We also looked at how the `sleep()` method can be used to pause a thread, and we saw that when an object goes to sleep, it holds onto any locks it acquired prior to sleeping.

We looked at five thread states: new, runnable, running, blocked/waiting/sleeping, and dead. You learned that when a thread is dead, it can never be restarted even if it's still a valid object on the heap. We saw that there is only one way a thread can transition to running, and that's from runnable. However, once running, a thread can become dead, go to sleep, wait for another thread to finish, block on an object's lock, wait for a notification, or return to runnable.

You saw how two threads acting on the same data can cause serious problems (remember Lucy and Fred's bank account?). We saw that to let one thread execute a method but prevent other threads from running the same object's method, we use the `synchronized` keyword. And we saw how the `wait()`, `notify()`, and `notifyAll()` methods can be used to coordinate activity between different threads.

TWO-MINUTE DRILL

Here are some of the key points from each certification objective in this chapter. Photocopy it and sleep with it under your pillow for complete absorption.

Defining, Instantiating, and Starting Threads (OCP Objective 10.1)

☐ Threads can be created by extending `Thread` and overriding the `public void run()` method.

☐ `Thread` objects can also be created by calling the `Thread` constructor that takes a `Runnable` argument. The `Runnable` object is said to be the *target* of the thread.

☐ A `Runnable` can be defined as an instance of a class that implements the `Runnable` interface. You can create a Runnable with a lambda expression, because `Runnable` is a functional interface.

☐ You can call `start()` on a `Thread` object only once. If `start()` is called more than once on a `Thread` object, it will throw a `IllegalThreadStateException`.

☐ It is legal to create many `Thread` objects using the same `Runnable` object as the target.

☐ When a `Thread` object is created, it does not become a *thread of execution* until its `start()` method is invoked. When a `Thread` object exists but hasn't been started, it is in the *new* state and is not considered *alive*.

Transitioning Between Thread States (OCP Objective 10.1)

☐ Once a new thread is started, it will always enter the runnable state.

☐ The thread scheduler can move a thread back and forth between the runnable state and the running state.

☐ For a single-processor machine, only one thread can be running at a time, although many threads may be in the runnable state.

☐ There is no guarantee that the order in which threads were started determines the order in which they'll run.

☐ There's no guarantee that threads will take turns in any fair way. It's up to the thread scheduler, as determined by the particular virtual machine implementation. If you want a guarantee that your threads will take turns, regardless of the underlying JVM, you can use the `sleep()` method. This prevents one thread from hogging the running process while another thread starves. (In most cases, though, `yield()` works well enough to encourage your threads to play together nicely.)

☐ A running thread may enter a blocked/waiting state by a `wait()`, `sleep()`, or `join()` call.

☐ A running thread may enter a blocked/waiting state because it can't acquire the lock for a synchronized block of code.

☐ When the sleep or wait is over, or an object's lock becomes available, the thread can only reenter the runnable state. It will *go* directly from waiting to runnable (well, for all practical purposes anyway).

☐ A dead thread cannot be started again.

Sleep, Yield, and Join (OCP Objective 10.1)

☐ Sleeping is used to delay execution for a period of time, and no locks are released when a thread goes to sleep.

☐ A sleeping thread is guaranteed to sleep for at least the time specified in the argument to the `sleep()` method (unless it's interrupted), but there is no guarantee as to when the newly awakened thread will actually return to running.

☐ The `sleep()` method is a `static` method that sleeps the currently executing thread's state. One thread *cannot* tell another thread to sleep.

☐ The `setPriority()` method gives `Thread` objects a priority of between 1 (low) and 10 (high). Priorities are not guaranteed, and not all JVMs recognize ten distinct priority levels—some levels may be treated as effectively equal.

☐ If not explicitly set, a thread's priority will have the same priority as the thread that created it.

☐ The `yield()` method *may* cause a running thread to back out if there are runnable threads of the same priority. There is no guarantee that this will happen, and there is no guarantee that when the thread backs out there will be a *different* thread selected to run. A thread might yield and then immediately reenter the running state.

❑ The closest thing to a guarantee is that at any given time, when a thread is running, it will usually not have a lower priority than any thread in the runnable state. If a low-priority thread is running when a high-priority thread enters runnable, the JVM will usually preempt the running low-priority thread and put the high-priority thread in.

❑ When one thread calls the `join()` method of another thread, the currently running thread will wait until the thread it joins with has completed. Think of the `join()` method as saying, "Hey, thread, I want to join on to the end of you. Let me know when you're done, so I can enter the runnable state."

Concurrent Access Problems and Synchronized Threads (OCP Objectives 10.2 and 10.3)

❑ `synchronized` methods prevent more than one thread from accessing an object's critical method code simultaneously.

❑ You can use the `synchronized` keyword as a method modifier or to start a synchronized block of code.

❑ To synchronize a block of code (in other words, a scope smaller than the whole method), you must specify an argument that is the object whose lock you want to synchronize on.

❑ While only one thread can be accessing synchronized code of a particular instance, multiple threads can still access the same object's unsynchronized code.

❑ When a thread goes to sleep, its locks will be unavailable to other threads.

❑ `static` methods can be `synchronized` using the lock from the `java.lang.Class` instance representing that class.

Communicating with Objects by Waiting and Notifying (OCP Objective 10.1)

❑ The `wait()` method lets a thread say, "There's nothing for me to do now, so put me in your waiting pool and notify me when something happens that I care about." Basically, a `wait()` call means "let me wait in your pool" or "add me to your waiting list."

❑ The `notify()` method is used to send a signal to one and only one of the threads that are waiting in that same object's waiting pool.

☐ The notify() method CANNOT specify which waiting thread to notify.

☐ The method notifyAll() works in the same way as notify(), only it sends the signal to *all* of the threads waiting on the object.

☐ All three methods—wait(), notify(), and notifyAll()—must be called from within a synchronized context! A thread invokes wait() or notify() on a particular object, and the thread must currently hold the lock on that object.

Deadlocked, Livelocked, and Starved Threads and Race Conditions (OCP Objective 10.2)

☐ Deadlocking is when thread execution grinds to a halt because the code is waiting for locks to be removed from objects.

☐ Deadlocking can occur when a locked object attempts to access another locked object that is trying to access the first locked object. In other words, both threads are waiting for each other's locks to be released; therefore, the locks will *never* be released!

☐ Deadlocking is bad. Don't do it.

☐ Livelocking is when thread execution grinds to a halt because the threads are too busy to make any progress. The threads are still working but can't get anywhere.

☐ Thread starvation is when a thread can't get access to a resource it needs so it starves. It's still alive, but barely.

☐ A race condition is when two threads race to get the same shared resource, and the result (often wrong) depends on which thread gets there first.

☐ Race conditions are bad. Don't allow them to happen. Use the volatile keyword to protect variables that should be atomic, and the synchronized keyword to make sure only one thread at a time can run code that manages a resource.

SELF TEST

The following questions will help you measure your understanding of the material presented in this chapter. If you have a rough time with some of these at first, don't beat yourself up. Some of these questions are long and intricate. Expect long and intricate questions on the real exam, too!

1. The following block of code creates a `Thread` using a `Runnable` target:

```
Runnable target = new MyRunnable();
Thread myThread = new Thread(target);
```

   Which of the following classes can be used to create the target so that the preceding code compiles correctly?

   A. `public class MyRunnable extends Runnable{public void run(){}}`
   B. `public class MyRunnable extends Object{public void run(){}}`
   C. `public class MyRunnable implements Runnable{public void run(){}}`
   D. `public class MyRunnable implements Runnable{void run(){}}`
   E. `public class MyRunnable implements Runnable{public void start(){}}`

2. Given:

```
3.  class MyThread extends Thread {
4.     public static void main(String [] args) {
5.        MyThread t = new MyThread();
6.        Thread x = new Thread(t);
7.        x.start();
8.     }
9.     public void run() {
10.       for(int i=0;i<3;++i) {
11.          System.out.print(i + "..");
12.       }
13.    }
14. }
```

   What is the result of this code?

   A. Compilation fails
   B. `1..2..3..`
   C. `0..1..2..3..`
   D. `0..1..2..`
   E. An exception occurs at runtime

3. Given:

```
3. class Test {
4.     public static void main(String [] args) {
5.         printAll(args);
6.     }
7.     public static void printAll(String[] lines) {
8.         for(int i=0;i<lines.length;i++){
9.             System.out.println(lines[i]);
10.            Thread.currentThread().sleep(1000);
11.        }
12.    }
13. }
```

The static method `Thread.currentThread()` returns a reference to the currently executing `Thread` object. What is the result of this code?

A. Each `String` in the array `lines` will output, with a one-second pause between lines

B. Each `String` in the array `lines` will output, with no pause in between because this method is not executed in a `Thread`

C. Each `String` in the array `lines` will output, and there is no guarantee that there will be a pause because `currentThread()` may not retrieve this thread

D. This code will not compile

E. Each `String` in the `lines` array will print, with at least a one-second pause between lines

4. Assume you have a class that holds two `private` variables: a and b. Which of the following pairs can prevent concurrent access problems in that class? (Choose all that apply.)

A. `public int read(){return a+b;}`
   `public void set(int a, int b){this.a=a;this.b=b;}`

B. `public synchronized int read(){return a+b;}`
   `public synchronized void set(int a, int b){this.a=a;this.b=b;}`

C. `public int read(){synchronized(a){return a+b;}}`
   `public void set(int a, int b){`
   `    synchronized(a){this.a=a;this.b=b;}}`

D. `public int read(){synchronized(a){return a+b;}}`
   `public void set(int a, int b){`
   `    synchronized(b){this.a=a;this.b=b;}}`

E. `public synchronized(this) int read(){return a+b;}`
   `public synchronized(this) void set(int a, int b){`
   `    this.a=a;this.b=b;}`

F. `public int read(){synchronized(this){return a+b;}}`
   `public void set(int a, int b){`
   `    synchronized(this){this.a=a;this.b=b;}}`

5. Given:

```
1. public class WaitTest {
2.     public static void main(String [] args) {
3.         System.out.print("1 ");
4.         synchronized(args){
5.             System.out.print("2 ");
6.             try {
7.                 args.wait();
8.             }
9.             catch(InterruptedException e){}
10.        }
11.        System.out.print("3 ");
12.    }
13. }
```

What is the result of trying to compile and run this program?

A. It fails to compile because the `IllegalMonitorStateException` of `wait()` is not dealt with in line 7

B. 1 2 3

C. 1 3

D. 1 2

E. At runtime, it throws an `IllegalMonitorStateException` when trying to wait

F. It will fail to compile because it has to be synchronized on the `this` object

6. Assume the following method is properly synchronized and called from a thread A on an object B:

```
wait(2000);
```

After calling this method, when will thread A become a candidate to get another turn at the CPU?

A. After object B is notified, or after two seconds

B. After the lock on B is released, or after two seconds

C. Two seconds after object B is notified

D. Two seconds after lock B is released

7. Which are true? (Choose all that apply.)

A. The `notifyAll()` method must be called from a synchronized context

B. To call `wait()`, an object must own the lock on the thread

C. The `notify()` method is defined in class `java.lang.Thread`

D. When a thread is waiting as a result of `wait()`, it releases its lock

E. The `notify()` method causes a thread to immediately release its lock

F. The difference between `notify()` and `notifyAll()` is that `notifyAll()` notifies all waiting threads, regardless of the object they're waiting on

8. Given this scenario: This class is intended to allow users to write a series of messages so that each message is identified with a timestamp and the name of the thread that wrote the message:

```
public class Logger {
    private StringBuilder contents = new StringBuilder();
    public void log(String message) {
        contents.append(System.currentTimeMillis());
        contents.append(": ");
        contents.append(Thread.currentThread().getName());
        contents.append(message);
        contents.append("\n");
    }
    public String getContents() { return contents.toString(); }
}
```

How can we ensure that instances of this class can be safely used by multiple threads?

A. This class is already thread-safe

B. Replacing `StringBuilder` with `StringBuffer` will make this class thread-safe

C. Synchronize the `log()` method only

D. Synchronize the `getContents()` method only

E. Synchronize both `log()` and `getContents()`

F. This class cannot be made thread-safe

9. Given:

```
public static synchronized void main(String[] args) throws InterruptedException {
    Thread t = new Thread();
    t.start();
    System.out.print("X");
    t.wait(10000);
    System.out.print("Y");
}
```

What is the result of this code?

A. It prints X and exits

B. It prints X and never exits

C. It prints XY and exits almost immediately

D. It prints XY with a 10-second delay between X and Y

E. It prints XY with a 10,000-second delay between X and Y

F. The code does not compile

G. An exception is thrown at runtime

10. Given:

```
class MyThread extends Thread {
  MyThread() {
    System.out.print("MyThread ");
  }
  public void run() {
    System.out.print("bar ");
  }
  public void run(String s) {
    System.out.print("baz ");
  }
}
public class TestThreads {
  public static void main (String [] args) {
    Thread t = new MyThread() {
      public void run() {
        System.out.print("foo ");
      }
    };
    t.start();
  } }
```

What is the result?

A. foo

B. MyThread foo

C. MyThread bar

D. foo bar

E. foo bar baz

F. bar foo

G. Compilation fails

H. An exception is thrown at runtime

11. Given:

```
public class ThreadDemo {
  synchronized void a() { actBusy(); }
  static synchronized void b() { actBusy(); }
  static void actBusy() {
    try {
      Thread.sleep(1000);
    } catch (InterruptedException e) {}
  }
  public static void main(String[] args) {
    final ThreadDemo x = new ThreadDemo();
    final ThreadDemo y = new ThreadDemo();
    Runnable runnable = () -> {
```

```
            int option = (int) (Math.random() * 4);
            switch (option) {
              case 0: x.a(); break;
              case 1: x.b(); break;
              case 2: y.a(); break;
              case 3: y.b(); break;
            }
        };
        Thread thread1 = new Thread(runnable);
        Thread thread2 = new Thread(runnable);
        thread1.start();
        thread2.start();
      }
    }
```

If the code compiles, which of the following pairs of method invocations could NEVER be executing at the same time? (Choose all that apply.)

A. x.a() in thread1, and x.a() in thread2

B. x.a() in thread1, and x.b() in thread2

C. x.a() in thread1, and y.a() in thread2

D. x.a() in thread1, and y.b() in thread2

E. x.b() in thread1, and x.a() in thread2

F. x.b() in thread1, and x.b() in thread2

G. x.b() in thread1, and y.a() in thread2

H. x.b() in thread1, and y.b() in thread2

I. Compilation fails due to an error in declaring the Runnable

12. Given:

```
public class TwoThreads {
  static Thread laurel, hardy;
  public static void main(String[] args) {
    laurel = new Thread() {
      public void run() {
        System.out.println("A");
        try {
          hardy.sleep(1000);
        } catch (Exception e) {
          System.out.println("B");
        }
        System.out.println("C");
      }
    };
    hardy = new Thread() {
      public void run() {
```

```
        System.out.println("D");
        try {
          laurel.wait();
        } catch (Exception e) {
            System.out.println("E");
        }
        System.out.println("F");
      }
    };
    laurel.start();
    hardy.start();
  }
}
```

Which letters will eventually appear somewhere in the output? (Choose all that apply.)

A. A

B. B

C. C

D. D

E. E

F. F

G. The answer cannot be reliably determined

H. The code does not compile

13. Given:

```
3. public class Starter implements Runnable {
4.   void go(long id) {
5.     System.out.println(id);
6.   }
7.   public static void main(String[] args) {
8.     System.out.print(Thread.currentThread().getId() + " ");
9.     // insert code here
10.  }
11.  public void run() { go(Thread.currentThread().getId()); }
12. }
```

And given the following five fragments:

```
I.   new Starter().run();
II.  new Starter().start();
III. new Thread(new Starter());
IV.  new Thread(new Starter()).run();
V.   new Thread(new Starter()).start();
```

When the five fragments are inserted, one at a time at line 9, which are true? (Choose all that apply.)

A. All five will compile

B. Only one might produce the output 4 4

C. Only one might produce the output 4 2

D. Exactly two might produce the output 4 4

E. Exactly two might produce the output 4 2

F. Exactly three might produce the output 4 4

G. Exactly three might produce the output 4 2

14. Given:

```
3. public class Leader implements Runnable {
4.   public static void main(String[] args) {
5.     Thread t = new Thread(new Leader());
6.     t.start();
7.     System.out.print("m1 ");
8.     t.join();
9.     System.out.print("m2 ");
10.  }
11.  public void run() {
12.    System.out.print("r1 ");
13.    System.out.print("r2 ");
14.  }
15. }
```

Which are true? (Choose all that apply.)

A. Compilation fails

B. The output could be r1 r2 m1 m2

C. The output could be m1 m2 r1 r2

D. The output could be m1 r1 r2 m2

E. The output could be m1 r1 m2 r2

F. An exception is thrown at runtime

15. Given:

```
3. class Dudes {
4.   static long flag = 0;
5.   // insert code here
6.     if(flag == 0) flag = id;
7.     for(int x = 1; x < 3; x++) {
8.       if(flag == id) System.out.print("yo ");
9.       else System.out.print("dude ");
10.    }
11.  }
12. }
```

```
13. public class DudesChat implements Runnable {
14.   static Dudes d;
15.   public static void main(String[] args) {
16.     new DudesChat().go();
17.   }
18.   void go() {
19.     d = new Dudes();
20.     new Thread(new DudesChat()).start();
21.     new Thread(new DudesChat()).start();
22.   }
23.   public void run() {
24.     d.chat(Thread.currentThread().getId());
25.   }
26. }
```

And given these two fragments:

```
I. synchronized void chat(long id) {
II. void chat(long id) {
```

When fragment I or fragment II is inserted at line 5, which are true? (Choose all that apply.)

A.   An exception is thrown at runtime

B.   With fragment I, compilation fails

C.   With fragment II, compilation fails

D.   With fragment I, the output could be yo dude dude yo

E.   With fragment I, the output could be dude dude yo yo

F.   With fragment II, the output could be yo dude dude yo

16.   Given:

```
 3. class Chicks {
 4.   synchronized void yack(long id) {
 5.     for(int x = 1; x < 3; x++) {
 6.       System.out.print(id + " ");
 7.       Thread.yield();
 8.     }
 9.   }
10. }
11. public class ChicksYack implements Runnable {
12.   Chicks c;
13.   public static void main(String[] args) {
14.     new ChicksYack().go();
15.   }
16.   void go() {
17.     c = new Chicks();
18.     new Thread(new ChicksYack()).start();
19.     new Thread(new ChicksYack()).start();
20.   }
```

```
21.  public void run() {
22.    c.yack(Thread.currentThread().getId());
23.  }
24. }
```

Which are true? (Choose all that apply.)

A. Compilation fails

B. The output could be 4 4 2 3

C. The output could be 4 4 2 2

D. The output could be 4 4 4 2

E. The output could be 2 2 4 4

F. An exception is thrown at runtime

17. Given:

```
3. public class Chess implements Runnable {
4.   public void run() {
5.     move(Thread.currentThread().getId());
6.   }
7.   // insert code here
8.     System.out.print(id + " ");
9.     System.out.print(id + " ");
10.  }
11.  public static void main(String[] args) {
12.    Chess ch = new Chess();
13.    new Thread(ch).start();
14.    new Thread(new Chess()).start();
15.  }
16. }
```

And given these two fragments:

```
I. synchronized void move(long id) {
II. void move(long id) {
```

When either fragment I or fragment II is inserted at line 7, which are true? (Choose all that apply.)

A. Compilation fails

B. With fragment I, an exception is thrown

C. With fragment I, the output could be 4 2 4 2

D. With fragment I, the output could be 4 4 2 3

E. With fragment II, the output could be 2 4 2 4

18. You have two threads, t1 and t2, attemping to access a shared resource, and t2 is always descheduled when it tries to access that resource. What is this kind of problem called?

    A. A race condition

    B. Deadlock

    C. Livelock

    D. Starvation

    E. Synchronization

    F. Multitasking

SELF TEST ANSWERS

1. ☑ **C** is correct. The class implements the `Runnable` interface with a legal `run()` method.
   ☒ **A** is incorrect because interfaces are implemented, not extended. **B** is incorrect because even though the class has a valid `public void run()` method, it does not implement the `Runnable` interface. **D** is incorrect because the `run()` method must be public. **E** is incorrect because the method to implement is `run()`, not `start()`. Note that we could replace the first line of code with:

   ```
   Runnable target = () -> {};
   ```

   and dispense with `MyRunnable` completely. (OCP Objective 10.1)

2. ☑ **D** is correct. The thread `MyThread` will start and loop three times (from 0 to 2).
   ☒ **A** is incorrect because the `Thread` class implements the `Runnable` interface; therefore, in line 6, `Thread` can take an object of type `Thread` as an argument in the constructor (this is NOT recommended). **B** and **C** are incorrect because the variable `i` in the `for` loop starts with a value of 0 and ends with a value of 2. **E** is incorrect based on the above. (OCP Objective 10.1)

3. ☑ **D** is correct. The `sleep()` method must be enclosed in a `try/catch` block, or the method `printAll()` must declare it throws the `InterruptedException`.
   ☒ **E** is incorrect, but it would be correct if the `InterruptedException` was dealt with (**A** is too precise). **B** is incorrect (even if the `InterruptedException` was dealt with) because all Java code, including the `main()` method, runs in threads. **C** is incorrect. The `sleep()` method is `static`; it always affects the currently executing thread. (OCP Objective 10.1)

4. ☑ **B** and **F** are correct. By marking the methods as `synchronized`, the threads will get the lock of the `this` object before proceeding. Only one thread will be setting or reading at any given moment, thereby assuring that `read()` always returns the addition of a valid pair.
   ☒ **A** is incorrect because it is not synchronized; therefore, there is no guarantee that the values added by the `read()` method belong to the same pair. **C** and **D** are incorrect; only objects can be used to synchronize on. **E** is incorrect because it fails to compile—it is not possible to select other objects (even `this`) to synchronize on when declaring a method as `synchronized`. (OCP Objectives 10.2 and 10.3)

5. ☑ **D** is correct. 1 and 2 will be printed, but there will be no return from the `wait` call because no other thread will notify the main thread, so 3 will never be printed. It's frozen at line 7.
   ☒ **A** is incorrect; `IllegalMonitorStateException` is an unchecked exception. **B** and **C** are incorrect; 3 will never be printed, since this program will wait forever. **E** is incorrect because `IllegalMonitorStateException` will never be thrown because the `wait()` is done on `args` within a block of code synchronized on `args`. **F** is incorrect because any object can be used to synchronize on, and `this` and `static` don't mix. (OCP Objective 10.3)

6. ☑ **A** is correct. Either of the two events will make the thread a candidate for running again.
☒ **B** is incorrect because a waiting thread will not return to runnable when the lock is released unless a notification occurs. **C** is incorrect because the thread will become a candidate immediately after notification. **D** is also incorrect because a thread will not come out of a waiting pool just because a lock has been released. (OCP Objective 10.3)

7. ☑ **A** is correct because `notifyAll()` (and `wait()` and `notify()`) must be called from within a synchronized context. **D** is a correct statement.
☒ **B** is incorrect because to call `wait()`, the thread must own the lock on the object that `wait()` is being invoked on, not the other way around. **C** is incorrect because `notify()` is defined in `java.lang.Object`. **E** is incorrect because `notify()` will not cause a thread to release its locks. The thread can only release its locks by exiting the synchronized code. **F** is incorrect because `notifyAll()` notifies all the threads waiting on a particular locked object, not all threads waiting on *any* object. (OCP Objectives 10.2 and 10.3)

8. ☑ **E** is correct because synchronizing the `public` methods is sufficient to make this safe, which is why **F** is incorrect. This class is not thread-safe unless some sort of synchronization protects the changing data.
☒ **B** is incorrect because although a `StringBuffer` is synchronized internally, we call `append()` multiple times, and nothing would prevent two simultaneous `log()` calls from mixing up their messages. **C** and **D** are incorrect because if one method remains unsynchronized, it can run while the other is executing, which could result in reading the contents while one of the messages is incomplete, or worse. (You don't want to call `toString()` on the `StringBuffer` as it's resizing its internal character array.) **F** is incorrect based on the information above.(OCP Objective 10.3)

9. ☑ **G** is correct. The code does not acquire a lock on `t` before calling `t.wait()`, so it throws an `IllegalMonitorStateException`. The method is `synchronized`, but it's not synchronized on `t` so the exception will be thrown. If the wait were placed inside a `synchronized(t)` block, then **D** would be correct.
☒ **A, B, C, D, E,** and **F** are incorrect based on the logic described above. (OCP Objective 10.3)

10. ☑ **B** is correct. In the first line of `main` we're constructing an instance of an anonymous inner class extending from `MyThread`. So the `MyThread` constructor runs and prints `MyThread`. Next, `main()` invokes `start()` on the new thread instance, which causes the overridden `run()` method (the `run()` method in the anonymous inner class) to be invoked.
☒ **A, C, D, E, F, G,** and **H** are incorrect based on the logic described above.
(OCP Objective 10.1)

11. ☑ **A, F,** and **H** are correct. **A** is correct because when `synchronized` instance methods are called on the same *instance,* they block each other. **F** and **H** can't happen because `synchronized static` methods in the same class block each other, regardless of which instance was used to call the methods. (An instance is not required to call `static` methods; only the class.)

    ☒ **C,** although incorrect, could happen because `synchronized` instance methods called on different instances do not block each other. **B, D, E,** and **G** are incorrect but also could all happen because instance methods and `static` methods lock on different objects and do not block each other. **I** is incorrect because the code compiles. (OCP Objectives 10.2 and 10.3)

12. ☑ **A, C, D, E,** and **F** are correct. This may look like `laurel` and `hardy` are battling to cause the other to `sleep()` or `wait()`—but that's not the case. Since `sleep()` is a `static` method, it affects the current thread, which is `laurel` (even though the method is invoked using a reference to `hardy`). That's misleading, but perfectly legal, and the `Thread laurel` is able to sleep with no exception, printing **A** and **C** (after at least a one-second delay). Meanwhile, `hardy` tries to call `laurel.wait()`—but `hardy` has not synchronized on `laurel`, so calling `laurel.wait()` immediately causes an `IllegalMonitorStateException`, and so `hardy` prints **D, E,** and **F**. Although the *order* of the output is somewhat indeterminate (we have no way of knowing whether **A** is printed before **D**, for example), it is guaranteed that **A, C, D, E,** and **F** will all be printed in some order, eventually—so **G** is incorrect.

    ☒ **B, G,** and **H** are incorrect based on the above. (OCP Objective 10.2)

13. ☑ **C** and **D** are correct. Fragment I doesn't start a new thread. Fragment II doesn't compile. Fragment III creates a new thread but doesn't start it. Fragment IV creates a new thread and invokes `run()` directly, but it doesn't start the new thread. Fragment V creates and starts a new thread.

    ☒ **A, B, E, F,** and **G** are incorrect based on the above. (OCP Objective 10.1)

14. ☑ **A** is correct. The `join()` must be placed in a `try/catch` block. If it were, answers **B** and **D** would be correct. The `join()` causes the main thread to pause and join the end of the other thread, meaning `"m2"` must come last.

    ☒ **B, C, D, E,** and **F** are incorrect based on the above. (OCP Objective 10.1)

15. ☑ **F** is correct. With Fragment I, the `chat` method is `synchronized`, so the two threads can't swap back and forth. With either fragment, the first output must be `yo`.

    ☒ **A, B, C, D,** and **E** are incorrect based on the above. (OCP Objective 10.3)

16. ☑ **F** is correct. When `run()` is invoked, it is with a new instance of `ChicksYack` and `c` has not been assigned to an object. If `c` were static, then because `yack` is `synchronized`, answers **C** and **E** would have been correct.

    ☒ **A, B, C, D,** and **E** are incorrect based on the above. (OCP Objectives 10.1 and 10.3)

17. ☑ **C** and **E** are correct. **E** should be obvious. **C** is correct because, even though `move()` is synchronized, it's being invoked on two different objects.

☒ **A, B,** and **D** are incorrect based on the above. (OCP Objective 10.3)

18. ☑ **D** is correct. Starvation occurs when one or more threads cannot get access to a resource.

☒ **A, B, C, E** and **F** are incorrect based on the above. (OCP Objective 10.2)

EXERCISE ANSWERS

Exercise 10-1: Creating a Thread and Putting It to Sleep

The final code should look something like this:

```
class TheCount extends Thread {
    public void run() {
        for(int i = 1;i<=100;++i) {
            System.out.print(i + "  ");
            if(i % 10 == 0)  System.out.println("Hahaha");
            try { Thread.sleep(1000); }
            catch(InterruptedException e) {}
        }
    }
    public static void main(String [] args) {
        new TheCount().start();
    }
}
```

Exercise 10-2: Synchronizing a Block of Code

Your code might look something like this when completed:

```
class InSync extends Thread {
  StringBuffer letter;
  public InSync(StringBuffer letter) { this.letter = letter; }
  public void run() {
    synchronized(letter) {        // #1
      for(int i = 1;i<=100;++i) System.out.print(letter);
      System.out.println();
      char temp = letter.charAt(0);
      ++temp;            // Increment the letter in StringBuffer:
      letter.setCharAt(0, temp);
    }      // #2
  }
```

```
public static void main(String [] args) {
  StringBuffer sb = new StringBuffer("A");
  new InSync(sb).start();  new InSync(sb).start();
  new InSync(sb).start();
}
}
```

Just for fun, try removing lines 1 and 2 and then run the program again. It will be unsynchronized—watch what happens.

11
Concurrency

CERTIFICATION OBJECTIVES

- Create Worker Threads Using Runnable, Callable and Use an ExecutorService to Concurrently Execute Tasks

- Use Synchronized Keyword and java.util .concurrent.atomic Package to Control the Order of Thread Execution

- Use java.util.concurrent Collections and Classes Including CyclicBarrier and CopyOnWriteArrayList

- Use Parallel Fork/Join Framework

- Use Parallel Streams Including Reduction, Decomposition, Merging Processes, Pipelines and Performance

- Identify Potential Threading Problems among Deadlock, Starvation, Livelock, and Race Conditions

✓ Two-Minute Drill

Q&A Self Test

Concurrency with the java.util.concurrent Package

As you learned in the previous chapter on threads, the Java platform supports multithreaded programming. Supporting multithreaded programming is essential for any modern programming language because servers, desktop computers, laptops, and most mobile devices contain multiple CPUs. If you want your applications to take advantage of all of the processing power present in a modern system, you must create multithreaded applications.

Unfortunately, creating efficient and error-free multithreaded applications can be a challenge. The low-level threading constructs such as `Thread`, `Runnable`, `wait()`, `notify()`, and synchronized blocks are too primitive for many requirements and force developers to create their own high-level threading libraries. Custom threading libraries can be both error prone and time consuming to create.

The `java.util.concurrent` package provides high-level APIs that support many common concurrent programming use cases. When possible, you should use these high-level APIs in place of the traditional low-level threading constructs (synchronized, wait, notify). Some features (such as the locking API) provide functionality similar to what existed already, but with more flexibility at the cost of slightly awkward syntax. Using the `java.util.concurrent` classes requires a solid understanding of the traditional Java threading types (`Thread` and `Runnable`) and their use (start, run, synchronized, wait, notify, join, sleep, etc.). If you are not comfortable with Java threads, you should return to the previous chapter before continuing with these high-level concurrency APIs.

CERTIFICATION OBJECTIVE

Apply Atomic Variables and Locks (OCP Objective 10.3)

10.3   Use synchronized keyword and java.util.concurrent.atomic package to control the order of thread execution.

The `java.util.concurrent.atomic` and `java.util.concurrent.locks` packages solve two different problems. They are grouped into a single exam objective simply because they are the only two packages below `java.util.concurrent`

and both have a small number of classes and interfaces to learn. The `java.util`
`.concurrent.atomic` package enables multithreaded applications to safely access
individual variables without locking, whereas the `java.util.concurrent.locks`
package provides a locking framework that can be used to create locking behaviors
that are the same or superior to those of Java's synchronized keyword.

Atomic Variables

Imagine a multiplayer video game that contains monsters that must be destroyed.
The players of the game (threads) are vanquishing monsters, while at the same time
a monster-spawning thread is repopulating the world to ensure players always have
a new challenge to face. To keep the level of difficulty consistent, you would need
to keep track of the monster count and ensure that the monster population stays
the same (a hero's work is never done). Both the player threads and the monster-
spawning thread must access and modify the shared monster count variable. If the
monster count somehow became incorrect, your players may find themselves with
more adversaries than they could handle.

The following example shows how even the seemingly simplest of code can lead
to undefined results. Here you have a class that increments and reports the current
value of an integer variable:

```
public class Counter {
  private int count;
  public void increment() {
    count++; // it's a trap!
            // a single "line" is not atomic
  }
  public int getValue() {
    return count;
  }
}
```

A `Thread` that will increment the counter 10,000 times:

```
public class IncrementerThread extends Thread {
  private Counter counter;
  // all instances are passed the same counter
  public IncrementerThread(Counter counter) {
    this.counter = counter;
  }
  public void run() {
    // "i" is local and therefore thread-safe
```

```
        for(int i = 0; i < 10000; i++) {
          counter.increment();
        }
      }
    }
```

Here is the code from within this application's main method:

```
Counter counter = new Counter();        // the shared object
IncrementerThread it1 = new IncrementerThread(counter);
IncrementerThread it2 = new IncrementerThread(counter);
it1.start(); // thread 1 increments the count by 10000
it2.start(); // thread 2 increments the count by 10000
it1.join();   // wait for thread 1 to finish
it2.join();   // wait for thread 2 to finish
System.out.println(counter.getValue()); // rarely 20000
                                        // lowest 11972
```

The trap in this example is that count++ looks like a single action when, in fact, it is not. When incrementing a field like this, what *probably* happens is the following sequence:

1. The value stored in count is copied to a temporary variable.
2. The temporary variable is incremented.
3. The value of the temporary variable is copied back to the count field.

We say "probably" in this example because while the Java compiler will translate the count++ statement into multiple Java bytecode instructions, you really have no control over what native instructions are executed. The JIT (Just In Time compiler)–based nature of most Java runtime environments means you don't know when or if the count++ statement will be translated to native CPU instructions and whether it ends up as a single instruction or several. You should always act as if a single line of Java code takes multiple steps to complete. Getting an incorrect result also depends on many other factors, such as the type of CPU you have. Do both threads in the example run concurrently or in sequence? A large loop count was used in order to make the threads run longer and be more likely to execute concurrently.

While you could make this code thread-safe with synchronized blocks, the act of obtaining and releasing a lock flag would probably be more time consuming than the work being performed. This is where the classes in the java.util .concurrent.atomic package can benefit you. They provide variables whose values can be modified atomically. An atomic operation is one that, for all intents and purposes, appears to happen all at once. The `java.util.concurrent.atomic` package provides several classes for different data types, such as `AtomicInteger`, `AtomicLong`, `AtomicBoolean`, and `AtomicReference`, to name a few.

Here is a thread-safe replacement for the `Counter` class from the previous example:

```
public class Counter {
  private AtomicInteger count = new AtomicInteger();
  public void increment() {
    count.getAndIncrement(); // atomic operation
  }
  public int getValue() {
    return count.intValue();
  }
}
```

In reality, even a method such as `getAndIncrement()` still takes several steps to execute. The reason this implementation is now thread-safe is something called CAS. CAS stands for Compare And Swap. Most modern CPUs have a set of CAS instructions. Following is a basic outline of what is happening now:

1. The value stored in `count` is copied to a temporary variable.
2. The temporary variable is incremented.
3. Compare the value currently in `count` with the original value. If it is unchanged, then swap the old value for the new value.

Step 3 happens atomically. If step 3 finds that some other thread has already modified the value of `count`, then repeat steps 1–3 until we increment the field without interference.

The central method in a class like `AtomicInteger` is the `boolean compareAndSet(int expect, int update)` method, which provides the CAS behavior. Other atomic methods delegate to the `compareAndSet` method. The `getAndIncrement` method implementation is simply:

```
public final int getAndIncrement() {
  for (;;) {
    int current = get();
    int next = current + 1;
    if (compareAndSet(current, next))
      return current;
  }
}
```

Locks

The java.util.concurrent.locks package is about creating (not surprisingly) locks. Why would you want to use locks when so much of java.util.concurrent seems geared toward avoiding overt locking? You use java.util.concurrent .locks classes and traditional monitor locking (the synchronized keyword) for roughly the same purpose: creating segments of code that require exclusive execution (one thread at a time).

Why would you create code that limits the number of threads that can execute it? While atomic variables work well for making single variables thread-safe, imagine if you have two or more variables that are related. A video game character might have a number of gold pieces that can be carried in his backpack and a number of gold pieces he keeps in an in-game bank vault. Transferring gold into the bank is as simple as subtracting gold from the backpack and adding it to the vault. If we have 10 gold pieces in our backpack and 90 in the vault, we have a total of 100 pieces that belong to our character. If we want to transfer all 10 pieces to the vault, we can first add 10 to the vault count and then subtract 10 from the backpack, or first subtract 10 from the backpack and then add 10 to the vault. If another thread were to try to assess our character's wealth during the middle of our transfer, it might see 90 pieces or 110 pieces, depending on the order of our operations, neither being the correct count of 100 pieces.

This other thread that is attempting to read the character's total wealth might do all sorts of things, such as increase the likelihood of your character being robbed or a variety of other actions to control the in-game economics. All game threads must correctly gauge a character's wealth even if there is a transfer in progress.

The solution to our balance inquiry transfer problem is to use locking. Create a single method to get a character's wealth and another to perform gold transfers. You should never be able to check a character's total wealth while a gold transfer is in progress. Having a single method to get a character's total wealth is also important because you don't want a thread to read the backpack's gold count before a transfer and then the vault's gold count after a transfer. That would lead to the same incorrect total as trying to calculate the total during a transfer.

Much of the functionality provided by the classes and interfaces of the java .util.concurrent.locks package duplicates that of traditional synchronized locking. In fact, the hypothetical gold transfer outlined earlier could be solved with either the synchronized keyword or classes in the java.util.concurrent .locks package. In Java 5, when java.util.concurrent was first introduced, the new locking classes performed better than the synchronized keyword, but there is no longer a vast difference in performance. So why would you use these newer locking classes? The `java.util.concurrent.locks` package provides

- The ability to duplicate traditional synchronized blocks.
- Nonblock scoped locking—obtain a lock in one method and release it in another (this can be dangerous, though).
- Multiple `wait`/`notify`/`notifyAll` pools per lock—threads can select which pool (`Condition`) they wait on.
- The ability to attempt to acquire a lock and take an alternative action if locking fails.
- An implementation of a multiple-reader, single-writer lock.

ReentrantLock

The `java.util.concurrent.locks.Lock` interface provides the outline of locking provided by the `java.util.concurrent.locks` package. Like any interface, the `Lock` interface requires an implementation to be of any real use. The `java.util.concurrent.locks.ReentrantLock` class provides that implementation. To demonstrate the use of `Lock`, we will first duplicate the functionality of a basic traditional synchronized block.

```
Object obj = new Object();
synchronized(obj) {    // traditional locking, blocks until acquired
                       // work
}                      // releases lock automatically
```

Here is an equivalent piece of code using the `java.util.concurrent` `.locks` package. Notice how `ReentrantLock` can be stored in a `Lock` reference because it implements the `Lock` interface. This example blocks on attempting to acquire a lock, just like traditional synchronization.

```
Lock lock = new ReentrantLock();
lock.lock();           // blocks until acquired
try {
    // do work here
} finally {            // to ensure we unlock
  lock.unlock();       // must manually release
}
```

It is recommended that you always follow the `lock()` method with a `try-finally` block, which releases the lock. The previous example doesn't really provide a compelling reason for you to choose to use a `Lock` instance instead of traditional synchronization. One of the very powerful features is the ability to attempt (and fail) to acquire a lock. With traditional synchronization, once you hit a synchronized block, your thread either immediately acquires the lock or blocks until it can.

```
Lock lock = new ReentrantLock();
boolean locked = lock.tryLock(); // try without waiting
if (locked) {
  try {
      // work
  } finally {                      // to ensure we unlock
    lock.unlock();
  }
}
```

The ability to quickly fail to acquire the lock turns out to be powerful. You can process a different resource (lock) and come back to the failed lock later instead of just waiting for a lock to be released and thereby making more efficient use of system resources. There is also a variation of the tryLock method that allows you to specify an amount of time you are willing to wait to acquire the lock:

```
Lock lock = new ReentrantLock();
try {
  boolean locked = lock.tryLock(3, TimeUnit.SECONDS);
  if (locked) {
    try {
                        // work
    } finally {        // to ensure we unlock
        lock.unlock();
    }
  }
} catch (InterruptedException ex) {
                        // handle
}
```

Another benefit of the tryLock method is deadlock avoidance. With traditional synchronization, you must acquire locks in the same order across all threads. For example, if you have two objects to lock against:

```
Object o1 = new Object();
Object o2 = new Object();
```

and you synchronize using the internal lock flags of both objects:

```
synchronized(o1) {
        // thread A could pause here
  synchronized(o2) {
        // work
  }
}
```

you should never acquire the locks in the opposite order because it could lead to deadlock. Although thread A has only the o1 lock, thread B acquires the o2 lock. You are now at an impasse because neither thread can obtain the second lock it needs to continue.

```
synchronized(o2) {
        // thread B gets stuck here
    synchronized(o1) {
        // work
    }
}
```

Looking at a similar example using a ReentrantLock, start by creating two locks:

```
Lock l1 = new ReentrantLock();
Lock l2 = new ReentrantLock();
```

Next, you acquire both locks in thread A:

```
boolean aq1 = l1.tryLock();
boolean aq2 = l2.tryLock();
try{
  if (aq1 && aq2) {
      // work
  }
} finally {
  if (aq2) l2.unlock(); // don't unlock if not locked
  if (aq1) l1.unlock();
}
```

Notice the example is careful to always unlock any acquired lock, but ONLY the lock(s) that were acquired. A ReentrantLock has an internal counter that keeps track of the number of times it has been locked/unlocked, and it is an error to unlock without a corresponding successful lock operation. If a thread attempts to release a lock that it does not own, an IllegalMonitorStateException will be thrown.

Now in thread B, the locks are obtained in the reverse order in which thread A obtained them. With traditional locking, using synchronized code blocks and attempting to obtain locks in the reverse order could lead to deadlock.

```
boolean aq2 = l2.tryLock();
boolean aq1 = l1.tryLock();
try{
  if (aq1 && aq2) {
      // work
```

```
    }
  } finally {
    if (aq1) l1.unlock();
    if (aq2) l2.unlock();
  }
```

Now, even if thread A was only in possession of the l1 lock, there is no possibility that thread B could block because we use the nonblocking tryLock method. Using this technique, you can avoid deadlocking scenarios, but you must deal with the possibility that both locks could not be acquired. Using a simple loop, you can repeatedly attempt to obtain both locks until successful (Note: This approach is CPU intensive; we'll look at a better solution later):

```
loop2:
while (true) {
  boolean aq2 = l2.tryLock();
  boolean aq1 = l1.tryLock();
  try {
    if (aq1 && aq2) {
      // work
      break loop2;
    }
  } finally {
    if (aq2) l2.unlock();
    if (aq1) l1.unlock();
  }
}
```

on the job

It is remotely possible that this example could lead to livelock. Imagine if thread A always acquires lock1 at the same time that thread B acquires lock2. Each thread's attempt to acquire the second lock would always fail, and you'd end up repeating forever, or at least until you were lucky enough to have one thread fall behind the other. You can avoid livelock in this scenario by introducing a short random delay with Thread.sleep(int) any time you fail to acquire both locks.

Condition

A Condition provides the equivalent of the traditional wait, notify, and notifyAll methods. The traditional wait and notify methods allow developers to implement an await/signal pattern. You use an await/signal pattern when you would use locking, but with the added stipulation of trying to avoid spinning (endless checking if it is okay to do something). Imagine a video game character who wants to buy something from a store, but the store is out of stock at the moment. The character's thread could repeatedly lock the store object and check for the desired item, but that would lead to unneeded system utilization. Instead, the character's thread can say, "I'm taking a nap, wake me up when new stock arrives."

The `java.util.concurrent.locks.Condition` interface is a replacement for the `wait` and `notify` methods. A three-part code example shows you how to use a condition. Part one shows that a `Condition` is created from a `Lock` object:

```
Lock lock = new ReentrantLock();
Condition blockingPoolA = lock.newCondition();
```

When your thread reaches a point where it must delay until another thread performs an activity, you "await" the completion of that other activity. Before calling `await`, you must have locked the `Lock` used to produce the `Condition`. It is possible that the awaiting thread may be interrupted, and you must handle the possible `InterruptedException`. When you call the `await` method, the `Lock` associated with the `Condition` is released. Before the `await` method returns, the lock will be reacquired. In order to use a `Condition`, a thread must first acquire a `Lock`. Part two of the three-part `Condition` example shows how a `Condition` is used to pause or wait for some event:

```
lock.lock();
try {
  blockingPoolA.await(); // "wait" here
                         // lock will be reacquired
    // work
} catch (InterruptedException ex) {
    // interrupted during await()
} finally {                 // to ensure we unlock
  lock.unlock();            // must manually release
}
```

In another thread, you perform the activity that the first thread was waiting on and then signal that first thread to resume (return from the `await` method). Part three of the `Condition` example is run in a different thread than part two. This part causes the thread waiting in the second piece to wake up:

```
lock.lock();
try {
  // work
  blockingPoolA.signalAll(); // wake all awaiting
                             // threads
} finally {
  lock.unlock();                 // now an awoken thread can run
}
```

The `signalAll()` method causes all threads awaiting on the same `Condition` to wake up. You can also use the `signal()` method to wake up a single awaiting thread. Remember that "waking up" is not the same thing as proceeding. Each awoken thread will have to reacquire the `Lock` before continuing.

One advantage of a `Condition` over the traditional wait/notify operations is that multiple `Conditions` can exist for each `Lock`. A `Condition` is effectively a waiting/blocking pool for threads.

```
Lock lock = new ReentrantLock();
Condition blockingPoolA = lock.newCondition();
Condition blockingPoolB = lock.newCondition();
```

By having multiple conditions, you are effectively categorizing the threads waiting on a lock and can, therefore, wake up a subset of the waiting threads.

`Conditions` can also be used when you can't use a `BlockingQueue` to coordinate the activities of two or more threads.

ReentrantReadWriteLock

Imagine a video game that was storing a collection of high scores using a non-thread-safe collection. With a non-thread-safe collection, it is important that if a thread is attempting to modify the collection, it must have exclusive access to the collection. To allow multiple threads to concurrently read the high score list or allow a single thread to add a new score, you could use a `ReadWriteLock`.

A `ReentrantReadWriteLock` is not actually a `Lock`; it implements the `ReadWriteLock` interface. What a `ReentrantReadWriteLock` does is produce two specialized `Lock` instances, one to a read lock and the other to a write lock.

```
ReentrantReadWriteLock rwl =
  new ReentrantReadWriteLock();
Lock readLock = rwl.readLock();
Lock writeLock = rwl.writeLock();
```

These two locks are a matched set—one cannot be held at the same time as the other (by different threads). What makes these locks unique is that multiple threads can hold the read lock at the same time, but only one thread can hold the write lock at a time.

This example shows how a non-thread-safe collection (an `ArrayList`) can be made thread-safe, allowing concurrent reads but exclusive access by a writing thread:

```
public class MaxValueCollection {
    private List<Integer> integers = new ArrayList<>();
    private ReentrantReadWriteLock rwl =
        new ReentrantReadWriteLock();
```

```
public void add(Integer i) {
    rwl.writeLock().lock(); // one at a time
    try {
        integers.add(i);
    } finally {
        rwl.writeLock().unlock();
    }
}

public int findMax() {
    rwl.readLock().lock(); // many at once
    try {
        return Collections.max(integers);
    } finally {
        rwl.readLock().unlock();
    }
}
}
```

Instead of wrapping a collection with Lock objects to ensure thread safety, you can use one of the thread-safe collections you'll learn about in the next section.

CERTIFICATION OBJECTIVE

Use java.util.concurrent Collections (OCP Objective 10.4)

10.4   Use java.util.concurrent collections and classes including CyclicBarrier and CopyOnWriteArrayList.

Imagine an online video game with a list of the top 20 scores in the last 30 days. You could model the high score list using a `java.util.ArrayList`. As scores expire, they are removed from the list, and as new scores displace existing scores, remove and insert operations are performed. At the end of every game, the list of high scores is displayed. If the game is popular, then a lot of people (threads) will be reading the list at the same time. Occasionally, the list will be modified—sometimes by multiple threads—probably at the same time that it is being read by a large number of threads.

A traditional `java.util.List` implementation such as `java.util.ArrayList` is not thread-safe. Concurrent threads can safely read from an `ArrayList` and possibly even modify the elements stored in the list, but if any thread modifies the structure of the list (add or remove operation), then unpredictable behavior can occur.

Look at the `ArrayListRunnable` class in the following example. What would happen if there were a single instance of this class being executed by several threads? You might encounter several problems, including `ArrayIndexOutOfBoundsException`, duplicate values, skipped values, and null values. Not all threading problems manifest immediately. To observe the bad behavior, you might have to execute the faulty code multiple times or under different system loads. It is important that you are able to recognize the difference between thread-safe and non-thread-safe code yourself, because the compiler will not detect thread-unsafe code.

```
public class ArrayListRunnable implements Runnable {
  // shared by all threads
  private List<Integer> list = new ArrayList<>();

  public ArrayListRunnable() {
    // add some elements
    for (int i = 0; i < 100000; i++) {
      list.add(i);
    }
  }

    // might run concurrently, you cannot be sure
    // to be safe you must assume it does
  public void run() {
    String tName = Thread.currentThread().getName();
    while (!list.isEmpty()) {
      System.out.println(tName + " removed " + list.remove(0));
    }
  }

  public static void main(String[] args) {
    ArrayListRunnable alr = new ArrayListRunnable();
    Thread t1 = new Thread(alr);
    Thread t2 = new Thread(alr); // shared Runnable
    t1.start();
    t2.start();
  }
}
```

To make a collection thread-safe, you could surround all the code that accessed the collection in synchronized blocks or use a method such as `Collections`.`synchronizedList(new ArrayList())`. Using synchronization to safeguard a collection creates a performance bottleneck and reduces the liveness of your application. The `java.util.concurrent` package provides several types of collections that are thread-safe but do not use coarse-grained synchronization. When a collection will be concurrently accessed in an application you are developing, you should always consider using the collections outlined in the following sections.

Problems in multithreaded applications may not always manifest—a lot depends on the underlying operating system and how other applications affect the thread scheduling of a problematic application. On the exam, you might be asked about the "probable" or "most likely" outcome. Unless you are asked to identify *every possible outcome of a code sample, don't get hung up on unlikely results. For example, if a code sample uses* `Thread .sleep(1000)` *and nothing indicates that the thread would be interrupted while it was sleeping, it would be safe to assume that the thread would resume execution around one second after the call to sleep.*

Copy-on-Write Collections

The copy-on-write collections from the `java.util.concurrent` package implement one of several mechanisms to make a collection thread-safe. By using the copy-on-write collections, you eliminate the need to implement synchronization or locking when manipulating a collection using multiple threads.

The `CopyOnWriteArrayList` is a `List` implementation that can be used concurrently without using traditional synchronization semantics. As its name implies, a `CopyOnWriteArrayList` will never modify its internal array of data. Any mutating operations on the `List` (add, set, remove, etc.) will cause a new modified copy of the array to be created, which will replace the original read-only array. The read-only nature of the underlying array in a `CopyOnWriteArrayList` allows it to be safely shared with multiple threads. **Remember that read-only (immutable) objects are always thread-safe.**

The essential thing to remember with a copy-on-write collection is that a thread that is looping through the elements in a collection must keep a reference to the same unchanging elements throughout the duration of the loop; this is achieved with the use of an `Iterator`. You want to keep using the old, unchanging collection that you began a loop with. When you use `list.iterator()`, the returned `Iterator` will always reference the collection of elements as it was when `list.iterator()` was called, even if another thread modifies the collection. Any mutating methods called on a copy-on-write–based `Iterator` or `ListIterator` (such as add, set, or remove) will throw an `UnsupportedOperationException`.

on the job

A `for-each` loop uses an `Iterator` when executing, so it is safe to use with a copy-on-write collection, unlike a traditional `for` loop.

```
for(Object o : collection) {}              // use this
for(int i = 0; i < collection.size(); i++) {} // not this
```

The `java.util.concurrent` package provides two copy-on-write-based collections: `CopyOnWriteArrayList` and `CopyOnWriteArraySet`. Use the copy-on-write collections when your data sets remain relatively small and the number of read operations and traversals greatly outnumber modifications to the collections. Modifications to the collections (not the elements within) are expensive because the entire internal array must be duplicated for each modification.

Concurrent Collections

The `java.util.concurrent` package also contains several concurrent collections that can be concurrently read and modified by multiple threads, but without the copy-on-write behavior seen in the copy-on-write collections. The concurrent collections include

- `ConcurrentHashMap`
- `ConcurrentLinkedDeque`
- `ConcurrentLinkedQueue`

- ConcurrentSkipListMap
- ConcurrentSkipListSet

Be aware that an `Iterator` for a concurrent collection is weakly consistent; it can return elements from the point in time the `Iterator` was created **or later**. This means that while you are looping through a concurrent collection, you might observe elements that are being inserted by other threads. In addition, you may observe only some of the elements that another thread is inserting with methods such as `addAll` when concurrently reading from the collection. Similarly, the `size` method may produce inaccurate results. Imagine attempting to count the number of people in a checkout line at a grocery store. While you are counting the people in line, some people may join the line and others may leave. Your count might end up close but not exact by the time you reach the end. This is the type of behavior you might see with a weakly consistent collection. The benefit to this type of behavior is that it is permissible for multiple threads to concurrently read and write a collection without having to create multiple internal copies of the collection, as is the case in a copy-on-write collection. If your application cannot deal with these inconsistencies, you might have to use a copy-on-write collection.

The `ConcurrentHashMap` and `ConcurrentSkipListMap` classes implement the `ConcurrentMap` interface. A `ConcurrentMap` enhances a `Map` by adding the atomic `putIfAbsent`, `remove`, and `replace` methods. For example, the `putIfAbsent` method is equivalent to performing the following code as an atomic operation:

```
if (!map.containsKey(key))
    return map.put(key, value);
  else
    return map.get(key);
```

`ConcurrentSkipListMap` and `ConcurrentSkipListSet` are sorted. `ConcurrentSkipListMap` keys and `ConcurrentSkipListSet` elements require the use of the `Comparable` or `Comparator` interfaces to enable ordering.

Blocking Queues

The copy-on-write and the concurrent collections are centered on the idea of multiple threads sharing data. Sometimes, instead of shared data (objects), you need to transfer data between two threads. A `BlockingQueue` is a type of shared collection that is used to exchange data between two or more threads while causing one or more of the threads to wait until the point in time when the data can be exchanged. One use case of a `BlockingQueue` is called the producer-consumer problem. In a producer-consumer scenario, one thread produces data, then adds it to a queue, and another thread must consume the data from the queue. A queue provides the means for the producer and the consumer to exchange objects. The `java.util.concurrent` package provides several `BlockingQueue` implementations. They include

- `ArrayBlockingQueue`
- `LinkedBlockingDeque`
- `LinkedBlockingQueue`
- `PriorityBlockingQueue`
- `DelayQueue`
- `LinkedTransferQueue`
- `SynchronousQueue`

General Behavior

A blocking collection, depending on the method being called, may cause a thread to block until another thread calls a corresponding method on the collection. For example, if you attempt to remove an element by calling `take()` on any `BlockingQueue` that is empty, the operation will block until another thread inserts an element. Don't call a blocking operation in a thread unless it is safe for that thread to block. The commonly used methods in a `BlockingQueue` are described in the following table.

Method	General Purpose	Unique Behavior
`add(E e)`	Insert an object.	Returns `true` if object added, false if duplicate objects are not allowed. Throws an `IllegalStateException` if the queue is bounded and full.
`offer(E e)`	Insert an object.	Returns `true` if object added, false if the queue is bounded and full.
`put(E e)`	Insert an object.	Returns `void`. If needed, will block until space in the queue becomes available.
`offer(E e, long timeout, TimeUnit unit)`	Insert an object.	Returns `false` if the object was not able to be inserted before the time indicated by the second and third parameters.
`remove(Object o)`	Remove an object.	Returns `true` if an equal object was found in the queue and removed; otherwise, returns `false`.

Method	General Purpose	Unique Behavior
`poll(long timeout, TimeUnit unit)`	Remove an object.	Removes the first object in the queue (the head) and returns it. If the timeout expires before an object can be removed because the queue is empty, a null will be returned.
`take()`	Remove an object.	Removes the first object in the queue (the head) and returns it, blocking if needed until an object becomes available.
`poll()`	Remove an object.	Removes the first object in the queue (the head) and returns it or returns null if the queue is empty.
`element()`	Retrieve an object.	Gets the head of the queue without removing it. Throws a `NoSuchElementException` if the queue is empty.
`peek()`	Retrieve an object.	Gets the head of the queue without removing it. Returns a null if the queue is empty.

Bounded Queues

`ArrayBlockingQueue`, `LinkedBlockingDeque`, and `LinkedBlockingQueue` support a bounded capacity and will block on `put(e)` and similar operations if the collection is full. `LinkedBlockingQueue` is optionally bounded, depending on the constructor you use.

```
BlockingQueue<Integer> bq = new ArrayBlockingQueue<>(1);
try {
  bq.put(42);
  bq.put(43); // blocks until previous value is removed
} catch (InterruptedException ex) {
  // log and handle
}
```

Special-Purpose Queues

A `SynchronousQueue` is a special type of bounded blocking queue; it has a capacity of zero. Having a zero capacity, the first thread to attempt either an insert or remove operation on a `SynchronousQueue` will block until another thread performs the opposite operation. You use a `SynchronousQueue` when you need threads to meet up and exchange an object.

A `DelayQueue` is useful when you have objects that should not be consumed until a specific time. The elements added to a `DelayQueue` will implement the java.util.concurrent.Delayed interface, which defines a single method: public long getDelay(TimeUnit unit). The elements of a DelayQueue can only be taken once their delay has expired.

The LinkedTransferQueue

A LinkedTransferQueue (added in Java 7) is a superset of ConcurrentLinkedQueue, SynchronousQueue, and LinkedBlockingQueue. It can function as a concurrent Queue implementation similar to ConcurrentLinkedQueue. It also supports unbounded blocking (consumption blocking) similar to LinkedBlockingQueue via the take() method. Like a SynchronousQueue, a LinkedTransferQueue can be used to make two threads rendezvous to exchange an object. Unlike a SynchronousQueue, a LinkedTransferQueue has internal capacity, so the transfer(E) method is used to block until the inserted object (and any previously inserted objects) is consumed by another thread.

In other words, a LinkedTransferQueue might do almost everything you need from a Queue.

Because a LinkedTransferQueue implements the BlockingQueue, TransferQueue, and Queue interfaces, it can be used to showcase all the different methods that can be used to add and remove elements using the various types of queues. Creating a LinkedTransferQueue is easy. Because LinkedTransferQueue is not bound by size, a limit to the number of elements CANNOT be supplied to its constructor.

```
TransferQueue<Integer> tq =
  new LinkedTransferQueue<>(); // not bounded
```

There are many methods to add a single element to a LinkedTransferQueue. Note that any method that blocks or waits for any period may throw an InterruptedException.

```
boolean b1 = tq.add(1);                 // returns true if added or throws
                                         // IllegalStateException if full
tq.put(2);                       // blocks if bounded and full
boolean b3 = tq.offer(3);                // returns true if added or false
                                         // if bounded and full
                                         // recommended over add

boolean b4 =
  tq.offer(4, 10, MILLISECONDS);         // returns true if added
                                         // within the given time
                                         // false if bound and full
tq.transfer(5);                  // blocks until this element is consumed
```

```
boolean b6 = tq.tryTransfer(6);          // returns true if consumed
                                         // by an awaiting thread or
                                         // returns false without
                                         // adding if there was no
                                         // awaiting consumer
boolean b7 =
  tq.tryTransfer(7, 10, MILLISECONDS);   // will wait the
                                         // given time for
                                         // a consumer
```

Shown next are the various methods to access a single value in a
`LinkedTransferQueue`. Again, any method that blocks or waits for any period
may throw an `InterruptedException`.

```
Integer i1 = tq.element();      // gets without removing
                                // throws NoSuchElementException
                                // if empty
Integer i2 = tq.peek();         // gets without removing
                                // returns null if empty
Integer i3 = tq.poll();         // removes the head of the queue
                                // returns null if empty
Integer i4 =
  tq.poll(10, MILLISECONDS);    // removes the head of the
                                // queue, waits up to the time
                                // specified before returning
                                // null if empty
Integer i5 = tq.remove();       // removes the head of the queue
                                // throws NoSuchElementException
                                // if empty
Integer i6 = tq.take();         // removes the head of the queue
                                // blocks until an element is ready
```

*Use a `LinkedTransferQueue` (added in Java 7) instead of another comparable
queue type. The other `java.util.concurrent` queues (introduced in Java 5)
are less efficient than `LinkedTransferQueue`.*

Controlling Threads with CyclicBarrier

Whereas blocking queues force threads to wait based on capacity or until a method
is called on the queue, a `CyclicBarrier` can force threads to wait at a specific
point in the execution until all threads reach that point before continuing. You can
think of that point in the execution as a *barrier:* no thread can proceed beyond that
point until all other threads have also reached it.

Imagine you have two threads that are processing data in arrays and you want to
copy the processed data from the arrays to a final `ArrayList` that contains data

from both threads. You can't have both threads accessing the final `ArrayList` because `ArrayList` is not thread-safe. It is better to wait until both threads are done processing the arrays and only then copy the data to the final `ArrayList` using one thread.

This is an example of the type of problem where `CyclicBarrier` can be useful. When you can break up a problem into smaller pieces that can be processed concurrently and then combine the data into a result at certain key points in the processing, using a `CyclicBarrier` ensures the threads wait for each other at those key points in the execution.

Let's take a look at some code to see how to use `CyclicBarrier` to force two threads to wait for each other. In this example, we'll use the optional `Runnable` that `CyclicBarrier` will take and run, once both threads reach the barrier point. This `Runnable` is run only one time, by the last thread to reach the barrier and before any of the threads can continue, ensuring the code in the `Runnable` is thread-safe. Each thread processes a small array and then ends, but imagine how this idea might be applied to threads processing large arrays a chunk at a time and continuing after a barrier is reached. In fact, that's exactly why `CyclicBarrier` is named "cyclic": the `CyclicBarrier` can be reused after the threads are released to continue running.

```
public class CB {
    List<String> result = new ArrayList<>();
    static String[] dogs1 = {"boi", "clover", "charis"};
    static String[] dogs2 = {"aiko", "zooey", "biscuit"};
    final CyclicBarrier barrier;                 // The barrier for the threads
    class ProcessDogs implements Runnable { // Each thread will process
        String dogs[];                           // an array of dogs
        ProcessDogs(String[] d) { dogs = d; }
// #4
        public void run() {                      // Convert first chars into
                                                 // uppercase
            for (int i = 0; i < dogs.length; i++) {
                String dogName = dogs[i];
                String newDogName = dogName.substring(0, 1).toUpperCase()
                                  + dogName.substring(1);
                dogs[i] = newDogName;
            }
            try {
// #5
                barrier.await();                 // Wait at the barrier
            } catch(InterruptedException | BrokenBarrierException e) {
                // The other thread must have been interrupted
                e.printStackTrace();
            }
```

```
// #7
            System.out.println(Thread.currentThread().getName() + " is done!");
        }
    }
    public CB() {
// #1    ------------------------- the 2nd argument code runs later
        barrier = new CyclicBarrier(2, () -> { // 2 threads, 1 Runnable
// #6
                                                    // Copy results to list
            for (int i = 0; i < dogs1.length; i++) {
                result.add(dogs1[i]);               // add dogs from array 1
            }
            for (int i = 0; i < dogs2.length; i++) {
                result.add(dogs2[i]);               // add dogs from array 2
            }
                                                    // print the thread name and
                                                    // result
            System.out.println(Thread.currentThread().getName() +
                            " Result: " + result);
        });
// #2
        Thread t1 = new Thread(new ProcessDogs(dogs1));
        Thread t2 = new Thread(new ProcessDogs(dogs2));
// #3
        t1.start();
        t2.start();
        System.out.println("Main Thread is done");
    }
    public static void main(String[] args) {
        CB cb = new CB();
    }
}
```

In this example, we have two arrays of dog names and the processing is
quite simple; we just convert the first letter of each dog name from lowercase to
uppercase. Once both arrays have been processed, we then combine the results into
an ArrayList of dog names. In the class CB, we define the result ArrayList,
where we'll write results when both threads have finished processing the two arrays,
dogs1 and dogs2. We also declare the CyclicBarrier that both threads will
use to wait for each other. Let's step through how the code executes (follow the
numbers in the code):

1. In the CB constructor, we create a new CyclicBarrier, passing in the
   number of threads that will wait at the barrier **and a Runnable that will
   be run by the last thread to reach the barrier.** Here, we're using a lambda
   expression for this Runnable.

2. We then create two threads, `t1` and `t2`, and pass each the `ProcessDogs` `Runnable`. When we create the `ProcessDogs Runnables` for the threads, we pass in the array that the thread will process: we pass `dogs1` to thread `t1` and `dogs2` to thread `t2`.

3. We then start both threads and print a message saying the main thread is done.

4. The two threads begin running and process their respective arrays. The `ProcessDogs run()` method simply iterates through the array and converts the first letter of the dog name to uppercase, storing the modified string back in the original array.

5. Once the loop is complete, the thread then waits at the barrier by calling the barrier's `await()` method. We'll come back and talk about the exception handling in a minute.

6. Once both threads reach the barrier, then the `Runnable` we passed to the `CyclicBarrier` constructor is executed by the last thread to reach the barrier. This adds all the items from both arrays to the `ArrayList result` and prints the `result`.

7. When the `Runnable` completes, then both threads are released and can continue executing where they left off at the barrier. In this example, each thread just prints a message to the console indicating it's done (with the thread name), but you can imagine that in a more realistic example, they could continue on to do more processing. Notice that neither thread can print out that it's done until *both* threads have reached the barrier and the barrier `Runnable` is complete.

If you have a machine with at least two cores and you run this code several times, you may see thread 0 displaying the result or you may see thread 1 displaying the result. It just depends on which thread gets to the barrier last. Also, notice that the main thread often finishes before the other threads, but not always. The most important point to notice is that *every time* you run this code, you will see the resulting `ArrayList` displayed *before* the messages from the threads that they are done. Why? Because both threads must wait at the barrier for the barrier `Runnable` to complete before they can continue!

```
Main Thread is done
Thread-0 Result: [Boi, Clover, Charis, Aiko, Zooey, Biscuit]
Thread-0 is done!
Thread-1 is done!
```

Now let's get back to the exception handling on the `barrier.await()` method. What if one of the threads gets stuck? If this happens, then all the other threads waiting at the barrier get an `InterruptedException` or a `BrokenBarrierException` and are all released. In that case, the barrier `Runnable` will not run and the remaining threads will continue.

You can reuse a `CyclicBarrier` or use multiple `CyclicBarriers` to coordinate threads at more than one barrier point. For example, you might have the thread `Runnable` execute some code, wait at barrier 1, then execute some more code, wait at barrier 2, and then finally execute more code and finish. To reset a barrier to its initial state, call the `reset()` method. If you need the main thread to also wait at the barrier, you can call `await()` on the barrier in the main thread, but don't forget to increase the number of threads allowed at the barrier by one when you create the `CyclicBarrier`.

CERTIFICATION OBJECTIVE

Use Executors and ThreadPools (OCP Objective 10.1)

10.1   Create worker threads using Runnable, Callable and use an ExecutorService to concurrently execute tasks.

`Executors` (and the `ThreadPools` used by them) help meet two of the same needs as `Threads` do:

1. Creating and scheduling some Java code for execution and
2. Optimizing the execution of that code for the hardware resources you have available (using all CPUs, for example)

With traditional threading, you handle needs 1 and 2 yourself. With `Executors`, you handle need 1, but you get to use an off-the-shelf solution for need 2. The `java.util.concurrent` package provides several different off-the-shelf solutions (`Executors` and `ThreadPools`), which you'll read about in this chapter.

on the **job**

When you have multiple needs or concerns, it is common to separate the code for each need into different classes. This makes your application more modular and flexible. This is a fundamental programming principle called "separation of concerns."

In a way, an `Executor` is an alternative to starting new threads. Using `Threads` directly can be considered low-level multithreading, whereas using `Executors` can be considered high-level multithreading. To understand how an `Executor` can replace manual thread creation, let us first analyze what happens when starting a new thread.

1. First, you must identify a task of some sort that forms a self-contained unit of work. You will typically code this task as a class that implements the `Runnable` interface.

2. After creating a `Runnable`, the next step is to execute it. You have two options for executing a `Runnable`:

   ■ **Option one**   Call the `run` method synchronously (i.e., without starting a thread). This is probably **not** what you would normally do.

   ```
   Runnable r = new MyRunnableTask();
   r.run(); // executed by calling thread
   ```

   ■ **Option two**   Call the method indirectly, most likely with a new thread.

   ```
   Runnable r = new MyRunnableTask();
   Thread t1 = new Thread(r);
   t1.start();
   ```

The second approach has the benefit of executing your task asynchronously, meaning the primary flow of execution in your program can continue executing, without waiting for the task to complete. On a multiprocessor system, you must divide a program into a collection of asynchronous tasks that can execute concurrently in order to take advantage of all of the computing power a system possesses.

Identifying Parallel Tasks

Some applications are easier to divide into separate tasks than others. A single-user desktop application may only have a handful of tasks that are suitable for concurrent execution. Networked multiuser servers, on the other hand, have a natural division of work. Each user's actions can be a task. Continuing our computer game scenario, imagine a computer program that can play chess against thousands of people simultaneously. Each player submits his or her move, the computer calculates its move, and finally it informs the player of that move.

Why do we need an alternative to new `Thread(r).start()`? What are the drawbacks? If we use our online chess game scenario, then having 10,000 concurrent players might mean 10,001 concurrent threads. (One thread awaits network connections from clients and performs a `Thread(r).start()` for each player.) The player thread would be responsible for reading the player's move, computing the computer's move, and making the response.

How Many Threads Can You Run?

Do you own a computer that can concurrently run 10,000 threads or 1,000 or even 100? Probably not—this is a trick question. A quad-core CPU (with four processors per unit) might be able to execute two threads per core for a total of eight concurrently executing threads. You can start 10,000 threads, but not all of them will be running at the same time. The underlying operating system's task scheduler rotates the threads so that they each get a slice of time on a processor. Ten thousand threads all competing for a turn on a processor wouldn't make for a very responsive system. Threads would either have to wait so long for a turn or get such small turns (or both) that performance would suffer.

In addition, each thread consumes system resources. It takes processor cycles to perform a context switch (saving the state of a thread and resuming another thread), and each thread consumes system memory for its stack space. Stack space is used for temporary storage and to keep track of where a thread returns to after completing a method call. Depending on a thread's behavior, it might be possible to lower the cost (in RAM) of creating a thread by reducing a thread's stack size.

To reduce a thread's stack size, the Oracle JVM supports using the nonstandard-Xss1024k option to the `java` command. Note that decreasing the value too far can result in some threads throwing exceptions when performing certain tasks, such as making a large number of recursive method calls.

Another limiting factor in being able to run 10,000 threads in an application has to do with the underlying limits of the OS. Operating systems typically have limits on the number of threads an application can create. These limits can prevent a buggy application from spawning countless threads and making your system unresponsive. If you have a legitimate need to run 10,000 threads, you will probably have to consult your operating system's documentation to discover possible limits and configuration options.

CPU-Intensive vs. I/O-Intensive Tasks

If you correctly configure your OS and you have enough memory for each thread's stack space plus your application's primary memory (heap), will you be able to run an application with 10,000 threads? It depends.... Remember that your processor can only run a small number of concurrent threads (in the neighborhood of 8 to 16 threads). Yet many network server applications, such as our online chess game, would have traditionally started a new thread for each connected client. A system might be able to run an application with such a high number of threads because most of the threads are not doing anything. More precisely, in an application like our online chess server, most threads would be blocked waiting on I/O operations such as `InputStream.read` or `OutputStream.write` method calls.

When a thread makes an I/O request using `InputStream.read` and the data to be read isn't already in memory, the calling thread will be put to sleep by the system until the requested data can be loaded. This is much more efficient than keeping the thread on the processor while it has nothing to do. I/O operations are extremely slow when compared to compute operations—reading a sector from a hard drive takes much longer than adding hundreds of numbers. A processor might execute hundreds of thousands, or even millions, of instructions while awaiting the completion of an I/O request. The type of work (either CPU intensive or I/O intensive) a thread will be performing is important when considering how many threads an application can safely run. Imagine your world-class-computer chess-playing program takes one minute of processor time (no I/O at all) to calculate each move. In this scenario, it would only take about 16 concurrent players to cause your system to have periods of maximum CPU utilization.

on the job

If your tasks will be performing I/O operations, you should be concerned about how increased load (users) might affect scalability. If your tasks perform blocking I/O, then you might need to utilize a thread-per-task model. If you don't, then all your threads may be tied up in I/O operations with no threads remaining to support additional users. Another option would be to investigate whether you can use nonblocking I/O instead of blocking I/O.

Fighting for a Turn

If it takes the computer player one minute to calculate a turn and it takes a human player about the same time, then each player only uses one minute of CPU time out of every two minutes of real time. With a system capable of executing 16 concurrent game threads, that means we could handle 32 connected players.

But if all 32 players make their turn at once, the computer will be stuck trying to calculate 32 moves at once. If the system uses preemptive multitasking (the most common type), then each thread will get preempted while it is running (paused and kicked off the CPU) so a different thread can take a turn (time slice). In most JVM implementations, this is handled by the underlying operating system's task scheduler. The task scheduler is itself a software program. The more CPU cycles spent scheduling and preempting threads, the less processor time you have to execute your application threads. Note that it would appear to the untrained observer that all 32 threads were running concurrently because a preemptive multitasking system will switch out the running threads frequently (millisecond time slices).

Decoupling Tasks from Threads

The best design would be one that utilized as many system resources as possible without attempting to overutilize the system. If 16 threads are all you need to fully utilize your CPU, why would you start more than that? In a traditional system, you start more threads than your system can concurrently run and hope that only a small number are in a running state. If we want to adjust the number of threads that are started, we need to decouple the tasks that are to be performed (our `Runnable` instances) from our thread creation and starting. This is where a `java.util` `.concurrent.Executor` can help. The basic usage looks something like this:

```
Runnable r = new MyRunnableTask();
Executor ex = // details to follow
ex.execute(r);
```

A `java.util.concurrent.Executor` is used to execute the `run` method in a `Runnable` instance much like a thread. Unlike a more traditional `new Thread(r).start()`, an `Executor` can be designed to use any number of threading approaches, including

- Not starting any threads at all (task is run in the calling thread)
- Starting a new thread for each task
- Queuing tasks and processing them with only enough threads to keep the CPU utilized

You can easily create your own implementations of an `Executor` with custom behaviors. As you'll see soon, several implementations are provided in the standard Java SE libraries. Looking at sample `Executor` implementations can help you to understand their behavior. This next example doesn't start any new threads; instead, it executes the Runnable using the thread that invoked the Executor.

```
import java.util.concurrent.Executor;
public class SameThreadExecutor implements Executor {
    @Override
    public void execute(Runnable command) {
        command.run(); // caller waits
    }
}
```

The following Executor implementation would use a new thread for each task:

```
import java.util.concurrent.Executor;
public class NewThreadExecutor implements Executor {
    @Override
    public void execute(Runnable command) {
        Thread t = new Thread(command);
        t.start();
    }
}
```

This example shows how an Executor implementation can be put to use:

```
Runnable r = new MyRunnableTask();
Executor ex = new NewThreadExecutor(); // choose Executor
ex.executor(r);
```

By coding to the Executor interface, the submission of tasks is decoupled from the execution of tasks. The result is that you can easily modify how threads are used to execute tasks in your applications.

on the
job

There is no "right number" of threads for task execution. The type of task (CPU intensive versus I/O intensive), number of tasks, I/O latency, and system resources all factor into determining the ideal number of threads to use. You should test your applications to determine the ideal threading model. This is one reason why the ability to separate task submission from task execution is important.

Several Executor implementations are supplied as part of the standard Java libraries. The Executors class (notice the "s" at the end) is a factory for Executor implementations.

```
Runnable r = new MyRunnableTask();
Executor ex = Executors.newCachedThreadPool(); // choose Executor
ex.execute(r);
```

The `Executor` instances returned by `Executors` are actually of type `ExecutorService` (which extends `Executor`). An `ExecutorService` provides management capability and can return `Future` instances that are used to obtain the result of executing a task asynchronously. We'll talk more about `Future` in a few pages!

```
Runnable r = new MyRunnableTask();
ExecutorService ex = Executors.newCachedThreadPool(); // subtype of Executor
ex.execute(r);
```

Three types of `ExecutorService` instances can be created by the factory methods in the `Executors` class: cached thread pool executors, fixed thread pool executors, and single thread pool executors.

Cached Thread Pools

```
ExecutorService ex = Executors.newCachedThreadPool();
```

A cached thread pool will create new threads as they are needed and reuse threads that have become free. Threads that have been idle for 60 seconds are removed from the pool.

Watch out! Without some type of external limitation, a cached thread pool may be used to create more threads than your system can handle.

Fixed Thread Pools—Most Common

```
ExecutorService ex = Executors.newFixedThreadPool(4);
```

A fixed thread pool is constructed using a numeric argument (4 in the preceding example) that specifies the number of threads used to execute tasks. This type of pool will probably be the one you use the most because it prevents an application from overloading a system with too many threads. Tasks that cannot be executed immediately are placed on an unbounded queue for later execution.

on the job

You might base the number of threads in a fixed thread pool on some attribute of the system your application is executing on. By tying the number of threads to system resources, you can create an application that scales with changes in system hardware. To query the number of available processors, you can use the `java.lang.Runtime` class.

```
Runtime rt = Runtime.getRuntime();
int cpus = rt.availableProcessors();
```

ThreadPoolExecutor

Both `Executors.newCachedThreadPool()` and `Executors`
`.newFixedThreadPool(4)` return objects of type `java.util.concurrent`
`.ThreadPoolExecutor` (which implements `ExecutorService` and
`Executor`). You will typically use the `Executors` factory methods instead of
creating `ThreadPoolExecutor` instances directly, but you can cast the fixed
or cached thread pool `ExecutorService` references if you need access to the
additional methods. The following example shows how you could dynamically
adjust the thread count of a pool at runtime:

```
ThreadPoolExecutor tpe = (ThreadPoolExecutor)Executors.newFixedThreadPool(4);
tpe.setCorePoolSize(8);
tpe.setMaximumPoolSize(8);
```

Single Thread Pools

```
ExecutorService ex = Executors.newSingleThreadExecutor();
```

A single thread pool uses a single thread to execute tasks. Tasks that cannot
be executed immediately are placed on an unbounded queue for later execution.
Unlike a fixed thread pool executor with a size of 1, a single thread executor
prevents any adjustments to the number of threads in the pool.

Scheduled Thread Pool

In addition to the three basic `ExecutorService` behaviors outlined
already, the Executors class has factory methods to produce a
`ScheduledThreadPoolExecutor`. A `ScheduledThreadPoolExecutor`
enables tasks to be executed after a delay or at repeating intervals. Here, we see
some thread-scheduling code in action:

```
ScheduledExecutorService ftses =
  Executors.newScheduledThreadPool(4);                       // multi-threaded
                                                              // version
ftses.schedule(r, 5, TimeUnit.SECONDS);                      // run once after
                                                              // a delay
ftses.scheduleAtFixedRate(r, 2, 5, TimeUnit.SECONDS);        // begin after a
                                                              // 2sec delay
    // and begin again every 5 seconds
ftses.scheduleWithFixedDelay(r, 2, 5, TimeUnit.SECONDS); // begin after
                                                              // 2sec delay
    // and begin again 5 seconds *after* completing the last execution
```

The Callable Interface

So far, the Executors examples have used a Runnable instance to represent the task to be executed. The java.util.concurrent.Callable interface serves the same purpose as the Runnable interface, but provides more flexibility. Unlike the Runnable interface, a Callable may return a result upon completing execution and may throw a checked exception. An ExecutorService can be passed a Callable instead of a Runnable.

on the job

Avoid using methods such as Object.wait, Object.notify, and Object .notifyAll in tasks (Runnable and Callable instances) that are submitted to an Executor or ExecutorService. Because you might not know what the threading behavior of an Executor is, it is a good idea to avoid operations that may interfere with thread execution. Avoiding these types of methods is advisable anyway since they are easy to misuse.

The primary benefit of using a Callable is the ability to return a result. Because an ExecutorService may execute the Callable asynchronously (just like a Runnable), you need a way to check the completion status of a Callable and obtain the result later. A java.util.concurrent.Future is used to obtain the status and result of a Callable. Without a Future, you'd have no way to obtain the result of a completed Callable and you might as well use a Runnable (which returns void) instead of a Callable. Here's a simple Callable example that loops a random number of times and returns the random loop count:

```java
import java.util.concurrent.Callable;
import java.util.concurrent.ThreadLocalRandom;
public class MyCallable implements Callable<Integer> {

  @Override
  public Integer call() {
    // Obtain a random number from 1 to 10
    int count = ThreadLocalRandom.current().nextInt(1, 11);
    for(int i = 1; i <= count; i++) {
      System.out.println("Running..." + i);
    }
    return count;
  }
}
```

Submitting a `Callable` to an `ExecutorService` returns a `Future` reference. When you use the `Future` to obtain the `Callable`'s result, you will have to handle two possible exceptions:

- **`InterruptedException`**   Raised when the thread calling the `Future`'s `get()` method is interrupted before a result can be returned
- **`ExecutionException`**   Raised when an exception was thrown during the execution of the `Callable`'s `call()` method

```
Callable<Integer> c = new MyCallable();
ExecutorService ex =
        Executors.newCachedThreadPool();
Future<Integer> f = ex.submit(c); // finishes in the future
try {
  Integer v = f.get(); // blocks until done
  System.out.println("Ran:" + v);
} catch (InterruptedException | ExecutionException iex) {
  System.out.println("Failed");
}
```

on the
ⓘ o b

I/O activities in your `Runnable` and `Callable` instances can be a serious bottleneck. In preceding examples, the use of `System.out.println()` will cause I/O activity. If this wasn't a trivial example being used to demonstrate `Callable` and `ExecutorService`, you would probably want to avoid repeated calls to `println()` in the `Callable`. One possibility would be to use `StringBuilder` to concatenate all output strings and have a single `println()` call before the `call()` method returns. Another possibility would be to use a logging framework (see `java.util.logging`) in place of any `println()` calls.

ThreadLocalRandom

The first `Callable` example used a `java.util.concurrent.ThreadLocalRandom`. `ThreadLocalRandom` was introduced in Java 7 as a new way to create random numbers. `Math.random()` and shared `Random` instances are thread-safe, but suffer from contention when used by multiple threads. A `ThreadLocalRandom` is unique to a thread and will perform better because it avoids any contention. `ThreadLocalRandom` also provides several convenient methods such as `nextInt(int, int)` that allow you to specify the range of possible values returned.

ExecutorService Shutdown

You've seen how to create `Executors` and how to submit `Runnable` and `Callable` tasks to those `Executors`. The final component to using an `Executor` is shutting it down once it is done processing tasks. An `ExecutorService` should be shut down once it is no longer needed to free up system resources and to allow graceful application shutdown. Because the threads in an `ExecutorService` may be nondaemon threads, they may prevent normal application termination. In other words, your application stays running after completing its main method. You could perform a `System.exit(0)` call, but it would preferable to allow your threads to complete their current activities (especially if they are writing data).

```
ExecutorService ex =
// …
ex.shutdown(); // no more new tasks
               // but finish existing tasks
try {
  boolean term = ex.awaitTermination(2, TimeUnit.SECONDS);
    // wait 2 seconds for running tasks to finish
} catch (InterruptedException ex1) {
  // did not wait the full 2 seconds
} finally {
  if(!ex.isTerminated()) // are all tasks done?
  {
    List<Runnable> unfinished = ex.shutdownNow();
    // a collection of the unfinished tasks
  }
}
```

For long-running tasks (especially those with looping constructs), consider using `Thread.currentThread().isInterrupted()` to determine if a `Runnable` or `Callable` should return early. The `ExecutorService` `.shutdownNow()` method will typically call `Thread.interrupt()` in an attempt to terminate any unfinished tasks.

CERTIFICATION OBJECTIVE

Use the Parallel Fork/Join Framework (OCP Objective 10.5)

10.5   Use the parallel Fork/Join Framework.

The Fork-Join Framework provides a highly specialized `ExecutorService`. The other `ExecutorService` instances you've seen so far are centered on the concept of submitting multiple tasks to an `ExecutorService`. By doing this, you provide an easy avenue for an `ExecutorService` to take advantage of all the

CPUs in a system by using threads to complete tasks. Sometimes, you don't have multiple tasks; instead, you have one really big task.

There are many large tasks or problems you might need to solve in your application. For example, you might need to initialize the elements of a large array with values. You might think that initializing an array doesn't sound like a large complex task in need of a framework. The key is that it needs to be a **large** task. What if you need to fill up a 100,000,000-element array with randomly generated values? The Fork/Join Framework makes it easier to tackle big tasks like this, while leveraging all of the CPUs in a system.

Divide and Conquer

Certain types of large tasks can be split up into smaller subtasks; those subtasks might, in turn, be split up into even smaller tasks. There is no limit to how many times you might subdivide a task. For example, imagine the task of having to repaint a single long fence that borders several houses. The "paint the fence" task could be subdivided so that each household would be responsible for painting a section of the fence. Each household could then subdivide their section into subsections to be painted by individual family members. In this example, there are three levels of recursive calls. The calls are considered recursive because at each step we are trying to accomplish the same thing: paint the fence. In other words, Joe, one of the home owners, was told by his wife, "paint that (huge) fence; it looks old." Joe decides that painting the whole fence is too much work and talks all the households along the fence into taking a subsection. Now Joe is telling himself "paint that (subsection of) fence; it looks old." Again, Joe decides that it is still too much work and subdivides his section into smaller sections for each member of his household. Again, Joe tells himself "paint that (subsection of) fence; it looks old," but this time, he decides that the amount of work is manageable and proceeds to paint his section of fence. Assuming everyone else paints their subsections (hopefully in a timely fashion), the result is the entire fence being painted.

When using the Fork/Join Framework, your tasks will be coded to decide how many levels of recursion (how many times to subdivide) are appropriate. You'll want to split things up into enough subtasks that you have adequate tasks to keep all of your CPUs utilized. Sometimes, the best number of tasks can be a little hard to determine because of factors we will discuss later. You might have to benchmark different numbers of task divisions to find the optimal number of subtasks that should be created.

Just because you can use Fork/Join to solve a problem doesn't always mean you should. If our initial task is to paint eight fence planks, then Joe might just decide to paint them himself. The effort involved in subdividing the problem and assigning those tasks to workers (threads) can sometimes be more than the actual work you want to perform. The number of elements (or fence planks) is not the only thing to consider—the amount of work performed on each element is also important. Imagine if Joe was asked to paint a mural on each fence plank. Because processing each element (fence plank) is so time consuming, in this case, it might be beneficial to adopt a divide-and-conquer solution even though there is a small number of elements.

ForkJoinPool

The Fork/Join `ExecutorService` implementation is `java.util.concurrent.ForkJoinPool`. You will typically submit a single task to a `ForkJoinPool` and await its completion. The `ForkJoinPool` and the task itself work together to divide and conquer the problem. Any problem that can be recursively divided can be solved using Fork/Join. Anytime you want to perform the same operation on a collection of elements (painting thousands of fence planks or initializing 100,000,000 array elements), consider using Fork/Join.

To create a `ForkJoinPool`, simply call its no-arg constructor:

```
ForkJoinPool fjPool = new ForkJoinPool();
```

The no-arg `ForkJoinPool` constructor creates an instance that will use the `Runtime.availableProcessors()` method to determine the level of parallelism. The level of parallelism determines the number of threads that will be used by the `ForkJoinPool`.

There is also a `ForkJoinPool(int parallelism)` constructor that allows you to override the number of threads that will be used.

ForkJoinTask

Just as with `Executors`, you must capture the task to be performed as Java code. With the Fork/Join Framework, a `java.util.concurrent.ForkJoinTask` instance (actually a subclass—more on that later) is created to represent the task that should be accomplished. This is different from other executor services that primarily used either `Runnable` or `Callable`. A `ForkJoinTask` concrete subclass has many methods (most of which you will never use), **but the following methods are important: `compute()`, `fork()`, and `join()`.**

A `ForkJoinTask` subclass is where you will perform most of the work involved in completing a Fork/Join task. `ForkJoinTask` is an abstract base class; we will discuss the two subclasses, `RecursiveTask` and `RecursiveAction`, later. The basic structure of any `ForkJoinTask` is shown in this pseudocode example:

```
class ForkJoinPaintTask {
  compute() {
    if(isFenceSectionSmall()) {   // is it a manageable amount of work?
      paintFenceSection();        // do the task
    } else {                      // task too big, split it
      ForkJoinPaintTask leftHalf = getLeftHalfOfFence();
      leftHalf.fork();            // queue left half of task
      ForkJoinPaintTask rightHalf = getRightHalfOfFence();
      rightHalf.compute();        // work on right half of task
      leftHalf.join();            // wait for queued task to be complete
    }
  }
}
```

Fork

With the Fork/Join Framework, each thread in the `ForkJoinPool` has a queue of the tasks it is working on; this is unlike most `ExecutorService` implementations that have a single shared task queue. The fork() method places a `ForkJoinTask` in the current thread's task queue. A normal thread does not have a queue of tasks—only the specialized threads in a `ForkJoinPool` do. This means that you can only call fork() if you are within a `ForkJoinTask` that is being executed by a `ForkJoinPool`.

Initially, only a single thread in a `ForkJoinPool` will be busy when you submit a task. That thread will begin to subdivide the tasks into smaller tasks. Each time a task is subdivided into two subtasks, you fork (or queue) the first task and compute the second task. In the event you need to subdivide a task into more than two subtasks, each time you split a task, you would fork every new subtask except one (which would be computed).

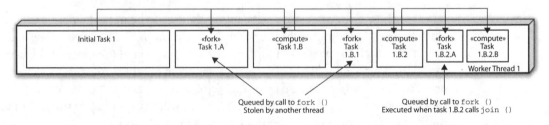

Work Stealing

Notice how the call to `fork()` is placed before the call to `compute()` or `join()`. A key feature of the Fork/Join Framework is work stealing. Work stealing is how the other threads in a `ForkJoinPool` will obtain tasks. When initially submitting a Fork/Join task for execution, a single thread from a `ForkJoinPool` begins executing (and subdividing) that task. Each call to `fork()` placed a new task in the calling thread's task queue. The order in which the tasks are queued is important. The tasks that have been queued the longest represent larger amounts of work. In the `ForkJoinPaintTask` example, the task that represents 100 percent of the work would begin executing, and its first queued (forked) task would represent 50 percent of the fence, the next 25 percent, then 12.5 percent, and so on. Of course, this can vary, depending on how many times the task will be subdivided and whether we are splitting the task into halves or quarters or some other division, but in this example, we are splitting each task into two parts: queuing one part and executing the second part.

The nonbusy threads in a `ForkJoinPool` will attempt to steal the oldest (and, therefore, largest) task from any Fork/Join thread with queued tasks. Given a `ForkJoinPool` with four threads, one possible sequence of events could be that the initial thread queues tasks that represent 50 percent and 25 percent of the work, which are then stolen by two different threads. The thread that stole the 50 percent task then subdivides that task and places a 25 percent task on its queue, which is then stolen by a fourth thread, resulting in four threads that each process 25 percent of the work.

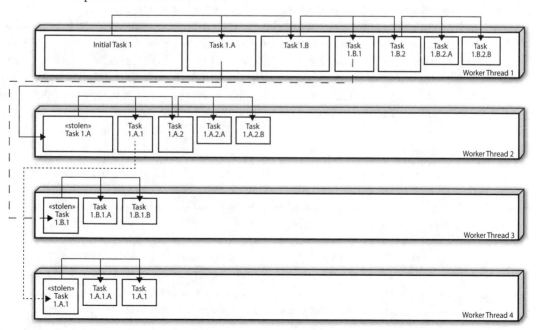

Of course, if everything was always this evenly distributed, you might not have as much of a need for Fork/Join. You could just presplit the work into a number of tasks equal to the number of threads in your system and use a regular `ExecutorService`. In practice, each of the four threads will not finish their 25 percent of the work at the same time—one thread will be the slow thread that doesn't get as much work done. There are many reasons for this: The data being processed may affect the amount of computation (25 percent of an array might not mean 25 percent of the workload), or a thread might not get as much time to execute as the other threads. Operating systems and other running applications are also going to consume CPU time. In order to finish executing the Fork/Join task as soon as possible, the threads that finish their portions of the work first will start to steal work from the slower threads—this way, you will be able to keep all of the CPU involved. If you only split the tasks into 25 percent of the data (with four threads), then there would be nothing for the faster threads to steal from when they finish early. In the beginning, if the slower thread stole 25 percent of the work and started processing it without further subdividing and queuing, then there would be no work on the slow thread's queue to steal. You should subdivide the tasks into a few more sections than are needed to evenly distribute the work among the number of threads in your `ForkJoinPools` because threads will most likely not perform exactly the same. Subdividing the tasks is extra work—if you do it too much, you might hurt performance. Subdivide your tasks enough to keep all CPUs busy, but not more than is needed. Unfortunately, there is no magic number to split your tasks into—it varies based on the complexity of the task, the size of the data, and even the performance characteristics of your CPUs.

Back to fence painting, make the `isFenceSectionSmall()` logic as simple as possible (low overhead) and easy to change. You should benchmark your Fork/Join code (using the hardware that you expect the code to typically run on) and find an amount of task subdivision that works well. It doesn't have to be perfect; once you are close to the ideal range, you probably won't see much variation in performance unless other factors come into play (different CPUs, etc.).

Join

When you call `join()` on the (left) task, it should be one of the last steps in the `compute` method, after calling `fork()` and `compute()`. Calling `join()` says, "I can only proceed when this (left) task is done." Several possible things can happen when you call `join()`:

- The task you call `join()` on might already be done. Remember you are calling `join()` on a task that already had `fork()` called. The task might have been stolen and completed by another thread. In this case, calling `join()` just verifies the task is complete and you can continue on.

- The task you call `join()` on might be in the middle of being processed. Another thread could have stolen the task, and you'll have to wait until the joined task is done before continuing.
- The task you call `join()` on might still be in the queue (not stolen). In this case, the thread calling `join()` will execute the joined task.

RecursiveAction

`ForkJoinTask` is an abstract base class that outlines most of the methods, such as `fork()` and `join()`, in a Fork/Join task. If you need to create a `ForkJoinTask` that does not return a result, then you should subclass `RecursiveAction`. `RecursiveAction` extends `ForkJoinTask` and has a single abstract compute method that you must implement:

```
protected abstract void compute();
```

An example of a task that does not need to return a result would be any task that initializes an existing data structure. The following example will initialize an array to contain random values. Notice that there is only a single array throughout the entire process. When subdividing an array, you should avoid creating new objects when possible.

```
public class RandomInitRecursiveAction extends RecursiveAction {
  private static final int THRESHOLD = 10000;
  private int[] data;
  private int start;
  private int end;

  public RandomInitRecursiveAction(int[] data, int start, int end) {
    this.data = data;
    this.start = start;              // where does our section begin?
    this.end = end;                  // how large is this section?
  }
  @Override
  protected void compute() {
    if (end - start <= THRESHOLD) {  // is it a manageable amount of work?
      // do the task
      for (int i = start; i < end; i++) {
        data[i] =  ThreadLocalRandom.current().nextInt();
      }
    } else {                             // task too big, split it
      int halfWay = ((end - start) / 2) + start;
      RandomInitRecursiveAction a1 =
        new RandomInitRecursiveAction(data, start, halfWay);
      a1.fork(); // queue left half of task
      RandomInitRecursiveAction a2 =
        new RandomInitRecursiveAction(data, halfWay, end);
```

```
      a2.compute();    // work on right half of task
      a1.join();       // wait for queued task to be complete
    }
  }
}
```

Sometimes, you will see one of the `invokeAll` methods from the `ForkJoinTask` class used in place of the fork/compute/join method combination. The `invokeAll` methods are convenience methods that can save some typing. Using them will also help you avoid bugs! The first task passed to `invokeAll` will be executed (compute is called), and all additional tasks will be forked and joined. In the preceding example, you could eliminate the three fork/compute/join lines and replace them with a single line:

```
invokeAll(a2, a1);
```

To begin the application, we create a large array and initialize it using Fork/Join:

```
public static void main(String[] args) {
  int[] data = new int[10_000_000];
  ForkJoinPool fjPool = new ForkJoinPool();
  RandomInitRecursiveAction action =
    new RandomInitRecursiveAction(data, 0, data.length);
  fjPool.invoke(action);
}
```

Notice that we do not expect any return values when calling invoke. A `RecursiveAction` returns nothing.

RecursiveTask

If you need to create a `ForkJoinTask` that does return a result, then you should subclass `RecursiveTask`. `RecursiveTask` extends `ForkJoinTask` and has a single abstract compute method that you must implement:

```
protected abstract V compute(); // V is a generic type
```

The following example will find the position in an array with the greatest value; if duplicate values are found, the first occurrence is returned. Notice that there is only a single array throughout the entire process. (Just like before, when subdividing an array, you should avoid creating new objects when possible.)

```
public class FindMaxPositionRecursiveTask extends RecursiveTask<Integer> {
  private static final int THRESHOLD = 10000;
  private int[] data;
  private int start;
  private int end;
```

```
public FindMaxPositionRecursiveTask(int[] data, int start, int end) {
  this.data = data;
  this.start = start;
  this.end = end;
}

@Override
protected Integer compute() {      // return type matches the <generic> type
  if (end - start <= THRESHOLD) { // is it a manageable amount of work?
    int position = 0;               // if all values are equal, return
                                    // position 0
    for (int i = start; i < end; i++) {
      if (data[i] > data[position]) {
        position = i;
      }
    }
    return position;
  } else { // task too big, split it
    int halfWay = ((end - start) / 2) + start;
    FindMaxPositionRecursiveTask t1 =
      new FindMaxPositionRecursiveTask(data, start, halfWay);
    t1.fork(); // queue left half of task
    FindMaxPositionRecursiveTask t2 =
      new FindMaxPositionRecursiveTask(data, halfWay, end);
    int position2 = t2.compute(); // work on right half of task
    int position1 = t1.join();    // wait for queued task to be complete
    // out of the position in two subsection which is greater?
    if (data[position1] > data[position2]) {
      return position1;
    } else if (data[position1] < data[position2]) {
      return position2;
    } else {
      return position1 < position2 ? position1 : position2;
    }
  }
}
}
```

To begin the application, we reuse the RecursiveAction example to create a large array and initialize it using Fork/Join. After initializing the array with random values, we reuse the ForkJoinPool with our RecursiveTask to find the position with the greatest value:

```
public static void main(String[] args) {
  int[] data = new int[10_000_000];
  ForkJoinPool fjPool = new ForkJoinPool();
  RandomInitRecursiveAction action =
    new RandomInitRecursiveAction(data, 0, data.length);
  fjPool.invoke(action);
  // new code begins here
```

```
FindMaxPositionRecursiveTask task =
    new FindMaxPositionRecursiveTask(data, 0, data.length);
Integer position = fjPool.invoke(task);
System.out.println("Position: " + position + ", value: " + data[position]);
}
```

Notice that a value is returned by the call to invoke when using a `RecursiveTask`.

If your application will repeatedly submit tasks to a `ForkJoinPool`, then you should reuse a single `ForkJoinPool` instance and avoid the overhead involved in creating a new instance.

Embarrassingly Parallel

A problem or task is said to be embarrassingly parallel if little or no additional work is required to solve the problem in a parallel fashion. Sometimes, solving a problem in parallel adds so much more overhead that the problem can be solved faster serially. The `RandomInitRecursiveAction` example, which initializes an array to random values, has no additional overhead because what happens when processing one subsection of an array has no bearing on the processing of another subsection. Technically, there is a small amount of overhead even in the `RandomInitRecursiveAction`; the Fork/Join Framework and the `if` statement that determines whether the problem should be subdivided both introduce some overhead. Be aware that it can be difficult to get performance gains that scale with the number of CPUs you have. Typically, four CPUs will result in less than a 4× speedup when moving from a serial to a parallel solution.

The `FindMaxPositionRecursiveTask` example, which finds the largest value in an array, does introduce a small additional amount of work because you must compare the result from each subsection and determine which is greater. This is only a small amount, however, and adds little overhead. Some tasks may introduce so much additional work that any advantage of using parallel processing is eliminated (the task runs slower than serial execution). If you find yourself performing a lot of processing after calling `join()`, then you should benchmark your application to determine if there is a performance benefit to using parallel processing. Be aware that performance benefits might only be seen with a certain number of CPUs. A task might run on one CPU in 5 seconds, on two CPUs in 6 seconds, and on four CPUs in 3.5 seconds.

The Fork/Join Framework is designed to have minimal overhead as long as you don't over-subdivide your tasks and the amount of work required to join results can be kept small. A good example of a task that incurs additional overhead but still benefits from Fork/Join is array sorting. When you split an array into two halves and sort each half separately, you then have to combine the two sorted arrays, as shown in the following example:

```java
public class SortRecursiveAction extends RecursiveAction {
  private static final int THRESHOLD = 1000;
  private int[] data;
  private int start;
  private int end;

  public SortRecursiveAction(int[] data, int start, int end) {
    this.data = data;
    this.start = start;
    this.end = end;
  }

  @Override
  protected void compute() {
    if (end - start <= THRESHOLD) {
      Arrays.sort(data, start, end);
    } else {
    int halfWay = ((end - start) / 2) + start;
    SortRecursiveAction a1 =
      new SortRecursiveAction(data, start, halfWay);
    SortRecursiveAction a2 =
      new SortRecursiveAction(data, halfWay, end);
    invokeAll(a1, a2);  // shortcut for fork() & join()
      if(data[halfWay-1] <= data[halfWay]) {
        return; // already sorted
      }
        // merging of sorted subsections begins here
        int[] temp = new int[end - start];
        int s1 = start, s2 = halfWay, d = 0;
        while(s1 < halfWay && s2 < end) {
          if(data[s1] < data[s2]) {
          temp[d++] = data[s1++];
        } else if(data[s1] > data[s2]) {
          temp[d++] = data[s2++];
        } else {
            temp[d++] = data[s1++];
          temp[d++] = data[s2++];
        }
      }
        if(s1 != halfWay) {
        System.arraycopy(data, s1, temp, d, temp.length - d);
```

```
      } else if(s2 != end) {
        System.arraycopy(data, s2, temp, d, temp.length - d);
      }
      System.arraycopy(temp, 0, data, start, temp.length);
    }
  }
}
```

In the previous example, everything after the call to invokeAll is related to merging two sorted subsections of an array into a single larger sorted subsection.

Because Java applications are portable, the system running your application may not have the hardware resources required to see a performance benefit. Always perform testing to determine which problem and hardware combinations see performance increases when using Fork/Join.

CERTIFICATION OBJECTIVE

Parallel Streams (OCP Objective 10.6)

10.6   Use parallel Streams including reduction, decomposition, merging processes, pipelines and performance.

Parallel streams are designed for problems you can divide and conquer, just like the problems described in the previous section. In fact, parallel streams are implemented with Fork/Join tasks under the covers, so you're essentially doing the same thing: that is, splitting up a problem into subtasks that can be executed on separate threads and then joining them back together to produce a result.

Unlike the code you write to take advantage of the Fork/Join Framework, parallel stream code is relatively easy to write. If you think writing RecursiveActions and RecursiveTasks is tricky (we do too!), you'll be pleased with how much easier parallel streams can be. That said, there are several gotchas to watch out for when using parallel streams, so even though the code is easier to write, you need to pay close attention.

And, like we said about using the Fork/Join Framework, just because you can use parallel streams to solve a problem doesn't always mean you should. The same concerns apply: the effort to create tasks that can run in threads can add enough overhead that using parallel streams is sometimes slower than using sequential streams. We'll do testing as we work through some parallel stream code and check our results as we go to make sure we get the performance gains we expect.

How to Make a Parallel Stream Pipeline

In Chapter 9, "Streams," we made a stream parallel by calling the `parallel()` method on the stream, like this:

```
List<Integer> nums = Arrays.asList(1, 2, 3, 4, 5, 6, 7, 8, 9, 10);
int sum = nums.stream()
        .parallel()         // make the stream parallel
        .mapToInt(n -> n)
        .sum();
System.out.println("Sum is: " + sum);
```

Here, we take a list of numbers, stream them, map each `Integer` to an `int`, and sum. To make this very simple stream pipeline parallel, we simply call the `parallel()` method on the stream.

Let's take a peek at how the tasks created by this parallel stream get split up and handled by workers in the `ForkJoinPool`. We can do that by adding a `peek()` into the pipeline and then printing the name of the thread handling each `Integer` in the stream:

```
List<Integer> nums = Arrays.asList(1, 2, 3, 4, 5, 6, 7, 8, 9, 10);
int sum = nums.stream()
        .parallel()         // make the stream parallel
        .peek(i ->          // print the thread for the worker
           System.out.println(i + ": "
             + Thread.currentThread().getName()))
        .mapToInt(n -> n)
        .sum();
System.out.println("Sum is: " + sum);
```

The output (on our computer) is

```
7: main
5: ForkJoinPool.commonPool-worker-5
8: ForkJoinPool.commonPool-worker-4
9: ForkJoinPool.commonPool-worker-2
3: ForkJoinPool.commonPool-worker-1
1: ForkJoinPool.commonPool-worker-6
10: ForkJoinPool.commonPool-worker-7
2: ForkJoinPool.commonPool-worker-3
6: main
4: ForkJoinPool.commonPool-worker-5
Sum is: 55
```

You will likely see different output (although the same final sum) because your computer may have a different number of cores, and the tasks will likely get split up differently. We ran this code on a computer with eight cores, and you can see that the computer used all eight. We might not actually want the computer to use all eight cores (especially for this simple sum), so we can tell the computer exactly how many workers to use by creating a custom `ForkJoinPool` and then submitting a task to the pool for execution:

```
ForkJoinPool fjp = new ForkJoinPool(2);
try {
   int sum =
       fjp.submit(                    // returns a Future (FutureTask)
           () -> nums.stream()        // a Callable (value returning task)
             .parallel()              // make the stream parallel
             .peek(i ->
                 System.out.println(i + ": " +
                     Thread.currentThread().getName()))
             .mapToInt(n -> n)
             .sum()
       ).get();                       // from Future; get() waits for
                                      // computation to complete and
                                      // gets the result
   System.out.println("FJP with 2 workers, sum is: " + sum);
} catch (Exception e) {
   System.out.println("Error executing stream sum");
   e.printStackTrace();
}
```

Here is our output now:

```
7: ForkJoinPool-1-worker-1
6: ForkJoinPool-1-worker-1
9: ForkJoinPool-1-worker-1
3: ForkJoinPool-1-worker-0
10: ForkJoinPool-1-worker-1
5: ForkJoinPool-1-worker-0
8: ForkJoinPool-1-worker-1
4: ForkJoinPool-1-worker-0
2: ForkJoinPool-1-worker-1
1: ForkJoinPool-1-worker-0
FJP with 2 workers, sum is: 55
```

We get the same sum, 55, but now we're using only two workers to do it. This is friendlier to the computer, which may want some cores to do other things while this task is running.

When we call the `submit()` method of the `ForkJoinPool`, we use this method:

```
<T> ForkJoinTask<T> submit(Callable<T> task)
```

and pass a lambda expression for the `Callable`. `Callable` is a functional interface, which is why we can express an instance of a class implementing that interface with the lambda expression. The functional method in `Callable` is `call()`, which "computes a result" (thus, the lambda we are supplying for the `Callable` is a `Supplier`: it takes no arguments and supplies a result).

You've seen how to create a parallel stream with `parallel()`; you can also combine the methods `stream()` and `parallel()` into one method, `parallelStream()`, like this:

```
List<Integer> nums = Arrays.asList(1, 2, 3, 4, 5, 6, 7, 8, 9, 10);
int sum = nums.parallelStream()          // make a parallel stream
        .peek(i -> System.out.println(i + ": "
            + Thread.currentThread().getName()))
        .mapToInt(n -> n)
        .sum();
System.out.println("Sum is: " + sum);
```

When we run this code (similar to the first version of the code above), we get the following output:

```
2: ForkJoinPool.commonPool-worker-3
3: ForkJoinPool.commonPool-worker-1
9: ForkJoinPool.commonPool-worker-2
7: main
8: ForkJoinPool.commonPool-worker-4
1: ForkJoinPool.commonPool-worker-6
5: ForkJoinPool.commonPool-worker-5
10: ForkJoinPool.commonPool-worker-7
6: ForkJoinPool.commonPool-worker-1
4: ForkJoinPool.commonPool-worker-3
Sum is: 55
```

Notice the ordering of the processing: the ordering is totally different from the first example above! When summing numbers, it doesn't matter in what order they are summed; we'll get the same result every time. In Chapter 9, you saw that if you display the result of a parallel stream pipeline, the ordering is not guaranteed, and you can see that mixed-up ordering in the output here, too.

You can check to see if a stream is parallel with the `isParallel()` method. This might come in handy if someone hands you a stream and you're not sure. For instance, the following code checks to see if `numsStream` is parallel:

```
List<Integer> nums = Arrays.asList(1, 2, 3, 4, 5, 6, 7, 8, 9, 10);
Stream<Integer> numsStream =           // create a parallel stream
    nums.parallelStream();
// Later...
System.out.println("Is numsStream a parallel stream?? "
    + numsStream.isParallel());
```

You should see the output:

```
Is numsStream a parallel stream?? true
```

What if you have a parallel stream and you want to make it not parallel (i.e., sequential)? You can do that with the `sequential()` method:

```
Stream<Integer> numsStreamSeq =     // make stream sequential
    numsStream.sequential();
System.out.println("Is numsStreamSeq a parallel stream?? "
    + numsStreamSeq.isParallel());
```

and get the output:

```
Is numsStreamSeq a parallel stream?? false
```

Note here that `parallel()`, `isParallel()`, and `sequential()` are methods of `BaseStream` (which is the superinterface of `Stream`), and `parallelStream()` is a method of the `Collection` interface. Table 11-1 summarizes the methods related to parallel streams that you are expected to know for the exam, which we'll cover in this chapter.

Embarrassingly Parallel, Take Two (with Parallel Streams)

Earlier we talked about how some problems are "embarrassingly parallel": that is, they're easily split up into independent pieces that can be computed separately and then combined. These are precisely the kinds of problems that work well

TABLE 11-1   Methods Related to Parallel Streams

Method	Of Interface	Description
`parallel()`	`BaseStream`	Creates a parallel stream from a stream
`parallelStream()`	`Collection`	Creates a parallel stream from the Collection source
`isParallel()`	`BaseStream`	Returns true if the stream is parallel (that is, if the stream would execute in parallel when a terminal operation is executed)
`sequential()`	`BaseStream`	Returns a sequential stream
`unordered()`	`BaseStream`	Creates an unordered stream
`forEachOrdered()`	`Stream`	Consumes elements from a stream and performs an action on those elements, in the encounter order of the original stream if that stream has an order

with parallel streams. The sum example we've been using in this section is a great example of an embarrassingly parallel problem: we can split up the stream into subsections, compute the sum of the subsection, and then combine the sums from each to make one total sum. We visualized this process in Chapter 9 with two images. The first illustrates how we compute a sum with a sequential stream:

```
1   2   3   4   5   6   7   8   9   10
    3   3   4   5   6   7   8   9   10
        6   4   5   6   7   8   9   10
           10   5   6   7   8   9   10
               15   6   7   8   9   10
                   21   7   8   9   10
                       28   8   9   10
                           36   9   10
                               45   10
                                   55
```

while the second image illustrates how we can compute a sum with a parallel stream that is using two workers:

```
     Thread 1              Thread 2

 1   2   3   4   5  ⋮  6   7   8   9   10
     3   3   4   5  ⋮ 13       8   9   10
         6   4   5  ⋮     21       9   10
            10   5  ⋮         30       10
                15  ⋮             40
            ‿‿‿‿‿‿‿‿‿‿‿‿‿‿‿‿‿‿‿‿
                       55
```

As you can see in the second illustration, the stream can be split in two and each sum computed completely independently from the other and then combined at the end. Again, this is precisely the kind of problem that works well with parallel streams.

We can summarize the conditions that make for successful parallel streams as follows: a problem is most suitable for parallel streams if the pipeline operations are *stateless,* the reduction operation used to compute the result is *associative* and *stateless,* and the stream is *unordered.*

Let's take a look at each of these.

Associative Operations

We talked about associative operations earlier in Chapter 9. Recall from that chapter that sum() is an example of an associative operation. That is, we can compute the sum of a + b, and then add c, or we can compute b + c, and then add a, and get the same result.

Some operations are definitely not associative. We discovered in Chapter 9 that computing the average of a stream of numbers is not associative. Recall that when we implemented our own average reduction operation, we got an incorrect result. Using the built-in average() method solved the problem in that chapter.

Because parallel streams are split up for processing in unpredictable ways, operations that aren't associative will probably fail. Just to reinforce how important associativity is in properly reducing a stream, let's review how computing the average fails when we don't use the built-in average() method:

```
List<Integer> nums = Arrays.asList(1, 2, 3, 4, 5, 6, 7, 8, 9, 10);
OptionalDouble avg = nums
    .parallelStream()                       // make a parallel stream
    .mapToDouble(n -> n)                     // make a stream of doubles
    .reduce((d1, d2) -> (d1 + d2) / 2); // reduce with (bad) average
avg.ifPresent((a) ->
    System.out.println("Average of parallel stream with reduce: " + a));
OptionalDouble avg2 = nums
    .parallelStream()                       // make a parallel stream
    .mapToDouble(n -> n)                     // make a stream of doubles
    .average();                             // reduce with built-in average
avg2.ifPresent((a) ->
    System.out.println("Average of parallel stream with average: " + a));
```

In the first stream pipeline, we make the stream parallel, then we map to a stream of doubles so we can compute the average and return a double value; then we reduce using our own reduction function, which sums two numbers from the stream and divides by 2.

In the second stream pipeline, we do the same except we reduce with the built-in average() stream method, which is implemented in a way to produce the correct result (accounting for the inherent nonassociativity of the average function).

We get the output:

```
Average of parallel stream with reduce: 5.125   // wrong!
Average of parallel stream with average: 5.5    // correct!
```

The point is, just as with sequential stream reductions, parallel stream reductions need to be associative. This is even more important for parallel streams given that we don't know how the system will split up and then recombine the stream results.

Stateless Operations (and Streams)

A stateless operation in a stream pipeline is an operation that does not depend on the context in which it's operating. Before we talk more about what stateless operations are, let's talk about what they are not.

There are two main ways you can create a state*ful* stream pipeline. The first is with *side effects*. We talked about this in Chapter 9, too; side effects occur when your result creates or depends on changes to state in the pipeline.

Side Effects and Parallel Streams   We already said not to ever modify the source of a stream from within the stream pipeline, so you haven't been—right? Right. That's one way you can create side effects, but you know not to do that.

Another way you can create side effects is to modify the field of an object. In sequential stream pipelines, you can get away with these kinds of side effects, and you may recall from Chapter 9 how we created a list of DVDs from a file input stream. However, in parallel stream pipelines, these kinds of side effects will fail unless the objects you're modifying from within the pipeline are synchronized (either via a synchronized accessor method or if the objects are a concurrent data type).

Here's an example: We're streaming integers between 0 and 50 (noninclusive), filtering to find integers divisible by 10 and then summing those. We're also attempting to count the integers as we go by updating the field of an object. Although we aren't allowed to update a plain variable counter from within a lambda (you'll get a compiler error if you try to do this), we are allowed to update the field of an object, as we're doing here:

```
public static void stateful() {
  class Count {                       // an object to hold our counter
    int counter = 0;
  }
  Count count = new Count();          // create an instance
  IntStream stream =                  // generate a stream of integers, 0-49
    IntStream.range(0, 50);
  int sum = stream
    .parallel()                       // make the stream parallel
    .filter(i -> {                    // filter the stream
      if (i % 10 == 0) {              // ...only count numbers divisible by 10
        count.counter++;              // ...there should be 5!
        return true;
      }
      return false;
    })
    .sum();                           // sum up the integers
  System.out.printf("sum: " + sum + ", count: " + count.counter);
}
```

The first time we ran this code, we got:

```
sum: 100, count: 5
```

The next time:

```
sum: 100, count: 4
```

Hmmm. We get the right sum (the sum doesn't depend on the counter and doesn't depend on the ordering), but the counter is not always correct (try a bigger number than 50 in the range if this code doesn't produce different counter values for you). That's because, when we are using a parallel stream, multiple threads are accessing the Count object to modify the counter field and Count is not thread-safe.

We could use a synchronized object to store our counter and that would solve the problem, but it would also defeat the purpose of using parallel streams in this example.

We can fix the code above by removing the count in the parallel stream pipeline and computing it separately from the sum.

Stateful Operations in the Stream Pipeline   Another way we can create stateful stream pipelines is with stateful stream operations. A stateful stream operation is one that requires some knowledge about the stream in order to operate. Take a look at the following stream pipeline:

```
IntStream stream = IntStream.range(0, 10);
long sum = stream.limit(5).sum();
System.out.println("Sum is: " + sum);
```

In this code, we are creating a stream of ten ints, limiting the stream to the first five of those ints (0–4) and summing those. The result, as you'd expect, is 10:

```
Sum is: 10
```

Now think about this operation, limit(5). This is a stateful operation. Why? Because it requires context: the stream has to keep some intermediate state to know when it has five items and can stop streaming from the source (that is, short circuit the stream). So adding parallel() to this stream will not improve performance and might even hurt performance because now that state has to be synchronized across threads.

Let's test this and see what performance we get. We'll create a stream of 100 million ints, limit the stream to the first 5 ints, and sum, like we just did above. We'll also time the operation:

```
final int SIZE = 100_000_000;
final int LIMIT = 5;
long sum = 0, startTime, endTime, duration;
```

```
IntStream stream = IntStream.range(0, SIZE);
startTime = Instant.now().toEpochMilli();
sum = stream
        .limit(LIMIT)
        .sum();
endTime = Instant.now().toEpochMilli();
duration = endTime - startTime;
System.out.println("Items summed in " + duration
    + " milliseconds; sum is: " + sum);
```

When we run this on our machine (eight cores), we get

```
Items summed in 29 milliseconds; sum is: 10
```

Running it several times takes 28 or 29 milliseconds each time.
    Now, let's make this a parallel stream and see what we get:

```
IntStream stream = IntStream.range(0, SIZE);
startTime = Instant.now().toEpochMilli();
sum = stream
        .parallel()
        .limit(LIMIT)
        .sum();
endTime = Instant.now().toEpochMilli();
duration = endTime - startTime;
System.out.println("Items summed in " + duration
    + " milliseconds; sum is: " + sum);
```

Running this, we get

```
Items summed in 34 milliseconds; sum is: 10
```

The performance is worse! Repeated runs yield running times of between
33 and 36 milliseconds each time. Increasing the SIZE to 400 million yields
similar results.
    One thing we should consider here is that the overhead of creating eight threads
might be contributing to the performance problem. To really test that a parallel
pipeline can hurt (or, at least, not help) when using limit(), we should try our
experiment with a custom ForkJoinPool and set the number of threads ourselves.
Let's do that.
    The code is similar to what you've seen before: we create a custom ForkJoinPool,
submit the task to the ForkJoinPool, get the result from the FutureTask that's
returned, and time the whole thing. We've bumped up the size of the stream to
400 million ints, but we're still limiting to 5 ints for the sum. For this initial test,

we've commented out the call to `parallel()` in the stream pipeline, so our first test will be on a sequential stream with one thread in the `ForkJoinPool`:

```
final int SIZE = 400_000_000;
final int LIMIT = 5;
long sum = 0, startTime, endTime, duration;
ForkJoinPool fjp = new ForkJoinPool(1);    // Limit FJP to 1 thread
IntStream stream = IntStream.range(0, SIZE);
try {
  startTime = Instant.now().toEpochMilli();
  sum =
    fjp.submit(
      () -> stream
              //.parallel()                     // test sequential first
              .limit(LIMIT)
              .sum()
    ).get();
  endTime = Instant.now().toEpochMilli();
  duration = endTime - startTime;
  System.out.println("FJP Stream data summed in "
      + duration + " milliseconds; sum is: " + sum);
} catch (Exception e) {
  System.out.println("Error executing stream sum");
  e.printStackTrace();
}
```

When we ran this code, we got

```
FJP Stream data summed in 35 milliseconds; sum is: 10
```

Now let's make the stream pipeline parallel and increase the number of threads to two:

```
ForkJoinPool fjp = new ForkJoinPool(2);   // Now use 2 threads
IntStream stream = IntStream.range(0, SIZE);
try {
  startTime = Instant.now().toEpochMilli();
  sum =
    fjp.submit(
      () -> stream
              .parallel()                      // make the stream parallel
              .limit(LIMIT)
              .sum()
    ).get();
  endTime = Instant.now().toEpochMilli();
  duration = endTime - startTime;
  System.out.println("FJP Stream data summed in "
      + duration + " milliseconds; sum is: " + sum);
```

```
} catch (Exception e) {
  System.out.println("Error executing stream sum");
  e.printStackTrace();
}
```

Run it again and we get

```
FJP Stream data summed in 36 milliseconds; sum is: 10
```

Now using parallel streams is not that much slower than running it sequential, but there's still no benefit to using parallel streams; our results from this test indicate that whether we use two threads or eight, the parallel pipeline runs no faster than the sequential pipeline.

Run some more experiments yourself. Change the number of workers in the ForkJoinPool; see what happens. Change the LIMIT to a much larger number, like 500,000, and see what happens. More than likely, you'll find that the parallel stream pipeline runs the same as or more slowly than the sequential stream pipeline for this operation, which is what we'd expect.

We've talked about a couple of ways that stream pipelines are stateful: that is, stream pipelines are stateful if we create side effects (modifying an object as we process the pipeline) or if we use a stateful stream operation, like limit(). Other stateful stream operations might be fairly obvious to you; they are skip(), distinct(), and sorted(). How do you know which stream operations are stateful? The documentation describing these methods says so. And if you think about it, each of these operations requires some knowledge about the stream in order for the stream to operate.

Stream operations that are not necessarily stateful include map(), filter(), and reduce() (among others), so there's a lot we can do with streams that is stateless, although, as with all things related to concurrency, we need to be careful. As you saw in the example above, when we tried to count numbers in the stream using a filter(), we can make filter() stateful by creating a side effect.

Just to revisit quickly a simple example of a parallel stream using map(), filter(), and reduce() stateless operations, here's a slightly modified take on our original example:

```
List<Integer> nums = Arrays.asList(1, 2, 3, 4, 5, 6, 7, 8, 9, 10);
long sum = nums.stream()
          .parallel()                  // make the stream parallel
          .mapToInt(n -> n)            // map from Integer to int
          .filter(i ->                 // filter the evens
              i % 2 == 0 ? true : false)
          .sum();                      // sum the evens
System.out.println("Sum of evens is: " + sum);
```

Run this and you should see the following:

```
Sum of evens is: 30
```

None of these stream operations requires any state in order to operate on the values in the stream pipeline. The map simply converts the type of the stream value from `Integer` to `int`; the filter simply determines if the value is even or odd, and the reduction (`sum()`) sums the values, which can happen in any order because `sum()` is associative, so this operation requires no state either. This is an example of a stateless stream pipeline...well almost.

Hopefully now, you can see the difference between a stateless and a stateful stream pipeline. We've mostly talked about what a stateless stream pipeline is by talking about what a stateful stream pipeline is. The short story is that a stateless stream pipeline is one that requires no underlying intermediate state to be stored and accessed by the thread(s) in order to execute properly. And that statelessness is what helps make parallel stream pipelines more efficient.

However, we need to do one more thing to make this stream pipeline completely stateless, as you'll see next.

Unordered Streams

Earlier we said a problem is suitable for parallel streams if the operations used to compute the result are associative and stateless and the stream is unordered. We've talked about the first two; what about unordered?

By default, many (but not all!) streams are ordered. That means there is an inherent ordering to the items in the stream. A stream of `int`s created by `range()` and a stream of `Integer`s created from a `List` of `Integer`s are both ordered streams. Intuitively that makes sense; technically, ordering is determined by whether the stream has an `ORDERED` *characteristic*. This is just a bit that is set on the underlying implementation of a stream. There are other characteristics of streams, including `SORTED` and `DISTINCT`, but you don't need to worry too much about characteristics of streams except to know that the characteristics of a stream can affect how that stream performs, especially if you make the stream parallel.

Sometimes we want our streams to retain their order; for instance, if we are mapping stream values from `int`s to `Integer`, filtering to extract the even numbers, and then displaying the results, we might want the ordering of the stream to be maintained so we see the results in order.

However, an ordered stream pipeline will not execute as efficiently in parallel. Again, it comes down to context: an ordered stream has to maintain some state—in this case, the ordering of the stream values—to keep the stream values in order, which adds overhead to the processing.

The characteristics of a stream can be inspected by using a `Spliterator`, *which is an object for traversing a source, like a collection or a stream, that can also split up that source for potential parallel processing.* `Spliterator` *and its characteristics are not on the exam, but if you want to explore how streams (and collections) are traversed and partitioned in more detail, you can study* `Spliterator` *in depth.*

Here's how you can use a stream's `spliterator()` *method to determine if that stream is ordered:*

```
List<Integer> nums = Arrays.asList(1, 2, 3, 4, 5, 6, 7, 8, 9, 10);
Stream<Integer> s = nums.stream();
System.out.println("Stream from List ordered? " +
   s.spliterator().hasCharacteristics(Spliterator.ORDERED));
```

In this case you'll see that, indeed, the stream of Integers we make from a `List` *is ordered.*

If a stream is ordered and we process it in parallel, the stream will remain ordered, but at the price of some efficiency. If we don't care about the ordering, as is the case when we are summing numbers, we might as well remove the ordering on the stream in scenarios where we are using a parallel stream pipeline. That way we get the extra performance benefits of working with an unordered stream in a situation where we shouldn't be concerned about the ordering anyway (because if we are, then the problem we're trying to solve probably isn't appropriate for a parallel stream pipeline).

So how do we make sure we're working with an unordered stream? We can explicitly tell the stream to not worry about remaining ordered by calling the `unordered()` stream method. Of course, we should do this *before* we call `parallel()` so we can maximize the efficiency of the parallel processing. Here's how we can modify the previous example to create an unordered stream pipeline:

```
List<Integer> nums = Arrays.asList(1, 2, 3, 4, 5, 6, 7, 8, 9, 10);
long sum = nums.stream()
            .unordered()      // make the stream unordered
            .parallel()
            .mapToInt(n -> n)
            .filter(i -> i % 2 == 0 ? true : false)
            .sum();
System.out.println("Sum of evens is: " + sum);
```

Calling `unordered()` doesn't change the ordering of the stream; it just unsets that `ORDERED` bit so the stream doesn't have to maintain the ordering state.

Depending on how the stream is processed in the parallel pipeline, you may find that the final stream (before the reduction) is in the same order as the source, or not. Note that an ordered stream is not the same thing as a sorted stream. Once you've made a stream unordered, there is no way to order it again, except by calling `sorted()`, which makes it sorted *and* ordered but not necessarily in the same order as it was in the original source.

Don't worry too much about ordering for the exam; do remember that ordering has an implication for performance and make sure to note which collections create ordered streams (e.g., `List`) and which create unordered streams (e.g., `HashSet`) when you call that collection's `stream()` method, so you know the performance implications.

To summarize: to make the most efficient parallel stream, you should:

- Make sure your reductions are associative and stateless.
- Avoid side effects.
- Make sure your pipeline is stateless by avoiding contextual operations such as `limit()`, `skip()`, `distinct()`, and `sorted()`.

forEach() and forEachOrdered()

As you know, `forEach()` is a terminal stream operation that takes a `Consumer` and consumes each item in the stream. We often use `forEach()` to show the values in a stream after a map and/or filter operation, for example:

```
dogs.stream().filter(d -> d.getAge() > 7).forEach(System.out::println);
```

will display any `Dog` in the stream whose age is > 7 in the order in which the values in the stream are encountered.

Imagine we have a `Dog` class and a `Dog` constructor that takes the name and age of a dog. You've seen the `Dog` class often enough that we probably don't have to repeat it. Given that `Dog` class, we can make some dogs, like this:

```
List<Dog> dogs = new ArrayList<>();
Dog aiko = new Dog("aiko", 10);
Dog boi = new Dog("boi", 6);
Dog charis = new Dog("charis", 7);
Dog clover = new Dog("clover", 12);
Dog zooey = new Dog("zooey", 8);
dogs.add(aiko); dogs.add(boi); dogs.add(charis);
dogs.add(clover); dogs.add(zooey);
```

Notice that we've added the dogs in alphabetical order on purpose, so we can watch the ordering of our stream when we use a sequential stream and when we use a parallel stream.

Running the code:

```
dogs.stream().filter(d -> d.getAge() > 7).forEach(System.out::println);
```

gives us the output:

```
aiko is 10 years old
clover is 12 years old
zooey is 8 years old
```

That is, we see all dogs whose age is > 7 in the order in which they are encountered in the stream (which is the order in which they are added to the List). This is because, by default, when we stream the List, we get a sequential, ordered stream.

Now, as you might expect at this point, when we make this a parallel stream, we get different results:

```
dogs.stream()
    .parallel()
    .filter(d -> d.getAge() > 7)
    .forEach(System.out::println);
```

This code produced the output:

```
zooey is 8 years old
aiko is 10 years old
clover is 12 years old
```

The output is unpredictable; if you run it again, you may get different results. Even though the stream is ordered (since we're streaming a List), we see the output in a random order because the stream is parallel, so the dogs can be processed by different threads that may finish at different times, and the forEach() Consumer is stateful: it is essentially creating a side effect by outputting data to the console, which is not thread-safe.

We can make sure we see the dogs in the order in which they appear in the original source by using the method forEachOrdered() instead:

```
dogs.stream().parallel().filter(d -> d.getAge() > 7)
    .forEachOrdered(System.out::println);      // enforce ordering
```

We can do this because the underlying stream is ordered (it's made from a List and its ORDERED characteristic is set), and the forEachOrdered() method will make sure the items are seen in the same order as they are encountered in the ordered stream. (Note that if we call `unordered()` on the stream, then the order will not be guaranteed!)

Of course, this takes a bit of overhead to perform, right? As we discussed earlier, an ordered stream is going to be less efficient when processed in parallel than an unordered stream. However, there may be times when you want to maintain the ordering of the stream when processing in parallel and you're willing to sacrifice a bit of efficiency.

Typically, you won't end up using `forEachOrdered()` much in the real world; you're sacrificing performance, and usually you don't want to see the results of a big data operation on a parallel stream; you want to collect the results in a new data structure or compute some final result like a sum. However, you will see `forEachOrdered()` on the exam, so make sure you understand how it works.

Also, note that `forEach()` (and `forEachOrdered()`) as well as `peek()` are stream operations that are designed for side effects. That is, they consume elements from the stream: `peek()` typically creates a side effect (say, printing the stream element passing through) and then passes the values on unchanged to the stream; `forEach()` consumes the stream values and produces a result (it's a terminal operation), and typically that result is output to the console or saves each item to the field of an object. So take care when using `forEach()`, `forEachOrdered()`, and `peek()` with parallel streams, remembering that stream pipelines with side effects (even just printing to the console) can change how the stream pipeline operates, and reduce the performance of parallel streams.

A Quick Word About findAny()

You might remember from Chapter 9 that we used the `findAny()` stream operation to find any value in the stream pipeline that matched a `filter()`. For instance, we can use `findAny()` to find any even `int` in a stream like this:

```
IntStream nums = IntStream.range(0, 20);
OptionalInt any = nums
        .filter(i ->                  // filter the evens
           i % 2 == 0 ? true : false)
        .findAny();                   // find any even int
any.ifPresent(i -> System.out.println("Any even is: " + i));
```

With a sequential stream, `findAny()` will likely return the first value in the stream, 0, every time, even though it's not guaranteed.

Now, let's parallelize this stream and see what happens. We'll add a `peek()`, so we can see the thread workers as they work on the problem:

```
IntStream nums = IntStream.range(0, 20);
OptionalInt any = nums
        .parallel()            // make the stream parallel
                               // peek at the thread name
        .peek(i -> System.out.println(i + ": "
            + Thread.currentThread().getName()))
            .filter(i ->      // filter the evens
            i % 2 == 0 ? true : false)
        .findAny();            // find any even int
any.ifPresent(i -> System.out.println("Any even is: " + i));
```

We run this and get

```
12: main
1: ForkJoinPool.commonPool-worker-6
5: ForkJoinPool.commonPool-worker-7
2: ForkJoinPool.commonPool-worker-3
6: ForkJoinPool.commonPool-worker-1
8: ForkJoinPool.commonPool-worker-5
17: ForkJoinPool.commonPool-worker-2
16: ForkJoinPool.commonPool-worker-4
Any even is: 12
```

Remember, our computer has eight cores, so this stream pipeline has been split up into eight workers, each tackling part of the stream. The `findAny()` method is short circuiting, so even though we still have 12 more values in the stream to process (since the stream has 20 values), we stop as soon as we find the first even number. In this run, we had several threads with even numbers: the main worker, worker-1, worker-4, and worker-5. It just so happens that the main thread probably got done first, and so as soon as that even number was found, everything else stopped, and that result, 12, was returned.

Run the code again, and you'll likely get a different answer.

This example illustrates that `findAny()` really does find any result, particularly when you're working with a parallel stream pipeline.

A Parallel Stream Implementation of a RecursiveTask

Let's write code to sum an array of `ints` with a `ForkJoinPool RecursiveTask`, and compare that code with a parallel stream (which, remember, uses `ForkJoinPool` under the covers). We'll also implement it with a plain-old `for` loop, so you can see not only how the code itself compares, but also how the performance compares. Much of this code should look familiar to you by now.

```
/*
 * Sum numbers in an array of SIZE random numbers
 * from 1 to MAX if number > NUM
 */
public class SumRecursiveTask extends RecursiveTask<Long> {
    public static final int SIZE = 400_000_000;
    public static final int THRESHOLD = 1000;
    public static final int MAX = 10;       // array of numbers, 1-10
    public static final int NUM = 5;        // sum numbers > 5
    private int[] data;
    private int start;
    private int end;
    public SumRecursiveTask(int[] data, int start, int end) {
        this.data = data;
        this.start = start;
        this.end = end;
    }
    @Override
    protected Long compute() {
        long tempSum = 0;
        if (end - start <= THRESHOLD) {
            for (int i = start; i < end; i++) {
                if (data[i] > NUM) {
                    vtempSum += data[i];
                }
            }
            return tempSum;
        } else {
            int halfWay = ((end - start) / 2) + start;
            SumRecursiveTask t1 = new SumRecursiveTask(data, start, halfWay);
            SumRecursiveTask t2 = new SumRecursiveTask(data, halfWay, end);
            t1.fork();                      // queue left half of task
            long sum2 = t2.compute(); // compute right half
            long sum1 = t1.join();    // compute left and join
            return sum1 + sum2;
        }
    }
    public static void main(String[] args) {
        int[] data2sum = new int[SIZE];
        long sum = 0, startTime, endTime, duration;
        // create an array of random numbers between 1 and MAX
        for (int i = 0; i < SIZE; i++) {
            data2sum[i] = ThreadLocalRandom.current().nextInt(MAX) + 1;
        }
        startTime = Instant.now().toEpochMilli();
        // sum numbers with plain old for loop
        for (int i = 0; i < data2sum.length; i++) {
            if (data2sum[i] > NUM) {
```

```
                sum = sum + data2sum[i];
        }
}
endTime = Instant.now().toEpochMilli();
duration = endTime - startTime;
System.out.println("Summed with for loop in " + duration
    + " milliseconds; sum is: " + sum);

// sum numbers with ResursiveTask
ForkJoinPool fjp = new ForkJoinPool();
SumRecursiveTask action =
    new SumRecursiveTask(data2sum, 0, data2sum.length);
startTime = Instant.now().toEpochMilli();
sum = fjp.invoke(action);
endTime = Instant.now().toEpochMilli();
duration = endTime - startTime;
System.out.println("Summed with recursive task in "
    + duration + " milliseconds; sum is: " + sum);

// sum numbers with a parallel stream
IntStream stream2sum = IntStream.of(data2sum);
startTime = Instant.now().toEpochMilli();
sum =
    stream2sum
        .unordered()
        .parallel()
        .filter(i -> i > NUM)
        .sum();
endTime = Instant.now().toEpochMilli();
duration = endTime - startTime;
System.out.println("Stream data summed in " + duration
    + " milliseconds; sum is: " + sum);

// sum numbers with a parallel stream, limiting workers
ForkJoinPool fjp2 = new ForkJoinPool(4);
IntStream stream2sum2 = IntStream.of(data2sum);
try {
    startTime = Instant.now().toEpochMilli();
    sum =
        fjp2.submit(
                () -> stream2sum2
                        .unordered()
                        .parallel()
                        .filter(i -> i > NUM)
                        .sum()
                ).get();
    endTime = Instant.now().toEpochMilli();
    duration = endTime - startTime;
    System.out.println("FJP4 Stream data summed in "
        + duration + " milliseconds; sum is: " + sum);
} catch (Exception e) {
```

```
                    System.out.println("Error executing stream average");
                    e.printStackTrace();
             }
        }
    }
```

This code first generates a large array of random numbers between 1 and 10 and then computes the sum of all numbers > 5 four different times (from the same data, so we should get the same answer each time): first, using a plain-old `for` loop; second, using a `RecursiveTask`, third, using a parallel stream on the default `ForkJoinPool` (that is, using all eight cores of our machine); and finally, using a parallel stream on a custom `ForkJoinPool` with four workers (using four cores). Here are our results:

```
Summed with for loop in 287 milliseconds; sum is: 399980957
Summed with recursive task in 267 milliseconds; sum is: 399980957
Stream data summed in 118 milliseconds; sum is: 399980957
FJP4 Stream data summed in 136 milliseconds; sum is: 399980957
```

We ran it again and this time we got

```
Summed with for loop in 292 milliseconds; sum is: 399927370
Summed with recursive task in 196 milliseconds; sum is: 399927370
Stream data summed in 184 milliseconds; sum is: 399927370
FJP4 Stream data summed in 138 milliseconds; sum is: 399927370
```

In the first run, the parallel stream running on all eight cores was the winner, slightly faster than the parallel stream running on four cores. Both parallel streams were far superior to the `RecursiveTask` and the `for` loop.

In the second run, this time the parallel stream running on four cores was the clear winner, with the `RecursiveTask` and the parallel stream running on eight cores about the same, both much faster than the `for` loop.

As you can see, your results will vary depending on the solution you choose as well as your underlying machine architecture. If you get an `OutOfMemoryError` when you run this, try reducing the `SIZE`.

Reducing Parallel Streams with reduce()

Let's say you want to reduce your stream to a value, but none of the built-in stream reduction methods (like `sum()`) suffice. You can build your own custom reduction with the `reduce()` function, as you saw in Chapter 9.

How about building a custom reduction that multiplies all the elements of a stream? It's a bit like computing the sum, except we're multiplying instead. This is known as computing the *product* (as compared to the sum). Before we write this reduction, we should check a few things. First, remember that a reduction produces an `Optional` value unless we provide an identity.

Recall the type signature of `reduce()`:

```
T reduce(T identity, BinaryOperator<T> accumulator)
```

Although the identity is optional, providing one is a good idea because it allows us to get a result (rather than an `Optional` result), and that identity value is also used to make the first result in the stream pipeline, and we want to make sure the correct identity is being used in our custom reduction.

For the sum, the identity value is 0 because any number added to 0 is that number. For the product, the identity is 1 because any number multiplied by 1 is that number. So, we'll use 1. That's easy enough.

The accumulator is a `BinaryOperator` that takes two values and produces one value. Remember that an `Operator` produces a value of the same type as its arguments. Our `BinaryOperator` is simple; it just takes two numbers and multiples them together, returning a number:

```
(i1, i2) -> i1 * i2
```

Another thing we should check is that our accumulator function is associative. Remember the trouble we ran into when we tried to reduce using a custom average function? We didn't get a correct result because our average function is not associative, so we had to use the built-in `average()` reduction method instead.

Is our product function associative? It is. That is, we can multiply a * b and then by c and get the same answer as when we multiply b * c and then by a.

Another quick check: Is our accumulator stateless? That is, does it rely on any additional state in the stream to be computed? If it's not stateless, then we could run into trouble; either we'll potentially get incorrect results or we'll drastically reduce the performance of the parallel stream (or both!). In this case, our reduction function is, indeed, stateless. There is no state needed in order to properly multiply two values from the stream and produce a result.

Okay! We've got our identity, and we've got our associative, stateless reduction function. Now we can write the code to reduce a parallel stream to the product of all values in the stream:

```
List<Integer> nums = Arrays.asList(1, 2, 3, 4, 5, 6, 7, 8, 9, 10);
int mult = nums.stream()
      .unordered()                          // unordered for efficiency
      .parallel()                           // make the stream parallel
      .reduce(1,  (i1, i2) -> i1 * i2);   // reduce to the product
System.out.println("Product reduction: " + mult);
```

Here, we start with a `List` of `Integer` values and create a stream. We call `unordered()` on that stream so we can get additional efficiency from parallel processing—and this works great, because just like addition, computing the product does not depend on the order of the values. We then make the stream parallel and call the `reduce()` terminal operation method, passing in our identity, 1, and our product accumulator. Here is the result we get:

```
Product reduction: 3628800
```

That's the correct answer (phew!). Running the code again several times produces the same result each time. It looks like we got the code correct.

As an exercise, you can try this reduction on a much larger stream of numbers and time the performance, comparing the parallel version with the sequential version. See what results you get!

Collecting Values from a Parallel Stream

As we've said before, when processing data with streams, you will most likely want to reduce the stream to a single value, like a sum or a product or a count, or you might want to collect results into a new collection with `collect()` (which is a reduction, too).

Consider again our `ArrayList` of dogs we used above, containing aiko, boi, charis, clover, and zooey.

If you forget that you aren't supposed to create side effects from a parallel stream pipeline, you might do something like this to collect dogs who are older than 7 into a new `List` collection:

```
List<Dog> dogsOlderThan7 = new ArrayList<>();
long count = dogs.stream()                    // stream the dogs
    .unordered()                              // make the stream unordered
    .parallel()                               // make the stream parallel
    .filter(d -> d.getAge() > 7)              // filter the dogs
    .peek(d -> dogsOlderThan7.add(d))         // save… with a side effect
    .count();
System.out.println("Dogs older than 7, via side effect: " + dogsOlderThan7);
```

Here, we're initializing a new `List`, `dogsOlderThan7`; we're streaming our original dogs `ArrayList`, making it unordered, making it parallel, filtering for dogs older than 7, and then making the mistake of saving those dogs older than 7 to our new `List` using a side effect from within a `peek()` lambda expression. We then terminate the pipeline with the `count()` operation.

The first time we ran this we got the following:

```
Dogs older than 7, via side effect: [null, aiko is 10 years old]
```

Hmm, definitely a problem there! Running it again, we got this:

```
Dogs older than 7, via side effect: [null, null, clover is 12 years old]
```

Clearly, as you should know well by now, this is not the way to collect results from a stream pipeline. The reason this fails is because we have multiple threads trying to access the `List dogsOlderThan7` at the same time and `dogsOlderThan7` is not thread-safe.

We could fix this code by using a synchronized list, like this:

```
List<Dog> dogsOlderThan7 =
    Collections.synchronizedList(new ArrayList<>());
```

Now, the `List` is thread-safe. The order of the dogs in the resulting `List` may not be the same as in the source, but at least you'll get the right set of dogs. However, you're also sacrificing some performance because you're forcing a synchronization of all the threads attempting to write to the synchronized `List`.

A better way to collect values from a parallel stream pipeline is to use `Collectors`, as we did in Chapter 9 with sequential streams. Here's how:

```
List<Dog> dogsOlderThan7 =
    dogs.stream()                          // stream the dogs
        .unordered()                       // make the stream unordered
        .parallel()                        // make the stream parallel
        .filter(d -> d.getAge() > 7)       // filter dogs older than 7
        .collect(Collectors.toList());     // collect older dogs into a List
System.out.println("Dogs older than 7: " + dogsOlderThan7);
```

When we run this code, we see the output:

```
Dogs older than 7: [aiko is 10 years old, clover is 12 years old,
zooey is 8 years old]
```

Now you might be thinking, "Didn't you just say that the `List` is not thread-safe? We're still using a `List` in the `collect()` method with `Collectors` `.toList()`, so how is this working?"

Good question. It turns out that the way `collect()` works under the covers is that each worker processing a piece of the stream collects its data into its own collection. Worker 1 will create a `List` of dogs older than 7; worker 2 will create a `List` of dogs older than 7; and so on. Each of these `List`s is separate, built from the pieces of the stream that each worker got when the stream was split up across the parallel workers. At the end, once each thread is complete, the separate `Lists` are merged together, in a thread-safe manner, to create one final `List` of dogs.

`Lists` are inherently ordered, so we will get a reduction in efficiency unless we make sure the stream is unordered, which we've done by adding a call to `unordered()` at the beginning of the pipeline. (Of course, this means the dogs may not be in the same order as they were in the source, but you expected that, right?). You can also collect values from a parallel stream with `toSet()` and `toMap()`, and a method `toConcurrentMap()` is there for additional efficiency since merging maps is expensive.

As we mentioned in Chapter 9, you can use the `collect()` method with your own supplier, accumulator, and combiner functions if you need a way to collect that isn't provided for by the `Collectors` class:

```
<R> R collect(Supplier<R> supplier,
              BiConsumer<R,? super T> accumulator,
              BiConsumer<R,R> combiner)
```

If you use a custom collector, just like with the custom reduction, you'll need to make sure that your accumulator is associative and stateless. In addition, your combiner should be stateless and thread-safe. Typically, the combiner will be adding values to a new collection, so using a concurrent collection here is a good idea.

CERTIFICATION SUMMARY

This chapter covered the required concurrency knowledge you'll need to apply on the certification exam. The `java.util.concurrent` package and its subpackages form a high-level multithreading framework in Java. You should become familiar with threading basics before attempting to apply the Java concurrency libraries, but once you learn `java.util.concurrent`, you may never extend `Thread` again.

`Callables` and `Executors` (and their underlying thread pools) form the basis of a high-level alternative to creating new `Threads` directly. As the trend of adding more CPU cores continues, knowing how to get Java to make use of them all concurrently could put you on easy street. The high-level APIs provided by `java.util.concurrent` help you create efficient multithreaded applications while eliminating the need to use low-level threading APIs such as `wait()`, `notify()`, and `synchronized`, which can be a source of hard-to-detect bugs.

When using an `Executor`, you will commonly create a `Callable` implementation to represent the work that needs to be executed concurrently. A `Runnable` can be used for the same purpose, but a `Callable` leverages generics to allow a generic return type from its `call` method. `Executor` or `ExecutorService` instances with predefined behavior can be obtained by calling one of the factory methods in the `Executors` class like so: `ExecutorService es = Executors.newFixedThreadPool(100);`.

Once you obtain an `ExecutorService`, you submit a task in the form of a `Runnable` or `Callable`, or a collection of `Callable` instances to the `ExecutorService` using one of the `execute`, `submit`, `invokeAny`, or `invokeAll` methods. An `ExecutorService` can be held onto during the entire life of your application if needed, but once it is no longer needed, it should be terminated using the `shutdown` and `shutdownNow` methods.

We looked at the Fork/Join Framework, which supplies a highly specialized type of `Executor`. Use the Fork/Join Framework when the work you would typically put in a `Callable` can be split into multiple units of work. The purpose of the Fork/Join Framework is to decrease the amount of time it takes to solve a problem by leveraging the additional CPUs in a system. You should only run a single Fork/Join task at a time in an application, because the goal of the framework is to allow a single task to consume all available CPU resources in order to be solved as quickly as possible. In most cases, the effort of splitting a single task into multiple tasks that can be operated on by the underlying Fork/Join threads will introduce additional overhead. Don't assume that applying Fork/Join will grant you a performance benefit for all problems. The overhead involved may be large enough that any benefit of applying the framework is offset.

When applying the Fork/Join Framework, first subclass either `RecursiveTask` (if a return result is desired) or `RecursiveAction`. Within one of these `ForkJoinTask` subclasses, you must implement the `compute` method. The `compute()` method is where you divide the work of a task into parts and then call the `fork` and `join` methods or the `invokeAll` method. To execute the task, create a `ForkJoinPool` instance with `ForkJoinPool pool = new ForkJoinPool();` and submit the `RecursiveTask` or `RecursiveAction` to the pool with the `pool.invoke(task)` method. Although the Fork/Join API itself is not that large, creating a correct and efficient implementation of a `ForkJoinTask` can be challenging.

Java 8 added parallel streams to make the Fork/Join Framework easier to use. Parallel streams are built on top of the Fork/Join Framework and allow you to split a task into parts more easily than when using the Fork/Join API directly. Simply create a stream and call `parallel()`, and your stream pipeline will be split into tasks that execute in separate threads. However, as you saw, you need to be aware of the potential issues with parallel streams and make sure you are using them to solve the appropriate kinds of problems.

We learned about the `java.util.concurrent` collections. There are three categories of collections: copy-on-write collections, concurrent collections, and blocking queues. The copy-on-write and concurrent collections are similar in use to the traditional `java.util` collections but are designed to be used efficiently in a thread-safe fashion. The copy-on-write collections (`CopyOnWriteArrayList` and `CopyOnWriteArraySet`) should be used for read-heavy scenarios. When attempting to loop through all the elements in one of the copy-on-write collections, always use an `Iterator`. The concurrent collections included

- `ConcurrentHashMap`
- `ConcurrentLinkedDeque`
- `ConcurrentLinkedQueue`
- `ConcurrentSkipListMap`
- `ConcurrentSkipListSet`

These collections are meant to be used concurrently without requiring locking. Remember that iterators of these five concurrent collections are weakly consistent. `ConcurrentHashMap` and `ConcurrentSkipListMap` are `ConcurrentMap` implementations that add atomic `putIfAbsent`, `remove`, and `replace` methods to the `Map` interface. Seven blocking queue implementations are provided by the `java.util.concurrent` package:

- `ArrayBlockingQueue`
- `LinkedBlockingDeque`
- `LinkedBlockingQueue`
- `PriorityBlockingQueue`
- `DelayQueue`
- `LinkedTransferQueue`
- `SynchronousQueue`

These blocking queues are used to exchange objects between threads— one thread will deposit an object and another thread will retrieve that object. Depending on which queue type is used, the parameters used to create the queue, and the method being called, an insert or a removal operation may block until it can be completed successfully. In Java 7, the `LinkedTransferQueue` class was added and acts as a superset of several blocking queue types; you should prefer it when possible.

Another way to coordinate threads is to use a `CyclicBarrier`. A `CyclicBarrier` creates a barrier where all threads must wait until all participating threads reach that barrier; once they do, then the threads can continue. You can have an optional `Runnable` run before the threads continue; the last thread to reach the barrier is the thread that's used to run that `Runnable`.

The `java.util.concurrent.atomic` and `java.util.concurrent.locks` packages contain additional utility classes you might consider using in concurrent applications. The `java.util.concurrent.atomic` package supplies thread-safe classes that are similar to the traditional wrapper classes (such as `java.lang.Integer`) but with methods that support atomic modifications. The `java.util.concurrent.locks.Lock` interface and supporting classes enable you to create highly customized locking behaviors that are more flexible than traditional object monitor locking (the `synchronized` keyword).

TWO-MINUTE DRILL

Here are some of the key points from the certification objectives in this chapter.

Apply Atomic Variables and Locks (OCP Objective 10.3)

☐ The `java.util.concurrent.atomic` package provides classes that are similar to volatile fields (changes to an atomic object's value will be correctly read by other threads without the need for synchronized code blocks in your code).

☐ The atomic classes provide a `compareAndSet` method that is used to validate that an atomic variable's value will only be changed if it matches an expected value.

☐ The atomic classes provide several convenience methods such as `addAndGet` that will loop repeatedly until a `compareAndSet` succeeds.

☐ The `java.util.concurrent.locks` package contains a locking mechanism that is an alternative to synchronized methods and blocks. You get greater flexibility at the cost of a more verbose syntax (such as having to manually call `lock.unlock()` and having an automatic release of a synchronization monitor at the end of a synchronized code block).

☐ The `ReentrantLock` class provides the basic Lock implementation. Commonly used methods are `lock()`, `unlock()`, `isLocked()`, and `tryLock()`. Calling `lock()` increments a counter and `unlock()` decrements the counter. A thread can only obtain the lock when the counter is zero.

☐ The `ReentrantReadWriteLock` class provides a `ReadWriteLock` implementation that supports a read lock (obtained by calling `readLock()`) and a write lock (obtained by calling `writeLock()`).

Use java.util.concurrent Collections (OCP Objective 10.4)

☐ Copy-on-write collections work well when there are more reads than writes because they make a new copy of the collection for each write. When looping through a copy-on-write collection, use an iterator (remember, `for-each` loops use an iterator).

☐ None of the concurrent collections make the elements stored in the collection thread-safe—just the collection itself.

☐ `ConcurrentHashMap`, `ConcurrentSkipListMap`, and `ConcurrentSkipListSet` should be preferred over synchronizing with the more traditional collections.

☐ `ConcurrentHashMap` and `ConcurrentSkipListMap` are `ConcurrentMap` implementations that enhance a standard Map by adding atomic operations that validate the presence and value of an element before performing an operation: `putIfAbsent(K key, V value)`, `remove(Object key, Object value)`, `replace(K key, V value)`, and `replace(K key, V oldValue, V newValue)`.

☐ Blocking queues are used to exchange objects between threads. Blocking queues will block (hence the name) when you call certain operations, such as calling `take()` when there are no elements to take. There are seven different blocking queues that have slightly different behaviors; you should be able to identify the behavior of each type.

Blocking Queue	Description
`ArrayBlockingQueue`	A FIFO (first-in-first-out) queue in which the head of the queue is the oldest element and the tail is the newest. An `int` parameter to the constructor limits the size of the queue (it is a bounded queue).
`LinkedBlockingDeque`	Similar to `LinkedBlockingQueue`, except it is a double-ended queue (deque). Instead of only supporting FIFO operations, you can remove from the head or tail of the queue.
`LinkedBlockingQueue`	A FIFO queue in which the head of the queue is the oldest element and the tail is the newest. An optional `int` parameter to the constructor limits the size of the queue (it can be bounded or unbounded).
`PriorityBlockingQueue`	An unbounded queue that orders elements using `Comparable` or `Comparator`. The head of the queue is the lowest value.
`DelayQueue`	An unbounded queue of `java.util.concurrent.Delayed` instances. Objects can only be taken once their delay has expired. The head of the queue is the object that expired first.
`LinkedTransferQueue`	Added in Java 7. An unbounded FIFO queue that supports the features of a `ConcurrentLinkedQueue`, `SynchronousQueue`, and `LinkedBlockingQueue`.
`SynchronousQueue`	A blocking queue with no capacity. An `insert` operation blocks until another thread executes a remove operation. A `remove` operation blocks until another thread executes an `insert` operation.

☐ Some blocking queues are bounded, meaning they have an upper bound on the number of elements that can be added, and a thread calling `put(e)` may block until space becomes available.

☐ `CyclicBarrier` creates a barrier at which threads must wait until all participating threads reach that barrier. Once all of the threads have reached the barrier, they can continue running. You can use `CyclicBarrier` to coordinate threads so that an action occurs only after another action is complete or to manage data in Collections that are not thread-safe.

☐ `CyclicBarrier` takes the number of threads that can wait at the barrier and an optional `Runnable` that is run after all threads reach the barrier, but before they continue execution. The last thread to reach the barrier is used to run this `Runnable`.

Use Executors and ThreadPools (OCP Objective 10.1)

☐ An `Executor` is used to submit a task for execution without being coupled to how or when the task is executed. Basically, it creates an abstraction that can be used in place of explicit thread creation and execution.

☐ An `ExecutorService` is an enhanced `Executor` that provides additional functionality, such as the ability to execute a `Callable` instance and to shut down (nondaemon threads in an `Executor` may keep the JVM running after your main method returns).

☐ The `Callable` interface is similar to the `Runnable` interface, but adds the ability to return a result from its `call` method and can optionally throw an exception.

☐ The `Executors` (plural) class provides factory methods that can be used to construct `ExecutorService` instances, for example: `ExecutorService ex = Executors.newFixedThreadPool(4);`.

Use the Parallel Fork/Join Framework (OCP Objective 10.5)

☐ Fork/Join enables work stealing among worker threads in order to keep all CPUs utilized and to increase the performance of highly parallelizable tasks.

☐ A pool of worker threads of type `ForkJoinWorkerThread` is created when you create a new `ForkJoinPool()`. By default, one thread per CPU is created.

☐ To minimize the overhead of creating new threads, you should create a single Fork/Join pool in an application and reuse it for all recursive tasks.

☐ A Fork/Join task represents a large problem to solve (often involving a collection or array).

☐ When executed by a `ForkJoinPool`, the Fork/Join task will subdivide itself into Fork/Join tasks that represent smaller segments of the problem to be solved.

☐ A Fork/Join task is a subclass of the `ForkJoinTask` class, either `RecursiveAction` or `RecursiveTask`.

☐ Extend `RecursiveTask` when the `compute()` method must return a value, and extend `RecursiveAction` when the return type is void.

☐ When writing a `ForkJoinTask` implementation's `compute()` method, always call `fork()` before `join()` or use one of the `invokeAll()` methods instead of calling `fork()` and `join()`.

☐ You do not need to shut down a Fork/Join pool before exiting your application because the threads in a Fork/Join pool typically operate in daemon mode.

Use Parallel Streams Including Reduction, Decomposition, Merging Processes, Pipelines, and Performance (OCP Objective 10.6)

☐ Parallel streams are built on top of the Fork/Join pool.

☐ Parallel streams provide an easier syntax for creating tasks in the Fork/Join pool.

☐ You can use the default Fork/Join pool, or create a custom pool and submit tasks expressed as parallel streams via a `Callable`.

☐ Parallel streams split the stream into subtasks that represent portions of the problem to be solved. Each subtask solution is then combined to produce a final result for the terminal operation of the parallel stream.

☐ Create a parallel stream by calling `parallel()` on a stream object or `parallelStream()` on a `Collection` object.

☐ Make a parallel stream sequential again by calling the `sequential()` method.

☐ Test to see if a stream is parallel with the `isParallel()` method.

- ☐ Parallel stream pipelines should be stateless, and for optimum performance, parallel streams should be unordered. Reduction operations on parallel streams should be associative and stateless.

- ☐ Stateful parallel stream pipelines will either create an error or unexpected results.

- ☐ Nonassociative reductions on streams will produce unexpected results.

- ☐ Just like sequential streams, parallel streams can have multiple intermediate operations and must have one terminal operation to produce a result.

- ☐ Test your parallel streams to verify you are getting the performance benefits you expect. The performance overhead of creating threads can be greater than the performance gain of a parallel stream in some situations.

- ☐ Stateful stream operations, such as `distinct()`, `limit()`, `skip()`, and `sorted()`, will limit the performance of your parallel streams.

- ☐ Collect results from a parallel stream pipeline with `collect()`, just as we did with sequential streams. The collecting happens in a thread-safe way, so you can use `collect()` with `Collectors.toList()`, `toSet()`, and `toMap()` safely.

SELF TEST

The following questions might be some of the hardest in the book. It's just a difficult topic, so don't panic. (We know some Java book authors who didn't do well with these topics and still managed to pass the exam.)

1. The following block of code creates a `CopyOnWriteArrayList`, adds elements to it, and prints the contents:

```
CopyOnWriteArrayList<Integer> cowList = new CopyOnWriteArrayList<>();
cowList.add(4);
cowList.add(2);
Iterator<Integer> it = cowList.iterator();
cowList.add(6);
while(it.hasNext()) {
  System.out.print(it.next() + " ");
}
```

What is the result?

A. 6

B. 12

C. 4 2

D. 4 2 6

E. Compilation fails

F. An exception is thrown at runtime

2. Given:

```
CopyOnWriteArrayList<Integer> cowList = new CopyOnWriteArrayList<>();
cowList.add(4);
cowList.add(2);
cowList.add(6);
Iterator<Integer> it = cowList.iterator();
cowList.remove(2);
while(it.hasNext()) {
  System.out.print(it.next() + " ");
}
```

Which shows the output that will be produced?

A. 12

B. 10

C. 4 2 6

D. 4 6

E. Compilation fails

F. An exception is thrown at runtime

3. Which methods from a `CopyOnWriteArrayList` will cause a new copy of the internal array to be created? (Choose all that apply.)

A. `add`

B. `get`

C. `iterator`

D. `remove`

4. Given:

```
ArrayBlockingQueue<Integer> abq = new ArrayBlockingQueue<>(10);
```

Which operation(s) can block indefinitely? (Choose all that apply.)

A. `abq.add(1);`

B. `abq.offer(1);`

C. `abq.put(1);`

D. `abq.offer(1, 5, TimeUnit.SECONDS);`

5. Given the following code fragment:

```
class SingletonTestDrive {
    public static void main(String args[]) {
        CyclicBarrier barrier = new CyclicBarrier(3, () -> {
            System.out.println(Singleton.INSTANCE.getValue());
        });
        Runnable r = () -> {
            for (int i = 0; i < 100; i++) {
                Singleton.INSTANCE.updateValue();
            }
            try {
                barrier.await();
            } catch (InterruptedException | BrokenBarrierException e) {
                e.printStackTrace();
            }
        };
        Thread t1 = new Thread(r);
        Thread t2 = new Thread(r);
        Thread t3 = new Thread(r);
        t1.start(); t2.start(); t3.start();
        System.out.println("Main thread is complete");
    }
}
enum Singleton {
    INSTANCE;
    int value = 0;
    private void doSomethingWithValue() {
        value = value + 1;
    }
```

```
    public synchronized int updateValue() {
        doSomethingWithValue();
        return value;
    }
        public int getValue() {
            return value;
        }
}
```

What do you expect the output to be, and which thread(s) will be responsible for the output? (Choose all that apply.)

A.

```
Main thread is complete
300
```

Main thread, thread t3

B.

```
300
Main thread is complete
```

thread t3, Main thread

C.

```
Main thread is complete
300
```

OR

```
300
Main thread is complete
```

Main thread, the last thread to reach the barrier

D.

The total value displayed could be any number because the Singleton is not thread-safe.

```
Main thread is complete
```

Main thread, the last thread to reach the barrier

E.

```
Main thread is complete
```

A BrokenBarrierException
Main thread, thread t1

6.   Given:

```
ConcurrentMap<String,Integer> ages = new ConcurrentHashMap<>();
ages.put("John", 23);
```

Which method(s) would delete John from the map only if his value was still equal to 23?

A. `ages.delete("John", 23);`

B. `ages.deleteIfEquals("John", 23);`

C. `ages.remove("John", 23);`

D. `ages.removeIfEquals("John", 23);`

7.   Which method represents the best approach to generating a random number between 1 and 10 if the method will be called concurrently and repeatedly by multiple threads?

A. ```
public static int randomA() {
    Random r = new Random();
    return r.nextInt(10) + 1;
}
```

B.  ```
private static Random sr = new Random();
    public static int randomB() {
    return sr.nextInt(10) + 1;
}
```

C. ```
public static int randomC() {
    int i = (int)(Math.random() * 10 + 1);
    return i;
}
```

D.  ```
public static int randomD() {
    ThreadLocalRandom lr = ThreadLocalRandom.current();
    return lr.nextInt(1, 11);
}
```

8.   Given:

```
AtomicInteger i = new AtomicInteger();
```

Which atomically increment i by 9? (Choose all that apply.)

A. `i.addAndGet(9);`

B. `i.getAndAdd(9);`

C. `i.set(i.get() + 9);`

D. `i.atomicIncrement(9);`

E. `i = i + 9;`

9. Given:

```
public class LeaderBoard {
  private ReadWriteLock rwl = new ReentrantReadWriteLock();
  private List<Integer> highScores = new ArrayList<>();
  public void addScore(Integer score) {
    // position A
    lock.lock();
    try {
      if (highScores.size() < 10) {
        highScores.add(score);
      } else if (highScores.get(highScores.size() - 1) < score) {
        highScores.set(highScores.size() - 1, score);
      } else {
        return;
      }
      Collections.sort(highScores, Collections.reverseOrder());
    } finally {
      lock.unlock();
    }
  }
  public List<Integer> getHighScores() {
    // position B
    lock.lock();
    try {
      return Collections.unmodifiableList(new ArrayList<>(highScores));
    } finally {
      lock.unlock();
    }
  }
}
```

Which block(s) of code best match the behavior of the methods in the LeaderBoard class? (Choose all that apply.)

A. Lock lock = rwl.reentrantLock(); // should be inserted at position A

B. Lock lock = rwl.reentrantLcock(); // should be inserted at position B

C. Lock lock = rwl.readLock(); // should be inserted at position A

D. Lock lock = rwl.readLock(); // should be inserted at position B

E. Lock lock = rwl.writeLock(); // should be inserted at position A

F. Lock lock = rwl.writeLock(); // should be inserted at position B

10. Given:

```
ReentrantReadWriteLock rwl = new ReentrantReadWriteLock();
rwl.readLock().unlock();
System.out.println("READ-UNLOCK-1");
rwl.readLock().lock();
System.out.println("READ-LOCK-1");
rwl.readLock().lock();
System.out.println("READ-LOCK-2");
rwl.readLock().unlock();
System.out.println("READ-UNLOCK-2");
rwl.writeLock().lock();
System.out.println("WRITE-LOCK-1");
rwl.writeLock().unlock();
System.out.println("WRITE-UNLOCK-1");
```

What is the result?

A. The code will not compile

B. The code will compile and output:

```
READ-UNLOCK-1
READ-LOCK-1
READ-LOCK-2
READ-UNLOCK-2
```

C. The code will compile and output:

```
READ-UNLOCK-1
READ-LOCK-1
READ-LOCK-2
READ-UNLOCK-2
WRITE-LOCK-1
WRITE-UNLOCK-1
```

D. A `java.lang.IllegalMonitorStateException` will be thrown

11. Which class contains factory methods to produce preconfigured `ExecutorService` instances?

A. `Executor`

B. `Executors`

C. `ExecutorService`

D. `ExecutorServiceFactory`

12. Given:

```
private Integer executeTask(ExecutorService service,
                        Callable<Integer> task) {
    // insert here
}
```

Which set(s) of lines, when inserted, would correctly use the `ExecutorService` argument to execute the `Callable` and return the `Callable`'s result? (Choose all that apply.)

A.
```
   try {
       return service.submit(task);
   } catch (Exception e) {
       return null;
   }
```

B.
```
   try {
       return service.execute(task);
   } catch (Exception e) {
       return null;
   }
```

C.
```
   try {
       Future<Integer> future = service.submit(task);
       return future.get();
   } catch (Exception e) {
       return null;
   }
```

D.
```
   try {
       Result<Integer> result = service.submit(task);
       return result.get();
   } catch (Exception e) {
       return null;
   }
```

13. Which are true? (Choose all that apply.)

A. A Runnable may return a result but must not throw an `Exception`
B. A Runnable must not return a result nor throw an `Exception`
C. A Runnable must not return a result but may throw an `Exception`
D. A Runnable may return a result and throw an `Exception`
E. A Callable may return a result but must not throw an `Exception`
F. A Callable must not return a result nor throw an `Exception`
G. A Callable must not return a result but may throw an `Exception`
H. A Callable may return a result and throw an `Exception`

14. Given:

```
public class IncrementAction extends RecursiveAction {
  private final int threshold;
  private final int[] myArray;
  private int start;
  private int end;
  public IncrementAction(int[] myArray, int start, int end, int threshold) {
    this.threshold = threshold;
    this.myArray = myArray;
    this.start = start;
    this.end = end;
  }
  @Override
  protected void compute() {
    if (end - start < threshold) {
      for (int i = start; i <= end; i++) {
        myArray[i]++;
      }
    } else {
      int midway = (end - start) / 2 + start;
      IncrementAction a1 = new IncrementAction(myArray, start,
                                        midway, threshold);
      IncrementAction a2 = new IncrementAction(myArray, midway + 1,
                                        end, threshold);
      // insert answer here
    }
  }
}
```

Which line(s), when inserted at the end of the compute method, would correctly take the place of separate calls to fork() and join()? (Choose all that apply.)

A.   compute();

B.   forkAndJoin(a1, a2);

C.   computeAll(a1, a2);

D.   invokeAll(a1, a2);

15. When writing a RecursiveTask subclass, which are true? (Choose all that apply.)

A.   fork() and join() should be called on the same task

B.   fork() and compute() should be called on the same task

C.   compute() and join() should be called on the same task

D.   compute() should be called before fork()

E.   fork() should be called before compute()

F.   join() should be called after fork() but before compute()

16. Given the following code fragment:

```
public static void sampleTest() {
    Stream<Integer> nums = Stream.of(10, 5, 3, 2);
    Optional<Integer> result =
        nums
            .parallel()
            .map(n -> n * 10)
            .reduce((n1, n2) -> n1 - n2);
    System.out.println("Result: " + result.get());
}
```

What is the result?

A. 0

B. 40

C. The result is unpredictable

D. Compilation fails

E. An exception is thrown at runtime

17. Given the following code fragment:

```
Stream<List<String>> sDogNames =
    Stream.generate(() ->
                    Arrays.asList("boi", "aiko", "charis", "zooey", "clover"))
        .limit(2).unordered();
sDogNames.parallel()
        .flatMap(s -> s.stream())
        .map(s -> s.toUpperCase())
        .forEach(s -> System.out.print(s + " "));
```

What is the result?

A. BOI AIKO CHARIS ZOOEY CLOVER BOI AIKO CHARIS ZOOEY CLOVER

B. Most likely, although not guaranteed:
    BOI AIKO CHARIS ZOOEY CLOVER BOI AIKO CHARIS ZOOEY CLOVER

C. A ConcurrentModificationException is thrown

D. Compilation fails

E. An exception other than ConcurrentModificationException is thrown at runtime

18. Given the following code fragment:

```
Stream<List<String>> sDogNames2 =
    Arrays.asList(
            Arrays.asList("boi", "aiko", "charis", "zooey", "clover"),
            Arrays.asList("boi", "aiko", "charis", "zooey", "clover"))
        .stream().unordered();
                    sDogNames2.parallel()
        .flatMap(s -> s.stream())
        .map(s -> s.toUpperCase())
        .forEach(s -> System.out.print(s + " "));
```

What is the result?

A. `BOI AIKO CHARIS ZOOEY CLOVER BOI AIKO CHARIS ZOOEY CLOVER`

B. The result is unpredictable

C. A `ConcurrentModificationException` is thrown

D. Compilation fails

E. An exception is thrown at runtime

19. Given the code fragment:

```
List<Integer> myNums = Arrays.asList(1, 2, 3, 4, 5);
OptionalInt aNum = myNums.parallelStream().mapToInt(i -> i * 2).findAny();
aNum.ifPresent(System.out::println);
```

What is the result?

A. 1

B. 2

C. The result is unpredictable; it could be any one of the numbers in the stream

D. A `ConcurrentModificationException` is thrown

E. Compilation fails

F. An exception is thrown at runtime

SELF TEST ANSWERS

1. ☑ **C** is correct. The Iterator is obtained before 6 is added. As long as the reference to the Iterator is maintained, it will only provide access to the values 4 and 2.
   ☒ **A, B, D, E,** and **F** are incorrect based on the above. (OCP Objective 10.4)

2. ☑ **C** is correct. Because the Iterator is obtained before remove() is invoked, it will reflect all the elements that have been added to the collection.
   ☒ **A, B, D, E,** and **F** are incorrect based on the above. (OCP Objective 10.4)

3. ☑ **A** and **D** are correct. Of the methods listed, only add and remove will modify the list and cause a new internal array to be created.
   ☒ **B** and **C** are incorrect based on the above. (OCP Objective 10.4)

4. ☑ **C** is correct. The add method will throw an IllegalStateException if the queue is full. The two offer methods will return false if the queue is full. Only the put method will block until space becomes available.
   ☒ **A, B,** and **D** are incorrect based on the above. (OCP Objective 10.4)

5. ☑ **C** is correct; you could see the output in either order because we don't know in advance if threads t1, t2, and t3 will complete before the main thread or if the main thread will complete first. However, in either case, t1, t2, and t3 will wait at the barrier until t1, t2, and t3 are all at the barrier, and the last thread to reach the barrier will display the output.
   ☒ **A, B, D,** and **E** are incorrect; **A** and **B** are incorrect because of the above. **D** is incorrect because the Singleton is thread-safe; enum singletons are guaranteed to be created in a thread-safe manner, and we have synchronized the updateValue() method. **E** is incorrect because it is highly unlikely one of these threads will get stuck or time out and none is accessing any collection that is not thread-safe. (OCP Objective 10.4)

6. ☑ **C** is correct; it uses the correct syntax.
   ☒ The methods for answers **A, B,** and **D** do not exist in a ConcurrentHashMap. A traditional Map contains a single-argument remove method that removes an element based on its key. The ConcurrentMap interface (which ConcurrentHashMap implements) added the two-argument remove method, which takes a key and a value. An element will only be removed from the Map if its value matches the second argument. A boolean is returned to indicate if the element was removed. (OCP Objective 10.4)

7. ☑ **D** is correct. The ThreadLocalRandom creates and retrieves Random instances that are specific to a thread. You could achieve the same effect prior to Java 7 by using the java.lang.ThreadLocal and java.util.Random classes, but it would require several lines of code. Math.random() is thread-safe, but uses a shared java.util.Random instance and can suffer from contention problems.
   ☒ **A, B,** and **C** are incorrect based on the above. (OCP Objective 10.1)

8. ☑ **A** and **B** are correct. The addAndGet and getAndAdd both increment the value stored in an AtomicInteger.

☒ Answer **C** is not atomic because in between the call to get and set, the value stored by i may have changed. Answer **D** is invalid because the atomicIncrement method is fictional, and answer **E** is invalid because auto-boxing is not supported for the atomic classes. The difference between the addAndGet and getAndAdd methods is that the first is a prefix method (++x) and the second is a postfix method (x++). (Objective 10.3)

9. ☑ **D** and **E** are correct. The addScore method modifies the collection and, therefore, should use a write lock, whereas the getHighScores method only reads the collection and should use a read lock.

☒ **A, B, C,** and **F** are incorrect; they will not behave correctly. (Objective 10.3)

10. ☑ **D** is correct. A lock counts the number of times it has been locked. Calling lock increments the count, and calling unlock decrements the count. If a call to unlock decreases the count below zero, an exception is thrown.

☒ **A, B,** and **C** are incorrect based on the above. (OCP Objective 10.3)

11. ☑ **B** is correct. Executor is the super-interface for ExecutorService. You use Executors to easily obtain ExecutorService instances with predefined threading behavior. If the Executor interface does not produce ExecutorService instances with the behaviors that you desire, you can always look into using java.util.concurrent.AbstractExecutorService or java.util.concurrent.ThreadPoolExecutor directly.

☒ **A, C,** and **D** are incorrect based on the above. (OCP Objective 10.1)

12. ☑ **C** is correct. When you submit a Callable to an ExecutorService for execution, you will receive a Future as the result. You can use the Future to check on the status of the Callable's execution, or just use the get() method to block until the result is available.

☒ **A, B,** and **D** are incorrect based on the above. (OCP Objective 10.1)

13. ☑ **B** and **H** are correct. Runnable and Callable serve similar purposes. Runnable has been available in Java since version 1. Callable was introduced in Java 5 and serves as a more flexible alternative to Runnable. A Callable allows a generic return type and permits thrown exceptions, whereas a Runnable does not.

☒ **A, C, D, E, F,** and **G** are incorrect statements. (Objective 10.1)

14. ☑ **D** is correct. The invokeAll method is a var-args method that will fork all Fork/Join tasks, except one that will be invoked directly.

☒ **A, B,** and **C** are incorrect; they would not correctly complete the Fork/Join process. (OCP Objective 10.5)

15. ☑ **A** and **E** are correct. When creating multiple `ForkJoinTask` instances, all tasks except one should be forked first, so they can be picked up by other Fork/Join worker threads. The final task should then be executed within the same thread (typically by calling `compute()`) before calling `join()` on all the forked tasks to await their results. In many cases, calling the methods in the wrong order will not result in any compiler errors, so care must be taken to call the methods in the correct order.

☒ **B, C, D,** and **F** are incorrect based on the above. (OCP Objective 10.5)

16. ☑ **C** is correct. The result is unpredictable because the reduction function is not associative and the stream is parallel.

☒ **A, B, D,** and **E** are incorrect based on the above (OCP Objective 10.6)

17. ☑ **B** is correct. Because of the `limit(2)`, we will see the dog names twice, most likely in order. The `limit()` forces the stream to maintain state about the source data, so it is likely the stream will retain the original source ordering (although that is not guaranteed) even though it's an unordered parallel stream.

☒ **A, C, D,** and **E** are incorrect based on the above (OCP Objective 10.6)

18. ☑ **B** is correct. Unlike the previous sample question, we have no `limit()` so we have a stateless stream pipeline. The stream is unordered, and the pipeline is executing in parallel, so we cannot predict the ordering of the output. Note that if we were using `forEachOrdered()` instead of `forEach()` as the terminal operation, it is likely, but not guaranteed, that we would see the results in the same ordering as the source.

☒ **A, C, D,** and **E** are incorrect based on the above (OCP Objective 10.6)

19. ☑ **C** is correct. For a parallel stream, any of the numbers can be multiplied by 2 and returned by `findAny()`.

☒ **A, B, D, E,** and **F** are incorrect based on the above (OCP Objective 10.6)

12
JDBC

- Describe the interfaces that Make Up the Core of the JDBC API Including the Driver, Connection, Statement, and ResultSet Interfaces and Their Relationship to Provider Implementations

- Identify the Components Required to Connect to a Database Using the DriverManager Class Including the JDBC URL

- Submit Queries and Read Results from the Database Including Creating Statements, Returning Result Sets, Iterating Through the Results, and Properly Closing Result Sets, Statements, and Connections

✓ Two-Minute Drill

Q&A Self Test

This chapter covers the JDBC API that was added for the Java SE 7 and 8 exams. The exam developers have long felt that this API is truly a core feature of the language, and being able to demonstrate proficiency with JDBC goes a long way toward demonstrating your skills as a Java programmer.

Interestingly, JDBC has been a part of the language since JDK version 1.1 (1997) when JDBC 1.0 was introduced. Since then, there has been a steady progression of updates to the API, roughly one major release for each even-numbered JDK release, with the last major update being JDBC 4.0, released in 2006 with Java SE 6. In Java SE 7 and 8, JDBC got some minor updates and is now at version 4.2. While the focus of the exam is on JDBC 4.*x*, there may be questions about the differences between loading a driver with a JDBC 3.0 and JDBC 4.*x* implementation, so we'll talk about that as well.

The good news is that the exam is not going to test your ability to write SQL statements. That would be an exam all by itself (maybe even more than one— SQL is a BIG topic!). But you will need to recognize some basic SQL syntax and commands, so we'll start by spending some time covering the basics of relational database systems and give you enough SQL to make you popular at database parties. If you feel you have experience with SQL and understand database concepts, you might just skim the first section or skip right to the first exam objective and dive right in.

Starting Out: Introduction to Databases and JDBC

When you think of organizing information and storing it in some easily understood way, a spreadsheet or a table is often the first approach you might take. A spreadsheet or a table is a natural way of categorizing information: The first row of a table defines the sort of information that the table will hold, and each subsequent row contains a set of data that is related to the key we create on the left. For example, suppose you wanted to chart your monthly spending for several types of expenses (Table 12-1).

TABLE 12-1

Chart of Expenses

Month	Gas	EatingOut	Utilities	Phone
January	$200.25	$109.87	$97.00	$45.08
February	$225.34	$121.08	$97.00	$23.36
March	$254.78	$130.45	$97.00	$56.09

From the data in the chart, we can determine that your overall expenses are increasing month to month in the first three months of this year. But notice that without the table, without a relationship between the month and the data in the columns, you would just have a pile of receipts with no way to draw out important conclusions, such as

- Assuming you drove the same number of miles per month, gas is getting pricey—maybe it is time to get a Prius.
- You are eating out more month to month (or the price of eating out is going up)—maybe it's time to start doing some meal planning.
- And maybe you need to be a little less social—that phone bill is high.

The point is that this small sample of data is the key to understanding a relational database system. A relational database is really just a software application designed to store and manipulate data in tables. The software itself is actually called a Relational Database Management System (RDBMS), but many people shorten that to just "database"—so know that going forward, when we refer to a database, we are actually talking about an RDBMS (the whole system). What the relational management system adds to a database is the ability to define relationships between tables. It also provides a language to get data in and out in a meaningful way.

Looking at the simple table in Table 12-1, we know that the data in the columns, Gas, EatingOut, Utilities, and Phone, are grouped by the months January, February, and so on. The month is unique to each row and identifies this row of data. In database parlance, the month is a "primary key." A primary key is generally required for a database table to identify which row of the table you want and to make sure that there are no duplicate rows.

Extending this a little further, if the data in Table 12-1 were stored in a database, I could ask the database (write a query) to give me all of the data for the month of January (again, my primary key is "month" for this table). I might write something like:

"Give me all of my expenses for January."

The result would be something like:

```
January: Gas: $200.25, EatingOut: $109.87, Utilities: $97.00, Phone: $45.08
```

This kind of query is what makes a database so powerful. With a relatively simple language, you can construct some really powerful queries in order to manipulate your data to tell a story. In most RDBMSs, this language is called the Structured

Query Language (SQL). The same query we wrote out in a sentence earlier would be expressed like this in SQL:

```
SELECT * FROM Expenses WHERE Month = 'January'
```

which can be translated to "select all of the columns (*) from my table named 'Expenses' where the month column is equal to the string `'January'`." Let's look a bit more at how we "talk" to a database and what other sorts of queries we can make with tables in a relational database.

Talking to a Database

There are three important concepts when working with a database:

- Creating a connection to the database
- Creating a statement to execute in the database
- Getting back a set of data that represents the results

Let's look at these concepts in more detail.

Before we can communicate with the software that manages the database, before we can send it a query, we need to make a connection with the RDBMS itself. There are many different types of connections, and a lot of underlying technology to describe the connection itself, but in general, to communicate with an RDBMS, we need to open a connection using an IP address and port number to the database. Once we have established the connection, we need to send it some parameters (such as a username and password) to authenticate ourselves as a valid user of the RDBMS. Finally, assuming all went well, we can send queries through the connection. This is like logging into your online account at a bank. You provide some credentials, a username and password, and a connection is established and opened between you and the bank. Later in the chapter, when we start writing code, we'll open a connection using a Java class called the `DriverManager`, and in one request, pass in the database name, our username, and password.

Once we have established a connection, we can use some type of application (usually provided by the database vendor) to send query statements to the database, have them executed in the database, and get a set of results returned. A set of results can be one row, as we saw before when we asked for the data from the month of January, or several rows. For example, suppose we wanted to see all of the Gas expenses from our Expenses table. We might query the database like this:

```
"Show me all of my Gas Expenses"
```

Or as a SQL query:

```
SELECT Gas FROM Expenses
```

The set of results that would "return" from my query would be three rows, and each row would contain one column.

$200.25
$225.34
$254.78

An important aspect of a database is that the data is presented back to you exactly the same way that it is stored. Since Gas expense is a column, the query will return three rows (one for January, one for February, and one for March). Note that because we did not ask the database to include the Month column in the results, all we got was the Gas column. The results do preserve the fact that Gas is a column and not a row and, in general, present the data in the same row-and-column order in which it is stored in the database.

SQL Queries

Let's look a bit more at the syntax of SQL, the language used to write queries in a database. There are really four basic SQL queries that we are going to use in this chapter and that are common to manipulating data in a database. In summary, the SQL commands we are interested in are used to perform CRUD operations.

Like most terms presented in all caps, CRUD is an acronym and means *Create, Read, Update,* and *Delete.* These are the four basic operations for data in a database. They are represented by four distinct SQL commands, detailed in Table 12-2.

Here is a quick explanation for the examples in Table 12-2:

- **INSERT**   Add a row to the table Expenses, and set each of the columns in the table to the values expressed in the parentheses.
- **SELECT with WHERE**   You have already seen the SELECT clause with a WHERE clause, so you know that this SQL statement returns a single row identified by the primary key—the Month column. Think of this statement as a refinement to Read—more like a Find or Find by primary key.
- **SELECT**   When the SELECT clause does not have a WHERE clause, we are asking the database to return every row. Further, because we are using an asterisk (*) following the SELECT, we are asking for every column. Basically, it is a dump of the data shown in Table 15-1. Think of this statement as a Read All.

TABLE 12-2 Example SQL CRUD Commands

"CRUD"	SQL Command	Example SQL Query	Expressed in English
Create	INSERT	`INSERT INTO Expenses VALUES ('April', 231.21, 29.87, 97.00, 45.08)`	Add a new row (April) to expenses with the following values....
Read (or Find)	SELECT	`SELECT * FROM Expenses WHERE Month="February"`	Get me all of the columns in the Expenses table for February.
Read All	SELECT	`SELECT * FROM Expenses`	Get me all of the columns in the Expenses table.
Update	UPDATE	`UPDATE Expenses SET Phone=32.36, EatingOut=111.08 WHERE Month='February'`	Change my Phone expense and EatingOut expense for February to....
Delete	DELETE	`DELETE FROM Expenses WHERE Month='April'`	Remove the row of expenses for April.

■ **UPDATE** Change the data in the Phone and EatingOut cells to the new data provided for February.

■ **DELETE** Remove a row altogether from the database where the Month is April.

Really, this is all the SQL you need to know for this chapter. There are many other SQL commands, but this is the core set. If we need to go beyond this set of four commands in the chapter, we will cover them as they come up. Now, let's look at a more detailed database example that we will use as the example set of tables for this chapter, using the data requirements of a small bookseller, Bob's Books.

on the **Job**

SQL commands, like SELECT, INSERT, UPDATE, and so on, are case-insensitive. So it is largely by convention (and one we will use in this chapter) that we use all capital letters for SQL commands and key words, such as WHERE, FROM, LIKE, INTO, SET, and VALUES. SQL table names and column names, also called identifiers, can be case-sensitive or case-insensitive, depending on the database. The example code shown in this chapter uses a case-insensitive database, so again, just for convention, we will use upper camel case, that is, the first letter of each noun capitalized and the rest in lowercase.

One final note about case—all databases preserve case when a string is delimited—that is, when it is enclosed in quotes. So a SQL clause that uses single or double quotation marks to delimit an identifier will preserve the case of the identifier.

Bob's Books, Our Test Database

In this section, we'll describe a small database with a few tables and a few rows of data. As we work through the various JDBC topics in this chapter, we'll work with this database.

Bob is a small bookseller who specializes in children's books. Bob has designed his data around the need to sell his books online using a database (which one doesn't really matter) and a Java application. Bob has decided to use the JDBC API to allow him to connect to a database and perform queries through a Java application.

To start, let's look at the organization of Bob's data. In a database, the organization and specification of the tables is called the database schema (Figure 12-1). Bob's is a relatively simple schema, and again, for the purposes of this chapter, we are going to concentrate on just four tables from Bob's schema.

This is a relatively simple schema that represents a part of the database for a small bookstore. In the schema shown, there is a table for Customer (Table 12-3). This table stores data about Bob's customers—a customer ID, first name and last name, an e-mail address, and phone number. Postal addresses and other information could be stored in another table.

The next three tables we will look at represent the data required to store information about books that Bob sells. Because a book is a more complex set of data than a customer, we need to use one table for information about books, one for information about authors, and a third to create a relationship between books and authors.

FIGURE 12-1   Bob's BookSeller database schema

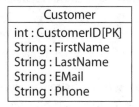

TABLE 12-3		Bob's Books Customer Table Sample Data		
CustomerID	**FirstName**	**LastName**	**Email**	**Phone**
5000	John	Smith	john.smith@verizon.net	555-340-1230
5001	Mary	Johnson	mary.johnson@comcast.net	555-123-4567
5002	Bob	Collins	bob.collins@yahoo.com	555-012-3456
5003	Rebecca	Mayer	rebecca.mayer@gmail.com	555-205-8212
5006	Anthony	Clark	anthony.clark@gmail.com	555-256-1901
5007	Judy	Sousa	judy.sousa@verizon.net	555-751-1207
5008	Christopher	Patriquin	patriquinc@yahoo.com	555-316-1803
5009	Deborah	Smith	debsmith@comcast.net	555-256-3421
5010	Jennifer	McGinn	jmcginn@comcast.net	555-250-0918

Suppose that you tried to store a book in a single table with a column for the ISBN (International Standard Book Number), title, and author name. For many books, this would be fine. But what happens if a book has two authors? Or three authors? Remember that one requirement for a database table is a unique primary key, so you can't simply repeat the ISBN in the table. In fact, having two rows with the same primary key will violate a key constraint in relational database design: the primary key of every row must be unique.

ISBN	Title	Author
ABCD	The Wonderful Life	Fred Smith
~~ABCD~~	~~The Wonderful Life~~	~~Tom Jones~~
1234	Some Enchanted Night	Paula Fredrick

Instead, there needs to be a way to have a separate table of books and authors and some way to link them together. Bob addressed this issue by placing Books in one table (Table 12-4) and Authors (Table 12-5) in another. The primary key for Books is the ISBN number, and therefore, each Book entry will be unique. For the Author table, Bob is creating a unique AuthorID for each author in the table.

TABLE 12-4	Bob's Books Sample Data for the "Books" Table				
ISBN	**Title**	**PubDate**	**Format**	**Price**	
142311339X	The Lost Hero (Heroes of Olympus, Book 1)	2010-10-12	Hardcover	10.95	
0689852223	The House of the Scorpion	2002-01-01	Hardcover	16.95	
0525423656	Crossed (Matched Trilogy, Book 2)	2011-11-01	Hardcover	12.95	
1423153627	The Kane Chronicles Survival Guide	2012-03-01	Hardcover	13.95	
0439371112	Howliday Inn	2001-11-01	Paperback	14.95	
0439861306	The Lightning Thief	2006-03-12	Paperback	11.95	
031673737X	How to Train Your Dragon	2010-02-01	Hardcover	10.95	
0545078059	The White Giraffe	2008-05-01	Paperback	6.95	
0803733428	The Last Leopard	2009-03-05	Hardcover	13.95	
9780545236	Freaky Monday	2010-01-15	Paperback	12.95	

To tie Authors to Books and Books to Authors, Bob has created a third table called Books_by_Author. This is a unique table type in a relational database. This table is called a *join* table. In a join table, there are no primary keys—instead, all the columns represent data that can be used by other tables to create a relationship. These columns are referred to as foreign keys—they represent a primary key in

TABLE 12-5	**AuthorID**	**FirstName**	**LastName**
Bob's Books Author Table Sample Data for the "Authors" Table	1000	Rick	Riordan
	1001	Nancy	Farmer
	1002	Ally	Condie
	1003	Cressida	Cowell
	1004	Lauren	St. John
	1005	Eoin	Colfer
	1006	Esther	Freisner
	1007	Chris	D'lacey
	1008	Mary	Rodgers
	1009	Heather	Hatch

AuthorID	ISBN
1000	142311339X
1001	0689852223
1002	0525423656
1000	1423153627
1003	031673737X
1004	0545078059
1004	0803733428
1008	9780545236
1009	9780545236

another table. Looking at the last two rows of this table, you can see that the Book with the ISBN 9780545236 has two authors: author id 1008 (Mary Rodgers) and 1009 (Heather Hatch). Using this join table, we can combine the two sets of data without needing duplicate entries in either table. We'll return to the concept of a join table later in the chapter.

A complete Bob's Books database schema would include tables for publishers, addresses, stock, purchase orders, and other data that the store needs to run its business. But for our purposes, this part of the schema is sufficient. Using this schema, we can write SQL queries using the SQL CRUD commands you learned earlier.

To summarize, before looking at JDBC, you should now know about connections, statements, and result sets:

- A connection is how an application communicates with a database.
- A statement is a SQL query that is executed on the database.
- A result set is the data that is returned from a SELECT statement.

Having these concepts down, we can use Bob's Books simple schema to frame some common uses of the JDBC API to submit SQL queries and get results in a Java application.

Core Interfaces of the JDBC API (OCP Objective 11.1)

11.1   Describe the interfaces that make up the core of the JDBC API including the Driver, Connection, Statement, and ResultSet interfaces and their relationship to provider implementations.

As we mentioned in the previous section, the purpose of a relational database is really threefold:

- To provide storage for data in tables
- To provide a way to create relationships between the data—just as Bob did with the Authors, Books, and Books_by_Author tables
- To provide a language that can be used to get the data out, update the data, remove the data, and create new data

The purpose of JDBC is to provide an application programming interface (API) for Java developers to write Java applications that can access and manipulate relational databases and use SQL to perform CRUD operations.

Once you understand the basics of the JDBC API, you will be able to access a huge list of databases. One of the driving forces behind JDBC was to provide a standard way to access relational databases, but JDBC can also be used to access file systems and object-oriented data sources. The key is that the API provides an abstract view of a database connection, statements, and result sets. These concepts are represented in the API as interfaces in the `java.sql` package: `Connection`, `Statement`, and `ResultSet`, respectively. What these interfaces define are the *contracts* between you and the implementing class. In truth, you may not know (nor should you care) *how* the implementation class works. As long as the implementation class implements the interface you need, you are assured that the methods defined by the interface exist and you can invoke them.

The `java.sql.Connection` interface defines the contract for an object that represents the connection with a relational database system. Later, we will look at the methods of this contract, but for now, an instance of a `Connection` is what we need to communicate with the database. How the `Connection` interface is implemented is vendor dependent, and again, we don't need to worry so much about the how—as long as the vendor follows the contract, we are assured that the object that represents a `Connection` will allow us to work with a database connection.

The `Statement` interface provides an abstraction of the functionality needed to get a SQL statement to execute on a database, and a `ResultSet` interface is an abstraction functionality needed to process a result set (the table of data) that is returned from the SQL query when the query involves a SQL SELECT statement.

The classes that implement `Connection`, `Statement`, `ResultSet`, and a number of other interfaces we will look at shortly are created by the vendor of the database we are using. The vendor understands their database product better than anyone else, so it makes sense that they create these classes. And it allows the vendor to optimize or hide any special characteristics of their product. The collection of the implementation classes is called the JDBC driver. A JDBC driver (lowercase "d") is the collection of classes required to support the API, whereas Driver (uppercase "D") is one of the implementations required in a driver.

A JDBC driver is typically provided by the vendor in a JAR or ZIP file. The implementation classes of the driver must meet a minimum set of requirements in order to be JDBC compliant. The JDBC specification provides a list of the functionality that a vendor must support and what functionality a vendor may optionally support.

Here is a partial list of the requirements for a JDBC driver. For more details, please read the specification (JSR-221). Note that the details of implementing a JDBC driver are NOT on the exam.

- Fully implement the interfaces: `java.sql.Driver`, `java.sql` `.DatabaseMetaData`, `java.sql.ResultSetMetaData`.
- Implement the `java.sql.Connection` interface. (Note that some methods are optional depending on the SQL version the database supports—more on SQL versions later in the chapter.)
- Implement `java.sql.Statement`, and `java.sql.PreparedStatement`.
- Implement the `java.sql.CallableStatement` interfaces if the database supports stored procedures. Again, more on this interface later in the chapter.
- Implement the `java.sql.ResultSet` interface.

Connect to a Database Using DriverManager (OCP Objective 11.2)

11.2   Identify the components required to connect to a database using the DriverManager class including the JDBC URL

Not all of the types defined in the JDBC API are interfaces. One important class for JDBC is the `java.sql.DriverManager` class. This concrete class is used to interact with a JDBC driver and return instances of `Connection` objects to you. Conceptually, the way this works is by using a Factory design pattern. Next, we'll look at `DriverManager` in more detail.

---

e x a m

ⓦ a t c h   *Let's take this opportunity to see the factory design pattern in use. In a factory pattern, a concrete class with static methods is used to create instances of objects that implement an interface. For example, suppose we wanted to create an instance of a* `Vehicle` *object:*

```
public interface Vehicle {
  public void start();  // Methods we think all vehicles should
  public void stop();   // support.
}
```

We need an implementation of `Vehicle` *in order to use this contract. So we design a* `Car`:

```
package com.us.automobile;
public class Car implements Vehicle {
  public void start() { }  // ... do start things
  public void stop() { }   // ... do stop things
}
```

(*continued*)

In order to use the `Car`, we could create one:

```
public class MyClass {
  public static void main(String args[]) {
    Vehicle ferrari =
      new com.us.automobile.Car(); // Create a Ferrari
    ferrari.start();              // Start the Ferrari
  }
}
```

However, here it would be better to use a factory—that way, we need not know anything about the actual implementation, and, as we will see later with `DriverManager`, we can use methods of the factory to dynamically determine which implementation to use at runtime.

```
public class MyClass {
  public static void main(String args[]) {
    Vehicle ferrari =
      CarFactory.getVehicle("Ferrari");     // Use a factory to
                                            // create a Ferrari
    ferrari.start();
  }
}
```

The factory in this case could create a different car based on the string passed to the static `getVehicle()` method—something like this:

```
public class CarFactory {
  public static Vehicle getVehicle(String type) {
    // ... create an instance of an object that represents the
    // type of car passed as the argument
  }
}
```

`DriverManager` uses this factory pattern to "construct" an instance of a `Connection` object by passing a string to its `getConnection()` method.

The DriverManager Class

The `DriverManager` class is a concrete, utility class in the JDBC API with static methods. You will recall that static or class methods can be invoked by other classes using the class name. One of those methods is `getConnection()`, which we look at next.

The `DriverManager` class is so named because it manages which JDBC driver implementation you get when you request an instance of a `Connection` through the `getConnection()` method.

There are several overloaded `getConnection` methods, but they all share one common parameter: a `String` URL. One pattern for `getConnection` is

```
DriverManager.getConnection(String url, String username, String password);
```

For example:

```
String url
    = "jdbc:derby://localhost:1521/BookSellerDB";   // JDBC URL
String user = "bookguy";   // BookSellerDB user name
String pwd = "$3lleR";     // BookSellerDB password
try {
  Connection conn
    = DriverManager.getConnection(url, user, pwd);  // Get an
                                                    // instance of a
                                                    // Connection
                                                    // object
} catch (SQLException se) { }
```

In this example, we are creating a connection to a Derby database, on a network, at a localhost address (on the local machine), at port number 1521, to a database called `"BookSellerDB"`, and we are using the credentials `"bookguy"` as the user id, and `"$3lleR"` as the password. Don't worry too much about the syntax of the URL right now—we'll cover that soon.

on the Job

It's a horrible idea to hard-code a username and password in the `getConnection()` method. Obviously, anyone reading the code would then know the username and password to the database. A more secure way to handle database credentials would be to separate the code that produces the credentials from the code that makes the connection. In some other class, you would use some type of authentication and authorization code to produce a set of credentials to allow access to the database. For simplicity in the examples in the chapter, we'll hard-code the username and password, but just keep in mind that on the job, this is not a best practice.

When you invoke the `DriverManager`'s `getConnection()` method, you are asking the `DriverManager` to try passing the first string in the statement, the driver URL, along with the username and password to each of the driver classes registered with the `DriverManager` in turn. If one of the driver classes recognizes the URL string, and the username and password are accepted, the driver returns an instance of a `Connection` object. If, however, the URL is incorrect, or the username and/or password are incorrect, then the method will throw a `SQLException`. We'll spend some time looking at `SQLException` later in this chapter.

How JDBC Drivers Register with the DriverManager

Because this part of the JDBC process is important to understand, and it involves a little Java magic, let's spend some time diagramming how driver classes become "registered" with the `DriverManager`, as shown in Figure 12-2.

First, one or more JDBC drivers, in a JAR or ZIP file, are included in the classpath of your application. The `DriverManager` class uses a service provider mechanism to search the classpath for any JAR or ZIP files that contain a file named `java.sql.Driver` in the META-INF/services folder of the driver jar or zip. This is simply a text file that contains the full name of the class that the vendor used to implement the `jdbc.sql.Driver` interface. For example, for a Derby driver, the full name is `org.apache.derby.jdbc.ClientDriver`.

The `DriverManager` will then attempt to load the class it found in the `java.sql.Driver` file using the class loader:

```
Class.forName("org.apache.derby.jdbc.ClientDriver");
```

When the driver class is loaded, its static initialization block is executed. Per the JDBC specification, one of the first activities of a driver instance is to "self-register"

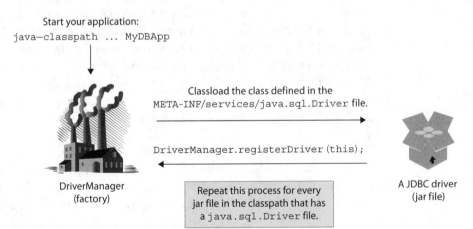

FIGURE 12-2

How JDBC drivers self-register with `DriverManager`

Start your application:
`java—classpath ... MyDBApp`

Classload the class defined in the
META-INF/services/java.sql.Driver file.

`DriverManager.registerDriver(this);`

DriverManager
(factory)

Repeat this process for every
jar file in the classpath that has
a `java.sql.Driver` file.

A JDBC driver
(jar file)

with the `DriverManager` class by invoking a static method on `DriverManager`. The code (minus error handling) looks something like this:

```
public class ClientDriver implements java.sql.Driver{
  static {
    ClientDriver driver = new ClientDriver();
    DriverManager.registerDriver(driver);
  }
  //...
}
```

This registers (stores) an instance of the `Driver` class into the `DriverManager`.

Now, when your application invokes the `DriverManager.getConnection()` method and passes a JDBC URL, username, and password to the method, the `DriverManager` simply invokes the `connect()` method on the registered `Driver`. If the connection was successful, the method returns a `Connection` object instance to `DriverManager`, which, in turn, passes that back to you.

If there is more than one registered driver, the `DriverManager` calls each of the drivers in turn and attempts to get a `Connection` object from them, as shown in Figure 12-3.

How the
`DriverManager`
gets a
`Connection`

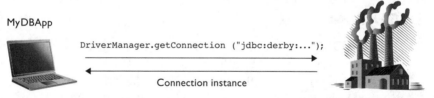

MyDBApp

`DriverManager.getConnection ("jdbc:derby:...");`

Connection instance

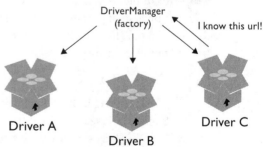

DriverManager
(factory)

I know this url!

Driver A

Driver B

Driver C

Pass the url, name, and password to each
of the registered drivers in turn until one
returns a non-null Connection.

The first driver that recognizes the JDBC URL and successfully creates a connection using the username and password will return an instance of a `Connection` object. If no drivers recognize the URL, username, and password combination, or if there are no registered drivers, then a `SQLException` is thrown instead.

To summarize:

- The JVM loads the `DriverManager` class, a concrete class in the JDBC API.

- The `DriverManager` class loads any instances of classes it finds in the META-INF/services/java.sql.Driver file of JAR/ZIP files on the classpath.

- Driver classes call `DriverManager.register(this)` to self-register with the `DriverManager`.

- When the `DriverManager.getConnection(String url)` method is invoked, `DriverManager` invokes the `connect()` method of each of these registered `Driver` instances with the URL string.

- The first `Driver` that successfully creates a connection with the URL returns an instance of a `Connection` object to the `DriverManager` `.getConnection` method invocation.

Let's look at the JDBC URL syntax next.

The JDBC URL

The JDBC URL is what is used to determine which driver implementation to use for a given `Connection`. Think of the JDBC URL (uniform resource locator) as a way to narrow down the universe of possible drivers to one specific connection. For example, suppose you need to send a package to someone. In order to narrow the universe of possible addresses down to a single unique location, you would have to identify the country, the state, the city, the street, and perhaps a house or address number on your package:

```
USA:California://SanJose:FirstStreet/15
```

This string indicates that the address you want is in the United States, California State, San Jose city, First Street, number 15.

JDBC URLs follow this same idea. To access Bob's Books, we might write the URL like this:

```
jdbc:derby://localhost:1521/BookSellerDB
```

The first part, `jdbc`, simply identifies that this is a JDBC URL (versus HTTP or something else). The second part indicates that driver vendor is `derby` driver. The third part indicates that the database is on the `localhost` of this machine (IP address 127.0.0.1), at port `1521`, and the final part indicates that we are interested in the `BookSellerDB` database.

Just like street addresses, the reason we need this string is because JDBC was designed to work with multiple databases at once. Each of the JDBC database drivers will have a different URL, so we need to be able to pass the JDBC URL string to the `DriverManager` and ensure that the `Connection` returned was for the intended database instance.

Unfortunately, other than a requirement that the JDBC URL begin with "jdbc," there is very little standard about a JDBC URL. Vendors may modify the URL to define characteristics for a particular driver implementation. The format of the JDBC URL is

```
jdbc:<subprotocol>:<subname>
```

In general, the subprotocol is the vendor name; for example:

```
jdbc:derby
jdbc:mysql
jdbc:oracle
```

e x a m

ⓦ a t c h   **There are two ways to establish a connection in JDBC. The first way is using one of the few concrete classes in the `java.sql` package, `DriverManager`. The `java.sql.DriverManager` class has been a part of the JDBC implementation since the beginning, and is the easiest way to obtain a connection from a Java SE application. The alternative way is with an instance of a class that implements `javax.sql.DataSource`, introduced in JDBC 2.0.**

Since a `DataSource` instance is typically obtained through a Java Naming and Directory Interface (JNDI) lookup, it is more often used in Java applications where there is a container that supports JNDI—for example, a Java EE application server. For the purposes of this chapter (and because `DataSource` is not on the exam), we'll focus on using `DriverManager` to obtain a connection, but in the end, both ways serve to give you an instance of a `Connection` object.

To summarize, `DriverManager` is on the exam and `DataSource` is not.

The subname field is where things get a bit more vendor specific. Some vendors use the subname to identify the hostname and port, followed by a database name. For example:

```
jdbc:derby://localhost:1521/MyDB
jdbc:mysql://localhost:3306/MyDB
```

Other vendors may use the subname to identify additional context information about the driver. For example:

```
jdbc:oracle:thin:@//localhost:1527/MyDB
```

In any case, it is best to consult the documentation for your specific database vendor's JDBC driver to determine the syntax of the URL.

JDBC Driver Implementation Versions

We talked about how the `DriverManager` will scan the classpath for JAR files that contain the `META-INF/services/java.sql.Driver` file and use a classloader to load those drivers. This feature was introduced in the JDBC 4.0 specification. Prior to that, JDBC drivers were loaded manually by the application.

If you are using a JDBC driver that is an earlier version, say, a JDBC 3.0 driver, then you must explicitly load the class provided by the database vendor that implements the `java.sql.Driver` interface. Typically, the database vendor's documentation would tell you what the driver class is. For example, if our Apache Derby JDBC driver were a 3.0 driver, you would manually load the `Driver` implementation class before calling the `getConnection()` method:

```
Class.forName("org.apache.derby.jdbc.ClientDriver");  // Class loads
                                                      // ClientDriver
try {
  Connection conn
    = DriverManager.getConnection(url, user, pwd);
```

Note that using the `Class.forName()` method is compatible with both JDBC 3.0 and JDBC 4.0 drivers. It is simply not needed when the driver supports 4.0.

Here is a quick summary of what we have discussed so far:

■ Before you can start working with JDBC, creating queries and getting results, you must first establish a connection.

■ In order to establish a connection, you must have a JDBC driver.

- If your JDBC driver is a JDBC 3.0 driver, then you are required to explicitly load the driver in your code using `Class.forName()` and the fully qualified path of the `Driver` implementation class.
- If your JDBC driver is a JDBC 4.0 driver, then simply include the driver (jar or zip) in the classpath.

Although the certification exam covers up through Java SE 8, the exam developers felt they ought to include some questions about obtaining a connection using both JDBC 3.0 and JDBC 4.0 drivers. So **keep in mind that for JDBC 3.0 drivers (and earlier), you are responsible for loading the class using the static `forName()` method from `java.lang.Class`.**

CERTIFICATION OBJECTIVE

Submit Queries and Read Results from the Database (OCP Objective 11.3)

11.3 Submit queries and read results from the database including creating statements, returning result sets, iterating through the results, and properly closing result sets, statements, and connections.

In this section, we'll explore the JDBC API in much greater detail. We will start by looking at a simple example using the `Connection`, `Statement`, and `ResultSet` interfaces to pull together what we've learned so far in this chapter. Then we'll do a deep dive into `Statements` and `ResultSets`.

All of Bob's Customers

Probably one of the most used SQL queries is SELECT * FROM <Table name>, which is used to print out or see all of the records in a table. Assume that we have a Java DB (Derby) database populated with data from Bob's Books. To query the database and return all of the Customers in the database, we would write something like the example shown next.

Note that to make the code listing a little shorter, going forward, we will use `out.println` instead of `System.out.println`. Just assume that means we have included a static import statement, like the one at the top of this example:

```
import static java.lang.System.*;   // Static import of the
                                     // System class methods.
                                     // Now we can use just 'out'
                                     // instead of System.out.
String url = "jdbc:derby://localhost:1521/BookSellerDB";
String user = "bookguy";
String pwd = "$3lleR";
try {
  Connection conn =
    DriverManager.getConnection(url, user, pwd);  // Get Connection
  Statement stmt = conn.createStatement();        // Create Statement
  String query = "SELECT * FROM Customer";
  ResultSet rs = stmt.executeQuery(query);        // Execute Query
  while (rs.next()) {                             // Process Results
    out.print(rs.getInt("CustomerID") + "  ");    // Print Columns
    out.print(rs.getString("FirstName") + "  ");
    out.print(rs.getString("LastName") + "  ");
    out.print(rs.getString("EMail") + "  ");
    out.println(rs.getString("Phone"));
  }
} catch (SQLException se) { }                      // Catch SQLException
```

Again, we'll dive into all of the parts of this example in greater detail, but here is what is happening:

- **Get connection** We are creating a `Connection` object instance using the information we need to access Bob's Books Database (stored on a Java DB Relational database, `BookSellerDB`, and accessed via the credentials "bookguy" with a password of "$3lleR").

- **Create statement** We are using the `Connection` to create a `Statement` object. The `Statement` object handles passing `String`s to the database as queries for the database to execute.

- **Execute query** We are executing the query string on the database and returning a `ResultSet` object.

- **Process results** We are iterating through the result set rows—each call to `next()` moves us to the next row of results.

- **Print columns** We are getting the values of the columns in the current result set row and printing them to standard out.

- **Catch SQLException** All of the JDBC API method invocations throw SQLException. A SQLException can be thrown when a method is used improperly or if the database is no longer responding. For example, a SQLException is thrown if the JDBC URL, username, or password is invalid. Or we attempted to query a table that does not exist. Or the database is no longer reachable because the network went down or the database went offline. We will look at SQLException in greater detail later in the chapter.

The output of the previous code will look something like this:

```
5000   John    Smith   John.Smith@comcast.net   555-340-1230
5001   Mary    Johnson   mary.johnson@comcast.net   555-123-4567
5002   Bob    Collins   bob.collins@yahoo.com   555-012-3456
5003   Rebecca   Mayer   rebecca.mayer@gmail.com   555-205-8212
5006   Anthony   Clark   anthony.clark@gmail.com   555-256-1901
5007   Judy   Sousa   judy.sousa@verizon.net   555-751-1207
5008   Christopher   Patriquin   patriquinc@yahoo.com   555-316-1803
5009   Deborah   Smith   debsmith@comcast.net   555-256-3421
5010   Jennifer   McGinn   jmcginn@comcast.net   555-250-0918
```

We'll take a detailed look at the Statement and ResultSet interfaces and methods in the next two sections.

Statements

Once we have successfully connected to a database, the fun can really start. From a Connection object, we can create an instance of a Statement object (or, to be precise, using the Connection instance we received from the DriverManager, we can get an instance of an object that implements the Statement interface). For example:

```
String url = "jdbc:derby://localhost:1521/BookSellerDB";
String user = "bookguy";
String pwd = "$3lleR";
try {
  Connection conn = DriverManager.getConnection(url, user, pwd);
  Statement stmt = conn.createStatement();
  // do stuff with SQL statements
} catch (SQLException se) { }
```

The primary purpose of a `Statement` is to execute a SQL statement using a method and return some type of result. There are several forms of `Statement` methods: those that return a result set, and those that return an integer status. The most commonly used `Statement` method performs a SQL query that returns some data, like the SELECT call we used earlier to fetch all the `Customer` table rows.

Constructing and Using Statements

To start, let's look at the base `Statement`, which is used to execute a static SQL query and return a result. You'll recall that we get a `Statement` from a `Connection` and then use the `Statement` object to execute a SQL statement, like a query on the database. For example:

```
Connection conn = DriverManager.getConnection(url, user, pwd);
Statement stmt = conn.createStatement();
ResultSet rs = stmt.executeQuery("SELECT * FROM Customer");
```

Because not all SQL statements return results, the `Statement` object provides several different methods to execute SQL commands. Some SQL commands do not return a result set, but instead return an integer status. For example, SQL INSERT, UPDATE, and DELETE commands, or any of the SQL Data Definition Language (DDL) statements like CREATE TABLE, return either the number of rows affected by the query or 0.

Let's look at each of the execute methods in detail.

public ResultSet executeQuery(String sql) throws SQLException   This is
the most commonly executed `Statement` method. This method is used when we know that we want to return results—we are querying the database for one or more rows of data. For example:

```
ResultSet rs = stmt.executeQuery("SELECT * from Customer");
```

Assuming there is data in the `Customer` table, this statement should return all of the rows from the `Customer` table into a `ResultSet` object—we'll look at `ResultSet` in the next section. Notice that the method declaration includes "throws SQLException." This means that this method must be called in a `try-catch` block or must be called in a method that also throws `SQLException`. Again, one reason that these methods all throw `SQLException` is that a connection to the database is likely **to a database on a network**. As with all things on the network, availability is not guaranteed, so one possible reason for `SQLException` is the lack of availability of the database itself.

public int executeUpdate(String sql) throws SQLException   This method is used for a SQL operation that affects one or more rows and does not return results—for example, SQL INSERT, UPDATE, DELETE, and DDL queries. These statements do not return results, but do return a count of the number of rows affected by the SQL query. For example, here is an example method invocation where we want to update the Book table, increasing the price of every book that is currently priced less than 8.95 and is a hardcover book:

```
String q = "UPDATE Book SET UnitPrice=8.95
          WHERE UnitPrice < 8.95 AND Format='Hardcover'";
int numRows = stmt.executeUpdate(q);
```

When this query executes, we are expecting some number of rows will be affected. The integer that returns is the number of rows that were updated.

Note that this `Statement` method can also be used to execute SQL queries that do not return a row count, such as CREATE TABLE or DROP TABLE and other DDL queries. For DDL queries, the return value is 0.

public boolean execute(String sql) throws SQLException   This method is used when you are not sure what the result will be—perhaps the query will return a result set and perhaps not. This method can be used to execute a query whose type may not be known until runtime—for example, one constructed in code. The return value is true if the query resulted in a result set and false if the query resulted in an update count or no results.

However, more often, this method is used when invoking a stored procedure (using the `CallableStatement`, which we'll talk about later in the chapter). A stored procedure can return a single result set or row count, or multiple result sets and row counts, so this method was designed to handle what happens when a single database invocation produces more than one result set or row count.

You might also use this method if you wrote an application to test queries—something that reads a `String` from the command line and then runs that `String` against the database as a query. For example:

```
ResultSet rs;
int numRows;
boolean status = stmt.execute("");   // True if there is a ResultSet
if (status) {                        // True
  rs = stmt.getResultSet();          // Get the ResultSet
  // Process the result set...
} else {                             // False
  numRows = stmt.getUpdateCount();   // Get the update count
  if (numRows == -1) {               // If -1, there are no results
    out.println("No results");
```

```
    } else {                              // else, print the number of
                                          // rows affected
      out.println(numRows + " rows affected.");
    }
  }
```

Because this statement may return a result set or may simply return an integer row count, there are two additional statement commands you can use to get the results or the count based on whether the execute() method returned true (there is a result set) or false (there is an update count or there was no result). The getResultSet() is used to retrieve results when the execute() method returns true, and the getUpdateCount() is used to retrieve the count when the execute() method returns false. Let's look at these methods next.

on the job

It is generally a very bad idea to allow a user to enter a query string directly in an input field or allow a user to pass a string to construct a query directly. The reason is that if a user can construct a query or even include a freeform string into a query, he or she can use the query to return more data than you intended or alter the database table permissions.

For example, assume that we have a query where the user enters his e-mail address and the string the user enters is inserted directly to the query:

```
String s = System.console().readLine("Enter your e-mail address: ");
ResultSet rs = stmt.executeQuery("SELECT * FROM Customer
                                WHERE EMail='" + s + "'");
```

The user of this code could enter a string like this:

```
tom@trouble.com' OR 'x'='x
```

The resulting query executed by the database becomes:

```
SELECT * FROM Customer WHERE Email='tom@trouble.com' OR 'x'='x'
```

Because the OR statement will always return true*, the result is that the query will return ALL of the customer rows, effectively the same as the query:*

```
SELECT * FROM Customer
```

And now this user of your code has a list of the e-mail addresses of every customer in the database.

This type of attack is called a SQL injection attack. It is easy to prevent by carefully sanitizing any string input used in a query to the database and/ or by using one of the other Statement *types:* PreparedStatement *and* CallableStatement. *Despite how easy it is to prevent, it happens frequently, even to large, experienced companies like Yahoo!*

public ResultSet getResultSet() throws SQLException   If the boolean value from the `execute()` method returns true, then there is a result set. To get the result set, as shown earlier, call the `getResultSet()` method on the `Statement` object. Then you can process the `ResultSet` object (which we will cover in the next section). This method is basically foolproof—if, in fact, there are no results, the method will return a null.

```
ResultSet rs = stmt.getResultSet();
```

public int getUpdateCount() throws SQLException   If the boolean value from the `execute()` method returns false, then there is a row count, and this method will return the number of rows affected. A return value of −1 indicates that there are no results.

```
int numRows = stmt.getUpdateCount();
if (numRows == -1) {
  out.println("No results");
} else {
  out.println(numRows + " rows affected.");
}
```

Table 12-7 summarizes the `Statement` methods we just covered.

TABLE 12-7   Important `Statement` Methods

Method (Each Throws SQLException)	Description
`ResultSet executeQuery(String sql)`	Execute a SQL query and return a `ResultSet` object, i.e., SELECT commands.
`int executeUpdate(String sql)`	Execute a SQL query that will only modify a number of rows, i.e. INSERT, DELETE, or UPDATE commands.
`boolean execute(String sql)`	Execute a SQL query that may return a result set OR modify a number of rows (or do neither). The method will return true if there is a result set or false if there may be a row count of affected rows.
`ResultSet getResultSet()`	If the return value from the `execute()` method was true, you can use this method to retrieve the result set from the query.
`int getUpdateCount()`	If the return value from the `execute()` method was false, you can use this method to get the number of rows affected by the SQL command.

ResultSets

When a query returns a result set, an instance of a class that implements the ResultSet interface is returned. The `ResultSet` object represents the results of the query—all of the data in each row on a per-column basis. Again, as a reminder, *how* data in a `ResultSet` are stored is entirely up to the JDBC driver vendor. It is possible that the JDBC driver caches the entire set of results in memory all at once, or that it uses internal buffers and gets only a few rows at a time. From your point of view as the user of the data, it really doesn't matter much. Using the methods defined in the `ResultSet` interface, you can read and manipulate the data and that's all that matters.

One important thing to keep in mind is that a `ResultSet` is a *copy* of the data from the database from the instance in time when the query was executed. Unless you are the only person using the database, you need to always assume that the underlying database table or tables that the `ResultSet` came from could be changed by some other user or application.

Because `ResultSet` is such a comprehensive part of the JDBC API, we are going to tackle it in sections. Table 12-8 summarizes each section so you can reference these later.

TABLE 12-8   `ResultSet` Sections

Section Title	Description
"Moving Forward in a ResultSet"	How to access each "row" of the result of a query.
"Reading Data from a ResultSet"	How to use `ResultSet` methods to access the individual columns of each "row" in the result set.
"Getting Information about a ResultSet"	How to use a `ResultSetMetaData` object to retrieve information about the result set: the number of columns returned in the results, the names of each column, and the Java type of each column.
"Printing a Report"	How to use the `ResultSetMetaData` methods to print a nicely formatted set of results to the console.
"Moving Around in ResultSets"	How to change the cursor type and concurrency settings on a `Statement` object to create a `ResultSet` that allows the row cursor to be positioned and allows the data to be modified.
"Updating ResultSets"	How to use the concurrency settings on a `Statement` object to create a `ResultSet` that allows you to update the results returned and later synchronize those results with the database.
"Inserting New Rows into a ResultSet"	How to manipulate a `ResultSet` further by deleting and inserting rows.
"Getting Information about a Database Using DatabaseMetaData"	How to use the `DatabaseMetaData` object to retrieve information about a database.

Moving Forward in a ResultSet

The best way to think of a `ResultSet` object is visually. Assume that in our BookSellerDB database we have several customers whose last name begins with the letter "C." We could create a query to return those rows "like" this:

```
String query = "SELECT FirstName, LastName, EMail from Customer
                WHERE LastName LIKE 'C%'";
```

The SQL operator LIKE treats the string that follows as a pattern to match, where the `%` indicates a wildcard. So, `LastName LIKE 'C%'` means "any LastName with a C, followed by any other character(s)."

When we execute this query using the `executeQuery()` method, the `ResultSet` returned will contain the `FirstName`, `LastName`, and `EMail` columns where the customer's `LastName` starts with the capital letter "C":

```
ResultSet rs = stmt.executeQuery (query);
```

The `ResultSet` object returned contains the data from the query as shown in Figure 12-4.

Note in Figure 12-4 that the `ResultSet` object maintains a cursor, or a pointer, to the current row of the results. When the `ResultSet` object is first returned from the query, the cursor is not yet pointing to a row of results—the cursor is pointing above the first row. In order to get the results of the table, you must always

| FIGURE 12-4 | A `ResultSet` after the `executeQuery` |

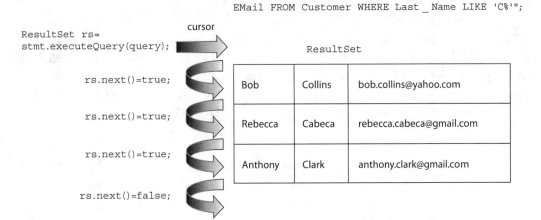

```
String query = "SELECT First _ Name, Last _ Name,
EMail FROM Customer WHERE Last _ Name LIKE 'C%'";
```

ResultSet rs=
stmt.executeQuery(query);

cursor

ResultSet

rs.next()=true;

| Bob | Collins | bob.collins@yahoo.com |

rs.next()=true;

| Rebecca | Cabeca | rebecca.cabeca@gmail.com |

rs.next()=true;

| Anthony | Clark | anthony.clark@gmail.com |

rs.next()=false;

call the next() method on the ResultSet object to move the cursor forward to the first row of data. By default, a ResultSet object is read-only (the data in the rows cannot be updated), and you can only move the cursor forward. We'll look at how to change this behavior a little later on.

So the first method you will need to know for ResultSet is the next() method.

public boolean next()   The next() method moves the cursor forward one row and returns true if the cursor now points to a row of data in the ResultSet. If the cursor points beyond the last row of data as a result of the next() method (or if the ResultSet contains no rows), the return value is false.

So in order to read the three rows of data in the table shown in Figure 12-4, we need to call the next() method, read the row of data, and then call next() again twice more. When the next() method is invoked the fourth time, the method will return false. The easiest way to read all of the rows from first to last is in a while loop:

```
String query = "SELECT FirstName, LastName, EMail FROM Customer
                WHERE LastName LIKE 'C%'";
ResultSet rs = stmt.executeQuery(query);
while (rs.next()) {  // Move the cursor from the current position
                     // to the next row of data - return true if the
                     // next row is valid data and false if the
                     // cursor has moved past the last row
    // ...
}
```

exam
ⓦatch   *Because the cursor is such a fundamental concept in JDBC, the exam will test you on the status of the cursor in a ResultSet. As long as you keep in mind that you must call the next() method*

before processing even one row of data in a ResultSet, then you'll be fine. Maybe you could use a memory device like this one: "When getting results, don't vex, always call next!" Okay, maybe not.

Reading Data from a ResultSet

Moving the cursor forward through the ResultSet is just the start of reading data from the results of the query. Let's look at the two ways to get the data from each row in a result set.

When a `ResultSet` is returned and you have dutifully called `next()` to move the cursor to the first actual row of data, you can now read the data in each column of the current row. As illustrated in Figure 12-4, a result set from a database query is like a table or a spreadsheet. Each row contains (typically) one or more columns, and the data in each column is one of the SQL data types. In order to bring the data from each column into your Java application, you must use a `ResultSet` method to retrieve each of the SQL column values into an appropriate Java type. So SQL INTEGER, for example, can be read as a Java int primitive, SQL VARCHAR can be read as a Java String, SQL DATE can be read as a `java.sql.Date` object, and so on. `ResultSet` defines several other types as well, but whether or not the database or the driver supports all of the types defined by the specification depends on the database vendor. For the exam, we recommend you focus on the most common SQL data types and the `ResultSet` methods shown in Table 12-9.

SQL has been around for a long time. The first formalized American National Standards Institute (ANSI)–approved version was adopted in 1986 (SQL-86). The next major revision was in 1992, SQL-92, which is widely considered the "base" release for every database. SQL-92 defined a number of new data types, including DATE, TIME, TIMESTAMP, BIT, and VARCHAR strings. SQL-92 has multiple levels; each level adds a bit more functionality to the previous level. JDBC drivers recognize three ANSI SQL-92 levels: Entry, Intermediate, and Full.

SQL-1999, also known as SQL-3, added LARGE OBJECT types, including BINARY LARGE OBJECT (BLOB) and CHARACTER LARGE OBJECT (CLOB). SQL-1999 also introduced the BOOLEAN type and a composite type, ARRAY and ROW, to store collections directly into the database. In addition, SQL-1999 added a number of features to SQL, including triggers, regular expressions, and procedural and flow control.

SQL-2003 introduced XML to the database, and importantly, added columns with auto-generated values, including columns that support identity, like the primary key and foreign key columns. Believe it or not, other standards have been proposed, including SQL-2006, SQL-2008, and SQL-2011.

The reason this matters is because the JDBC specification has attempted to be consistent with features from the most widely adopted specification at the time. Thus, JDBC 3.0 supports SQL-92 and a part of the SQL-1999 specification, and JDBC 4.0 supports parts of the SQL-2003 specification. In this chapter, we'll try to stick to the most widely used SQL-92 features and the most commonly supported SQL-1999 features that JDBC also supports.

One way to read the column data is by using the names of the columns themselves as string values. For example, using the column names from Bob's

Book table (Table 12-4), in these `ResultSet` methods, the `String` name of the column from the Book table is passed to the method to read the column data type:

```
String query = "SELECT Title, PubDate, Price FROM Book";
ResultSet rs = stmt.executeQuery(query);
while (rs.next()) {
    String title = rs.getString("Title");    // Read the data in the
                                             // column named "Title"
                                             // into a String
    Date PubDate = rs.getDate("PubDate");    // Read the data in the
                                             // "PubDate" column into
                                             // a java.sql.Date object
    float price = rs.getFloat("Price");      // Read the data in the
                                             // column "Price"
                                             // into a float
    // ....
}
```

Note that although here the column names were retrieved from the `ResultSet` row in the order they were requested in the SQL query, they could have been processed in any order.

`ResultSet` also provides an overloaded method that takes an integer index value for each of the SQL types. This value is the integer position of the column in the result set, numbered from 1 to the number of columns returned. So we could write the same statements earlier like this:

```
String title = rs.getString(1); // Title is first column
Date PubDate = rs.getDate(2);   // PubDate is second column
float price = rs.getFloat(3);   // Price is third column
```

Using the positional methods shown earlier, the order of the column in the `ResultSet` does matter. In our query, Title is in position 1, PubDate is in position 2, and Price is in position 3.

exam

ⓦatch

Remember: Column indexes start with 1.

It is important to keep in mind that when you are accessing columns using integer index values, the column indexes always start with 1, not 0 as in traditional arrays. If you attempt to access a column with an index of less than 1 or greater than the number of columns returned, a `SQLException` will be thrown. You can get the number of columns returned in a `ResultSet` through the result set's metadata object. See the section on `ResultSetMetaData` to learn more.

What the database stores as a type, the SQL type, and what JDBC returns as a type are often two different things. It is important to understand that the JDBC specification provides a set of standard mappings—the best match between what the database provides as a type and the Java type a programmer should use with that type. Rather than repeating what is in the specification, we encourage you to look at Appendix B of the JDBC (JSR-221) specification.

The most commonly used `ResultSet` get methods are listed next. Let's look at these methods in detail.

public boolean getBoolean(String columnLabel)   This method retrieves the value of the named column in the `ResultSet` as a Java boolean. Boolean values are rarely returned in SQL queries, and some databases may not support a SQL BOOLEAN type, so check with your database vendor. In this contrived example here, we are returning employment status:

```
if (rs.getBoolean("CURR_EMPLOYEE")) {
    // Now process the remaining columns
}
```

public double getDouble(String columnLabel)   This method retrieves the value of the column as a Java double. This method is recommended for returning the value stored in the database as SQL DOUBLE and SQL FLOAT types.

```
double cartTotal = rs.getDouble("CartTotal");
```

public int getInt(String columnLabel)   This method retrieves the value of the column as a Java int. Integers are often a good choice for primary keys. This method is recommended for returning values stored in the database as SQL INTEGER types.

```
int authorID = rs.getInt("AuthorID");
```

public float getFloat(String columnLabel)   This method retrieves the value of the column as a Java float. It is recommended for SQL REAL types.

```
float price = rs.getFloat("UnitPrice");
```

public long getLong(String columnLabel)   This method retrieves the value of the column as a Java long. It is recommended for SQL BIGINT types.

```
long socialSecurityNumber = rs.get("SocSecNum");
```

public java.sql.Date getDate(String columnLabel) This method retrieves the value of the column as a Java `Date` object. Note that `java.sql.Date` extends `java.util.Date`. One difference between the two is that the `toString()` method of `java.sql.Date` returns a date string in the form: "yyyy mm dd." This method is recommended for SQL DATE types.

```
java.sql.Date pubDate = rs.getDate("PubDate");
```

public java.lang.String getString(String columnLabel) This method retrieves the value of the column as a Java `String` object. It is good for reading SQL columns with CHAR, VARCHAR, and LONGVARCHAR types.

```
String lastName = rs.getString("LastName");
```

public java.sql.Time getTime(String columnLabel) This method retrieves the value of the column as a Java `Time` object. Like `java.sql.Date`, this class extends `java.util.Date`, and its `toString()` method returns a time string in the form: "hh:mm:ss." TIME is the SQL type that this method is designed to read.

```
java.sql.Time time = rs.getTime("FinishTime");
```

public java.sql.Timestamp getTimestamp(String columnLabel) This method retrieves the value of the column as a `Timestamp` object. Its `toString()` method formats the result in the form: yyyy-mm-dd hh:mm:ss.fffffffff, where fffffffff is nanoseconds. This method is recommended for reading SQL TIMESTAMP types.

```
java.sql.Timestamp timestamp = rs.getTimestamp("ClockInTime");
```

public java.lang.Object getObject(String columnLabel) This method retrieves the value of the column as a Java `Object`. It can be used as a general-purpose method for reading data in a column. This method works by reading the value returned as the appropriate Java wrapper class for the type and returning that as a Java `Object` object. So, for example, reading an integer (SQL INTEGER type) using this method returns an object that is a `java.lang.Integer` type. We can use `instanceof` to check for an `Integer` and get the int value:

```
Object o = rs.getObject("AuthorID");
if (o instanceof java.lang.Integer) {
    int id = ((Integer)o).intValue();
}
```

TABLE 12-9	SQL Types and JDBC Types	

SQL Type	Java Type	ResultSet get methods
BOOLEAN	boolean	getBoolean(String columnName) getBoolean(int columnIndex)
INTEGER	int	getInt(String columnName) getInt(int columnIndex)
DOUBLE, FLOAT	double	getDouble(String columnName) getDouble(int columnIndex)
REAL	float	getFloat(String columnName) getFloat(int columnIndex)
BIGINT	long	getLong(String columnName) getLong(int columnIndex)
CHAR, VARCHAR, LONGVARCHAR	String	getString(String columnName) getString(int columnIndex)
DATE	java.sql.Date	getDate(String columnName) getDate(int columnIndex)
TIME	java.sql.Time	getTime(String columnName) getTime(int columnIndex)
TIMESTAMP	java.sql.Timestamp	getTimestamp(String columnName) getTimestamp(int columnIndex)
Any of the above	java.lang.Object	getObject(String columnName) getObject(int columnIndex)

Table 12-9 lists the most commonly used methods to retrieve specific data from a `ResultSet`. For the complete and exhaustive set of `ResultSet` get methods, see the Java documentation for `java.sql.ResultSet`.

ⓦatch *The exam is not going to test your knowledge of all of the `ResultSet` `get` and `set` methods for SQL types. For the exam, just remember the basic Java types: `String` and `int`. Each `ResultSet` getter method is named by its closest Java type, so,*

for example, to read a database column that holds an integer into a Java `int` type, you invoke the `getInt()` method with either the `String` column or the column index of the column you wish to read.

Getting Information about a ResultSet

When you write a query using a string, as we have in the examples so far, you know the name and type of the columns returned. However, what happens when you want to allow your users to dynamically construct the query? You may not always know in advance how many columns are returned and the type and name of the columns returned.

Fortunately, the ResultSetMetaData class was designed to provide just that information. Using ResultSetMetaData, you can get important information about the results returned from the query, including the number of columns, the table name, the column name, and the column class name—the Java class that is used to represent this column when the column is returned as an Object. Here is a simple example, and then we'll look at these methods in more detail:

```
String query = "SELECT AuthorID FROM Author";
ResultSet rs = stmt.executeQuery(query);
ResultSetMetaData rsmd = rs.getMetaData();
rs.next();
int colCount = rsmd.getColumnCount();   // How many columns in this
                                        // ResultSet?
out.println("Column Count: " + colCount);
for (int i = 1; i <= colCount; i++) {
  out.println("Table Name:   " + rsmd.getTableName(i));
  out.println("Column Name:  " + rsmd.getColumnName(i));
  out.println("Column Size:  " + rsmd.getColumnDisplaySize(i));
}
```

Running this code using the BookSeller database (Bob's Books) produces the following output:

```
Column Count: 1
Table Name:    AUTHOR
Column Name:   AUTHORID
Column Size:   11
```

ResultSetMetaData is often used to generate reports, so here are the most commonly used methods. For more information and more methods, check out the JavaDocs.

public int getColumnCount() throws SQLException   This method is probably the most used ResultSetMetaData method. It returns the integer count of the number of columns returned by the query. With this method, you can iterate through the columns to get information about each column.

```
try {
  conn = DriverManager.getConnection(...);
  stmt = conn.createStatement();
  String query = "SELECT * FROM Author";
```

```
        ResultSet rs = stmt.executeQuery(query);
        ResultSetMetaData rsmd = rs.getMetaData(); // Get the meta data
                                                   // for this ResultSet
        int columnCount = rsmd.getColumnCount();   // Get the number
                                                   // of columns in this
        ...                                        // ResultSet
    } catch (SQLException se) { }
```

The value of `columnCount` for the `Author` table is 3. We can use this value to iterate through the columns using the methods illustrated next.

public String getColumnName(int column) throws SQLException   This method returns the `String` name of this column. Using the `columnCount`, we can create an output of the data from the database in a report-like format. For example:

```
String colData;
ResultSet rs = stmt.executeQuery(query);
ResultSetMetaData rsmd = rs.getMetaData();
int cols = rsmd.getColumnCount();
for (int i = 1; i <= cols; i++) {
  out.print(rsmd.getColumnName(i)+ " ");       // Print each column name
}
out.println();
while (rs.next()) {
  for (int i = 1; i <= cols; i++) {
    if (rs.getObject(i) != null) {
      colData = rs.getObject(i).toString();    // Get the String value
                                               // of the column object
    } else {
      colData = "NULL";                        // or NULL for a null
    }
    out.print(colData);                        // Print the column data
  }
  out.println();
}
```

This example is somewhat rudimentary, as we probably need to do some better formatting on the data, but it will produce a table of output:

```
AUTHORID FIRSTNAME LASTNAME
1000 Rick Riordan
1001 Nancy Farmer
1002 Ally Condie
1003 Cressida Cowell
1004 Lauren St. John
1005 Eoin Colfer
...
```

public String getTableName(int column) throws SQLException   The method returns the `String` name of the table that this column belongs to. This method is useful when the query is a join of two or more tables and we need to know which table a column came from. For example, suppose that we want to get a list of books by author's last name:

```
String query = "SELECT Author.LastName, Book.Title
                FROM Author, Book, Books_By_Author
                WHERE Author.AuthorID = Books_By_Author.AuthorID
                AND Book.isbn = Books_By_Author.isbn"
```

With a query like this, we might want to know which table the column data came from:

```
ResultSetMetaData rsmd = rs.getMetaData();
int cols = rsmd.getColumnCount();
for (int i = 1; i <= cols; i++) {
  out.print(rsmd.getTableName(i) + ":" +
                    rsmd.getColumnName(i) + " ");
}
```

This code will print the name of the table, a colon, and the column name. The output might look something like this:

```
AUTHOR:LASTNAME BOOK:TITLE
```

public int getColumnDisplaySize(int column) throws SQLException   This method returns an integer of the size of the column. This information is useful for determining the maximum number of characters a column can hold (if it is a VARCHAR type) and the spacing that is required between columns for a report.

Printing a Report

To make a prettier report than the one in the `getColumnName` method earlier, for example, we could use the display size to pad the column name and data with spaces. What we want is a table with spaces between the columns and headings that looks something like this when we query the Author table:

```
AUTHORID    FIRSTNAME            LASTNAME
1000        Rick                 Riordan
1001        Nancy                Farmer
1002        Ally                 Condie
1003        Cressida             Cowell
1004        Lauren               St. John
1005        Eoin                 Colfer
...
```

Using the methods we have discussed so far, here is code that produces a pretty report from a query:

```
ResultSet rs = stmt.executeQuery(query);
ResultSetMetaData rsmd = rs.getMetaData();
int cols = rsmd.getColumnCount();
String col, colData;
for (int i = 1; i <= cols; i++) {
  col = leftJustify(rsmd.getColumnName(i),          // Left justify
                    rsmd.getColumnDisplaySize(i));  // column name
  out.print(col);                                   // padded with
}                                                   // size spaces
out.println(); // Print a linefeed
while (rs.next()) {
  for (int i = 1; i <= cols; i++) {
    if (rs.getObject(i) != null) {
      colData = rs.getObject(i).toString(); // Get the data in the
                                            // column as a String
    } else {
      colData = "NULL";                     // If the column is null
                                            // use "NULL"
    }
    col = leftJustify(colData,
                      rsmd.getColumnDisplaySize(i)));
    out.print(col);
  }
  out.println();
}
```

A couple of things to note about the example code: first, the `leftJustify` method, which takes a string to print left-justified and an integer for the total number of characters in the string. The difference between the actual string length and the integer value will be filled with spaces. This method uses the `String` `format()` method and the "-" (dash) flag to return a `String` that is left-justified with spaces. The `%1$` part indicates the flag should be applied to the first argument. What we are building is a format string dynamically. If the column display size is 20, the format string will be `%1$-20s`, which says "print the argument passed (the first argument) on the left with a width of 20 and use a string conversion."

Note that if the length of the string passed in and the integer field length (n) are the same, we add one space to the length to make it look pretty:

```
public static String leftJustify(String s, int n) {
  if (s.length() <= n) n++;  // Add an extra space if the length of
                             // the String s is less than or equal to
                             // the length of the column n
  return String.format("%1$-" + n + "s", s);  // Pad to the right of
                                              // the String by n
                                              // spaces
}
```

Second, databases can store NULL values. If the value of a column is NULL, the object returned in the `rs.getObject()` method is a Java null. So we have to test for null to avoid getting a null pointer exception when we execute the `toString()` method.

Notice that we don't have to use the `next()` method before reading the `ResultSetMetaData`—we can do that at any time after obtaining a valid result set. Running this code and passing it a query like "SELECT * FROM Author" returns a neatly printed set of authors:

```
AUTHORID    FIRSTNAME          LASTNAME
1000        Rick               Riordan
1001        Nancy              Farmer
1002        Ally               Condie
1003        Cressida           Cowell
1004        Lauren             St. John
1005        Eoin               Colfer
...
```

Moving Around in ResultSets

So far, for all the result sets we looked at, we simply moved the cursor forward by calling `next()`. The default characteristics of a `Statement` are cursors that only move forward and result sets that do not support changes. The `ResultSet` interface actually defines these characteristics as static int variables: TYPE_FORWARD_ONLY and CONCUR_READ_ONLY. However, the JDBC specification defines additional static `int` types (shown next) that allow a developer to move the cursor forward, backward, and to a specific position in the result set. In addition, the result set can be modified while open and the changes written to the database. Note that support for cursor movement and updatable result sets is not a requirement on a driver, but most drivers provide this capability. In order to create a result set that uses positionable cursors and/or supports updates, you must create a `Statement` with the appropriate scroll type and concurrency setting, and then use that `Statement` to create the `ResultSet` object.

The ability to move the cursor to a particular position is the key to being able to determine how many rows are returned from a result set—something we will look at shortly. The ability to modify an open result set may seem odd, particularly if you are a seasoned database developer. After all, isn't that what a SQL UPDATE command is for?

Consider a situation in which you want to perform a series of calculations using the data from the result set rows, then write a change to each row based on some criteria, and finally write the data back to the database. For example, imagine a database table that contains customer data, including the date they joined as a customer, their purchase history, and the total number of orders in the last two months. After reading this data into a result set, you could iterate over each customer record and modify it based on business rules: set their minimum discount higher if they have been a customer for more than a year with at least one purchase per year or set their preferred credit status if they have been purchasing more than $100 per month. With an updatable result set, you can modify several customer rows, each in a different way, and commit the rows to the database without having to write a complex SQL query or a set of SQL queries—you simply commit the updates on the open result set.

Let's look at how to modify a result set in more detail. There are three `ResultSet` cursor types:

- **TYPE_FORWARD_ONLY**   The default value for a `ResultSet`—the cursor moves forward only through a set of results.

- **TYPE_SCROLL_INSENSITIVE**   A cursor position can be moved in the result forward or backward, or positioned to a particular cursor location. Any changes made to the underlying data—the database itself—are not reflected in the result set. In other words, the result set does not have to "keep state" with the database. This type is generally supported by databases.

- **TYPE_SCROLL_SENSITIVE**   A cursor can be moved in the results forward or backward, or positioned to a particular cursor location. Any changes made to the underlying data are reflected in the open result set. As you can imagine, this is difficult to implement and is, therefore, not implemented in a database or JDBC driver very often.

JDBC provides two options for data concurrency with a result set:

- **CONCUR_READ_ONLY**   This is the default value for result set concurrency. Any open result set is read-only and cannot be modified or changed.

- **CONCUR_UPDATABLE**   A result set can be modified through the `ResultSet` methods while the result set is open.

Because a database and JDBC driver are not required to support cursor movement and concurrent updates, the JDBC provides methods to query the database and driver using the DatabaseMetaData object to determine if your driver supports these capabilities. For example:

```
Connection conn = DriverManager.getConnection(...);
DatabaseMetaData dbmd = conn.getMetaData();
if (dbmd.supportsResultSetType(ResultSet.TYPE_FORWARD_ONLY)) {
  out.print("Supports TYPE_FORWARD_ONLY");
  if (dbmd.supportsResultSetConcurrency(
      ResultSet.TYPE_FORWARD_ONLY,
      ResultSet.CONCUR_UPDATABLE)) {
    out.println(" and supports CONCUR_UPDATABLE");
  }
}

if (dbmd.supportsResultSetType(ResultSet.TYPE_SCROLL_INSENSITIVE)) {
  out.print("Supports TYPE_SCROLL_INSENSITIVE");
  if (dbmd.supportsResultSetConcurrency(
      ResultSet.TYPE_SCROLL_INSENSITIVE,
      ResultSet.CONCUR_UPDATABLE)) {
    out.println(" and supports CONCUR_UPDATABLE");
  }
}
if (dbmd.supportsResultSetType(ResultSet.TYPE_SCROLL_SENSITIVE)) {
  out.print("Supports TYPE_SCROLL_SENSITIVE");
  if (dbmd.supportsResultSetConcurrency(
      ResultSet.TYPE_SCROLL_SENSITIVE,
      ResultSet.CONCUR_UPDATABLE)) {
    out.println("Supports CONCUR_UPDATABLE");
  }
}
```

Running this code on the Java DB (Derby) database, these are the results:

```
Supports TYPE_FORWARD_ONLY and supports CONCUR_UPDATABLE
Supports TYPE_SCROLL_INSENSITIVE and supports CONCUR_UPDATABLE
```

In order to create a ResultSet with TYPE_SCROLL_INSENSITIVE and CONCUR_UPDATABLE, the Statement used to create the ResultSet must be created (from the Connection) with the cursor type and concurrency you want. You can determine what cursor type and concurrency the Statement was created with, but once created, you can't change the cursor type or concurrency of an existing Statement object. Also, note that just because you set a cursor type or concurrency setting, that doesn't mean you will get those settings. As you will see in the section on exceptions, the driver can determine that the database doesn't support one or both of the settings you chose and it will throw a warning and (silently) revert to its default settings, if they are not supported. You will see how to detect these JDBC warnings in the section on exceptions and warnings.

```
Connection conn = DriverManager.getConnection(...);
Statement stmt =
  conn.createStatement(ResultSet.TYPE_SCROLL_INSENSITIVE,
                       ResultSet.CONCUR_UPDATABLE);
```

Besides being able to use a `ResultSet` object to update results, which we'll look at next, being able to manipulate the cursor provides a side benefit—we can use the cursor to determine the number of rows returned in a query. Although it would seem like there ought to be a method in `ResultSet` or `ResultSetMetaData` to do this, this method does not exist.

In general, you should not need to know how many rows are returned, but during debugging, you may want to diagnose your queries with a stand-alone database and use cursor movement to read the number of rows returned.

Something like this would work:

```
ResultSet rs = stmt.executeQuery(query);  // Get a ResultSet
if (rs.last()) {                          // Move the very last row
    int rowCount = rs.getRow();           // Get row number (the count)
    rs.beforeFirst();                     // Move to before the 1st row
}
```

Of course, you may also want to have a more sophisticated method that preserves the current cursor position and returns the cursor to that position, regardless of when the method was called. Before we look at that code, let's look at the other cursor movement methods and test methods (besides `next`) in `ResultSet`. As a quick summary, Table 12-10 lists the methods you use to change the cursor position in a `ResultSet`.

Let's look at each of these methods in more detail.

public boolean absolute(int row) throws SQLException This method positions the cursor to an absolute row number. The contrasting method is relative. Passing 0 as the row argument positions the cursor to before the first row. Passing a negative value, like -1, positions the cursor to the position after the last row minus one—in other words, the last row. If you attempt to position the cursor beyond the last row, say at position 22 in a 19-row result set, the cursor will be positioned beyond the last row, the implications of which we'll discuss next. Figure 12-5 illustrates how invocations of `absolute()` position the cursor.

TABLE 12-10	`ResultSet` Cursor Positioning Methods

Method	Effect on the Cursor and Return Value
`boolean next()`	Moves the cursor to the next row in the `ResultSet`. Returns `false` if the cursor is positioned beyond the last row.
`boolean previous()`	Moves the cursor backward one row. Returns `false` if the cursor is positioned before the first row.
`boolean absolute(int row)`	Moves the cursor to an absolute position in the `ResultSet`. Rows are numbered from 1. Moving to row 0 moves the cursor to before the first row. Moving to negative row numbers starts from the last row and works backward. Returns `false` if the cursor is positioned beyond the last row or before the first row.
`boolean relative(int row)`	Moves the cursor to a position relative to the current position. Invoking `relative(1)` moves forward one row; invoking `relative(-1)` moves backward one row. Returns `false` if the cursor is positioned beyond the last row or before the first row.
`boolean first()`	Moves the cursor to the first row in the `ResultSet`. Returns `false` if there are no rows in the `ResultSet` (empty result set).
`boolean last()`	Moves the cursor to the last row in the `ResultSet`. Returns `false` if there are no rows in the `ResultSet` (empty result set).
`void beforeFirst()`	Moves the cursor to before the first row in the `ResultSet`.
`void afterLast()`	Moves the cursor to after the last row in the `ResultSet`.

FIGURE 12-5	

Absolute cursor
positioning

```
String query = "SELECT * FROM Author";
```

The `absolute()` method returns `true` if the cursor was successfully positioned within the `ResultSet` and `false` if the cursor ended up before the first or after the last row. For example, suppose you wanted to process only every other row:

```
ResultSet rs = stmt.executeQuery(query);
for (int i = 1; ; i += 2) {
  if (rs.absolute(i)) {  // The absolute method moves to the row
                         // passed as the integer value and returns
                         // true if the move was successful
                         // ... process the odd row
  } else {
    break;
  }
}
```

public int getRow() throws SQLException   This method returns the current row position as a positive integer (1 for the first row, 2 for the second, and so on) or 0 if there is no current row—the cursor is either before the first row or after the last row. This is the only method of this set of cursor methods that is optionally supported for TYPE_FORWARD_ONLY `ResultSets`.

public boolean relative(int rows) throws SQLException   The `relative()` method is the cousin to `absolute`. Get it, cousin? Okay, anyway, `relative()` will position the cursor either before or after the current position of the number of rows passed in to the method. So if the cursor is on row 15 of a 30-row `ResultSet`, calling `relative(2)` will position the cursor to row 17, and then calling `relative(-5)` positions the cursor to row 12. Figure 12-6 shows how the cursor is moved based on calls to `absolute()` and `relative()`.

Like absolute positioning, attempting to position the cursor beyond the last row or before the first row simply results in the cursor being after the last row or before the first row, respectively, and the method returns false. Also, calling relative with an argument of 0 does exactly what you might expect—the cursor remains where it is. Why would you use relative? Let's assume you are displaying a fairly long database table on a web page using an HTML table. You might want to allow your user to be able to page forward or backward relative to the currently selected row—maybe something like this:

```
public boolean getNextPageOfData (ResultSet rs, int pageSize) throws
SQLException{
  return rs.relative(pageSize);
}
```

FIGURE 12-6

String query = "SELECT * FROM Author";

Relative cursor
positioning
(Circled numbers
indicate order of
invocation.)

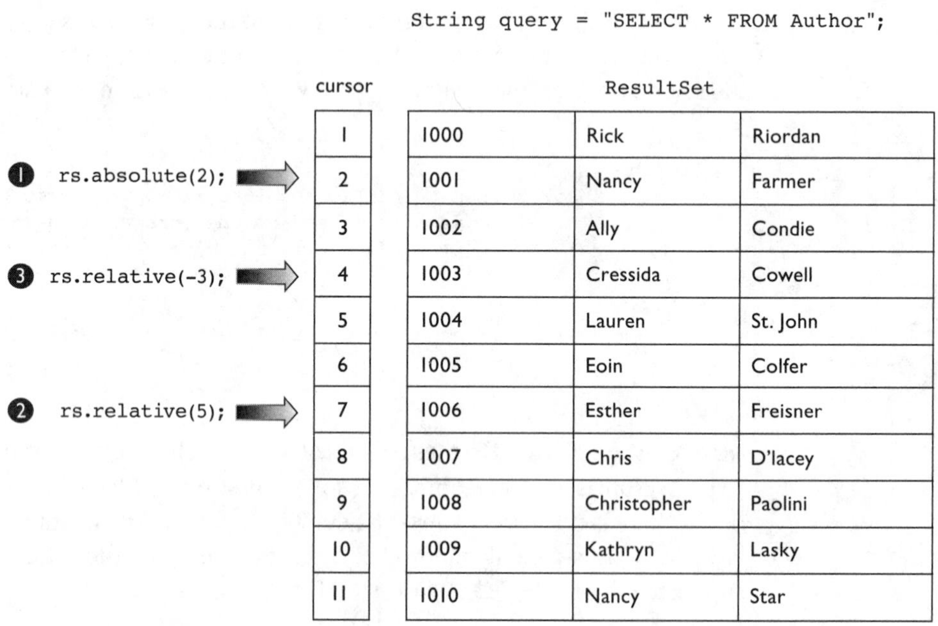

cursor		ResultSet	
I	1000	Rick	Riordan
2	1001	Nancy	Farmer
3	1002	Ally	Condie
4	1003	Cressida	Cowell
5	1004	Lauren	St. John
6	1005	Eoin	Colfer
7	1006	Esther	Freisner
8	1007	Chris	D'lacey
9	1008	Christopher	Paolini
10	1009	Kathryn	Lasky
II	1010	Nancy	Star

❶ rs.absolute(2);

❸ rs.relative(-3);

❷ rs.relative(5);

public boolean previous() throws SQLException The previous() method
works exactly the same as the next() method, only it backs up through the
ResultSet. Using this method with the afterLast() method described next,
you can move through a ResultSet in reverse order (from last row to first).

public void afterLast() throws SQLException This method positions the
cursor after the last row. Using this method and then the previous() method,
you can iterate through a ResultSet in reverse. For example:

```
public void showFlippedResultSet(ResultSet rs) throws SQLException {
    rs.afterLast();          // Position the cursor after the last row
    while (rs.previous()) {  // Back up through the ResultSet
                             // process the result set
    }
}
```

Just like next(), when previous() backs up all the way to before the first
row, the method returns false.

public void beforeFirst() throws SQLException   This method will return the cursor to the position it held when the `ResultSet` was first created and returned by a `Statement` object.

```
rs.beforeFirst(); // Position the cursor before the first row
```

public boolean first() throws SQLException   The `first()` method positions the cursor on the first row. It is the equivalent of calling `absolute(1)`. This method returns `true` if the cursor was moved to a valid row and `false` if the `ResultSet` has no rows.

```
if (!rs.first()) {
   out.println("No rows in this result set");
}
```

public boolean last() throws SQLException   The `last()` method positions the cursor on the last row. This method is the equivalent of calling `absolute(-1)`. This method returns `true` if the cursor was moved to a valid row and `false` if the `ResultSet` has no rows.

```
if (!rs.last()) {
   out.println("No rows in this result set");
}
```

A couple of notes on the exceptions thrown by all of these methods:

- A `SQLException` will be thrown by these methods if the type of the `ResultSet` is TYPE_FORWARD_ONLY, if the `ResultSet` is closed (we will look at how a result set is closed in an upcoming section), or if a database error occurs.

- A `SQLFeatureNotSupportedException` will be thrown by these methods if the JDBC driver does not support the method. This exception is a subclass of `SQLException`.

- Most of these methods have no effect if the `ResultSet` has no rows—for example, a `ResultSet` returned by a query that returned no rows.

The following methods return a boolean to allow you to "test" the current cursor position without moving the cursor. Note that these are not on the exam but are provided to you for completeness:

- `isBeforeFirst()`   True if the cursor is positioned before the first row
- `isAfterLast()`   True if the cursor is positioned after the last row

- **isFirst()**   True if the cursor is on the first row
- **isLast()**   True if the cursor is on the last row

So now that we have looked at the cursor positioning methods, let's revisit the code to calculate the row count. We will create a general-purpose method to allow the row count to be calculated at any time and at any current cursor position. Here is the code:

```
public static int getRowCount(ResultSet rs) throws SQLException {
  int rowCount = -1;
  int currRow = 0;

  if (rs != null) {                    // make sure the ResultSet is not null
    currRow = rs.getRow();             // Save the current row position:
                                       // zero indicates that there is no
                                       // current row position - could be
                                       // beforeFirst or afterLast
    if (rs.isAfterLast()) {            // afterLast, so set the currRow negative
        currRow = -1;
    }
    if (rs.last()) {                   // move to the last row and get the position
                                       // if this method returns false, there are no
                                       // results
      rowCount = rs.getRow();          // Get the row count
                                       // Return the cursor to the position it
                                       // was in before the method was called.
      if (currRow == -1) {             // if the currRow is negative, the cursor
                                       // position was after the last row, so
                                       // return the cursor to the last row
        rs.afterLast();
      } else if (currRow == 0) {  // else if the cursor is zero, move
                                       // the cursor to before the first row
        rs.beforeFirst();
      } else {                         // else return the cursor to its last position
        rs.absolute(currRow);
      }
    }
  }
  return rowCount;
}
```

Looking through the code, you notice that we took special care to preserve the current position of the cursor in the ResultSet. We called getRow() to get the current position, and if the value returned was 0, the current position of the ResultSet could be either before the first row or after the last row, so we used the isAfterLast() method to determine where the cursor was. If the cursor was after the last row, then we stored a -1 in the currRow integer.

We then moved the cursor to the last position in the `ResultSet`, and if that move was successful, we get the current position and save it as the `rowCount` (the last row and, therefore, the count of rows in the `ResultSet`). Finally, we use the value of `currRow` to determine where to return the cursor. If the value of the cursor is `-1`, we need to position the cursor after the last row. Otherwise, we simply use `absolute()` to return the cursor to the appropriate position in the `ResultSet`.

While this may seem like several extra steps, we will look at why preserving the cursor can be important when we look at updating `ResultSets` next.

Updating ResultSets

Please note that you might not get any questions on the real exam for this section and the subsections that follow.

If you have casually used JDBC, or are new to JDBC, you may be surprised to know that a `ResultSet` object can do more than just provide the results of a query to your application. Besides just returning the results of a query, a `ResultSet` object may be used to modify the contents of a database table, including update existing rows, delete existing rows, and add new rows.

In a traditional SQL application, you might perform the following SQL queries to raise the price of all of the hardcover books in inventory that are currently 10.95 to 11.95 in price:

```
UPDATE Book SET UnitPrice = 11.95 WHERE UnitPrice = 10.95
                                AND Format = 'Hardcover'
```

Hopefully, by now you feel comfortable creating a `Statement` to perform this query using a SQL UPDATE:

```
// We have a connection and we are in a try-catch block...
Statement stmt = conn.createStatement();
String query = "UPDATE Book SET UnitPrice = 11.95 " +
               "WHERE UnitPrice = 10.95 AND Format = 'Hardcover'";
int rowsUpdated = stmt.executeUpdate(query);
```

But what if you wanted to do the updates on a book-by-book basis? What if you only want to increase the price of your bestsellers, rather than every single book?

You would have to get the values from the database using a SELECT, then store the values in an array indexed somehow (perhaps with the primary key), then construct the appropriate UPDATE command strings, and call `executeUpdate()` one row at a time. Another option is to update the `ResultSet` directly.

When you create a `Statement` with concurrency set to CONCUR_
UPDATABLE, you can modify the data in a result set and then apply your changes
back to the database without having to issue another query.

In addition to the `getXXXX` methods we looked at for `ResultSet`—methods
that get column values as integers, `Date` objects, `Strings`, etc.—there is an
equivalent `updateXXXX` method for each type. And, just like the `getXXXX`
methods, the `updateXXXX` methods can take either a `String` column name or
an integer column index.

Let's rewrite the previous update example using an updatable `ResultSet`:

```
// We have a connection and we are in a try-catch block...
Statement stmt =                                          // Scrollable
  conn.createStatement(ResultSet.TYPE_SCROLL_SENSITIVE, // and
                       ResultSet.CONCUR_UPDATABLE);      // updatable
String query = "SELECT UnitPrice from Book " +
               "WHERE Format = 'Hardcover'";
ResultSet rs = stmt.executeQuery(query);        // Populate the ResultSet
while (rs.next()) {
    if (rs.getFloat("UnitPrice") == 10.95f) { // Check each row: if
                                               // unitPrice = 10.95
        rs.updateFloat("UnitPrice", 11.95f);   // set it to 11.95
        rs.updateRow();                        // and update the row
                                               // in the database

    }
}
```

Notice that after modifying the value of `UnitPrice` using the `updateFloat()`
method, we called the method `updateRow()`. This method writes the current row
to the database. This two-step approach ensures that all of the changes are made to
the row before the row is written to the database. And you can change your mind
with a `cancelRowUpdates()` method call.

Table 12-11 summarizes methods that are commonly used with updatable
`ResultSets` (whose concurrency type is set to CONCUR_UPDATABLE).

Let's look at the common methods used for altering database contents through
the `ResultSet` in detail.

public void updateRow() throws SQLException   This method updates
the database with the contents of the current row of the `ResultSet`. There are
a couple of caveats for this method. First, the `ResultSet` must be from a SQL
SELECT statement on a single table—a SQL statement that includes a JOIN or a
SQL statement with two tables cannot be updated. Second, the `updateRow()`
method should be called *before* moving to the next row. Otherwise, the updates to
the current row may be lost.

TABLE 12-11   Methods Used with Updatable `ResultSets`

Method	Purpose
void updateRow()	Updates the database with the contents of the current row of this `ResultSet`.
void deleteRow()	Deletes the current row from the `ResultSet` and the underlying database.
void cancelRowUpdates()	Cancels any updates made to the current row of this `ResultSet` object. This method will effectively undo any changes made to the `ResultSet` row. If the `updateRow()` method was called before `cancelRowUpdates`, this method will have no effect.
void moveToInsertRow()	Moves the cursor to a special row in the `ResultSet` set aside for performing an insert. You need to move to the insert row before updating the columns of the row with update methods and calling `insertRow()`.
void insertRow()	Inserts the contents of the insert row into the database. Note that this method does not change the current `ResultSet`, so the `ResultSet` should be read again if you want the `ResultSet` to be consistent with the contents of the database.
void moveToCurrentRow()	Moves the cursor back to the current row from the insert row. If the cursor was not on the insert row, this method has no effect.

So the typical use for this method is to update the contents of a row using the appropriate `updateXXXX()` methods and then update the database with the contents of the row using the `updateRow()` method. For example, in this fragment, we are updating the `UnitPrice` of a row to $11.95:

```
rs.updateFloat("UnitPrice", 11.95f); // Set the price to 11.95
rs.updateRow();                      // Update the row in the DB
```

public boolean rowUpdated() throws SQLException   This method returns true if the current row was updated. Note that not all databases can detect updates. However, JDBC provides a method in `DatabaseMetaData` to determine if updates are detectable, `DatabaseMetaData.updatesAreDetected(int type)`, where the type is one of the `ResultSet` types—TYPE_SCROLL_INSENSITIVE, for example. We will cover the `DatabaseMetaData` interface and its methods a little later in this section.

```
if (rs.rowUpdated()) {            // Has this row been modified?
  out.println("Row: " + rs.getRow() + " updated.");
}
```

public void cancelRowUpdates() throws SQLException   This method allows you to "back out" changes made to the row. This method is important, because the updateXXXX methods should not be called twice on the same column. In other words, if you set the value of UnitPrice to 11.95 in the previous example and then decided to switch the price back to 10.95, calling the updateFloat() method again can lead to unpredictable results. So the better approach is to call cancelRowUpdates() before changing the value of a column a second time.

```
boolean priceRollback = ...;  // Price rollback set somewhere else
while (rs.next()) {
  if (rs.getFloat("UnitPrice") == 10.95f) {
    rs.updateFloat("UnitPrice", 11.95f);
  }
  if (priceRollback) {          // If priceRollback is true
    rs.cancelRowUpdates();      // Rollback changes to this row
  } else {
    rs.updateRow();             // else, commit this row to the DB
  }
}
```

public void deleteRow() throws SQLException   This method will remove the current row from the ResultSet and from the underlying database. The row in the database is removed (similar to the result of a DELETE statement).

```
rs.last();
rs.deleteRow();  // Delete the last row.
```

What happens to the ResultSet after a deleteRow() method depends on whether the ResultSet can detect deletions. And this ability depends on the JDBC driver.

The DatabaseMetaData interface can be used to determine if the ResultSet can detect deletions:

```
int type = ResultSet.TYPE_SCROLL_INSENSITIVE; // Scrollable ResultSet
DatabaseMetaData dbmd = conn.getMetaData();    // Get meta data about
                                               // the driver and DB
if (dbmd.deletesAreDetected(type)) {           // Returns false if deleted rows
                                               // are removed from the ResultSet
  while (rs.next()) {                          // Iterate through the ResultSet
    if (rs.rowDeleted()) {                     // Deleted rows are flagged, but
      continue;                                // not removed, so skip them
    } else {
     // process the row
    }
  } else {
   // Close the ResultSet and re-run the query
  }
```

In general, to maintain an up-to-date `ResultSet` after a deletion, the `ResultSet` should be re-created with a query.

Deleting the current row does not move the cursor—it remains on the current row—so if you deleted row 1, the cursor is still positioned at row 1. However, if the deleted row was the last row, then the cursor is positioned after the last row. Note that there is no undo for `deleteRow()`, at least, not by default.

public boolean rowDeleted() throws SQLException   As described earlier, when a `ResultSet` can detect deletes, the `rowDeleted()` method is used to indicate a row has been deleted but remains as a part of the `ResultSet` object. For example, suppose that we deleted the second row of the Customer table. Printing the results (after the delete) to the console would look like Figure 12-7.

So if you are working with a `ResultSet` that is being passed around between methods and shared across classes, you might use `rowDeleted()` to detect if the current row contains valid data.

Updating Columns Using Objects   An interesting aspect of the `getObject()` and `updateObject()` methods is that they retrieve a column as a Java object.

FIGURE 12-7

A `ResultSet` after `deleteRow()` is called on the second row

```
String query = "SELECT * FROM Customer";
ResultSet rs = stmt.executeQuery(query);
rs.next();
rs.next();
rs.deleteRow();
```

ResultSet

5000	John	Smith	john.smith@verizon.net	555-340-1230
null	null	null	null	null
5002	Bob	Collins	bob.collins@yahoo.com	555-012-3456
5003	Rebecca	Mayer	rebecca.mayer@gmail.com	555-205-8212
5006	Anthony	Clark	anthony.clark@gmail.com	555-256-1901
5007	Judy	Sousa	judy.sousa@verizon.net	555-751-1207
5008	Christopher	Patriquin	patriquinc@yahoo.com	555-316-1803
5009	Deborah	Smith	deb.smith@comcast.net	555-256-3421
5010	Jennifer	McGinn	jmcginn@comcast.net	555-250-0918

And because every Java object can be turned into a String using the object's toString() method, you can retrieve the value of any column in the database and print the value to the console as a String, as you saw in the section "Printing a Report."

Going the other way, toward the database, you can also use Strings to update almost every column in a ResultSet. All of the most common SQL types—integer, float, double, long, and date—are wrapped by their representative Java object: Integer, Float, Double, Long, and java.sql.Date. Each of these objects has a method valueOf() that takes a String.

The updateObject() method takes two arguments: the first, a column name (String) or column index; and the second, an Object. We can pass a String as the Object type, and as long as the String meets the requirements of the valueOf() method for the column type, the String will be properly converted and stored in the database as the desired SQL type.

For example, suppose that we are going to update the publish date (PubDate) of one of our books:

```
// We have a connection and we are in a try-catch block...
Statement stmt =
  conn.createStatement(ResultSet.TYPE_SCROLL_INSENSITIVE,
                       ResultSet.CONCUR_UPDATABLE);
String query = "SELECT * FROM Book WHERE ISBN='142311339X'";
ResultSet rs = stmt.executeQuery(query);
rs.next();
rs.updateObject("PubDate", "2005-04-23"); // Update PubDate using
                                          // a String date
rs.updateRow();                           // Update this row
```

The String we passed meets the requirements for java.sql.Date, "yyyy-[m]m-[d]d," so the String is properly converted and stored in the database as the SQL Date value: 2005-04-23. Note this technique is limited to those SQL types that can be converted to and from a String, and if the String passed to the valueOf() method for the SQL type of the column is not properly formatted for the Java object, an IllegalArgumentException is thrown.

Inserting New Rows Using a ResultSet

In the last section, we looked at modifying the existing column data in a ResultSet and removing existing rows. In our final section on ResultSets, we'll look at how to create and insert a new row. First, you must have a valid ResultSet open, so typically, you have performed some query. ResultSet provides a special row, called the insert row, that you are actually modifying (updating) before performing the insert. Think of the insert row as a buffer where you can modify an empty row of your `ResultSet` with values.

Inserting a row is a three-step process, as shown in Figure 12-8: First (1) move to the special insert row, then (2) update the values of the columns for the new row, and finally (3) perform the actual insert (write to the underlying database). The existing `ResultSet` is not changed—you must rerun your query to see the underlying changes in the database. However, you can insert as many rows as you like. Note that each of these methods throws a `SQLException` if the concurrency type of the result set is set to CONCUR_READ_ONLY. Let's look at the methods before we look at example code.

public void moveToInsertRow() throws SQLException   This method moves the cursor to insert a row buffer. Wherever the cursor was when this method was called is remembered. After calling this method, the appropriate updater methods are called to update the values of the columns.

```
rs.moveToInsertRow();
```

FIGURE 12-8   The `ResultSet` insert row

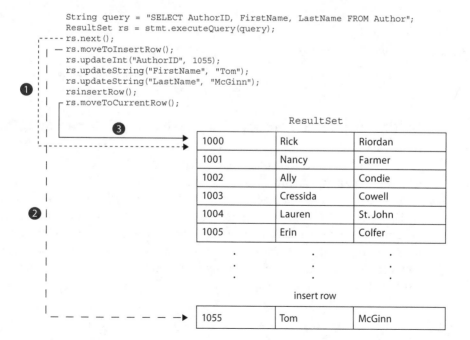

public void insertRow() throws SQLException This method writes the insert row buffer to the database. Note that the cursor must be on the insert row when this method is called. Also, note that each column must be set to a value before the row is inserted in the database or a SQLException will be thrown. The insertRow() method can be called more than once—however, the insertRow follows the same rules as a SQL INSERT command. Unless the primary key is auto-generated, two inserts of the same data will result in a SQLException (duplicate primary key).

```
rs.insertRow();
```

public void moveToCurrentRow() throws SQLException This method returns the result set cursor to the row the cursor was on before the moveToInsertRow() method was called.

Let's look at a simple example, where we will add a new row in the Author table:

```
// We have a connection and we are in a try-catch block...
Statement stmt = conn.createStatement(ResultSet.TYPE_SCROLL_INSENSITIVE,
                                      ResultSet.CONCUR_UPDATABLE);
ResultSet rs = stmt.executeQuery("SELECT AuthorID, FirstName, LastName
                                  FROM Author");
rs.next();
rs.moveToInsertRow();                   // Move the special insert row
rs.updateInt("AuthorID", 1055);         // Create an author ID
rs.updateString("FirstName", "Tom");    // Set the first name
rs.updateString("LastName", "McGinn");  // Set the last name
rs.insertRow();                         // Insert the row into the database
rs.moveToCurrentRow();                  // Move back to the current row in
                                        // ResultSet
```

Getting Information about a Database Using DatabaseMetaData

Note: On the real exam, you might not get any questions about DatabaseMetaData.

In the example we are using in this chapter, Bob's Books, we know quite a lot about the tables, columns, and relationships between the tables because we had that nifty data model earlier. But what if that were not the case? This section covers DatabaseMetaData, an interface that provides a significant amount of information about the database itself. This topic is fairly advanced stuff and is not on the exam, but it is provided here to give you an idea about how you can use metadata to build a model of a database without having to know anything about the database in advance.

Recall that the `Connection` object we obtained from `DriverManager` is an object that represents an actual connection with the database. And while the `Connection` object is primarily used to create `Statement` objects, there are a couple of important methods to study in the `Connection` interface. A `Connection` can be used to obtain information *about* the database as well. This data is called "metadata," or "data about data."

One of `Connection`'s methods returns a `DatabaseMetaData` object instance, through which we can get information about the database, about the driver, and about transaction semantics that the database and JDBC driver support.

To obtain an instance of a `DatabaseMetaData` object, we use `Connection`'s `getMetaData()` method:

```
String url = "jdbc:derby://localhost:1521/BookSellerDB";
String user = "bookguy";
String pwd = "$3lleR";
try {
  Connection conn = DriverManager.getConnection(url, user, pwd);
  DatabaseMetaData dbmd = conn.getMetaData(); // Get the database
                                             // metadata
} catch (SQLException se) { }
```

`DatabaseMetaData` is a comprehensive interface, and through an object instance, we can determine a great deal about the database and the supporting driver. Most of the time, as a developer, you aren't coding against a database blindly and know the capabilities of the database and the driver before you write any code. Still, it is helpful to know that you can use `getObject` to return the value of the column, regardless of its type—very useful when all you want to do is create a report. We'll look at an example.

Here are a few methods we will highlight:

- **getColumns()** Returns a description of columns in a specified catalog and schema

- **getProcedures()** Returns a description of the stored procedures in a given catalog and schema

- **getDriverName()** Returns the name of the JDBC driver

- **getDriverVersion()** Returns the version number of the JDBC driver as a string

- **supportsANSI92EntryLevelSQL()** Returns a boolean true if this database supports ANSI92 entry-level grammar

It is interesting to note that `DatabaseMetaData` methods also use `ResultSet` objects to return data about the database. Let's look at these methods in more detail.

public ResultSet getColumns(String catalog, String schemaPattern, String tableNamePattern, String columnNamePattern) throws SQLException   This method is one of the best all-purpose data retrieval methods for details about the tables and columns in your database. Before we look at a code sample, it might be helpful to define catalogs and schemas. In a database, a schema is an object that enforces the integrity of the tables in the database. The schema name is generally the name of the person who created the database. In our examples, the BookGuy database holds the collection of tables and is the name of the schema. Databases may have multiple schemas stored in a catalog.

In this example, using the Java DB database as our sample database, the catalog is null and our schema is "BOOKGUY", and we are using a SQL catch-all pattern "%" for the table and column name patterns, like the "*" character you are probably used to with file systems like Windows. Thus, we are going to retrieve all of the tables and columns in the schema. Specifically, we are going to print out the table name, column name, the SQL data type for the column, and the size of the column. Note that here we used uppercase column identifiers. These are the column names verbatim from the JavaDoc, but in truth, they are not case-sensitive either, so "Table_Name" would have worked just as well. Also, the JavaDoc specifies the column index for these column headings, so we could have also used `rs.getString(3)` to get the table name.

```
String url = "jdbc:derby://localhost:1521/BookSellerDB";
String user = "bookguy";
String pwd = "$3lleR";
try {
  Connection conn = DriverManager.getConnection(url, user, pwd);
  DatabaseMetaData dbmd = conn.getMetaData();
  ResultSet rs
   = dbmd.getColumns(null, "BOOKGUY", "%", "%"); // Get a ResultSet
                                                 // for any catalog (null)
                                                 // in the BOOKGUY schema
                                                 // for all tables (%)
                                                 // for all columns (%)
  while (rs.next()) {
    out.print("Table Name:  " + rs.getString("TABLE_NAME") + " ");
    out.print("Column_Name: " + rs.getString("COLUMN_NAME") + " ");
    out.print("Type_Name:   " + rs.getString("TYPE_NAME") + " ");
    out.println("Column Size  " + rs.getString("COLUMN_SIZE"));
  }
} catch (SQLException se) {
  out.println("SQLException: " + se);
}
```

Running this code produces output something like this:

```
Table Name:  AUTHOR Column_Name: AUTHORID Type_Name:   INTEGER Column Size
10 Primary Key
Table Name:  AUTHOR Column_Name: FIRSTNAME Type_Name:   VARCHAR Column Size
20
Table Name:  AUTHOR Column_Name: LASTNAME Type_Name:   VARCHAR Column Size
20
Table Name:  BOOK Column_Name: ISBN Type_Name:   VARCHAR Column Size  10
Primary Key
Table Name:  BOOK Column_Name: TITLE Type_Name:   VARCHAR Column Size  100
Table Name:  BOOK Column_Name: PUBDATE Type_Name:   DATE Column Size  10
Table Name:  BOOK Column_Name: FORMAT Type_Name:   VARCHAR Column Size  30
Table Name:  BOOK Column_Name: UNITPRICE Type_Name:   DOUBLE Column Size  52
Table Name:  BOOKS_BY_AUTHOR Column_Name: AUTHORID Type_Name:   INTEGER
Column Size  10
Table Name:  BOOKS_BY_AUTHOR Column_Name: ISBN Type_Name:   VARCHAR Column
Size  10
Table Name:  CUSTOMER Column_Name: CUSTOMERID Type_Name:   INTEGER Column
Size  10 Primary Key
Table Name:  CUSTOMER Column_Name: FIRSTNAME Type_Name:   VARCHAR Column Size
30
Table Name:  CUSTOMER Column_Name: LASTNAME Type_Name:   VARCHAR Column Size
30
Table Name:  CUSTOMER Column_Name: EMAIL Type_Name:   VARCHAR Column Size  40
Table Name:  CUSTOMER Column_Name: PHONE Type_Name:   VARCHAR Column Size  15
```

public ResultSet getProcedures(String catalog, String schemaPattern, String procedureNamePattern) throws SQLException   Stored procedures are functions that are sometimes built into a database and often defined by a database developer or database admin. These functions can range from data cleanup to complex queries. This method returns a result set that contains descriptive information about the stored procedures for a catalog and schema. In the example code, we will use null for the catalog name and schema pattern. The null indicates that we do not wish to narrow the search (effectively, the same as using a catch-all "%" search). Note that this example is returning the name of every stored procedure in the database. A little later, we'll look at how to actually call a stored procedure.

```
try {
   Connection conn = ...
   DatabaseMetaData dbmd = conn.getMetaData();
   ResultSet rs =
       dbmd.getProcedures(null, null, "%");    // Get a ResultSet of all
                                                // the stored procedures
                                                // in any catalog (null)
                                                // in any schema (null)
                                                // with wildcard name (%)
```

```
while(rs.next()) {
  out.println("Procedure Name: " + rs.getString("PROCEDURE_NAME"));
}
} catch (SQLException se) { }
```

Note that the output from this code fragment is highly database dependent. Here is sample output from the Derby (JavaDB) database that ships with the JDK:

```
Procedure Name: INSTALL_JAR
Procedure Name: REMOVE_JAR
Procedure Name: REPLACE_JAR
Procedure Name: SYSCS_BACKUP_DATABASE
Procedure Name: SYSCS_BACKUP_DATABASE_AND_ENABLE_LOG_ARCHIVE_MODE
Procedure Name: SYSCS_BACKUP_DATABASE_AND_ENABLE_LOG_ARCHIVE_MODE_NOWAIT
Procedure Name: SYSCS_BACKUP_DATABASE_NOWAIT
Procedure Name: SYSCS_BULK_INSERT
```

public String getDriverName() throws SQLException   This method simply returns the name of the JDBC driver as a string. This method would be useful to log at the start of the application, as you'll see in the next section.

```
System.out.println("getDriverName: " + dbmd.getDriverName());
```

Obviously, the name of the driver depends on the JDBC driver you are using. Again, with the Derby database and JDBC driver, the output from this method looks something like this:

```
getDriverName: Apache Derby Network Client JDBC Driver
```

public String getDriverVersion() throws SQLException   This method returns the JDBC driver version number as a string. This information and the driver name would be good to log in at startup of an application.

```
Logger logger = Logger.getLogger("com.cert.DatabaseMetaDataTest");
Connection conn = ...
DatabaseMetaData dbmd = conn.getMetaData();
logger.log(Level.INFO, "Driver Version: {0}", dbmd.getDriverVersion());
logger.log(Level.INFO, "Driver Name: {0}", dbmd.getDriverName());
```

Statements written to the log are generally recorded in a log file, but depending on the IDE, they can also be written to the console. In NetBeans, for example, the log statements look something like this in the console:

```
Sep 23, 2012 3:55:39 PM com.cert.DatabaseMetaDataTest main
INFO: Driver Version: 10.8.2.2 - (1181258)
Sep 23, 2012 3:55:39 PM com.cert.DatabaseMetaDataTest main
INFO: Driver Name: Apache Derby Network Client JDBC Driver
```

public boolean supportsANSI92EntryLevelSQL() throws SQLException   This method returns true if the database and JDBC driver support ANSI SQL-92 entry-level grammar. Support for this level (at a minimum) is a requirement for JDBC drivers (and, therefore, the database).

```
Connection conn = ...
DatabaseMetaData dbmd = conn.getMetaData();
if (!dbmd.supportsANSI92EntryLevelSQL()) {
    logger.log(Level.WARNING, "JDBC Driver does not meet minimum
               requirements for SQL-92 support");
}
```

When Things Go Wrong—Exceptions and Warnings

Whenever you are working with a database using JDBC, there is a possibility that something can go wrong. A JDBC connection is typically through a socket to a database resource on the network. So already we have at least two possible points of failure—the network can be down and/or the database can be down. And that assumes everything else you are doing with your database is correct, that all your queries are perfect! Like other Java exceptions, SQLException is a way for your application to determine what the problem is and take action if necessary.

Let's look at the type of data you get from a SQLException through its methods.

public String getMessage()   This method is actually inherited from java.lang.Exception, which SQLException extends from. This method returns the detailed reason why the exception was thrown. Often, the message contents SQLState and error code provide specific information about what went wrong.

public String getSQLState()   The String returned by getSQLState provides a specific code and related message. SQLState messages are defined by the X/Open and SQL:2003 standards; however, it is up to the implementation to use these values. You can determine which standard your JDBC driver uses (or if it does not) through the DatabaseMetaData.getSQLStateType() method. Your implementation may also define additional codes specific to the implementation, so in either case, it is a good idea to consult your JDBC driver and database documentation. Because the SQLState messages and codes tend to be specific to the driver and database, the typical use of these in an application is limited to either logging messages or debugging information.

public int getErrorCode()   Error codes are not defined by a standard and are thus implementation specific. They can be used to pass an actual error code or severity level, depending on the implementation.

public SQLException getNextException()   One of the interesting aspects of SQLException is that the exception thrown could be the result of more than one issue. Fortunately, JDBC simply tacks each exception onto the next in a process called chaining. Typically, the most severe exception is thrown last, so it is the first exception in the chain.

You can get a list of all of the exceptions in the chain using the getNextException() method to iterate through the list. When the end of the list is reached, getNextException() returns a null. In this example, the SQLExceptions, SQLState, and vendor error codes are logged:

```
Logger logger = Logger.getLogger("com.example.MyClass");
try {
  // some JDBC code in a try block
  // ...
} catch (SQLException se) {
  while (se != null) {
    logger.log(Level.SEVERE, "------ SQLException ------");
    logger.log(Level.SEVERE, "SQLState: " + se.getSQLState());
    logger.log(Level.SEVERE, "Vendor Error code: " +
                    se.getErrorCode());
    logger.log(Level.SEVERE,"Message: " + se.getMessage());
    se = se.getNextException();
  }
}
```

Warnings

Although SQLWarning is a subclass of SQLException, warnings are silently chained to the JDBC object that reported them. This is probably one of the few times in Java where an object that is part of an exception hierarchy is not thrown as an exception. The reason is that a warning is not an exception per se. Warnings can be reported on Connection, Statement, and ResultSet objects.

For example, suppose that we mistakenly set the result-set type to TYPE_SCROLL_SENSITIVE when creating a Statement object. This does not create an exception; instead, the database will handle the situation by chaining a SQLWarning to the Connection object and resetting the type to TYPE_FORWARD_ONLY (the default) and continue on. Everything would be fine, of course, until we tried to position the cursor, at which point a SQLException would be thrown. And, like SQLException, you can retrieve warnings from the SQLWarning object using the getNextWarning() method.

```
Connection conn =
  DriverManager.getConnection("jdbc:derby://localhost:1527/BookSellerDB",
  "bookguy", "$3lleR");
Statement stmt =
  conn.createStatement(ResultSet.TYPE_SCROLL_SENSITIVE,
                       ResultSet.CONCUR_UPDATABLE);
String query = "SELECT * from Book WHERE Book.Format = 'Hardcover'";
ResultSet rs = stmt.executeQuery(query);
SQLWarning warn = conn.getWarnings();      // Get any SQLWarnings
while (warn != null) {                     // If there is a SQLWarning, print it
  out.println("SQLState: " + warn.getSQLState());
  out.println("Message: " + warn.getMessage());
  warn = warn.getNextWarning();            // Get the next warning
}
```

Connection objects will add warnings (if necessary) until the Connection is closed or until the clearWarnings() method is called on the Connection instance. The clearWarnings() method sets the list of warnings to null until another warning is reported for this Connection object.

Statements and ResultSets also generate SQLWarnings, and these objects have their own clearWarnings() methods. Statement warnings are cleared automatically when a statement is reexecuted, and ResultSet warnings are cleared each time a new row is read from the result set.

The following sections summarize the methods associated with SQLWarnings.

SQLWarning getWarnings() throws SQLException   This method gets the first SQLWarning object or returns null if there are no warnings for this Connection, Statement, or ResultSet object. A SQLException is thrown if the method is called on a closed object.

void clearWarnings() throws SQLException   This method clears and resets the current set of warnings for this Connection, Statement, or ResultSet object. A SQLException is thrown if the method is called on a closed object.

Properly Closing SQL Resources
In this chapter, we have looked at some very simple examples where we create a Connection and Statement and a ResultSet all within a single try block

and catch any SQLExceptions thrown. What we have not done so far is properly close these resources. The reality is that it is probably less important for such small examples, but for any code that uses a resource, like a socket, or a file, or a JDBC database connection, closing the open resources is a good practice.

It is also important to know when a resource is closed automatically. Each of the three major JDBC objects—Connection, Statement, and ResultSet—has a close() method to explicitly close the resource associated with the object and explicitly release the resource. We hope by now you also realize that the objects have a relationship with each other, so if one object executes close(), it will have an impact on the other objects. The following table should help explain this.

Method Call	Has the Following Action(s)
Connection.close()	Releases the connection to the database. Closes any Statement created from this Connection.
Statement.close()	Releases this Statement resource. Closes any open ResultSet associated with this Statement.
ResultSet.close()	Releases this ResultSet resource. Note that any ResultSetMetaData objects created from the ResultSet are still accessible.
Statement.executeXXXX()	Any ResultSet associated with a previous Statement execution is automatically closed.

It is also a good practice to minimize the number of times you close and re-create Connection objects. As a rule, creating the connection to the database and passing the username and password credentials for authentication is a relatively expensive process, so performing the activity once for every SQL query can cause code to execute slowly. In fact, typically, database connections are created in a pool and connection instances are handed out to applications as needed, rather than allowing or requiring individual applications to create them.

Statement objects are less expensive to create. There are ways to precompile SQL statements using a PreparedStatement, which reduces the overhead associated with creating SQL query strings and sending those strings to the database for execution, but understanding PreparedStatement is no longer on the exam.

ResultSets are the least expensive of the objects to create, and as you saw in the section "ResultSets," for results from a single table, you can use the ResultSet to update, insert, and delete rows, so it can be very efficient to use a ResultSet.

Let's look at one of our previous examples, where we used a `Connection`, a `Statement`, and a `ResultSet`, and rewrite this code to close the resources properly.

```
Connection conn = null;
String url, user, pwd;      // These are populated somewhere else
try {
  conn = DriverManager.getConnection(url, user, pwd);
  Statement stmt = conn.createStatement();
  ResultSet rs = stmt.executeQuery("SELECT * FROM Customer");
  // ... process the results
  // ...
  if (rs != null && stmt != null) {
    rs.close();               // Attempt to close the ResultSet
    stmt.close();             // Attempt to close the Statement
  }
} catch (SQLException se) {
  out.println("SQLException: " + se);
} finally {
  try {
    if (conn != null) {
      conn.close();           // Close the Connection
    }
  } catch (SQLException sec) {
    out.println("Exception closing connection!");
  }
}
```

Notice all the work we have to go through to close the `Connection`—we first need to make sure we actually got an object and not a null, and then we need to try the `close()` method inside of another `try` inside of the `finally` block! Fortunately, there is an easier way....

Using try-with-resources to Close Connections, Statements, and ResultSets

One of the most useful changes in Java SE 7 (JDK 7) was a number of small modifications to the language, including a new `try` statement to support automatic resource management. This language change is called `try`-with-resources, and its longer name belies how much simpler it makes writing code with resources that should be closed. The `try`-with-resources statement will automatically call the `close()` method on any resource declared in the parentheses at the end of the `try` block.

There is a caveat: A resource declared in the `try`-with-resource statement must implement the `AutoCloseable` interface. One of the changes for JDBC in Java SE 7 (JDBC 4.1) was the modification of the API so that `Connection`, `Statement`, and `ResultSet` all extend the `AutoCloseable` interface and support automatic resource management. So we can rewrite our previous code example using `try`-with-resources:

```
String url, user, pwd;  // These are populated somewhere else
try (Connection conn = DriverManager.getConnection(url, user, pwd)){
  Statement stmt = conn.createStatement();
  ResultSet rs = stmt.executeQuery("SELECT * FROM Customer");
  // ... process the results
  // ...
  if (rs != null && stmt != null) {
    rs.close();        // Attempt to close the ResultSet
    stmt.close();      // Attempt to close the Statement
  }
} catch (SQLException se) {
  out.println("SQLException: " + se);
}
```

Notice that we must include the object type in the declaration inside of the parentheses. The following will throw a compilation error:

```
try (conn = DriverManager.getConnection(url, user, pwd);) {
```

The `try`-with-resources can also be used with multiple resources, so you could include the `Statement` declaration in the `try` as well:

```
try (Connection conn = DriverManager.getConnection(url, user, pwd);
     Statement stmt = conn.createStatement()) {
```

Note that when more than one resource is declared in the `try`-with-resources statement, the resources are closed in the reverse order of their declaration—so `stmt.close()` will be called first, followed by `conn.close()`.

It probably makes sense that, if an exception is thrown from the `try` block, the exception will be caught by the `catch` statement, but what happens to exceptions thrown as a result of closing the resources in the `try`-with-resources statement? Any exceptions thrown as a result of closing resources at the end of the `try` block are suppressed, if there was also an exception thrown in the `try` block. These exceptions can be retrieved from the exception thrown by calling the `getSuppressed()` method on the exception thrown.

For example:

```
} catch (SQLException se) {
  out.println("SQLException: " + se);
  Throwable[] suppressed = se.getSuppressed(); // Get an array of
                                               // suppressed
                                               // exceptions
  for (Throwable t: suppressed) {  // Iterate through the array
    out.println("Suppressed exception: " + t);
  }
}
```

CERTIFICATION SUMMARY

Core JDBC API

Remember that the JDBC API is a set of interfaces with one important concrete class, the `DriverManager` class. You write code using the well-defined set of JDBC interfaces, and the provider of your JDBC driver writes code implementations of those interfaces. The key (and, therefore, required) interfaces a JDBC driver must implement include `Driver`, `Connection`, `Statement`, and `ResultSet`.

The driver provider will also implement an instance of `DatabaseMetaData`, which you use to invoke a method to query the driver for information about the database and JDBC driver. One important piece of information is if the database is SQL-92 compliant, and there are a number of methods that begin with "supports" to determine the capabilities of the driver. One important method is `supportsResultSetType()`, which is used to determine if the driver supports scrolling result sets.

DriverManager

The `DriverManager` is one of the few concrete classes in the JDBC API, and you will recall that the `DriverManager` is a factory class—using the `DriverManager`, you construct instances of `Connection` objects. In reality, the `DriverManager` simply holds references to registered JDBC drivers, and when you invoke the `getConnection()` method with a JDBC URL, the `DriverManager` passes the URL to each driver in turn. If the URL matches a valid driver, host, port number, username, and password, then that driver returns an instance of a `Connection` object. Remember that the JDBC URL is simply a string that encodes the information required to make a connection to a database.

How a JDBC driver is registered with the `DriverManager` is also important. In JDBC 4.0 and later, the driver jar file simply needs to be on the classpath, and the `DriverManager` will take care of finding the driver's `Driver` class implementation and load that. JDBC 3.0 and earlier, require that the driver's `Driver` class implementation be manually loaded using the `Class.forName()` method with the fully qualified class name of the class.

Statements and ResultSets

The most important use of a database is clearly using SQL statements and queries to create, read, update, and delete database records. The `Statement` interface provides the methods needed to create SQL statements and execute them. Remember that there are three different `Statement` methods to execute SQL queries: one that returns a result set, `executeQuery()`; one that returns an affected row count, `executeUpdate()`; and one general-purpose method that returns a boolean to indicate if the query produced a result set, `execute()`.

`ResultSet` is the interface used to read columns of data returned from a query, one row at a time. `ResultSet` objects represent a snapshot (a copy) of the data returned from a query, and there is a cursor that points to just above the first row when the results are returned. Unless you created a `Statement` object using the `Connection.createStatement(int, int)` method that takes `resultSetType` and `resultSetConcurrency` parameters, `ResultSets` are not updatable and only allow the cursor to move forward through the results. However, if your database supports it, you can create a `Statement` object with a type of `ResultSet.TYPE_SCROLL_INSENSITIVE` and/or a concurrency of `ResultSet.CONCUR_UPDATABLE`, which allows any result set created with the `Statement` object to position the cursor anywhere in the results (scrollable) and allows you to change the value of any column in any row in the result set (updatable). Finally, when using a `ResultSet` that is scrollable, you can determine the number of rows returned from a query—and this is the only way to determine the row count because there is no "rowCount" method.

`SQLException` is the base class for exceptions thrown by JDBC, and because one query can result in a number of exceptions, the exceptions are chained. To determine all of the reasons a method call returned a `SQLException`, you must iterate through the exception by calling the `getNextException()` method. JDBC also keeps track of warnings for methods on `Connection`, `Statement`, and `ResultSet` objects using a `SQLWarning` exception type. Like `SQLException`, `SQLWarning` is silently chained to the object that caused the warning—for example, suppose that you attempt to create a `Statement` object that supports the scrollable `ResultSet`, but the database does not support that type. A `SQLWarning` will be added to the `Connection` object (the `Connection.createStatement(int, int)` method creates a `Statement` object). The `getWarnings()` method is used to return any `SQLWarnings`.

One of the important additions to Java SE 7 was the `try`-with-resources statement, and all of the JDBC interfaces have been updated to support the new `AutoCloseable` interface. However, bear in mind that there is an order of precedence when closing `Connections`, `Statements`, and `ResultSets`. So when a `Connection` is closed, any `Statement` created from that `Connection` is also closed, and likewise, when a `Statement` is closed, any `ResultSet` created using that `Statement` is also closed. And attempting to invoke a method on a closed object will result in a `SQLException`!

TWO-MINUTE DRILL

Here are some of the key points from the certification objectives in this chapter.

Core Interfaces of the JDBC API (OCP Objective 11.1)

■ To be compliant with JDBC, driver vendors must provide implementations for the key JDBC interfaces: `Driver`, `Connection`, `Statement`, and `ResultSet`.

■ `DatabaseMetaData` can be used to determine which SQL-92 level your driver and database support.

■ `DatabaseMetaData` provides methods to interrogate the driver for capabilities and features.

Connect to a Database Using DriverManager (OCP Objective 11.2)

■ The JDBC API follows a factory pattern, where the `DriverManager` class is used to construct instances of `Connection` objects.

■ The JDBC URL is passed to each registered driver, in turn, in an attempt to create a valid `Connection`.

■ Identify the Java statements required to connect to a database using JDBC.

■ JDBC 3.0 (and earlier) drivers must be loaded prior to their use.

■ JDBC 4.0 drivers just need to be part of the classpath, and they are automatically loaded by the `DriverManager`.

Submit Queries and Read Results from the Database (OCP Objective 11.3)

■ The `next()` method must be called on a `ResultSet` before reading the first row of results.

■ When a `Statement execute()` method is executed, any open `ResultSets` tied to that `Statement` are automatically closed.

■ When a `Statement` is closed, any related `ResultSets` are also closed.

■ `ResultSet` column indexes are numbered from 1, not 0.

- The default `ResultSet` is not updatable (read-only), and the cursor moves forward only.

- A `ResultSet` that is scrollable and updatable can be modified, and the cursor can be positioned anywhere within the `ResultSet`.

- `ResultSetMetaData` can be used to dynamically discover the number of columns and their type returned in a `ResultSet`.

- `ResultSetMetaData` does not have a row count method. To determine the number of rows returned, the `ResultSet` must be scrollable.

- `ResultSet` fetch size can be controlled for large data sets; however, it is a hint to the driver and may be ignored.

- `SQLExceptions` are chained. You must iterate through the exceptions thrown to get all of the reasons why an exception was thrown.

- `SQLException` also contains database-specific error codes and status codes.

- The `executeQuery` method is used to return a `ResultSet` (SELECT).

- The `executeUpdate` method is used to update data, to modify the database, and to return the number of rows affected (INSERT, UPDATE, DELETE, and DDLs).

- The `execute` method is used to perform any SQL command. A boolean `true` is returned when the query produces a `ResultSet` and `false` when there are no results, or if the result is an update count.

- There is an order of precedence in the closing of `Connections`, `Statements`, and `ResultSets`.

- Using the `try`-with-resources statement, you can close `Connections`, `Statements`, and `ResultSets` automatically (they implement the new `AutoCloseable` interface in Java SE 7).

- When a `Connection` is closed, all of the related `Statements` and `ResultSets` are closed.

SELF TEST

1. Given:

   ```
   String url = "jdbc:mysql://SolDBServer/soldb";
   String user = "sysEntry";
   String pwd = "foOB3@r";
   // INSERT CODE HERE
   Connection conn = DriverManager.getConnection(url, user, pwd);
   ```

   Assuming "org.gjt.mm.mysql.Driver" is a legitimate class, which line, when inserted at
   // INSERT CODE HERE, will correctly load this JDBC 3.0 driver?

   A. `DriverManager.registerDriver("org.gjt.mm.mysql.Driver");`

   B. `Class.forName("org.gjt.mm.mysql.Driver");`

   C. `DatabaseMetaData.loadDriver("org.gjt.mm.mysql.Driver");`

   D. `Driver.connect("org.gjt.mm.mysql.Driver");`

   E. `DriverManager.getDriver("org.gjt.mm.mysql.Driver");`

2. Given that you are working with a JDBC 4.0 driver, which three are required for this JDBC
   driver to be compliant?

   A. Must include a `META-INF/services/java.sql.Driver` file

   B. Must provide implementations of `Driver`, `Connection`, `Statement`, and `ResultSet`
      interfaces

   C. Must support scrollable `ResultSets`

   D. Must support updatable `ResultSets`

   E. Must support transactions

   F. Must support the SQL99 standard

   G. Must support `PreparedStatement` and `CallableStatement`

3. Which three are available through an instance of `DatabaseMetaData`?

   A. The number of columns returned

   B. The number of rows returned

   C. The name of the JDBC driver

   D. The default transaction isolation level

   E. The last query used

   F. The names of stored procedures in the database

4. Given:

```
try {
  Statement stmt = conn.createStatement();
  String query =
        "SELECT * FROM Author WHERE LastName LIKE 'Rand%'";
  ResultSet rs = stmt.executeQuery(query);   // Line X
  if (rs == null) {                          // Line Y
    System.out.println("No results");
  } else {
    System.out.println(rs.getString("FirstName"));
  }
} catch (SQLException se) {
  System.out.println("SQLException");
}
```

Assuming a `Connection` object has already been created (conn) and that the query produces a valid result, what is the result?

A. Compiler error at line X

B. Compiler error at line Y

C. No result

D. The first name from the first row that matches 'Rand%'

E. `SQLException`

F. A runtime exception

5. Given the SQL query:

```
String query = "UPDATE Customer SET EMail='John.Smith@comcast.net'
                WHERE CustomerID = 5000";
```

Assuming this is a valid SQL query and there is a valid `Connection` object (conn), which will compile correctly and execute this query?

A. `Statement stmt = conn.createStatement();`
   `stmt.executeQuery(query);`

B. `Statement stmt = conn.createStatement(query);`
   `stmt.executeUpdate();`

C. `Statement stmt = conn.createStatement();`
   `stmt.setQuery(query);`
   `stmt.execute();`

D. `Statement stmt = conn.createStatement();`
   `stmt.execute(query);`

E. `Statement stmt = conn.createStatement();`
   `ResultSet rs = stmt.executeUpdate(query);`

6. Given:

```
try {
  ResultSet rs = null;
  try (Statement stmt = conn.createStatement()) {   // line X
    String query = "SELECT * from Customer";
    rs = stmt.executeQuery(query);                   // line Y
  } catch (SQLException se) {
    System.out.println("Illegal query");
  }
  while (rs.next()) {
    // print customer names
  }
} catch (SQLException se) {
  System.out.println("SQLException");
}
```

And assuming a valid `Connection` object (conn) and that the query will return results, what is the result?

A. The customer names will be printed out

B. Compiler error at line X

C. Illegal query

D. Compiler error at line Y

E. `SQLException`

F. Runtime exception

7. Which interfaces must a vendor implement to be JDBC compliant? (Choose all that apply.)

A. Query

B. Driver

C. ResultSet

D. Statement

E. Connection

F. SQLException

8. Given this code fragment:

```
Statement stmt = conn.createStatement();
ResultSet rs;
String query = "<QUERY HERE>";
stmt.execute(query);
if ((rs = stmt.getResultSet()) != null) {
  System.out.println("Results");
}
if (stmt.getUpdateCount() > -1) {
  System.out.println("Update");
}
```

Assuming each query is valid and that all tables have valid row data, which query statements entered into <QUERY HERE> produce the output that follows the query string (in the following answer? (Choose all that apply.)

A. `"SELECT * FROM Customer"`
   Results
B. `"INSERT INTO Book VALUES ('1023456789', 'One Night in Paris', '1984-10-20',`
   `   'Hardcover', 13.95)"`
   Update
C. `"UPDATE Customer SET Phone = '555-234-1021' WHERE CustomerID = 101"`
   Update
D. `"SELECT Author.LastName FROM Author"`
   Results
E. `"DELETE FROM Book WHERE ISBN = '1023456789'"`
   Update

9. Which are true about queries that throw `SQLExceptions`? (Choose all that apply.)

A. A single query either executes correctly or throws a single exception
B. A single query can throw many exceptions
C. If a single query throws many exceptions, the exceptions can be captured by invoking `SQLException.getExceptions()`, which returns a `List`
D. If a single query encounters more than one exception-worthy problem, a `SQLException` is created for each problem encountered
E. If a single query throws many exceptions, the exceptions can be captured by iterating through the exceptions using `SQLException.getNextException()`

10. Which are true about the results of a query?

A. The results are stored in a `ResultSet` object
B. The results are stored in a `List` of type `Result`
C. By default, the results remain synchronized with the database
D. The results are accessed via iteration
E. Once you have the results, you can retrieve a given row without needing to iterate
F. The results are stored in a `List` of type `ResultSet`

SELF TEST ANSWERS

1. ☑ **B** is correct. Prior to JDBC 4.0, JDBC drivers were required to register themselves with the `DriverManager` class by invoking `DriverManager.register(this);` after the driver was instantiated through a call from the classloader. The `Class.forName()` method calls the classloader, which, in turn, creates an instance of the class passed as a `String` to the method.
   ☒ **A** is incorrect because this method is meant to be invoked with an instance of a `Driver` class. **C** is incorrect because `DatabaseMetaData` does not have a `loadDriver` method, and the purpose of `DatabaseMetaData` is to return information about a database connection. **D** is incorrect because, again, while the method sounds right, the arguments are not of the right types, and this method is actually the one called by `DriverManager.getConnection` to get a `Connection` object. **E** is incorrect because although this method returns a `Driver` instance, one has to be loaded and registered with the `DriverManager` first. (OCP Objective 11.2)

2. ☑ **A, B,** and **E** are correct. To be JDBC 4.0 compliant, a JDBC driver must support the ability to autoload the driver by providing a file, `META-INF/services/java.sql.Driver`, that indicates the fully qualified class name of the `Driver` class that `DriverManager` should load on startup. The JDBC driver must implement the interfaces for `Driver`, `Connection`, `Statement`, `ResultSet`, and others. The driver must also support transactions.
   ☒ **C** and **D** are incorrect. It is not a requirement to support scrollable or updatable `ResultSets`, although many drivers do. If, however, the driver reports that through `DatabaseMetaData` it supports scrollable and updatable `ResultSets`, then the driver must support all of the methods associated with cursor movement and updates. **F** is incorrect. The JDBC requires that the driver support SQL92 entry-level grammar and the SQL command DROP TABLE (from SQL92 Transitional Level). **G** is incorrect. Although JDBC 4.0 drivers must support `PreparedStatement`, `CallableStatement` is optional and only required if the driver returns true for the method `DatabaseMetaData.supportsStoredProcedures`. (OCP Objective 11.2)

3. ☑ **C, D,** and **F** are correct. `DatabaseMetaData` provides data about the database and the `Connection` object. The name, version, and other JDBC driver information are available, plus information about the database, including the names of stored procedures, functions, SQL keywords, and more. Finally, the default transaction isolation level and data about what transaction levels are supported are also available through `DatabaseMetaData`.
   ☒ **A** and **B** are incorrect, as they are really about the result of a query with the database. Column count is available through a `ResultSetMetaData` object, but a row count requires that you, as the developer, move the cursor to the end of a result set and then evaluate the

cursor position. **E** is incorrect. There is no method defined to return the last query in JDBC. (OCP Objective 11.1)

4. ☑ **E** is correct. When the `ResultSet` returns, the cursor is pointing before the first row of the `ResultSet`. You must invoke the `next()` method to move to the next row of results *before* you can read any data from the columns. Trying to read a result using a `getXXXX` method will result in a `SQLException` when the cursor is before the first row or after the last row.
   ☒ **A, B, D,** and **F** are incorrect based on the above. Note about **C**: the `ResultSet` returned from `executeQuery` will never be null. (OCP Objective 11.3)

5. ☑ **D** is correct.
   ☒ Note that answer **E** is close, but will not compile because the `executeUpdate(query)` method returns an integer result. **A** will compile correctly, but throw a `SQLException` at runtime—the `executeQuery` method cannot be used on INSERT, UPDATE, DELETE, or DDL SQL queries. **B** will not compile because the `createStatement` method does not take a `String` argument for the query. **C** is incorrect because `Statement` does not have a `setQuery` method and this fragment will not compile. (OCP Objective 11.3)

6. ☑ **E** is correct. Recall that the `try`-with-resources statement on line X will automatically close the resource specified at the close of the `try` block (when the closing curly brace is reached) and closing the `Statement` object automatically closes any open `ResultSets` associated with the `Statement`. The `SQLException` thrown is that the `ResultSet` is not open. To fix this code, move the `while` statement into the `try`-with-resources block.
   ☒ **A, B, C, D,** and **F** are incorrect based on the above. (OCP Objective 11.3)

7. ☑ **B, C, D,** and **E** are correct.
   ☒ **A** and **F** are incorrect. They are not interfaces required by JDBC. To query a database, the `Statement` interface is used, not the plausibly named, but mythical, `Query` interface. (OCP Objective 11.1)

8. ☑ All of the answers are correct (**A, B, C, D, E**). SELECT statements will produce a `ResultSet` even if there are no rows. INSERT, UPDATE, and DELETE statements all produce an update count, even when the number of rows affected is 0. (OCP Objective 9.3)

9. ☑ **B, D,** and **E** are correct.
   ☒ **A** is incorrect because a single query can throw many exceptions. **C** is incorrect; when many exceptions are thrown, you must use `getNextException()` to iterate through them. (OCP Objective 11.3)

10. ☑ **A, D,** and **E** are correct. For **E** you can use, for example, `getRow()`.

 ☒ **B** is incorrect; results are stored in a `ResultSet` object. **C** is incorrect; once a `ResultSet` is created, it does NOT stay synchronized with the database unless the `ResultSet` was created with one of the `CONCUR_XXX` cursor types. **F** is incorrect based on the above. (OCP Objective 11.3)

A

About the CD-ROM
and Online Content

T he CD-ROM accompanying this book comes with a link to the Total Seminars Training Hub, instructions to access customizable practice exam software with 170 practice exam questions, and a secured PDF of the book. The CD-ROM also contains additional files covering objectives for upgrading to OCP Java SE 8 Programmer II from OCP Java SE 7 and OCP Java SE 6 that are not otherwise included in the book.

> **NOTE:** If you do not have a CD-ROM drive or wish to access the online practice exam directly, please refer to the details in the following sections. To receive the supplemental material on upgrade objectives without accessing the CD-ROM, go to http://mhprofessional.com/mediacenter/; enter product ISBN **9781260117370**; click Find Product; enter your e-mail address as prompted; and click Send Me My Download.

System Requirements

We recommend and support the current and previous major versions of Chrome, Firefox, Microsoft Edge, and Safari. These browsers update frequently, and sometimes an update may cause compatibility issues with the Total Tester Online or other content hosted on the Training Hub. If you run into a problem using one of these browsers, please try using another one until the problem is resolved.

Single User License Terms and Conditions

Online access to the digital content included with this book is governed by the McGraw-Hill Education License Agreement outlined next. By using this digital content, you agree to the terms of that license.

Access   To register and activate your Total Seminars Training Hub account and access your online practice exam, simply follow these easy steps:

1. Go to **hub.totalsem.com/mheclaim**.
2. To register and create a new Training Hub account, enter your e-mail address, name, and password. No further information (such as credit card number) is required to create an account.

3. If you already have a Total Seminars Training Hub account, select Log In and enter your e-mail and password.

4. Enter your Product Key: `m2gw-4nj6-k3zd`

5. Click to accept the user license terms.

6. Click Register And Claim to create your account. You will be taken to the Training Hub and have access to the content for this book.

Duration of License   Access to your online content through the Total Seminars Training Hub will expire one year from the date the publisher declares the book out of print.

Your purchase of this McGraw-Hill Education product, including its access code, through a retail store is subject to the refund policy of that store.

The Content is a copyrighted work of McGraw-Hill Education and McGraw-Hill Education reserves all rights in and to the Content. The Work is © 2018 by McGraw-Hill Education, LLC.

Restrictions on Transfer   The user is receiving only a limited right to use the Content for user's own internal and personal use, dependent on purchase and continued ownership of this book. The user may not reproduce, forward, modify, create derivative works based upon, transmit, distribute, disseminate, sell, publish, or sublicense the Content or in any way commingle the Content with other third-party content, without McGraw-Hill Education's consent.

Limited Warranty   The McGraw-Hill Education Content is provided on an "as is" basis. Neither McGraw-Hill Education nor its licensors make any guarantees or warranties of any kind, either express or implied, including, but not limited to, implied warranties of merchantability or fitness for a particular purpose or use as to any McGraw-Hill Education Content or the information therein or any warranties as to the accuracy, completeness, currentness, or results to be obtained from, accessing or using the McGraw-Hill Education content, or any material referenced in such content or any information entered into licensee's product by users or other persons and/or any material available on or that can be accessed through the licensee's product (including via any hyperlink or otherwise) or as to non-infringement of third-party rights. Any warranties of any kind, whether express or implied, are disclaimed. Any material or data obtained through use of the McGraw-Hill Education content is at your own discretion and risk and user understands that it will be solely responsible for any resulting damage to its computer system or loss of data.

Neither McGraw-Hill Education nor its licensors shall be liable to any subscriber or to any user or anyone else for any inaccuracy, delay, interruption in service, error or omission, regardless of cause, or for any damage resulting therefrom.

In no event will McGraw-Hill Education or its licensors be liable for any indirect, special or consequential damages, including but not limited to, lost time, lost money, lost profits or good will, whether in contract, tort, strict liability or otherwise, and whether or not such damages are foreseen or unforeseen with respect to any use of the McGraw-Hill Education content.

Total Tester Online

Total Tester Online access with this book provides you with a simulation of the Java SE 8 Programmer II (1Z0-809) exam. Exams can be taken in Practice Mode or Exam Mode. Practice Mode provides an assistance window with hints, references to the book, explanations of the correct and incorrect answers, and the option to check your answer as you take the test. Exam Mode provides a simulation of the actual exam. The number of questions, the types of questions, and the time allowed are intended to be an accurate representation of the exam environment. The option to customize your quiz allows you to create custom exams from selected domains or chapters, and you can further customize the number of questions and time allowed.

To take a test, follow the instructions provided in the previous section to register and activate your Total Seminars Training Hub account. When you register, you will be taken to the Total Seminars Training Hub. From the Training Hub Home page, select your exam from the Study drop-down list at the top of the page or from the list of Products You Own on the Home page. You can then select the option to customize your quiz and begin testing yourself in Practice Mode or Exam Mode. All exams provide an overall grade and a grade broken down by domain.

Technical Support

For questions regarding the Total Tester software or operation of the Training Hub, visit **www.totalsem.com** or e-mail **support@totalsem.com**.

For questions regarding book content, e-mail **hep_customer-service @mheducation.com**. For customers outside the United States, e-mail **international_cs@mheducation.com**.

INDEX

F

Beta Test Oracle Software

Get a first look at our newest products—and help perfect them. You must meet the following criteria:

- ✓ Licensed Oracle customer or Oracle PartnerNetwork member

- ✓ Oracle software expert

- ✓ Early adopter of Oracle products

Please apply at: pdpm.oracle.com/BPO/userprofile

If your interests match upcoming activities, we'll contact you. Profiles are kept on file for 12 months.

Join the Largest Tech Community in the World

 Download the latest software, tools, and developer templates

 Get exclusive access to hands-on trainings and workshops

 Grow your professional network through the Oracle ACE Program

 Publish your technical articles – and get paid to share your expertise

**Join the Oracle Technology Network
Membership is free. Visit community.oracle.com**

@OracleOTN   facebook.com/OracleTechnologyNetwork

Push a Button
Move Your Java Apps to the Oracle Cloud

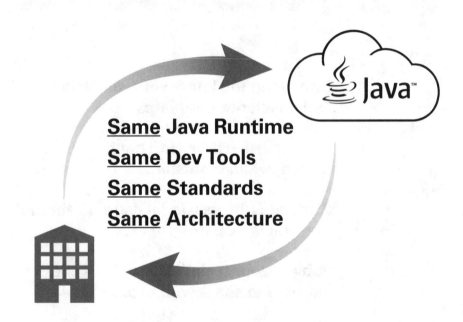

<u>Same</u> Java Runtime
<u>Same</u> Dev Tools
<u>Same</u> Standards
<u>Same</u> Architecture

... or Back to Your Data Center

Reach More than 640,000 Oracle Customers with Oracle Publishing Group

Connect with the Audience that Matters Most to Your Business

Oracle Magazine
The Largest IT Publication in the World
Circulation: 325,000
Audience: IT Managers, DBAs, Programmers, and Developers

Profit
Business Insight for Enterprise-Class Business Leaders to Help Them Build
a Better Business Using Oracle Technology

Circulation: 90,000
Audience: Top Executives and Line of Business Managers

Java Magazine
The Essential Source on Java Technology, the Java Programming Language,
and Java-Based Applications

Circulation: 225,00 and Growing Steady
Audience: Corporate and Independent Java Developers, Programmers,
and Architects

For more information
or to sign up for a FREE
subscription: Scan the
QR code to visit Oracle
Publishing online.

Single User License Terms and Conditions

Online access to the digital content included with this book is governed by the McGraw-Hill Education License Agreement outlined next. By using this digital content you agree to the terms of that license.

Access To register and activate your Total Seminars Training Hub account, simply follow these easy steps.

1. Go to **hub.totalsem.com/mheclaim.**
2. To Register and create a new Training Hub account, enter your email address, name, and password. No further information (such as credit card number) is required to create an account.
3. If you already have a Total Seminars Training Hub account, select "Log in" and enter your email and password.
4. Enter your Product Key: `m2gw-4nj6-k3zd`
5. Click to accept the user license terms.
6. Click "Register and Claim" to create your account. You will be taken to the Training Hub and have access to the content for this book.

Duration of License Access to your online content through the Total Seminars Training Hub will expire one year from the date the publisher declares the book out of print.

Your purchase of this McGraw-Hill Education product, including its access code, through a retail store is subject to the refund policy of that store.

The Content is a copyrighted work of McGraw-Hill Education and McGraw-Hill Education reserves all rights in and to the Content. The Work is © 2018 by McGraw-Hill Education, LLC.

Restrictions on Transfer The user is receiving only a limited right to use the Content for user's own internal and personal use, dependent on purchase and continued ownership of this book. The user may not reproduce, forward, modify, create derivative works based upon, transmit, distribute, disseminate, sell, publish, or sublicense the Content or in any way commingle the Content with other third-party content, without McGraw-Hill Education's consent.

Limited Warranty The McGraw-Hill Education Content is provided on an "as is" basis. Neither McGraw-Hill Education nor its licensors make any guarantees or warranties of any kind, either express or implied, including, but not limited to, implied warranties of merchantability or fitness for a particular purpose or use as to any McGraw-Hill Education Content or the information therein or any warranties as to the accuracy, completeness, currentness, or results to be obtained from, accessing or using the McGraw-Hill Education content, or any material referenced in such content or any information entered into licensee's product by users or other persons and/or any material available on or that can be accessed through the licensee's product (including via any hyperlink or otherwise) or as to non-infringement of third-party rights. Any warranties of any kind, whether express or implied, are disclaimed. Any material or data obtained through use of the McGraw-Hill Education content is at your own discretion and risk and user understands that it will be solely responsible for any resulting damage to its computer system or loss of data.

Neither McGraw-Hill Education nor its licensors shall be liable to any subscriber or to any user or anyone else for any inaccuracy, delay, interruption in service, error or omission, regardless of cause, or for any damage resulting therefrom.

In no event will McGraw-Hill Education or its licensors be liable for any indirect, special or consequential damages, including but not limited to, lost time, lost money, lost profits or good will, whether in contract, tort, strict liability or otherwise, and whether or not such damages are foreseen or unforeseen with respect to any use of the McGraw-Hill Education content.

LICENSE AGREEMENT

THIS PRODUCT (THE "PRODUCT") CONTAINS PROPRIETARY SOFTWARE, DATA AND INFORMATION (INCLUDING DOCUMENTATION) OWNED BY McGRAW-HILL EDUCATION AND ITS LICENSORS. YOUR RIGHT TO USE THE PRODUCT IS GOVERNED BY THE TERMS AND CONDITIONS OF THIS AGREEMENT.

LICENSE: Throughout this License Agreement, "you" shall mean either the individual or the entity whose agent opens this package. You are granted a non-exclusive and non-transferable license to use the Product subject to the following terms:

(i) If you have licensed a single user version of the Product, the Product may only be used on a single computer (i.e., a single CPU). If you licensed and paid the fee applicable to a local area network or wide area network version of the Product, you are subject to the terms of the following subparagraph (ii).

(ii) If you have licensed a local area network version, you may use the Product on unlimited workstations located in one single building selected by you that is served by such local area network. If you have licensed a wide area network version, you may use the Product on unlimited workstations located in multiple buildings on the same site selected by you that is served by such wide area network; provided, however, that any building will not be considered located in the same site if it is more than five (5) miles away from any building included in such site. In addition, you may only use a local area or wide area network version of the Product on one single server. If you wish to use the Product on more than one server, you must obtain written authorization from McGraw-Hill Education and pay additional fees.

(iii) You may make one copy of the Product for back-up purposes only and you must maintain an accurate record as to the location of the back-up at all times.

COPYRIGHT; RESTRICTIONS ON USE AND TRANSFER: All rights (including copyright) in and to the Product are owned by McGraw-Hill Education and its licensors. You are the owner of the enclosed disc on which the Product is recorded. You may not use, copy, decompile, disassemble, reverse engineer, modify, reproduce, create derivative works, transmit, distribute, sublicense, store in a database or retrieval system of any kind, rent or transfer the Product, or any portion thereof, in any form or by any means (including electronically or otherwise) except as expressly provided for in this License Agreement. You must reproduce the copyright notices, trademark notices, legends and logos of McGraw-Hill Education and its licensors that appear on the Product on the back-up copy of the Product which you are permitted to make hereunder. All rights in the Product not expressly granted herein are reserved by McGraw-Hill Education and its licensors.

TERM: This License Agreement is effective until terminated. It will terminate if you fail to comply with any term or condition of this License Agreement. Upon termination, you are obligated to return to McGraw-Hill Education the Product together with all copies thereof and to purge all copies of the Product included in any and all servers and computer facilities.

DISCLAIMER OF WARRANTY: THE PRODUCT AND THE BACK-UP COPY ARE LICENSED "AS IS." McGRAW-HILL EDUCATION, ITS LICENSORS AND THE AUTHORS MAKE NO WARRANTIES, EXPRESS OR IMPLIED, AS TO THE RESULTS TO BE OBTAINED BY ANY PERSON OR ENTITY FROM USE OF THE PRODUCT, ANY INFORMATION OR DATA INCLUDED THEREIN AND/OR ANY TECHNICAL SUPPORT SERVICES PROVIDED HEREUNDER, IF ANY ("TECHNICAL SUPPORT SERVICES"). McGRAW-HILL EDUCATION, ITS LICENSORS AND THE AUTHORS MAKE NO EXPRESS OR IMPLIED WARRANTIES OF MERCHANTABILITY OR FITNESS FOR A PARTICULAR PURPOSE OR USE WITH RESPECT TO THE PRODUCT. McGRAW-HILL EDUCATION, ITS LICENSORS, AND THE AUTHORS MAKE NO GUARANTEE THAT YOU WILL PASS ANY CERTIFICATION EXAM WHATSOEVER BY USING THIS PRODUCT. NEITHER McGRAW-HILL EDUCATION, ANY OF ITS LICENSORS NOR THE AUTHORS WARRANT THAT THE FUNCTIONS CONTAINED IN THE PRODUCT WILL MEET YOUR REQUIREMENTS OR THAT THE OPERATION OF THE PRODUCT WILL BE UNINTERRUPTED OR ERROR FREE. YOU ASSUME THE ENTIRE RISK WITH RESPECT TO THE QUALITY AND PERFORMANCE OF THE PRODUCT.

LIMITED WARRANTY FOR DISC: To the original licensee only, McGraw-Hill Education warrants that the enclosed disc on which the Product is recorded is free from defects in materials and workmanship under normal use and service for a period of ninety (90) days from the date of purchase. In the event of a defect in the disc covered by the foregoing warranty, McGraw-Hill Education will replace the disc.

LIMITATION OF LIABILITY: NEITHER McGRAW-HILL EDUCATION, ITS LICENSORS NOR THE AUTHORS SHALL BE LIABLE FOR ANY INDIRECT, SPECIAL OR CONSEQUENTIAL DAMAGES, SUCH AS BUT NOT LIMITED TO, LOSS OF ANTICIPATED PROFITS OR BENEFITS, RESULTING FROM THE USE OR INABILITY TO USE THE PRODUCT EVEN IF ANY OF THEM HAS BEEN ADVISED OF THE POSSIBILITY OF SUCH DAMAGES. THIS LIMITATION OF LIABILITY SHALL APPLY TO ANY CLAIM OR CAUSE WHATSOEVER WHETHER SUCH CLAIM OR CAUSE ARISES IN CONTRACT, TORT, OR OTHERWISE. Some states do not allow the exclusion or limitation of indirect, special or consequential damages, so the above limitation may not apply to you.

U.S. GOVERNMENT RESTRICTED RIGHTS: Any software included in the Product is provided with restricted rights subject to subparagraphs (c), (1) and (2) of the Commercial Computer Software-Restricted Rights clause at 48 C.F.R. 52.227-19. The terms of this Agreement applicable to the use of the data in the Product are those under which the data are generally made available to the general public by McGraw-Hill Education. Except as provided herein, no reproduction, use, or disclosure rights are granted with respect to the data included in the Product and no right to modify or create derivative works from any such data is hereby granted.

GENERAL: This License Agreement constitutes the entire agreement between the parties relating to the Product. The terms of any Purchase Order shall have no effect on the terms of this License Agreement. Failure of McGraw-Hill Education to insist at any time on strict compliance with this License Agreement shall not constitute a waiver of any rights under this License Agreement. This License Agreement shall be construed and governed in accordance with the laws of the State of New York. If any provision of this License Agreement is held to be contrary to law, that provision will be enforced to the maximum extent permissible and the remaining provisions will remain in full force and effect.